Sixth Edition

COGNITION

Gabriel A. Radvansky
University of Notre Dame

Mark H. Ashcraft
University of Nevada, Las Vegas

PEARSON

Boston   Columbus   Indianapolis   New York   San Francisco   Upper Saddle River
Amsterdam   Cape Town   Dubai   London   Madrid   Milan   Munich   Paris   Montréal   Toronto
Delhi   Mexico City   São Paulo   Sydney   Hong Kong   Seoul   Singapore   Taipei   Tokyo

Acquisitions Editor: Amber Chow
Program Manager: Diane Szulecki
Editorial Assistant: Alexis Rodriguez
Marketing Manager: Kelly May
Managing Editor: Linda Behrens
Project Manager: Crystal McCarthy
Sr. Manufacturing Manager: Mary Fischer
Senior Operations Specialist: Diane Peirano
Cover Design Manager: Jayne Conte
Cover Designer: Bruce Kenselaar
Cover Photo: www.shutterstock.com
Digital Media Director: Brian Hyland
Digital Media Editor: Michael Halas
Digital Media Project Manager: Pamela Weldin
Full-Service Project Management: Jogender Taneja, Aptara®, Inc.
Composition: Aptara®, Inc.
Printer/Binder: Courier Westford
Text Font: ITC Garamond

Credits and acknowledgements borrowed from other sources and reproduced, with permission, in this textbook appears beginning on C-1.

Library of Congress Cataloging-in-Publication Data
Ashcraft, Mark H.
  [Human memory and cognition]
  Cognition/Gabriel A. Radvansky, University of Notre Dame, Mark H.
Ashcraft, University of Nevada, Las Vegas.—Sixth edition.
    pages cm
  Previous editions published as: Human memory and cognition/Mark H. Ashcraft.
  Includes bibliographical references and index.
  ISBN-13: 978-0-205-98580-7 (alk. paper)
  ISBN-10: 0-205-98580-7 (alk. paper)
  1. Memory.   2. Cognition.   I. Radvansky, Gabriel A. II. Title.
  BF371.A68 2014
  153—dc23   2013023536

10 9 8 7 6 5 4 3 2 1

PEARSON

Student Edition:
ISBN-10:   0-205-98580-7
ISBN-13: 978-0-205-98580-7

Books A la Carte:
ISBN-10:   0-205-98623-4
ISBN-13: 978-0-205-98623-1

BRIEF CONTENTS

CONTENTS

PREFACE

TO THE STUDENT

The psychology of human memory and cognition is fascinating, dealing with questions and ideas that are inherently interesting: how we think, reason, remember, and use language, to name just a few. When cognitive psychologists talk research at conventions, they are agitated, intense, and full of energy. In contrast to this enthusiasm, however, undergraduate texts often portray the field as dull, too concerned with the minutiae of experimental method and technical jargon and not concerned enough with the interesting issues. Without slighting the empirical foundation of the field, we have tried to capture some of the excitement of the area. All professors want their students to understand the material, of course, but we also want you to appreciate cognitive psychology as one of the most interesting and memorable topics of your student career. Several features of the text are designed to accomplish this:

- To engage your interest and understanding, examples of the main points are sprinkled throughout the text. Each of the chapters has a box that asks you to "Prove It." This feature gives you a demonstration project that can be done quickly to illustrate the points being made.
- Mastering the terminology of a new field can be difficult. To help you with the jargon, critical terms are boldfaced in the text and defined immediately in italicized print. Each chapter's terms are listed at the end of the chapter.
- Each major section of a chapter ends with a brief Section Summary. This, along with the listing of glossary terms at the end of each chapter, should help you check your understanding and memory as you study. Note that some people find it helpful to read the Section Summaries first as a preview of the section's content.
- We use a more colloquial style than is customary in the field (or in texts in general), using the first person, posing direct questions to you, inserting parenthetical commentary, and so on. Our students have told us that these features make the text more enjoyable to read; one said, "It's interesting—not like a textbook," which we take as a compliment. Some professors may expect a more formal, detached style, of course. We would rather have you read and remember the material than have you cope with a text selected because of a carefully pedantic style. Besides, you will have plenty of time to deal with boring texts in graduate school.
- Although "how people think" is a topic that is likely to be of basic interest to just about everyone, most of you will not end up being cognitive scientists. So, although the material is written to be useful to people going on to a career some field of cognition, the exposition is also written to given insights to applications outside of formal cognitive science, in careers that more of you are likely to pursue.

TO THE INSTRUCTOR

Like the first five editions, this sixth edition is directed primarily toward under-graduates at the junior and senior level, who are probably taking their first basic course in memory and cognition. It has also been used successfully in introductory graduate surveys, especially when first-year students need a more thorough back-ground in memory and cognition. There is much continuity between the fifth edition of *Cognition* and this one: The foundation areas in cognition are still covered thoroughly, as you'll see in the Table of Contents.

But this revision has several new features that you'll want to note:

- There continue to be tremendous increases in the study of memory and cognition with the technologies and perspectives of cognitive neuroscience. This was reflected in prior editions, and this emphasis continues to grow in the sixth edition. There is now a chapter largely devoted to issues of cognitive neuropsychology. These discussions of neuroscience are further integrated within the individual chapter topics, along with a reference to Brodmann areas to help students more easily understand where processes may be occurring in the cortex.

- **Two new chapters** have been added to the text to cover emerging emphases in the field. **Chapter 13** covers cognition and emotion, and **Chapter 14** is on cognitive development. These are capstone chapters that recapitulate the topics in the text and can be used as desired, or not, by individual instructors wanting to give different flavors or emphases in their course. These chapters are also added because they cover topics that will be of interest to a broader range of students. **Chapter 14** is an online-only chapter: it is exclusively available within MyPsychLab (0-205-98653-6) and in all eText versions of *Cognition* 6th ed.

- The text has been thoroughly updated, adding and expanding on important topics and developments that are central to the field across a range of topics. As always, there has also been some careful pruning of topics and streamlining of presentation to make room for the new material. Specific example changes include:

  Chapter 1: More concise presentation of the history of cognitive psychology; inclusion of a broad overview of cognitive science, and how cognitive psychology relates to the wider range of topic areas.

  Chapter 2: More in-depth and extensive introduction to issues and methods of cognitive neuroscience; reference to brain areas by using Brodmann areas that are illustrated inside the front cover, and referenced throughout the text; introduction to connectionism placed here.

  Chapter 3: Neuroimaging links to Gestalt grouping principles; links to dorsal stream processing in pattern perception; influences of embodied cognition on perception expanded.

  Chapter 4: Updated discussion of attention capture processes; inclusion of inhibition of return concept, and its relation to embodied cognition; discussion of mind wandering.

  Chapter 5: Deeper consideration of the regulation of working memory resources; embodied effects of mental rotation; evidence of changes in working memory abilities.

Chapter 6: Inclusion of the benefits of survival processing on memory; consideration of the testing effect; discussion of the HERA model.

Chapter 7: Expanded discussion of embodied semantic memory; connectionism moved to integrate with the rest of the chapter.

Chapter 8: Discussion of propositions tightened up; discussion of the process of reconsolidation; discussion of cultural schemas for the reminiscence bump.

Chapter 9: Added material on tongue twisters.

Chapter 10: Expanded discussions of gesture and conversation.

Chapter 11: Update perspectives on the SNARC effect; text on automatic decision making.

Chapter 12: Inclusion of embodied influences on problem solving; expanded discussion of analogical reasoning.

- As in the first five editions, we have tried to strike a balance between basic, core material and cutting-edge topics. As cognitive psychology continues to evolve, it is important to maintain some continuity with older topics and evidence. Students need to understand how we got here, and instructors cannot be expected to start from scratch each time they teach the course. I've preserved the overall outline and organization of the text, while updating the sections to reflect newer material.

INSTRUCTOR SUPPLEMENTS

- An updated and expanded **Instructor's Manual** (ISBN 0-205-98699-4), **Test Item File** (ISBN 0-205-98689-7), and set of lecture **PowerPoint presentations** (ISBN 0-205-98701-X) are available on for download on www.pearson-highered.com or by contacting your local Pearson sales representative.
- The test item file comes with the **Pearson MyTest (ISBN** 0-205-98700-1**)**, a powerful assessment generation program that helps instructors easily create and print quizzes and exams. Questions and tests can be authored online, allowing instructors ultimate flexibility and the ability to efficiently manage assessments anytime, anywhere. For more information, go to www.pearsonmytest.com.
- **MyPsychLab (ISBN:** 0-205-98653-6**).** Available at www.mypsychlab.com, this learning and assessment tool can be used to supplement a traditional lecture course or to administer a course entirely online. Instructors decide the extent of integration—from independent self-assessment for students to total course management. Students benefit from an easy-to-use site where they can test themselves on key content, track their progress, and make use of individually tailored study plans. MyPsychLab is an all-inclusive tool, including a Pearson eText, plus teaching and learning resources organized by chapter in the form of videos, simulations, animations, assessments, and other tools to engage students and reinforce learning. Fully customizable and easy to use, MyPsychLab meets the individual teaching and learning needs of every instructor and every student. To package MyPsychLab with the student text, use ISBN 0-205-99165-3.
- **Simulations.** Students participate in virtual classic psychology experiments and research-based inventories with the MyPsychLab Simulations. The simulations help reinforce your classroom teachings and textbook.

- **MyClassPrep.** Available for instructors within MyPsychLab, this exciting new instructor resource makes lecture preparation easier and less time consuming. MyClassPrep collects the very best class preparation resources—art and figures from our leading texts, videos, lecture activities, classroom activities, demonstrations, and much more—in one convenient online destination. You can search through MyClassPrep's extensive database of tools by content topic or by content type. You can select resources appropriate for your lecture, many of which can be downloaded directly; or you can build your own folder of resources and present from within MyClassPrep.

STUDENT SUPPLEMENTS

- **MyPsychLab.** With this exciting new tool students are able to self-assess using embedded diagnostic tests and instantly view results along with a customized study plan.

  The customized study plan will focus on the student's strengths and weaknesses, based on the results of the diagnostic testing, and present a list of activities and resources for review and remediation, organized by chapter section. Some study resources intended for use with portable electronic devices are made available exclusively through MyPsychLab, such as key terms flashcards and video clips. Students will be able to quickly and easily analyze their own comprehension level of the course material and study more efficiently, leading to exceptional exam results!

  An access code is required and can be purchased at www.pearsonhighered.com or at www.mypsychlab.com.

- **CourseSmart eTextbook (ISBN:** 0-205-98709-5**).** CourseSmart offers students an online subscription to *Cognition, 6th edition* at up to 60% savings. With the CourseSmart eTextbook, students can search the text, make notes online, print out reading assignments that incorporate lecture notes, and bookmark important passages. Ask your Pearson sales representative for details or visit www.coursesmart.com.

We hope that the balance between classic research and current topics, the style we have adopted, and the standard organization we have used will make the text easy to teach from and easy for students to read and remember. More important, we hope that you will find our portrayal of the field of cognitive psychology useful. As always, we are delighted to receive the comments and suggestions of those who use this text, instructors and students alike. You can contact G.A. Radvansky by writing in care of the Department of Psychology, University of Notre Dame, Notre Dame, IN 46556, or e-mail him at gradvans@nd.edu. You can contact Mark Ashcraft by writing in care of the Psychology Department, University of Nevada Las Vegas, 4505 S. Maryland Pkwy, Box 455030, Las Vegas, NV 89154-5030, or e-mail him at mark.ashcraft@unlv.edu.

ACKNOWLEDGMENTS

The list of students, colleagues, and publishing professionals who have helped shape this project continues to grow.

For editorial support and assistance, we thank Amber Chow, Acquisitions Editor; Diane Szulecki, Program Manager; Crystal McCarthy, Project Manager; Alexis Rodriguez, Editorial Assistant; and Nicole Kunzmann, Marketing Manager.

Professional colleagues who have assisted across the years include R. Reed Hunt, John Jonides, Michael Masson, James S. Nairne, Marjorie Reed, Gregory B. Simpson, Richard Griggs, Richard Jackson Harris, Donald Homa, Paul Whitney, Tom Carr, Frances Friedrich, Dave Geary, Mike McCloskey, Morton Gernsbacher, Art Graesser, Keith Holyoak, George Kellas, Mark Marschark, Randy Engle, Fred Smith, Pamela Ansburg, Jeremy Miller, J.L. Nicol, Jennie Euler, Bob Slevc, and Joe Magliano.

And, in addition to our undergraduate classes, who have tested many of the ideas and demonstrations in the text, we'd like to thank a few special students who have helped in a variety of ways, from reading and critiquing to duplicating and checking references: Mike Faust, David Fleck, Elizabeth Kirk, David Copeland, Don Seyler, Tom Wagner, Paul Korzenko, and Jeremy Krause. We're very grateful to all.

Gabriel A. Radvansky
Mark H. Ashcraft

1

Cognitive Psychology

An Introduction

> *What a piece of work is man. How noble in reason! How infinite in faculty! In form and moving how express and admirable! In action how like an angel! In apprehension, how like a god!*
>
> (ACT 2, SCENE 2, OF SHAKESPEARE'S HAMLET)

This text is about human memory and cognition, and specifically about the scientific study of human memory and cognition. For the moment, consider memory and cognition to be the mental events and knowledge we use when we recognize an object, remember a name, have an idea, understand a sentence, or solve a problem. In this text, we consider a broad range of subjects, from basic perception through complex decision making, from seemingly simple mental acts such as recognizing a letter of the alphabet to very complicated acts such as having a conversation. We ask questions such as "How do we read for meaning?" "How

1

do we memorize facts?" "What does it mean to forget something?" "How do we know that we don't know something?" The unifying theme behind all this is one of the most fascinating and important questions of all time: How do people think?

Here we are interested in a scientific approach to memory and thought. This is cognitive psychology. One of the central features of modern cognitive psychology is its allegiance to objective, empirical methods of investigation. We are experimentalists, and this is the approach you will read about here. However, although we do present a lot of studies, we also try to make connections with your everyday experiences and how they are relevant to the issues being discussed.

Within the boundaries of science, cognitive psychology is asking a wide range of fascinating questions. There has been an explosion of interest in cognition both in and outside of psychology proper. Questions that were on the back burner for too long—such as "How do we read?" or "How do we use language?"— are now active areas of research. The pent-up interest in these questions, unleashed during the **cognitive revolution** of the late 1950s, has yielded tremendous progress. Furthermore, we now acknowledge, seek, and sometimes participate in the important contributions of disciplines such as linguistics, computer science, and the neurosciences. This interdisciplinary approach is called **cognitive science**, *the scientific study of thought, language, and the brain—in short, the scientific study of the mind.*

The most basic aim of this text is to tell you what has been discovered about human memory and cognition, and to share the insights those discoveries provide about human thought. Human memory—your memory, with its collection of mental processes—is the most highly sophisticated, flexible, and efficient computer available. How does it work? As amazing as electronic computers are, their abilities are primitive compared with what you do routinely in even a single minute of thinking. The need to understand ourselves is basic, and this includes an understanding of how our minds work.

Another aim of this text is to describe how cognitive psychology has made these discoveries. You'll better appreciate this information if you also understand how research is done and how new knowledge is acquired. Few of you will become cognitive scientists, but presumably most of you are majoring in psychology or a related field. Because the cognitive approach influences many areas of psychology—indeed, cognitive psychology is at the core and is "the most prominent school" of thought in psychology (Robins, Gosling, & Craik, 1999)—your mastery of psychology as a whole will be enhanced by understanding cognitive psychology.

A final aim of this text is to illustrate the pervasiveness of cognitive psychology and its impact on fields outside of psychology. Cognitive science is a multidisciplinary field. This fusion and cross-pollination of ideas stems from the conviction that researchers in linguistics, artificial intelligence, the neurosciences, economics, and even anthropology can contribute important ideas to psychology and vice versa. Psychology has a long tradition of influencing educational practice, and the potential for cognitive psychology to continue this is obvious and important. Even fields as diverse as medicine, law, and business use findings from cognitive psychology—for example, a cognitive psychologist named Kahneman won the Nobel Prize in Economics in 2003 for his work on decision making. But it should not be surprising that cognitive psychology is relevant to so many other fields. After all, what human activity doesn't involve thought?

THINKING ABOUT THINKING

Let's begin to develop a feel for our topic by considering three examples. For all three, you should read and answer the question, but more importantly try to be as aware as possible of the thoughts that cross your mind as you consider the question. The first question is easy:

1. *How many hands did Aristotle have?*

Here we are not particularly interested in the correct answer, "two." We are more interested in the thoughts you had as you considered the question. Most students report a train of thoughts something like this: "Dumb question. Of course he had two hands. Wait a minute—why would a professor ask such an obvious question? Maybe Aristotle had only one hand. Nah, I would have heard of it if he had had only one hand—he must have had two." An informal analysis will uncover some of the thoughts you had. This is tracked with the list in Table 1-1. Bear in mind that Table 1-1 illustrates the intuitive analysis and is not a full description of these processes.

TABLE 1-1 Summary of the Intuitive Cognitive Analysis	
Processes	**Topic and Chapter**
Sensory and perceptual	
Focus eyes on print	Visual perception, sensory memory: Chapter 3
Encode and recognize printed material	Pattern recognition, reading: Chapters 3 and 10
Memory and retrieval	
Look up and identify words in memory	Memory retrieval: Chapters 5–8
Retrieve word meanings	
Comprehension	
Combine word meanings to yield sentence meaning	Semantic retrieval, comprehension: Chapters 7–10
Evaluate sentence meaning, consider alternative meanings	Comprehension: Chapters 9 and 10
Judgment and decision	
Retrieve answer to question	Semantic retrieval: Chapters 8 and 9
Determine reasonableness of question	Comprehension, conversation: Chapters 9 and 10
Judge speaker's intent and knowledge	Decision making and reasoning: Chapter 11
Computational (Question 2)	
Retrieve factual knowledge	Semantic retrieval: Chapter 7
Retrieve knowledge of how to divide and execute procedure	Procedural knowledge: Chapters 6, 11, and 12

First, perceptual processes were used for the written words of the question to focus your eyes on the printed line, then move your focus across the line bit by bit, registering the material into a memory system. Smoothly and rapidly, other processes took the material into memory to identify the letters and words. Of course, few college readers consciously attend to the nuts and bolts of perceiving and identifying words unless the vocabulary is unfamiliar or the print is bad. Yet your lack of awareness does not mean that these processes didn't happen; ask any first-grade teacher about the difficulties children have identifying letters and putting them together into words.

We have encountered two important lessons already. First, mental processes can occur with little conscious awareness, especially if they are highly practiced, such as reading. Second, even though these processes can operate very quickly, they are complex. Their complexity makes it even more amazing how efficient, rapid, and seemingly automatic they are.

As you identified the words in the question, you were looking up their meanings and fitting them together to understand the question. Surely, you weren't consciously aware of looking up the meaning of *hands* in a mental dictionary. But just as surely, you did find that entry, along with your general knowledge about the human body.

Now we are getting to the meat of the process. With little effort, we retrieve information from memory that *Aristotle* refers to a human being, a historical figure from the past. Many people know little about Aristotle beyond the fact that he was a Greek philosopher. Yet this seems to be enough, combined with what we know about people in general, to determine that he was probably just like everyone else: He had two hands.

At a final (for now) stage, people report thoughts about the reasonableness of the question. In general, people do not ask obvious questions, at least not of other adults. If they do, it is often for another reason—a trick question, maybe, or sarcasm. So, students report that for a time they decided that maybe the question wasn't so obvious after all. In other words, they returned to memory to see whether there was some special knowledge about Aristotle that pertains to his hands. The next step is truly fascinating. Most students claim to think to themselves, "No, I would have known about it if he had had only one hand," and decide that it was an obvious question after all. This lack-of-knowledge reasoning is fascinating because so much everyday reasoning is done without benefit of complete knowledge. In an interesting variation, if students are asked, "How many hands did Beethoven have?" their knowledge of Beethoven's musical fame typically leads to the following inference: "Because he was a musician, he played the piano, and he could not possibly have been successful at it with only one hand; therefore he must have had two." An occasional student goes even further with "Two, but he did go deaf before he died."

Now *that's* interesting! Someone found a connection between the disability implied by the question "How many hands?" and a related idea in memory, Beethoven's deafness. Such an answer shows how people can also consider implications, inferences, and other unstated connections as they reason: A great deal of knowledge can be considered, and this illustrates the role of prior knowledge in reasoning, where richer knowledge about Beethoven can lead to an inference.

One other thing to note from this example is that there are different cognitive processes that are all operating at the same time or similar times—perception, attention, memory, language comprehension, and so forth. These processes are also providing input and influencing one another. In essence, cognition is a complex and interactive thing, and it is going to take a lot of time and effort to tease it all apart and understand how it works.

2. *What is 723 divided by 6?*

This question uses your knowledge of arithmetic. Just as with the first question, many of your mental processes happened more or less automatically: identifying the digits, accessing knowledge of arithmetic procedures, and so on. Yet you may be aware of the steps in doing long division: Divide 6 into 7, subtract 6 from 7 to get the first remainder, bring down the 2, then divide 12 by 6, and so on. These steps are mentioned at the bottom of Table 1-1, "Computational," which includes your knowledge of how to do long division. Cognitive psychology is also interested in your mental processing of arithmetic problems and knowledge you acquired in school, not just the kind of reasoning you used in the Aristotle question (see Chapter 12 for more on the cognitive psychology of arithmetic and math).

3. *Does a robin have wings?*

Most adults have little to say about their train of thought when answering this question. Many people insist, "I just knew the answer was yes." The informal analysis for Question 1 showed how much of cognition occurs below awareness. The assertion that "I just knew it" is not useful, however certain you are that no other thoughts occurred. You had to read the words, find their meanings in memory, check the relevant facts, and make your decision as in the previous examples. Each of these steps is a mental act, the very substance of cognitive psychology. Furthermore, each step takes some amount of time to complete. Question 3 takes adults about one second to answer; the question "Does a robin have feet?" takes a little longer, around 1.2 or 1.3 seconds. Even small time differences can give us a wealth of information about cognition and memory. What is different for Question 3 is that most of the mental processes do not require much conscious activity; the question seems to be processed automatically. Because such automatic processes are so pervasive, we are particularly interested in understanding them.

Section Summary

- Cognitive psychology is the scientific study of human mental processes. This includes perceiving, remembering, using language, reasoning, and solving problems.
- Intuitive analysis of examples such as "How many hands did Aristotle have?" and "Does a robin have wings?" indicates that many mental processes occur automatically (very rapidly and below the level of conscious awareness).

MEMORY AND COGNITION DEFINED

Now that you have an idea of the topics in the area of cognitive psychology, we need more formal definitions of the terms *memory* and *cognition*. Most of us have a good idea of what the term *memory* means, something like "being able to remember or recall some information" or "the act of recalling previously learned facts or events." Note that both of these definitions are hopelessly circular; memory is "being able to remember" or "the act of recalling." However, the definitions do point to several critical ideas.

First, the information recalled from memory is from the past. The past could be a childhood memory from years ago or something that happened only moments ago. Second, *memory* is a process of storing information or recovering it for current use. Note that *retrieval* includes both the conscious, intentional recalling to mind and the more automatic (or even unaware) retrieval of the earlier examples.

Finally, *memory* is also a place where all the knowledge of a lifetime is stored. This is evident in theories of cognition that rely on divisions such as short-term and long-term memory. Although there is some physical location in your brain for storage, "location" is often taken metaphorically; regardless of *where* it happens, there is some memory system that holds information. With the advent of neuroimaging, we are making progress in understanding where functions and processes occur in the brain.Chapter 2 introduces you to some of this new methodology.

A formal definition of *memory* captures these essential ingredients. Consider **memory** to be *the mental processes of acquiring and retaining information for later retrieval and the mental storage system that enables these processes*. Memory is demonstrated whenever the processes of retention and retrieval influence behavior or performance in some way, even if we are unaware of it. Furthermore, this definition includes retention not just across hours, weeks, or years, but even across very brief spans of time, in any situation in which the original event is no longer present. Note that memory refers to three kinds of mental activities: acquisition (also called learning or encoding), retention, and retrieval (Melton, 1963). Because all three are needed to demonstrate remembering, we include them in our broader definition.

The term *cognition* is a much richer term. In Neisser's landmark book *Cognitive Psychology* (1967), he stated that cognition "refers to all the processes by which the sensory input is transformed, reduced, elaborated, stored, recovered, and used . . . [including] such terms as sensation, perception, imagery, retention, recall, problem solving, and thinking" (p. 4). For the present, we use the following definition: **Cognition** is *the collection of mental processes and activities used in perceiving, remembering, thinking, and understanding, as well as the act of using those processes*.

Cognitive psychology is largely, though not exclusively, interested in what might be everyday, ordinary mental processes. These processes are entirely commonplace—not simple, by any means, but certainly routine. Our definition should not include only "normal" mental activities. Although cognitive psychology generally does not deal with psychologically "abnormal" states, such as schizophrenia, such "nonnormal" processes, although unusual or rare, may enrich our science.

Most cognitive research deals with the sense modalities of vision and hearing and focuses heavily on language. Some people have been bothered by the reliance on seemingly sterile experimental techniques and methods, techniques that ask simple questions that may yield overly simple-minded views about cognition. This reflects a concern that cognitive research lacks **ecological validity**, or *generalizability to the real-world situations in which people think and act* (e.g., Neisser, 1976). To some this criticism was sensible, but to many it was premature. Cognition is complex, even when using artificially simple tasks. At our current level of sophistication, we would be quickly overwhelmed if tasks were very complex or if we tried to investigate the full range of a behavior in all its detail and nuance. In the early stage of investigation it is reasonable for scientists to take an approach called **reductionism**, *attempting to understand complex events by breaking them down into their components*. An artificially simple situation can reveal an otherwise obscure process. Of course, scientists eventually put the pieces back together and deal with the larger event as a whole.

Section Summary

- Memory is composed of the mental processes of acquiring and retaining information for later use (encoding), the mental retention system (storage), and then using that information (retrieval).
- Cognition is the complex of mental processes and activities used in perceiving, remembering, and thinking and the act of using those processes.

AN INTRODUCTORY HISTORY OF COGNITIVE PSYCHOLOGY

Let's now turn to cognitive psychology's history and development (for an excellent history of cognitive psychology, see Mandler, 2007). Figure 1-1 summarizes the main patterns of influence that produced cognitive psychology and cognitive science, along with approximate dates.

To a remarkable extent, the bulk of the scientific work on memory and cognition is quite recent, although some elements, and many experimental tasks, appeared even in the earliest years of psychology. However, interest in memory and cognition—thinking—is as old as recorded history. Aristotle, born in 384 BC, considered the basic principles of memory and proposed a theory in his treatise *De Memoria* (*Concerning Memory;* Hothersall, 1984). Even a casual reading of ancient works such as Homer's *Iliad* or *Odyssey* reveals that people have always wondered how the mind works and how to improve it (in Plato's *Phaedrus*, Socrates fretted that the invention of written language would weaken reliance on memory and understanding, just as modern parents worry about television and computers). Philosophers of every age have considered the nature of thought. Descartes even decided that the proof of human existence is our awareness of our own thought: *Cogito ergo sum,* "I think, therefore I am" (Descartes, 1637, p. 52).

The critical events at the founding of psychology, in the mid- to late 1800s, converged most strongly on one man, Wilhelm Wundt, and on one place, Leipzig,

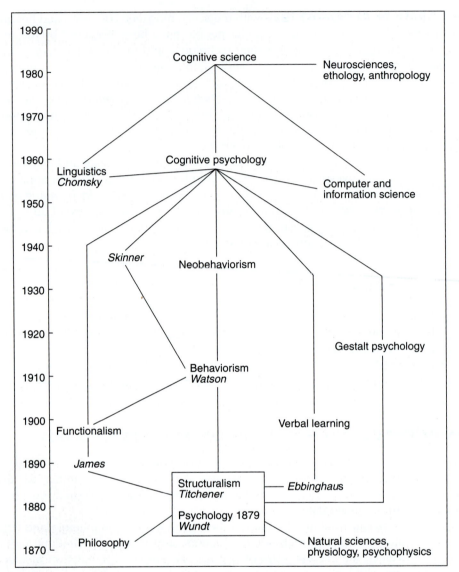

FIGURE 1-1   The main patterns of influence that produced cognitive psychology and cognitive science.

Germany. In 1879, Wundt established the first laboratory for psychological experiments, at the University of Leipzig, although several people had already been doing psychological research (e.g., Weber's and Fechner's work in psychophysics, Helmholtz's studies of the speed of neural impulses, and Broca's and Wernicke's identification of linguistic brain regions). A laboratory was even established by American psychologist William James in 1875, although apparently it was used more for classroom demonstrations than for genuine experiments. Still, the consensus is that 1879 is the beginning of the discipline of psychology, separate from philosophy and physiology.

Anticipations of Psychology

Aristotle, for two reasons, is one of the first historical figures to advocate an empirically based, natural science approach. Although he was certainly not the only great thinker to insist on *observation as the basis for all science,* he was the first to express this—a position known as **empiricism**. Second, Aristotle's inquiry into the nature of thought led him to a reasonably objective explanation of how learning and memory take place. The basic principles of association he identified have figured prominently in many psychological theories. Equally important was *Aristotle's insistence that the mind is a "blank slate" at birth*, a **tabula rasa**, or clean sheet of paper (Watson, 1968). The idea is that experience, rather than inborn factors, "writes" a record onto the blank paper.

There have been many fits and starts in the study of memory over time since Aristotle. For example, St. Augustine, in Chapter 10 of his *Confessions*, presents a surprisingly modern account of memory. Most other anticipations of psychology date from the Renaissance and later periods and are largely developments in scientific methods and approaches. By the mid-1800s, more observational or empirical methods were adopted. By the time psychology appeared, the general procedures of scientific inquiry were well developed. Given the progress in scientific fields such as physics, biology, and medicine by the mid-1800s, it is not surprising that the early psychologists thought the time was ripe for a science of the mind.

Early Psychology

Simulate
*Closer Look:
A History of
Psychology* in
MyPsychLab

Four early psychologists are of particular interest for cognitive psychology. They are Wilhelm Wundt, Edward Titchener, Hermann von Ebbinghaus, and William James.

WILHELM WUNDT   To a large extent, the early psychologists were students of Wilhelm Wundt (1832–1920) (Benjamin, Durkin, Link, Vestal, & Acord, 1992). Beginning in 1875, Wundt directed more than 200 doctoral theses on psychological topics (Leahey, 2000). Wundt continually updated his book *Principles of Physiological Psychology*, reporting new results from his laboratory. He also founded the first psychology journal, *Philosophical Studies* (neither of these titles matches its modern connotations). Unfortunately, Wundt's later interests went largely unrecognized until recently (Leahey, 2000). His work on language, child psychology, and other applied topics foreshadowed some modern insights but was rejected or ignored at the time.

In terms of psychology, Wundt believed that the study of psychology was "of conscious processes and immediate experience"—what today we consider areas of sensation, perception, and attention. To study these, in addition to extensive use of response time measures, Wundt used the method of *Selbst-Beobachtung*. Translated literally as "self-observation," this generally is known as **introspection**, *a method in which one looks carefully*

Wilhelm Wundt

inward, reporting on inner sensations and experiences. Wundt intended this to be a careful, reliable, and scientific method in which the observers (who were also the participants) needed a great deal of training to report only the elements of experience that were immediate and conscious. Reports in which memory intruded were to be excluded.

EDWARD TITCHENER   For American psychology in Wundt's tradition, the most important figure was Edward Titchener, an Englishman who came to Cornell University in 1892. Working with Wundt convinced Titchener that psychology's progress depended critically on introspection. Topics such as mental illness and educational and social psychology (including Wundt's broader interests) were "impure" because they could not be studied this way. Titchener insisted on rigorous training for his introspectors, who had to avoid "the stimulus error" of describing the physical stimulus rather than the mental experience of it. Moreover, Titchener made himself the final authority on whether introspection reports were correct or not. By these means, Titchener studied *the structure of the conscious mind, the sensations, images, and feelings that were the very elements of the mind's structure.* He called this **structuralism**, an early movement or school of psychological thought (see Figure 1-1). Such a system was destined for difficulties. It is unscientific that one person, Titchener, would be the ultimate authority to validate observations. As other researchers used introspective methods, differences and contradictory results began to crop up, producing disputes, hastening the decline of Titchener's once-powerful structuralism.

Hermann von
Ebbinghaus

HERMANN VON EBBINGHAUS   In contrast to Titchener's structuralism, there was the theoretically modest but eventually more influential work of Hermann von Ebbinghaus (see Chapter 6). Ebbinghaus was a contemporary of Wundt in Germany, although he never studied with Wundt in person. Ebbinghaus's achievements in studying memory and forgetting are all the more impressive because he worked outside the establishment of the time. Historical accounts suggest that Ebbinghaus read Wundt's book, decided that a study of the mind by objective methods *was* possible, and set about the task of figuring out how to do it.

Lacking a formal laboratory and in an academic position with no like-minded colleagues, Ebbinghaus had to rely on his own resources, even to the extent that he alone served as a subject in his research. Ebbinghaus's aim was to study memory in a "pure" form. To do this, he needed materials that had no preexisting associations, so he constructed lists of *nonsense syllables,* consonant–vowel–consonant (CVC) trigrams that, by definition, had *no* meaning. Ebbinghaus would learn a list (e.g., of 16 items) to a criterion of mastery (e.g., two perfect recitations), then set the list aside. Later, he would relearn the same list, noting how many fewer trials he needed to relearn it. His measure of learning was the "savings score," the number (or proportion) of trials that had been saved in memory between the first and second sessions. With this method, Ebbinghaus studied forgetting as a function of time, degree of learning or over-learning, and even the effect of nonsense versus meaningful material (he compared forgetting curves for nonsense syllables and meaningful poetry).

Ebbinghaus's work, described in his 1885 book, was acclaimed widely as a model of scientific inquiry into memory; for instance, Titchener praised Ebbinghaus's work as the most significant progress since Aristotle (1919; cited in Hall, 1971). It is difficult to point to another psychologist of his day whose contributions or methods continue to be used. The field of verbal learning owed a great deal to Ebbinghaus. The Ebbinghaus tradition, depicted in Figure 1-1, is one of the strongest influences on cognitive psychology.

WILLIAM JAMES American philosopher and psychologist William James, a contemporary of Wundt, Titchener, and Ebbinghaus, provided at Harvard an alternative to Titchener's rigid system. His approach, **functionalism**, was influenced by the writings of Darwin, in which *the functions of consciousness, rather than its structure, were of interest.* Thus, James asked questions such as "How does the mind function?" and "How does it adapt to new circumstances?"

James's informal analyses led to some useful observations. For example, he suggested that memory consists of two parts: an immediately available memory that we are currently aware of and a larger memory that is the repository for past experience. The idea of memory being divided into parts, based on different functions, is popular today. Indeed, the first serious models of human cognition included the two kinds of memory James discussed in 1890.

Probably because of his personal distaste for experimentation and his far-reaching interests, James did not do much research. However, his far-reaching ideas were more influential than any of Titchener's work, as evidence by his classic 1890 book *Principles of Psychology.* James's influence on the psychology of memory and cognition was delayed, however, for it was John B. Watson, in 1913, who solidified a new direction in American psychology away from both the structuralist and functionalist approaches. This new direction was behaviorism.

William James

Behaviorism and Neobehaviorism

Not all of American psychology from 1910 through the 1950s was behaviorist. The fields of clinical, educational, and social psychology, to name a few, continued in their own development in parallel to behaviorism. Furthermore, there were changes within behaviorism that smoothed the transition to cognitive psychology. This was a kind of neobehaviorism with some unobservable, mediating variables. Nonetheless, it was still a behaviorist environment.

Most people who take introductory psychology know of John B. Watson, the early behaviorist who stated in his 1913 "manifesto" that observable, quantifiable behavior was the proper topic of psychology, not the fuzzy and unscientific concepts of thought, mind, and consciousness. Attempts to understand the "unobservables" of mind were inherently unscientific, in his view, and he pointed to the unresolved debates in structuralism as evidence. Thus psychology was redefined as *the scientific study of observable behavior,* the program of **behaviorism**. There was no room for mental processes because they were not observable behaviors.

Why did such a radical redefinition of psychology's interests have such broad appeal? Part of this was a result of the work that Pavlov and others were doing on conditioning and learning. Here was a scientific approach that was going somewhere compared to the endless debates in structuralism. Furthermore, the measurement and quantification of behaviorism mirrored successful sciences such as physics. Modeling psychology on the methods of these sciences might help it become more scientific (Leahey, 2000, calls this mentality "physics envy"). One of behaviorism's greatest legacies was the emphasis on methodological rigor and observables, traditions continued to this day.

During the behaviorist era, there were a few psychologists who pursued cognitive topics—Bartlett of Great Britain, for example—but most American experimental psychology focused on observable, learned behaviors, especially in animals (but see Dewsbury, 2000, for a history of research on animal cognition during the behaviorist era). Even the strongly cognitive approach of Tolman—whose article "Cognitive Maps in Rats and Men" (1948), a molar (as opposed to molecular) approach to behaviorism, is still worth reading—included much of the behaviorist tradition: concern with the learning of new behaviors, animal studies, and interpretation based closely on observable stimuli. Gestalt psychology, which emigrated to the United States in the 1930s (Mandler & Mandler, 1969), always maintained an interest in human perception, thought, and problem solving but never captured the imaginations of many American experimentalists.

Thus the behaviorist view dominated American experimental psychology until the 1940s, when B. F. Skinner emerged as a vocal, even extreme, advocate. In keeping with Watson's earlier sentiments, Skinner also argued that mental events such as thinking have no place in the science of psychology—not that they are not real, but that they are unobservable and hence unnecessary to a scientific explanation of behavior.

Emerging Cognition: The Winds of Change

It is often difficult to determine precisely when historical change takes place. Still, many psychologists look kindly on the idea that there was a cognitive revolution in the mid- to late 1950s, with a relatively abrupt change in research activities, interests, and the scientific beliefs, a definitive break from behaviorism (Baars, 1986). Because of the nature and scope of these changes, the current approach is seen by some as a revolution in which behaviorism was rejected and replaced with cognitive psychology, although some historians claim that this was not a true scientific revolution but merely "rapid, evolutionary change" (see Leahey, 1992). In either case, the years from 1945 through 1960 were a period of rapid reform in experimental psychology. The challenges to neobehaviorism came both from within its own ranks and from outside, prodding psychologists to move in a new direction.

WORLD WAR II Lachman, Lachman, and Butterfield (1979) made a point about this growing dissatisfaction among the neobehaviorists. They noted that many academic psychologists were involved with the U.S. war effort during World War II. Psychologists accustomed to studying animal learning in the laboratory were "put to work on the practical problems of making war . . . trying to understand problems of perception, judgment, thinking, and decision mak-

Tasks, such as the vigilance needed for air traffic control, require cognitive processes at a fundamental level.

ing" (p. 56). Many of these problems arose because of soldiers' difficulties with sophisticated technical devices: skilled pilots who crashed their aircraft, radar and sonar operators who failed to detect or misidentified enemy blips, and so on.

Lachman et al. (1979) were very direct in their description of this situation:

> *Where could psychologists turn for concepts and methods to help them solve such problems? Certainly not to the academic laboratories of the day. The behavior of animals in mazes and Skinner boxes shed little light on the performance of airplane pilots and sonar operators. The kind of learning studied with nonsense syllables contributed little to psychologists trying to teach people how to operate complex machines accurately. In fact, learning was not the central problem during the war. Most problems arose after the tasks had already been learned, when normally skillful performance broke down. The focus was on performance rather than learning; and this left academic psychologists poorly prepared.* (pp. 56–57)

As Bruner, Goodnow, and Austin (1956) put it, the "impeccable peripheralism" of stimulus–response (S–R) behaviorism became painfully obvious in the face of such practical concerns.

To deal with practical concerns, wartime psychologists were forced to conceive of human behavior differently. The concepts of attention and vigilance, for instance, were important to understand sonar operators' performance; experiments on the practical and theoretical aspects of vigilance began (see especially Broadbent, 1958, Chapter 6). Decision making was a necessary part of this performance, too, and from this came such developments as signal detection theory. These wartime psychologists rubbed shoulders with professionals from different fields—those in communications engineering, for instance—from whom they gained new outlooks and perspectives on human behavior. Thus these psychologists returned to their laboratories after the war determined to broaden their own research interests and those of psychology as well.

VERBAL LEARNING   **Verbal learning** was *the branch of experimental psychology that dealt with humans as they learned verbal material, composed of letters, nonsense syllables, or words.* The groundbreaking research by Ebbinghaus started the verbal learning tradition (see Chapter 6), which derives its name from the behaviorist context it found itself in. Thus, verbal learning was defined as the use of verbal materials in various learning paradigms. Throughout the 1920s and 1930s there was a large body of verbal learning research, with well-established methods and procedures. Tasks such as serial learning, paired-associate learning, and, to an extent, free recall were the accepted methods.

Verbal learners were similar to the behaviorists. For example, they agreed on the need to use objective methods. There also was widespread acceptance of the central role of learning, conceived as a process of forming new associations, much like the learning of new associations by a rat in a Skinner box. From this perspective, a theoretical framework was built that used a number of concepts that are accepted today. For example, a great deal of verbal learning was oriented around accounts of interference among related but competing newly learned items.

The more moderate view in verbal learning circles made it easy for people to accept cognitive psychology in the 1950s and 1960s: There were many indications that an adequate psychology of learning and memory needed more than just observable behaviors. For instance, the presence of meaningfulness in "nonsense" syllable had been acknowledged early on; Glaze (1928) titled his paper "The Association Value of Nonsense Syllables" (and apparently did so with a straight face). At first, such irksome associations were controlled for in experiments, to avoid contamination of the results. Later, it became apparent that the memory processes that yielded those associations were more interesting.

In this tradition, Bousfield (1953; Bousfield & Sedgewick, 1944) reported that, with free recall, words that were associated with one another (e.g., *car* and *truck*) tended to cluster together, even though they were arranged randomly in a study list. There were clear implications that existing memory associations led to the reorganization. Such evidence of processes occurring between the stimulus and the response—in other words, mental processes—led verbal learners to propose a variety of mental operations such as rehearsal, organization, storage, and retrieval.

The verbal learning tradition led to the derivation and refinement of laboratory tasks for learning and memory. They borrowed from Ebbinghaus's example of careful attention to rigorous methodology to develop tasks that measured the outcomes of mental processes in valid and useful ways. Some of these tasks were more closely associated with behaviorism, such as the paired-associate learning task that lent itself to tests of S–R associations in direct ways. Nonetheless, verbal learning gave cognitive psychology an objective, reliable way to study mental processes—research that was built on later (e.g., Stroop, 1935)—and a set of inferred processes such as storage and retrieval to investigate. The influence of verbal learning on cognitive psychology, as shown in Figure 1-1, was almost entirely positive.

LINGUISTICS   The changes in verbal learning were a gradual shifting of interests and interpretations that blended almost seamlessly into cognitive psychology. In contrast, 1959 saw the publication of an explicit, defiant challenge to behaviorism. Watson's 1913 article was a behaviorist manifesto, crystallizing the view against introspective methods. To an equal degree, Noam Chomsky's 1959 article was a cognitive manifesto, a rejection of purely behaviorist explanation of the most human of all behaviors: language.

A bit of background is needed. In 1957, B. F. Skinner published a book titled *Verbal Behavior,* a treatment of human language from the radical behaviorist standpoint of reinforcement, stimulus–response associations, extinction, and so on. His central point was that the psychology of learning—that is, the conditioning of new behavior by means of reinforcement—provided a useful and scientific account of human language. In oversimplified terms, Skinner's basic idea was that human language, "verbal behavior," followed the same laws that had been discovered in the animal learning laboratory: A reinforced response increased in frequency, a nonreinforced response should extinguish, a response conditioned to a stimulus should be emitted to the same stimulus in the future, and so on. In principle, then, human language, a learned behavior, could be explained by the same mechanisms given knowledge of the current reinforcement contingencies and past reinforcement history of the individual.

Noam Chomsky, a linguist at the Massachusetts Institute of Technology, reviewed Skinner's book in the journal *Language* in 1959. The first sentence of his review noted that many linguists and philosophers of language "expressed the hope that their studies might ultimately be embedded in a framework provided by behaviorist psychology" and therefore were interested in what Skinner had to say. Chomsky alluded to Skinner's optimism that the problem of verbal behavior would yield to behavioral analysis because the principles discovered in the animal laboratory "are now fairly well understood . . . [and] can be extended to human behavior without serious modification" (Skinner, 1957, cited in Chomsky, 1959, p. 26).

Noam Chomsky

But by the third page of his review, Chomsky stated that "the insights that have been achieved in the laboratories of the reinforcement theorist, though quite genuine, can be applied to complex human behavior only in the most gross and superficial way. . . . The magnitude of the failure of [Skinner's] attempt to account for verbal behavior serves as a kind of measure of the importance of the factors *omitted* from consideration" (p. 28, emphasis added). The fighting words continued. Chomsky asserted that if the terms *stimulus, response, reinforcement,* and so on are used in their technical, animal laboratory sense, then "the book covers almost no aspect of linguistic behavior" (p. 31) of interest. To Chomsky, Skinner's account used the technical terms in a nontechnical, metaphorical way, which "creates the illusion of a rigorous scientific theory [but] is no more scientific than the traditional approaches to this subject matter, and rarely as clear and careful" (pp. 30–31).

To illustrate his criticism, Chomsky noted the operational definitions that Skinner provided in the animal laboratory, such as for the term *reinforcement.* But unlike the distinct and observable pellet of food in the Skinner box, Skinner claimed that reinforcement for human verbal behavior could even be administered by the person exhibiting the behavior, that is, self-reinforcement. In some cases, Skinner continued, reinforcement could be delayed for indefinite periods or never be delivered at all, as in the case of a writer who anticipates that her work may gain her fame for centuries to come. When an explicit and immediate reinforcer in the laboratory, along with its effect on behavior, is generalized to include nonexplicit and nonimmediate (and even nonexistent) reinforcers in the real world, it seems that Skinner had brought along the vocabulary of scientific explanation but left the substance behind. As Chomsky bluntly put it, "A mere terminological revision, in which a term borrowed from the laboratory is used with the full vagueness of the ordinary vocabulary, is of no conceivable interest" (p. 38).

Chomsky's own view of language, emphasizing its novelty and the internal rules for its use, is discussed in Chapter 9; there, the influence of linguistics on cognitive psychology (Figure 1-1) is described in detail. For now, the essential message is the impact of Chomsky's review. Language *was* an important behavior—and a learned one at that—to be understood by psychology. An approach that offered no help in understanding this was useless.

To a significant number of people, Chomsky's arguments summarized the dissatisfactions with behaviorism that had become so apparent. The irrelevance of behaviorism to the study of language, and, by extension, any significant human behavior, was now painfully obvious. In combination with the other developments—the wartime fling with mental processes, the expansion of the catalog of such processes by verbal learning, and the disarray within behaviorism itself—it was clear that the new direction for psychology would take hold.

Section Summary

- The modern history of cognitive psychology began in 1879 with Wundt and the beginnings of experimental psychology as a science.
- The behaviorist movement rejected the use of introspections and substituted the study of observable behavior.
- Modern cognitive psychology, which dates from approximately 1960, rejected much of the behaviorist position but accepted its methodological rigor. Many diverse viewpoints, assumptions, and methods converged to help form cognitive psychology. This was at least a rapid, evolutionary change in interests, if not a true scientific revolution.

COGNITIVE PSYCHOLOGY AND INFORMATION PROCESSING

If we had to pick a date that marks the beginning of cognitive psychology, we might pick 1960. This is not to say that significant developments were not present before this date, for they were. This is also not to say that most experimental psychologists who studied humans became cognitive psychologists that year, for they did not. As with any major change, it takes a while for the new approach to catch on and for people to decide that the new direction is worth following. However, several significant events clustered around 1960 that were significant departures from what came before.

Just as 1879 is considered the formal beginning of psychology, and 1913 the beginning of behaviorism, so 1960 approximates the beginning of cognitive psychology.[1]

Let's pick up the threads of what came before this date. One significant thread was Chomsky's 1959 review, a forceful argument against a purely behaviorist position. Chomsky argued that the truly interesting part of language was exactly what Skinner had omitted: mental processes and cognition. Language users follow rules when they generate language, rules that are stored in memory and operated on by mental processes. In Chomsky's view, it was exactly there, *in* the organism, that the key to understanding language would be found.

Researchers in verbal learning and other fields were making the same claim. As noted, Bousfield (1953) found that people cluster or group words together on the basis of the associations among them. Memory and a tendency to reorganize clearly were involved. Where were these associations? Where was this memory? And where was this tendency to reorganize? They were in the person, in memory and mental processes.

During the 1950s, there were reports on attention, first from British researchers such as Colin Cherry and Donald Broadbent, that were related to the wartime concerns of attention and vigilance. Again, mental processes were being isolated and investigated—no one could deny their existence any longer, even though they were unseen, mental processes. A classic paper, Sperling's monograph on visual sensory memory, appeared in 1960. (MacLeod [1991] noted an increase around 1960 of citations to the rediscovered Stroop [1935] task.)

Another startling development of this period was the invention of the modern digital computer. At some point in the 1950s, some psychologists realized the relevance of computing to psychology. In some interesting and possibly useful ways, computers behave like people (not surprising, according to Norman, 1986, p. 534, because "the architecture of the modern digital computer . . . was heavily influenced by people's naive view of how the mind operated"). They take in information, do something with it internally, then produce some observable product. The product gives clues to what went on internally. The operations done by the computer were not unknowable because they were internal and unobservable. They were under the control of the computer program, the instructions given to the machine to tell it what to do.

The realization that human mental activity might be understood by analogy to this machine was a breakthrough. The computer was an existence proof for the idea that unobservable processes could be studied and understood. Especially important was the idea of symbols and their internal manipulation. A computer

---

[1]Gardner (1985, p. 28) stated, "There has been nearly unanimous agreement among the surviving principals that cognitive science was officially recognized around 1956. The psychologist George A. Miller . . . has even fixed the date, 11 September 1956." Miller recalled a conference from September 10 to 12, 1956, at MIT, attended by leading researchers in communication and psychology. On the second day of the conference, there were papers by Newell and Simon on the "Logic Theory Machine," by Chomsky on his theory of grammar and linguistic transformations, and by Miller himself on the capacity limitations of short-term memory. Others whom Gardner cited suggest that, at a minimum, the five-year period 1955 to 1960 was the critical time during which cognitive psychology emerged as a distinct and new approach. By analogy to psychology's selection of 1879 as the starting date for the whole discipline, 1960 is special in Gardner's analysis: In that year, Jerome Bruner and George Miller founded the Center for Cognitive Studies at Harvard University.

is a symbol-manipulating machine. The human mind might also be a symbol-manipulating system, an idea attributed to Allen Newell and Herb Simon. According to Lachman et al. (1979), their conference in 1958 had a tremendous impact on those who attended. Newell and Simon presented an explicit analogy between information processing in the computer and that in humans. This important work was the basis for the Nobel Prize awarded to Simon in 1978 (see Leahey, 2003, for a full account of Simon's contributions).

Among the indirect results of this conference was the 1960 publication of a book by Miller, Galanter, and Pribram called *Plans and the Structure of Behavior*. The book suggested that human problem solving could be understood as a kind of planning in which mental strategies or plans guide behavior toward its goal. The mentalistic plans, goals, and strategies in the book were not just unobservable, hypothetical ideas. Instead, they were ideas that in principle could be specified in a program running on a lawful, physical device: the computer.

MEASURING INFORMATION PROCESSES

Getting Started

The aim of cognitive psychology is to reverse engineer the brain in much the same way that engineers reverse engineer devices that they can't get into. Putting it simply, we want to know: What happens in there? What happens in the mind—or in the brain, if you prefer—when we perceive, remember, reason, and solve problems? How can we peer into the mind to get a glimpse of the cognition that operates so invisibly? What methods can we use to obtain some scientific evidence on mental processes?

Guiding Analogies

With the development of cognitive psychology, the seemingly unrelated fields of communications engineering and computer science supplied psychology with some intriguing ideas and useful analogies that were central to developing the cognitive science.

CHANNEL CAPACITY   To highlight one, psychologists found the concept of **channel capacity** from communications engineering useful (a similar, more popular term would be *bandwidth*). In the design of telephone systems, for instance, one of the built-in limitations is that *any channel—any physical device that transmits messages or information—has a limited capacity*. In simple terms, one wire can carry just so many messages at a time, and it loses information if capacity is exceeded. Naturally, engineers tried to design equipment and techniques to get around these limitations to increase overall capacity.

Psychologists noticed that, in several ways, humans are limited-capacity channels, too. There is a limit on how many things you can do, or think about, at a time. This insight lent a fresh perspective to human experimental psychology. It makes sense to ask questions such as: How many sources of information can people pay attention to at a time? What information is lost if we overload the system? Where is the limitation, and can we overcome it?

THE COMPUTER ANALOGY   Even more influential than communications engineering was computer science. Computer science developed a machine that reflected the essence of the human mind. Because those things are unseen when both computers and humans do them, there was good reason for drawing the **computer analogy** to cognition. Basically, this analogy said that human information processing may be similar to the steps and operations in a computer program, similar to the flow of information from input to output. If so, then thinking about how a computer does various tasks gives some insights into how people process information.

IN DEPTH
Interpreting Graphs

If you're good at interpreting data in graphs, do not bother with the rest of this box; just study the figures. Some students struggle with graphs, not understanding what is being shown. Because you will encounter a lot of graphs in this text, you need to understand what you are looking at and what it means. Take a moment to go through these graphs to see how they are put together and what to pay attention to.

Figure 1-2 (see on page 20), is a graph of response time data, the time it takes to respond to an item. We abbreviate response time as RT, and it is usually measured in milliseconds (ms), thousandths of a second (because thought occurs so fast). In the figure, the label on the y-axis is "Vocal RT"; these people were making vocal responses (speaking), and we measured the time between the onset of a multiplication problem and the vocal response. The numbers on the y-axis show you the range of RTs that were observed. The dependent variable is always the measure of performance we collected—here it is vocal RT—and it always goes on the y-axis.

The x-axis in the left panel is labeled "Multiplication problems," and we've plotted two problems, 2×3 and 6×9. It is customary to show a more general variable than this on the x-axis, as shown in the right panel. There you see a point for a whole set of small multiplication problems, from 2×3 up to 4×5; a set of medium-size problems such as 2×7 and 8×3; and a set of large problems, such as 6×8 and 9×7. So the x-axis label in the right panel says "Size of problem." Notice that the y-axis is now in whole seconds, to save some space.

Now the data. The points in the graph are often a mean or average of the dependent variable, RT in this case. Both panels show two curves or lines each, one for college students and one for fourth-grade students (Campbell & Graham, 1985), for multiplication problems. Notice that the curves for fourth-graders are higher. Looking at the y-axis in the left panel, the average fourth-grader took 1,940 ms to answer "6" to the problem 2×3, compared to 737 ms for the average college student. In the right panel, the average fourth-grader took about 2,400 ms to respond to small problems, 4,100 ms to medium, and 4,550 ms to large. Compare this much greater increase in RT as the problems get larger with the pattern for college students: There was still an increase, but only from 730 ms to about 900 ms.

Why did Campbell and Graham find that fourth-graders were slower? No doubt because college students have had more practice in doing multiplication problems than fourth-graders. In other words, college students know multiplication better, have the facts stored more strongly in memory, and so can retrieve them more rapidly. It is a sensible, cognitive effect that the strength of information in memory influences the speed of retrieval. And it is easily grasped by looking at and understanding the graphed results.

Time and Accuracy Measures

How we peer into the mind to study cognition depends on using acceptable measurement tools to assess otherwise unseen, unobservable mental events. Other than Wundt's method of introspection, what can be used? There are many measures, but two of the most prominent behavioral measures are (a) the *time* it takes to do some task and (b) the *accuracy* of that performance. Because these measures are so pervasive, it is important to discuss them at the outset.

RESPONSE TIME   Many research programs in cognitive psychology rely heavily on **response time (RT)**, *a measure of the time elapsed between some stimulus and the person's response to the stimulus* (RT is typically measured in milliseconds, abbreviated *ms;* a millisecond is one thousandth of a second). Why is this so important, especially when the actual time differences can seem so small, say, on the order of 40 to 50 ms?

It has been known for a long time that individual differences among people can be revealed by RT measures. In 1868, the Dutch physiologist Donders (1868/1969) observed that RT is more informative and can be used to study the "Speed of Mental Processes." A moment's reflection reveals why cognitive psychology uses response times: *Mental events take time.* That's important—the mental processes and events we want to understand occur in real time and can be studied by measuring how long they take. Thus, we can "peer into the head" by looking at how long it takes to complete certain mental processes.

Here's an example of this kind of reasoning from measuring RTs. Research in mathematical cognition studies how we remember and use mathematical knowledge. Consider two simple arithmetic problems, such as $2 \times 3 = ?$ and $6 \times 9 = ?$ The left panel of Figure 1-2 shows the time it took some fourth-graders and some college

Simulate
Implicit Association Test: Cats and Dogs in **MyPsychLab**

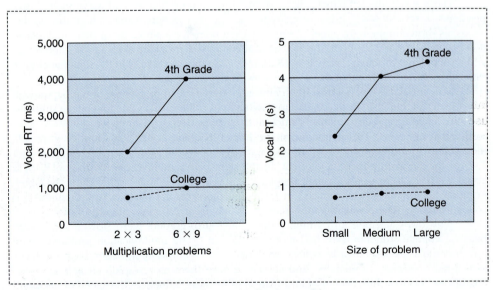

FIGURE 1-2   Vocal response times (RTs) to multiplication problems.

Source: Data from Campbell and Graham (1985).

adults to solve these problems (Campbell & Graham, 1985). There are two important effects: an obvious age difference in which children were slower than adults, and an effect related to the problems, longer RT for 6 × 9 than for 2 × 3. The right panel shows comparable functions for a range of multiplication problems, from small ones such as 2 × 3 to medium (e.g., 7 × 3) and large (e.g., 6 × 9) problems. For both age groups, the curves increase as the size of the problems increases, commonly known as the problem size effect (e.g., Stazyk, Ashcraft, & Hamann, 1982).

Think of the basic assumption again: Mental processes take time. The implication is that longer time is evidence that some process or subprocess took longer in one case than in the other. What could account for that? Most adults agree that 6 × 9 is harder than 2 × 3, but that by itself is not very useful; of course a harder decision will take longer to make. But why would 6 × 9 be harder? After all, we learned our multiplication facts in grade school. Haven't we had sufficient experience since then to equalize all the basic facts, to make them pretty much the same in difficulty? Apparently not.

So what accounts for the increase in RT? It is unlikely that it takes longer to perceive the numbers in a larger problem—and also unlikely that it takes longer to start reporting the answer once you have it. One possibility is that smaller problems have a memory advantage, perhaps something to do with knowing them better. This might date back to grade school, such as the fact that problems with smaller numbers (from 2 to 4) occur more frequently in grade-school textbooks (Ashcraft & Christy, 1995; Clapp, 1924). Another possibility is that smaller problems are easier to figure out or compute in a variety of ways. Aside from simply remembering that 2 × 3 is 6, you could also count up by 2s or 3s easily and rapidly. But counting up by 6s or 9s would take longer and be more error prone (LeFevre et al., 1996).

The point here is not to explain exactly why solving one kind of problem takes longer than another (see Ashcraft, 1995 or Geary, 1994). Instead, the point is to show how we can use time-based measures to address interesting questions about mental processing (for an exposition of how to use more than just the mean response time to explore cognition, see Balota & Yap, 2011).

ACCURACY   In addition to RT measures, we are often interested in **accuracy**, broadly defined. The earliest use of accuracy as a measure of cognition was the seminal work by Ebbinghaus, published in 1885. As you will read in Chapter 6, Ebbinghaus compared correct recall of information in a second learning session with recall of the same material during original learning as a way of measuring how much material had been saved in memory.

Figure 1-3 is a classic serial position graph, showing the percentage of items correctly recalled. The x-axis indicates each item's original position in the list. In this experiment (Glanzer & Cunitz, 1966), the list items were shown one at a time, and people had to wait 0, 10, or 30 seconds before they could

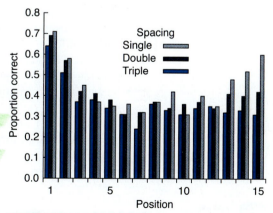

FIGURE 1-3   Serial position curves, showing the decrease in accuracy at the end of the list when 0, 10, or 30 seconds of backward counting intervenes between study and recall.

(Based on Glanzer & Cunitz, 1966.)

recall the items. Making it even more difficult, the retention interval was filled with counting backward by threes (see Chapter 5 for details). Here, it is clear that memory was influenced by an item's position in the list—recall was better for early items than for those in the middle. Also notice the big effect that delaying recall with backward counting had at late positions. So, we cannot conclude that early list items *always* had an advantage over late list items—look how accurately the very last items were recalled when there was no delay. Instead, the overall bowed shape of the graph tells us something complex and diagnostic about memory: Recalling the items from the end of the list may depend on a different kind of memory than recalling the early words, and maybe that memory that can be disrupted by activity-filled delays.

More modern variations on simple list-learning tasks look not only at proportion correct on a list, but also at incorrect responses, such as any recalled words that were not on the studied list (called *intrusions*). Did the person remember a related word such as *apple* rather than the word that was studied, *pear?* Was an item recalled because it resembles the target in some other way, such as remembering *G* instead of *D* from a string of letters? Of course, this approach is similar to the Piagetian tradition of examining children's errors in reasoning, such as failure to conserve quantity or number, to examine their cognitive processes.

In more complex situations, *accuracy* takes on richer connotations. For instance, if we ask people to read and paraphrase a paragraph, we do not score the paraphrase according to verbatim criteria. Instead, we score it based on its meaning, on how well it preserves the ideas and relationships of the original. Preserving the gist is something memory does well (e.g., Neisser, 1981). However, remembering exact, verbatim wording is something we seldom do well, perhaps because this level of detail is often not needed (see Chapter 8).

Section Summary

- Although channel capacity was an early, useful analogy in studying information processing, a more influential analogy was later drawn between humans and computers: that human mental processing might be analogous to the sequence of steps and operations in a computer program. Computers still provide an important tool for theorizing about cognitive processes.
- Measuring information processes, the mental processes of cognition, has relied heavily on time and accuracy measures. Differences in response time (RT) can yield interpretations about the speed or difficulty of mental processes, leading to inferences about cognitive processes and events. Accuracy of performance, whether it measures correct recall of a list or accurate paraphrasing of text, also offers evidence about underlying mental processes.

Explore
*Key Processes
in Stages of
Memory* in
MyPsychLab

INFORMATION PROCESSING AND COGNITIVE SCIENCE

Here we present a standard theory of human cognition along with major outlines that are widely accepted.

FIGURE 1-4 Information flow through the memory system in the Atkinson and Shiffrin (1968, 1971) model, the original standard theory in the information-processing approach.

The Standard Theory

Figure 1-4 illustrates the **standard theory** of memory (Atkinson & Shiffrin, 1968, 1971), often called the modal model. It is one of the first models to receive widespread acceptance. The basic system includes three components: **sensory memory**, **short-term memory**, and **long-term memory**. At the input end, environmental stimuli enter the system, with each sense modality having its own sensory register or memory. Some of this information is selected and forwarded to short-term memory, a temporary working memory system with several **control processes** at its disposal. The short-term store can transmit information to and retrieve information from long-term memory. It was also the component responsible for response output, for communicating with the outside world. If consciousness is anywhere in the system, it is here.

Let's use the multiplication example described earlier to trace the flow of processing through Figure 1-5. You read "2 × 3 = ?" and encode the visual stimulus into a visual sensory register; **encoding** is *the act of taking in information and converting it to a usable mental form.* Because you are paying attention, the encoded stimulus is passed to short-term memory (STM). This STM is a working memory system where the information you are aware of is held and manipulated. For this example, the system may search long-term memory (LTM) for the answer. A control process in working memory initiates this search, while others maintain the problem until processing is completed. After the memory search, LTM "sends" the answer, 6, to STM, where the final response is prepared and output, say by speech.

Each step in this sequence consumes some amount of time. By comparing these times, we start to get an idea of the underlying mental processing. As you saw in Figure 1-2, a problem such as 2 × 3 takes about 700 ms to answer, compared to more than 1,000 for 6 × 9 (values are taken from Campbell & Graham, 1985). The additional 300 ms might be due to long-term memory retrieval, say because of differences in how easily the problems can be located in LTM.

FIGURE 1-5 **A.** A general process model, adapted from Sternberg (1969). **B.** A list of the memory components and processes that operate during separate stages of the process model. **C.** A process analysis of the lexical decision task, where RT to each letter string is the sum of the durations of the separate stages. Note that for the three-word trials, the only systematic difference arises from the search stage; encoding, decision, and response times should be the same for all three-word trials, according to the logic of process models and the assumptions of sequential and independent stages of processing.

A Process Model

Although the modal model provided a useful summary, we often needed something more focused to explain our results. A common technique is to conceptualize performance in terms of a process model, a small-scale model that delineated the mental steps involved in a task and made testable predictions. Formally, a **process model** is *a hypothesis about the specific mental processes that take place when a particular task is performed.*

A PROCESS MODEL FOR LEXICAL DECISION A task that is often used in research in cognitive psychology to explore process models is the **lexical decision task**, *a timed task in which people decide whether letter strings are or are not English words* (see Meyer, Schvaneveldt, & Ruddy, 1975; this task and representative results are discussed further in Chapter 7). In this task people are shown a series of letter strings. The task is to decide on each trial whether they form a word. So, the letter string might be a word, such as MOTOR, or a nonword, such as MANTY. People are asked to respond rapidly but accurately, and response time is the main dependent measure.

Logically, what sequence of events must happen in this task? In the process model shown in Figure 1-5, the first stage involves *encoding*, taking in the visually presented letter string and transferring it to working memory. Working memory polls long-term memory to assess whether the letter string is stored there. Some kind of *search* through long-term memory takes place. The outcome of the search is returned to working memory and forms the basis for a *decision,* either "yes, it's a word," or "no, it's not." If the decision is yes, then one set of motor *responses* is prepared and executed, say, pressing the button on the left; the alternative set of responses is prepared and executed for pressing the other button.

LEXICAL DECISION AND WORD FREQUENCY   Say that our results revealed a relationship between RT and the frequency of the words (word frequency is almost always an influence on RT in lexical decision). We might test words at low, medium, and high levels of frequency in the language: ROBIN occurs infrequently, about twice per million words; MOTOR is of moderate frequency, occurring 56 times per million; and OFFICE is of high frequency, occurring 255 times per million (Kucera & Francis, 1967; the most frequent printed word in English is THE, occurring 69,971 times per million). *It takes longer to judge words of lower frequency than higher-frequency words* (Allen & Madden, 1990; Whaley, 1978). This is the **word frequency effect**. Other variables also affect response times, but word frequency is enough for our example.

For the sake of argument, say that average responses to low-frequency words, such as ROBIN, took 650 ms; those to medium-frequency words, such as MOTOR, took 600 ms; and those to high-frequency words such as OFFICE took 550 ms. What does the process model in Figure 1-5 tell us about such a result? Logically, we would not expect that word encoding would be influenced by frequency, with high-frequency words being easier to see. So, we assume that encoding is unaffected by word frequency and is relatively constant.

Likewise, all three cases will net a successful search. So, we would not expect time differences in the decision stage because the decision is the same (yes). And finally, "yes" responses should all take about the same amount of time for any word. Thus, the encoding, decision, and response stage times are constants, regardless of word frequency.

The only stage left is the search stage. On reflection, this seems likely to be influenced by word frequency. For instance, it could easily be that words used more frequently are stored more strongly in memory, or stored repeatedly (e.g., Logan, 1988); either possibility could yield shorter search times. Thus, we can tentatively conclude that word frequency has an effect on the search stage. Any factor that affects long-term memory search should influence this stage and should produce a time or accuracy difference. Using the numbers from earlier, the search process would take an extra 50 ms for each change from high to medium to low word frequency.

Revealing Assumptions

There are several assumptions that are made when doing a process analysis. It is important for you to understand such assumptions to better appreciate how theories and models of cognition are derived. We'll use the foregoing example as a guide.

The first was the assumption of **sequential stages of processing**. It was assumed that there is *a sequence of stages or processes,* such as those depicted in

Figure 1-5, *that occur on every trial, a set of stages that completely account for mental processing.* Importantly, the order of the stages was treated as fixed on the grounds that each stage provides a result that is used for the next one. More to the point, this assumption implies that one and only one stage can be done at a time, which may not be the case in reality. The influence of the computer analogy is very clear here. Computers have achieved high speeds of operation, but are largely serial processors: They do operations one by one, in a sequential order. And yet there is no *a priori* reason to expect that human cognition has this quality in all situations.

The second assumption is that the stages were **independent and non-overlapping**. That is, *any single stage was assumed to finish its operation before the next stage could begin, and the duration of any single stage had no bearing or influence on the others.* Thus, at the beginning of a trial, encoding starts, completes its operations, and passes its result to the search stage. Then and only then could the search stage begin, followed after its completion by the decision and response stages. With these assumptions, the total time for a trial could be interpreted as the sum of the durations for each stage; because mental processes take time and because each stage is a separate, the total time could be viewed as the sum of the times for all the individual stages. In our earlier example, then, the 50-ms differences between ROBIN, MOTOR, and OFFICE were attributed to the search stage.

PARALLEL PROCESSING   As research has been done, evidence has accumulated that casts doubt on the assumptions of serial, nonoverlapping stages of processing. Instead, there is some evidence that multiple mental processes can operate *simultaneously*—which is termed **parallel processing**. One example involves typing. Salthouse (1984) did a study of how skilled typists type and how performance changes with age. His data argued for a four-process model; the input stage encoded the to-be-typed material, a parsing stage broke large reading units (words) into separate characters, a translation stage transformed the characters into finger movements, and an execution stage triggered the keystrokes. Significantly, his evidence indicated that these stages operate in parallel: While one letter is typed, another is translated into a finger movement, and the input stage is encoding upcoming letters, even as many as eight characters in advance of the one being typed. Moreover, older adults counteracted the tendency toward slower finger movements by increasing their "look ahead" span at the upcoming letters (see Townsend & Wenger, 2004, for a thorough discussion of serial versus parallel processing).

In moving away from the simpler computer analogy, the cognitive science approach embraced the ideas that cognition needs to be understood with some reference to the brain. An important lesson we have learned from neuroscience is that the brain shows countless ways in which different cognitive components and processes operate simultaneously, in parallel. Furthermore, there is now ample neurological evidence that different regions of the brain are more specialized for different processing tasks, such as encoding, responding, memory retrieval, and controlling the stream of thought (Anderson, Qin, Jung, & Carter, 2007).

CONTEXT EFFECTS A second difficulty with the early assumptions of sequential stages and nonoverlapping processes arose when **context effects** were taken into account. A simple example of this is the speedup in deciding—that you are faster to decide MOTOR is a word if you have seen MOTOR recently (see "repetition priming" in Chapters 6 and 7). A more compelling demonstration comes from work on lexical ambiguity—the fact that many words have more than one meaning. As an example, Simpson (1981) had people do a modified lexical decision task, judging letter strings such as DUKE or MONEY (or MANTY or ZOOPLE) after they had read a context sentence. When the letter string and sentence were related—for instance, "The vampire was disguised as a handsome count," followed by DUKE—the lexical decision on DUKE was faster than normal. The reason involved priming (see Chapters 6 and 7), the idea that concepts in memory become activated and hence easier to process. In this case, because the context sentence primed the royalty sense of the word *count*, the response time to DUKE was speeded up.

This was an issue for earlier cognitive models because there was no mechanism to account for priming. Look again at Figure 1-5; is there any component that allows a context sentence to influence the speed of the processes? No, you need a meaning-based component to keep track of recently activated meanings that would speed up the search process when meanings matched but not when they were unrelated.

Let's look more deeply at the influence of context on cognition. Information that is active in long-term memory, for example, can easily have an effect *right now* on sensory memory, the input stage for external stimuli. Here is a simple example:

> As you read a sentence or paragraph, you begin to develop a feel for its meaning. Often you understand well enough that you can then skim through the rest of the material, possibly reading so rapidly that lower-level processes such as proofreading and noticing typograpical errors may not function as accurately as they usually do. *Did you see the mistake?*

What? Mistake? If you fell for it, you failed to notice the missing *h* in the word *typographical*, possibly because you were skimming but probably because the word *typographical* was expected, predictable based on meaning. You may have even "seen" the missing *h* in a sense. Why? Because your understanding of the passage, its meaningfulness to you, may have been strong enough that the missing *h* was supplied by your long-term memory.

We call such influences **top-down** or **conceptually driven processing** *when existing context or knowledge influences earlier or simpler forms of mental processes.* It's one of the recurring themes in cognition (see Table 1-2). For another example, adapted from Reed (1992), read the following sentence:

FINISHED FILES ARE THE RESULT OF YEARS OF SCIENTIFIC STUDY COMBINED WITH THE EXPERIENCE OF MANY YEARS.

Now, read it a second time, counting the number of times the letter F occurs.

If you counted fewer than six, try again—and again, if necessary. Why is this difficult? Because you know that function words such as *of* carry very little meaning, your perceptual, input processes are prompted to pay attention only to the content words. Ignoring function words, and consequently failing to see the letter *F* in a word such as OF, is a clear-cut example of conceptually driven processing (for an explanation of the "missing letter effect," see Greenberg, Healy, Koriat, & Kreiner, 2004).

OTHER ISSUES   Another issue involves other, often slower mental processes that cognitive psychology is interested in. Some process models are aimed at accuracy-based investigations—percentage correct or the nature of one's errors in recall. In a similar vein, many cognitive processes are slower and more complex. As you will learn in Chapters 11 and 12, studies of decision making and problem solving often involve processing that takes *much* longer than most RT tasks; for example, some cryptarithmetic problems (substitute digits for letters in the problem SEND + MORE; see Chapter 12) can take 15 to 20 minutes! A more meaningful measure of these mental processes involve a verbal report or **verbal protocol** procedure, in which people *verbalize their thoughts as they solve the problems.* This type of measure in cognitive research is less widely used than time and accuracy measures, but is important nonetheless (see Ericsson & Simon, 1980 for the usefulness of verbal protocols).

Cognitive Science

Cognitive psychology is now firmly embedded in a larger, multidisciplinary effort, focused on the study of mind. This broader perspective is called *cognitive science.* As noted earlier, cognitive science draws from, and influences, a variety of disciplines such as computer science, linguistics, and neuroscience, and even such far-flung fields as law and anthropology (e.g., Spellman & Busey, 2010). It is a true study of the mind, in a broad sense, as illustrated in Figure 1-6. In general, cognitive science is *the study of thought, using available scientific techniques and including all relevant scientific disciplines for exploring and investigating cognition.* One of the strongest contributions to this expanded body of evidence has been the consideration of the neurological bases and processes that underlie thought. We devote all of Chapter 2 to these neurological issues.

Section Summary

- The modal model of memory suggested that mental processing can be understood as a sequence of independent processing stages, such as the sensory, short-term, and long-term memory stages.
- Process models are appropriate for fairly simple, rapid tasks that are measured by response times, such as the lexical decision task.
- There is substantial evidence to suggest that cognition involves parallel processing and is influenced by context; for example, research on skilled typing

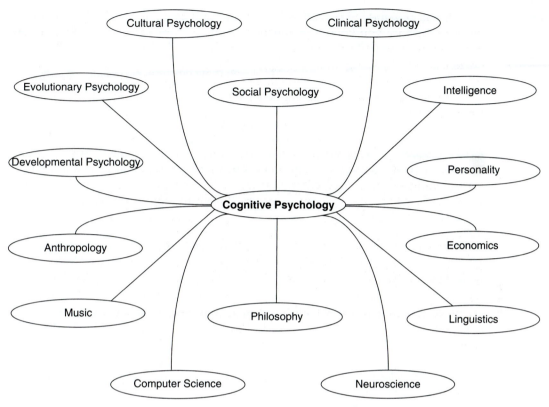

FIGURE 1-6 Cognitive psychology and the various fields of psychology and other disciplines to which it is related.

shows a high degree of parallel processing. Also, slower, more complex mental processes, such as those in the study of decision making and problem solving, may be studied using verbal protocols.

- Cognitive psychology is better understood as residing within the context of a broader cognitive science. This approach describes cognition as the coordinated, often parallel operation of mental processes within a multicomponent system. The approach is deliberately multidisciplinary, accepting evidence from all the sciences interested in cognition.

THEMES

Across the various topics in cognition, there are a number of themes that appear repeatedly. You won't find sections in this text labeled with them. Instead, they crop up across several areas of cognitive science, in different contexts. If you can read a chapter and identify and discuss the themes that pertain to it, then you probably have a good understanding of the material. Table 1-2 provides a list and brief description of seven important themes that occur throughout the text.

TABLE 1-2   Seven Themes of Cognition

Attention. This is an all-important but poorly understood mental process. It is limited in quantity, essential to most processing, but only partially under our control. Is it a mechanism? A limited pool of mental resources? If attention controls mental processing, what controls attention? Why do some processes occur automatically, whereas others require conscious, attentive processing? How does attention make some things more available in mind, and others less so?

Data-driven processing versus conceptually driven processing. Some processes rely heavily on information from the environment (data-driven or bottom-up processing). Others rely heavily on our existing knowledge (conceptually driven or top-down processing). Conceptually driven processing can be so powerful that we often make errors, from mistakes in perception up through mistakes in reasoning. But could we function without it?

Representation. How is information mentally represented? Can different kinds of knowledge all be formatted in the same mental code, or are there separate codes for the different types of knowledge? How do we use different types of representation together?

Implicit versus explicit memory. We have direct and explicit awareness of certain types of memories; you remember the experience of buying this text, for example. But some processes are implicit; they are there but not necessarily with conscious awareness. This raises all sorts of interesting issues about the unconscious and its role in cognition; for instance, how do unconscious processes affect your behavior and thinking?

Metacognition. This is our awareness of our own thoughts, cognition, knowledge, and insight into how the system works. It is the awareness that prompts us to write reminders to ourselves to avoid forgetting. How accurate is this awareness and knowledge? Does it sometimes mislead us?

Brain. Far more than the cognitive psychology of the past, brain–cognition relationships and questions are a primary concern. It is important to understand how our neural hardware works to produce the kinds of thinking that we are capable of, and what its limitations are.

Embodiment. An emerging awareness in cognitive psychology is that the way we think about and represent information reflects the fact that we need to interact physically with the world—it's called "embodied cognition." How do we capture the world in our mental life? How do the ways that our bodies interact with the world influence our thinking? How do we incorporate and take into account physical realities in how we think about and process information?

Key Terms

accuracy (p. *21*)
attention (p. *30*)
behaviorism (p. *12*)
channel capacity (p. *18*)
cognition (p. *6*)
cognitive psychology
   (p. *5*)
cognitive revolution
   (p. *2*)
cognitive science (p. *2*)
computer analogy
   (p. *19*)
conceptually driven
   processing (p. *27*)

context effects (p. *27*)
control processes
   (p. *23*)
data-driven processing
   (p. *30*)
ecological validity (p. *7*)
embodiment (p. *30*)
empiricism (p. *9*)
encoding (p. *23*)
functionalism (p. *11*)
independent and
   nonoverlapping
   (p. *26*)
introspection (p. *9*)

lexical decision task
   (p. *24*)
long-term memory
   (p. *23*)
memory (p. *6*)
metacognition (p. *30*)
parallel processing
   (p. *26*)
process model (p. *24*)
reductionism (p. *7*)
response time (RT)
   (p. *20*)
sensory memory
   (p. *23*)

sequential stages
   of processing
   (p. *25*)
short-term memory
   (p. *23*)
standard theory
   (p. *23*)
structuralism (p. *10*)
tabula rasa (p. *9*)
verbal learning (p. *14*)
verbal protocol
   (p. *28*)
word frequency effect
   (p. *25*)

2

Cognitive Neuroscience and Cognitive Science

How can a three-pound mass of jelly that you can hold in your palm imagine angels, contemplate the meaning of infinity, and even question its own place in the cosmos? Especially awe inspiring is the fact that any single brain, including yours, is made up of atoms that were forged in the hearts of countless, far-flung stars billions of years ago. These particles drifted for eons and light-years until gravity and change brought them together here, now. These atoms now form a conglomerate—your brain—that can not only ponder the very stars that gave it birth but can also think about its own ability to think and wonder about its own ability to wonder. With the arrival of humans, it has been said, the universe has suddenly become conscious of itself. This, truly, it the greatest mystery of all.

(RAMACHANDRAN, 2011, PP. 4–5)

As noted in Chapter 1, an important aspect of modern cognitive science is an understanding of neural processes and how they relate to thought. In Chapter 2, we provide you with a basic understanding of the fundamental principles of neural processing, and various brain structures that are important for a wide range of cognitive processes. We begin with an exposition of the characteristics of individual neurons, how they communicate information, and the influence of some basic classes of neurotransmitters. After this we provide an overview of various structures of the brain and outline the major regions of the cortex. This is followed by coverage of some of the major methods of assessing how the neural processing corresponds to cognitive processing. Finally, we discuss a computational approach, called neural network or connectionist modeling, which tries to capture the basic principles of neural processing in computer-based mathematical models of thought.

COGNITIVE NEUROSCIENCE: THE BRAIN AND COGNITION TOGETHER

We start with a stunning story of cognitive disruption to motivate our interest in cognitive neuroscience. Tulving (1989) described a patient he called K. C., a young man who sustained brain damage in a motorcycle accident. Some nine years after the accident, he still showed pervasive disruption of long-term memory. The fascinating thing about his memory impairment was that it was selective: K. C. remains perfectly competent at language, his intelligence is normal, and he is able to converse on a number of topics. But when he is asked about an experience from his own past, he doesn't remember; in Tulving's words, "he cannot remember, in the sense of bringing back to conscious awareness, a single thing that he has ever done or experienced in the past" (p. 362). For example, even though he remembers how to play chess, he does not remember ever having played it before. He knows his family had a vacation house on a lake, but he doesn't have any recollections of being there. K. C.'s brain damage seemed to destroy his ability to access what we'll call episodic memory, his own autobiographical knowledge, while leaving his general knowledge system—his semantic memory—intact. This pattern is called a **dissociation**, *a disruption in one component of mental functioning but no impairment of another.* Can these two forms of long-term memory, episodic and semantic memory, be the same, given K. C.'s dissociation between the two? Probably not. So we now ask a more general question: How must the cognition be organized neurologically for disruptions such as these to take place?

As important as the evidence from brain damage is, we also need other kinds of evidence—for example, information about the neurochemical and neurobiological activities that support normal learning and thought, or about the changes in the brain that accompany aging. We are therefore interested in contributions from all the various neurosciences—neurochemistry, neurobiology, neuroanatomy, and so on—as they relate to human cognition.

Understanding cognitive handicaps is an obvious goal; no one can dispute the importance of rehabilitation and retraining for patients with brain damage. But our interest in cognitive science goes a step further. We want to understand *normal* cognition from the standpoint of the human brain. That is, we want to learn

IN DEPTH
Dissociations and Double Dissociations

The concept of dissociation—the opposite of association—is important, so we should spend a little more time on it.

Consider two mental processes that "go together" in some cognitive task, called process A and process B. By looking at these processes as they may be disrupted in brain damage, we can determine how separable the processes are.

Complete separation is a double dissociation. Evidence of a double dissociation requires at least two patients, with "opposite" or reciprocal deficits. For example,

- Patient X has a brain lesion that has disrupted process A. His performance on tasks that use process B is intact, not disrupted at all.
- Patient Y has a lesion that has damaged process B, but tasks that use process A are normal, not disrupted by the damage.

Think of a double dissociation as illustrated in this simple diagram and refer back to it later in the text as you read about processes that are dissociated. If these circles depicted actual brain regions, such as those used in language processes (Chapter 9), then damage to either one of them could easily leave the other one unaffected.

- In a simple dissociation, process A could be damaged while process B remains intact, yet no other known patient has the reciprocal pattern. For example, semantic retrieval (retrieving the meaning of a concept) could be intact while lexical retrieval (finding the name for the concept) could be disrupted; this is called anomia (see Chapter 7). In this situation, lexical retrieval is dissociated from semantic retrieval, but it is probably impossible to observe the opposite pattern; how can you name a concept if you can't retrieve the concept in the first place?
- In a full or complete association (lack of dissociation), disruption of one of the processes always accompanies disruption in the other process. This pattern implies that processes A and B rely on the same region or brain mechanism, such as recognizing objects and recognizing pictures of those objects (see Chapter 3).

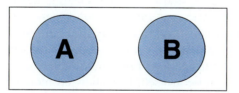

---

about normal cognition through any means available. Toward this goal, more and more investigators are examining the behavioral and cognitive effects of brain damage (e.g., McCloskey, 1992), using those observations to develop and refine theories of normal cognition (Martin, 2000). As you will see throughout this text, sometimes the great misfortune of brain damage leads to a clearer understanding of normal processes.

Likewise, cognitive science is now putting to good use the new, high-tech brain imaging capabilities we have adopted from medicine. We can now use brain images based on positron emission tomography (PET) scans and magnetic resonance imaging (MRI) to localize regions of activity during different kinds of cognitive processing, testing not just brain-damaged individuals but normal, intact ones as well (see Poldrack & Wagner, 2004; Sarter, Berntson, & Cacioppo, 1996).

Just as the cognitive influence on neuroscience has been a rejuvenating one, the cross-fertilization for cognition has been crucial and will become more so with time. What has become clear is that cognition and neuroscience are highly interlinked. This is particularly evident when you consider how embodied views of cognition critically depend on neurological accounts of perceptual and motor process and how they influence even seemingly abstract tasks, such as using semantic memory or solving problems (Marshall, 2009). We focus only on a few of the many highlights in the interrelation of cognition and neuroscience.

NEURONS: THE BASIC BUILDING BLOCKS

Basic Neurology

At birth, the human brain weighs approximately 400 g (about 14 oz). It grows to an average of 1,450 g in adults, slightly more than 3 lb, and is roughly the size of a ripe grapefruit. The basic building block of the brain, indeed of the entire nervous system, is the **neuron**, *a cell that is specialized for receiving and transmitting a neural impulse.* Neurons are the components that form nerve tracts throughout the body and in all brain structures. How many neurons are there in the brain? Available estimates vary. Williams and Herrup (1988) reported that there are about 100 billion neurons in the brain, although humans will lose about 10% of this mass over the course of a lifetime. To put that figure in perspective, consider that the Milky Way galaxy has about 100 billion stars. Moreover, there is a very high degree of interconnectivity in the brain among these cells, with these neurons making about 100 trillion connections. Talk about a complex mental machine. Note that there are many additional cells of other types in the brain, including glial cells and connective and circulatory tissue.

Neurons

Figure 2-1A illustrates an idealized or prototypical neuron. The details of structure vary, but each neuron within the nervous system has the same general features. At one end of the neuron, many small branchlike fingers called **dendrites** gather a neural impulse into the neuron itself. In somewhat more familiar terms, the dendrites are the *input* structures of the neuron, taking in the message that is being passed along in a particular neural tract.

The central portion of each neuron is the cell body, or **soma**, where the biological activity of the cell is regulated. Extending from the cell body is a longish extension or tube, the **axon**, which ends in another set of branchlike structures called *axon terminals* or sometimes *terminal arborizations;* the latter term derives from the tree-like form of these structures. The axon terminals are the *output* end of the neuron, the place where the neural impulse ends within the neuron itself. Obviously, this is the location where an influence on the next neuron in the pathway must take place.

Some neurons also have a fatty coating on the axon. This coating is called the **myelin sheath**, and this serves as an insulator for the axon. The myelin sheath is typically not continuous, but has gaps along the way. These gaps are

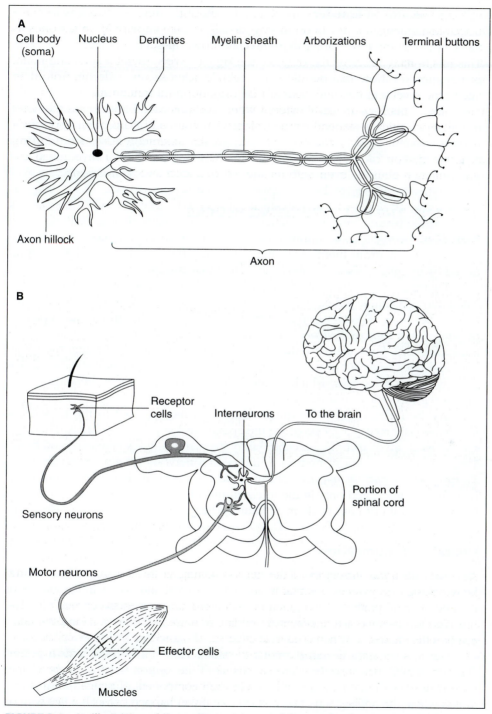

FIGURE 2-1 An illustration of the various structures of the neuron. Note that the lower diagram illustrates a sensory–motor reflex arc.

called the **nodes of Ranvier**. An important job of the myelin sheath is to speed neural communication. It can do this by having a nerve impulse jump from one of these nodes to the next, rather than traveling down the entire length of the axon. This functionally shortens the distance the signal travels, thereby speeding neural communication. Note that people with multiple sclerosis are suffering from damage to the myelin that would normally be present on their neurons.

Not all neurons are myelinated. Often, myelin is found in neurons that need to transmit signals a relatively long distance, such as out in the periphery of the nervous system. Most of the cortical neurons that cognition arises from are not myelinated. You can easily see differences between bundles of myelinated and unmyelinated neurons even without the aid of a microscope. Neurons that have myelin sheaths appear to be white, because the myelin is made of fat, whereas neurons that do not have a myelin sheath appear to be gray. So, when people talk about "white matter" and "gray matter' in a person's brain, they are talking about bundles of myelinated and unmyelinated neurons, respectively. Also, it should be noted that the neurons themselves do not produce the myelin. Instead, this is produced by the glial cells in the nervous system that support the neurons.

Figure 2-1B is a diagram of the elements of the nervous system that are activated during a simple reflex, such as jerking your arm away when you accidentally touch a hot stove. *Receptor cells* react to the physical stimulus and trigger a pattern of firing down *sensory neurons*. These neuron tracts pass the message along into the spinal cord. For a simple reflex, the message loops quickly through the spinal cord and goes back out to the arm muscles through a tract of *motor neurons* that terminate at *effector cells,* which connect directly to the muscle fibers and cause the muscles to pull your arm away.

As the reflex triggers the quick return of a message out to the muscles, it simultaneously routes a message up the spinal cord and into the brain. Thus, the second route involves only the central nervous system—the spinal cord and brain. There is only one kind of neuron in the central nervous system, called an *interneuron* or *association neuron*. Because we are concerned only with the brain here, we are interested only in the interneurons of the central nervous system. For simplicity, we'll just refer to them as neurons here.

Neural Communication

As noted earlier, the primary job of neuron is to communicate information. This is done by two basic components, one that is primarily electrical and occurs in the interior of the neuron, and another that is primarily chemical and occurs between neurons. The first type involves the action potential and is discussed in this section, and the other involves the synapse and neurotransmitters and is discussed in the following sections.

Again, the electrical part of neural communication is called the **action potential**, which is a change in the electrical charge of the neuron (relative to the charge outside of it). We're all familiar with the electrical component of neural transmission. This is where the tingling sensation comes from if you happen to touch a live wire or touch your tongue on both poles at the end of a 9-volt battery. When a neuron is not being stimulated, it has a resting electrical charge of −70 mV (millivolts). When a neuron is stimulated, there is a depolarization of its electrical potential, and the neuron is said to "fire" (see Figure 2-2). At this point there is a change in the charge of the neuron to +40 mV. Note that the entire neuron does not change its electrical charge. Instead, the action potential is **propagated** from the dendrites down the axon over time, almost like a wave of electrical charge. After the neuron has fired, there is a recovery period where the neuron resets itself and is ready to fire again. It should be noted that action potentials follow the **all-or-none principle**. That is, there is either an action potential, which is always the same anywhere in the nervous system, or there is no action potential. It is *not* the case that some action potentials are larger or smaller than others.

FIGURE 2-2 Action potential.

Be aware that an action potential does not occupy the entire body of the neuron at once. Instead, a wave of electrical charge flows down the axon, with sodium ions entering the interior of the cell as the ion gates on the cell membrane open in sequence. These sodium ions have a positive electrical charge, thereby causing the action potential to be electrically positive. Behind this wave of sodium ions, there is a second wave of potassium ions being forced out of the cell. Potassium is also positively charged. However, because it is being pushed out of the neuron, it renders the base charge of the neuron negative again.

There may be relatively few or many axon terminals emanating from a single neuron. In either case, these terminals in the brain are adjacent to dendrites from many other neurons. Thus, the impulse of the action potential within a neuron terminates at the axon terminals and is taken up by the dendrites of the next neurons in the pathway, the neurons whose dendrites are adjacent to the axon terminals. The *region where the axon terminals of one neuron and the dendrites of another come together* is the **synapse**. For the most part, the neurons do not actually touch one another (some regions of the brain contradict this rule). They are essentially islands unto themselves. The synapses in the nervous system are extremely small physical gaps or clefts between the neurons. Each synapse is 100 to 200 angstroms wide, with an angstrom being one ten-thousandth of a millimeter. Note that the word *synapse* is also used as a verb: A neuron is said to synapse on another, meaning that it passes its message on to that other neuron.

A general law of the nervous system, especially in the brain, is that any single neuron synapses on a large number of other neurons. The evidence for this *divergence* is that a typical neuron synapses on anywhere from 100 to as many as 15,000 other neurons. Likewise, many different neurons can synapse on a single destination neuron, a principle known as *convergence*. So, as you can see, there is a great deal of complexity in how neurons connect to one another. This complexity is important in regulating the flow of the vast different types of knowledge that our brains need to handle at any one time.

Explore
*Neuronal
Transmission* in
MyPsychLab

For the bulk of the nervous system, the bridge across the synaptic cleft involves chemical activity within the synaptic cleft itself. A neuron releases a chemical transmitter substance, or simply a *neurotransmitter,* from small *buttons* or *sacs* in the axon terminals. This chemical fits into specific receptor sites on the dendrites of the next neuron and thereby causes some effect on that next neuron. The relationship between those chemicals and the receptor sites is like a key-and-lock system in which different chemicals bond only with certain receptor sites. Two general effects of these chemicals are possible, excitation and inhibition. That is, the effect can be excitatory, in which the neurotransmitters encourage the next neuron to fire, or they can be inhibitory, in which the neurotransmitters encourage the postsynaptic neuron to not fire.

So, why do we have both excitatory and inhibitory neurotransmitters? One reason is that one of the ways that the nervous system codes information is by the pattern of activation across a wide set of neurons, with some neurons needing to fire and others not. As a rough analogy, computers code information as a pattern of 1s (on) and 0s (off), although the nervous system does this differently and with much greater complexity. You really don't want to have all of your neurons firing at once. This would be like having all of the bits in your computer set to 1; it doesn't convey any meaningful information. The closest your brain gets to having all of the neurons fire is if you have a seizure.

It is also important to keep in mind that neurotransmitters do not operate alone, but work in conjunction with other chemicals, such as with neuromodulators, which accentuate or diminish the effects of neurotransmitters. For example, a neuromodulator may accentuate the effect of a neurotransmitter, making an excitatory neurotransmitter more excitatory, or making an inhibitory neurotransmitter more inhibitory. Conversely, a neuromodulator may diminish the effect of a neurotransmitter, making an excitatory neurotransmitter less excitatory, or making an inhibitory neurotransmitter less inhibitory. The operation of such neuromodulators is just one of the many ways that the human brain differs from a computer and illustrates some of the limitations of the computer analogy of human cognition.

By some counts, more than 100 different neurotransmitters have been identified in the human brain. Many seem to have rather ordinary functions, maintaining the physical integrity of the living organism, for instance. Others, especially **acetylcholine** and possibly **norepinephrine**, seem to have major influences on cognitive processes such as learning and memory (Drachman, 1978; Sitaran, Weingartner, Caine, & Gillin, 1978; Squire, 1987). For example, acetylcholine can enhance memory (Mishkin & Appenzellar, 1987). Acetylcholine may do this by enhancing the strength of synaptic potentials during long-term potentiation (see later discussion). Also, decreased levels of acetylcholine have been found in the brains of people with Alzheimer's disease, with very low levels of acetylcholine associated with more severe dementia (Samuel, 1999). It is tempting to suggest this as part of the explanation for the learning and memory deficits observed among such patients, although it could be a side effect of the disease instead of a cause (e.g., Banich, 2004; Riley, 1989). In either case, the result suggests that acetylcholine plays some kind of essential role in normal learning and memory processes.

Another important neurotransmitter for human cognition is **glutamate**, which is an excitatory neurotransmitter. This is important for creating or strengthening the connections between neurons. This is how we learn, by changing how neurons are connected to one another, and glutamate is an important neurotransmitter for doing this. An important neurotransmitter that is derived from glutamate is *gamma-aminobutyric acid*. However, rather than remembering such a long name, most neuroscientists simply refer to this neurotransmitter as **GABA**. GABA is an inhibitory neurotransmitter that works by weakening the connections between neurons, and so, in some sense, it is the opposite of glutamate.

Neurons and Learning

So, what exactly is changed by these neurotransmitters when learning occurs? Although it is not completely understood, the basic process is something called **long-term potentiation (LTP)** (Bliss & Collingridge, 1993; Bliss & Lomo, 1973; Gustafsson & Wigstrom, 1988). LTP is the process by which connections between neurons are strengthened. This strengthening essentially changes the ease with which two connected neurons will fire. More specifically, how strongly the presynaptic neuron encourages the postsynaptic neuron to fire is a function of LTP.

Let's look at the processes that bring about LTP during learning in a bit more detail, following work done by Pittenger and Kandel (2003). The process described here is illustrated in Figure 2-3. When a neuron is stimulated, it can release glutamate into the synapse. This is taken up by the next neuron. Some of these glutamate neurons are taken up by what are known as *AMPA receptors*. These are fast-acting receptor sites that will result in a depolarization of the neuron at that particular moment and may cause it to fire. What is more interesting here is that some of the glutamate

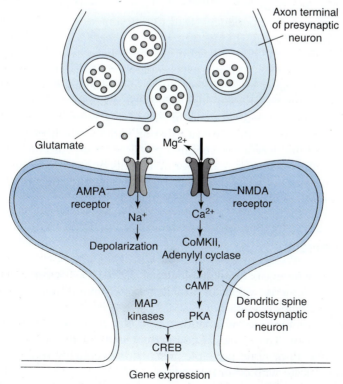

FIGURE 2-3 Short- and long-term effects of glutamate on a postsynaptic neuron, which can result in LTP.

will also be taken up by what are known as *NMDA receptors*. The consequence of these is a series of chemical and genetic reactions that ultimately results in the creation of new AMPA receptors. When these new AMPA receptors do is to make it more likely that the neuron will take up glutamate that is released in the future, making it more likely that the neuron will fire. In other words, a simple way of thinking about this is that the AMPA receptors cause the neuron to fire, but the NMDA receptors lead to a strengthening of the connection between the neurons. This idea of changing the strength of the connection between neurons will be important when we discuss the development of connectionist models of cognition later in the chapter.

Often LTP can last for days or weeks. However, we need to be able to remember things for longer periods of time. This is accomplished by a process known as **consolidation** (Abraham, 2006), which takes place over long periods of time lasting days, weeks, and years. Consolidation makes memories more and more permanent over time. Interestingly, this consolidation process can be aided by one of the processes that occur when we sleep. People have been shown to remember more information if they slept during the delay between study and test than if they had not (Hu, Stylos-Allan, & Walker, 2006), particularly if they experienced slow-wave (stages 3 and 4) sleep, as compared to REM (dreaming) sleep (Rasch & Born, 2008).

At a small scale, LTP captures change in individual neural connections. At a larger scale, consolidation captures changes in assemblies of neurons over long periods of time. At an even larger scale, changes in brain connections as a result of experience lead to different ways of processing information over a person's lifetime, even to the point where different cultures—and hence different collections and complexes of experience—lead to different ways of neurologically processing information (Park & Huang, 2010).

Before we leave the neural level of the nervous system, note that significant research is being done on various psycho-biochemical properties of the neural system, such as the direct influence of various chemical agents on neurotransmitters and the resulting behavioral changes. As an example, Abraham (2006) and Thompson (1986) described progress in identifying neural changes believed to underlie memory storage and retrieval. Just as various psychoactive drugs affect the functioning of the nervous system in a physical sense, current research is now identifying the effects of drugs and other treatments on the functioning of the nervous system in a psychological or cognitive sense (e.g., the effect of alcohol intoxication; Nelson, McSpadden, Fromme, & Marlatt, 1986).

Section Summary

- Neurons are the basic building blocks of the nervous system. Understanding how these elements work can provide a better understanding of the machinery that underlies cognition.
- Neurons communicate information via an electrical component and a chemical component. The electrical component is the action potential by which, obeying the all-or-none principle, a signal is eventually sent down the axon to communicate with other neurons.
- The chemical component involves neurotransmitters released at the synapse. There are a wide variety of neurotransmitters, each involved in a different

type of neural process. Some of these neurotransmitters are excitatory, stimulating the postsynaptic neuron, and some are inhibitory, suppressing the postsynaptic neuron.

- Information is stored in the nervous system via a pattern of interconnections among neurons and how strong these interconnections are. Early on in memory formation, adjustments to this pattern are affected by processes such as long-term potentiation, but later memory solidification is affected by a process of consolidation.

NEUROANATOMY: IMPORTANT PARTS OF THE BRAIN

Brain Anatomy

Ignoring many levels of intermediate neural functioning and complexity, we now take a tremendous leap from the level of single neurons to the level of the entire brain, the awesomely complex "biological computer." To account for all human behavior, including bodily functions that occur involuntarily (e.g., digestion), entails an extensive discussion of the central and peripheral nervous systems. But to explore cognitive neuroscience, we can limit ourselves to just the central nervous system—the brain and spinal cord. In fact, our discussion even omits much of the central nervous system, save for the **neocortex** (or cerebral cortex), which sits at the top of the human brain, and a few other nearby structures.

In Figure 2-4, the physically lower brain structures are collectively called the old brain or brain stem. This portion of the brain is older in terms of evolution, for

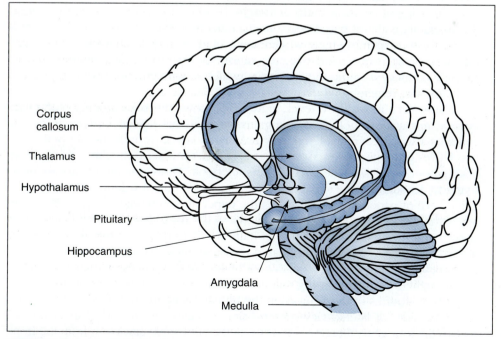

FIGURE 2-4 Lower brain structures.

the most part governing basic, primitive functions (e.g., digestion, heartbeat, and breathing). The old brain structures are present in even very primitive animals.

There are a number of these subcortical (meaning "below the cortex") structures that are important in understanding cognition. Let's consider four of them here. First, deep inside the brain is the **thalamus**, meaning "inner room" or "chamber." It is often called the gateway to the cortex because almost all messages entering the cortex come through the thalamus (a portion of the olfactory sense of smell is one of the very few exceptions). In other words, the thalamus is the major relay station from the sensory systems of the body into the neocortex. The ability to coordinate information from different parts of the brain, such as remembering what was said and who said it, involves effective functioning in the thalamus.

Just above the thalamus is a broad band of nerve fibers called the **corpus callosum**. As described later, the corpus callosum ("callous body") is the primary bridge across which messages pass between the left and right halves—the hemispheres—of the cortex. This is the broadband connection of the brain that allows the two halves to communicate and pass information between each other.

The third structure is the **hippocampus**, from the Latin word for "sea horse," referring to its curved shape. The hippocampus is located immediately interior to the temporal lobes, that is, underneath the temporal lobes but in the same horizontal plane. Research on the effects of hippocampal damage is described later in the text (especially in Chapter 6), including one of the best-known case histories in cognitive neuroscience, that of patient H. M. The hippocampus is crucially important in long-term memory processes, especially for memories that are conscious.

Finally, a fourth structure that will be mentioned from time to time in this text, especially in Chapter 13, is the **amygdala**. This is an almond-shaped structure adjacent to one end of the hippocampus. The amygdala is critically important in the processing of emotional information in the brain. One of the unique aspects of the amygdala is that it gets nearly direct inputs from the olfactory nerves (Herz & Engen, 1996), which is why how something smells can be strongly associated with emotional responses (e.g., love, relaxation, or disgust). The amygdala is also strongly connected to the hippocampus, which is why emotional experience can sometimes be remembered very well.

Now, let's move up a level. Figure 2-5 shows the **neocortex**, or **cerebral cortex**, *the top layer of the brain, responsible for higher-level mental processes*. The cortex is a wrinkled, convoluted structure that nearly surrounds the old brain. The two halves or hemispheres cover about 2,500 cm^2 and are from about 1.5 to 3 mm thick, about as thick as the cover of this textbook. The wrinkling comes about by trying to get such a large surface area in a small volume. It is kind of like trying to get a piece of paper into a cup. To get the paper in, you wrinkle it up. The neocortex is the most recent structure to have evolved in the human brain (*neo* means "new") and is much larger in humans than in other animals; compare the average weight in humans, 1,450 g, with that in the great apes, 400 g. In addition, because the neocortex is primarily responsible for higher mental processes such as language and thought, it is not surprising that it is so large relative to the rest of the brain— about three-fourths of the neurons in the human brain are in the neocortex.

The side, or lateral, view (*lateral* simply means "to the side") in Figure 2-5 reveals the four general regions, or *lobes,* of the neocortex; clockwise from the front,

Simulate
*The Human
Cerebrum* in
MyPsychLab

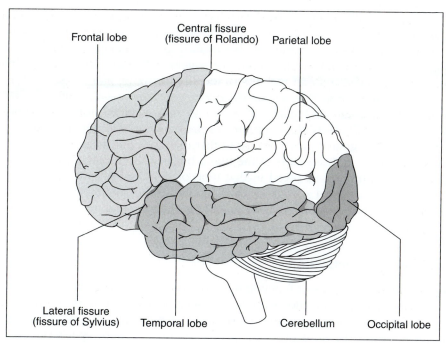

Frontal lobe

**Central fissure
(fissure of Rolando)**

Parietal lobe

**Lateral fissure
(fissure of Sylvius)**   **Temporal lobe**   **Cerebellum**   **Occipital lobe**

FIGURE 2-5   The four lobes of the neocortex.

these are the **frontal lobe**, **parietal lobe**, **occipital lobe**, and **temporal lobe**, named after the skull bones on top of them (e.g., the temporal lobes lie beneath your temples). Note that these lobes are not separate from one another in the brain. Instead, each hemisphere of the neocortex is a single sheet of neural tissue. The lobes are formed by the larger folds and convolutions of the cortex, with the names used as convenient reference terms for the regions. As an example, the central fissure, or fissure of Rolando, shown in the figure is merely one of the deeper folds in the brain, serving as a convenient landmark between the frontal and parietal lobes.

It should be noted that the lobes of the cortex are generally specialized for processing different kind of information. For example, the occipital lobe is used for visual processing; the temporal lobe for auditory, linguistic, and memory processing; the parietal lobe for spatial and sensory processing; and the frontal lobes for cognitive control. Throughout this text, we may refer to mental functions critically involving different lobes of the cortex. However, we know that a more fine-grained consideration of the localization of different brain activities than at the level of just the four lobes is needed. Rather than have you memorize a large number of names and terms in this text, whenever we refer to a particular part of the cortex as being involved in cognition, we will also give you some numbers. These numbers refer to what are called **Brodmann's areas**. If you look at the front endpapers of this text, you will find maps of the outside and inside of the cortex laid out with the different areas numbered accordingly. So, for example, if you were to read that attention can involve activity in the anterior cingulate cortex (B.A. 24), you would know that you could look on the Brodmann maps to know just where this is.

More generally, it should be noted that as different topics are covered in this text, various smaller areas of the cortex will be identified as being critically involved for doing specific tasks. For example, the fusiform face area (B.A. 37) is important for the processing of human faces, and damage in this area can lead to a deficit known as prosopagnosia (an inability to identify faces). Similarly, the parahippocampal place area (also B.A. 37) is important when processing spatial locations, and damage there can lead to an inability to process location information (Epstein & Kanwisher, 1998). Thus, different parts of the brain are critically involved in different types of cognitive processes. Note that this does not mean that those processes occur *only* in those parts of the brain, but that those parts of the brain are important and critically involved in that type of thinking. An analogy would be with a car. The gas pedal is critically involved in the speed of the car, but by itself it doesn't make the car go (you need an engine, wheels, and many other components for that).

Principles of Functioning

Two important principles of functioning in the neocortex are described here. This is necessary background knowledge for understanding the effects of brain function on cognitive processes—that is, how the mind relates to the brain. These principles involve the ideas of contralaterality and hemispheric specialization.

CONTRALATERALITY   When viewed from the top, the neocortex is divided into two mirror-image halves—the left and right cerebral hemispheres. This follows a general law of anatomy, that with the exception of internal organs such as the heart, the body is basically bilaterally symmetrical. What is somewhat surprising, however, is that *the receptive and control centers for one side of the body are in the opposite hemisphere of the brain.* This is **contralaterality** (*contra* means "against" or "opposite"). In other words, for evolutionary reasons that will probably remain obscure, the right hemisphere of the brain receives its input from the left side of the body and also controls the left side. Likewise, the left hemisphere receives input from and controls output to the right side of the body. As an example, people who have a stroke in the left hemisphere will often have some paralysis in the right half of the body. There are a few exceptions, such as the olfactory nerves, in which there are ipsilateral (same side) connections.

Different parts of the brain are more or less involved depending on the kind of activity a person is engaged in.

HEMISPHERIC SPECIALIZATION   The second issue concerning lateralization involves different specializations within the two cerebral hemispheres. Despite their mirror-image appearance, the two hemispheres do not completely mirror one another's abilities. Instead, each hemisphere tends to specialize in different abilities and tends to process different kinds of information. This is the full principle of

cerebral lateralization and specialization: *Different functions or actions within the brain tend to rely more heavily on one hemisphere or the other or tend to be performed differently in the two hemispheres.* This is not to say that a process or function can happen *only* in one particular hemisphere. It merely says that there is often a tendency, sometimes strong, for one or the other hemisphere to be especially dominant in different processes or functions.

The most obvious evidence of lateralization in humans is the overwhelming incidence of right-handedness across all cultures and apparently throughout the known history of human evolution (Corballis, 1989). Accompanying this tendency toward right-handedness is a particularly strong left-hemispheric specialization in humans for language. That is, for the majority of people, language ability is especially lateralized in the left hemisphere; countless studies have demonstrated this general tendency (see Provins, 1997, for a review of the handedness–speech relationship). Note that the left lateralization of language in the brain also applies to many left-handers, so handedness and brain lateralization are not completely synched.

In contrast to the left hemisphere, the right hemisphere seems to be somewhat more specialized for nonverbal, spatial, and more perceptual information processing (see Banich, 2004, and Moscovitch, 1979, for reviews of such left–right hemisphere characterizations). For instance, the evidence suggests that face recognition (Ellis, 1983) and mental rotation (Deutsch, Bourbon, Papanicolaou, & Eisenberg, 1988), both requiring spatial and perceptual processing, are especially dependent on the right cerebral hemisphere. Table 2-1 provides a summary of data on cerebral lateralization.

Many people have heard of these "left brain versus right brain" issues, often from the popular press. Such treatments are notorious for exaggerating and over-simplifying laterality and specialization. For instance, in these descriptions the left hemisphere ends up with the rational, logical, and symbolic abilities—the boring ones—whereas the right hemisphere gets the holistic, creative, and intuitive processes—the sexy ones! Corballis (1989, p. 501) noted that the right hemisphere achieves "a certain cult status" in some treatments.

TABLE 2-1   Summary of Data on Cerebral Lateralization

Function	Left Hemisphere	Right Hemisphere
Visual system	Letters, words	Complex geometric patterns, faces
Auditory system	Language-related sounds	Nonlanguage environmental sounds, music
Somatosensory system	?	Tactile recognition of complex patterns, Braille
Movement	Complex voluntary movement	Movements in spatial patterns
Memory	Verbal memory	Nonverbal memory
Language	Speech	Prosody
	Reading	Narrative
	Writing	Inference
	Arithmetic	
Spatial processes		Geometry, sense of direction, mental rotation of shapes

Note: These functions of the respective hemispheres are mediated predominantly by one hemisphere in right-handed people.

But even ignoring that oversimplification, it is far too easy to misunderstand the principles of lateralization and specialization, too easy to say "process X happens in *this* hemisphere, process Y in *that* one." Even the simplest act of cognition, say naming a picture, involves multiple components, distributed widely across both hemispheres, and complex coordination of the components. Disruption of any one of those could disrupt picture naming. Thus several different patients, each with dramatically different localized brain damage, could show an inability to name a picture, each for a different reason relating to different lateralized processes.

Nonetheless, there is a striking division of labor in the neocortex, in which the left cerebral hemisphere is specialized for language. This is almost always true; it characterizes up to 85% or 90% of the population. The percentages are this high, however, only if you are a right-handed male with no family history of left-handedness and if you write with your hand in a normal rather than inverted position (Friedman & Polson, 1981). If you are female, if you are left-handed, if you write with an inverted hand position, and so on, then the "left hemisphere language rule" is not quite as strong. In such groups, the majority of people have the customary pattern, but the percentages are not as high; for example, Bryden's (1982) review indicated that 79% of women have language lateralized to the left hemisphere. Thus directing language input to the left cerebral hemisphere is optimal and efficient for many people, but not for all. (For simplicity, however, we rely on the convenient fiction that language is processed in the left hemisphere for most people; see Banich, 2004, for useful discussions.)

Split-Brain Research and Lateralization

Despite the exaggerated claims you often read, there has been a good deal of careful work on the topic of lateralization and specialization of different regions in the two hemispheres. Among the best known is the research on split-brain patients.

Simulate
Split-Brain in
MyPsychLab

Before about 1960, evidence of hemispheric specialization was rather indirect; neurologists and researchers simply noted the location and kind of head injury that was sustained and the kind of behavioral or cognitive deficit that was observed after the injury. Sperry (1964; Gazzaniga & Sperry, 1967), however, put the facts of anatomy together with a surgical procedure for severe epilepsy. In this operation, the corpus callosum is completely severed to restrict the epileptic seizure to just one of the cerebral hemispheres. For patients who had this radical surgery, a remarkably informative test could be administered, one that could reveal the different abilities and actions of the two hemispheres. That is, from the standpoint of brain functioning, when a patient's corpus callosum is surgically cut, the two hemispheres cannot communicate internally with each other—information in one hemisphere cannot cross over to the other. Sperry's technique was to test such people by directing sensory information to one side or the other of the body (e.g., by placing a pencil in the left or right hand of such a patient or presenting a visual stimulus to the left or right visual field), then observing their behavior.

For example, if a patient had a pencil placed in the left hand (the patients were prevented from seeing the objects and their hands, of course), the neural impulse went to the right hemisphere but then could not cross over into the left hemisphere. The patients usually were able to demonstrate how to use the object when the sensation was sent to the right hemisphere—for example, they could make the appropriate hand movements as if they were writing with the pencil. But they usually could not name the object unless it was placed in the right hand. This is exactly what would be expected from someone whose knowledge of language is localized in the left hemisphere but whose perceptual, nonverbal knowledge is localized in the right hemisphere. Similar effects were obtained with purely visual stimuli as well, that is, when the left half of a picture was projected to the right hemisphere and vice versa. A caveat to this work is that these patients all had long-term, severe epilepsy, and this condition may have altered the organization of their mental abilities, although some of the basic separation of abilities revealed is likely to be accurate. (Incidentally, Sperry earned the Nobel Prize for medicine in 1981 for his research; the award was made jointly to him and to Hubel and Wiesel, whose research on specialized feature detectors in the visual cortex is described in Chapter 3.)

Although the principle of laterality has been a mainstay of neurological research for a long time, recent evidence suggests that lateralization usually is not as absolute as was previously believed (e.g., in the area of language and speech; see Chapter 9). For such reasons, current researchers usually subscribe to the less extreme version of this principle. For instance, we say that different functions tend to occur more or less efficiently in one hemisphere or the other, or they tend to occur somewhat differently in one side or the other (Banich, 2004; Friedman & Polson, 1981; Moscovitch, 1979), or that the two hemispheres contribute different components to an ability or process (see Gardner, 1985; Gazzaniga, 1995).

Although we have discussed some localization of function in this chapter, implying that different hemispheres, lobes, or parts of the brain are largely responsible for different types of cognition, it should be kept in mind that there is some individual variability in this. Some people are different. For example, some people have the distribution of processes associated with the left and right hemisphere reversed (and it is not just being left handed that does this). Also, there can be influences of culture on cognitive neurological processing (Ambday & Bharucha, 2009). For example, Tang et al. (2006) found that whereas English speakers tended to use more language areas when processing Arabic numerals, Chinese speakers tended to use more visual/spatial areas of the brain, suggesting that different cultures can lead people to use different parts of the brain to process the same kinds of information.

Cortical Specialization

Not only are the different hemispheres of the cortex differentially able to do different things, but the different parts of the cortex are tuned for different kinds of processes. Again, as with lateralization of brain function, the fact that a part of the brain is implicated in a certain kind of mental process, such as remembering, does not mean that that part of the brain does only that process, nor does it mean that other parts of the brain are not involved in that activity. The localization or specialization of function in the cortex means that that part of the brain is critically important for a certain kind of cognition. There will be numerous examples of the

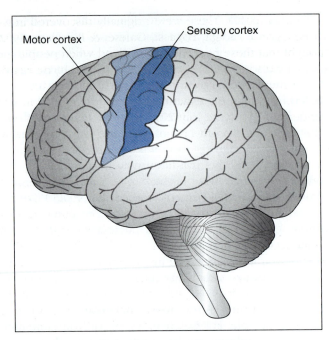

FIGURE 2-6   The locations of the sensory and motor cortices.

localization of function throughout this text for different types of cognition. To give you a better feel for this, we'll cover three types of cortical specialization, and the implications they have for human thought.

First of all, let's consider a kind of cortical specialization in which a section of cortex is specialized for a certain type of processing. As you know, your brain is connected to the rest of your body (obviously). When you sense things touching your body or move part of your body, this involves specific parts of your cortex. These are called the sensory and motor cortices, respectively, and are shown in Figure 2-6. The **sensory cortex** is a band of cortex at the front of the parietal lobes, just behind the central sulcus (B.A.s, 1, 2, & 3), and it is responsible for processing sensory information from throughout the body. In comparison, the **motor cortex** is a band of cortex at the back of the frontal lobe, just in front of the central sulcus (B.A. 4), and is responsible for controlling all of your voluntary muscle movements. But it is not the case that the whole of the sensory or motor cortices are responsible for any and all sensations and voluntary movements you make. Instead, there are different places along these cortices that are specialized for different parts of the body, such as the fingers, leg, or mouth. So, not only is there a localization of sensory and motor processes in the brain, but there is even a localization of different body parts within each of those parts of the cortex.

A second kind of specialization in the cortex does not involve a region of the brain, but certain kinds of neurons that seem to be involved in a specific kind of mental processing. Here, this specialization is with neurons found in association with processing in or near the motor cortex. These neurons are active when a person is performing an action, or, more interestingly, watching another person do something (see Glenberg, 2011). These were originally discovered in work involving monkeys (Di Pellegrino, Fadiga, Fogassi, Galese, & Rizzolatti, 1992). Because it was initially thought that these neurons are involved when people mentally imitate or mirror another person's actions, they were called **mirror neurons**. These neurons appear in a number of places in the cortex, such as the inferior frontal cortex (B.A. 44 & 45). Although the exact nature and role of mirror neurons is not yet completely understood (see the July 2011 issue of *Perspectives on Psychological Science* for a lively debate on the issue), they are used in some way to plan and execute movements and to understand what people are doing.

A third type of specialization of function in the cortex does not involve certain regions of the cortex, or certain types of cells, but a chain or sequence of cells and areas that are all working toward a particular processing goal. A good example of this involves the visual pathways in the cortex and the processing of different types of visual information. Many initial, early visual processes occur at the back of the brain in the occipital lobe, a region called V1 (for "visual 1") (B.A. 17). The visual pathways that emerge from the early visual processing done in this and subsequent areas diverge into two pathways, depending on the type of visual information being processed (Mishkin, Ungerleider, & Macko, 1983; Ungerleider & Haxby, 1994), as shown in Figure 2-7. One of these is the **dorsal pathway**, which moves along the top of the cortex across the parietal lobes. The dorsal pathway is primarily involved in determining *where* things are in space. As such, it is also called the "where" system in vision. The other of these is the **ventral pathway**, which moves along the bottom of the cortex into the temporal lobes. The ventral pathway is primarily involved in determining *what* things are. As such, it is also called the "what" system in visual. Although it seems odd when you first come across this fact, the visual system does process where a thing is and what it is differently, although the system does bring this information together later on. More on this is in Chapters 3 and 4.

FIGURE 2-7   The dorsal and ventral pathways.

Levels of Explanation and Embodied Cognition

Although understanding how neurons communicate with each other is important for a deeper understanding of human cognition, it is not necessarily the case that all of our understanding of thought can be reduced to understanding how neurons do their job. Instead, assemblies of neurons working together can produce cognitive processes that are **emergent properties**: They are present when neurons work together but are absent in the individual neurons (Minsky, 1986). A more everyday example of an emergent property is that of containment. Although no piece of wood has the property of containment, if you arrange a number of them into a box shape, then the property of containment emerges out of this. Similarly, some aspects of cognition are emergent properties of collections of neurons working together.

Because of this, cognitive science will often use levels of explanation to capture how a process is operating. Thus, we can sometimes understand how problem solving may be progressing without knowing what the individual neurons are doing (let alone the individual molecules, protons, quarks, and such). That said, cognitive scientists understand that there are important bridges across these different levels, and that understanding what is happening at one level can help explain and give an understanding of what is happening at another level. For example, lacking appropriate levels of a certain neurotransmitter may have dramatic consequences on a person's ability to think clearly (see Marshall, 2009, for a clear exposition of these ideas).

One example of how understanding how the brain processes information can inform our understanding of how cognition works comes from research on embodied or grounded cognition. As a reminder, one of the basic tenets of ideas about embodied cognition is that the way we think about things is a reflection of how our bodies work and interact with objects in the world. Research in cognitive neuroscience has observed that much of cognition is oriented around allowing us to use our bodies effectively in the environments we find ourselves in—after all, the body is an action-oriented system made to do things. Consistent with an embodied cognition perspective, it has been reported that certain parts of the motor cortex (B.A. 4, a band of tissue at the back of the frontal lobes, responsible for controlling various muscles throughout the body) become activated when people are motionless, but processing words that refer to actions. Moreover, different parts of the motor cortex become active for different kinds of verbs. For example, a verb like "kick" would be more likely to activate the part of the cortex responsible for controlling the feet, whereas a verb like "punch" would be more likely to activate the part responsible for the hand (e.g., Kemmerer, Castillo, Talavage, Patterson, & Wiley, 2008).

Section Summary

- Many subcortical structures have a meaningful contribution to cognition, including the thalamus, the corpus callosum, the hippocampus, and the amygdala.
- The cerebral cortex is the largest brain structure in humans and is the seat of many cognitive functions. The cortex is divided into four lobes and two hemispheres, with some localization of function in these various brain

regions, such as the occipital lobe being primarily involved in visual processing. Damage to certain areas of the brain can cause specific cognitive deficits, such as prosopagnosia.

- There are contralateral connections of the brain with the body, as well as some lateralization of cognitive function in the two hemispheres. This separation of different mental tasks by the two halves of the cortex is most clearly illustrated in split-brain patients who had the corpus callosum cut, thereby separating the two hemispheres.
- Although there are different levels of analysis and explanation, a good understanding of neurophysiology can be very helpful in understanding human cognition. A good example of this is how embodied cognition processes may involve neural processes used in actual physical action.

NEUROIMAGING: LOOKING AT THE BRAIN

There are a number of ways to look at the brain and how it processes information. In this part of the chapter we review a number of these, many of which are referred to in later chapters where these methods are used to help understand how thinking works in one context or another. We divide our discussion into four basic areas: (a) structural measures that look at the structure of the brain itself, (b) electrical measures that capitalize on the electrical properties of the action potential when neurons talk to one another, (c) processing measures that assess changes in metabolic processes, such as blood flow, as a consequence of different types of thinking, and (d) other neuroimaging measures.

Structural Measures

One of the first things we may be interested in is the structure of the brain itself. This is of particular interest if there is reason to believe that there has been some sort of brain damage or disease, or if there is some reason to suspect that someone may have a brain structure that is unusually small or large. The simplest way of doing this, of course, is to open up the skull and look at the brain. However, this is a rather dramatic line of action, and, fortunately there are other, less invasive methods.

One way to do this is by taking **computerized axial tomography (CT)** scans. With this technique, people place their heads in a big mechanical doughnut that takes a series of x-ray images. These images are then assembled by a computer to allow various "slices" of the brain to be studied as x-ray images. This is a fairly common technique that allows for a quick assessment of general brain structure. Another way of taking images like this is by using **magnetic resonance imaging (MRI)** scans. Again, people put their heads in a big mechanical doughnut, but instead of taking a collection of x-ray images, what happens is that the machine creates a very strong magnetic field. This is then used to look at the distribution of molecules of a certain type. For example, if you were interested in brain structure, you might look at the distribution of water molecules. What you get back is a detailed image of the structure of the brain that is clearer than with a CT scan. An MRI scan can give you surprisingly clear images of a living brain,

FIGURE 2-8   The clarity of a magnetic resonance imaging view (**B.**) of the brain as compared with a photograph of a dissected brain (**A.**).

as shown in Figure 2-8. Another advantage of this technique is that you do not need to subject a person's brain to a high dose of x-rays. A disadvantage to this technique is that it cannot be used with people who have certain kinds of metal implants because of the magnetic field produced by the scanner.

Electrical Measures

Although it is sometimes important to know about the structure of the brain, in terms of memory, cognition, and thinking, it is often important to know about *how* the brain is processing information. One way of getting at this issue is to look at the amount of activity in different parts of the cortex. This can be done by capitalizing on the change in electrical charge that occurs during an action potential. The most basic way this is done is by inserting a microelectrode into the brain to record the activity of a single cell. This, simply enough, is called *single cell recording.* What is done here is to look at how the firing rate of an individual cell changes, by seeing if it fires more or less often as a function of the given task. Because of the invasiveness of this procedure, it is typically used with animals. This is the method used to map visual cells in the occipital lobe, as discussed in Chapter 3.

There are less invasive ways to measure neural activity. This can be done by measuring brain wave patterns using electroencephalogram (EEG) recordings. In this technique, electrodes are placed on the person's scalp, and the device records the patterns of brain waves. Typically, researchers have focused on **event-related potentials (ERPs)**, *the momentary changes in electrical activity of the brain when a particular stimulus is presented to a person* (e.g., Donchin, 1981; Rugg & Coles, 1995). As an example, read the following sentence (adapted from Banich, 2004, based on Kutas & Hillyard, 1980): "Running out the door, Patty grabbed her jacket, her baseball glove, her cap, a softball, and a skyscraper." Of course you noticed that *skyscraper* does not fit the context of the sentence; it's called a semantic anomaly. What is fascinating is that the ERP recording of your brain wave activities would show a marked change about 400 ms after you read *skyscraper,* an electrically

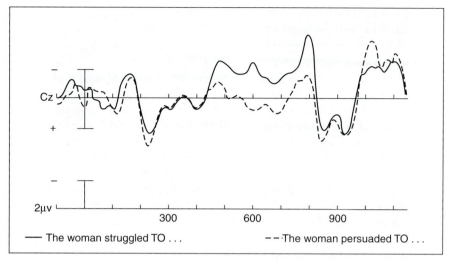

FIGURE 2-9 Mean ERPs to syntactically acceptable sentences (solid curve) and syntactically anomalous sentences (dotted curve). The P600 component, shown as a dip in the dotted curve, shows the effect of detecting the syntactic anomaly. Note that in this figure, positive changes go downward.

Source: Reprinted with permission from "Introduction and Overview" by E. D. Bigler, R. A. Yeo, and F. Turkheimer, in *Neuropsychological Function and Brain Imaging* (p. 10), edited by E. D. Bigler, R. A. Yeo, and E. Turkheimer, 1989, New York, Plenum Press.

negative wave called N4 or N400. The N4 would be present, though smaller, if the last word in the sentence had been *lamp* and at baseline if the last word were *bat*.

Osterhout and Holcomb (1992) found this N4 effect for semantic anomalies and also a similar effect when the grammar or syntax of the sentence violated normal language rules. They showed their participants control sentences along with sentences that contained grammatical or syntactic anomalies:

> *(Control) John told the man to leave.*
>
> *(Anomalous) John hoped the man to leave.*

With this manipulation of syntactic anomaly, Osterhout and Holcomb found a pronounced P6 or P600 effect, an electrically positive change in activity, roughly 600 ms after reading the word *to* (the word that signals the syntactic violation). Figure 2-9 shows their result. Clearly, our language comprehension system reacts differently—and very quickly—when we encounter unusual or incorrect sentences.

ERP technology is especially good at telling *when* mental mechanisms operate in an online task, but assessments of *where* this process occurs is much trickier and not very precise. By carefully controlling surrounding

A person having his EEGs recorded for an ERP study.

conditions and measuring the elapsed time since a stimulus was presented, we can begin to see how the electrical activity of the brain changes moment by moment when the person is processing a stimulus.

Another way of capitalizing on the electrical aspect of neural processing is to use a method known as **transcranial magnetic stimulation (TMS)**. With this technique, the apparatus is positioned near a person's head with a particular part of the brain targeted. Then, when the machine is turned on, it produces a magnetic field that disrupts the electrical activity in a particular part of a person's brain. Think of this as inducing a mild seizure in a person's brain. In essence, this process is like giving a person a temporary lesion by temporarily knocking out part of the brain, and assessing the effects on cognition when that part of the brain is no longer operating. As one example of this, Grafman et al. (1994) used TMS to disrupt the ability of people to recall lists of words when the TMS stimulation was applied over temporal-lobe and frontal-lobe areas of the brain.

Metabolic Measures

Other things that change in the brain when we think, in addition to electrical activity, are metabolic processes, such as blood flow. For example, when a part of the brain is working hard, the neurons there need more energy, such as what comes from oxygen, to keep working. This change in demands of different part of the brain can be reflected in the amount of blood flowing through the capillaries to that part of the brain. What the metabolic measures can do is tap into this information to help figure out what parts of the brain are more active under various circumstances.

One means of doing this is with a method called **positron emission tomography (PET)** scans. With PET scans, a person is injected with a radioactive isotope that is taken up by the bloodstream. This isotope has a very short half-life, so the impact of the radiation on the body is fairly minimal. After the isotope is injected, the person is placed into a scanner and asked to do a particular kind of task. What is found is that certain parts of the brain will work harder than they normally do, and after an analysis is done, that part of the brain will "light up" in the PET scan image, suggesting that that part of the cortex is more involved in that type of thinking.

Another exciting technique that yields images of the *functioning* of the brain is **functional MRI (fMRI)**. Here, rather than injecting a person with a radioactive isotope, the MRI magnet is used to isolate molecules such as oxygen to assess where the blood is flowing to in the brain, thereby indicating heightened neural activity. This is the blood oxygenation level–dependent or **BOLD** signal. The logic is straightforward: If a region becomes active because of mental processing, the metabolic rate of that region increases, so increases in oxygenated blood flow are seen (for an excellent and thorough introduction to the fMRI technique, see Huettel, Song, & McCarthy, 2004). An example of this logic is a study by Davachi, Mitchell, and Wagner (2003). People were presented with a series of words and were later given a recognition test for their memory of those words. The learning phase of the study was done while a person was in the MRI scanner, and brain activity was recorded at this time. After the recognition memory test, the researchers went back to see if there were any differences in the fMRI data collected during learning. What they found, as shown in Figure 2-10, was that items that were remembered later, during recognition, showed greater activity during learning in the perirhinal cortex (B.A.s 35 and 36), compared to items that were later forgotten. So, this shows that we can look at brain activity and make reliable connections to how people think.

An advantage to these techniques, at least from the perspective of cognitive science, is that they show the brain in action rather than just the physical structures. Such scans are called *functional* because they show the brain as it is functioning, as it performs some mental task. A second advantage is that they can be applied with (apparently) minimal risk to normal people.

The set of color pictures from a PET scan study assessing the processing of different types of information (i.e., language and/or music) (see the endpapers of this text) relied on a similar procedure, computer-assisted detection of blood flow patterns in a patient injected with an irradiated substance that binds to oxygen in the blood. Note, however, that imaging techniques that measure blood flow have a time lag drawback; the increase in metabolic activity can lag anywhere from several hundred milliseconds to several seconds after the cognitive activity.

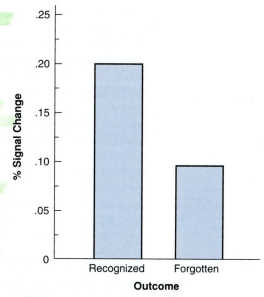

FIGURE 2-10   Percent signal change in fMRI recordings of words that were later remembered or forgotten.

Source: From Davachi, Mitchell, and Wagner (2003).

Neuroimaging data can be used not only to verify and expand theories of cognition, but also to help solve more applied and clinical problems. Take the example of dyslexia. Some work has shown that people with dyslexia show different patterns of neural processing as revealed by various neuroimaging technologies (Shaywitz, Mody, & Shaywitz, 2006). For example, some people have a genetically based form of dyslexia in which there are problems in the occipital-temporal region (where the occipital and temporal lobes meet) of the left hemisphere, a region that is strongly associated with language processing. Specifically, there appears to be a disruption of processing in this region of the brain that makes it difficult to accurately assemble sets of letters into words. In comparison, another group of dyslexics show very adequate processing in the left occipital-temporal region. Their dyslexia, instead, seems environmentally based, related to poorer educational support and other factors, and shows a stronger connection to the right hemisphere prefrontal region, which is associated with memory retrieval. In essence, rather than mentally sounding words out, they treat words more as wholes, attempting to retrieve word meanings directly. As a result, less frequent and new words become much more difficult to process, and dyslexics of this type show persistent difficulties with reading of a very different sort.

Other Methods

Apart from looking at the structure of the brain, or the electrical or metabolic activity that a person exhibits when doing a certain kind of thinking, there are other methods that are available to cognitive neuroscientists to relate mental function to the underlying brain structures. In this section we consider a few of these, including lesions, electrical stimulation, and special populations.

Any example of the investigation technique used by Sperry, discussed earlier in the section on lateralization and split brain patients, involved deliberate **lesioning** of the brain. Although such techniques are limited in their usefulness, they can sometimes be revealing of the secrets of cognitive processing. Lesions are used with only two kinds of subjects—laboratory animals and patients with medical conditions requiring brain surgery. A long-standing tradition, however, reports case studies of people or groups of people who by disease or accident have experienced damage or lesions to the brain. Much of the evidence described throughout this text comes from victims of strokes, diseases, aneurysms, head injuries, and other accidental circumstances. In all cases, the site and extent of the brain lesion are important guides to the kind of disruption in behavior that is observed and vice versa (a clear description of the lesion method is found in Damasio & Damasio, 1997).

Another technique that has been used to study localization of function in the brain is the method of **direct stimulation**, pioneered by Penfield, the famous Canadian neurosurgeon. In Penfield's technique, the patient remained conscious during the brain surgery, with only a local anesthetic used to prevent pain in the scalp. The surgeon then applied minute electrical charges to the exposed brain, thus triggering very small regions. The patient was then asked to answer questions or report out loud the thoughts and memories that entered awareness. By comparing the patient's reports with the different regions that are stimulated, a map of cerebral functioning can be developed.

Generally, the patients in Penfield's procedure reported ideas or episodes that had a dreamlike quality. Although they occasionally reported seemingly distinct memories, it was seldom possible to check on the accuracy of these reports. Their dreamlike nature suggests that they were heavily influenced by reconstructive processes; that is, they may not have been genuine memories. On the other hand, by stimulating different regions of the exposed brain, a great deal was discovered about the localization of different functions, kinds of knowledge, and so on, in different parts of the neocortex (e.g., Ojemann, 1982; Ojemann & Creutzfeldt, 1987; Penfield & Jasper, 1954; Penfield & Milner, 1958; for an update on such methods, see Gordon, Hart, Boatman, & Lesser, 1997).

Although such research often yields fascinating evidence, it has some clear difficulties. For one, it is restricted to clinical settings (i.e., patients needing brain surgery). Second, there is the caveat again that at least some evidence shows that the organization of a patient's brain function may differ substantially from the normal pattern, perhaps because they are epileptic, and epilepsy can have noticeable consequences for memory (e.g., Butler, Muhlert, & Zeman, 2010), thus limiting the generalizability of such results.

Finally, another technique that has been used to study how neurological structures relate to cognitive processing is to look at **special populations**. These are groups of people whose neurological condition is known to differ in regular ways from some standard. For example, these could be people with a known neurological disease or syndrome, such as people with the cognitive deficits that occur with Alzheimer's disease, or people with the amnesia that accompanies Korsakoff's syndrome. Alternatively, some developmental studies compare people of different age groups, keeping in mind that the neurological machinery changes in regular ways at different ages. For example, by studying older adults, whose brains are systematically different from those of college students, a cognitive neuroscientist can make assumptions about how certain parts of the brain are involved in cognition by looking at how performance changes in some tasks as a function of age.

Section Summary

- There are a number of neurological measures for assessing how brain structure and function relate to cognitive processes. These provide insight into how the mind and the brain interact.
- Structural measures, such as CT and MRI scans, allow evaluation of the structure of living brains. These measures are useful in identifying brain abnormalities. The consequences of such abnormalities, such as from a stroke, tumor, or other trauma, may affect thinking in principled ways.
- Electrical measures, such as single cell recording, ERPs, and TMS, take advantage of the electrical component of neural transmission. Neurological measures based on these kinds of signals have the potential to provide moment-to-moment information about the intensity of neural processes.
- Metabolic imaging methods take advantage of changes in blood flow to assess how hard different regions of the brain are working. The great advantage of this kind of imaging technology is that it allows us to more precisely pinpoint when different regions in a person's brain are active for different types of mental activity.
- There are numerous other ways of assessing neurological function and how it relates to cognition. This includes looking at people who have sustained a lesion to the brain, direct stimulation of the cortex, case studies, and testing special populations, among many others that are not discussed here. Each of these different approaches has the potential to reveal new and interesting aspects of human cognition.

NEURAL NET MODELS: CONNECTIONISM

We conclude the chapter with a brief presentation on connectionism, an important computer-based method in cognitive science. Although you will encounter connectionist modeling at several points in this text, it will be useful to learn a few general characteristics now, especially because of the strong similarities between this approach and that of cognitive neuroscience.

Connectionist models are also called **neural net models** or **parallel distributed processing (PDP) models**; for our purposes the three terms are treated as synonymous. They refer to *a computer-based technique for modeling complex systems that is inspired by the structure of the nervous system.* A fundamental principle in connectionist models is that the simple nodes or units that make up the system are interconnected. Knowledge, all the way from the simplest to the most complex, is represented in these models as simple interconnected units. The connections between units can either be excitatory or inhibitory; that is, the connections can have positive or negative weights. The basic units receive positive and negative activation from other units; depending on these patterns, they in turn transmit activation to yet other units. Furthermore, the interconnectedness of these basic units usually is described as "massive" because there is no particular restriction on the number of interconnections any unit can have. That is, in principle, any bit of knowledge or information can be connected or related to an almost limitless number of other units.

   Figure 2-11 illustrates an early connectionist model by McClelland and Rumelhart (1981), a model that dealt with word recognition. The bottom row of nodes or units represents simple features, simple patterns such as a horizontal line and a vertical line, each connected to letters at the next higher level, which in turn are connected to words at the top level. For simplicity, look at the feature on the

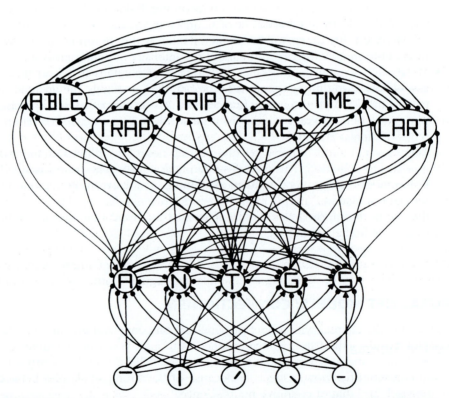

FIGURE 2-11   An illustration of part of McClelland and Rumelhart's (1981) PDP model of feature, letter, and word recognition. From "An Interactive Activation Model of Context Effects in Letter Perception: Part 1. An Account of Basic Findings" by J. L. McClelland and D. E. Rumelhart (1981), *Psychological Review, 88,* p. 30. Copyright 1981 by the American Psychological Association. Reprinted by permission.

far left, the horizontal line. The connection directly up from that to the capital let-ter *A* would be a positive, excitatory connection because the letter *A* has two horizontal lines. The connection from this feature up to the letter *N*, however, would be a negative, inhibitory one: If the feature detection system detects a hori-zontal line, this works against recognition of the letter *N*. In the same fashion, the capital *A* would have a positive connection up to the word ABLE because *A* is in the first position there, but it would have a negative, inhibitory connection to TRAP because TRAP does not begin with the letter *A*.

Referring to such models by the term *parallel distributed processing* high-lights a different facet of the brain and the computer system. Mental processes operate in a thoroughly parallel fashion and are widely distributed across the brain; likewise, processing in a PDP model is thoroughly parallel and distributed across multiple levels of knowledge. As an example, even as the feature detectors at the bottom of the model are being matched to an incoming stimulus, word units at the top of the model may already be activated. Thus, activation from higher levels may influence processing at lower levels, even as the lower levels affect activation at higher levels.

Consider how the system would recognize the word TRAP in the sentence "After the bear attacked the visiting tourists, hunters went into the forest to set a trap." Even as the feature and letter detector units would be working on the *T*, then the *R*, and so forth, word units at the top would have already received activa-tion based on the meaning and context of the sentence; with bears attacking tour-ists and hunters going into the forest, the word TRAP is highly predictable from the context, but CART would not be (just as "bat" was predictable but "skyscraper" wasn't in the example given earlier). Given this context, TRAP would be more eas-ily recognized, perhaps because the features within the letters would have been activated by the context already. In this fashion, the comprehension and word recognition systems would be operating in parallel with the feature and letter detection systems, each system making continuing, simultaneous contributions to the other systems and to overall mental processing.

The similarity of the connectionist scheme to the functioning of the brain is obvious and vitally important—it is widely believed that connectionist models oper-ate on the same, or at least very similar, basic principles as the brain (McClelland, Rumelhart, & Hinton, 1986). In other words, the connectionist framework may give us an excellent way of modeling and simulating cognitive processes (for a more recent example, see Monaghan & Pollmann, 2003).

Section Summary

- The notion that human cognition is analogous to processing in a computer system has been abandoned at the detailed level, especially because of evi-dence of widespread parallel processing in humans. Connectionist (neural net, PDP) models can simulate such parallel processes and therefore may be excellent ways of modeling human cognitive processes.

Key Terms

acetylcholine (p. *38*)

action potential (p. *36*)

all-or-none principle (p. *37*)

amygdala (p. *42*)

axon (p. *34*)

Brodmann's areas (p. *43*)

BOLD (p. *54*)

cerebral cortex (p. *42*)

cerebral lateralization (p. *45*)

computerized axial tomography (CT) (p. *51*)

connectionist models (p. *57*)

consolidation (p. *40*)

contralaterality (p. *44*)

corpus callosum (p. *42*)

direct stimulation (p. *56*)

dissociation (p. *32*)

dendrites (p. *34*)

dorsal pathway (p. *49*)

emergent properties (p. *50*)

event-related potentials (ERPs) (p. *52*)

frontal lobe (p. *43*)

functional MRI (fMRI) (p. *54*)

GABA (p. *39*)

glutamate (p. *38*)

hippocampus (p. *42*)

lesioning (p. *56*)

long-term potentiation (LTP) (p. *39*)

magnetic resonance imaging (MRI) (p. *51*)

mirror neurons (p. *49*)

motor cortex (p. *48*)

myelin sheath (p. *34*)

neocortex (p. *41*)

neural net models (p. *57*)

neuron (p. *34*)

nodes of Ranvier (p. *36*)

norepinephrine (p. *38*)

occipital lobe (p. *43*)

parallel distributed processing (PDP) models (p. *57*)

parietal lobe (p. *43*)

positron emission tomography (PET) (p. *54*)

propagated (p. *36*)

sensory cortex (p. *48*)

soma (p. *34*)

special populations (p. *56*)

synapse (p. *37*)

temporal lobe (p. *43*)

thalamus (p. *42*)

transcranial magnetic stimulation (TMS) (p. *54*)

ventral pathway (p. *49*)

Sensation and Perception

*Even psychologists who ought to know better have acted as if they
believed (1) that the person's visual experience directly mirrors the
stimulus pattern; (2) that his visual experience begins when the pattern
is first exposed and terminates when it is turned off; (3) that his
experience, itself a passive—if fractional—copy of the stimulus, is in
turn mirrored by his verbal report.*

(NEISSER, 1967, P. 16)

It's a wonder we can see or hear anything at all. The structure of the eye is so implausible,
even backward, and the ear so indirect and unlikely. Yet, we can see the flame of a single
candle, on a dark night, from a distance of 20 miles; we can hear a watch ticking 20 feet
away in a large, quiet room; and (some of you please note!), we can smell a single drop of perfume diffused into the entire volume of a six-room apartment (Galanter, 1962). Even this

sensitivity is exceeded by the complexity of mental processing of perception. Because we "understand" what we have seen so quickly, with so little effort, "we can be deceived into thinking that vision should therefore be fairly simple to perform" (Hildreth & Ullman, 1989). Over and over, this chapter (and this book) emphasizes the fact that a rapid and unconscious process is not necessarily simple, or simple to investigate. If anything, just the opposite is probably true.

This chapter presents a basic study of perception in vision and hearing. We focus on the visual and auditory sensory registers because they are our most prominent intersections with the world (some animals make more use of other senses, such as the sense of smell in dogs). Several theories are covered, including an elaboration of the connectionist model you were presented in Chapter 2. In the final section, we consider brain-related disruptions in perception. We see what perceptual deficits tell us about the normal processes we take for granted.

VISUAL SENSATION AND PERCEPTION

Figure 3-1 illustrates the basic sensory equipment of human vision. Light waves enter the eye, are focused and inverted by the lens, and are projected onto the **retina**. The retina has three layers of neurons: *rods and cones, bipolar cells,* and *ganglion cells* (see Figure 3-1B). The rods and cones are neurons stimulated by light, beginning the process of vision. Patterns of neural firing from these are passed on to a second layer, the bipolar cells, which collect the messages and move them along to a third layer, the ganglion cells. The axons of the ganglion cells converge at the rear of the eye, forming the bundle of fibers that makes up the optic nerve. This signal exits the eye and continues through various structures, eventually projecting to the visual cortex of the occipital lobe, in the lower rear portion of the brain.

A brief explanation is in order about how the eyes transmit information to the brain. The contralaterality principle is not as simple as "left eye to right hemisphere." Instead, each eye transmits to *both* hemispheres. Importantly, each half of the retina gathers information from the *contra*lateral visual field. As shown in Figure 3-2, where you are looking is your fixation point. The left half of the retina in each eye receives images from the right visual field (the house), and the right half of each retina receives images from the left visual field (the tree). Thus, the right *visual field*—the solid lines in the figure—projects to the left half of the retina in both eyes, and this is then transmitted to the left hemisphere. Similarly, stimuli in the left *visual field*—the dotted lines—project to the right half of both retinas, and are then sent to the right hemisphere.

At each step—from rods to bipolar cells, then from bipolar cells to ganglia—there is some loss of information. To put it another way, there is a great deal of *compression* in the early stages of vision. Thus, the message that finally reaches the cortex is an already processed and summarized record of the original stimulus (Haber & Hershenson, 1973). There are about 120 million rods on each retina and about 7 million cones. Most of the cones are in a *small area* known as the **fovea**, *which provides our most accurate, precise vision.* Some of the cones in the fovea have "private" bipolar cells for relaying impulses: *One* cone synapses with *one* bipolar cell. In contrast, in peripheral vision, tens to hundreds of rods converge on

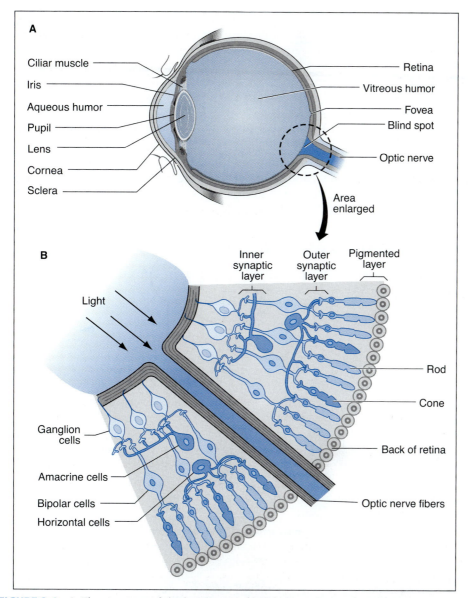

A

Ciliar muscle
Iris
Aqueous humor
Pupil
Lens
Cornea
Sclera

Retina
Vitreous humor
Fovea
Blind spot
Optic nerve

Area
enlarged

B

Inner
synaptic
layer

Outer
synaptic
layer

Pigmented
layer

Light

Rod

Cone

Back of retina

Ganglion
cells

Amacrine cells

Bipolar cells

Horizontal cells

Optic nerve fibers

FIGURE 3-1 **A.** The structure of the human eye, foveal pit, optic nerve, and other structures. **B.** The retina, rods and cones, and ganglion cells. Based on Hothersall, 1985.

a single bipolar cell. Such convergence results in a loss of information because a bipolar cell cannot "know" which of its many rods triggered it. Finally, about 1 million ganglion cells combine to form the optic nerve. So, essentially, vision is compressed from 120 million bits of information down to 1 million. Thus, the messages reaching the brain have been reduced and summarized to an enormous degree. Despite this compression, human vision is still amazingly sensitive and acute. Like all good summaries, the visual system preserves the most useful information, the edges, contours, and any kind of change, and omits the less useful, steady-state information.

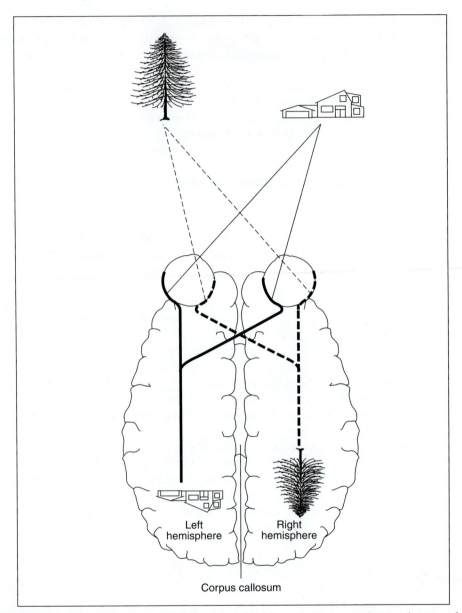

FIGURE 3-2   Binocular pathways of information flow from the eyes into the visual cortex of the brain. The patterns of stimulus-to-brain pathways demonstrate the contralaterality of the visual system.

Although much of the coverage here is on the visual processing of individual objects, it should be kept in mind that sensory and perceptual processes influence cognition even based on general visual properties or impressions of a scene as a whole. As an example of this, there is some evidence to suggest that rooms with lighter colored ceilings and/or walls (but not floors) are experienced and perceived as being higher than rooms with darker ceilings or walls (Oberfeld, Hecht, & Gamer, 2010). Thus, sensation and perception is not just about bits and pieces of a scene; ultimately, all of the information is integrated into a greater whole that influences cognition on a broad scale.

With regard to early visual processing in the retina and optic nerve, we are talking about **sensation**, *the reception of stimulation from the environment and the encoding of it into the nervous system.* Our primary interest of course is in what we *do* with this information. This is **perception**, *the process of interpreting and understanding sensory information.* As such, we need to explore the stages of visual perception. We begin with how the eye gathers information from the world, and then turn to the memory that retains that information, visual sensory memory.

Gathering Visual Information

To start out, let's eliminate an apparently common misunderstanding about vision right away. Winer, Cottrell, Gregg, Fournier, and Bica (2002) asked college students "How does vision work?" using several variations of the task. In *every* variation, they found a substantial percentage of college students exhibited "extramission," the belief that that vision involves some kind of ray or wave going out from the eyes to the object being perceived (think of the rays emanating from Superman's eyes). For instance, 69% of the students drew outward-pointing arrows on diagrams. Another 33% gave extramission responses when asked about looking at a shining light bulb, where the correct answer should be obvious (the bulb emits light, which goes to the eyes). Because this is a common misunderstanding, we correct it here—vision is *not* the result of anything coming out from our eyes *toward* the thing we're looking at. Instead, it is triggered when the reflection of light from an object hits our eyes.

A more subtle misbelief is that we take in visual information in a continuous fashion whenever our eyes are open. After all, our visual experience is of a connected, coherent visual scene that we scan and examine at will. This is largely an illusion. Watch people's eyes as they read. You will see that their eyes do not sweep smoothly across the page. Instead, they jerk, bit by bit, with pauses between successive movements.

PROVE IT

Yogi Berra supposedly once said something to the effect that "you can observe a lot just by watching." Very little of the evidence you're reading about in this chapter can be observed easily without specialized apparatus; for instance, you need to present visual stimuli in a highly controlled, precise fashion. But you can make some important and revealing observations just by watching someone's eyes (this also relates to material you will read in Chapter 9).

Get close to a friend and watch as he or she reads a passage of text silently and as he or she looks at a photo or drawing, maybe something like the photo in Figure 3-3. At a minimum, what you'll see—the fast, jerky saccades of the eye movements—disproves the intuition that the eyes move smoothly and regularly across a line of print or around a photograph or picture.

Observer asked to view the image

●	**Fixations:** points where the eye pauses and visual information is taken in
—	**Saccades:** fast movements when the eye sweeps from one point to the other (eye does not encode visual information)

Hypothetical tracking of fixations and saccades.

Observer will have different fixation points and saccades when considering different aspects of the image.

FIGURE 3-3   On the bottom are hypothetical Saccade and fixation paths of a person looking at the painting on the top. Note that there would be an emphasis of looking times at psychologically meaningful information, such as people's faces, and salient objects. Less time, if any, would be spent fixating on uninformative locations, such as a blank spot on a wall or floor.

Here are the facts. The *eyes sweep from one point to another in fast movements* called **saccades** (French for "jerk," pronounced "*suh-KAHD*"). These movements are interrupted by *pauses* called **fixations** (Figure 3-3). A saccade is quite rapid, but also quite variable, taking anywhere from 25 ms to 175 ms (Rayner, 1998). Furthermore, it takes up to 200 ms just to plan and start the movement (Haber & Hershenson, 1973), and this planning involves area MT (B.A. 19) along the dorsal stream of visual processing. So, assume something in the range of 250 to 300 ms for an entire fixation–saccade cycle. At that rate, there are three or four visual cycles per second. Each cycle registers a separate visual scene. During the saccade, there is suppression of the normal visual processes, even those that do not involve the current scene. In essence, some types of thinking stop when we move our eyes. For example, if given a task of rotating mental images, people cease rotating the images during a saccade (Irwin & Brockmole, 2004).

For the most part we take in visual information only during a fixation. It is almost as if we are blind during the actual saccade (if the eye did encode information during the saccade, we'd see a smear). As a quick demonstration of this, try to watch your own eyes make saccades while looking in a mirror. You can't do it. You can only see the part of the visual field you are looking directly at. In confirmation of this, several investigations show what is called **change blindness**, our *failure to notice changes in visual stimuli (e.g., photographs) when those changes occur during a saccade* (e.g., Henderson & Hollingworth, 2003; Simons & Ambinder, 2005).

A final detail concerns the triggering of saccades and the engagement of visual attention. As Allport (1989) noted, there is a competition-like situation in visual attention. On the one hand, attention must be interruptible. That is, we need to be able to react quickly to the unexpected, as when sudden movement alerts us to a possibly dangerous situation (a car running a red light as you drive through the intersection). While you are focusing your attention on one stimulus, the visual system must be able to react to other visual inputs, those outside the focus of attention, to at least some degree (e.g., Theeuwes, Kramer, Hahn, & Irwin, 1998). As you will read later, much of this low-level processing occurs in parallel with other visual processing (Treisman & Gelade, 1980).

On the other hand, visual attention should not be *too* interruptible. We cannot constantly be switching from one thing to another—from the words in this sentence to your desk lamp to the scene outside your window to the color of the wall. If attention switched that frequently and erratically, visual (and mental) continuity would be destroyed. Balancing these competing tendencies is an ongoing process; we evaluate the importance of current activity, of maintaining visual attention, relative to the importance of things outside the current attentional focus.

Several studies have shown that *we sometimes fail to see an object we are looking at directly because attention is directed elsewhere* (Mack, 2003); this **inattention blindness** is due, in some sense, to our lack of attention to an object. In a dramatic demonstration of this, Haines (1991) tested experienced pilots in flight simulators. A few of them proceeded to land the simulator, paying attention to the gauges and dials on the instrument panel but failing to notice that another airplane was blocking the runway (see Mack & Rock, 1998). That's a dramatic example, but it's indicative of our mental processing, nonetheless.

Visual Sensory Memory

We turn now to visual sensory memory. Because this memory system has such a short duration, we have few useful intuitions about its operation. Unusual circumstances, however, can give us some clues. We begin with such a circumstance.

Everyone has seen a flash of lightning. Think about that for a moment, and make a guess as to the duration of a bolt of lightning. Most people guess that the flash of light lasts a little more than a half second or so, maybe closer to a whole second. If your estimate was in this neighborhood, then it is reasonable—but wrong. The bolt of lightning is actually three or four separate bolts. Each one lasts about 1 millisecond (ms), and there is a separation of about 50 ms between bolts. Thus the entire lightning strike lasts no more than about 2/10 of a second, or 200 ms, and is composed of several individual flashes (Trigg & Lerner, 1981).

Our perception of lightning is a mental event that reflects visual persistence.

Given that it was so off, what was reasonable about your estimate? It was your *perception* of a flash of light that extended in time. This is called **visual persistence**, the *apparent persistence of a visual stimulus beyond its physical duration*. The neural activity on the retina that is caused by the lightning flash does not outlast the flash itself. The eye does not continue to send "lightning" messages after the flash is over. Your perception of the lightning is a mental event that reflects visual persistence in that you perceive a lighted scene that then fades away. Because any persistence of information beyond its physical duration defines the term *memory*, the processes of visual perception (as opposed to sensation) must begin with memory, a *temporary visual buffer that holds visual information for brief periods of time*. This memory is called **visual sensory memory** or **iconic memory** (Neisser, 1967).

AMOUNT AND DURATION OF STORAGE The classic research on the characteristics and processes of visual sensory memory was reported by Sperling and his coworkers (Averbach & Sperling, 1961; Sperling, 1960). Sperling presented a visual stimulus for a controlled period of time, usually on the order of milliseconds, to study "the information available in brief visual presentations," the title of his paper in 1960. A typical iconic memory experiment presented arrays of letters and digits to people for brief durations. In all cases, the task was to report what could be remembered from the display. For example, people were shown a series of trials, each with a 3 × 4 array of letters (three rows, four letters per row). The array was shown for 50 ms and was followed by a blank postexposure field. Finally, a signal was given to report the letters. See Figure 3-4 for a schematic diagram of a typical trial.

Sperling found that people generally reported no more than 4 or 5 items correctly. Furthermore, this level of accuracy is essentially the same for exposures as long as 500 ms and as short as 5 ms (Sperling, 1963). It seemed that an average of 4.5 items correct reflected a default strategy. People said they could not remember all 12 letters, because the display seemed to fade from view too rapidly. Their level of performance, about 4 or 5 items, was what is expected based on the **span of**

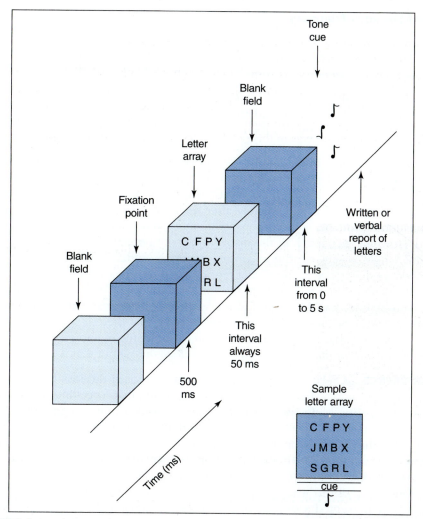

FIGURE 3-4   A schematic diagram of a typical trial in Sperling's (1960) experiments. After a fixation point appears for 500 ms, the letter array is displayed. The visual field after the display is blank. The tone cue can occur at the same time as the postfield, or it can be delayed up to 5s. Data from Sperling (1960).

apprehension, *the number of items recallable after any short display* (also known as the *span of attention* or the *span of immediate memory*; see Chapters 4 and 5).

What distinguished Sperling's research was a condition he developed to contrast with these results. The condition just described, in which *people are to report any letters they can,* is called the **whole report condition** because the whole display is to be reported. The condition Sperling created is called the **partial report condition**, *in which only one of the rows was to be reported.* Sperling reasoned that *all* the letters of the display might be available initially but then might be lost faster than they can be reported (note that Zhang & Luck, 2009, suggest that these representations do not fade, but are lost). If so, then people should be accurate on any of the rows the experimenter might choose if they are told which row to report before too much loss took place. So in the partial report condition, he had a signal: A high tone, sounded right after the display went off, was a cue for reporting the top row, a medium tone for the middle row, and a low tone for the bottom row. Importantly, people had no way of knowing which row they would be responsible for, so they had to be prepared to report any of them.

Given that the array should still be available because of visual persistence, the person should be able to focus attention on whichever row was cued, and read out those letters accurately. This is exactly what happened. When the tone followed the display immediately, performance was 76% correct, regardless of row. By extension, if performance was 76% on any randomly selected row, then visual memory of the *entire* display must also be around 76%.[1]

This suggests that immediately after seeing a visual display, a great deal of information is available in visual sensory memory, much more than can be reported aloud. However, this much of the display does not remain available for long. After all, the whole report condition almost never exceeded four or five items. As expected, performance in the partial report group declines as the iconic memories are lost. As more time passed until the tone sounded, performance dwindled further. With a 1-second delay, partial report performance was back down to 36% (Sperling, 1960). So, results such as these indicate that there is a large amount of information available in the **icon** (the contents of iconic memory often are called the icon, *the visual image that resides in iconic memory*) but that it is lost quickly.

INTERFERENCE   A related series of experiments explored the loss of information from iconic memory. The original research suggested that forgetting was *a passive process like fading* or **decay**; that is, the mere passage of time degraded the icon. But, in normal vision we look around continuously, shifting our gaze from one thing to another. What happens to iconic memory when one visual scene immediately follows another? The answer, in short, is **interference**, *forgetting caused by the effects of intervening stimulation or mental processing*.

One study of this was by Averbach and Coriell (1961; reprinted in Coltheart, 1973). They presented a display of two rows of letters, eight letters per row, for 50 ms. A blank white postexposure field, varying in duration, followed the display and was itself followed by a partial report cue. Unlike Sperling, Averbach and Coriell used a visual cue, either a vertical bar marker or a circle marker. The bar marker was just above (or below) the position of the to-be-reported letter, and the circle marker surrounded the position where the to-be-reported letter had just been. With the bar marker, the results that were similar to those obtained by Sperling, such as higher performance with short delays of the cues. But the results with the circle marker were different. With the circle marker, accuracy was lower than with the bar marker, especially when the target letter resembled the circle marker (for instance, when the letter c had been shown at that position).

These results suggest that the circle had in some way disrupted the memory trace for the letter in that position. Thus, a later visual stimulus interfered with the

---

[1]Professors use the same logic. We tell our class, "You are going to be tested on Chapters 1 through 3," then we ask questions only from Chapter 2. If a student scores 76% on this test, we infer that student also could have gotten about 76% on either of the other two chapters. Thus it seems that 76% of the total amount of information was available to the student on the test.

memory for the prior stimulus at that location. This is called **backward masking**. The masking stimulus, if it occurs soon enough after the display, interferes with the perception of the earlier image at the same spot. In some backward masking studies, people claim that they saw *only* the mask, even though their performance indicates that sensation did indeed register the first stimulus (data on this go back as far as Werner, 1935; see Kahneman, 1968, for a review).

The Early Parts of a Fixation

The evidence by Sperling, Averbach and Coriell, and many others led cognitive psychology to propose that iconic memory existed and that it was the first phase in visual perception (Neisser, 1967). But newer evidence is showing even more fascinating results. A study by Rayner, Inhoff, Morrison, Slowiaczek, and Bertera (1981) is a good example. They examined performance during reading (see Chapter 10 for more research on the process of reading), using an eye tracker for precise timing measurements. After people had fixated a word for a mere 50 ms, the word was replaced with an irrelevant stimulus, which remained in view for another 175 ms to fill up the rest of the fixation time. Surprisingly, this did not affect reading at all—people often did not notice that the word had even changed!

This is important—this is very important, so you should stop and think about it for a moment. Despite what it feels like, as you read these words on this page, you are not viewing them continuously. You are seeing them in brief bursts, extracting information quickly and then devoting mental energy to processing them further, unaware of your "down time" during the fixation and of your blindness during the following saccade.

Several investigators have also collected evidence on what might be called "dynamic icons," that is, iconic images that contain movement (see Finke & Freyd, 1985; Irwin, 1991, 1992; Loftus & Hanna, 1989). Treisman, Russell, and Green (1975) presented a brief (100 ms) display of six moving dots and asked people to report the direction of movement. Partial report performance was superior to whole report performance, and accuracy under partial report declined across time. In short, the moving images of the dots were decaying just as the static letter grid had in Sperling's procedures. Visual perception, therefore, is not a process of flipping through successive snapshots, with three or four snapshots per second. Instead, it is a process of focusing on the visually attended elements of successive fixations, where each fixation encodes a dynamic segment of the visual environment.

In fact, integration across brief intervals of time can occur even *without* eye movements. Loftus and Irwin (1998) showed that temporal integration—perceiving two separate events as if they had occurred at the same time—happens seamlessly when visual events occur within about 20 ms of each other. This happens without any conscious awareness that two separate events have occurred. Events separated by 40 ms or more, or separate events that themselves last for 40 ms or more, tend not to be integrated as completely, however. With these longer durations, people can more easily detect that two separate events happened rather than just one.

A Summary for Visual Sensory Memory

How do all these different results make sense: the wholesale input of visual stimulation; the persistence, decay, interference, and integration of information; and the concept of visual attention? The entire sequence of encoding visual information—selecting part of it for further processing, planning subsequent eye movements, and so on—is very active and rapid. The visual continuity we experience, our feeling that we see continuously, is due to the constant updating of visual sensory memory and to our focus on attended information. As we attend to a visual stimulus, we are examining the readout from iconic memory. In the meantime, a new visual scene is being registered in iconic memory. Our mental processes then pick up the thread of the newly registered scene, providing a smooth transition from one display to the next.

Focal attention was Neisser's (1967) term for this *mental process of visual attention,* such as the mental redirection of attention when the partial report cue is presented. It seems that focal attention, or simply *visual attention,* helps bridge between successive scenes in visual sensory memory. This prevents us from sensing the blank space of time occupied by the eye's saccades by directing focal attention to elements of the icon. Although we *sense* a great deal of visual information, what we *perceive* is the part of a visual scene selected for focal, visual attention. To exaggerate a bit, what you are perceiving right now is not the printed page in front of you, but the processed and attended portions that were registered in sensory memory, your iconic trace, as processed by visual attention.

Trans-saccadic Memory

To build up an understanding of the visual world, we need to move our eyes, head, and body, gathering in visual information across each successive fixation. How do we put all of these fixations together? This is done using iconic memory in a way known as **trans-saccadic memory** (e.g., Irwin, 1996), *the memory that is used across a series of eye movements.* How does iconic memory track information to figure out how to put together information from different fixations? It does not use retinal coordinates (where the images fall on the eyes) or spatial coordinates (where things are in space) to do this (Irwin, Yantis, & Jonides, 1983). Instead, trans-saccadic memory works by using what are called *object files* (Kahneman, Triesman, & Gibbs, 1992), which are *iconic representations of individual objects used to track what is going on in the world.* Evidence for their use comes from studies in which people are asked to detect changes in objects after a saccadic eye movement (Henderson & Anes, 1994)—for example, detecting whether a letter changed to a plus sign in a display. In general, people are fairly accurate at noticing changes in objects they focused on. This does not occur for all objects in a visual scene, but only those that a person is attending to. Our brain assumes that everything that we are not attending to is more or less stable, which is why we may miss those changes.

Section Summary

- The eye sweeps across the visual field in short, jerky movements called saccades, taking in information during brief fixations. The information encoded in these fixations is stored in visual sensory memory for no more than about 250 ms. This iconic image, which may include movement, is lost rapidly or can be interfered with by subsequent visual stimulation. More information is stored in visual sensory memory than can be reported immediately. Information that is reported has been selected by focal attention.

- We do not continuously extract information from the visual scene around us, but instead extract most of the information we need within the first 50 ms of fixation. Thus, visual sensory memory is a fast-acting and rapidly adapting system, ideally suited for processing information in real time in a continuously dynamic world.
- To build up a complete mental representation of the world, we use transsaccadic memory. This integration tracks the various entities in the world using object files of what they are doing and how they might be changing. However, this also requires that a person be actively attending to those objects.

PATTERN RECOGNITION

We turn now to one of the most intriguing and debated topics in visual perception, the identification of patterns and objects. As you will see, pattern recognition does not occur instantly, although it does happen automatically and spontaneously. Perceptual pattern recognition is, in many ways, a problem-solving process, with much of the mental work occurring subconsciously and very rapidly. Essentially, during perception a person needs to identify the nature of the *distal* objects in the world based on the *proximal* images reaching the retina. Often these images are compromised in some way, such as being occluded by another object or being against a complex visual background. There are a number of ways that vision parses the visual image to extract information about the objects that are actually present, and there are a number of principles that it follows in doing this.

Gestalt Grouping Principles

Perhaps the best-known and established of these perceptual principles are the Gestalt grouping principles laid out by the Gestalt psychologists (see Chapter 1) in the early to mid 20th century. These principles identify those characteristics of perception in which ambiguities in a stimulus are resolved to help determine which objects are present. They are also aimed more at processing information about the whole of an object, rather than simply, and only, building up a mental representation from more basic elements. This approach has been supported by fMRI neuroimaging work (Kubilius, Wagemans, & Op de Beeck, 2011) that has shown that some parts of the brain, namely the lateral occipital lobe (B.A. 19) and the posterior fusiform gyrus (B.A. 37), are involved in the processing of whole objects, apart from the occipital brain areas involved in processing individual elements (see the section on feature detection later).

One of these Gestalt principles is the *figure-ground* principle. When viewing an image, part of the image is treated as the figure or foreground (the object identified), which is segregated from the visual information upon which it is set (the background). Classic examples illustrating difficulties in determining figure-ground

Simulate
Distinguishing Figure-Ground Relationships in
MyPsychLab

FIGURE 3-5   An illustration of the Gestalt figure-ground perceptual grouping principle.

Simulate
Gestalt Laws of Perception in
MyPsychLab

are reversible figures, such as the one shown in Figure 3-5 in which a person shifts back and forth between what is the foregrounded object, and what is the background. At one moment it might be two faces, whereas in the next it might be a vase.

Some Gestalt grouping principles are aimed at providing a more complete percept from an incoming image that may be fragmentary or incomplete. They follow the principle of *closure*, in which a person "closes up" an image that has gaps or parts missing, perhaps because they are being occluded (blocked) by some other object. An example of closure can be seen in Figure 3-6C. Although there are just a collection of dashed lines here, they can be joined using the principle of closure to give the impression of a circle and a square.

Additional Gestalt principles included *proximity*, in which elements that are near to one another tend to be grouped together. This is shown in Figure 3-6A. Because of this principle, you see a flight of geese as forming a classic V. Another is *similarity*, in which elements that are visually similar in some way, such as having a similar color or texture, tend to be grouped together. This is shown in Figure 3-6B. An example of the use of similarity is when you see the individual dots on a television or computer screen as being part of the same object if they have a similar color or visual texture.

Finally, some grouping principles take into account some form of trajectory. In some cases, the trajectory is the edge of an object. The principle of *good continuation* assumes that when an edge is interrupted, people assume that it continues along in a

FIGURE 3-6 An illustration of the Gestalt perceptual grouping principles of proximity (A), similarity (B), closure (C), and good continuation (D).

regular fashion. In the example shown in Figure 3-6D people tend to organize this as lines from A to B and from C to D, not A to D, B to C, etc. Finally, with *common fate,* entities that move together are grouped together. For example, when an animal moves in the forest, it is easier to spot than if it remains motionless. This is because the movement allows perception to group those points together because they are moving together.

Although we use Gestalt grouping principles to some degree, we need to go deeper to understand how a visual stimulus is recognized as a familiar pattern. How does cognition manage to input a visual stimulus such as *G* or *tree* and end up recognizing them as familiar and meaningful? How do we recognize patterns of handwriting, or different printed fonts, despite incredible variability? The following sections present some ideas about how this occurs, by looking at the case of written language.

The Template Approach

As Neisser (1967) pointed out, pattern recognition would be simplified, though still thorny, if all the equivalent patterns we saw were identical. That is, pattern recognition would be easier to explain if there were one and only one way for the capital letter *G* to appear. But, the visual environment is not like this. An enormous variety of visual patterns, in countless combinations of orientation and size, are all categorized as the capital letter *G*, and likewise for all other letters, figures, shapes, and so on.

Perhaps this categorization is done by means of **templates**, *stored models of all categorizable patterns*. When the computer at your bank reads your checking account number, it is using a template matching process, making physical identity matches between the numbers on your check and its stored templates for the digits 0 through 9. When the computer recognizes a pattern, it has matched it to one of its stored templates (think bar codes).

The template approach has simplicity and economy on its side, and we do have preferred viewing angles for many objects (called the *canonical view*), such as preferring to view a cow from the side, rather than from above or in front. However, beyond this simplicity and economy, it has little else to recommend it, and it has some serious flaws. We have already covered the primary reason, the enormous variability in the patterns that we can recognize. Also, just think of how long would it take you to learn the infinite number of possible patterns (for all of the objects in the world, the different orientations they can be in, the various distances they can be from you, etc.) and search through those patterns in memory. Would you have time left for anything else?

Visual Feature Detection

An improvement over the template approach is **feature analysis** or **feature detection**. A feature is a *very simple visual element that can appear in combination with other features* across a variety of stimulus patterns. A good example of a visual feature might be a straight, horizontal line, which appears in capital letters *A*, *G*, *H*, *L*, and so on; others would be vertical or diagonal lines, curves, and so on. In Chapter 2, you read about a connectionist model of word recognition (refer back to Figure 2-12); the lowest level of representation in that model was at this feature level. In general, feature theories claim that we recognize patterns by first identifying their features. Rather than matching an entire template-like pattern for capital *G*, we identify the elemental features that are present in the *G*. When "circle opening right" and "horizontal straight" segments are detected, the features match with those stored in memory for capital *G*.

Several investigators have proposed theories of feature-based pattern recognition. We'll discuss one such model, Pandemonium, in detail. Understanding Pandemonium will also help you understand the reasons behind interactive, connectionist approaches.

PANDEMONIUM   Selfridge (1959), an early advocate of feature detection, described a model of pattern recognition he called **Pandemonium**; an illustration of the model is shown in Figure 3-7. In Selfridge's imaginative description, the mechanisms involved were little mental *demons* who shout out loud as they attempt to identify patterns. As the figure shows, a pattern is encoded by a set of *data demons*. Next, the *computational demons* begin to act. They are the feature analyzers in Selfridge's model; each one has a single, simple feature it is trying to

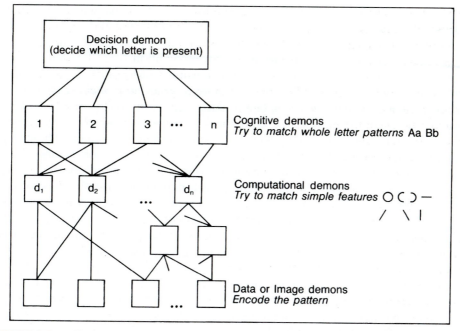

FIGURE 3-7   Selfridge's (1959) Pandemonium model. The image demons encode the visual pattern. The feature demons try to match the simple features present in the pattern. Cognitive demons represent the combination of features that are present in different letters of the alphabet; each tries to match the several computational demons that match the stimulus input. Finally, the decision demon identifies the pattern by selecting the loudest cognitive demon, the one whose features most nearly match the pattern being presented. Adapted from Selfridge(1959).

match in the stimulus pattern. For instance, one demon might be trying to match a simple horizontal line, another would try to match a vertical line, another a curve opening to the right, and so on. When a computational demon matches a stimulus feature, it begins to shout excitedly.

At the next level up, listening to all this shouting is a set of *cognitive demons*. They represent the different letters of the alphabet, one for each letter. Each one is listening for a particular combination of demons: For instance, the *G*-demon is listening for the "open curve" and the "horizontal bar" feature analyzers or demons to shout. Any evidence from the computational demons that suggests a match with the stimulus causes the cognitive demon to begin shouting as well: Based on the feature analysis evidence, it thinks that *it* is the matching pattern. Several of the cognitive demons will be shouting at once because several letters usually share some features (e.g., *C* and *G*). Thus the one who shouts the loudest is the one whose pattern most nearly matched the stimulus. The loudest cognitive demon is heard by the *decision demon*. This demon has the final say in recognizing and categorizing the pattern.

THREE IMPORTANT IDEAS   Aside from the vividness of the model's description of scores of shouting demons producing a noisy Pandemonium, Selfridge's model incorporates several ideas that are important for pattern recognition. First, at base, it is a feature detection model. The features that are detected and reported by the demons are elementary, simple features. There are several related lines of evidence for feature detection in visual pattern recognition (e.g., Pritchard, 1961). Especially convincing are neurophysiological studies showing that special visual cortex cells exist for simple visual features. These are found in area V1 (B.A. 17) of the occipital lobe, where "V" stands for "visual." The most widely known evidence of this kind comes from research pioneered by Hubel and Wiesel (1962). Using electrode implant procedures, these researchers found neurons in cats' brains that respond only to vertical lines, others that respond only to diagonals, and so on. On the assumption that the human brain is not radically different from a cat's (at least for vision), this suggests that feature detection may even have a physiological status in the nervous system. Furthermore, it means that psychological theories must be compatible with this neurological evidence.

A second important idea in Selfridge's model was parallel processing: The computational demons all work at the same time, each one trying to match its own feature while the others are doing the same thing. With this aspect of his model, Selfridge was pointing out that feature analysis is a parallel process. Neisser, Novick, and Lazar (1963) found evidence consistent with parallel feature processing when their participants could scan for the presence of 10 different letters just as quickly as they could scan for 1.

The third important idea captured by Pandemonium was that perception is, in a very real sense, a problem-solving process. The world presents the visual system with bits and pieces of features and relations. The visual system must put these together to accurately identify the objects that are out there in the world. Often the system gets this correct. However, occasionally errors do occur, as with visual illusions, or when you mistakenly identify one object as something else, such as when you are driving and swerve to avoid hitting a chipmunk, only to discover a moment later that it is only a dead leaf.

Simulate
*Muller-Lyer
Illusion* in
MyPsychLab

The inadequacy of template approaches, and the advantage of feature-based approaches, is further emphasized when you think about how we interact with the world. Specially, we are often in motion, walking, running, driving, and so on. Moreover, the things we are looking at are often moving as well. Thus, our views of objects can be constantly shifting. The area of the brain that leads us to see objects as constant and stable across such movement and different viewing angles is area MT (B.A. 19), part of the dorsal stream of visual processing, at the conjunction of the occipital, parietal, and temporal lobes. This area is also involved in the perception of apparent movement (Larsen & Bundesen, 2009), as well as real movement, when cognition must make inferences about what goes on in between—such as when you are watching a movie or television, which involves a series of still pictures presented to you in rapid fashion, one after the other. The pictures change faster than your iconic memory can decay, replacing one another. Your brain fills in any jumps in position, producing the illusion of motion. This mental perception of illusory motion is **beta movement** (Wertheimer, 1912). A related, perceptual illusion occurs when you see lights moving or flowing around on a movie marquee or chasing Christmas lights. This is the **phi phenomenon** (Wertheimer, 1912). Essentially, when iconic memory receives visual images in relatively close proximity in space and time, it will infer virtual movement.[2] So, in essence, beta movement occurs when making inferences from one picture to the next, as in a movie, but phi movement involves illusory tracking of an object in space.

Beyond Features: Conceptually Driven Pattern Recognition

Even Selfridge knew that Pandemonium was missing an important ingredient. Basically, Pandemonium was a completely **bottom-up**, **data-driven processing system** in which *processing is driven by the stimulus pattern, the incoming data.* The patterns to be recognized came in to the image demons at the bottom, then were processed at higher and higher levels until the top-level demon finally recognized the pattern. And yet, Selfridge presented examples like those shown in Figure 3-8, showing that context influences pattern recognition. How adequate is the bottom-up approach as a sole explanation of visual pattern recognition? Did you "see" the words WENT and EVENT despite the fact that the way they are written in the two sentences is identical? So what was the missing ingredient in Selfrige's model?

The missing ingredient was *context* and a person's expectations. Such effects are called top-down, or **conceptually driven effects**, in which *context and higher-level knowledge influence lower-level processes* (remember "typographical"?). In Figure 3-8 your knowledge of English words and your understanding of the meaning of sentences leads you to perceive what is written as either the word WENT or EVENT, depending on the context. Let's examine some evidence that supports the feature theory approach but also makes the case for conceptually driven processing.

In Neisser's (1964) classic work on visual search, people saw pages of characters, 50 lines of printed letters, with four to six letters per line. The task was to scan the page as rapidly as possible to find the one occurrence of a prespecified

FIGURE 3-8   As an illustration of the power of top-down processing, consider these two sentences. If you look carefully, the way the word "went" is written in the first sentence is identical to the way the word "event" is written second sentence. Although they are perceptually identical, your expectations based on the context bias you to see the beginning part as either a "w" or an "e" and a "v."

---

[2]The phi phenomenon was important in the establishment of automated railroad crossings. Back in the day, important railroad crossings had a railroad employee who would swing a lantern to warn vehicles that they were approaching a crossing. The automated crossings were designed with two lights that would blink at the appropriate rate to produce the Phi phenomenon and produce the perception of a swinging lamp. However, when the first automated crossings were built, they got the timing off—it just looked like two lights alternating on and off. Nevertheless, the railroad companies stuck with that timing.

A. Search for *Z*	B. Search for line without *P*	C. Search for *K*	D. Search for *K*
EHYP	ZVMLBP	ODUGQR	IVMXEW
SWIQ	HSPJMF	QCDUGO	EWVMIX
UFCJ	ZTJVPR	CQOGRD	EXWMVI
WBYH	RDPTFM	QUGCDR	IXEMWV
OGTX	TPVRSX	URDGQO	VXWEMI
GWVX	MSVRPX	GRUQDO	MXVEWI
TWLN	ZHPBTL	DUKGRO	XVWMEI
XJBU	ZJTPXL	UCGROD	MWXVIE
UDXI	LHPVXM	DQRCGU	VIMEXW
HSFP	FVPHMS	QDOCGU	EXVWIM
XSCQ	MTSDPL	CGUROQ	VWMIEX
SDJU	TZDFPB	OCDURQ	VMWIEX
PODC	PLHBMZ	UOCGQD	XVWMEI
KVBP	PMXBJD	RGQCOU	WXVEMI
PEVK	RVZHSP	GRUDQO	XMEWIV
SLRA	STFMPZ	GODUCQ	MXIVEW
JCEN	RVXSPM	QCURDO	VEWMIX
KLRD	MPBJFT	DUCOQG	EMVXWI
XBOD	MVZXLP	CGRDQU	IVWMEX
PHMU	RTBXPH	UDRCOQ	IEVMWX
KHFZ	BLPSZX	GQCORU	WVKMXE
PNJW	PSVFDJ	GOQUCD	XEMIWV
CQXT	FLDVZT	GDQUOC	WXIMEV
GHNR	BPHMDX	URDCGO	EMWIVX
IXYD	BMFDPH	GODROC	IVEMXW
QSVB	PHLJZT		
GUCH	TPSHRL		
OWBN	BMPHZJ		
BVQN	RTBJZP		
FOAS	FPDLXH		
ITKN	XJHSVP		
VYLD	MZRJDP		
LRYK	XVPRMB		
IJXE	PMXLSD		
RBOE	DSZHPR		
DVUS	FJPSMV		
BIAJ	RSBMDP		
ESGF	LBMPFX		
QGKI	FDMVPJ		
KWNE	HPZTXB		
QBVC	VBPSRF		
VARP	PHSVDZ		
LRPA	HVPBFL		
SGHL	HSRPZV		
MVRJ	DPVXFB		
GADB	RXJPSM		
PCME	MPZFVD		
KODW	ZJLRTP		
HDBR	SHMVTP		
BVDK	PXFBRJ		

FIGURE 3-9 Neisser's (1964) search lists. In list A, the target is the letter *Z;* in list B, the target is the line without the letter *P;* in lists C and D, the target is the letter *K.*

letter (in other tasks, people had to find the line *without* a certain letter). As an illustration, do the visual searches presented in Figure 3-9, timing yourself as you find the targets. Notice how hard it is to find a line *without* a specified letter and to find a letter that is physically similar to the distractor letters.

Finding the *Z* in the angular-letter column is hard because the features that define *Z* are also sprinkled throughout the angular letters. Likewise, finding the *K* in the third column is easier than in the fourth, because the third column contains mostly rounded-feature letters that can be ignored (see also Duncan & Humphreys, 1989). Aha—*there's* the shortcoming: We have to "shut off" some feature detectors to explain fast search for *Z* in the round-letter condition. But where did the instruction to shut off those detectors come from? Not from the feature detectors themselves. Feature detectors do only one thing—they detect visual features. Instead, this instruction came from some place "higher up," something that "realizes" you can ignore the dissimilar letter shapes. This is the contribution of your existing knowledge to the lower-level process of feature detection—it's conceptually driven processing.

To be sure, pattern recognition starts by processing the incoming pattern, a bottom-up process. Nonetheless, this bottom-up emphasis slights the contribution of top-down processes. It misses the effect of **context**, the *surrounding information and your own knowledge.* The influence of knowledge and expertise on perception is fairly common. Think of the ability of people who are experts at reading x-rays, tasting wines, or identifying fingerprints (e.g., Busey & Parada, 2010) to detect subtle variations and detect things that for most people are very hard to notice. Still, there is some expertise that you have, and this is in your ability to read. As an example, we often identify a pattern that is *not* in original stimulus at all, such as the word *the* in

Without context.

the last clause. You misread that sentence, didn't you? And now you know where the missing *the* came from: It came from you, from your knowledge of language. Top-level conceptual knowledge in memory augments or assists lower-level processes such as pattern recognition.

Here's a set of sentences (from Morris & Harris, 2002) that illustrate top-down processing.

When she spilled the ink there was ink all over.

She ran her best time yet in the rice last week.

I broke a wine class in my class yesterday.

In the first sentence, the word *ink* is repeated. When the sentence is presented word-by-word at a rapid rate (this is called the *RSVP method*, for *Rapid Serial Visual Presentation*), a surprising result is obtained, called *repetition blindness*. People often fail to report the second occurrence of *ink*—even though it makes the sentence ungrammatical, people report having seen "When she spilled the ink there was all over" (see also Kanwisher, 1987, 1991). **Repetition blindness** is *the tendency to not perceive a pattern, whether a word, a picture, or any other visual stimulus, when it is quickly repeated.* The basic explanation is that cognition has just identified the stimulus, so it "expects" *not* to see the same thing again.

Another interesting effect noted by Morris and Harris (2002) was a misreading effect, a tendency to read a word that *should* be in the sentence, based on context, such as *race* instead of *rice,* and *glass* instead of *class* in the other two sentences. Morris and Harris found that repetition blindness and misreading can

With context.

combine. For example, in "ink–ink" trials, a strong repetition blindness effect occurred—the second "ink" was reported less than 50% of the time, compared to a control sentence such as "When she dropped the box there was ink all over," where "ink" was reported over 80% of the time. The percentages were similar in the "class–class" sentences—but only when the first "class" was read correctly. When the context led people to read "wine glass," however, there was no repetition blindness—reports of "class" were correct on about 70% of the trials. So, even in cases ("class–class") that should produce repetition blindness, the critical variable was what word ("glass") the person had understood.

Note that top-down, conceptually driven processing can be influenced not just by things like your knowledge of a language or the context of a sentence. Even one's culture can influence perception to some degree. For example, there is evidence suggesting that when Westerners view a scene, they are more likely to focus perceptual processes on a foreground object and its visual properties. Eastern Asians, by comparison, are more likely to focus on the context and the background of the scene, taking into account the relations among the various elements (e.g., Nisbett & Masuda, 2003). This conclusion is supported by evidence of different levels of neural activity in perceptual processing regions of the brain (Gutchess, Welsh, Boduroglu, & Park, 2006).

Conceptually driven *and* data-driven processes work in combination in most pattern recognition situations, not to mention more complex cognitive processes such as language comprehension. And an excellent way to model this, to explore how this combination works, is within the connectionist model introduced in Chapter 2. Think of this model as Pandemonium Plus, a bottom-up model like Selfridge's with an added top-down processing effect.

Connectionist Modeling

Connectionist modeling is a computational approach that is often used in cognitive science. Connectionist models involve a *massive* number of mathematical computations. Essentially, each unit in a connectionist layer is massively connected with many or all of the units in the next layer. The impact of each experience on each of these connections needs to be computed. Even if the number of units is fairly small, the number of separate computations in a single run of the model is staggeringly large because of massive number of connections among the units.

To flesh out the word recognition model (McClelland & Rumelhart, 1981; Rumelhart & McClelland, 1986), we'll use a model that recognizes four-letter words, such as *TREE*. We start with some of the basics of connectionist modeling, including some of the vocabulary. Table 3-1 provides a list of basic terms and assumptions, with some explanations to help you. Consult Table 3-1 and Figure 3-10 frequently as you read the next section.

TABLE 3-1   A Primer of Connectionist Terminology and Assumptions

Basic Statement of PDP Principles

- Complex mental operations are the combined effects of the massively parallel processing that characterizes a network. The processing is distributed across all the levels of the network (hence the term *parallel distributed processing,* or PDP).

- A network is composed of (often) three levels of units: the input level, hidden level, and output level. The internal "hidden" layer is invisible to an outsider. Units in each of these levels are interconnected (hence the term *connectionism*). The connections are either positively or negatively weighted.

- Positive connection weights pass excitatory activation to the connected unit; negatively weighted connections pass inhibition. A unit transmits its activation to connected units if it has received enough positive activation to reach threshold. The analog here is excitatory and inhibitory neurotransmitters, which play a similar role in the nervous system.

- Connection weights are varied as a function of training, in which feedback as to correctness or incorrectness leads to a mathematical adjustment of weights. When a network is given this procedure and the weights have stabilized, the network is said to have been trained up. Back propagation is a commonly used training method, although others exist.

- The similarities between PDP models and the neurological structures and activities in the brain are intentional; connections sometimes are called synapses, excitation and inhibition parallel those processes in the cortex, and the approach is known as *neural net modeling.*

Lexicon of Other Connectionist Terms

Back propagation	A commonly used training procedure, in which the weight-adjusting phase proceeds from the output units back in to the other layers, each unit propagating a series of computations.
Delta rule	The mathematical rule for adjusting weights during training, where delta (Δ) stands for "change."
Distributed representation	The representation for a letter, word, concept, and so on is distributed because the knowledge is spread widely across the units and their weights.
Local minima	Occasionally during training, the system finds a stable baseline value for the weights, the global minimum; think of the global minimum as the deepest "valley." But the system may just be trapped in a local minimum or valley.
Massively parallel processing	Almost all units in the system have a role in processing, and all units operate simultaneously.

INPUT UNITS   Let's build the simple model illustrated in Figure 3-10 piece by piece. Here there are three levels of units. At the bottom are the *input units.* These are elementary "cells" that receive input from the environment. Our example is visual word recognition, so our input units are simple visual detectors. That is, we have nine input units, each of which responds to different visual features of the letters of the alphabet. To build on what you already understand, consider the input units to have the same function as the data and computational demons in Pandemonium shown in Figure 3-7. Our input units encode and respond to simple visual features in letters of the alphabet. Thus the input-unit level in this illustration is the feature-detector level.

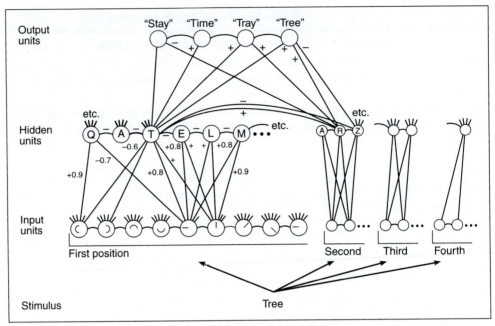

FIGURE 3-10 A portion of the PDP network for recognizing four-letter words. The bulk of the illustration involves identifying the first letter of the word.

HIDDEN UNITS   When a stimulus is presented to the input level, one or more of the units matches the features in the stimulus. When this happens, each unit that matches activates a set of connected units in the middle, *hidden unit* level; *hidden* here simply means that this level is internal, always one step removed from either input or output. Note that the activation is sent across the connections that link the units together; *these* are the connections in connectionism.

The connections have a weight that represents the relationship between the linked units. Some weights are positive, and some are negative. So, in Figure 3-10 the horizontal straight bar feature has positive weights connecting it to the letters *T, E,* and *L* because they all contain that feature (to minimize confusion, many of the connections have not been drawn fully, and only a few numerical weights are given). Conversely, the weights between the horizontal straight bar feature and the letters *C, O, Q,* and so on are negative. Likewise, all the curved features at the input level have positive weights to curved letters and negative weights to angular letters. Eventually, after all the weights have been factored into the computational formulae, activations at the output level come into play.

OUTPUT UNITS   Where is this getting us? Imagine that you were building a machine (programming a computer) that could identify visually presented words. What you see in Figure 3-10 is the connectionist network for the first position in four-letter words. Three more sets of connections, shown in reduced form at the right of the figure, duplicate the same connections again, once for each position. Given these additional positions, we can now talk about the *output units.*

For simplicity, only a handful of four-letter words are shown in the figure. Note, however, that three of the word-level units are consistent with the letter detection performed on *T* in the first position; that is, three of the words begin with a *T*. Now think about the fuller model that identifies four-letter words. Each of the four input unit segments performs as described earlier, forwarding both activation and inhibition to the hidden units, these in turn forwarding activation and inhibition to the output units. At the end, one of the several output units will have received enough activation to exceed its threshold. When this happens, that unit responds by answering the question, "What is this word?"

One more complexity is needed to get top-down effects into the model. Reflect for a moment on how likely the spelling pattern *TZ* is at the beginning of English words. Not very likely, is it? On the other hand, *TA, TE, TI,* and other consonant–vowel pairs are likely, as are a few consonant–consonant pairs such as *TH* and *TR*. These likelihoods are represented in the network; to distinguish them visually from the other connections, they are shown with curve-shaped connections. The overall effect of these letter-to-letter weights is that the activations in the system can make up for missing features at the perceptual level.

Figure 3-11 shows the final levels of activation for three possible words, given the partially obscured stimulus pattern at the bottom. This shows an important feature of connectionist models: Enough knowledge is represented in the system, in the weights for letter-to-letter sequences, that the model identifies the word *fork* even when the last letter could also be an *R*.

Why is this important? It is important because it illustrates the general theme of top-down, conceptually driven processing. If you saw the partially obscured pattern in Figure 3-11, you would identify the word as *fork*, based on your knowledge that *forr* is not an English word. Your knowledge of English assists your

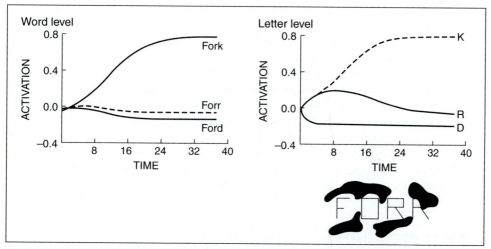

FIGURE 3-11   A possible display that might be presented in the connectionist model of word recognition and the resulting activations of selected letter and word units. The letter units are for the letters indicated in the fourth position of a four-letter display. Based on Rumelhart & McClelland (1986).

perception. This is what happens in the connectionist model; higher-level knowledge, coded as weighted connections in the network, participates in the lower-level task of identifying letters.

Note that the weights of the connections change with experience. Every experience you have changes you, because the connections among the neurons are changed, even if in very subtle ways. As an example of this, in a study by Hussain, Sekuler, and Bennett (2011), people were presented with long series of faces or patterns. The task was to select which of eight options was seen before. As people progressed through the task, their performance improved—they gained expertise in this kind of perceptual processing. When they started, their accuracy was around 20% to 40% correct, but after two days of practice, their accuracy was up to around 60 to 80%. Importantly, this change was not temporary. When the same people were asked to do the task over a year later, their performance only dropped 10% to 20% for items they had seen before, and some more for new items. The point is that they did not have to start back from the beginning. The experience of being in this study changed the connections between their neurons that persisted for over a year (and probably longer).

Such connectionist models satisfy a difficulty you read about earlier: the need for top-down processing. In Figure 3-10, the top-down effect is prominent in the curved connections, which represent mutual excitation and inhibition. As you will read at several points in this text, connectionist accounts of a whole range of processes can provide new insights into ways of modeling and understanding human cognition. Indeed, connectionist models are finding applications in a stunningly large number of fields (e.g., see Corder, 2004, on a neural net application to landing a crippled airliner).

Section Summary

- Recognizing visual patterns follows principles that have been known for quite some time. The most familiar of these are the Gestalt grouping principles, including figure-ground segregation, closure, proximity, similarity, good continuation, and common fate.
- Recognition of visual patterns is not a process of matching stored templates to a visual stimulus. Feature detection is a much more convincing account where the features being detected are elementary patterns that can be combined to form more complex visual stimuli.
- A feature detection account of pattern recognition, such as Pandemonium, must be augmented by conceptually driven processes to account for the effects of context in visual recognition. Current models of this sort include the connectionist approach.

OBJECT RECOGNITION AND AGNOSIA

How does this approach to identifying letters and words extend to other objects, to recognizing a tree, a briefcase, a human face, or a knife hidden in a carry-on bag going through airport security (McCarley, Kramer, Wickens, Vidoni, & Boot, 2004;

Smith, Redford, Washburn, & Taglialatela, 2005)? Some of the most significant work on the topic of object recognition involves a process very similar to the feature detection ideas you have been studying.

Recognition by Components

The idea in Biederman's (1987, 1990) recognition by components (RBC) theory is that we recognize objects by breaking them down into their parts, and then look up this combination in memory to see which object matches it. Here, pattern recognition has a small number of *basic "primitives," simple three-dimensional geometric forms* like those shown in Figure 3-12. These forms are called **geons**, a combined form of *geometric ions* (remember *ions* from chemistry?). Recognizing a briefcase, for example, involves analyzing the object into its two geons, the rectangular box (geon 2 in the figure) and the curved cylinder (geon 5). By itself, the rectangular box geon would match the memory for "brick" or "box." When that component and the curved part on top are detected, the combination matches the memory for "briefcase" or "suitcase."

Biederman (1987) argued that mental representations of three-dimensional objects are composed of geons, much as written language is composed of letters, combined and recombined in different ways. Thus, when we recognize objects, we break them down (*parse* is the technical term) into their components and note where the components join together. This pattern is then matched to information stored in memory to yield recognition. Two aspects of these patterns are particularly important. First, we find the edges of objects. This enables us to determine which edges maintain the same relationships to one another regardless of viewing orientation; however you look at a brick, the three long edges that are visible remain parallel to one another.

Second, we scan regions of the pattern where the lines intersect (vertices), usually places where deep concave angles are formed. Look at the deep concave angles on the briefcase in Figure 3-12, where the curved component joins the

FIGURE 3-12 Geons (components) and the objects they make. From Biederman, 1990.

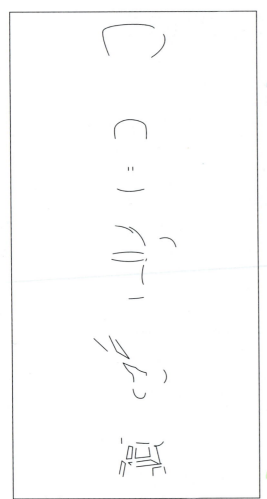

FIGURE 3-13 Nonrecoverable objects. From Biederman, 1987.

rectangle. Examining the edges and the areas of intersection enables us to determine which components are present in the pattern: rectangular solid joined on the upper surface by a curved segment. This description is then compared with stored descriptions in memory, something like "Briefcase: rectangular solid joined on the upper surface by a curved segment." When we find a match between the identified components and the stored representation, we have recognized the pattern.

EVIDENCE FOR RBC In his investigations of the RBC model, Biederman discovered several facts about object recognition. For one, the emphasis on the importance of vertices turns out to be critical. If a pattern is degraded, it matters *where* it was degraded. If segments of the smooth, continuous edges are missing, it is relatively easy to fill in the missing parts and recognize the pattern. Alternatively, if the parts that are missing are in important locations, at the vertices, recognition is more difficult.

Figure 3-13 shows several drawings for which people either cannot recover from the deletions or take longer before recognizing the object. Look at these carefully now and try to figure out what the objects are. It is difficult because the vertices have been deleted. Now look at Figure 3-14. Here you see recoverable versions of the drawings that were degraded to the same degree as the images in Figure 3-13. However, in this case, it was parts of the continuous edges that were deleted, leaving the vertices still visible. Here it is relatively easy to identify the original objects (you *can* identify them, can't you?). In Biederman's data (Biederman & Blickle, 1985), people never made more than 30% errors in identifying recoverable patterns, even when 65% of the continuous line contours were deleted and the pattern was shown for only 100 ms. But when the same percentage of the junctions or intersections were deleted, as in Figure 3-13, people made errors in the 100-ms condition almost 55% of the time.

SHORTCOMINGS OF RBC AND EMBODIED PERCEPTION As useful as it is, RBC is incomplete. A difficulty is that it is tied to bottom-up processing, and object recognition is strongly influenced by context and prior knowledge (e.g., Biederman, Glass, & Stacy, 1973; Palmer, 1975). For example, Tanaka and Curran (2001) tested people with some expertise, "bird experts" and "dog experts," people who had more than 20 years of experience in local bird and dog organizations. These people showed neurological evidence of enhanced, early recognition in their areas of expertise, compared to how they recognized objects outside of those areas (e.g., plants).

There is also evidence that retrieval of an object's identity (at least in terms of the category it belongs to) occurs as fast as identifying that there is even something there—that is, that a stimulus is being presented (Grill-Spector & Kanwisher, 2005; but see Bowers & Jones, 2008). Indeed, Dell'acqua and Job (1998) claimed that object recognition is automatic, given that judgments of a perceptual feature (is this picture elongated horizontally or vertically?) were strongly affected by the top-down knowledge of the identity of the object in that picture.

Second, the model suggests that perceiving components is the first major step in object recognition, thus claiming that the whole is perceived by first identifying the components. There are data, however, that show that people can perceive the overall shape of an object as rapidly and as accurately as the components (e.g., Cave & Kosslyn, 1989). And, again, there are even data from Dell'acqua and Job (1998) indicating that the whole object is recognized automatically using stored knowledge about it, without necessarily identifying components or features. All of these contradict the features-first aspect of the model.

Finally, neuropsychological evidence shows that object recognition is a joint effort between two mental processes and two different regions of the brain, one for features and components—"bits and pieces," as it were—and another for overall shape and global patterns—the *Gestalt,* or overall form. Most of this neuropsychological evidence comes from studying people who, because of some kind of brain damage, have lost the fundamental ability we have been discussing here: the ability to look at something and rapidly recognize what it is. We'll consider these sorts of people in more detail after we take a more in-depth look at the impact of context and embodied cognition on perceptual processes.

FIGURE 3-14 Recoverable objects. From Biederman, 1987.

Context and Embodied Perception

As noted in Chapter 1, one idea that has had an influence across a broad range of thinking about cognition is the influence of embodied processes—that is, how the structure of our bodies and how we interact with the world influence how we think. At first, it might seem that this would not be relevant to perception. After all, perception is about taking in information from the environment, not acting on it. However, even if a person does not actually do anything, there are clear embodied influences on perception (Tipper, 2010). Most of these have to do with the motor programs (patterns of muscle movements) that a person would engage in if they were actually interacting with what they are seeing.

As noted in Chapter 2, there are a number of neural systems for programming motor activity, including the motor cortex and mirror neurons. Work on perception has shown that these areas are activated under a variety of circumstances when people are looking at objects, including when you are perceiving and predicting the actions of other people (Wilson & Knoblich, 2005). So, when you are watching another person, you arrive at a perceptual understanding in part because you are mentally simulating how you would perform that activity, and, perhaps, what you would be trying to accomplish by doing those things. To put it differently, we vicariously experience or enact what we see other people doing. This is why we may feel elated when we see a particularly good catch in a football game, or wince when we see a particularly hard tackle.

There is also behavioral evidence that people activate mental representations of the muscle activities they would engage in if they were to interact with an object or the environment. For example, in one study Tucker and Ellis (1998) had people respond to pictures of objects, such as a coffee cup. Importantly, these objects were shown so that the part of the object that would normally be grasped, such as the handle of a cup, were on either the left or the right of the picture. People then had to make a response using either their left or their right hand. An illustration of the data from one of their experiments is shown in Figure 3-15. What they found was people responded faster when the hand they responded with matched the accessible side of the object in the picture—for example, if the cup had the handle on the right, people responded faster if they were using their right hand to respond than if they had to use their left hand. Moreover, the ease with which objects are identified can be influenced by the actions people would take to use them (Desmarais, Dixon & Roy, 2007). So, over and above the visual features that compose an object's shape, people also use their knowledge of what the object is, and how they would interact with it, to help identify what it is. In other words, the perception of the object was influenced, in an embodied way, by how a person might reach out and us that object, even though they couldn't actually do so.

This embodied aspect of perception also influences how we look at our immediate environment. As an example, people view hills as being steeper and distances walked as being longer if they are wearing a heavy backpack, and perceive balconies as being higher if they have a fear of heights (Proffitt, 2006). Also, objects that are within your grasp are perceived as being closer than objects that you cannot reach out and touch (Bloesch, Davoli, Roth, Brockmole, & Abrams, 2012; Witt, Proffitt, & Epstein, 2005; Yang & Beilock, 2011), even if all you're touching it with is a laser pointer (Davoli, Brockmole, & Witt, 2012). Moreover, this perception is also influenced by characteristics of people themselves, and their abilities. For instance, people who are doing well at hitting a ball in a softball game report that the ball perceptually seems larger than someone who is not doing so well (Witt, 2011).

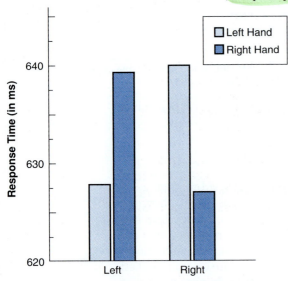

FIGURE 3-15 Response times to verify pictures of objects as a function of hand usage. From Tucker & Ellis, 1998.

Agnosia

You've been reading about perception, studying how mental mechanisms such as feature detection and top-down processing are used to recognize objects around us. But we have not questioned *that* it happens, never thought that there might be problems in actually recognizing a simple, ordinary object. It is amazing to learn that a person can lose the ability to glance at something and immediately know what it is. There's an object, say a cup, sitting on the kitchen counter, or a briefcase sitting on the floor. We encode the stimulus, the set of features or geons, into the visual system. It is then an automatic, seemingly instantaneous step from encoding to identification: You see the thing, and you immediately *know* that it's a cup—right?

Wrong. What you'll read about now is a deficit, caused by brain damage, in which people can no longer do the seemingly instantaneous mental steps of pattern recognition. There are certainly types of brain damage that can disrupt the recognition of printed language, letters, and words, and you will read about some of this in Chapter 10, after the section on reading. But for now, we look at a different kind of disruption of recognition, when the recognition of objects—real-world *things*—is disrupted. We're talking about **agnosia**, defined as *a failure or deficit in recognizing objects,* either because the pattern of features cannot be synthesized into a whole or because the person cannot then connect the whole pattern to meaning (from the prefix *a,* meaning "not," and the Greek root *gnostic,* meaning "to know"). Often this is associated with damage to the left occipital and/or temporal lobes (B.A. 37).

When this disruption affects a person's recognition of faces, sometimes while leaving object recognition intact, it is called **prosopagnosia**, *a disruption of face recognition.* This often is a result to damage to the fusiform gyrus (also B.A. 37), also along the ventral stream. The fact that there are separate conditions involving objects and faces is important because it shows that perception is complex, and that different brain areas emphasize different qualities of information. Perception is not a one-size-fits-all system, but is a number of specialty systems that typically work in seamless harmony.

Bear in mind that when we talk about agnosia and agnosics (patients with agnosia), we are not talking about people whose basic sensory systems are damaged. When an agnosic patient is tested, that the person can see and can detect visual stimuli; this is not blindness. Instead, it is a cognitive, mental loss. The agnosic can input the basic visual stimulus, but then cannot do anything with that encoded information.

A famous case of agnosia—and prosopagnosia, too—is the title story in *The Man Who Mistook His Wife for a Hat* (Sacks, 1970), about an elderly music professor (called Dr. P.) who had lost his ability to recognize objects and faces. At the end of a session with his doctor, he reached over and grasped his wife's head as if reaching to pick up his hat. In another meeting with the doctor, he was able to describe the components or elementary features of an object yet was unable to identify the object he was looking at:

> "About six inches in length," he commented. "A convoluted red form with a linear green attachment."
> "Yes," I said encouragingly, "and what do you think it is, Dr. P.?"
> "Not easy to say." . . .

"Smell it," I suggested.

"Beautiful!" he exclaimed. "An early rose. What a heavenly smell!"

(Sacks, 1970, pp. 13–14)

Dr. P. mistook the grandfather clock in the hall for a person and started with outstretched hand to greet it. Although he could describe the parts of an object (there were five "out-pouchings," and so forth), he could not identify a glove that the doctor held in front of him. Dr. P. had a serious and pervasive visual agnosia, a profound loss in the ability to visually recognize things.

Although agnosia is not limited to vision—there can be auditory agnosias, for example—an agnosia is modality specific. That is, a person with visual agnosia has disrupted recognition of objects presented visually but no disruption of hearing, touch, or other sensory systems (Dr. P. recognized the rose by smelling it). Likewise, there are subtypes of visual agnosia, each with a somewhat different type of deficit, each involving different regions of the brain.

One form of visual agnosia is **apperceptive agnosia**, *a disruption in perceiving patterns.* That is, although the ability to process rudimentary visual features, say color or brightness, is not disrupted, "the ability to coalesce this basic visual information into a percept, an entity, or a whole is lost" (Banich, 2004, p. 195). The region usually associated with apperceptive agnosia is in the right hemisphere, in the parietal lobe. If the agnosia is severe, the person has almost no ability to discriminate between objects, for instance between a square and a rectangle, and is unable to copy or match simple shapes. In less severe cases, there can still be difficulties with patterns like those in Figure 3-14, the patterns that you probably had little or no difficulty identifying (Warrington & James, 1988). People with apperceptive agnosia somehow cannot fill in the missing contours to perceive the whole form or pattern.

In **associative agnosia**, the person is not able to construct a mental percept; he or she can combine the perceived features into a whole pattern, but *cannot associate the pattern with meaning,* with stored knowledge about its identity. Again, this often involves B.A. 37, along with damage to the corpus callosum, consistent with the idea that there is a disruption in the access to associative meanings in some way. For example, a person tested by Ratcliff and Newcombe (1982) copied a drawing of a ship's anchor quite well and was able to give a verbal definition of an anchor. The patient could not, however, identify the drawing, nor could he draw an anchor from memory. In Gazzaniga, Ivry, and Mangun (1998, pp. 164–165), a patient known as P. T. who had associative agnosia was shown a drawing of a combination lock. He perceived the round shape and the number markings around the edge, but guessed that the object was a telephone or a clock. Finally, he finally identified the lock, but only because he noticed that he had been twirling his fingers around, as if pantomiming how to open a combination lock.

Implications for Cognitive Science

What do these neurological disruptions mean for our understanding of normal perception? How does evidence like this advance our understanding of cognition?

Start with the deficits known as apperceptive agnosia, where the *a* prefix to *perceptive* denotes some kind of perceptual failure. Here we have a serious disruption in an early stage of perception. It is a disorder of feature detection, a malfunction in the process of extracting features from visual stimuli. Biederman's (1990) geons, for instance, are not being identified or at least not processed much beyond noticing small segments or junction points. Furthermore, it may be important that apperceptive agnosia seems to result from damage in the right hemisphere, in the parietal region; there is growing evidence that the right hemisphere is more involved in global processing, to include forming global patterns, and that the left hemisphere plays more of a role in local processing (i.e., processing small components and features). If so, then it seems reasonable to talk about a disrupted mechanism for forming a *Gestalt* from the features, where this disrupted mechanism would correspond to the symptoms of apperceptive agnosia.

Associative agnosia is a deeper dysfunction: The *Gestalt* or pattern has been formed but seems to have lost the pathway to the meaning and name of the object. The damaged regions in associative agnosia are lower, more toward the temporal lobe, and in both hemispheres. This pathway, from the vision centers in the occipital lobe forward and down toward the temporal lobe, is commonly called the *"what" pathway,* the pathway that is activated when you look at something to decide *what* it is. The temporal lobes are particularly associated with language and word meaning. Connecting from a perceived pattern to its meaning and name is the impairment in associative agnosia.

In conclusion, the varieties of agnosia tell us at least three important things about the perception. First, detecting the features in a visual stimulus is a separate (and later) process from sensation. The basic features—whether horizontal lines in a capital *A*, geons, or something else—must be extracted from the sensory signal. Second, detecting visual features is critical in constructing a perceived pattern, a percept. If the features cannot be extracted, then the person cannot "get" the *Gestalt,* cannot form an overall pattern or percept. Finally, there is a separate step for hooking up the pattern with its meaning and name in memory. This is different from knowing the meaning and name of an object in verbal form. Indeed, given that P. T. only later realized what his pantomime meant, the visual association path can be isolated from all of the other ways of knowing about objects and patterns.

In short, simple, "immediate" recognition of objects—the cup, the briefcase—is neither simple nor immediate. The disruptions of agnosia, whether caused by difficulties in feature detection or in associating patterns with meaning, provide additional evidence of the complexity of perception.

Section Summary

- The recognition by components theory claims that we recognize objects by extracting or detecting three-dimensional components, geons, from visual stimuli, then accessing memory to determine what real-world objects contain those components. The most informative parts of objects tend to be where the components join together; people have difficulty recognizing objects when the intersections are degraded.

- Studies of patients with visual agnosia demonstrate the complexity of perception. Patients with apperceptive agnosia sometimes are unable to detect even elementary features and therefore have difficulty in perceiving a whole pattern or *Gestalt*. Those with associative agnosia can perceive the whole but still cannot associate the pattern with stored knowledge.

AUDITORY PERCEPTION

Auditory stimuli consist of sound waves moving the air. Human hearing responds to these stimuli using an awkward combination of components, a Rube Goldberg–type mechanism that translates the sound waves into a neural message. (Google *Rube Goldberg* if you don't know about the contraptions he drew.) First, the sound waves are funneled into the ear, causing the tympanic membrane, or eardrum, to vibrate. This in turn causes the bones of the middle ear to move, which then sets in motion the fluid in the ear's inner cavity. The moving fluid then moves the tiny hair cells along the basilar membrane, generating the neural message, which is sent along the auditory nerve into the cerebral cortex (e.g., Forgus & Melamed, 1976). Thus, from the unpromising elements of funnels, moving bones and fluid, and the like (Figure 3-16) comes our *sense of hearing* or **audition**.

Interestingly, both ears project auditory information to both cerebral hemispheres, although the majority of the input obeys the principle of contralaterality. The primary auditory cortex, a region in the superior (upper) medial (midway back) temporal lobe, also extends somewhat further rearward in the brain, into the parietal lobe. Auditory input to the brain is sent primarily to this auditory cortex, although at least four other nearby zones and several secondary areas are also affected.

The sensitivity of our hearing defines our auditory world. A pure tone, such as that generated by a tuning fork, is a traveling sound wave with a regular frequency, a smooth pattern of up-and-down cycles per unit of time. Generally, humans are sensitive to patterns as low as 20 cps (cycles per second) and as high as 20,000 cps—although the upper limits decline with age, which is why older adults cannot hear very high pitches. Most of the sound patterns we are interested in, such as those in spoken speech or music, are very complex, combining dozens of different frequencies that vary widely in intensity or loudness. In terms of the sound wave patterns, these different frequencies are superimposed and can be summarized in a spectrum (see examples under "Phonology" in Chapter 9).

In one sense, human hearing is not that impressive: Dogs, for instance, are sensitive to higher frequencies than humans. In quite a different sense, our hearing is very complex. For instance, we can accurately discriminate between highly similar sounds even from birth: The slight difference between the sounds "pah" and "bah" is noticed by newborns (Eimas, 1975). Also, we routinely convert the continuous stream of sounds in speech into a meaningful message with little or no effort, at a rate of about two or three words per second. How does audition work? How does it coordinate with our knowledge of language to work so rapidly?

Auditory Sensory Memory

Auditory sensory memory is also called **echoic memory** (Neisser, 1967). Both terms refer to a *brief memory system that receives auditory stimuli and preserves*

FIGURE 3-16   Gross structure of the human ear and a close-up of the middle and inner ear structures. From Price, 1987.

them for some amount of time. Neisser's argument on the existence of echoic memory is still airtight: "Perhaps the most fundamental fact about hearing is that sound is an intrinsically temporal event. Auditory information is always spread out in time; no single millisecond contains enough information to be very useful. If information were discarded as soon as it arrived, hearing would be all but impossible. Therefore, we must assume that some 'buffer,' some medium for temporary storage, is available in the auditory cognitive system" (1967, pp. 199–200). The function of echoic memory is to encode sensory stimulation into memory and hold it just long enough for the rest of the mental system to gain access to it.

AMOUNT AND DURATION OF STORAGE What is the duration of echoic memory? This question was answered by Darwin, Turvey, and Crowder (1972; see also Moray, Bates, & Barnett, 1965) using an auditory analog of Sperling's work. They used a task that presents auditory stimuli briefly, in different locations, so that we can cue selected parts for partial report. Darwin et al. used what they called the "three-eared man" procedure, in which three different spoken messages came from three distinct locations. People heard recorded letters and digits through stereo headphones, with one message played to the left ear, one message to the right ear, and the final message was played into both ears. The message played into both ears seemed to be localized in the middle of the head, at the "third ear." Each of the messages had three stimuli, say, *T 7 C* on the left ear, *4 B 9* on the right ear, and so on. Each sequence lasted 1 second on the recording, and all three sequences were played simultaneously. Thus in the space of 1 second, three different sequences of letter and digit combinations were played, for a total of nine separate stimuli.

After the messages were presented, people in the whole report condition reported as many of the nine items as they could remember. Their performance was about four items correct, as shown in Figure 3-17. People in the partial report condition were shown a visual cue, prompting recall of the left, right, or center message. When the cue was given immediately after the stimuli had been heard, performance on the cued location was well above 50%, suggesting that nearly five items out of the original nine were still available. The advantage of partial report over whole report was maintained even with a 4-second delay in presenting the cue, although performance did decline during that period (also shown in Figure 3-17). The decline in accuracy suggested a decrease in the useful contents of auditory sensory memory, presumably because of a passive loss of information across longer delays.

PERSISTENCE AND INTERFERENCE OF AUDITORY INFORMATION Without the process of redirected attention, the echoic memory degrades with the passage of time,

FIGURE 3-17
Partial report results in the "three-eared man" procedure. The average number of items recalled correctly is shown for the first, second, and third items in the three lists, across varying delay in the presentation of the partial report cue. Based on Darwin et al. (1972).

similar to the loss in iconic memory. However, remember that there is also another kind of forgetting in iconic memory, due to interference by subsequent stimuli. Is there any evidence of this in auditory sensory memory? In a word, yes, although a straightforward parallel with iconic persistence and interference may be misleading. We consider the original evidence, then discuss the controversy over the current status and understanding of auditory sensory memory.

The best-known evidence on auditory persistence was done by Crowder and Morton (1969; also Crowder, 1970, 1972). In their work, a list of nine digits was presented visually, at the fairly rapid rate of two items per second. In a Silent Vocalization condition, people saw the nine numbers and read them silently as they appeared. In the Active Vocalization condition, people not only saw the list, but were also asked to name the digits aloud. In the Passive Vocalization condition, people heard an accompanying recording that named the digits for them.

For recall, Crowder and Morton found hardly any errors for the last item in the Active and Passive Vocalization groups. Errors here, as shown in Figure 3-18, were below 10%. These people had actually heard that last item, so they could simply read it out of echoic memory (in fact, the last three positions showed this advantage). In other words, there was a lingering trace for the last sounds that were heard. However, the Silent group had many errors for the last items, around 50%, because there was no auditory memory trace. (Recall for the earlier positions presumably resulted from a combination of short- and long-term memory—rehearsal of some sort—and so is

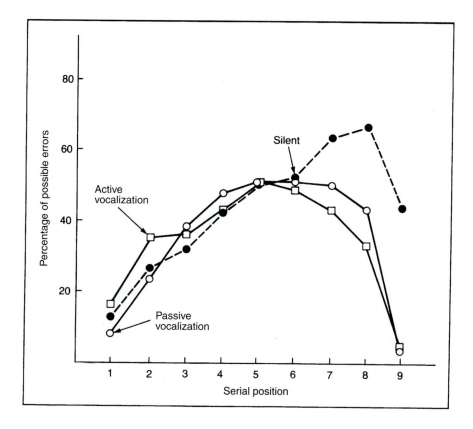

FIGURE 3-18 The number of errors in recall as a function of position in the list of items to be recalled. Note that the two vocalization groups show almost no errors on the last item, compared with the silent group, which had no auditory trace of the list.

not of interest here.) Crowder suggested that the Vocalization groups' recall for the last items was assisted by still-present traces in echoic memory. This is the **modality effect**, *superior recall of the end of the list when heard instead of seen.* Crowder (1972) argued that this supports two ideas: (a) the existence of auditory sensory memory and (b) the persistence of auditory traces across a short interval of time.

Having established that auditory traces persist, Crowder went on to investigate auditory interference. After people heard the items in the list, people in the *suffix* groups then heard an additional auditory stimulus: the word *zero* or a simple tone. Both groups were told that this final item was merely a cue to begin recalling the list. In reality, the auditory *suffix* was intended to interfere with the lingering auditory trace for the last items in the list. As predicted, the verbal suffix group showed a higher error rate on the last items. However, the tone-suffix group had very few errors. The auditory suffix had degraded the auditory trace for the last digits in the list when the suffix was similar to the list. Figure 3-18 summarizes this program of research.

This **suffix effect** is *inferior recall of the end of the list in the presence of an additional, meaningful, nonlist auditory stimulus.* In general, the more a suffix is like the information on the list, the greater the effect (Ayers, Jonides, Reitman, Egan, & Howard, 1979). It is also important what the person thinks the suffix is. In a study by Neath, Surprenant, and Crowder (1993), people heard a "baa" sound at the end of a list of words. If they were told that the sound was made by a person, there was a larger suffix effect than if they were told it was made by a sheep.

In summary, auditory sensory memory is generally similar to visual sensory memory. Both register sensory information and hold it for a brief period of time: 250 to 500 ms in vision but 2,000 to 4,000 ms in audition. This duration for auditory sensory memory, however, varies with the complexity of stored information. Generally, more information is encoded than can be reported. The items held in both sensory systems are prone to loss over short periods of time. Finally, if attention is redirected during the retention interval, information can be sent to short-term memory, preventing it from being lost. Just as in vision, our auditory world usually is one of continuous stimulation, not bursts of sound followed by empty intervals.

Auditory Pattern Recognition

We postpone an in-depth discussion of auditory pattern recognition until later after our discussion of attention (Chapter 4) and language (Chapter 9). So here is a brief discussion, with just enough to propel you into Chapter 4 and a full treatment of the topic of attention.

TEMPLATES   Attempts to understand how we recognize sounds, especially language, have paralleled the work on visual pattern recognition. That is, there were attempts at explaining auditory pattern recognition by using stored templates in memory. These attempts were quickly abandoned. For example, in language not only do different people produce different language sounds, but even the same sound produced by the same speaker varies widely from time to time. Moreover, the "same" sound varies from word to word, even when spoken by the same speaker. In psycholinguistics this is called the **problem of invariance**; the problem is that *the sounds of speech are not invariant from one time to the next.* Instead, any particular sound changes depending on the sounds that precede and follow it in a word. As another example, consider melodies in music. If the identification of a melody were done using a template, then when the melody is transposed up or down in pitch, and all of the notes change, people should not recognize it as the same melody. But, they clearly do.

FEATURE DETECTION   Parallel to work in vision, feature detection models were more successful. Research on feature detection in audition leads to the same conclusion as it did in vision: loads of evidence that *context*—in other words conceptually driven processing—plays a decisive role.

CONCEPTUALLY DRIVEN PROCESSING   Let's take two classic examples of the effects of context and conceptually driven processing effects. In the first, Pollack and Pickett (1964) recorded the idle conversations of volunteers who were waiting to be in a research project. The recordings were then played to other people to see if they could identify the words, which they could. But in a more interesting condition, individual words were spliced out and played in isolation. Here, only about half of all the words could be identified. Removing words from their normal context made it extremely difficult to recognize the words. By inference, then, context plays an important role in spoken word identification.

In the second example, Warren and Warren (1970) played speech to people and asked them to report what they had heard. The recordings were engineered so that one specific *language sound* (the technical term is **phoneme**) was removed from a single word. People heard the altered sentences shown in Table 3-2, where an asterisk indicates the sound that was removed. The word they recognized is shown at the right of each sentence. For instance, even though they heard "*eel," hearing the rest of the sentence, "on the axle," was sufficient for them to perceive the word *wheel*. In fact,

PROVE IT

The influence of top-down processing on perception is very powerful, and we typically do not notice it. In cognitive psychology we can manipulate whether people use top-down knowledge by giving some people knowledge they can later use, and others not. However, there are cases in our everyday lives when the influence of knowledge is clear, such as when we listen to songs.

Whereas the lyrics of many songs are clear from the first time you hear them, there are also songs when it takes some time to figure out just what the singer is singing. Everyone has had the experience of listening to a song for the first time. However, after you read the lyrics in the liner notes, it can be amazing how clear the words seem when you hear the song the next time. You can demonstrate this with some of your friends by playing songs to each other that you know are difficult to get the first time around, and then having a second listen after reading the lyrics. What happens here is that your prior knowledge (top-down processing) can now help organize the incoming auditory perceptual stream, allowing you to correctly parse the lyrics.

We don't always have a lyric sheet to help us figure out what a singer is singing, and we are left with other knowledge we have to figure the words out. Although we usually get this right, we can get it wrong, sometimes with hilarious results. There is a web site of misheard lyrics (sometimes called "mondegreens") that chronicles the failures of top-down processing on auditory perception (www.kissthisguy.com).

TABLE 3-2   Warren and Warren's (1970) Sentences and Participants' Responses

Participant Reports	Participant Hears
He knows that the *eel was on the orange.	peel
He knows that the *eel was on the shoe.	heel
He knows that the *eel was on the table.	meal
He knows that the *eel was on the axle.	wheel

Note: The asterisks represent a deleted sound.

most never even noticed anything strange at all about what they heard; it all sounded completely natural. It's a simple but powerful demonstration: Perception and identification of speech are heavily dependent on context, on top-down processing. It's also a nice reminder of the difference between sensation and perception, the physical, sensory nature of sensation but the overwhelmingly cognitive nature of perception.

Section Summary

- Auditory stimulation is stored briefly in auditory sensory memory, for periods up to 4 seconds or so for language-based information.
- Generally, the last items in a list presented auditorially are recalled better than items presented visually (the modality effect); furthermore, a suffix added to the end of the list degrades performance on the last list items, demonstrating erasure from echoic memory.
- Theories of auditory pattern recognition resemble those in vision; that is, they involve feature detection plus a substantial role for top-down processing.

Key Terms

agnosia (p. 91)
apperceptive agnosia (p. 92)
associative agnosia (p. 92)
audition (p. 94)
auditory sensory memory (p. 94)
backward masking (p. 71)
beta movement (p. 78)
change blindness (p. 67)
conceptually driven effects (p. 79)

connectionist modeling (p. 82)
context (p. 81)
data-driven processing system (p. 79)
decay (p. 70)
echoic memory (p. 94)
feature analysis (p. 76)
feature detection (p. 76)
fixation (p. 67)
focal attention (p. 72)
fovea (p. 62)
geons (p. 87)
icon (p. 70)
iconic memory (p. 68)

inattention blindness (p. 67)
interference (p. 70)
modality effect (p. 98)
Pandemonium (p. 76)
partial report condition (p. 69)
perception (p. 65)
phi phenomenon (p. 78)
phoneme (p. 99)
problem of invariance (p. 98)
prosopagnosia (p. 91)
repetition blindness (p. 81)

retina (p. 62)
saccades (p. 67)
sensation (p. 65)
span of apprehension (p. 68)
suffix effect (p. 98)
templates (p. 76)
trans-saccadic memory (p. 72)
visual persistence (p. 68)
visual sensory memory (p. 68)
whole report condition (p. 69)

4   Attention

Everyone knows what attention is. It is the taking possession by the mind, in clear and vivid form, of one out of what seem several simultaneously possible objects or trains of thought. Focalization, concentration of consciousness are of its essence. It implies withdrawal from some things in order to deal effectively with others.

(JAMES, 1890, PP. 381–382)

As he did every morning after waking, Bill went into the bathroom to begin his morning ritual. After squeezing toothpaste onto his toothbrush, he looked into the mirror and began to brush his teeth. Although he brushed the teeth on the right side of his mouth quite vigorously, for the most part he ignored those on the left side. . . . He shaved all the stubble from the right side of his face impeccably but did a spotty job on the left side. . . . [After eating at a diner,] when Bill asked for the check, the waitress placed it on the left side of the table. After a few minutes, he waved the waitress over and complained, saying "I asked for my tab 5 minutes ago. What is taking so long?"

(BANICH, 1997, P. 235)

Attention—one of cognitive psychology's most important topics and one of our oldest puzzles. What does it mean to pay attention to something? To direct your attention to something? To be unable to pay attention because of boredom, lack of interest, or fatigue? What sorts of things grab or capture our attention? How much control do we have over our attention? (Cognitive science says "attend to," meaning "pay attention," even though some dictionaries say that is an archaic usage.) We have to work at paying attention to some things (most topics in a faculty meeting, for example). But for other topics, it seems effortless: A good spy novel can rivet your attention.

MULTIPLE MEANINGS OF ATTENTION

Attention is one of the thorniest topics in cognitive psychology, possibly because we mean so many different things by the term. We use the term *attention* to describe a wide range of phenomena, from the basic idea of arousal and alertness all the way up to consciousness and awareness. Some attention processes are extremely rapid, so that we are aware only of their outcomes, if that, and others are slow enough that we seem to be aware of them—and able to control them—throughout. In some cases, attention is reflexive. Even when we deliberately concentrate on something, that concentration can be disrupted and redirected by an unexpected, attention-grabbing event, such as the sudden loud noise in the otherwise quiet library. In other cases, we are frustrated that our deliberate attempts to focus on some task are so easily disrupted by another train of thought; you try very hard to pay attention to a lecture, only to find yourself daydreaming about last weekend's party.

Table 4-1 presents six different connotations of the term *attention*. For organizational purposes, this chapter is structured around that list to impose some coherence on the field, to help you see the forest and prevent your getting lost in the trees (the final type of attention in the table is nearly synonymous with short-term or working memory, so it is not discussed until the next chapter). Although other organizational schemes are possible, this approach should help you develop an understanding of attention and see how some topics flow into others. The list

TABLE 4-1 Six Meanings of Attention

Input Attention	Controlled Attention
Alertness or arousal	Selective attention
Orienting reflex or response	Mental resources and conscious processing
Spotlight attention and search	Supervisory attentional system

will also help avoid some confusion that arises when the term *attention* is used for processes or mechanisms more precisely described by another term, such as *arousal*.

Moreover, this list tends to map on to different parts of the brain that are involved in different kinds of attention (Posner & Rothbart, 2007). For example, *alertness* is associated with the neurotransmitter norepinephrine, and with activity in the brain stem, the right frontal lobe, and portions of the parietal cortex. *Orienting* is associated with the neurotransmitter acetylcholine, and with activity in the tectum (in the midbrain), the superior parietal lobe (B.A. 7), and the temporal parietal junction (B.A. 19). Finally, *executive attention*, which encompasses spotlight, selective, and resource attention, is associated with the neurotransmitter dopamine, and with activity in the anterior cingulate (B.A. 24), the prefrontal cortex (B.A. 10), and the basal ganglia.

At every turn in considering attention, we confront four interrelated ideas. *First,* we are constantly presented with more information than we can attend to. *Second,* there are serious limits in how much we can attend to at once. *Third,* we can respond to some information and perform some tasks with little if any attention. And *fourth,* with sufficient practice and knowledge, some tasks become less and less demanding of our attention.

BASICS OF ATTENTION

Let's start by giving two general metaphors for *attention*, both of which apply throughout the list in Table 4-1.

ATTENTION AS A MENTAL PROCESS   **Attention** can be thought of as *the mental process of concentrating effort on a stimulus or a mental event.* By this, we mean that attention is an activity that occurs within cognition. This activity focuses a mental resource—effort—on either an external stimulus or an internal thought. When it refers to an external stimulus, attention is the mental mechanism by which we actively process information in the sensory registers pertaining to that entity. When you examine a picture like that in Figure 4-1, you focus your mental energies on an external stimulus, the splotches and patches of black and white in a photograph. If you have never seen this before, you struggle to identify it, to recognize the pattern in it. Your focus in the attempt to identify the pattern was attention. Sustained attention then led, after some time, to identify the Dalmatian. In fact, iconic memory and spatial visual attention use the same neural substrates, such as a shared frontal-parietal network (Ruff, Kristkjánsson, & Driver, 2007). Moreover, although much of this chapter discusses the use of attention in perceptual processes, such as vision and hearing, this neural network of attention is involved in other cognitive processes, such as memory retrieval, that require attention (Nee & Jonides, 2008).

In principle, the focusing of your attention on a visual stimulus is no different than when you focus attention on a word, idea, or concept. For example, your professor says something unexpected (e.g., describing an idea as "green"), and you puzzle over the remark, trying to find a way to interpret it that makes sense. (Can an idea that promotes conservation and ecology be described as "green"? See also Chapter 9.) It is this concentration of attention we are illustrating

FIGURE 4-1 First identification of the pattern relies almost exclusively on data-driven processing, whereas later identification relies heavily on conceptually driven processing.

here: attention focused on and driving the mental event of remembering, searching for information stored in memory, and attempting to comprehend.

ATTENTION AS A LIMITED MENTAL RESOURCE   Now consider attention as a mental resource, a kind of mental fuel. In this sense, attention is *the limited mental energy or resource that powers cognition*. It is a mental commodity, the stuff that gets used when we pay attention. According to this metaphor, attention is the all-important mental resource needed to run cognition.

A fundamentally important idea here is that of limitations: Attention is limited, finite. We usually state this by talking about the limited capacity of attention. Countless experiments, to say nothing of everyday experiences, reveal the limits of our attention, the capacity to attend to stimuli, to remember events that just happened, to remember things we are supposed to do. In short, there is a limit to how many different things we can attend to and do at once.

It does not take long to think of everyday situations that reveal these limitations. You can easily drive down an uncrowded highway in daylight while carrying on a conversation. You can easily listen to the news on the radio under normal driving conditions. In the middle of a heavy rainstorm, however, you can't talk to the person sitting in the passenger seat; in rush hour traffic, you can't (and shouldn't try to) do business on the cell phone. Under such demanding circumstances, the radio or the conversation are annoyances or irritating—and dangerous—distractions, and you have to turn down the volume, or turn off the phone.

Watch *IT Video:*
Cell Phones in
MyPsychLab

BASIC INPUT ATTENTIONAL PROCESSES

We'll start with a section on the more basic types of attention listed in Table 4-1, those occurring early in the stream of processing. These are the processes that seem either reflexive or automatic, are low-level in terms of informational content, and occur rapidly. They are especially involved in *getting sensory information into the cognitive system,* so they can generally be called forms of **input attention**.

Alertness and Arousal

It almost seems axiomatic to say that part of what we mean by *attention* involves the basic capacity to respond to the environment. This most basic sense refers to alertness and arousal as a necessary state of the nervous system: The nervous system must be awake, responsive, and able to interact with the environment. It seems intuitive that the nervous system must be aroused in order to pay attention. You cannot attend to something while you are unconscious, although certain things can impinge on us and rouse us to a conscious state (e.g., alarm clocks, smoke detectors, or other loud noises).

Although consciousness is important, to some degree there also needs to be an element of alertness. That is, we need to monitor the environment for new, interesting, and/or important events. Sometimes this can be difficult, especially when this alertness needs to be strung out over a long period of time during which nothing much happens. The *maintenance of attention for infrequent events over long periods of time* is known as **vigilance** or **sustained attention**. The study of vigilance began during World War II with British radar operators (Mackworth, 1948). However, vigilance is important in many other domains, including air traffic control, sonar detection, and nuclear power plant operations (Warm, 1984). Even quality inspections in a factory involve some degree of vigilance as workers constantly monitor for important but relatively infrequent flaws in products (Wiener, 1984).

There are a number of fundamental vigilance phenomena that have been observed over the years (see See, Howe, Warm, & Dember, 1995, for a review). For instance, there is a decline in performance as time on the task wears on, showing that people have difficulty maintaining attention on a single task over long periods of time. This decline takes place in about 20 to 35 minutes. Interestingly, the problems that occur with a decline in vigilance do not appear to involve people failing to notice the signal in the task they are doing. Instead, people have difficulty making the decision to respond that they have detected something, a shift in response bias. Vigilance is also affected by the neurological and physiological state of the person, such as a whether people are too hot or cold, their level of arousal, or if they have been taking drugs (Warm, 1984). Finally, there are also a number of aspects of the task that can influence how effective people are, such as how long the signal is (longer is better), how often there is a signal (more frequent is better), and how busy the background is (less busy is better) (Warm & Jerison, 1984). Interestingly, there is also some evidence that meditation training can improve vigilance performance (MacLean et al., 2010).

Although nobody disputes that arousal and alertness are a necessary precondition for most cognitive processes, this may overemphasize a kind of thinking known as **explicit processing**. That is, explicit processes are those *involving conscious awareness that a task is being performed, and usually conscious awareness of the outcome.* The opposite is known as **implicit processing**, *processing with no necessary involvement of conscious awareness* (Schacter, 1989, 1996). As you will see, the distinction between implicit and explicit is often in terms of memory performance, especially long-term memory. When you are asked to learn a list of words and then name them back, that's an explicit memory task: You are consciously aware of being tested and aware that you are remembering words you just studied. By contrast, you can also demonstrate memory for information *without* awareness, which is implicit memory. For example, you can reread a text more rapidly than you read it the first time, even if you have no recollection of ever reading it before (Masson, 1984).

There is some evidence showing that some mental processing can be done with only minimal attention. Much of this is discussed later. For now, consider a study by Bonebakker et al. (1996; see Andrade, 1995, for a review of learning under anesthesia) in which they played recorded lists of words to surgery patients, one list just before and another during surgery, and then tested memory up to 24 hours later. Despite the fact that all the patients were given general anesthesia, and so were unconscious during the surgery itself, they nonetheless showed memory for words they heard. Keep in mind, however, that they were only remembering 6% to 9% more words compared to a control condition of new words. They certainly did not learn any complex ideas. So, you do need to pay attention to learn well. It's just that small amounts of learning can sometimes occur unconsciously.

A powerful part of the study was that performance was based on an implicit memory task, the *word stem completion task*. Patients were given word stems and told to complete them with the first word they thought of. To ensure that the task was measuring implicit memory, patients were further asked to exclude any words they explicitly remembered hearing, such as the words they remembered hearing before receiving anesthesia. For example, say that they heard *BOARD* before surgery and *LIGHT* during surgery. When tested 24 hours after surgery, the patients completed the word stems (e.g., *LI_ _ _*) with words they had heard during surgery *(LIGHT)* more frequently than they did with presurgery words *(BO_ _ _)* or with control words that had never been presented. In other words, they remembered hearing *BOARD* and excluded it on the word stem task. Because they did not explicitly remember *LIGHT*, they finished *LI_ _ _* with *GHT*, presumably because their memory of *LIGHT* was implicit. The results demonstrated that the patients had implicit memory of the words they had heard while under the anesthesia.

So that you understand this procedure, and because it occurs in later chapters, here is a more focused version of the task. Imagine that you saw a list of words including *SCHOOL* and *SHELF*. Relying on explicit memory, you would probably complete the stem *SCH_ _ _* with *SCHOOL*. But if I asked you to exclude words you explicitly remembered, you would find another way of completing that stem, say *SCHEME;* likewise, you might exclude *SHELF* and write *SHELL*. By chance, you might complete the stem *CRA_ _ _* with *CRADLE* or *CRAYON,* neither of which you saw before. Here is the implicit part. Try it yourself. Complete the following word stems with the first word that comes to your mind: *PAP_ _; GRE_ _*. *PAPER* is a pretty common completion for the first one, probably because paper is a fairly common word (it has not appeared in this chapter yet). But if you completed the second word stem as *GREEN* without explicitly remembering that you read about "green ideas" earlier, then that probably was an implicit memory effect.

Orienting Reflex and Attention Capture

Now consider another kind of attention, the kind caused by a reflexive response in the nervous system. In a quiet room, an unexpected noise grabs your attention away from what you were doing and may involve a reflexive turning of your head toward the source of the sound. In vision, of course, you move your eyes and head toward the unexpected stimulus, the flash of light or sudden movement in your peripheral vision. This is the **orienting reflex**, *the reflexive redirection of attention toward the unexpected stimulus.* This response is found at all levels of the animal kingdom and is present very early in life. Although a host of physiological changes accompany the orienting reflex, including changes in heart rate and respiration (Bridgeman, 1988), we focus on its more mental aspects. The cognitive manifestation of all of this is a redirection of attention toward something, even if the eyes and body do not actually move toward the source. As such, we refer to this process as **attention capture**, which is *the spontaneous redirection of attention to stimuli in the world based on physical characteristics.*

The orienting reflex is a location-finding response of the nervous system. That is, an unexpected stimulus, a noise or a flash of light, triggers the reflex so that you can locate the stimulus—find where it is in space. This allows you to protect yourself against danger, in the reflexive, survival sense; after all, what if the unexpected movement is from a rock thrown at you or some other threat (e.g., Öhman, Flykt, & Esteves, 2001)? Note that this system also allows you to monitor for more positive survival stimuli, such as noticing a baby's face (Brosch, Sander, Pourtois, & Scherer, 2008). Given that the response helps you locate the stimulus, it is not surprising that some of the neural pathways involved correspond to the *"where" pathway* (as compared to the "what" pathway). As noted in Chapter 2, the "where" pathway projects from the visual cortex to upper (superior) rearward (dorsal) regions of the parietal lobe (and the "what" pathway is also called the ventral pathway).

Note also that attention is not only directed by objects and entities in the environment, but it can also be directed by social cues. Perhaps the biggest cue is noticing where other people are looking (Birmingham, Bischof, & Kingstone, 2008; Kingstone, Smilek, Ristic, Friesen, & Eastwood, 2003). In fact, it has been suggested that our face and eyes have evolved in such a way to communicate this sort of attention-directing information (Emery, 2000). Even our language can influence how we direct attention. For example, a study by Estes, Verges, and Barsalou (2008) showed that attention can be directed based on the meanings of words activated in long-term memory. In this study, people saw a cue word in the middle of the screen, which was soon followed by either an X or an O at either the top or the bottom of the screen. The task was to indicate which of these two letters was seen, by pressing one of two buttons. They found that people were faster to respond to a letter probe if the meaning of the cue word signified a direction consistent with the location of the letter. So, if the cue word was *hat*, people would respond to the letters faster if they were on the top of the screen rather than the bottom. Similarly, if the word was *boot*, the opposite was true.

We also orient toward things when something *unexpected* occurs: the unexpected sound in the quiet library, sudden and unexpected movement (Abrams &

A clearer picture of the image in Figure 4-1 in case you had trouble identifying the object.

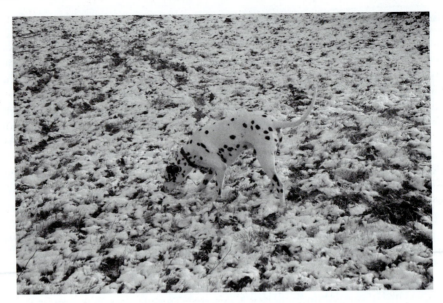

Christ, 2003; Franconeri & Simons, 2003), the abrupt onset of a new object (Davoli, Suszko, & Abrams, 2007; Yantis & Jonides, 1984), a change in the color of an object (Lu & Zhou, 2005), an animate object moving (Pratt, Radulescu, Guo, & Abrams, 2010), the change in pitch in a professor's voice during a lecture, maybe the word *different* in italics in a textbook paragraph. Notice that what seems to capture attention is the occurrence of something *unexpected*, not just something *new* (Vachon, Hughes, & Jones, 2012). Thus, not all visual changes capture attention equally. Moreover, visual offsets, when something suddenly disappears from a scene, are much less likely to capture attention than a visual onset, something suddenly appearing (e.g., Cole & Kuhn, 2010).

Orienting focuses us so that we can devote deliberate attention to the stimulus if warranted; Cowan (1995) called these *voluntary attentive processes*. In this sense, orienting is a preparatory response, one that prepares the system for further voluntary processing. In visual attention, fMRI (functional magnetic resonance imaging) neurological scanning has shown that the attention capture process itself seems to involve retinotopic (specific places on the retina in your eye) portions of the occipital lobe, the part of the brain dedicated to vision. This is in contrast to more controlled aspects of attention that involve portions of the dorsal parietal and frontal cortex, further down the stream of neural activity in the brain (Serences et al., 2005; Yantis, 2008).

If the stimulus that triggers an orienting reflex occurs over and over again, however, it is no longer novel or different; now it has become part of the normal, unchanging background. The process of **habituation** begins to take over, *a gradual reduction of the orienting response back to baseline*. For example, if the unexpected noise in the quiet library is the ventilation fan coming on, you first notice it but then grow accustomed to it. You have oriented to it, and then that response habituates, to the point that you will probably orient again when the fan *stops* running. When the constant noise stops, *that* is a change that triggers the orienting response.

Spotlight Attention and Visual Search

The last sense of *attention* to be considered among the input attentional processes is a kind of visual attention. It is related to perceptual space, that is, the spatial arrangement of stimuli in your visual field and the way you search that space. It is different from the orienting response in that there is no necessary movement of the eyes or head, although there is a strong correlation with eye movements (researchers often exploit this relationship to have a general idea of where attention is directed, using eye-tracking devices). Instead, there is a mental shift of attentional focus, as if a spotlight beam were focused on a region of visual space, enabling you to pick up information in that space more easily (think of a "Superman beam").

A large amount of work on this kind of visual attention has been reported, including some work that has found regions of the brain that seem to be involved in focused, visual attention.

THE SPOTLIGHT OF VISUAL ATTENTION Consider Figure 4-2, which depicts three kinds of displays in Posner's spatial cuing task (Posner, Nissen, & Ogden, 1978; Posner, Snyder, & Davidson, 1980). People in this task are first asked to fixate the

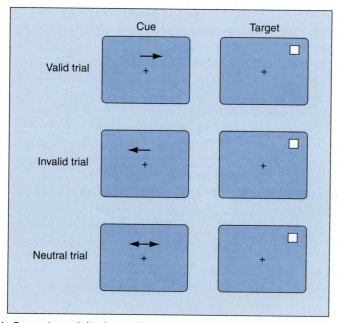

FIGURE 4-2 In Posner's spatial cuing task, the person fixates on the plus sign in the center of the screen, then sees an arrow pointing left or right or a two-headed arrow. For the targets shown in the figure, with a target appearing on the right, the right-pointing arrow is a valid cue, the left-pointing arrow an invalid cue, and the two-headed arrow a neutral cue. In this experiment, one-headed arrow cues were valid on 80% of the trials.

centered plus sign on the display, are then shown a directional cue, and finally see a simple target (the thing they are supposed to respond to). The task had people press a button when they detected the target. For 80% of the cued trials, the arrow pointed to the direction where the target actually did appear 1 second later. On the remaining 20% of the cued trials, however, the cue was invalid: It pointed to the wrong side. Neutral trials provided an uninformative cue, a two-headed arrow indicating that the target would appear equally often on the left or right. Throughout the task, people were required to maintain fixation on the plus sign. That is, they could shift only their *mental* attention to the space where they thought the target might appear, but were not allowed to move their eyes.

The results, shown in Figure 4-3, were very clear. When people shifted their visual attention to the correct area (the Valid 80% point in the figure), response time (RT) to detect the target was significantly faster than the neutral, uncued condition. This speedup is known as a **benefit or facilitation**, *a faster-than-baseline response resulting from useful advance information*. When the target appeared in the unexpected location, however, there was a significant **cost**, *a response slower than baseline because of a misleading cue*. Interestingly, further analysis suggested that the cost of having directed their attention to the wrong place resulted from a three-part process: (a) disengaging attention from its current focus, (b) moving the attentional spotlight to the target's true location, then (c) engaging attention at that new location.

Posner et al. (1980) concluded from this and related experiments that the attentional focus being switched was a cognitive phenomenon; it was not tied to eye movements but to an internal, mental mechanism. They suggested that attention is like a spotlight that highlights objects and events that it shines on. Thus,

FIGURE 4-3
Consider the response time (RT) points in the neutral condition to be baseline performance on detecting targets. When a valid cue was presented, there was a reduction in RT for targets in both the left and right visual fields ("Valid 80%"). When the cue was invalid, there was a slow-down in detecting the target in both visual fields ("Invalid 20%").

Source: From Posner, Snyder, & Davidson (1980).

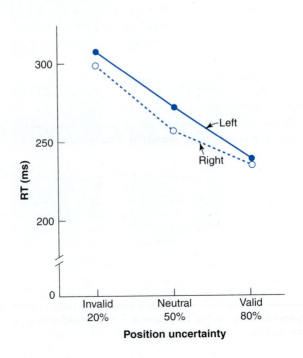

spotlight attention is *the mental attention-focusing mechanism that prepares you to encode stimulus information.* Furthermore, Posner et al. suggested that this shift in attention is essentially the same as the redirection of attention in the orienting reflex, with one big difference: It is voluntary. Therefore, it can happen before a stimulus occurs and can be triggered by cognitive factors such as expectations.

As Cave and Bichot (1999) pointed out, countless studies of visual attention, many of them inspired by Posner's work, have adopted the spotlight metaphor. Much of that work has explored the characteristics and limits of visual attention, attempting to evaluate how useful the metaphor is. The evidence suggests that the mental spotlight does not sweep, enhancing the intermediate locations along the way, but instead it jumps (much as the saccade does). On the other hand, there is also supportive evidence for the similarity between a real spotlight and spotlight attention. For example, it appears that the size of the spotlight beam can be altered, depending on circumstances (see Cave & Bichot, 1999, for an extensive review).

VISUAL SEARCH   Look at Figure 4-4, and do these quick demonstrations. In the first panel, search for *either* a letter *T* or a boldface letter; in the other two panels, search for a boldface *T.* As you did these visual searches, you surely noticed that searching for *T* in the first panel was stunningly simple; it hardly seemed like a search, did it? Instead, didn't the *T* just "pop out" at you? In contrast, searching for *T* in the middle panel probably was a slow process, and finding it in the last panel probably took even longer. A classic, everyday example of difficult visual search can be found in the *Where's Waldo?* children's books.

A series of studies by Treisman and her associates (Treisman, 1982, 1988, 1991; Treisman & Gelade, 1980) examined visual search. Typically, people were told to search a visual display for either of two simple features (e.g., letter *S* or a blue letter) or a conjunction of two features (e.g., a green *T*). The search for a simple feature was called a **feature search**: People responded "yes" when they detected the presence of either of the specified features, either a letter *S* or a blue letter. In the **conjunction search** condition, they had to search for the combination of two features, *T* and the color green. In the searches you did, the first were feature searches, and the last panel illustrated a conjunction search (the target had to be both boldfaced and a *T*).

In the typical result (Treisman & Gelade, 1980, Experiment 1), people could search rapidly for an item identified by the presence of a unique feature. It made little or no difference whether they searched through a small or a large display; for

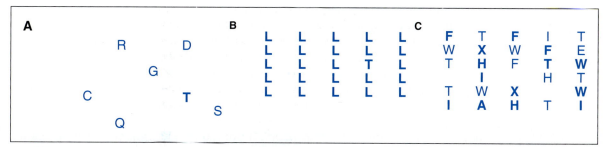

FIGURE 4-4   In panel **A**, search either for a capital *T* or a boldface letter. In panels **B** and **C**, search for a boldface capital *T*.

FIGURE 4-5 Search times when targets were of a specified color or shape. The dashed lines are for the disjunction search conditions (e.g., search for either a capital *T* or a boldface letter). The solid lines show search times for the conjunction condition (e.g., search for a boldface *T*). The important result is that disjunctive search times did not increase as the display size grew larger, but the conjunction search times did.

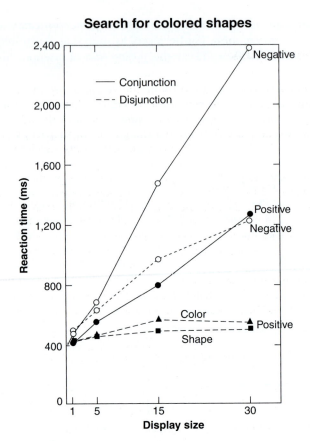

Search for colored shapes

instance, people were able to search through as few as 5 items or as many as 30 in about the same amount of time, approximately 500 ms. The target object just seemed to "pop out" of the display, and so this is called a **pop-out effect**. Because there was no increase in RT across the display sizes, Treisman and Gelade concluded that visual search for a dimension such as shape or color occurs in parallel across the entire region of visual attention. Such a search must be largely automatic and must represent very early visual processing. In the results, shown in Figure 4-5, this is the flat, low function of the graph.

But when people had to do a conjunction search, such as a green *T*, they took more time, up to 2,400 ms, as more and more distractors filled the display (distractors for both conditions were brown *T*s and green *X*s). Such conjunction search seems a more serial, one-by-one process and a far more conscious, deliberate act. This is the steeply increasing function in Figure 4-5.

Because a visual search can be complex, people need a way to keep track of what they have already checked and what they have not. A big problem would occur if a person kept checking the same, useless items over and over again, and never checking others. To help people from returning to inappropriate locations, there is a special attention process. This is called **inhibition of return** (Klein, 2000; Posner & Cohen, 1984), in which *recently checked locations are mentally*

PROVE IT
The Visual Search Task

Here we have a fairly simple task to do with your friends and a stopwatch that illustrates the difference between feature and conjunction searches in visual attention. Using two different colors of marker pens, make up a few sheets of paper, or some 4 × 6 index cards, on which you draw letters in two distinct colors, say red and green. For simplicity's sake, let's restrict ourselves to Xs and Ts. In all cases, we'll have your participants search for a *green T*.

For the *feature* search trials, you will have a number of red Xs and Ts all over the paper. On the "yes" sheets, you'll put a green T in one spot on the paper; on the "no" sheets, you'll just have red Xs and Ts. Make a separate sheet, one for "yes" trials and one for "no" trials, with 4 Xs and Ts, then do the same for 6 Xs and Ts, then 8, 10, and 12 (don't forget to go back and put the green T in for your "yes" trials). For the *conjunction* trials, in addition to the green T for the "yes" sheets, you'll put green Xs and red Ts on the sheets; as before, you'll also have "no" sheets that only have green Xs and red Ts.

Tell your participants that the task is to find the green T as fast as possible. When they find the green T, have them raise their right hand. However, if they don't think the green T is there, have them raise their left hand. Time people (the second hand/display on your watch is fine) each time. The standard result is that the feature search items should show a fairly constant retrieval rate regardless of the number of distractors. This is because the target letter should pop out under these circumstances. In comparison, for the conjunction search items should be an average increase in response time as the number of distractors increases.

marked by attention as places that the search would not return to. This process appears to be guided by the operations of the superior colliculus (a.k.a. the tectum) and the parietal lobe (Klein, 2000; Vivas, Humphreys, & Fuentes, 2006), consistent with the idea that inhibition of return is an important visual process (involving the superior colliculus) as well as knowledge of where things are in space, the "where" neural pathway (involving the parietal lobe). Note that when people are not searching for something, but are simply scanning or memorizing a picture, the opposite is shown, with people being *more* likely to return to a previously fixated location—a facilitation of return (Dodd, Van der Stigchel, & Hollingworth, 2009).

In some sense, the locations are inhibited from or kept out of the search pattern. These items were highly activated in cognition because they were attended to, and what inhibition of return does is turn this activation down. So, you only continue to search through those locations that are likely to still have the item you're looking for. A consequence of this is that people are slower to respond to events (such as a change in brightness) in locations that have recently been searched, and inhibited, relative to other locations. It's similar to searching for a friend at the airport when many people are arriving from many different flights. You search visually through the faces as they come out of security, but you don't keep scanning those same faces over and over again. What inhibition of return does is keep you from returning to those already scanned faces, having your visual search move on to other faces, ideally allowing you to find your friend faster.

Although this description of visual search places a heavy emphasis on the influence of visual features, and the bottom-up processes that can use such features, most of our real-world, everyday searching is not this difficult. For example, when you walk into a new kitchen and are looking for the sink, not only do you scan the room for objects with sinklike features, but you also draw on your prior knowledge of how things are organized in space (Huang & Grossberg, 2010). The sink is more likely to be on an outside wall, perhaps by a window, than somewhere else. Thus, this is a top-down influence of *what* an object is on the *where* tracking system involved in visual search. Note, also, that attention can be influenced by embodied characteristics. For example, people find it easier to spot a target during visual search when their hands are placed near the display as compared to when they are further away (Davoli, Brockmole, & Goujon, 2012). The idea is that where our hands are correspond to locations in space that can be easily manipulated, as so is a more likely place for attention to be directed to, facilitating even tasks that do not require manipulating the environment, such as visual search.

Contrasting Input and Controlled Attention

Treisman's two conditions provide clear evidence of both a very quick, automatic attentional process—essentially the capture of attention due to "pop-out"—and a much slower, more deliberate attention, the type used for the conjunction search. In line with Johnston, McCann, and Remington's (1995) suggestion, we use the term *input attention* for the fast, automatic process of attention, the type of process we have been talking about in this section. The slower one, in Johnston et al.'s terms, is *controlled attention,* to which we turn in a moment. It is important to note that research has suggested that these two forms of attention operate with some degree of independence (Berger, Henik, & Rafal, 2005).

Consider the early, rapid stages of feature detection as relying on spotlight attention (Posner & Cohen, 1984). The spotlight is directed toward a visual display and enhances the detection of objects and events within it (Kanwisher & Driver, 1992). It provides the encoding route into the visual system. It is this attentional focus mechanism that provides early, extremely rapid feature detection for the ensuing process of pattern recognition. It is especially visual; for instance, it has been called posterior attention because the earliest stages of visual perception occur in the posterior region of the brain, in the occipital lobe, as illustrated in Figure 4-6 (see also the inside front cover illustration of neural activity in the occipital lobe when a visual stimulus is presented), as well as involving the superior colliculus, a midbrain structure (Berger et al., 2005).

The spotlight attention we are talking about—and we presume there is an equivalent mechanism for other senses—appears to be rapid, automatic, and perceptual. It is distinguished from the slower, controlled or conscious attention process that matches the more ordinary connotation of the term *attention*. The "regular" kind is the conscious attention that we have loosely equated with awareness. Based on some neurophysiological evidence, we might even call this frontal or anterior attention because activity in the frontal regions of the brain seems to accompany elements of conscious awareness, such as awareness of the meaning of a word (Posner et al., 1992).

FIGURE 4-6 The top two drawings show lateral (side) views of the left and right hemispheres of the brain, and the bottom two show medial views, as if the hemispheres had been split down the center from front to back, showing inner portions of the cortex. The geometric shapes refer to different regions of the brain that are involved in attention; squares denote regions involved in the attentional network, the triangle denotes a region related to vigilance, and the diamond denotes a part of the anterior attentional network; the circle and oval denote word processing regions for semantic associates and visual word forms, respectively.

Source: From Solso (1998).

Conscious or controlled attention prepares us to respond in a deliberate way to the environment. It is slower, operates in a more serial fashion, and is especially influenced by conceptually driven processes. Spotlight attention, however, is a basic, rapid attentional mechanism that seems to operate in parallel across the visual field, in a highly automatic fashion. It is especially data driven, funneling aspects of the environment into the cognitive system. Conscious attention then enables us to respond to that environment.

Hemineglect: An Attention Deficit

In many cases, cognitive science has gained insight into a process when there has been some disruption to the system, as can happen with brain damage. The study of attention is no exception. Go back to the beginning of the chapter and reread the quotation from Banich (1997) about Bill. Bill suffers from *hemineglect*, a syndrome that leads to such behavior as brushing only the teeth on his right, washing only his right arm, and shaving only the right side of his face. To many people, this phenomenon is almost too bizarre to believe, maybe because the processes of mental attention have always been so closely tied to perception and voluntary movement and so automatic that we think they are indivisible parts of the same process. Look at yourself in a mirror, then look at the left side of your face—no problem, you merely move your eyes, shift your direction of gaze, and look at it. If I ask you to stare straight ahead and then attend to something in your left field of vision, say the letter *X* on a computer screen, your normal response is to shift your eyes toward the left and focus on the target. You simply look at the *X* and pay attention to it. You can even shift your mental attention to the left without moving your eyes.

The syndrome known as **hemineglect** (or hemi-inattention) is a disruption in the ability to refocus your attention to one side of your face or the other, to the *X* on the left of the computer screen. It is a *disruption or decreased ability to attend to something in the (often) left field of vision. Hemi* means "half," and *neglect* mean "to ignore" or "to fail to perceive." Thus, hemineglect is a disorder of attention in which one half of the perceptual world is neglected to some degree and cannot be attended to as completely or accurately as normal. Some form of hemineglect is often observed in stroke victims, even if it is in a more limited and temporary form. Very often, the neglect is of the left visual field, for stimuli to the left of the current fixation, the current focus of attention. And because of the principle of contralaterality, it is not surprising that the brain damage leading to hemineglect is often in the right hemisphere, in particular, certain regions of the right parietal lobe (see Intriligator & Cavanagh, 2001, for evidence that localizes selective attention in the parietal lobe).

Here are the facts (see Banich, 1997, or Rafal, 1997, for complete treatments). A patient with hemineglect cannot voluntarily direct attention to half of the perceptual world, whether the to-be-perceived stimulus is visual, auditory, or any other type of sensation. In some cases, the neglect is nearly total, as if half of the perceptual world has simply vanished, is simply not there in any normal sense of the word. In other cases, the neglect is partial, so for such people it is more accurate to say that they are *less able* to redirect their attention than are normal people. In either case, there is a disruption in the ability to control attention. Note that this is not a case of sensory damage like blindness or deafness. The patient with hemineglect receives input from both sides of the body and can make voluntary muscle movements on both sides. And in careful testing situations, such patients can also respond to stimuli in the neglected field. But somehow, the deliberate devotion of controlled attention to one side is deficient.

Bisiach and Luzatti (1978) present a compelling description of hemineglect. The afflicted individuals were from Milan, Italy, which they were quite familiar with before their brain damage. This study focused on the main piazza in town, a broad open square with buildings and shops along the sides and a large cathedral at one end. These patients were asked to imagine themselves standing at one end of the piazza, facing the cathedral, and to describe what they could see. They uniformly described only the buildings and shops on the right side of the piazza. When asked to imagine themselves standing on the steps of the cathedral, facing back the opposite way, they once again described what was on their right side. From this second view, of course, what they described was exactly what they had omitted from their earlier descriptions. Likewise, they now omitted what they had described earlier.

Critically important here is the observation that these reports, based on memory, were exactly the kind of reports patients with hemineglect give when actually viewing a scene; if these patients had been taken to the piazza, they probably would have seen and described it the same way as they did from memory. (For a

Model   Patient's copy

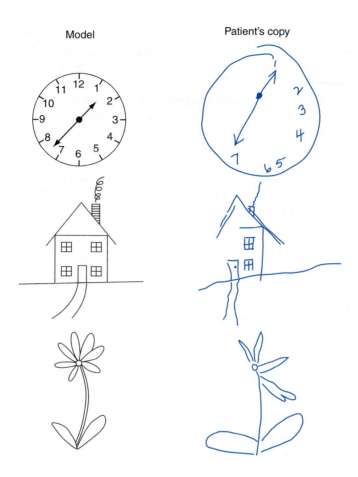

FIGURE 4-7
Drawings copied
by a patient with
contralateral
neglect.

Source: From F. E.
Bloom & A. Lazerson.
*Brain, Mind, and
Behavior,* 2nd ed. New
York: W. H. Freeman
and Co., p. 300.
Copyright © 1988.
Reprinted with
permission of W. H.
Freeman and Co.

similar account, see "Eyes Right!" in Sacks, 1970; the patient there eats the right half of everything on her dinner plate, then complains about not getting enough food.) Figure 4-7 shows some drawings made by patients with hemineglect. Here, patients were asked to copy drawings or to draw from memory, but the nature of their drawings was no different in either case. These drawings show a dramatic neglect for the left-hand sides of objects: a flower with no petals on the left, a clock face with no numbers on the left. In the standard line bisection task ("draw a slash through the middle of a horizontal line"), hemineglect patients position the slash too far to the right, as if bisecting only the right half of the entire horizontal line.

A careful analysis of the disruptions seen in patients with hemineglect has been provided by Duncan et al. (1999) in the context of the Theory of Visual Attention (Bundesen, 1990). Duncan et al. noted that several important advances in understanding hemineglect have been made, especially when the patients are tested with some standardized cognitive tasks such as Posner's spatial cuing task, which you read about earlier. For example, it turns out that patients with hemineglect often can attend to stimuli in the neglected field, but only if nothing else is displayed that might attract their attention. That is, they can detect a simple stimulus in the left visual field (the field contralateral to their brain damage), even if that is the portion of the world they normally neglect. The ability to detect the same stimulus is dramatically reduced if a stimulus in the right visual field (ipsilateral to their brain damage) is presented at the same time (see Danziger, Kingstone, & Rafal, 1998, for evidence of an orienting response in the neglected field).

This tendency to ignore the contralateral field when a competing stimulus is presented in the ipsilateral field is called *extinction*. It appears to be caused by something like attention capture. When a right-side (ipsilateral) stimulus is presented, it captures the person's attention and prevents attention from being devoted to the left (contralateral). In a sense, then, hemineglect patients may neglect one side only because there is usually something on the other side that captures their attention. In a very real sense, Bill might have been able to focus on shaving the left side of his face if he had not been able to see his right side.

In a way, hemineglect seems to disrupt both input and controlled attention. First, input attention is devoted largely or exclusively to a stimulus in the "good" or preserved field, the ipsilateral field (the term *ipsilesional* is also used, meaning "same side as the brain lesion"). The stimulus in this field captures the patient's input attention. But then it appears that hemineglect patients cannot disengage attention from that ipsilateral stimulus. Because attention toward the right cannot be disengaged, they cannot shift their attention voluntarily to the left. Thus, capture of attention on one side has disrupted a shift of controlled attention toward the other side.

In their analysis, Duncan et al. (1999) noted that their patients with hemineglect showed standard deficits in attention to the contralateral side but also some rather strong bilateral deficits related to attentional capacity; in other words, there were accuracy deficits on the neglected side but capacity difficulties on both sides. Interestingly, there was little evidence that the conceptually driven aspects of their attention were affected. It may be some time before such results and their implications for the normal processes of attention are fully understood. But even now, it is clear that such fractionation of performance—some abilities preserved, some disrupted—will be important in our further understanding of attention (for a neural net modeling approach to hemineglect, see Monaghan & Shillcock, 2004).

Section Summary

- Attention is a pervasive and complex topic, with meanings and connotations ranging from alertness and arousal up through the notions of automatic and conscious processing. Attention can be thought of as a mental process or mechanism or as a limited mental resource.
- Three basic senses of the term *attention* refer to alertness and arousal, the orienting reflex, and the spotlight of attention. These correspond to input attention, a fast process involved in encoding environmental stimuli into the mental system. Interestingly, in vision, the mental spotlight of attention can be shifted without any movement of the eyes, confirming the mental rather than perceptual nature of attention.
- A disorder known as hemineglect shows how attention can be affected by brain damage, thus informing us about normal attention. In hemineglect, a

patient is unable to direct attention voluntarily to one side of space, so he or she neglects stimuli presented in that side. The evidence suggests that this arises from an inability to disengage attention from a stimulus on the non-neglected side, hence disrupting the process of shifting attention to the opposite side.

CONTROLLED, VOLUNTARY ATTENTION

We turn now to several senses of the term *attention* that point to the controlled, voluntary nature of attention. **Controlled attention**, in contrast to what you've just been studying, refers to *a deliberate, voluntary allocation of mental effort or concentration. You* decide to pay attention to this stimulus and ignore others, and paying attention this way involves effort.

Cognitive psychology has always been intrigued by the fact that at any moment, scores of different sensory messages are impinging on us. We can't attend to all of them (we would be overwhelmed instantly), nor can we afford for our attention to be captured by one, then another, then another of the multiple sensory inputs (we would lose all coherence, all continuity). Therefore, it makes sense to ask questions about **selective attention**, *the ability to attend to one source of information while ignoring other ongoing stimuli around us.* How do we do this? How do you screen out the surrounding noises to focus on just one? How can you listen covertly to the person on your right, who is gossiping about someone you know, while overtly pretending to listen to a conversational partner on your left? (And how did you notice in the first place that the person on your right was gossiping?) Somewhat the converse of selective attention is the topic of divided attention: How do we divide or share our attentional capacity across more than one source of information at a time, and how much information are we picking up from the several sources?

Dangerously divided attention.

In a classroom situation, students must constantly filter out the unimportant from the important details. This is an example of selective attention in auditory perception.

Simulate
Selective Attention in
MyPsychLab

A modern example of how these questions involve real-world problems is the issue of whether we can really talk (or text message) on a cell phone and drive at the same time, dividing our attention between two demanding tasks (Kunar, Carter, Cohen, & Horowitz, 2008; Spence & Read, 2003; Strayer & Johnston, 2001). In short, the general answer is, "No, we really can't." Talking on the cell phone can lead to *inattention blindness,* in which people fail to attend to or process information about traffic, even if they are looking directly at it. This is equally true for both handheld and hands-free cell phone conversations, but not for listening to the radio or music (Strayer & Drews, 2007). This is because you are actively involved in cell phone conversations, but not in what is going on over the radio. In these studies, people drive a simulator while having their eye movements monitored (so the experimenter knows what they are looking at and for how long). Under these circumstances, people who are having phone conversations are less likely to recognize road signs or other important traffic events, even when they look directly at them. This is even revealed in electroencephalographic (EEG) recordings of drivers' brains, not just what they consciously report. What is happening is that when you are actively involved and interacting in a conversation, your limited-capacity attention is drawn away from your immediate environment. You have less attention to devote to driving, so as a consequence, your driving suffers and becomes more dangerous. At a more general level, the question is, when do we start reaching the limits of our attentional capacity?

Selective Attention and the Cocktail Party Effect

When there are many stimuli or events around you, you may try to focus on just one. The ones you are trying to ignore are distractions that must be excluded. *The mental process of eliminating those distractions* is called **filtering** or **selecting**.

Some aspect of attention seems to filter out unwanted, extraneous sources of information so we can select the one source we want to attend.

The process of selective attention seems straightforward in vision: You move your eyes, thereby selecting what you attend to. As you just saw, however, attention is separate from eye movements: You can shift your attention even without eye movements. But in hearing, attention has no outward, behavioral component analogous to eye movements, so cognitive psychology has always realized that selective attention in hearing was thoroughly cognitive. This accounts for the heavy investment in filter theories of auditory perception. If we cannot avoid hearing something, we then must select among the stimuli by some mental process, filtering out the unimportant and attending to the important.

DUAL TASK OR DUAL MESSAGE PROCEDURES   A general characteristic of many attention experiments involves the procedure of *overload*. Briefly, we can overload a sensory system by presenting more information than it can handle at once and then test accuracy for some part of the information. This has usually involved a **dual task procedure**. *Two tasks are presented such that one task captures attention as completely as possible*. Because attentional resources are consumed by the primary task, there are few if any resources left over for attention to the other tasks. By varying the characteristics or content of the messages, we can make the listener's job easier or harder. For instance, paying attention to a message spoken in one ear while trying to ignore the other ear's message is more difficult when both messages are spoken by the same person.

Going a step further, when we examine performance to the attended task, we can ask about the accuracy with which a message is perceived and about the degree of interference caused by a second message. We can also look at accuracy for information that was not in the primary message, the unattended message in the other ear. If there is any evidence of remembering the unattended message, or even some of its features, we can discuss how unattended information is processed and registered in memory.

SHADOWING EXPERIMENTS   Some of the earliest cognitive research on auditory selective attention was done by E. Colin Cherry (1953; Cherry & Taylor, 1954). Cherry was interested in speech recognition and attention. Cherry characterized his research procedures, and for that matter the question he was asking, as the cocktail party problem (although you can think of it as a dorm party problem): How do we pay attention to and recognize what one person is saying when we are surrounded by other spoken messages? To simulate this real-world situation in the laboratory, Cherry (see also Broadbent, 1952) devised the workhorse task of auditory perception research, the **shadowing task**. In this task, Cherry recorded spoken messages of different sorts, then played them to a person who was wearing headphones. The task was to "shadow" the message coming into the right ear, that is, *to repeat the message out loud as soon as it was heard*. In most of the experiments, people were also told to ignore the other message, the one coming to the left ear. (It makes no difference which ear is shadowed or ignored. For simplicity, assume that the right ear gets the to-be-shadowed attended message and the left ear gets the unattended message.)

Although this sounds simple, it takes a surprising amount of attention and concentration to shadow a message accurately. People were quite accurate in producing "shadows," although they spoke in a monotone, with little intonational stress, and lagged behind the message by a second or so. Interestingly, people seem unaware of the strangeness of their spoken shadows and usually cannot remember much of the content of the shadowed message once the task is over.

This task consumed enough attention to leave little, if any, for other purposes. In a typical session, the recording began with a continuous coherent message presented to the right (attended) ear and another coherent message to the left (unattended) ear. Once the person began to shadow, the message in the left ear was changed. After some amount of time, people were interrupted and asked what, if anything, they could report about the unattended message. They could report accurately on a variety of physical characteristics, such as if it changed from human speech to a tone. They also usually detected a change from a male to a female voice. However, when the unattended message was changed to reversed speech, only a few people noticed "something queer about it." Changes from English to a different language generally went unnoticed, and, overall, people were unable to identify words or phrases in the unattended message. In a dramatic confirmation of this last result, Moray (1959) found that even a word presented 35 times in the unattended message was never recalled (see also Wood & Cowan, 1995b).

Selection Models

It appears that a physical difference between the messages permits people to distinguish between them and eases the job of selectively attending to the target task (Johnston & Heinz, 1978). Investigators routinely call this early selection. This refers to the some of the earliest phases of perception, an acoustic analysis based on physical features of the message. The evidence is that people can select a message based on sensory information, such as loudness, location of the sound source, or pitch (Egan, Carterette, & Thwing, 1954; Spieth, Curtis, & Webster, 1954; Wood & Cowan, 1995a).

EARLY SELECTION THEORY   This evidence, indicating that people could somehow tune their attention to one message over the other, prompted Donald Broadbent (1958) to propose an **early selection theory** of attention. In this view, attention acts as a selective filter, as shown in Figure 4-8. Regardless of how many competing channels or messages are coming in, the filter can be tuned, or switched, to any one of them, based on characteristics such as loudness or pitch. Note that only one message can pass through the filter at a time. In other words, despite the many incoming signals, only one message can be sent through the filter into the "limited-capacity decision channel" (essentially short-term memory). Only the information on the attended, "passed along" message affects performance, in Broadbent's view, because only it gets past the filtering mechanism.

It was soon realized that the filter idea had serious problems. For one, intuition tells us that we often notice information from a message we are not attending, as when you hear your name in a crowded, noisy place. Moray (1959) found evidence for this: Although people did not recall a word presented 35 times to the

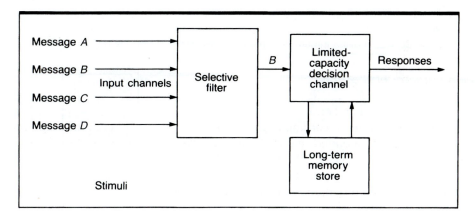

FIGURE 4-8
Broadbent's filter theory of selective attention. Four messages are presented, yet only one is selected and passed to the limited-capacity decision mechanism.

Source: Adapted from Broadbent (1958).

unattended ear, a third of the people heard their own name (see Wood & Cowan, 1995b, for a recent replication of this effect). Not everyone detects their name easily. Conway, Cowan, and Bunting (2001) found that people with less cognitive capacity (a.k.a. working memory; see Chapter 5) were more likely to detect their name. In other words, people who were less able to focus on a task, such as remembering a list of letters, appear to be more prone to distraction and are more likely to process and detect information that they are supposed to ignore, such as information on an unattended channel in this task.

More generally, these findings have implications about the nature of attention. If Broadbent's early filter theory were correct, then only the attended and passed-along information should be available, where attention is directed by physical cues. Yet clear evidence is available that unattended information can somehow slip past the filter (but see Lachter, Forster, & Ruthruff, 2004, who argue that some small amount of attention had been devoted to the "unattended" stimuli).

LATE SELECTION THEORY Treisman (1960, 1964) did a series of studies to explore this slippage more closely. She used the standard shadowing task but varied the nature of the unattended message across a more subtle range of differences. She first replicated Cherry's findings that selective attention was easy when physical differences existed. Then she turned to the situation in which physical differences were absent—both messages were recorded by the same speaker. Because the same pitch, intonation, stress, and so on were in both messages, early selection should not be possible. Yet she found that people could shadow accurately. The basis for the selection was *message content,* what the message was *about* rather than what it sounded like. In this situation, the grammatical and semantic features are the basis for selection (*semantic* refers to meaning). Because attentional selection occurs after all the initial processing of the message is done, this is called *late selection.* It is later in the stream of processing than early selection based on sensory features, yet before the moment of having to respond aloud with the shadowed speech.

To show the power of late selection, Treisman did a study now considered a classic (1960); the setup is depicted in Figure 4-9. Treisman arranged the recording

FIGURE 4-9 The shadowing task. Two messages are played simultaneously into different ears; then, at the slash, the ear-of-arrival is switched for the two messages.

Source: Adapted from Lindsay & Norman (1977).

Right ear:
While Bill was walking through the forest/a bank can lend you the money.

Left ear:
If you want to buy a car/a tree fell across his path.

"through the forest, a tree fell—uh . . . ."

so that the coherent message being shadowed was unexpectedly shifted to the unattended channel. That is, the sentence that was being said switched from the right to the left ear. Despite the high degree of practice and concentration needed, people routinely switched to the unattended message, although they did not continue to shadow the "wrong" ear for long. Clearly, there must be some processing of the unattended message. Semantic elements of the unattended channel must be receiving some analysis or there would be no basis for preferring it when the sentences switched ears.

Based on such results, Treisman claimed that all incoming messages receive some amount of low-level analysis. When the unattended messages yield no useful or important information, they are attenuated; they are reduced not in their volume or physical characteristics but in their informational importance to ongoing processing. In the process of shadowing, we arrive at an identification of the words and phrases on the attended message.

Treisman (1965) felt that it was during this process of semantic analysis that we make our selection among messages, selection at a "late" stage. This permits attention to be affected by the semantic aspects of the message—that is, a top-down effect. A more extreme view, by Deutsch and Deutsch (1963), claimed that selection takes place only after *all* messages have received full acoustic and semantic analysis (i.e., just before the response stage).

So the evidence is that quite a bit of information is getting into cognition: the meaning of the words on the unattended channel, for example, in Treisman's study (1960; see also Lewis, 1970; Carr, McCauley, Sperber, & Parmalee, 1982, found comparable results for visual stimuli). Intrusion of the word *tree* into the shadow, as shown in Figure 4-9, makes sense only if *tree* has been recognized as related to the forest theme of the shadowed message, an effect that implies some rapid process of accessing the meanings of words. More recent work has shown that information that is not actively attended, and subject to inattention blindness, is processed if it is consistent with our goals and intentions (Koivisto & Revonsuo, 2007; Marsh, Cook, Meeks, Clark-Foos, & Hicks, 2007; Most, Scholl, Clifford, & Simons, 2005). In all of the cases in which unattended information was processed, it was consistent with some enduring or temporal goal a person had, such as hearing their own name, completing the idea conveyed by a sentence, or whatever may be satisfying a person's goals at the time. This is why when you are hungry, images of food are so hard to ignore, even if you are trying to concentrate on something else.

So, on the one hand, it seems that people use attention by means of an early filter based on physical qualities, such as spatial location or loudness. On the other hand, it also seems that people use attention by means of a later filter that relies on semantic meaning. Which of these is correct? There seems to be evidence for both. Some researchers, such as Lavie (2010), have suggested that an early attention filter is more likely to be used when there is a lot of perceptual information that needs to be sorted through, as in most shadowing situations, leading attention to select information based on physical features and qualities, if possible. However, a later filter is more likely to be used when attention is not being overly taxed, leading it to select information based on meaning.

INHIBITION AND NEGATIVE PRIMING   Most of the discussion of attention to this point has focused on what gets attended to and activated in cognition, as well as some filter to keep irrelevant information from entering the stream of processing. At this point, we would like to discuss a cognitive mechanism that has been proposed that goes beyond the idea of a filter that keeps out irrelevant information and only allows selected information to be processed further. This is the cognitive attention mechanism of **inhibition**. Inhibition is thought to *actively suppress mental representations of salient but irrelevant information so that the information's activation level is reduced, perhaps below the resting baseline level.* You encountered an example of this already, when we discussed inhibition of return. In this section we look further at how inhibition may be operating to help people select relevant information and filter out irrelevant information.

In order for inhibition to operate, there needs to be a salient source of interfering and irrelevant information. That is, the irrelevant information needs to be strong and wrong. Under those circumstances, inhibition will be involved. A classic demonstration of this was provided in a study by Tipper (1985). In this study, people were presented with a series of pairs of line drawings of objects, with one object presented in green and the other in red. The task was to name the red object as quickly as possible. The important condition here involved target trials on which the red object had appeared in green on the previous trial (called the *prime* trial). What was observed was that people were slower to respond to the target trials (red object) when they had been preceded by the to-be-ignored distractor primes (same object in green) compared to control trials where the ignored object on the prime trial was some other object. This response time slow-down is called **negative priming** (Neill, 1977; Tipper, 1985).

The explanation for this is that when people are looking at the display, in addition to their processing of the red object, there is some activation and processing of the green object as well, because people are looking directly at it. That is, the mental representation of the object becomes activated. However, because the identity of this object is irrelevant to the task—it was green, so it didn't need to be named—attention actively inhibited and suppressed the object's representation. Then, when the person needed this information on the next trial (because it was not the red object), it took longer to activate and use because it had been inhibited.

So the inhibition process slowed down the person's response time (however, see Mayr & Buchner, 2006; and Neill, Valdes, & Terry, 1995; for alternative accounts of negative priming that do not involve an active inhibitory mechanism).

The idea that inhibition is an important part of attention has been extended to many other areas of psychology, particularly those dealing with individual differences. For example, in developmental psychology, attentional inhibition is thought to develop slowly with age (Diamond & Gilbert, 1989), meaning that it is difficult, especially for young children, to maintain focus. In contrast, in older adults there is increased difficulty suppressing irrelevant information (Hasher & Zacks, 1988). Inhibitory problems are also thought be present in schizophrenia (Beech, Powell, McWilliams, & Claridge, 1989), with schizophrenics having trouble keeping unwanted thoughts out of consciousness. In less extreme cases, people who are depressed also have trouble inhibiting irrelevant information (MacQueen, Tipper, Young, Joffe, & Levitt, 2000), leading them to have trouble with focusing on the task at hand.

Section Summary

- Controlled or conscious attention is slower and more voluntary. Selective attention, the ability to focus on one incoming message while ignoring other incoming stimuli, is a complex ability, one investigated since the beginnings of modern cognitive science. The evidence shows that we can select one message, and reject others, based on physical characteristics or on more semantic characteristics. The later the process of selection acts, the more demanding it is of the limited capacity of the attention mechanism.
- We are able to use the attention process of inhibition to keep information that would otherwise be highly active, but is irrelevant, out of the current stream of processing. Keeping inappropriate information out helps us focus on whatever it is that we want to be processing.

ATTENTION AS A MENTAL RESOURCE

An important and far-reaching meaning of the term *attention*—this one may be closer to our everyday meaning—treats attention as mental effort, as a mental resource that fuels cognitive activity. If we selectively attend to one particular message, we are deliberately focusing mental energy on that message, concentrating on it to the exclusion of other messages (clearly what James had in mind in the quotation at the beginning of the chapter). This sense involves the idea that attention is a limited resource, that there is only so much mental fuel to be devoted here or there at any one time (Kahneman, 1973, also suggested that capacity might be elastic, in that increasing the task load might also increase a person's arousal, thus making additional resources available). Approaches that emphasize this meaning of attention are called resource theories.

A corollary to this idea of limited capacity is that attention, loosely speaking, is the same as consciousness or awareness. After all, if you can be consciously aware of only one thing at a time, doesn't that illustrate the limited capacity of attention? Even on a smaller scale, when we process very simple stimuli, there is evidence of this limit to attention. If you are asked to respond to a stimulus and then immediately to a second one, your second response is delayed a bit. This is the **psychological refractory period** or **attentional blink**, which is *a brief slow-down in processing due to having processed another very recent event* (e.g., Barnard, Scott, Taylor, May, & Knightley, 2004; Pashler & Johnson, 1998). The implication is that allocating attention to a first stimulus momentarily deprives you of the attention needed for a second stimulus. However, this blink can be overcome if the target item that occurs during the period of the blink is particularly important, such as predicting what to do on the next trial (Livesey, Harris, & Harris, 2009). Also, the strain on attention can be reduced when people view nature scenes (which only subtly demand attention) as compared to urban scenes (which have many elements that grab our attention), thereby freeing up attention for other tasks (Berman, Jonides, & Kaplan, 2008).

A related idea, which you encountered in the previous section, is that this kind of attention is deliberate, willful, intended—*controlled attention. You* decide to pay attention to a signal, or you decide *not* to attend to it. *You* decide to pay attention to the lecture instead of your memory of last night's date, and when you realize your attention has wandered, you redirect it to the lecture, determined *not* to daydream about last night until class is over.

The James quotation at the beginning of this chapter is also interesting because of another insight he had about attention: the idea that we may do more than one thing at a time if the other processes are habitual. When processes are less automatic, however, then attention must oscillate among them if they are done simultaneously, with no consequent gain of time. The key point is the idea of automatic processes—that some mental events can happen without draining the pool of resources: attention. Putting it simply, the germ of James's idea, automaticity, has become central to cognitive psychology's views on attention, pattern recognition, and a host of other topics. Cognitive science has devoted a huge effort to recasting James's ideas about automaticity and attention into more formal, quantifiable concepts.

Automatic and Conscious Processing

In place of the former approach, the limited-capacity attentional mechanism and the need for filtering in selective attention, the current view is that a variety of cognitive processes can be done automatically, *with little or no necessary conscious involvement*. Two such theories of **automaticity** have been proposed, one by Posner and Snyder (1975) and one by Shiffrin and Schneider (1977; Schneider & Shiffrin, 1977). These theories differ in some of their details but are similar in their overall message (see also Logan & Etherton, 1994; for discussions that oppose the idea of mental resources, see Navon, 1984, and Pashler, 1994).

AUTOMATIC PROCESSING Posner and Snyder described three diagnostic criteria for an automatic process, listed in Table 4-2. First, an automatic process occurs without intention; in other words, you can't prevent it from happening, and once it does start, you can't stop it. A compelling example of this is the **Stroop effect** (named after the task described in Stroop, 1935). Words such as *RED GREEN BLUE*

TABLE 4-2 Diagnostic Criteria for Automatic and Conscious Processing	
Automatic	**Conscious**
The process occurs without intention, without a conscious decision.	The process occurs only with intention, with a deliberate decision.
The mental process is not open to conscious awareness or introspection.	The process is open to awareness and introspection.
The process consumes few if any conscious resources; that is, it consumes little if any conscious attention.	The process uses conscious resources; that is, it drains the pool of conscious attentional capacity.
(Informal) The process operates very rapidly, usually within 1 second.	(Informal) The process is slow, taking more than a second or two for completion.

YELLOW were presented visually, written in mismatching colors of ink (e.g., *RED* printed in green ink). When people have to name the ink color, they must ignore the printed words themselves. This leads to tremendous interference, a slowing of the ink color naming, caused by the mismatching information and the contradictory impulses to name the word and the ink color (this is an extremely easy demonstration to do, by the way). This is another case where inhibition is operating during attention, as the highly salient, but irrelevant, semantic meaning of the word must be suppressed. Note that this requires that a person be able to automatically read. People who are illiterate would not show a Stroop effect. That said, it is also the case that poor readers tend to show larger Stroop effects than good readers (Protopapas, Archonti, & Skaloumbakas, 2007), perhaps because better readers have greater executive control over their attentional resources.

In Posner and Snyder's terms, accessing the meaning of the written symbol *RED* is automatic: It requires no intention, it happens whether you want it to or not. In the research that demonstrates automatic access to word meaning, the term we use is **priming**. A word *activates* or primes its meaning in memory and, as a consequence, primes or activates meanings closely associated with it. This priming makes related meanings easier to access: Because of priming, they are boosted up, or given an extra advantage or head start (just as well water is pumped more easily when you prime the pump; see Dunbar & MacLeod, 1984, and MacLeod, 1991, for an explanation of Stroop interference based on priming).

Second, an automatic process does not reveal itself to conscious awareness. You cannot describe the mental processes of looking up the word *RED* in memory. Contrast this with the awareness you had when you answered the Aristotle or division questions in Chapter 1.

The third criterion of automaticity is that an automatic process consumes few if any resources. Such a process should not interfere with other tasks, certainly not those that rely on conscious resources.[1] As an example, walking is so automatic

---

[1]Interference in the Stroop task occurs because the two automatic processes, reading the word and detecting the ink color, compete with one another when it is time to make a response. That is, both processes are trying to output their results to the same speech mechanism, but the responses are incompatible ("red," "green"). When we say that an automatic process generally does not interfere with other processes, it is assumed that we are referring to situations in which the two processes are not competing for the same response mechanism.

PROVE IT
The Stroop Task

An almost fail-safe demonstration of automaticity, in particular the automatic nature of accessing word meaning, involves the Stroop task. With several different colors of marker pens, write a dozen or so color names on a sheet of paper, making sure to use a *different* color of ink than the word signifies (e.g., write *red* in green ink); alternatively, create a deck of 3 × 5 cards, with one word per card. Make a control list of noncolor words (e.g., *hammer, card, wall*), again in colored inks. (And try it yourself right now—name the color of the ink for the words at the top of the color plate, inside the back cover of the book.)

Explain to your participant that the task is to name the *ink color* as rapidly as possible. Time the person (the second hand/display on your watch is more than sufficient; or keep track of naming errors, another way to measure the Stroop interference) on each kind of list. The standard result is that the color word list will require substantially longer for ink color naming than the control list. Other useful control lists are simple blotches of color, to check on the speed of naming the colors, and pseudowords ("manty," "zoople," and the like) written in different ink colors.

According to several studies (e.g., Besner & Stolz, 1999; Manwell, Roberts, & Besner, 2004; Vecera, Behrmann, & McGoldrick, 2000), you should be able to eliminate the Stroop effect by getting people to focus on just *part* of the word or to say the first letter position (this might be easier if you used the 3 × 5 card method) or by printing only one letter in color. This work suggests that reading the whole word is a kind of "default" setting for visual attention, which might be changed depending on the task and instructions, and that our selective attention mechanism can select either whole objects (words) or their parts (letters) as the focus.

Simulate
Stroop Test in
MyPsychLab

for adults that it does not interfere with other processes; you can walk and talk at the same time.

A fourth criterion is that automatic processes tend to be fast; as a rule, a response taking no more than 1 second is heavily automatic. (For evidence of slow automatic processing, in a person with brain damage, see Wingfield, Goodglass, & Lindfield, 1997.)

CONTROLLED PROCESSING   Let's contrast these diagnostic criteria for automaticity with those for conscious or controlled processing (see Table 4-2). First, controlled processes occur only with intention. They are optional and can be deliberately performed or not. Second, conscious processes are open to awareness; we know they are going on, and, within limits, we know what they consist of. Finally, and of greatest importance, conscious processes use *attention*. They consume some of the limited attentional resources we have.

A demanding controlled process should leave few resources available for a second task that also uses controlled processing. Driving during a hard rainstorm consumes too many resources for you to listen simultaneously to the news on the radio. Alternatively, you may stop walking if you are thinking about something that requires intense thought. Of course, if the second task can be done fairly automatically, then both tasks may proceed without interference; for example, you can easily walk and carry on a casual conversation at the same time.

INTEGRATION WITH CONCEPTUALLY DRIVEN PROCESSES   We can go one step further, integrating this explanation into the idea of conceptually driven processing. Think back to the shadowing research you read about. Attending to one of two incoming messages, and shadowing that message aloud, demands controlled attention. Such a process is under direct control, the person is aware of doing the process, and it consumes most of a person's available mental resources. Presumably, no other conscious process can be done simultaneously with the shadowing task without affecting performance in one or the other task (or both). When the messages are acoustically similar, then people must use differences of content to keep them separate. But by tracking the meaning of a passage, the person's conceptually driven processes come into play in an obvious way. Just as people "restored" the missing sound in "the *eel was on the axle" (Warren & Warren, 1970), the person in the shadowing task "supplies" information about the message from long-term memory. Once you have begun to understand the content of the shadowed message, then your conceptually driven processes assist you by narrowing down the possible alternatives, by suggesting what might come next.

Saying that conceptually driven processes "suggest what might come next" is an informal way of referring to priming. You shadow, "While Bill was walking through the forest." Your semantic analysis primes related information and thereby suggests the likely content of the next clause in the sentence; it is likely to be about trees, and it is unlikely to be about banks and cars. At this instant in time, your "forest" knowledge is primed or activated in memory. It is ready (indeed, almost *eager*) to be perceived because it is so likely to be contained in the rest of the sentence. Then *tree* occurs on the unattended channel. Because we access the meanings of words in an automatic fashion, the extra boost given to *tree* by the priming process pushes it over into the conscious attention mechanism. Suddenly, you're saying "a tree fell across" rather than sticking with the right-ear message. Automatic priming of long-term memory has exerted a top-down influence on the earliest of your cognitive processes, auditory pattern recognition and attention.

THE ROLE OF PRACTICE AND MEMORY   If accessing word meaning is automatic, then you might wonder about some of the shadowing research described earlier in which people failed to detect a word presented 35 times, the reversed speech, and so on. If word meaning access is automatic, why didn't these people recognize the words on the unattended channel? A plausible explanation is practice. It seems likely that the inability to be influenced by the unattended message was caused by a lack of practice on the shadowing task. With greater degrees of practice, even a seemingly complex and attention-consuming task becomes easy, or less demanding of attention's full resources. In fact, Logan and Klapp (1991; see also Zbrodoff & Logan, 1986) suggested that the effect of practice is to store the relevant information in memory; that is, that the necessary precondition for automatic processing is memory. Interestingly, once a process or procedure has become automatic, devoting explicit attention to it can even lead to worse performance (e.g., Beilock & Carr, 2001; Logan & Crump, 2009).

One way that you can sometimes help yourself and avoid the automatic processing of irrelevant material is to close your eyes (Perfect, Andrade, & Eagan, 2011). When you close your eyes, your brain stops automatically processing much of the information in the environment, even if that information is not even visual, such as noises, and your thinking becomes better.

One of the compelling strengths of the Shiffrin and Schneider (1977) theory of automatic and controlled processing is the role they award to old-fashioned, repetitive practice. They asked people to detect one or more targets in successively presented displays (e.g., hold targets *2* and *7* in memory, then search for either of them in successively presented displays). For some people, the targets were consistent across hundreds of trials, always digits, for instance. This was called Consistent Mapping. For people in the Varied Mapping groups, the targets were varied across trials (e.g., *2* and *7* might be targets on one trial, *3* and *B* on another, *M* and *Z* on yet another).

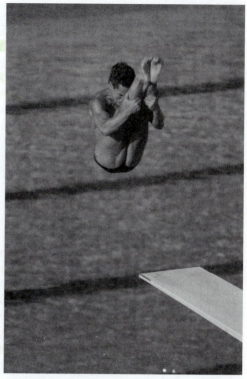

The essential ingredient here is practice. Unlike the Varied Mapping groups, people in the Consistent Mapping groups had enormous amounts of practice with the same targets. People in the Consistent Mapping conditions developed quick automatic detection processes for their unchanging targets. People in the Varied Mapping conditions, however, needed longer search times (Schneider & Shiffrin, 1977). They had not developed automatic detection processes because the stimuli they had to detect kept changing. In short, their search used controlled processing.

The role of practice in automaticity.

A Synthesis for Attention and Automaticity

Attention, in its usual, everyday sense, is equivalent to conscious mental capacity. We can devote attention to only one demanding task at a time or to two somewhat less demanding tasks simultaneously, as long as they do not exceed the total capacity available. This devotion of resources means that few, if any, additional resources are available for other demanding tasks. Alternatively, if a second task is performed largely at the automatic level, then it can occur simultaneously with the first because it does not draw from the conscious resource pool (or, to change the metaphor, the automatic process has achieved a high level of skill; see Hirst & Kalmar, 1987). The more automatically a task can be done, the more resources are available for other tasks.

The route to automaticity, it appears, is practice and memory. With repetition and overlearning comes the ability to perform automatically what formerly needed conscious processing. A particularly dramatic illustration of the power of practice was done by Spelke, Hirst, and Neisser (1976). With extensive practice, two people were able to read stories at normal rates and with high comprehension, while

The demands on attention and memory in flying a jet airplane are enormous. The pilot must simultaneously pay conscious attention to multiple sources of information while relying on highly practiced, automatic processes and overlearned actions to respond to others.

they simultaneously copied words at dictation or even categorized the dictated words according to meaning. Significantly, once practice has yielded automatic performance, it seems especially difficult to undo the practice, to overcome what has now become an automatic and, in a sense, autonomous process (Zbrodoff & Logan, 1986).

Disadvantages of Automaticity

We have been talking as if automaticity is always a positive, desirable characteristic, as if anything that reduces the drain on the limited available mental capacity is a good thing. This is not entirely true, however. There are several situations in which achieving automaticity can lead to difficulties (Reason, 1990). You may experience **action slips**, which are *unintended, often automatic, actions that are inappropriate for the current situation* (Norman, 1981).

Action slips can occur for a number of reasons, each involving a lapse of attention; the action seems foolish, and you wouldn't have done it if you had been paying more attention. In some cases, the environment has been altered from the way it would normally be, such as pressing a button to open a door that is already (unusually) propped open. Sometimes action slips are brought about by a change that requires people to relearn something they have become accustomed to doing another way. For example, your new car may have some of its controls in a different location from where they were on the older one, so you have to overcome the habit of reaching to the left dashboard to turn on the lights (this is why some controls, e.g., accelerator and brake pedals, do not change position). Often action slips occur when people have started something, but are distracted (Botvinick & Bylsma, 2006). They then lapse into a more automatic pattern of behavior of doing the wrong thing, or forgetting a needed step, such as turning on the coffee machine.

In other cases, people start doing something that they frequently do, but at an inappropriate time. A classic example involves the man whose wife told him to go back to the bedroom and change his tie one evening. When he did not return after a suitable amount of time, she went to the bedroom to find out what was keeping him. When she got there, she found that he had undressed and was in bed. What had happened was that there were a number of stimuli in the environment that triggered a more automatic pattern of action. Specifically, when he normally went to his room at night and took off his tie, this was the beginning of his routine that ended in his going to bed. This automatic pattern of behavior was triggered by these stimuli (it may sound like brain damage, but it's not—we all do things like this at one time or another). Another, more common example is when you find yourself driving to work or school when you meant to go someplace you go less often.

Sometimes we *should* be consciously aware of information or processes that have become too routine and automatic. Barshi and Healy (1993) provided an excellent example, using a proofreading procedure that mimics how we use checklists. People in their study scanned pages of simple multiplication problems. Five mistakes such as "7 × 8 = 63" were embedded in the pages of problems. People saw the same sets of 10 problems over and over. But in the fixed order condition, the problems were in the same order each time; in the varied order condition, the problems were in a different order each time. Those tested in the fixed order condition missed more of the embedded mistakes than those in the varied order condition; an average of 23% missed in fixed order, but only 9% missed with varied orders. Figure 4-10 shows this result across the five embedded errors. Performance did improve in the fixed order condition, as more and more of the mistakes were encountered. But the first multiplication error was detected only 55% of the time, compared with the 90% detection rate for the varied order group.

The fixed order of problems encouraged automatic proofreading, which disrupted accuracy at detecting errors. In fact, it took either an earlier error that *was* detected or a specific alerting signal (Experiment 3) to overcome the effects of routine, automatic proofreading.

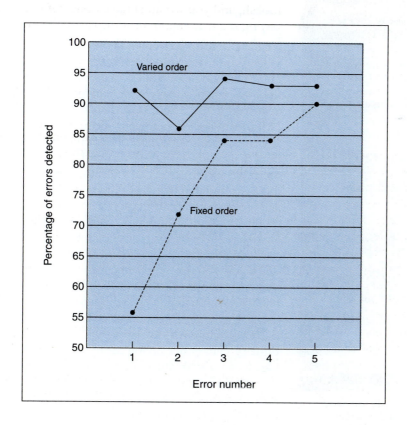

FIGURE 4-10

Results of Barshi and Healy's experiment, showing the percentage of participants detecting the five embedded errors in proofreading multiplication problems. Problems were presented in fixed or varied order.

Data from Barshi & Healy (1993).

The implications of this kind of result should be clear. Pilots are required to go through checklist procedures, say for landing an airplane, to ensure safety. Yet because the items on the checklist are in a fixed order, repeated use of the list probably leads to a degree of automaticity and probably a tendency to miss errors. This is exactly what happened in March 1983: A plane landed in Casper, Wyoming, without its landing gear down, even though the flight crew had gone through its standard checklist procedure and had "verified" that the wheels were down. In Barshi and Healy's words, this incident "reminded the crew and the rest of the aviation community that the countless repetition of the same procedure can lead to a dangerous automatization" (1993, P. 496). It's interesting to wonder which is worse, too much automatization of procedures, as exemplified by the Barshi and Healy study, or too much attention paid to the procedures, as in the Haines (1991) study you read about in Chapter 3 (hint: experienced pilots in flight simulators).

MIND WANDERING Perhaps one of the most obvious and ubiquitous examples of not being able to use our attention the way that we want to is when our minds drift from the task that we are supposed to be focusing on to some other, irrelevant idea. **Mind wandering** is *the situation in which a person's attention and thoughts wander from the current task to some other, inappropriate line of thought.* We all regularly experience mind wandering, such as when we start to daydream during a boring lecture, start thinking about a significant other when sitting at a

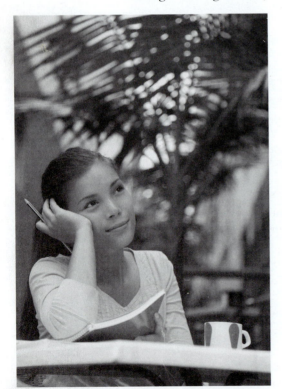

Sometimes when we are trying to do one task, attention disengages and our minds wander.

traffic light, or get to the bottom of a page and realize that we have no idea what we just read. In these cases, we have decoupled our attention from the environment to focus more exclusively on our own internal thoughts, often without an awareness that our mind is wandering until we catch ourselves (Smallwood, McSpadden, & Schooler, 2007, 2008); this idea is now supported by ERP (event-related potential) recordings (Barron, Riby, Greer, & Smallwood, 2011). During reading, we can now detect when a person is mind wandering because their eye movements become more erratic, eyeblinks increase, and their eye movements are less tied to characteristics that should influence their reading patterns (such as word frequency) (Reichle, Reineberg, & Schooler, 2010; Smilek, Carriere, & Cheyne, 2010).

As you know, your mind is more likely to wander when you are bored than when you are engaged and absorbed in something. Essentially, when you are really concentrating, all of your attention is engaged in the task you are focused on, and it is difficult for distractions to lure it away. However, when your intended primary task is not taking all of your attention, other ideas can break through and take attention away (Smallwood & Schooler, 2006). Under these circumstances, attention will drift from what you are supposed to be thinking about to something else, leaving your memory for what you are supposed to be doing much poorer. The surprising prediction here is that people with *more* working memory capacity are more likely to mind wander. This is because they will be more likely to have capacity available over and above what is required by the current task. These people get distracted by things that are in the environment, but are not part of what they are supposed to be attending. Such a proneness to mind wander impedes cognition, such as the ability to learn things in school (Smallwood, Fishman, & Schooler, 2007). Because mind wandering involves a loss of attentional control, in some sense, it is not surprising that mind wandering is more likely when a person is under the influence of alcohol (Sayette, Reichle, & Schooler, 2009) or craving a cigarette (Sayette, Schooler, & Reichle, 2010).

An important point to note is that your mind does not wander randomly. Instead, you are more likely to disengage from the current task and mind wander by thinking about things that are current concerns for you, or are relevant to your long-term goals. If you think about those cases where your mind wanders, you'll find that you are often daydreaming about things that are important to you in one way or another. Often, there may be something in the environment, such as a person you see, a word that you hear or read, or a smell of perfume, that directs your attention away from what you need to be doing and toward something else.

Section Summary

- When attention is viewed as a limited mental resource, issues of task complexity become concerned with how automatic or controlled different mental processes are. Automatic processes are rapid, are not dependent on intent, are unavailable to conscious awareness, and place few if any demands on limited attentional resources. Conscious or controlled processes are the opposite: rather slow, requiring intention, open to conscious awareness, and heavily demanding of attentional resources.
- Mental processes become more automatic as a function of practice and overlearning. A disadvantage of automaticity is that it is difficult to reverse the effects of practice in an automated task, and automaticity can lead to errors of inattention, including action slips.
- When our attention is not fully engaged, our minds can wander off topic. Mind wandering is more likely to occur when there is mental capacity left over and available. Moreover, when we mind wander, the things that we allow our attention to drift to are typically things that we have enduring concerns about, such as things we are anxious or excited about.

Key Terms

action slips (p. *132*)
attention (p. *103*)
attention capture
  (p. *107*)

attentional blink
  (p. *127*)
automaticity
  (p. *127*)

benefit or facilitation
  (p. *110*)
conjunction search
  (p. *111*)

controlled
  attention
  (p. *119*)
cost (p. *110*)

5

Short-Term Working Memory

Elementary memory makes us aware of . . . the just past. The objects we feel in this directly intuited past differ from properly recollected objects. An object which is recollected, in the proper sense of that term, is one which has been absent from consciousness altogether, and . . . is brought back . . . from a reservoir in which, with countless other objects, it lay buried and lost from view. But an object of primary memory is not thus brought back; it never was lost; its date was never cut off in consciousness from that of the immediately present moment. In fact it comes to us as belonging to the rearward portion of the present space of time, and not to the genuine past.

(JAMES, 1890, PP. 643–647)

Primary memory, elementary memory, immediate memory, short-term memory (STM), short-term store (STS), temporary memory, supervisory attention system (SAS), working memory (WM)—all these terms refer to the same general type of memory where the "immediately present moment," in James's explanation, is held in consciousness. It is the seat of conscious attention discussed in Chapter 4. This is where comprehension occurs: short-term, working memory. What it is, what it does, and how it does it are the topics of this chapter.

A short-term working memory is the memory we are conscious of. Many of our intuitions and introspections about it match what has been discovered empirically. However, some mental processes of short-term working memory are not open to consciousness: They are automatic. These processes yield no useful introspections; indeed, people often feel that they do not exist. (This is why short-term working memory is only *roughly* the same as consciousness. We are aware of its contents, but not necessarily the *processes* that occur in it.)

Modern research on short-term working memory came hard on the heels of selective attention studies of the mid-1950s.[1] George Miller's (1956) classic article, which we discuss shortly, is an excellent example of this upsurge in interest. A common observation, that we can remember only a small number of isolated items presented rapidly, began to take on new significance as psychology groped toward a new approach to human memory. Miller's insightful remarks were followed shortly by the Brown (1958) and Peterson and Peterson (1959) reports. Amazingly, simple three-letter stimuli, such as *MHA*, *GPR*, or *JMW*, were forgotten almost completely within 15 seconds if the person's attention was diverted by a distractor task of counting backward by threes. Such reports were convincing evidence that the limited capacity of memory was finally being pinned down and given an appropriate name: short-term memory.

As we proceed, we will shift from the term *short-term memory* to *working memory*. Why the two terms? Basically, they have different connotations. *Short-term memory* conveys a simpler idea. It is the label we use to focus on the input and storage of new information. For example, when a rapidly presented series of digits is tested for immediate recall, we generally refer to short-term memory. Likewise, when we focus on the role of rehearsal, we are examining the short-term memory maintenance of new information. Short-term memory is observed whenever short retention is tested—no more than 15 or 20 seconds—and when little, if any, transfer of new information to long-term memory is involved.

Working memory, in comparison, is the newer term and has the connotation of a mental workbench, a place where mental effort is applied (Baddeley, 1992a, b; Baddeley & Hitch, 1974). Thus, when word meanings are retrieved from long-term memory and put together to understand a sentence, working memory is where this happens. Traditional immediate memory tasks are a subset of working

---

[1]There was also some research on short-term memory before the behaviorist period. For instance, Mary W. Calkins, the first woman to serve as president of the American Psychological Association, conducted work in the 1890s and reported several important effects that were "discovered" in the 1950s and 1960s. See Madigan and O'Hara (1992) for an account of the "truly remarkable legacy" (p. 174) of this pioneering woman.

memory research but usually are only secondary to reasoning, comprehension, or retrieval processes. For example, the short-term memory responsible for digit span performance is but a single component of the more elaborate working memory system.

SHORT-TERM MEMORY: A LIMITED-CAPACITY BOTTLENECK

If you hear a string of 10 digits, read at a rapid rate, and are asked to reproduce them in order, generally you cannot recall more than about 7. The same result is found with unrelated words (see the "Prove It" projects on page 147 for sample lists and try testing a few volunteers). This is roughly the amount you can say aloud in about 2 seconds (Baddeley, Thomson, & Buchanan, 1975) or the amount you can recall in 4 to 6 seconds (Dosher & Ma, 1998; see also Cowan et al., 1998). This limit has been recognized for so long, it was included in the earliest intelligence tests (e.g., Binet's 1905 test; see Sattler, 1982). Young children and people of subnormal intelligence generally have a shorter span of apprehension, or memory-span. In the field of intelligence testing, it is almost unthinkable to devise a test *without* a memory-span component. Note that this is a general aspect of short-term memory, not something special about spoken words or digits. For example, a similar finding is observed with letters in American Sign Language (ASL) (Wilson & Emmorey, 2006; Wilson & Fox, 2007), which clearly is more visual/motor relative to spoken English.

Short-Term Memory Capacity

Simulate
Digit Span in
MyPsychLab

For our purposes, the importance of this limitation is that it reveals something fundamental about human memory. Our immediate memory cannot encode vast quantities of new information and hold it accurately. It has a severe limit. Miller stated this limit aptly in the title of his 1956 paper: "The Magical Number Seven, Plus or Minus Two: Some Limits on Our Capacity for Processing Information." However, more recent work suggests that the situation is worse than this—that people can maintain only four plus or minus one units of information (e.g., Cowan, 2010), and that seven plus or minus two is actually a result of some chunking. We process large amounts of information in the sensory memories, and we can hold vast quantities of knowledge in permanent long-term memory. Yet, short-term memory is the narrow end of a funnel, the four-lane bridge with only one open tollgate; it is the bottleneck in our information-processing system.

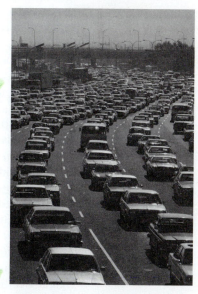

Toll booths force a bottleneck in a highway's traffic flow.

OVERCOMING THE BOTTLENECK   And so this limitation remains unless what we are trying to remember is made richer and more complex by grouping it in some way, as in the 3–3–4 grouping of a telephone number or the 3–2–4 grouping of a Social Security number. In Miller's terms, a *richer, more complex item* is called a **chunk** of information. By chunking items together into groups, we can overcome this limitation.

The following is a simple example of the power of chunking:

BYGROUPINGITEMSINTOUNITSWEREMEMBERBETTER

No one can easily remember 40 letters correctly if they are treated as 40 separate, unrelated items. But by chunking the letters into groups, we can retain more information. You can more easily remember the eight words because they are familiar ones that combine grammatically to form a coherent thought. You can remember a Social Security number more easily by grouping the digits into the 3–2–4 pattern. And you can remember a telephone number more easily if you group the last four digits into two two-digit numbers (of course the point generalizes beyond U.S. Social Security and phone numbers).

The term for this *process of grouping items together, then remembering the newly formed groups* is **recoding**. By recoding, people hear not the isolated dots and dashes of Morse code but whole letters, words, and so on. The principle behind recoding is straightforward: Recoding reduces the number of units held in short-term memory by increasing the richness, the information content, of each unit. Try recoding the longest digit list in the "Prove It" lists, at the end of the chapter, into two-digit numbers (28, 43, and so on). This illustrates the mental effort needed for recoding (in fact, Brooks & Watkins, 1990, suggested that there is already a subgrouping effect in the memory span, with the first half enjoying an advantage over the second).

Two conditions are important for recoding. First, we can recode if there is sufficient time or resources to use a recoding scheme. Second, we can recode if the scheme is well learned, as Morse code becomes with practice. In a dramatic demonstration of this, over the period of a few months, one person in a study by Chase and Ericsson (1982) could recall 82 digits in order by applying a highly practiced recoding scheme he invented for himself. But what about situations when an automatic recoding scheme is not available? What is the fate of items in short-term memory? Can we merely hold the usual small number of items?

Explore *Delay Interference* in **MyPsychLab**

Forgetting from Short-Term Memory

In addition to having a limited capacity, information in short-term memory, as the name says, is only around for a short period of time. Research by Brown (1958) and Peterson and Peterson (1959) provided a compelling demonstration of this. The central idea was that *forgetting might be caused simply by the passage of time before testing*—in other words, forgetting caused by **decay**. In their experiments, a simple three-letter trigram (e.g., *MHA*) was presented to people, followed by a three-digit number (e.g., *728*). People were told to attend to the letters, then to begin counting backward by threes from the number they were given. The counting was done aloud, in rhythm with a metronome clicking twice per second. The essential ingredient here is the distractor task of backward counting. This requires a great deal of attention (if you doubt this, try it yourself, making sure to count twice per second). Furthermore, it prevents rehearsal of the three letters because rehearsal uses the same cognitive mechanism as the backward counting. At the end of a variable period of time, the people reported the trigram. The results were so unexpected, and the number of researchers eager to replicate them so large, that the task acquired a name it is still known by—the **Brown–Peterson task**.

The surprising result was that memory of the three-letter trigram was only slightly better than 50% after 3 seconds of counting; accuracy dwindled to about 5% after 18 seconds (Figure 5-1). The letters were forgotten so quickly even though short-term memory was not overloaded—a 50% loss after only 3 seconds (assuming perfect recall with a zero-second delay). On the face of it, this seems evidence of a simple decay function: With an increasing period of time, less and less information remains in short-term memory.

Later research, especially by Waugh and Norman (1965), questioned some of the assumptions made. Waugh and Norman thought that the distractor task itself might be a source of interference. If the numbers spoken during backward counting interfered with the short-term memory trace, then longer counting intervals would have created more interference. Waugh and Norman's reanalysis of several studies confirmed their suspicion. Especially convincing were the results of their own probe digit task. People heard a list of 16 digits, read at a rate of either 1 or 4 per second. The final item in each list was a repeat of an earlier item, and it was the probe or cue to recall the digit that had *followed* the probe in the original list.

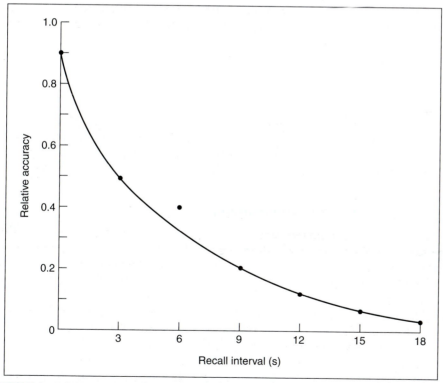

FIGURE 5-1 Relative accuracy of recall in the Brown–Peterson task across a delay interval from 0 to 18 seconds. People had to perform backward counting by threes during the interval.

Source: From Peterson & Peterson (1959).

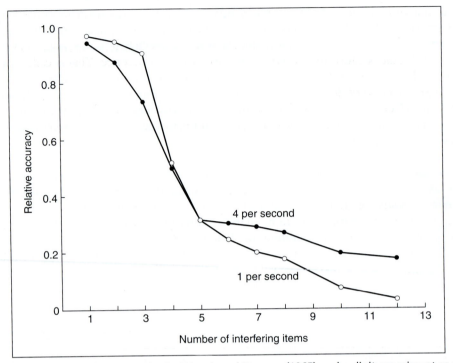

FIGURE 5-2 Relative accuracy in the Waugh and Norman (1965) probe digit experiment as a function of the number of interfering items spoken between the target item and the cue to recall; rate of presentation was either 1 or 4 digits per second.

For instance, if the sequence *7 4 6 9* had been presented, then the probe *4* would have cued recall of the *6*.

The important part of their study was the time it took to present the 16 digits. This took 16 seconds for one group (a long time) but only 4 seconds (a short time) for the other group. If forgetting were caused by decay (a time-based process), then the groups should have differed markedly in their recall because so much more time had elapsed in the 16 seconds group. Yet, as Figure 5-2 shows, the two groups differed little. This suggests that forgetting was influenced by the number of intervening items, not simply the passage of time. In other words, forgetting in short-term memory was caused by interference, not decay (for cross-species evidence of interference, see Wright & Roediger, 2003). Although it has been decades since the original work, the issue of decay versus interference explanations for forgetting in short-term memory continues to be of interest to cognitive psychologists (e.g., Unsworth, Heitz, & Parks, 2008). Some interesting recent work suggests that while the bulk of the forgetting is due to interference, there is still a small amount that can be attributed to a decay process as well (Altmann & Gray, 2002; Altmann & Schunn, in press; Berman, Jonides, & Lewis, 2009).

PROACTIVE AND RETROACTIVE INTERFERENCE (PI AND RI) Shortly after the Peterson and Peterson report, Keppel and Underwood (1962) challenged the decay explanation for forgetting in short-term memory. They found that people forgot at a dramatic rate only after several trials. On the first trial, memory for the trigram was almost perfect. Keppel and Underwood's explanation was that as you experience more and more trials in the Brown–Peterson task, recalling the trigram becomes more difficult because the *previous* trials generate interference. This is called **proactive interference (PI)**, *when older material interferes forward in time with your recollection of the current stimulus.* This is the opposite of **retroactive interference (RI)**, in which *newer material interferes backward in time with your recollection of older items.* The loss of information in the Brown–Peterson task was caused by proactive interference.

RELEASE FROM PI   An important adaptation of the interference task was done by Wickens (1972; Wickens, Born, & Allen, 1963). He gave people three Brown–Peterson trials, using three words or numbers rather than trigrams. On the first trial, accuracy was near 90%, but it fell to about 40% on Trial 3. At this point Wickens changed to a different kind of item for Trial 4. People who had heard three words per trial were given three numbers, and vice versa. The results were dramatic. When the nature of the items was changed, performance on Trial 4 returned to the 90% level of accuracy (Wickens also included a control group who got the same kind of stimulus on Trial 4 as they had gotten on the first three trials, to make sure performance continued to fall, which it did). Figure 5-3 shows this result.

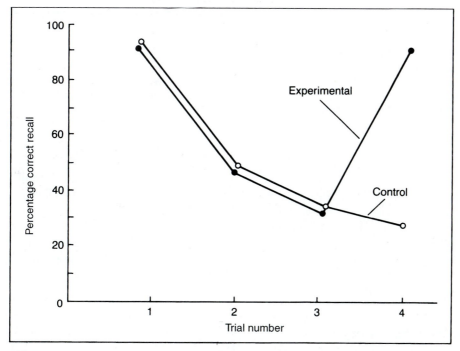

FIGURE 5-3   Recall accuracy in a release from PI experiment by Wickens, Born, and Allen (1963). Triads of letters are presented on the first three trials, and proactive interference begins to depress recall accuracy. On Trial 4, the control group gets another triad of letters; the experimental group gets a triad of digits and shows an increase in accuracy, known as release from PI.

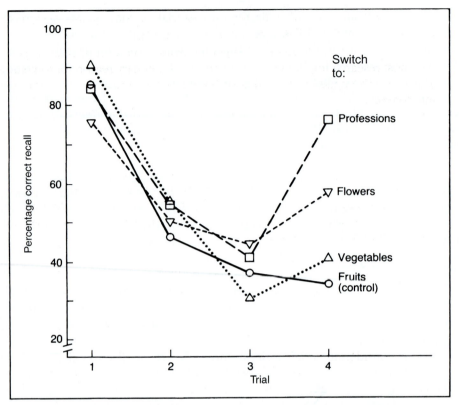

FIGURE 5-4 Recall accuracy in a release-from-PI experiment by Wickens and Morisano (reported in Wickens, 1972). All participants received word triads from the fruit category on Trial 4. On Trials 1 through 3, different groups received triads from the categories *fruits* (control condition), *vegetables, flowers,* and *professions.*

The interference interpretation is clear. Performance deteriorates because of the buildup of proactive interference. If the to-be-remembered information changes, then you are released from the interference. Thus, **release from PI** occurs *when the decline in performance caused by proactive interference is reversed because of a switch in the to-be-remembered stimuli.* Release from PI also occurs when the change is semantic, or meaning-based, as when the lists switched from one semantic category to another (see Figure 5-4). However, note that the more related the items on the fourth list were to the original category, the less release from PI was experienced. Thus, short-term memory, to some degree, uses semantic information.

Section Summary

- Short-term or working memory is an intermediate system between the sensory and long-term memories. Its capacity for holding information is limited, by some accounts, to only 7 ± 2 units of information, although other accounts suggest that it may only be able to hold 4 ± 1 chunks of information. The processes of chunking and recoding, grouping more information into a single unit, are ways of overcoming this limit or bottleneck.

• Whereas a decay explanation of forgetting from short-term memory is possible, most research implicates interference as the primary reason for forgetting. The research suggests two kinds of interference: retroactive and proactive interference.

SHORT-TERM MEMORY RETRIEVAL

In this section we consider retrieval from short-term memory. This refers to the act of bringing knowledge to the foreground of thinking, and perhaps reporting it. Our focus is on two aspects of retrieval. These are the serial position curve and studies of the retrieval process itself.

Serial Position Effects

Simulate *Serial Position Effect* in **MyPsychLab**

To start with, a **serial position curve** is a *graph of item-by-item accuracy on a recall task. Serial position* simply refers to the original position an item had in a study list. Figure 5-5 shows several serial position curves (which you encountered briefly in Chapter 1).

Before considering serial position curves per se, we'll cover the two tasks used to test people: **free recall** and **serial recall**. In free recall, people are free to *recall the list items in any order,* whereas in serial recall, people *recall the list items in their original order of presentation.* Not surprisingly, serial recall is the more difficult. Recalling items in order requires people to rehearse them as they are shown, trying to hold on to not only the information itself but also its position in the list. The more items there are, the harder the task becomes. In comparison, with free recall, people can recall the items in any order.

The early list positions are called the *primacy portion* of a serial position curve. *Primacy* here has its usual connotation of "first": It is the first part of the list that was studied. **Primacy effect**, then, refers to the *accuracy of recall for the early list positions.* A strong primacy effect means good, accurate recall of the early list items, usually because of rehearsal. The final portion of the serial position curve is the *recency portion.* **Recency effect** refers to *the level of correct recall on the final items of the originally presented list. High recency* means "high accuracy," and *low recency* means that this portion of the list was hardly recallable at all.

As Figure 5-5A shows, a strong recency effect is found across a range of list lengths; Murdock (1962) presented 20-, 30-, and 40-item lists at a rate of one item per second. Note that there is a slight primacy effect for each list length, but that the middle part had low recall accuracy. Apparently, the first few items were rehearsed enough to transfer them to long-term memory, but not enough time was available for rehearsing items in the middle of the list. For all lists, though, the strong recency effect can be attributed to recall from short-term memory.

The way to eliminate the recency effect should be no surprise. Glanzer and Cunitz (1966) showed people 15-item lists. For some people, after a list they needed to do an attention-consuming counting task for either 10 or 30 seconds

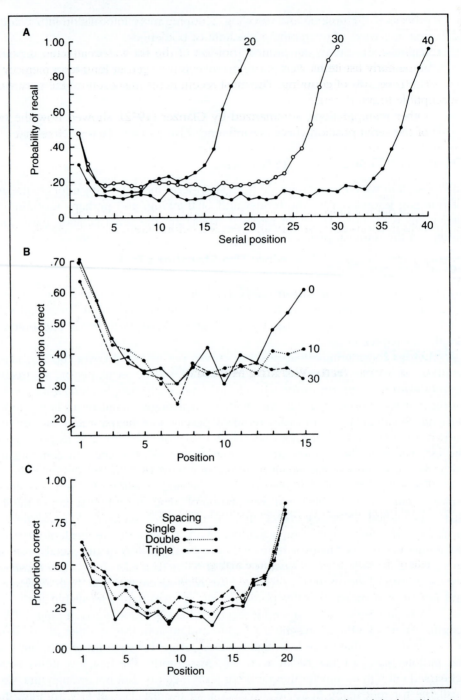

FIGURE 5-5 **A.** Serial position curves showing recall accuracy across the original positions in the learned list. Rate of presentation was one item per second. **B.** Serial position curves showing the decrease in recency when 10 or 30 seconds of backward counting is interpolated between study and recall. **C.** Three different rates of presentation: single (3 seconds), double (6 seconds), and triple (9 seconds).

before recalling the items. In contrast to people who gave immediate recall (0 seconds delay), the people who had to do a counting task showed very low recency (Figure 5-5B). However, the primacy portion of the list was unaffected. In other words, the early list items were more permanently stored in long-term memory to endure 30 seconds of counting. The most recent items in short-term memory were susceptible to interference.

Other manipulations, summarized by Glanzer (1972), showed how the two parts of the serial position curve are influenced by different factors. Note that providing more time per item during study (spacing of 3 versus 6 versus 9 seconds, in the figure) had almost no influence on recency but did alter the primacy effect (Figure 5-5C; from Glanzer & Cunitz, 1966). Additional time for rehearsal allowed people to store the early items more strongly in long-term memory. Moreover, additional time did not help the immediate recall of the most recent items. These items were held in short-term memory and recalled before interference could take place.

Short-Term Memory Scanning: The Sternberg Task

We turn now to a different question: How do we access or retrieve the information from short-term memory? To answer this question, we turn to another memory task: recognition.

PROVE IT
Tests of Short-Term, Working Memory

Several tests of short-term, working memory can be given with little difficulty, to confirm the various effects you are reading about in this chapter. Here are some suggestions.

Simple Memory Span

Make several lists, being sure that the items do not form unintended patterns; use digits, letters, or unrelated words. Read the items at a fairly constant and rapid rate (no slower than one item per second) and have the participant name them back in order. Your main dependent variable will be the number or percentage correct. See sample lists at the end of the chapter.

Try a few of these variations:

- To illustrate the importance of interference, have people do an interference task on half of the trials. On an interference trial, give them a number like 437 and have them count backward by threes, aloud, for 15 seconds, before recalling the list items.
- Keeping list length constant, give different retention intervals before asking for recall (e.g., 5 seconds, 10 seconds, 20 seconds), either with or without backward counting.
- Vary the presentation rate (e.g., one word per second versus one word per 3 seconds) to see how the additional time for rehearsal influences recall.

Working Memory Span

Follow the examples given in the text to construct a working memory span test—for example, from one to six unrelated sentences, each followed by an unrelated word, where the participant must process the sentence and then, at the end of the set, recall the unrelated words that appeared. Span size will be the number of words recalled correctly, assuming that the sentences were comprehended.

Essentially, a recognition test is one in which a person is presented with items and is asked to indicate whether or not the items were part of what had been studied before. A person would select "Yes" to indicate "Yes, I recognize that as being studied." Similarly, a person would select "No" to indicate "No, I didn't study that item." Making these decisions requires you to access stored knowledge, then compare the items to that knowledge. The important angle is that we can time people as they make their "yes/no" recognition decisions, and infer the underlying mental processes used on the basis of how long they took. It was this procedure Saul Sternberg used in addressing the question of how we access information in short-term memory.

Sternberg (1966, 1969, 1975) began by noting that the use of response time (RT) to infer mental processes had a venerable history, dating back at least to Donders in the 1800s. Donders proposed a subtractive method for determining the time for simple mental events. For example, if your primary task involves processes A, B, and C, you devise a comparison task that has only processes A and C in it. After giving both tasks, you subtract the A + C time from the A + B + C time. The difference should be a measure of the duration of process B because it is the process that was subtracted from the primary task.

Sternberg pointed out a major difficulty with Donders's subtractive method. It is virtually impossible to make sure that the comparison task, the A + C task, contains *exactly* the same A and C processes as in the primary task. There is always the possibility that the A and C components were altered when you remove process B. If so, then subtracting one from the other can't be justified. Sternberg's solution was to arrange it so that the critical process would have to *repeat* some number of times during a single trial. Across an entire study there would be many trials on which process B had occurred only once, many on which it occurred two times, three times, and so forth. He then examined the RTs for these conditions, and inferred the nature of process B by determining how much time was *added* to response times for each repetition of process B. This is referred to as the *additive factors* method.

THE STERNBERG TASK   The task Sternberg devised was a short-term memory scanning task, now simply called a Sternberg task. People were given a short list of letters, one at a time, at the rate of one per second, called the memory set. People then saw a single letter, the probe item, and responded "yes" or "no" depending on whether the probe was in the memory set. So, for example, if you stored the set *l r d c* in short-term memory and then saw the letter *d*, you would respond "yes." However, if the probe were *m* you would respond "no."

In a typical experiment, people saw several hundred trials, each consisting of these two parts, memory set then probe, as shown in Table 5-1. Memory sets were from one to six letters or digits long, within the span of short-term memory, and were changed on every trial. Probes changed on every trial, too, and were selected so that the correct response was "yes" on half the trials and "no" on the other half. This is illustrated by Trials 2 and 3 in Table 5-1. Take a moment to try several of these trials, covering the probe until you have the memory set in short-term memory, then covering the memory set and uncovering the probe, then make your "yes/no" judgment. (For a better demonstration, have someone read the memory sets and probe to you aloud.)

TABLE 5-1	Sample Sternberg Task		
Trial	**Memory Set Items**	**Probe Items**	**Correct Response**
1	R	R	Yes
2	LG	L	Yes
3	SN	N	Yes
4	BKVJ	M	No
5	LSCY	C	Yes

Figure 5-6 illustrates the **process model** that Sternberg (1969) proposed, simply *a flowchart of the four separate mental processes that occurred during the timed portion of every trial.* At the point marked "Timer starts running here," the person encodes the probe. Then, the search or scan through short-term memory begins and the mentally encoded probe is compared with items in memory to see whether there was a match. A simple "yes" or "no" decision could then be made by pressing one of two buttons.

In Sternberg's task, it was the search process of the contents of short-term memory that was of interest. Notice—this is critical—that it was *this* process that was repeated different numbers of times, depending on how many items were in the memory set. Thus, by manipulating memory set size, Sternberg influenced the number of cycles through the search process. And by examining the slope of the RT results, he could determine how much time was needed for each cycle.

STERNBERG'S RESULTS   Figure 5-7 shows Sternberg's (1969) results. There was a linear increase in RT as the memory set got larger, and this increase was nearly the same for both "yes" and "no" trials. The equation at the top of the figure shows that the y-intercept of this RT function was 397.2 ms. Hypothetically, if there had been zero items in short-term memory, the y-intercept would be the combined time for the encoding, decision, and response stages (refer back to Figure 5-6). More importantly, the slope of the equation was 37.9 ms; for each additional item in the memory set, the mental scanning process took 37.9 ms. Putting it slightly differently, the search through short-term memory is approximately 38 ms per item—*very* fast.

FIGURE 5-6   The four-stage process model for short-term memory scanning. Adapted from Sternberg (1969).

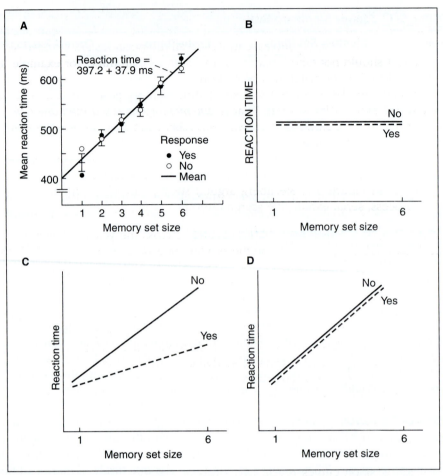

FIGURE 5-7   Reaction time in the short-term memory scanning task, for "yes" (shaded circles) and "no" (unshaded circles) responses. Reaction time increases linearly at a rate of 37.9 ms per additional item in the memory set.

What kind of mental search would produce these results? Sternberg considered three possibilities. The most intuitively appealing was a *serial self-terminating search* in which the positions in short-term memory are scanned one by one, and the scan stops when a match is found; this is how you search for a lost object, say your car keys. The idea is that, on the average, the slope of the RT trials for "yes" responses should be smaller than the slope for "no" responses. On the "no" trials, all positions have to be searched before you can decide that the probe was not in the set. But on "yes" trials, people would encounter matches at all positions in the memory set, sometimes early, sometimes late, with equal frequencies at all positions. This would yield a pattern similar to that of the visual search task you read about in Chapter 4; in Figure 4-5, the slopes of the positive curves ("yes, I found the target") were always smaller than those of the negative curves ("no, the target was not in the display"). However reasonable such a search seems, Sternberg's data did not match the prediction—he found the same slope for both kinds of trials.

The second possibility was a *parallel search*, in which each position in the memory set is scanned simultaneously. If short-term memory is scanned in parallel, then there should be no increase in RT—if all the positions are scanned simultaneously, it should not take longer to scan six items than three, for example. But again, the data did not match this prediction.

Instead, Sternberg inferred that short-term memory is searched in a fashion called **serial exhaustive search**. That is, *the memory set is scanned one item at a time (serial), and the entire set is scanned on every trial, whether or not a match is found (exhaustive).* Notice that exhaustive search has to be correct for "no" trials because the positions have to be scanned exhaustively before you can confidently and accurately make a "no" decision. Because of the similarity of the "yes" and "no" curves in Figure 5-7, Sternberg argued strongly that both reflect the same mental process, serial exhaustive search (Sternberg, 1969, 1975).

LIMITATIONS TO STERNBERG'S CONCLUSIONS   Across the years, it has been suggested that increasing RTs could be the product of a parallel search in which each additional item slows down the rate of scanning for all items (much as a battery can run several motors at once, but each runs more slowly when more motors are connected; see Baddeley, 1976, for a review). Others have objected to the assumption that the several stages or processes are sequential and that one must be completed before the next one begins. For instance, McClelland (1979) proposed that the mental stages might overlap partially, in cascade fashion. Still, Sternberg's work pushed the field toward more useful ways of studying cognition. Most research based on RT tasks (e.g., visual search tasks and many long-term memory tasks) owes credit, even if only indirectly, to Sternberg's ground-breaking and insightful work.

Section Summary

- Serial position curves reveal two kinds of memory. Early positions in a list are sensitive to deliberate rehearsal that transfers information into long-term memory, whereas later positions tend to be recalled with high accuracy in the free recall task; this latter effect is called the recency effect and is due to the strategy of recalling the most recent items first. Asking people to do a distractor task before recall usually eliminates the recency effect because the distractor task prevents them from maintaining the most recent items in short-term memory.
- Sternberg's paradigm, short-term memory scanning, provided a way to investigate how we search through short-term memory. Sternberg's results indicated that this search is a serial exhaustive process occurring at a rate of about 38 ms per item to be searched.

WORKING MEMORY

Working memory can be viewed as an augmentation of short-term memory. By the mid-1970s, all sorts of functions were being attributed to short-term memory in tasks of problem solving, comprehension, reasoning, and the like. Yet, as Baddeley pointed out, remarkably little work had actually demonstrated those functions in STM (Baddeley, 1976; Baddeley & Hitch, 1974; Baddeley & Lieberman, 1980). For example, pay attention to how you solve the following problem:

$$\frac{(4 + 5) \times 2}{3 + (12/4)}$$

How can a simple limited-capacity system capture the problem-solving processes here? Didn't you compute part of the expression, hold that intermediate answer in memory while computing the next part, then hold the updated intermediate value, and so on? Likewise, sentence comprehension can sometimes tax short-term memory almost palpably; for instance:

I know that you are not unaware of my inability to speak German.

Can you feel the burden on your controlled processing when you have to figure out—almost translate—the meaning of a sentence piece by piece, then put the pieces together? ("not unaware" equals "aware," "inability to speak German" means "cannot speak German," and so on). But ideas such as the burden or load on short-term memory, or switching between processing and remembering, are not addressed by simple approaches that emphasize a small number of "slots" or "chunks."

Going beyond intuitive examples, Baddeley and Hitch (1974) documented their position by describing a dramatic case study, originally reported by Warrington and Shallice (1969; also Shallice & Warrington, 1970; Warrington & Weiskrantz, 1970) of a patient "who by all normal standards, has a grossly defective STS. He has a digit span of *only two items,* and shows grossly impaired performance on the Peterson short-term forgetting task. If STS does indeed function as a central working memory, then one would expect this patient to exhibit grossly defective learning, memory, and comprehension. No such evidence of general impairment is found either in this case or in subsequent cases of a similar type" (Baddeley & Hitch, 1974, pp. 48–49, emphasis added; also Baddeley & Wilson, 1988; Vallar & Baddeley, 1984). In a similar vein, McCarthy and Warrington (1984) reported on a patient who had a memory span of only one word, but could nonetheless report back six- and seven-word sentences with about 85% accuracy. Despite the fact that both types of lists relied on short-term memory, performance on one type was seriously affected by the brain damage, and the other only minimally.

Baddeley and Hitch reasoned that the problem lies with a simple maintenance theory of STM. STM is but one component of a larger, more elaborate system, **working memory**.

The Components of Working Memory

A description of Baddeley's working memory model provides a useful context for the studies described later; (see Baddeley & Hitch, 1974; Salame & Baddeley, 1982; Baddeley, 2000a). Baddeley's model, shown in Figure 5-8, has four major components. The main part is the *central executive* (or sometimes *executive control*), assisted by two auxiliary systems: the *phonological loop* and the *visuo-spatial sketch pad*. Both of these had specific sets of responsibilities, assisting the central executive by doing some of the lower-level processing. Thus, in the arithmetic problem mentioned earlier, the central executive would be responsible for retrieving values from memory $(4 + 5, 9 \times 2)$ and applying the rules of arithmetic; a subsystem, the phonological loop, would then hold the intermediate value 18 in a rehearsal-like buffer until it was needed again. More recently, a third auxiliary system, the *episodic buffer*, was added (Baddeley, 2000a). This part is used to integrate information already in working memory with information retrieved from long-term memory. It is where different types of information are bound together to form a complete memory, such as storing together the sound of someone's voice with an image of his/her face.

The idea of working memory being divided into components is supported by neurological evidence. Smith and Jonides (1999; also Smith, 2000) reviewed a number of brain imaging studies to identify regions of heightened activity in various working memory tasks. In general, the thinking is that those brain regions involved in perception are also recruited by working memory for the storage of information, regions toward the posterior (back) of the brain, and that the rehearsal and processing of information is controlled by those aspects of the

FIGURE 5-8 An overview of Baddeley's working memory model, including the central executive, the phonological loop, the visuo-spatial sketchpad, and the episodic buffer. Based on Baddeley (2000a).

brain involved in motor control and attention (Jonides, Lacey, & Nee, 2005). For the Sternberg task, the scanning evidence showed strong activations in a left hemisphere parietal region, noted at the numbered area 40 in the figure, and three frontal sites, Broca's area (B.A. 44), and the left supplementary motor area (SMA) and premotor area (B.A. 6).

As you will read in Chapter 9, Broca's area is important in the production of language, so finding increased activity here was not surprising. Alternatively, tasks that emphasize executive control, such as switching from one task to another, tend to show strong activity in the dorsolateral prefrontal cortex (DLPFC) (B.A. 46) (for an argument that task switching does not involve executive control, see Logan, 2003). This area is central to understanding executive attention (Kane & Engle, 2002). The neurological basis for executive control is also supported by work showing that executive functions in cognition may have a significant genetic basis (Friedman et al., 2008).

Other studies have shown specific brain regions involved in visuo-spatial working memory. In one (Jonides et al., 1993), people saw a pattern of three random dots; the dots were then removed for 3 seconds, and a circle outline appeared; the task was to decide whether the circle surrounded a position where one of the dots had appeared earlier. In a control condition, the dots remained visible while the circle was shown, thus eliminating the need to remember the locations. Positron emission tomography (PET) scans revealed that three right hemisphere regions showed heightened activity and so were involved in spatial working memory. They were a portion of the occipital cortex, a posterior parietal lobe region, and the premotor and DLPFC region of the frontal lobe (see also Courtney, Petit, Maisog, Ungerleider, & Haxby, 1998). In related work, when the task required spatial information for responding, it was the premotor region that was more active; when the task required object rather than spatial location information, the DLPFC was more active (Jonides et al., 1993; see also Miyake et al., 2000, for a review of various executive functions attributed to working memory).[2]

The Central Executive

The *central executive* is the heart of working memory. It's like a large corporation, in which the chief executive is in charge of the tasks of planning, initiating activities, and making decisions. Likewise in working memory, the **central executive** is in charge of *planning future actions, initiating retrieval and decision processes as necessary,* and *integrating information coming into the system.* Let's take an example to illustrate some of this. To continue with the arithmetic example, the central executive triggers the retrieval of facts such as "4 + 5 = 9" and invokes the problem-solving rules such as "how to multiply and divide." Furthermore, the central executive also "realizes" that the intermediate value 18 must be held momentarily while further processing occurs. Accordingly, it activates the phonological loop, sending it the value 18 to rehearse for a few moments until that value is needed again.

Each of the subsystems has its own pool of attentional resources, but the pools are limited. Give any of the subsystems an undemanding task, and it can proceed without disrupting activities occurring elsewhere in working memory. However, if a subsystem is given a particularly difficult task, then either it falters or it must drain additional resources from the central executive. To some degree, working memory resources are shared across processing domains, such as verbal or visual (Vergauwe, Barrouillet, & Camos, 2010). This is why closing your eyes can help you think by reducing distractions from the external environment (Vredeveldt, Hitch, & Baddeley, 2011).

The central executive has its own pool of resources that can be depleted if overtaxed. For example, people who do something that places a strain on the central executive, such as ignoring distracting information as it scrolls across the bottom of a television screen or exaggerating their emotional expressions, have greater difficulty with central executive processing immediately thereafter (Schmeichel, 2007). Moreover, damage to portions of the frontal lobes, such as the medial frontal lobes (B.A. 32) and the polar regions (B.A. 10) can disrupt working memory executive function (Banich, 2009). This produces dysexecutive syndrome, in which patients continue to pursue goals that are no longer relevant, and experience heighted distractibility when they do not have clear goals (Gevins, Smith, McEvoy, & Yu, 1997).

---

[2]The procedure of subtracting patterns in the control condition from those obtained in the experimental condition is straightforward conceptually, although the computations are mind boggling. But notice that conceptually it rests on the same type of logic that Donders used (and Sternberg rejected): finding a control task that contains all of the experimental tasks' components except the one of interest. It will be surprising if this method does not come under attack again, in its newer application to brain imaging.

The Phonological Loop

The **phonological loop** is *the speech- and sound-related component responsible for rehearsal of verbal information and phonological processing.* This component recycles information for immediate recall, including articulating the information in auditory rehearsal (see Baddeley, 2000b; Jones, Macken, & Nicholls, 2004; and Mueller, Seymour, Kieras, & Meyer, 2003, for a debate on the articulatory versus phonological basis of this subsystem).

There are two components of the phonological loop, the phonological store and the articulatory loop. The **phonological store** is essentially *a passive store component of the phonological loop.* This is the part that holds on to verbal information. However, information in the phonological store is forgotten unless it is actively rehearsed and refreshed. Thus, rehearsal is the role of the **articulatory loop**, *the part of the phonological loop involved in the active refreshing of information in the phonological store.* One way of thinking about these two components of the phonological loop is that the phonological store is like your inner ear—you can hear yourself talk to yourself, or imagine hearing music. Similarly, the articulatory loop is like your inner voice, when you mentally say things to yourself.

Researchers have found a number of effects that provide insight into how the phonological loop works. We cover two of them here: the articulatory suppression and phonological similarity effects. The **articulatory suppression effect** is *the finding that people have poorer memory for a set of words if they are asked to say something while trying to remember the words* (Murray, 1967). This effect is not complicated; it occurs even when you say something simple, like repeating the word "the" over and over again. What happens here is that the act of speaking consumes resources in the articulatory loop. As a result, words in the phonological store cannot be refreshed and are lost. A related phenomenon is the irrelevant speech effect (Colle & Welsh, 1976). It is hard to keep information in the phonological loop when there is irrelevant speech in the environment. This irrelevant speech intrudes on the phonological loop, consuming resources and causing you to forget verbal information. This is why it is so difficult to read (and then remember what you read) when you are in a room with other people talking. (So, try to study somewhere quiet.)

The **phonological similarity effect** is *the finding that memory is poorer when people need to remember a set of words that are phonologically similar, compared to a set of words that are phonologically dissimilar* (Baddeley, 1966; Conrad & Hull, 1964). For example, it is harder to remember the set "boat," "bowl," "bone," and "bore," compared to the set "stick," "pear," "friend," and "cake." This is because words that sound similar can become confused in the phonological store. One thing that happens is that, because the words sound similar, it is hard to keep track of what was rehearsed and what wasn't. As a consequence, some words may not get rehearsed and so are forgotten (Li, Schweickert, & Gandour, 2000). In addition, as bits and pieces of them become forgotten or lost, people need to reconstruct them. As a result, people are more likely to make a mistake by misremembering a word that sounded like it should have been in the set, but wasn't—for example, recalling the word "bold" in the first set of words. In general, when people misremember words in working memory, they tend to be words that sound similar, rather than having a similar meaning. This suggests that this aspect of working memory relies primarily on phonological rather than semantic information.

Although we have spent a great deal of time covering phonological aspects of the phonological loop, there is some evidence that there are broader aspects of this part of working memory. For example, it has been found that memory for musical pitches shows similar characteristics to language, in that working memory has a limited capacity for what can be remembered, and people become confused by similar pitches, much like the phonological similarity effect (Williamson, Baddeley, & Hitch, 2010). Also, in a very clever study, Shand (1982) tested people who were congenitally deaf and skilled at American Sign Language (ASL). They were given five-item lists for serial recall, presented as either written English words or ASL signs. One list contained English words that were phonologically similar *(SHOE, THROUGH, NEW)* though not similar in terms of the ASL signs. Another list contained words that were cherologically similar in ASL—that is, similar in the hand movements necessary for forming the sign (e.g., wrist rotation in the vicinity of the signer's face), although they did not rhyme in English. Recall memory showed confusions based on the cherological relatedness. In other words, the deaf people were recoding the written words into an ASL-based code and holding *that* in working memory. Their errors naturally reflected the physical movements of that code rather than verbal or auditory features of the words.

The Visuo-Spatial Sketch Pad

The **visuo-spatial sketch pad** is *a system for visual and spatial information,* maintaining that kind of information in a short-duration buffer. If you must generate and hold a visual image for further processing, the visuo-spatial sketch pad is at work. In general, there is some support for the idea that the visuo-spatial sketchpad shares some of the same neural processes when manipulating mental images as are used during active perception (Broggin, Savazzi, & Marzi, 2012; Kosslyn et al., 1993).

The operation of the visuo-spatial sketch pad can be illustrated by a study by Brooks (1968). People were asked to hold a visual image in working memory, a large block capital *F*, then scan that image clockwise, beginning at the lower left corner. In one condition, people said "yes" aloud if the corner they reached while scanning was at the extreme top or bottom of the figure and "no" otherwise; this was the "image plus verbal" condition. The other condition was an "image plus visual" search condition: While people scanned the mental image, they also had to search through a printed page, locating the column that listed the "yes" or "no" decisions in the correct order. Thus, two different secondary tasks were combined with the primary task of image scanning; all the tasks used the visuo-spatial sketch pad of working memory. The result was that making verbal responses—saying "yes" or "no"—was easy and yielded few errors. However, visual scanning of printed columns was more difficult and yielded substantial errors. This is because scanning the response columns forced the visuo-spatial sketch pad to divide its resources between two tasks, and performance suffered.

A number of effects have been observed that illustrate basic qualities of the visuo-spatial sketch pad. One of the overarching principles of this aspect of working memory is the influence of embodied cognition. As you will see, processing in the visuo-spatial sketch pad acts as if a person were actively interacting with objects in the world. It is not an abstract code, but a dynamic system that allows a person to predict what would happen next if he or she were actually involved in a situation.

The most dramatic evidence for the visuo-spatial sketch pad comes from work on mental rotation (Cooper & Shepard, 1973; Shepard & Metzler, 1971). **Mental rotation** involves people *mentally turning, spinning, or rotating objects in the visuo-spatial sketch pad of working memory.* In one study, people were shown drawings of pairs of three-dimensional objects and they had to judge whether they were the same shape. The critical factor was the degree to which the second drawing was "rotated" from the orientation of the first. To make accurate judgments, people had to mentally transform one of the objects, mentally rotating it into the same orientation as the other so they could judge it "same" or "different." Figure 5-9 displays several such pairs of drawings and the basic findings of the study.

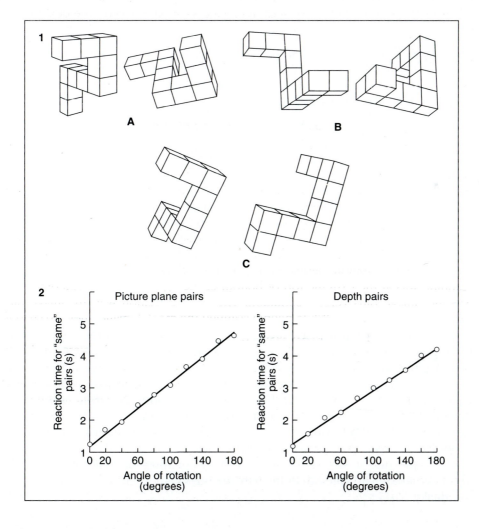

FIGURE 5-9

1. Three pairs of drawings are shown. For each, rotate the second drawing and decide whether it is the same figure as the first drawing. The *A* pair differs by an 80-degree rotation in the picture plane, and the *B* pair differs by 80 degrees in depth; the patterns in *C* do not match. **2.** The RTs to judge "same" are shown as a function of the degrees of rotation necessary to bring the second pattern into the same orientation as the first. Reaction time is a linear function of the degree of rotation.

One of the mainstays of research on the phonological loop is the articulatory suppression task. For this task people are asked to repeat words aloud over and over again while trying to remember another set of verbal/linguistic information. The basic idea is that the repeated talking consumes the resources of the articulatory loop, making it difficult to maintain other information. On the face of it, the articulatory suppression task sounds very easy, and that it should not be too difficult. However, actually doing it is a humbling experience that shows how limited our working memory capacity is, and how poor our ability is to do more than one thing at a time when the same part of working memory needs to be used.

To illustrate the powerful influence of articulatory suppression, following are two lists of 10 words each. Copy them down onto a set of note cards. These are just examples, and you can make more lists if you want. Then find a few people to be your participants. Have them read each list of cards by allowing them to see each one for 1 second before moving on to the next. When the end of the list is reached, the person should write down as many words as can be remembered. For one list, have the people simply read the words. However, for the other list, the articulatory suppression list, have them say the word "the" over and over again (the, the, the, . . .) while reading the words; have them keep saying "the the the" until the end of the list is reached. What you should find is that performance is worse under articulatory suppression than when they can read in peace and quiet.

Across	Figure
Result	Action
Center	Mother
Reason	Became
Effect	Making
Period	Really
Behind	Either
Having	Office
Cannot	Common
Future	Moment

The overall result was that people took longer to make their judgments as the angular rotation increased. In other words, a figure that needed to be rotated 120 degrees took longer to judge than one needing only 60 degrees of rotation, much as what would be found if a person were to manually turn the objects. In fact, performance can be enhanced if people are given tactile feedback (by holding an object in their hands) when the object is the same shape and moves in the same way (Wraga, Swaby, & Flynn, 2008), consistent with an embodied interpretation. Moreover, also consistent with an embodied influence, people find it harder to mentally rotate pictures of easily manipulated objects compared to ones that are hard to physically manipulate (Flusberg & Boroditsky, 2011).

In the Cooper and Shepard (1973) report, people were shown the first figure and were told how much rotation to expect in the second figure. This advance information on the degree of rotation permitted people to do the mental rotation ahead of time. Interestingly, the mental processes seem much the same if you ask people to retrieve an image from long-term memory, then hold it in working memory while performing mental rotation on that image. That is, researchers have found regular time-based effects of rotation, and activation in the visual (parietal) lobes, when people are asked to retrieve an image from long-term memory and rotate it mentally in working memory (Just, Carpenter, Maguire, Diwadkar, & McMains, 2001).

Another illustration of properties of the visuo-spatial sketch pad is **boundary extension**, in which *people tend to misremember more of a scene than was actually viewed, as if the boundaries of an image were extended further out* (Intraub & Richardson, 1989; for a review, see Hubbard, Hutchison, & Courtney, 2010). In boundary extension studies, people see a series of pictures. Later, memory is tested for what was seen in the pictures. This can be done by having people either draw what they remember, or identify the image they saw earlier. What is typically found is that people tend to misremember having viewed the picture from further back than was the case. That is, people misremember information from beyond the bounds of the actual picture (for example, if a person saw a picture of a stuffed animal on a set of steps, he or she will misremember more steps than were actually seen). What is going on here is that visuo-spatial working memory adds knowledge of what is beyond the picture boundary, based on previous world knowledge of what is likely to be there. This is then stored in long-term memory. So, when you think back to a show you've seen on television or at the movies, you tend to remember the events as if you were actually there, with no edge to the world. You don't typically remember the image as it appeared on the screen (or even remember sitting there watching the show).

The last of the visuo-spatial phenomena considered here (and there are many more) is **representational momentum**, which is *the phenomenon of misremembering the movement of an object further along its path of travel than where it actually was when it was last seen* (Hubbard, 1995, 2005). In a typical representational momentum study, people see an object moving along a computer screen. At some point the object disappears. The task is to indicate the point on the screen where the object was last seen. The typical results show a bias to misremember the object as being further along its path of travel than it actually was (Freyd & Finke, 1984; Hubbard, 1990). It is as if visuo-spatial working memory is simulating the movement as if it were happening in the world, predicting where that object will be next. This prediction then enters into the decision process, and people place the object further along its path.

Representational momentum can be influenced by other embodied aspects of the situation as well. For example, there is also a bias to remember objects as being farther down than they actually were, as if they were being drawn down by gravity (Hubbard, 1990). There is also evidence that visuo-spatial working memory takes into account friction (Hubbard, 1990), centripetal, and impetus forces (Hubbard, 1996), even if physics has shown these ideas to be wrong, as in the case of impetus. Finally, if an object is moving in an oscillating motion, back and forth like a pendulum, and it disappears just before it is about to swing back, people will mis-remember it as having started its backswing (Verfaille & Y'dewalle, 1991).

Overall, it should be clear that there is a lot of active cognition in the visuo-spatial sketch pad. This part of working memory is doing a lot of work, even if you are not consciously aware of much of it. Moreover, this work is oriented around capturing physical aspects of the world (accurately or not) to help predict what objects will do next, so that you can better interact with them, such as intercepting or avoiding them, with a minimum of conscious cognitive mental effort.

The Episodic Buffer

As mentioned earlier, the **episodic buffer** is *the portion of working memory where information from different modalities and sources is bound together to form new episodic memories* (Baddeley, 2000a). In other words, this is the part of working memory where the all-important chunking process occurs, but it also includes perceptual processes, such as the integration of color with shape in visual memory (Allen, Baddeley, & Hitch, 2006).

One study that may clarify the workings of the episodic buffer was done by Copeland and Radvansky (2001). In this study, people were given a working memory span test (these sorts of tests are described in detail later). People read a series of sentences and had to remember the last word of the sentences in a given set. What was manipulated was the phonetic similarity of the words in a set. Sometimes, the words were phonologically similar, and other times not. The phonological similarity effect described earlier in the phonological loop section predicts that working memory performance would be worse for the phonologically similar items. However, because the words were presented at the end of meaningful sentences, rather than alone, people could use their semantic understanding of the sentences and bind this with their memory for the words. The result was that, under these circumstances, memory for the phonologically similar words was better than for the dissimilar words, much as you would find with poetry or song lyrics. Thus, the episodic buffer's use of the meanings of the words trumped the normal loss of information that happens in the phonological loop.

Another study, by Jefferies, Lambdon Ralph, and Baddeley (2004), illustrates the capacity needed for integrating information in the episodic buffer. In their study, people were given lists of words, lists of unrelated sentences, and lists of sentences that formed a coherent story. People were asked to learn these lists either alone or under a more demanding dual task situation (see later) that involved pressing buttons on a keyboard when an asterisk appeared on the computer screen. They found that working memory resources were important for remembering the lists of words and the lists of unrelated sentences; when working memory resources were consumed by the dual task, memory for the words and unrelated sentences was compromised. In other words, the working memory capacity needed to chunk the information for words and unrelated sentences was being consumed by the secondary task. But for the related sentences, because the meaningful interrelations among them were easily derived, memory performance was relatively unaffected by the dual task. The ease of integrating the sentences into a coherent story reduced the demand for working memory resources.

Section Summary

- Working memory consists of a central executive and three major subsystems: the phonological loop for verbal and auditory information, the visuo-spatial sketch pad for visual and spatial information, and the episodic buffer for integrating or binding information from different parts of working memory and/or long-term memory.
- The various components of working memory are thought to operate relatively independently of one another, perhaps by using different neural substrates, although there can be some overlap for demanding tasks.
- There are capacity limits in the system. Dual task methods can be used to study strains on individual components, or on the overall capacity of working memory. For example, the subsystems may drain extra needed capacity from the central executive in situations of high working memory demands.

ASSESSING WORKING MEMORY

In general, there are two ways of assessing working memory: the dual task method and measures of working memory span. In the first case, performance is examined by having a person do a secondary task, one that consumes working memory resources at the same time as some primary task. This is the dual task method, often used to see how disruptive the secondary task is. In comparison, for working memory span tests, we get a measure of a person's working memory capacity. Across a range of people and abilities, we compare the span scores to performance on other tasks, to see what relationships emerge. Let's go over each of these methods in turn.

Dual Task Method

For the **dual task method**, one of the tasks done by a person is identified as the primary task we are most interested in. The other is a secondary task that is done simultaneously with the first. Both tasks must rely to some significant degree on working memory. In general, we are interested in how the two tasks can be done together and whether there is any competition or interference between them. Any two tasks that are done simultaneously may show complete independence, complete dependence, or some intermediate level of dependency. If neither task influences the other, then we infer that they rely on separate mental mechanisms or resources. If one task always disrupts the other, then they presumably use the same mental resources.

Finally, if the two tasks interfere with each other in some circumstances but not others, then there is evidence

One man band.

for a partial sharing of mental resources. Usually such interference is found when the difficulty of the tasks reaches some critical point at which the combination of the two becomes too demanding. Researchers manipulate the difficulty of the two tasks just as you would adjust the volume controls on a stereo, changing the left and right knobs independently until the combination hits some ideal setting. In research, we vary the difficulty of each task separately—we crank up the "difficulty knobs" on the two tasks, so to speak—and observe the critical point at which performance starts to suffer.

An important aspect of working memory that the dual task method highlights is that information processed in one component may not interfere with processing in another. For example, thinking that uses central executive resources will be relatively unaffected by processing that consumes resources in one of the subsystems.

Here's an example. In one experiment (Baddeley & Hitch, 1974, Experiment 3), people were asked to do a reasoning task. They were shown an item such as *AB* and were timed as they read and responded "yes" or "no" to sentences about it. A simple sentence here would be "*A* precedes *B*," an active affirmative sentence. An equivalent meaning is expressed by "*B* is preceded by *A*," but it's more difficult to verify because of the passive construction. There were also negative sentences, such as "*B* does not precede *A*," and "*A* is not preceded by *B*" (as well as false sentences, e.g., "*B* precedes *A*"). The sentence difficulty was a way of manipulating how much the central executive was needed. While doing the reasoning task, people also had to do one of three secondary tasks: (a) articulatory suppression, (b) repeating the numbers 1 through 6, or (c) repeating a random sequence of digits (the sequence was changed on every trial). Note how the amount of articulation in the three tasks was about the same (a speaking rate of four to five words per second was enforced), but the demands on the central executive steadily increased. There was also a control condition in which there was no concurrent articulation.

Figure 5-10 shows the reasoning times for these four conditions. The control condition showed that even when reasoning was done alone, it took more time to respond to the difficult sentences. Adding articulatory suppression or repeated counting added more time to reasoning but did not change the pattern of times to any great degree; the curves for "the the the" and "one two three . . ." in the figure have roughly the same slope as the control group. This is because these tasks do not strongly consume working memory resources. However, the random digit condition yielded a different pattern. As the sentences grew more difficult, the added burden of reciting a random sequence of digits took its toll. In fact, for the hardest sentences in the reasoning task, correct judgments took nearly 6 seconds in the random digit condition, compared with only 3 seconds in the control condition. When the secondary task is difficult, the articulatory loop must drain or borrow some of the central executive's resources, thereby slowing down or sacrificing accuracy.

This dual task interference has been shown in a variety of tasks, including showing that dividing attention during driving, such as talking on a cell phone, disrupts the ability to make important judgments, such as when to brake. In general, dual task processing leads to much slower braking (Levy, Pashler, & Boer, 2006). In

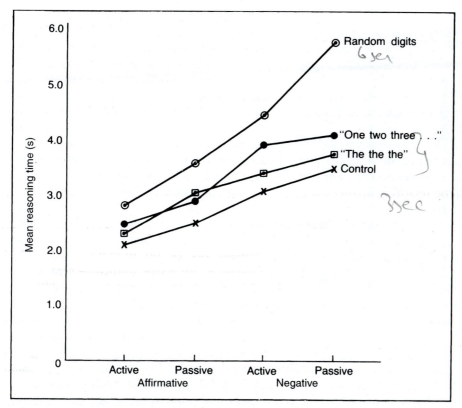

FIGURE 5-10 Average reasoning time is shown as a function of two variables: the grammatical form of the reasoning problem and the type of articulatory suppression task that was performed simultaneously with reasoning. In the random digits condition, a randomly ordered set of six digits had to be repeated out loud during reasoning; in the other two suppression tasks, either "the the the" or "one two three four five six" had to be repeated out loud during reasoning.

other words, when you tax working memory resources, the ability of the central executive to effectively process information is compromised.

Similar research has also been reported comparing the visuo-spatial sketch pad and the phonological loop. As one example, Logie, Zucco, and Baddeley (1990; but see Morey & Cowan, 2004, for a contrasting view) selected two different primary tasks: a visual memory span task and a letter span task. These were paired with two secondary tasks, one involving mental addition and the other visual imagery. In the visual memory span task, people saw a grid of squares on the computer screen, with a random half filled in. After a moment, the grid disappeared and was followed by an altered grid where one of the previously filled squares was now empty. People had to point to the square that was changed, using their visuo-spatial memory of the earlier pattern. In contrast, the letter memory span task, the other primary task, should use the phonological loop.

For the secondary tasks, Logie et al. used a mental addition task thought to be irrelevant to the visuo-spatial processing and an imaging task thought to be

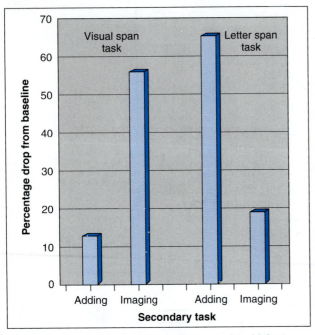

FIGURE 5-11 Results from Logie, Zucco, and Baddeley's (1990) experiment on the visuo-spatial sketch pad. Two secondary tasks, adding and imaging, were combined with two primary tasks, a visual span or a letter span task. The results are shown in terms of the percentage drop in performance measured from baseline; the larger the drop, the more disruption there was from the secondary task.

irrelevant to the phonological loop. The results are shown in Figure 5-11. First, look at the left half of the graph, which reports the results of the visual span (grid pattern) task. Each person did the span task alone, to determine baseline, then along with the secondary tasks. The graph shows the percentage *drop* in dual task performance as compared to baseline. For instance, visual span performance dropped about 15% when the addition task was paired with it; so, dual task performance was at 85% of the single-task baseline. In other words, mental addition disrupted visual memory only modestly. But when the secondary task was visual imagery, as shown by the second bar in the graph, visual memory span dropped about 55%. This is a large interference effect, suggesting that the visuo-spatial sketch pad was stretched beyond its limits.

The right half of the figure shows performance on the letter span task. Here, the outcome was reversed; mental addition was very disruptive to the letter span task, leading to a 65% decline, whereas the imaging task depressed letter span scores only a modest 20%. Thus, only minor declines were observed when the secondary task used a different part of working memory. But substantial declines occurred when the two tasks used the same pool of resources (see Baddeley & Lieberman, 1980, for some of the original research on the visuo-spatial sketch pad). Other work suggests that the impact dual tasks such as these are having is on the encoding aspect of a task, rather than the retention of information in working memory per se (Cowan & Morey, 2007).

Working Memory Span

A different way to study working memory is an individual differences approach. As in any area of psychology, when we speak of individual differences, we're talking about characteristics of individuals—anything from height to intelligence—that differ from one person to the next and can be measured and related to other factors.

Individual differences in working memory are related to various cognitive processes. In this research, people are first given a test to assess their working memory spans. They are then given standard cognitive tasks. Consider a program of research by Engle and his coworkers (Engle, 2001; Rosen & Engle, 1997; see Engle, 2002, for an excellent introduction). First, people are given a **working memory span** task. The task requires simultaneous mental processing and storage of information in working memory. For example, a person might see arithmetic statements along with a word, one at a time (from Turner & Engle, 1989):

$$(6 \times 2) - 2 = 10? \; SPOT$$
$$(5 \times 3) - 2 = 12? \; TRAIL$$
$$(6 \times 2) - 2 = 10? \; BAND$$

People first read the problem aloud, indicated whether the answer was correct, and then said the capitalized word, followed by the second problem and word, then the third. At that point, people tried to recall the three capitalized words, showing that they had stored them in working memory. Scores on this span task are based on the number of capitalized words recalled. Thus, someone who recalled "*SPOT TRAIL BAND*" and answered the arithmetic questions correctly would have a memory span of 3. In another version of the working memory span task, we use sentences instead of arithmetic problems. But both involve *processing* and *storage*: processing the problem or sentence for meaning, and storing the word for recall.

Many investigators have used span tasks to measure working memory capacity. The original work that used this method (Daneman & Carpenter, 1980) examined reading comprehension as a function of span. There were significant correlations between span scores and performance on the comprehension tasks. One of the most striking correlations was between span and verbal Scholastic Aptitude Test (SAT) scores; it was .59, whereas simple span scores seldom correlated significantly with SATs. (As a reminder, simple span tasks, such as remembering a string of digits, test only the storage of items, whereas working memory span tasks involve both storage and processing.) This strong correlation means that there is an important underlying relationship between one's working memory span and the verbal processing measured by the SAT.

The strongest correlation in Daneman and Carpenter's work was a .90 correlation between memory span and performance on a pronoun reference test. Here, people read sentences one by one and at some point confronted a pronoun that referred back to a previous noun. In the hardest condition, the noun had occurred up to six or seven sentences earlier. The results are shown in Figure 5-12. Here, people with the highest working memory span of 5 scored 100% correct on the pronoun test, even in the "seven sentences ago" condition. People with the lowest spans (of 2) got 0% correct. Thus, people with

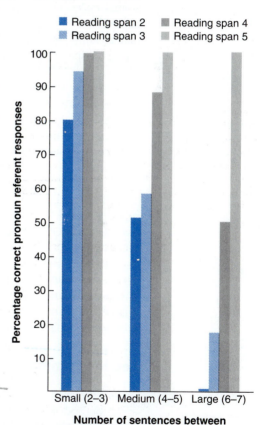

FIGURE 5-12 The percentage of correct responses to the pronoun reference task when the antecedent noun occurred a small, medium, or large number of sentences before the pronoun, as a function of participants' working memory (reading) span.

Source: From Daneman & Carpenter (1980).

higher working memory spans were able to keep more relevant information active in working memory as they comprehended the sentences.

Research since this has extended these findings. Basically, if a task relies on a need to control attention, scores on the task correlate strongly with working memory span. In fact, Engle (e.g., 2002) argued that working memory capacity *is* executive attention and offers the equation "WM = STM + controlled attention"—that is, working memory is the combination of traditional short-term memory plus our controlled attention mechanism (Kane & Engle, 2003; see also Daneman & Merikle, 1996; Engle, 2002; Miyake & Shah, 1999; Unsworth & Spillers, 2010). This involves both the maintenance of information in the short term as well as the ability to access needed information in long-term memory (Unsworth & Engle, 2007).

There is also some evidence that working memory abilities can change with practice. For example, women tend to perform less well than males on visuo-spatial tasks. However, with some training, such as 10 hours experience playing action-based video games, the performance of females can reach the levels of males (Feng, Spence, & Pratt, 2007). Such experience can also boost performance on visuo-spatially based scientific thinking, such as understanding plate tectonics (Sanchez, 2012). Also, it has been suggested that musical training can boost verbal intelligence (Moreno et al., 2011). Finally, there is some evidence that certain kinds of Buddhist meditation can also improve mental imagery abilities (Kozhevnikov, Louchakova, Josipovic, & Motes, 2009). Overall, this work, along with the research by Chase and Ericsson (1982) described earlier (as well as others, e.g., Verhaeghen, Cerella, & Basak, 2004), suggests that people can develop strategies to more efficiently and effectively use their working memories over and above any base level of capacity they may have.

That said, memory span scores do not provide insight into all aspects of cognitive abilities. For example, a study by Copeland and Radvansky (2004b) gave people a variety of memory span tasks, and also assessed performance at more complex levels of comprehension, such as remembering event descriptions, drawing inferences about causes and effects, and detecting inconsistencies in a text. The results showed little evidence of a relation between working memory span and performance. Thus, although memory span highlights important cognitive abilities, it is not the complete story. There is individual variation that can be attributed to other factors as well.

Section Summary

- One common method for assessing working memory is to use dual task methodologies. In these tasks, people are asked to simultaneously do at least two tasks. Researchers then assess how performance on the primary task is affected by the addition of the secondary task, and the theoretical relationship between the two.
- An alternative research strategy is to test working memory span, then examine differences in performance as a function of span scores. This has revealed a number of tasks that show a relationship between span and performance. The implication is that working memory span assesses controlled attentional processes, which are significant aspects of performance.

WORKING MEMORY AND COGNITION

As noted earlier, working memory does not exist or operate independently of other aspects of cognition. It is the vital nerve center of a great deal of activity. In the next few sections, we discuss ways in which working memory influences processing in a variety of domains, including attention, long-term memory, and reasoning.

Working Memory and Attention

Conway, Cowan, and Bunting (2001) examined working memory span and its relation to the classic cocktail party effect of hearing one's own name while paying attention to some other message. About 65% of the people with low memory spans detected their name in a dichotic listening task, versus only 20% of people with high spans. The idea was that high-span people were selectively attending to the shadowed message more effectively than the low-span people, so weren't as likely to detect their names on the unshadowed message. In contrast, the low-span people had difficulty blocking out or inhibiting attention to the distracting information in the unattended message—so they were more likely to hear their own names (see Kane et al., 2007, for evidence that high-span people are better at concentrating more generally and are less likely to engage in mind wandering).

In a similar demonstration, Kane and Engle (2003) used the classic Stroop task (see the "Prove It" box in Chapter 4)—you remember, name the ink color a word like RED is printed in, when the ink color mismatches. There was a strong Stroop effect, of course—approximately a 100-ms slowdown on mismatching items. More to the point, there was no difference in the Stroop effect for high- and low-span groups when the words were always in a mismatching color (*GREEN* printed in red ink) or when half of the words were presented that way; everyone remembered the task goal—ignore the word—in these conditions. But when only 20% of the words were in mismatching colors, low-span people made nearly twice as many errors as high-span people. Because mismatching trials were rarer, the low-span people seemed less able to maintain the task goal in working memory. High-span individuals had less difficulty maintaining that goal.

In a more everyday example, Sanchez and Wiley (2006) tested people with different memory spans, giving them texts to read that included illustrations. These illustrations were often irrelevant to the main points of the text, such as having a picture of snow in a passage about ice ages—the snow is related to the topic, but does not provide or support any new information. As such, performance is better if working memory capacity were to focus on the relevant details in the text. What was found was that people with lower memory spans were more likely to be "seduced" by the irrelevant details in the pictures. That is, they had more difficulty controlling the contents of their current stream of thought, and were more likely to be led astray by attractive, but unhelpful, sources of knowledge that served as a distraction.

Working Memory and Long-Term Memory

Long-term memory function can also depend on working memory. Rosen and Engle (1997), for instance, had high- and low-span people do a verbal fluency task: Generate members of the animal category as rapidly as possible for up to 15 minutes. High-span people outperformed their low-span counterparts, a difference noticeable

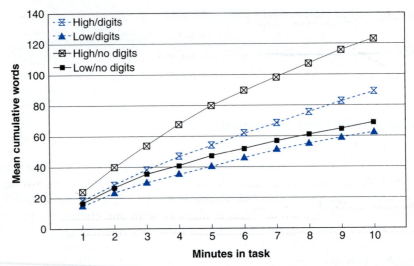

FIGURE 5-13 The cumulative number of animal names generated by participants of high (open points) or low (filled points) working memory span. Dashed lines indicate performance when participants performed the secondary task of monitoring a stream of digits while generating animal names.

Source: From Rosen & Engle (1997).

even 1 minute into the task. Intriguingly, in a second experiment, both groups were tested in the fluency task alone and in a dual-task setting. While naming animals, people had to simultaneously monitor the digits that showed up, one by one, on the computer monitor and press a key whenever three odd digits appeared in the sequence. This task reduced performance on the animal naming task, but only for the high-span people, as shown in Figure 5-13. Low-span people showed no decrease in performance.

Rosen and Engle suggested that the normal, automatic long-term memory search for animal names was equivalent in both groups. But high-span people were able to augment this with a conscious, controlled strategic search; in other words, along with regular retrieval, the high-span people could deliberately ferret out additional, hard-to-find animal names using a controlled attentional process. This additional "ferreting" process used working memory. As a consequence, the added digit monitoring task used up the working memory resources that had been devoted to the strategic search. This made the high-span group perform more like the low-span group when they had to perform the dual task.

Other studies have also shown the importance of working memory. For instance, Kane and Engle (2000) found that low-span people experience more proactive interference (PI) in the Brown–Peterson task than do high-span people. High-span people used their controlled attentional processes to combat PI, so they showed an increase in PI when they had to do a simultaneous secondary task (see Bunting, Conway, & Heitz, 2004; Cantor & Engle, 1993; and Radvansky & Copeland, 2006a; for an exploration of the role of working memory span in managing asso- ciative interference during retrieval). More generally, low-span people appear to search a wider range of knowledge, making them more prone to having irrelevant information intrude on retrieval (Unsworth, 2007). In Hambrick and Engle (2002; see also Hambrick & Meinz, 2011), high-span people had better performance than low-span people on a long-term memory retrieval task, even when both groups were equated for the rather specialized domain knowledge being tested (what a nice experiment to participate in—people listened to simulated radio broadcasts of baseball games).

Working Memory and Reasoning

The idea that working memory involves controlled attention can also be tied to general issues of cognitive and behavioral control, such as those needed in problem solving. People with lower memory span scores may be less effective at controlling their thought processes. One example of this is a study by Moore, Clark, and Kane (2008) that looked at working memory span and choices on moral reasoning problems. For example, suppose that there is a runaway trolley car. If you let it go, it will kill four unaware people a bit down the track. Alternatively, you could push a very large person next to you in front of the trolley; it will kill him, but derail the trolley and save the other four people. So, how morally acceptable is each of these choices? Moore et al. found that moral reasoning of this type was mediated by a person's working memory capacity, with high working memory capacity people making choices on a more consistent (i.e., principled) basis.

The influence of memory span is also seen on more traditional sorts of mental reasoning, such as solving logic problems like categorical syllogisms (see Chapter 11). In a study by Copeland and Radvansky (2004a; see also Markovits & Doyon, 2004), people with various working memory spans were asked to solve a set of logic problems. There were two primary findings. First, people with greater memory spans solved more syllogisms than people with smaller memory spans. Moreover, working memory span was also related to the strategies people used to reason; people with smaller memory spans used simpler strategies. It may be that having more working memory capacity allows one to keep more information active in memory, allowing a person to explore different alternatives when trying to reason and draw conclusions.

Sometimes Small Working Memory Spans Are Better

Intuitively, it would seem that people with more working memory capacity, or those who engage working memory resources more effectively, are more likely to succeed, and generally this is true. However, there are some interesting exceptions. One of these is illustrated in a study by Beilock and DeCaro (2007). In this study, high- and low-span people were given math problems to solve. Under normal conditions, high-span people tended to do better. However, people were then placed in a high-pressure situation; they were told that they were being timed, that their performance would be videotaped so math experts could evaluate them, that they would be paid for improving their performance, and so forth. In this high-pressure condition, working memory capacity was consumed with task-irrelevant anxiety-induced thoughts, and performance in both the high- and low-span groups was equivalent (and lower). Thus, when people have their working memory capacity consumed by irrelevant thoughts, they are more likely to use simpler, less effective strategies. This shift to simpler strategies equated people by causing the high-span people to solve the problems more like the low-span people, who were using simpler strategies in the first place.

Of particular interest, in a second experiment, people were asked to do a series of word problems that required a complex series of steps (i.e., B − A − 2 × C). Then under low- or high-pressure conditions, people were given a series of new problems, some of which required a simpler solution (i.e., A − C). Beilock and DeCaro (2007) found that the low-span people were actually more likely to use the simpler, correct solution than the high-span people. The explanation was that low-span people are less likely to derive rule-based strategies for solving problems (because they have less capacity to do so) and are more likely to draw from previous similar experiences. Thus, when given problems with the simpler solutions, the low-span people were less dependent on a complex, rule-based strategy they derived earlier, and so were more likely to use the more appropriate, simpler strategy (for other examples of better performance by people with smaller memory spans, see Colflesh & Conway, 2007; Cokely, Kelley, & Gilchrist, 2006).

Overview

The general conclusion from all these studies is that *working memory* is a more suitable name for the attention-limited workbench system. Working memory is responsible for the active mental effort of regulating attention, for transferring information into and from long-term memory.

Importantly, there is a limit to the mental resources available to working memory; when extra resources are drained by the subsystems, the central executive suffers along with insufficient resources for its own work. Naturally, as processes become more automatic, fewer resources are tied down (e.g., working memory is unrelated to counting when there are only two or three things to count but is influenced for larger quantities; Tuholski, Engle, & Baylis, 2001).

The "Engle tradition" emphasizes the general nature of working memory capacity as a measure of executive attention and de-emphasizes the multicomponent working memory approach advocated by Baddeley. Part of the reason for this is the generality of the working memory effects. Working memory span predicts performance on a variety of tasks. Of particular importance, working memory span routinely correlates with measures of intelligence, especially so-called fluid intelligence (Fukuda, Vogel, Mayr, & Awh, 2010; Kane et al., 2004; Salthouse & Pink, 2008; Shelton, Elliot, Matthews, Hill, & Gouvier, 2010), and more so if metacognitive control is taken into account (McCabe, 2010). The relationship between working memory and intelligence is that people who have greater cognitive control, and can manage sources of interference better, score better on intelligence tests. This is even supported by neuroimaging data in which people with higher working memory span and intelligence scores show better interference control in cortical areas tied to these processes, such as the dorsolateral prefrontal cortex (B.A. 9) and portions of the parietal cortex (B.A.s 7 and 40) (Burgess, Gray, Conway, & Braver, 2011).

Common to both the Baddeley and the Engle approaches, however, is a central set of principles. Working memory is intimately related to executive control, to the deliberate allocation of attention to a task, and to the maintenance of efficient, effective cognitive processing and behavior. There is a limitation, however, in the amount of attention available at any one time. Furthermore, the ability to deliberately focus and allocate attention, and to suppress or inhibit attention to extraneous factors, is key to higher-order cognitive processing.

Section Summary

- Working memory abilities and performance are critical to many tasks assessed by cognitive psychologists. For example, working memory capacity is strongly related to the ability to engage attention. It has also been shown to be strongly related to the efficiency with which simple facts can be retrieved from long-term memory.
- Although larger working memory capacity is associated with superior cognitive performance, there are cases where circumstances favor smaller working memory capacity. These are typically circumstances where it is better not to devote too much attention to a task.
- Although there is no clear view on exactly what working memory is, as evidenced by the Baddeley multicomponent model and the Engle attentional control view, there are a number of agreed-on characteristics of what working memory is able to do. These include its limited capacity, the ability to simultaneously handle certain types of noninterfering forms of information, the fact that people differ in their working memory capacities and abilities, and that these individual differences are related to performance on a variety of tasks.

Key Terms

articulatory loop (p. *155*)
articulatory suppression effect (p. *155*)
boundary extension (p. *159*)
Brown–Peterson task (p. *141*)
central executive (p. *154*)
chunk (p. *139*)

decay (p. *140*)
dual task method (p. *161*)
episodic buffer (p. *160*)
free recall (p. *145*)
mental rotation (p. *157*)
phonological loop (p. *155*)
phonological similarity effect (p. *155*)
phonological store (p. *155*)

primacy effect (p. *145*)
proactive interference (PI) (p. *143*)
process model (p. *149*)
recency effect (p. *145*)
recoding (p. *140*)
release from PI (p. *144*)
representational momentum (p. *159*)
retroactive interference (RI) (p. *143*)

serial exhaustive search (p. *151*)
serial position curve (p. *145*)
serial recall (p. *145*)
visuo-spatial sketch pad (p. *156*)
working memory (p. *152*)
working memory span (p. *164*)

Sample Lists for Simple Memory Span Tests

Digits
8 7 0 3 1 4
7 1 5 0 5 4 3 6
2 8 4 3 6 1 2 9 7 5
Words
leaf gift car fish rock
paper seat tire horse film beach forest brush
bag key book wire box wheel banana floor bar pad block radio boy

6

Learning and Remembering

> *Memory is the most important function of the brain; without it life would be a blank. Our knowledge is all based on memory. Every thought, every action, our very conception of personal identity, is based on memory. . . . Without memory, all experience would be useless.*
>
> (EDRIDGE-GREEN, 1900)

This is the first of three chapters devoted to long-term memory, the storage vault for a lifetime's worth of knowledge and experience. Why three chapters? First, as indicated in the quotation above: Long-term memory is fundamental to nearly every mental process, to almost every act of cognition. You cannot understand cognition unless you understand long-term mcmory. Second, long-term memory is an enormous research area—there's a lot to know

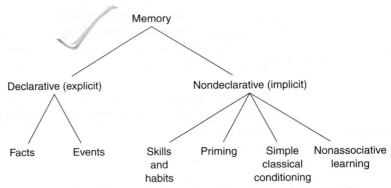

FIGURE 6-1 A taxonomy of long-term memories. Adapted from Squire (1993).

about. Third, people are curious about their own memories. Who has not complained, at some time, about forgetfulness or the unreliability of memory?

Long-term memory is divided and subdivided in various ways. Look at Figure 6-1, a taxonomy suggested by Squire (1986, 1993). As the figure shows, a distinction can be made between **declarative memory** (or **explicit memory**) and **nondeclarative memory** (or **implicit memory**). Here, declarative or explicit memory is *long-term memory knowledge that is retrieved and reflected on consciously*. The two types of declarative knowledge, episodic and semantic memory, are the topics of this chapter and the next. In contrast, nondeclarative or implicit memory is *knowledge that influences thought and behavior without any necessary involvement of consciousness*. The key to this distinction is conscious awareness—one has it, one doesn't.

Here's a brief example to help clarify the distinction between episodic and semantic memory. If you were asked what happened when you took your driver's license test, you retrieve knowledge from **episodic memory**, that is, *memory of the personally experienced events*. When you retrieve that information, you are conscious of it, you can talk about it, and so on. Episodic memory enables you to record your personal history. Alternatively, if you were asked what a driver's license is, you retrieve from **semantic memory**, your *general world knowledge*. You retrieve the concept of a driver's license, and it is now in your conscious awareness. Notice that whereas episodic memory is your mental slide show, semantic memory is your mental encyclopedia, and both involve knowledge that you can be consciously aware of (Tulving, 1972, 1983, 1993).

But there is more going on than what rises to the level of conscious awareness. As you read this sentence, you encounter the term *license* again. Although you are not conscious of it, you are faster at reading that term than you were the first time; the rereading speedup is called repetition priming. This happens at the nondeclarative, implicit level. Likewise, if we gave you some word stems an hour from now and asked you to fill in the blanks with the first word that comes to mind, you would be more likely than chance to complete "LIC___ " as "LICENSE" because you encountered it recently. Importantly, this happens even if you do not consciously recall having seen the word *license* (but teasing apart conscious and unconscious influences is no simple matter; see Buchner & Wippich, 2000; Jacoby, 1991; Jacoby, Toth, & Yonelinas, 1993).

An important aspect of episodic memories is that they are integrated mental representations. Different bits and pieces of information from different parts of our conscious and unconscious mental worlds are woven together. In Chapter 5 we introduced the episodic buffer, the part of working memory that integrates different types of knowledge together to form episodic memories. Although many of the examples given here use linguistic materials, such as word lists, episodic memories integrate various types of information, including sensory, motor, spatial, language, emotional, and narrative information, as well as other various encoding and retrieval processes (Rubin, 2007). Even this is not an exhaustive list. So, as you can see, episodic memory uses a rich variety of information about a broad range of human experience.

The main focus of this chapter is on episodic memory, although we also cover some issues about implicit memory as well. We progress, covering what is known about how storage and retrieval influence how we learn and remember. In the final section we discuss implicit memory along with a discussion of evidence about memory and amnesia.

PRELIMINARY ISSUES

Let's start by considering three preliminary issues. First, we talk about a classic, ancient approach to memory, mnemonic devices. We then spend time on the first systematic research on human memory, by Ebbinghaus, published in 1885. These topics suggest that people have always been aware of some of the workings—and failings—of memory. Such awareness is called **metamemory**, a type of **metacognition**. Here's a warning: As you read the chapters on long-term memory, keep in mind that just as your frustrations over your own memory problems probably are exaggerated, so is your certainty about remembering. It's a paradox; our memories are better than we often give ourselves credit for, and worse than we are often willing to believe or admit.

Mnemonics

The term *mnemonic* (pronounced *"ne-MAHN-ick"*) means "to help the memory"; it comes from the same Indo-European base word as *remember*, *mind*, and *think*. A **mnemonic** is an *active, strategic learning device or method*. Formal mnemonics use preestablished sets of aids and considerable practice. The strengths of mnemonics include: (1) The material to be remembered is practiced repeatedly, (2) the material is integrated into an existing memory framework, and (3) the mnemonic provides a way to retrieve the material. Let's consider two traditional mnemonics.

CLASSIC MNEMONICS   The first historical mention of mnemonics is in Cicero's *De oratore,* a treatise on rhetoric (the art of public speaking, which in those days meant speaking from memory). The power of mnemonics is tremendous; among other things, mnemonics enabled Greek orators to memorize and recite epics such as *The Iliad* and *The Odyssey.* Cicero describes a technique, based on visual imagery and memorized locations, called the **method of loci** (*loci* is the plural of *locus,* meaning "a place"; pronounced *"LOW-sigh"*). There are two steps to this method.

TABLE 6-1 The Method of Loci

Set of Loci	Word to Be Remembered	Grocery List and Images
Driveway	Grapefruit	Grapefruit instead of rocks along side of driveway
Garage door	Tomatoes	Tomatoes splattered on garage door
Front door of house	Lettuce	Lettuce leaves hanging over door instead of awning
Coat closet	Oatmeal	Oatmeal oozing out the door when I hang up my coat
Fireplace	Milk	Fire got out of control, so spray milk instead of water
Easy chair	Sugar	Throw pillow is a 5-7lb bag of sugar
Television	Coffee	Mrs. Olson advertising coffee
Dining-room table	Carrots	Legs of table are made of carrots

First, choose a known set of locations that can be recalled easily and in order, such as locations you encounter in a walk across campus, or as you arrive home. Now form a mental image of the first thing you want to remember and mentally place it into the first location, the second item in the second location, and so on (see Table 6-1) for examples. When it's time to recall the items, you mentally stroll through your set of locations, "looking" at the places and "seeing" the items you have placed there.

Another mnemonic is the **peg word mnemonic** (Miller, Galanter, & Pribram, 1960), in which *a prememorized set of words serves as a sequence of mental "pegs" onto which the to-be-remembered material can be "hung."* The peg words rely on rhymes with the numbers one through ten, such as "One is a bun, two is a shoe," and so on (Table 6-2). The to-be-learned material is then hung on the pegs, making sure that the rhyming word and the to-be-remembered item form a mental image. For the list "cup, flag, horse, dollar, . . ." create a visual image of a flattened tin cup, dripping with ketchup, inside your hamburger bun; for flag, conjure up a

TABLE 6-2 The Peg Word Mnemonic Device

Numbered Pegs	Word to Be Learned	Image
One is a bun	Cup	Hamburger bun with smashed cup
Two is a shoe	Flag	Running shoes with flag
Three is a tree	Horse	Horse stranded in top of tree
Four is a door	Dollar	Dollar bill tacked to front door
Five is a hive	Brush	Queen bee brushing her hair
Six is sticks	Pan	Boiling a pan full of cinnamon sticks
Seven is Heaven	Clock	St. Peter checking the clock at the gates of Heaven
Eight is a gate	Pen	A picket fence gate with ballpoint pens as pickets
Nine is a vine	Paper	Honeysuckle vine with newspapers instead of blossoms
Ten is a hen	Shirt	A baked hen on the platter wearing a flannel shirt

visual image of your running shoes with little American flags fluttering in the breeze as you run; and so on. Now at recall, all you have to do is first remember what peg word rhymes with one, then retrieve the bun image you created, looking inside to see a cup. Similarly, what peg word rhymes with *two,* and what image do you find along with *shoe?*

Mnemonic effectiveness involves three principles. First, it provides a structure for acquiring the information. The structure may be elaborate, like a set of 40 loci, or simple, like rhyming peg words. It can even be arbitrary if the material is not extensive. (The mnemonic *HOMES* for the names of the five Great Lakes—Huron, Ontario, Michigan, Erie, and Superior—isn't related to the to-be-remembered material, but it is simple.) Second, using visual images, rhymes, or other kinds of associations and the effort and rehearsal to form them, this helps create a durable and distinctive memories (what's sticking out of your running shoes?). So, a mnemonic helps safeguard against forgetting (but see Thomas & Wang, 1996, for less optimistic long-term benefits of mnemonics). Finally, the mnemonic guides you through retrieval by providing cues for recalling information. This function is important because much of forgetting is often a case of retrieval difficulty. In fact, it can't be stressed enough how the active use of retrieval cues—and practicing retrieval—are important for successful remembering (extended practice was the key in Chaffin & Imreh's [2002] study of how a pianist learned, remembered, and performed a challenging piece).

This three-step sequence may sound familiar. It is the sequence we talk about every time we consider learning and memory: the *encoding* of new information, its *retention* over time, and *retrieval* of the information (Melton, 1963). Performance in any situation that involves memory depends on all three steps. A fault along any one of the three might account for poor performance. A good mnemonic, including those you invent for yourself (e.g., Wenger & Payne, 1995), ensures success at each of the three stages. (Incidentally, don't count on a magic bullet to enhance your memory. Research has found little if any evidence that ginkgo biloba, or any other "memory enhancer," has any real effect; Gold, Cahill, & Wenk, 2002, 2003; Greenwald, Spangenberg, Pratkanis, & Eskenazi, 1991; McDaniel, Maier, & Einstein, 2002).

The Ebbinghaus Tradition

We turn now to the first systematic research on human memory, done by the German psychologist Hermann von Ebbinghaus. As noted in Chapter 1, the Ebbinghaus tradition began with the publication of *Über das Gedächtnis* (1885; the 1964 English translation is titled *Memory: A Contribution to Experimental Psychology*). Ebbinghaus used himself as the only subject in his studies. He also had to invent his own memory task, his own stimuli, and his own procedures for testing and data analysis. Few could do as well today. In devising how to analyze his results, he even came close to inventing a within-groups *t* test (Ebbinghaus, 1885/1913, footnote 1, p. 67).

It is helpful to consider *why* Ebbinghaus felt compelled to invent and use nonsense syllables. His rationale was that he wanted to study the properties of memory and forgetting apart from the influence of prior knowledge. As such, words would complicate his results. If he had used words it would be less clear whether performance reflected the simple use of memory, or the influence of prior knowledge. Putting it simply, *learning* implies acquiring *new* information. Yet, words are not new. And a control factor he adopted, to reduce the possible intrusion of mnemonic factors, was the rapid presentation rate of 2.5 items per second.

The task Ebbinghaus devised was the **relearning task**, in which *a list is originally learned, set aside for a period of time, then later relearned to the same criterion of accuracy.* In most cases, this was one perfect recitation of the list, without hesitations. After relearning the list, Ebbinghaus computed a **savings score** as the measure of learning; the savings score was *the reduction in the number of trials (or the time) necessary for relearning, compared to original learning.* Thus, if it took 10 trials to originally learn a list but only 6 for relearning, there was a 40% savings (4 fewer trials on relearning divided by the 10 original trials). By this method, *any* information that was left over in memory from original learning could have an influence, conscious or not (see Nelson, 1978, 1985; Schacter, 1987). Work by MacLeod (1988) indicates that relearning seems to help retrieve information that was stored in memory yet is not recallable.

Figure 6-2 presents Ebbinghaus's forgetting curve (actually a retention curve), showing the reduction in savings as a function of time until relearning (as Slamecka, 1985, points out, for the data in Figure 6-2, Ebbinghaus used more than 1,200 lists of nonsense syllables). Ebbinghaus relearned the lists after one of seven intervals: 20 minutes, 1 hour, 9 hours, 1 day, 2 days, 6 days, or 31 days. As is clear

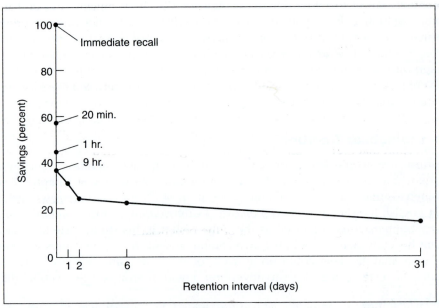

FIGURE 6-2 The classic forgetting curve from Ebbinghaus (1885/1913). The figure shows the reduction in savings across increasing retention intervals (time between original learning and relearning).

from the figure, the most dramatic forgetting occurs early after original learning. This is followed by a decrease in the rate of forgetting (technically, a negatively accelerating power function; Wixted & Ebbesen, 1991) and is found for a variety of other memory tests. That said, as outlined in a nice review by Erdelyi (2010), note that although generally and overall there is a loss of memories over time, it is possible for items that were previously forgotten to be remembered later (*reminiscence*). There are even cases when the rate of reminiscence may be greater than the rate of forgetting, and a person remembers more over time, a phenomenon called *hypermnesia.*

Other fundamentals Ebbinghaus found were impressive not because they were surprising, but because he first demonstrated them. For example, he studied the effects of repetitions, studying one list 32 times and another 64 times. Upon relearning, the more frequently repeated list showed about twice the savings of the less frequently repeated list; in other words, *overlearning* yields a stronger record in memory. Longer lists took more trials to learn than shorter lists but showed higher savings upon relearning. So, although it is harder to learn a long list originally, the longer list is remembered better, because there was more opportunity to overlearn it (there were more trials in learning before mastery of the whole list). The connection between learning difficulty and memory has been confirmed repeatedly (e.g., Schneider, Healy, & Bourne, 2002).

Finally, in one study, Ebbinghaus continued to relearn the same set of lists across a five-day period. The savings scores showed no forgetting at all. Ebbinghaus also reported his results on relearning passages of poetry (kept at 80 syllables). After the fourth day, the savings was 100%.

Beyond the idea of overlearning, there are issues involved with how people repeatedly study to learn something. Specifically, how quickly and effectively something is learned varies as a function of whether study sessions are grouped together, or spread out over time. If *study time is grouped together into one long session*, this is called **massed practice**, although many students know this better as *cramming*. In comparison, if *study time is spread out over many, shorter sessions*, this is called **distributed practice**. This distinction between these two types of studying is important because memory is much better with distributed practice than with massed practice (Glenberg & Lehmann, 1980), although many students incorrectly believe the opposite (Zechmeister & Shaughnessy, 1980). Students often report that they feel like they are working harder when they cram than when they study consistently throughout the term. And in general, that is true—people are working harder with massed practice. The problem is that a person is not learning much. So, you can save yourself a lot of time, and do better in your course work, if you spread your studying out across the term than if you cram (note that cramming also denies you of the beneficial effects of sleep on memory improvement). These benefits can even be seen a year later (Pashler, Rohrer, Cepeda, & Carpenter, 2007).

Metamemory

Think about these two issues, mnemonics and Ebbinghaus's work, from a larger perspective: They both involve intuitions about memory, what makes remembering easier or harder. This self-awareness about memory is **metamemory**, *knowledge about (meta) one's own memory, how it works or fails to work.* Research on this topic has raised at least two important issues. First is the importance of metacognitive awareness. A number of studies have focused on metamemory, such as people's "judgments-of-learning" and "feeling-of-knowing" estimates (Leonesio & Nelson, 1990; Nelson, 1988). Part of a person's behavior in a learning task involves self-monitoring, assessing how well one is doing and adjusting study strategies (e.g., Son, 2004). For example, these metacognitions guide people to know when to change their answers on multiple-choice exams (Higham & Garrard, 2005). However, metamemory can occasionally mislead us, leading to either over- or underconfidence that we've learned something (e.g., Koriat, Sheffer, & Ma'ayan, 2002).

The second issue involves self-regulation. If you realize you are not doing some task particularly well, what do you do to improve? Some of the research on metacognition gives some insight into some difficulties people have. For example, Mazzoni and Cornoldi (1993) report that people often "labor in vain," that is, devote more study time to difficult items, and yet do not improve much at all (see also Metcalfe, 2002; Nelson, 1993). Alternatively, Thiede (1999; see also Metcalfe & Kornell, 2003) argues that when study time is used appropriately, a positive, sensible relationship between monitoring and self-regulation emerges. This is what Son and Metcalfe (2000) call the *region of proximal learning*, studying information that is just beyond one's current knowledge and saving the more difficult material for later. The problem is that people are often poor judges of what they have and have not learned and make choices about what to study based on this inaccurate information (Metcalfe & Finn, 2008).

Section Summary

- Long-term memory is a divided between declarative memories and nondeclarative memories. Declarative memory consists of episodic and semantic memories; nondeclarative memory includes priming and procedural or motor learning. Declarative memories can be verbalized, but nondeclarative memories cannot; conscious awareness of the memory is unnecessary for implicit memory tasks but does accompany explicit memory tasks.
- A classic method for improving memory involves mnemonics. Mnemonics, such as the method of loci, use a variety of techniques, especially visual imagery, to improve performance.
- Ebbinghaus was the first person to extensively study memory and forgetting. Working on his own, he invented methods for doing so. The relearning task revealed a sensitivity to the demands of simple recall tasks—that they measure consciously retrievable information but underestimate the amount of information learned and remembered. The classic forgetting curve he obtained, along with his results on practice effects, inspired the tradition of verbal learning and, later, cognitive psychology.

STORING INFORMATION IN EPISODIC MEMORY

How do people store information in episodic memory? And how can we measure this storage? Ebbinghaus investigated one storage variable, repetition, and one memory task, relearning. He found that increasing the number of repetitions led to a stronger memory, a *trace* of the information in memory that could be relearned faster. Thus, frequency is a fundamental influence on memory: Information that is presented more frequently is stored more strongly.

A corollary of this is that people are good at remembering how frequently something has occurred (e.g., how many movies you've seen in the past month). Hasher and Zacks (1984) summarize a large body of research on how sensitive people are to event frequency. Because people's estimates of frequency generally are good, they proposed that frequency information is automatically encoded into memory, with no deliberate effort or intent. Although just how automatic this has been disputed (Greene, 1986; Hanson & Hirst, 1988; Jonides & Jones, 1992), there is no doubt that event frequency has an impact on long-term memory.

The flip side of frequency is distinctiveness. It is easier to remember unusual, unexpected, or distinctive events. This is technically called the **isolation effect**, but is more commonly known as the **von Restorff effect**, named after the woman who did the first study (von Restorff, 1933). The effect is simply *better memory for information that is distinct from the information around it*, such as printing one word in a list in red ink or changing its size (Cooper & Pantle, 1967; Kelley & Nairne, 2001). The isolation effect relies on memory for the distinctive item to be noticed as distinctive. Generally, the occurrence of unexpected and distinctive items can produce increased processing in the hippocampus (e.g., Axmacher et al., 2010). Thus, damage to the hippocampus should reduce or eliminate the von Restorff effect. In a study by Kishiyama, Yonelinas, and Lazzara (2004), people who were amnesic (as a result of damage to their medial temporal lobes and hippocampus) did not show a von Restorff effect (see Figure 6-3). That is because they could not remember the other items in the list very well, they could not identify the isolated item as unique, and so it did not stand out in memory. Thus, distinctiveness was not effective for this group of people.

But what about more typical situations, when the world doesn't highlight material to make it more frequent or more distinctive? How do you learn and remember something new? There are three important steps here: rehearsal, organization, and imagery. A summary of these will then lead us to the topic of retrieval and a discussion of forgetting.

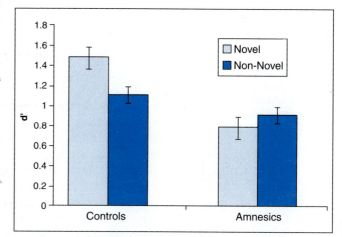

FIGURE 6-3 Accuracy data from Kishiyama, Yonelinas, and Lazzara (2004) (using the signal detection measure of d') showing memory for a novel distinctive item (the von Restorff effect) for normal controls on the left and amnesics on the right. Notice that performance is better for the novel information for the normal controls, but not for the amnesics.

Why do we rehearse?

Rehearsal

In Atkinson and Shiffrin's (1968) important model of human memory, information in short-term memory was subject to **rehearsal**, *a deliberate recycling or practicing of information in the short-term store.* They proposed two effects of rehearsal. First, rehearsal maintains information in the short-term store. Second, the longer an item is held in short-term memory, the more likely it will be stored in long-term memory, with the strength of the item's long-term memory trace depending on the amount of rehearsal it received. In short, rehearsal transfers information into long-term memory (see also Waugh & Norman, 1965).

Frequency of Rehearsal

What evidence is there of this? Aside from Ebbinghaus, many experiments have shown that rehearsal leads to better long-term retention. For example, Hellyer (1962) used the Brown–Peterson task, with CVC trigrams, and with an arithmetic task between study and recall. On some trials the trigram had to be spoken aloud one, two, four, or eight times. Figure 6-4 shows the results. The more frequently an item was rehearsed, the better it was retained. However, although rehearsal does improve memory, other work suggests that it is not repeated study that produces the primary memory benefit, but the repeated attempts at trying to remember (Karpicke & Roediger, 2007).

FIGURE 6-4
Hellyer's (1962) recall accuracy results as a function of the number of rehearsals afforded the three-letter nonsense syllable and the retention interval.

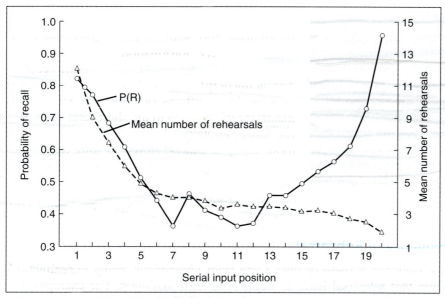

FIGURE 6-5 In the figure, the probability of recall, P(R), is plotted against the left axis, and the number of rehearsals afforded an item during storage is plotted against the right axis. The similar pattern of these two functions across the primacy portion of the list indicates that rehearsal is the factor responsible for primacy effects.

REHEARSAL AND SERIAL POSITION More evidence on the effects of rehearsal was provided in a series of studies by Rundus (1971; Rundus & Atkinson, 1970). In these experiments, Rundus had people learn 20-item lists of words, presenting them at a rate of 5 seconds per word. People were told to rehearse aloud as they studied the lists, repeating whatever words they cared to during each 5-second presentation. Rundus then tabulated the number of times each word was rehearsed and compared this to the likelihood of later recalling the word. Figure 6-5 shows his most telling results. In the early primacy portion of the serial position effect, there was a positive relationship between the frequency of rehearsal and the rate of recall. In other words, the primacy effect depended on rehearsal. The early items are rehearsed more frequently and so are recalled better. High recall of the late positions, the recency effect, was viewed as recall from short-term memory, which is why they were recalled so well despite being rehearsed so little.

Although we discussed serial position curves in Chapter 5, similar curves are observed in long-term memory. That is, given an event of a certain type, such as going to the movies, people are likely to remember their first and last experiences better, and not so much those in the middle (e.g., Sehulster, 1989). This even applies to semantic information, such as knowledge of the presidents of the United States (Roediger & Crowder, 1976). Although some people have argued that the cognitive processes involved in long-term memory are different from those involved in short-term memory (Davelaar, Goshen-Gottstein, Ashkenazi, Haarman, & Usher, 2005), there has also been some suggestion that the same principles are driving the serial position curves in both the short- and long-term memory (e.g., Brown, Neath, & Chater, 2007).

Depth of Processing

A more refined idea is that there are two kinds of rehearsal (Craik & Lockhart, 1972). **Maintenance rehearsal** is *a low-level, repetitive information recycling*. This is the rehearsal you use to recycle a phone number to yourself until you dial it. Once you stop rehearsing, the information is lost. In Craik and Lockhart's view, maintenance rehearsal holds information at a particular level in memory, without storing it permanently. As long as information is maintained, it can be retrieved. Once rehearsal stops, however, it will likely vanish.

Elaborative rehearsal is *a more complex rehearsal that uses the meaning of the information to store and remember it*. Information that is elaboratively rehearsed is stored more deeply in memory and is remembered better. You might include imagery or mnemonic elaboration in your elaborative rehearsal, you might try to construct sentences from the words in a list, you might impose an organization on the list, or you might even convert nonsense syllables like BEF into more meaningful items like BEEF. Stating it differently, maintenance rehearsal maintains an item at its current level of storage, whereas elaborative rehearsal moves the item more deeply, and more permanently, into memory.

Simulate
Depth of Processing in **MyPsychLab**

Craik and Lockhart (1972) proposed a theory of memory different from the stage approach of sensory, short-, and long-term memory. They embedded their two kinds of rehearsal into what they called the **levels of processing**, or **depth of processing**, framework. The essence of this is as follows. Information receives some amount of mental processing. Some items that get only incidental attention are processed at a shallow level (as in hearing the sounds of the words without attending to their meaning, as a daydreamer might do during a lecture). Other items get more intentional and meaningful processing that elaborates the memory of that item—for example, by drawing relationships between already-known information and what is being processed.

Several predictions from the depth of processing framework were tested with a fair degree of initial success. For example, if information is shallowly processed, using only maintenance rehearsal, then the information should not be well remembered later; if it is only maintained, then it should not be stored at a deep, meaningful level in long-term memory. This was the kind of result that was obtained. As an example, Craik and Watkins (1973) devised a monitoring task; people heard a long list of words but only had to keep track of the most recent word beginning with, say, a *G*. In a surprise recall test, people showed no recall differences for "*G*-words" held a long time versus those maintained only briefly (see also Craik & Tulving, 1975).

Challenges to Depth of Processing

As research continued on the depth of processing framework, some difficulties cropped up. One example was Baddeley's (1978) review paper "The Trouble with Levels." A major point in this review was the problem of defining levels independently of retention scores (see Glenberg & Adams, 1978; Glenberg, Smith, & Green, 1977). In essence, there is no method for deciding ahead of time whether a particular kind of rehearsal would lead to shallow or deep processing. Instead, we had to wait and see whether it improved recall. If it did, it must have been elaborative rehearsal; if it did not, it must have been maintenance rehearsal. The circularity of this reasoning should be obvious and was a serious problem for depth of processing ideas of memory retention.

TASK EFFECTS   A second point in Baddeley's (1978) review concerned task effects. That is, a difficulty arose with the levels of processing approach when different memory tasks were used. The reason was simply that very different results were obtained using one or another task.

   We have known since Ebbinghaus that different memory tasks reveal different things about the variables that affect performance. Ebbinghaus used a relearning task, so that even material that was hard to retrieve might still influence memory performance. In a similar vein, a substantial difference is found between performance on recall and **recognition** tasks. In recognition, people are shown items that were originally studied, known as "old" or target items, as well as items that were not studied, known as "new," lure, or distractor items. They must then decide which are targets and which are distractors (multiple-choice tests are recognition tests, by the way). Recognition accuracy usually is higher than recall accuracy (see Table 6-3 for a description of these tasks). Furthermore, recognition is influenced by two different factors, recollection—the actual remembering of the information—and familiarity—the general sense that you've experienced the information before (e.g., Curran, 2000; Yonelinas, 2002). Indeed, studies on false memory that you'll read about in Chapter 8 often ask people whether they actually "remember" experiencing an event or whether they just "know" that it happened.

   Recognition is easier than recall, in part because the answer is presented to a person, who then only has to make a new versus old decision. Because more information is stored in memory than can be retrieved easily, recognition shows greater sensitivity to the influence of stored information (the issue of *how much* easier recognition is than recall is difficult to resolve; see research by Craik, Govoni, Naveh-Benjamin, & Anderson, 1996, and by Hicks & Marsh, 2000).

   The relevance of this to the depth of processing framework is that most of the early research that supported it used recall tasks. When recognition was used, however, maintenance rehearsal had clear effects on long-term memory. A clever set of studies by Glenberg et al. (1977) confirmed this. They used a Brown–Peterson task, asking people to remember a four-digit number as the (supposedly) primary task. During retention intervals that varied in duration, people had to repeat either one or three words aloud as a distractor task (don't confuse the distractor task here with distractor items, items in a recognition test that were not shown originally). Because people believed that digit recall was the important task, they devoted only minimal effort to the word repetitions, and so probably used only maintenance rehearsal. After the supposedly "main" part of the task was done, people were given a surprise recall task; the results showed the standard effect. But when they were given a surprise recognition task, the amount of time spent rehearsing *did* influence performance; words rehearsed for 18 seconds were recognized better than those rehearsed for shorter intervals. Thus, the generalization that maintenance rehearsal does not lead to improved memory performance was disconfirmed—it did not apply when memory was tested with a recognition task.

TABLE 6-3   Standard Memory Tasks and Terminology

Relearning Task

1. Original learning: Learn list items (e.g., list of unrelated words) to some accuracy criterion.
2. Delay after learning the list.
3. Learn the list a second time.

Dependent variables: The main dependent variable is the savings score: how many fewer trials are needed during relearning relative to number of trials for the original learning. If the original learning took 10 trials and relearning took 6, then relearning took 4 fewer trials. Savings score = 4/10; expressed as a percentage, savings was 40%.

Independent or control variables: Presentation rate, list item types, list length, accuracy criterion.

Paired-Associate Learning Task

1. A list of pairs is shown, one pair at a time. The first member of the pair is the stimulus, and the second member is the response (e.g., for the pair "ice–brush," "ice" is the stimulus term and "brush" is the correct response).
2. After one study trial, the stimulus terms are shown, one at a time, and the person tries to name the correct response term for that stimulus.
3. Typically, the task involves several successive attempts at learning, each including first a study trial, then a test trial; the order of the pairs is changed each time. In the anticipation method, there is one continuous stream of trials, each consisting of two parts, presenting the stimulus alone, then presenting the stimulus and response together. Across repetitions, people begin to learn the correct pairings.

Dependent variables: Typically the number of study test trials to achieve correct responding to all stimulus terms ("trials to criterion") is the dependent variable.

Independent and control variables: Presentation rate, length of list, the types of items in the stimulus and response terms, and the types of connections between them. Commonly, once a list had been mastered, then either the stimulus or response terms are changed, or the item pairings rearranged (e.g., "ice–brush" and "card–floor" in the first list, then "ice–floor" and "card–brush" on the second list).

Recall Task

Serial Recall Task: Learn a list of items, and then recall them in the original order of presentation.
Free Recall Task: Learn the list information, and then recall the items in any order.

1. Learn list items.
2. Optional delay or distractor task during delay.
3. Recall list items.

Dependent variables: The main dependent variable is the number (or proportion) of items recalled correctly. For serial recall, accuracy is scored as a function of the original position of the items in the list. Occasionally, other dependent variables involve speed, or organization of recall (e.g., items recalled by category—"apple, pear, banana, orange"—before items from a different category are recalled).

Independent or control variables: Rate of presentation (usually experimenter paced), type of list items, length of list.

Recognition Task (Episodic)

1. Learn list items.
2. Optional delay or distractor task during delay.
3. Make yes/no decisions to the items in a test list: "Yes," the item was on the list, or "no," it was not. This is often refers to deciding whether an item is "old"—that is, on the original list—or is "new" and not on the original list. Old items are also called targets, and new items are also called distractors or lures.

Dependent variables: The dependent variable usually is accuracy, such as the proportion correct. Correct "yes" responses to old items are called *hits*, and incorrect "yes" responses to new items are called *false alarms*.

Independent or control variables: Same as with recall tasks.

Generation and Enactment

An overarching idea in the depth of processing framework is that the more you do with information, the better it is remembered. There are numerous examples of this "hard work has its rewards" principle. In this section we look at four examples of this—four ways in which how information is processed, and the amount of effort a person puts into encoding it, affects performance. These are the self-reference effect, the generation effect, the impact of enactment on memory, and the consequences of taking a survival-based perspective.

The **self-reference effect** is the finding that *memory is better for information that you relate to yourself in some way* (e.g., Bellezza, 1992; Gillihan & Farah, 2005; Rogers, Kuiper, & Kirker, 1977; Symons & Johnson, 1997). If you think about it, you know a lot about yourself, and you tend to be motivated by such information. When you relate something to yourself, say a detail you're trying to remember, you link the new knowledge up with the old, yielding a more complex structure, an elaborative encoding (for example, the locations given earlier for the method of loci—driveway, garage door, etc.—were the memorized locations one of this book's authors used for his own mnemonic device for years, based on his own house). Thus, the elaborated structure becomes more memorable.

The **generation effect** is the finding that *information you generate or create yourself is better remembered compared to information you only heard or read.* This was first reported by Slamecka and Graf (1978). In their study, for the *read* condition, people simply read words printed on cards. However, for the *generate* condition, people needed to generate the word on their own. This was done by giving a word and the first letter of the word that was to be recalled, with the instruction that the to-be-generated word had to be related to the first word. For example a person might see Long-S_____ where the word "short" needed to be generated. The results showed that people remembered words better when they were generated as compared to when they were just read.

In their review of work on the generation effect, Bertsch, Peta, Wiscott, and McDaniel (2007) reported that this robust finding was more likely to occur with free recall, and that the effect grew larger over longer delays. Importantly, the generation effect not only applies to lists of words, but also to textbook material (e.g., de Winstanley & Bjork, 2004). In short, the generation effect is another example that the more effort you put into mentally processing information, the more likely you will remember it later, and for a longer time.

Another way to engage in deep encoding is to take advantage of the **enactment effect**, in which there is *improved memory for participant-performed tasks, relative to those that are not.* In such studies, actually doing some activity is compared with just watching someone else doing it. For example, a person might be told to "break the match," "point at the door," or "knock on the table," or to watch someone else do those actions. In general, people remember things better if they do them themselves (e.g., Engelkamp & Dehn, 2000; Saltz & Donnenwerth-Nolan, 1981). In essence, the additional mental effort needed to do the task is another form of deep processing. Even saying something aloud (the production effect) can improve memory (MacLeod, 2011; MacLeod, Gopie, Hourihan, Neary, & Ozubko, 2010).

The value of enactment can be seen in the practical application of learning lines of dialogue. There is evidence that even untrained nonactors (i.e., novice actors) learn dialogue, as in the script of a play, better when the dialogue and stage movements are rehearsed together (Noice & Noice, 2001; see also Freeman & Ellis, 2003, and Shelton & McNamara, 2001, for other multimodality effects on learning). Physical movement, in other words, can be part of an enhanced mnemonic. Enactment improves memory by helping people better organize and structure information about the actions that they do (Koriat & Pearlman-Avnion, 2003).

Finally, for memory to be of value to us, and be better remembered, it needs to give us something useful. It should help us survive in the world. The survival motivation is strong, and knowledge of what can either increase or decrease our survival is important. Thus, if a person can bring a survival perspective to bear on what they are learning, it can improve performance. This was shown in a study by Nairne, Thompson, and Pandeirada (2007; see also Nairne, Pandeirada, & Thompson, 2008; Weinstein, Bugg, & Roediger, 2008). In this study, people were given lists of words. During the first part of the study, people rated the words for pleasantness, relevance to moving to a foreign land, personal relevance, or survival value (e.g., finding food and water or avoiding predators). Words that were rated high on survival value were more likely to be remembered later. The survival angle has such a strong impact that it can outperform the effects of other well-known memory-enhancing strategies such as imagery, self-reference, and generation (Nairne, Pandeirada, & Thompson, 2008). So, if we think about how information relates to our ability to survive, endure, or otherwise be useful, this takes advantage of our fundamental motivations, and we can leverage these to improve memory (Wurm, 2007; Wurm & Seaman, 2008).

Organization in Storage

Another important piece of the storage puzzle involves **organization**, *the structuring of information as it is stored in memory*. Well-organized material can be stored and retrieved with impressive levels of accuracy. The earliest work on organization (or clustering) was done by Bousfield. In his earliest study (Bousfield & Sedgewick, 1944), he asked people to name, for example, as many birds as they could. The result was that people tended to name the words in subgroups, such as "robin, bluejay, sparrow—chicken, duck, goose—eagle, hawk." To study this further, Bousfield (1953) gave people a 60-item list to be learned for **free recall**. Unlike other work at that time, Bousfield used related words for his lists, 15 words each from the categories *animals, personal names, vegetables,* and *professions*. Although the words were shown in a random order, people tended to recall them by category; for instance, "dog, cat, cow, pea, bean, John, Bob."

Where did this organizing come from? Obviously, people noticed that several words were drawn from the same categories. They used the strategy of grouping the items together on the basis of category (this has a nice metamemory effect as well). The consequence of this reorganization was straightforward: The way the material had been stored governed how it was recalled.

Baddeley (1978) was one of the critics of the depth of processing framework, concluding that it was valuable only at a rough, intuitive level but not as a scientific theory. Although that may be true, it is hard to beat Craik and Lockhart's insights if you're looking for a way to improve your own memory. Think of maintenance versus elaborative rehearsal as simple recycling in short-term memory versus meaningful study and transfer into long-term memory.

Apply this to your own learning. When you are introduced to someone, do you merely recycle that name for a few seconds, or do you think about it, use it in conversation, and try to find mnemonic connections to help you remember it? When you read, do you merely process the words at a simple level of understanding, or do you actively elaborate when you are reading, searching for connections and relationships that make the material more memorable? In other words, use the depth of processing ideas in your own metacognition. Try inventing a mnemonic (this invokes the generation effect), applying elaborative rehearsal principles, or actively doing something with the information, such as drawing a diagram (this invokes the enactment effect) to something you may need for this course, such as the seven themes of cognition presented in Chapter 1.

The power of organization for improving storage in long-term memory was demonstrated by Bower, Clark, Lesgold, and Winzenz (1969). Four hierarchies of words were presented in the organized condition, arranged as lists with headers (one of the four hierarchies is shown in Figure 6-6); for instance, under *stones* was *precious,* and under that were *sapphire, emerald, diamond,* and *ruby.* The control group was shown words in the same physical arrangements, but the words were randomly assigned to their positions. People got four trials to learn all 112 words; their performance is shown in Table 6-4. Presenting the words in the organized fashion led to 100% accuracy on Trials 3 and 4, an amazing feat given the number of words. In contrast, the control group managed to recall only 70 words out of 112 by Trial 4, 62% accuracy.

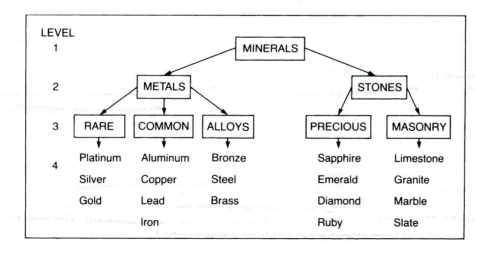

FIGURE 6-6 One of the hierarchies presented by Bower et al. (1969).

TABLE 6-4 Average Percentage of Words Recalled over Four Trials as a Function of Organization				
Conditions	**1**	**2**	**3**	**4**
Organized	65%	94.7%	100%	100%
Random	18.3	34.7	47.1	62.5

Source: Adapted from Bower et al., 1969.

This organizational principle, if used effectively, can lead to astounding feats of memory. People with exceptional memories, such as those who memorize *pi* out to insane numbers of digits, are essentially using some organizational strategy (e.g., Ericsson, Delaney, Weaver, & Mahadevan, 2004), along with other basic memory skills, such as imagery (e.g., Takahashi, Shimizu, Saito, & Tomoyori, 2006). This not only applies to words and numbers, but to complex sets of information. As Anderson (1985) pointed out, a chapter outline can serve the same function as the Bower et al. hierarchies, with obvious implications for students' study strategies (*there's* a hint).

Another reason for clustering studies was that they demonstrated people's strategies for learning in an objective fashion. Many studies used a free recall task, then examined the effects of different degrees of list organization, different numbers of categories, different numbers of items within categories, and so on. Clustering and organization were then examined in terms of a creative array of dependent variables, such as order of recall, degree of clustering, speed and patterning of pauses during recall, and rehearsal (see reviews by Johnson, 1970; Mandler, 1967, 1972). As an example, Ashcraft, Kellas, and Needham (1975) had people rehearse aloud as they studied clustered or randomized lists. Their results suggested that recalling the words by category was due to reorganization during rehearsal. That is, people tended to rehearse by category; for instance, when "horse" was presented, this would trigger the rehearsal of "dog, cat, cow, horse" together. When sufficient time is provided, people can reorganize the words as they store them in memory. Furthermore, the number of times a word had been rehearsed during study is predictive of recall order; more frequently rehearsed categories, as well as words within those categories, are recalled earlier than categories and words that received less rehearsal.

SUBJECTIVE ORGANIZATION   Don't misunderstand the previous section: Organization is *not* limited to sets of items with obvious, known categories. A study by Tulving (1962) showed that people can and do use subjective organizations—literally, organization imposed by the participant (for an update, see Kahana & Wingfield, 2000). Tulving used a multitrial free recall task, in which the same list of words is presented repeatedly across several trials, where each trial had a new reordering of the words. His analysis looked at the regularities that developed in the recall orders. For example, a person might recall the words "dog, apple, lawyer, brush" together on several trials. This consistency suggested that the person had formed a cluster or chunk composed of those four items using some idiosyncratic basis. For example, a person might link the words together in a sentence or story: "The dog brought an apple to the lawyer, who brushed the dog's hair." Regardless of how they were formed, the clusters were used repeatedly during recall, serving as a kind of organized unit. Tulving called this **subjective organization**, that is, *organization developed by a person for structuring and remembering information.* In other words, even "unrelated" items become organized through the mental activity of a person imposing an organization.

Imagery

The last storage variable considered here is **visual imagery**, *the mental picturing of a stimulus that affects later recall or recognition.* Of course, we have discussed some imagery effects already, such as mental rotation, and the imagery-based mnemonic devices. What we focus on now is its effect on the storage of information in long-term memory, and the boost that it gives to material you are trying to learn.

An early contributor to understanding of how imagery impacts memory was Alan Paivio. Paivio (1971) reviewed scores of studies that showed the generally beneficial effects of imagery on memory. These effects are beyond those caused by other variables, such as word- or sentence-based rehearsal, or meaningfulness (Bower, 1970; Yuille & Paivio, 1967). One example is a **paired-associate learning** study by Schnorr and Atkinson (1969; see Table 6-5). The task is to *learn the list so that the correct response item can be reproduced whenever the stimulus item is presented.* Thus, if you saw "elephant–book" during study, you would be tested during recall by seeing the term "elephant" and your correct response would be "book" (the later section on interference describes this task in more detail). Schnorr and Atkinson had people study half of a list by forming a visual image of the two terms together. The other half of the list was studied by rote repetition. On immediate recall, the pairs learned by imagery were recalled at better than 80% accuracy, compared to about 40% for the rote repetition pairs. The superiority of imagery was found even one week later. It is also important to note that the creation of mental images is not automatic. It requires attention and effort, which is part of the reason for the benefit it provides.

Studies such as this led Paivio to propose the **dual coding hypothesis** (Paivio, 1971), which states that *words that denote concrete objects, as opposed to abstract words, can be encoded into memory twice,* once in terms of their verbal attributes and once in terms of their imaginal attributes. Thus a word like *book* enjoys an advantage in memory—because it can be recorded twice, once as a word and once as a visual image, there are two ways it can be retrieved from memory, one way for each code. A term such as *idea,* however, has only a verbal code because there is no obvious image that it evokes. (This is not to say that people cannot create an image for *idea,* such as a light bulb, but only that the image is much more available and natural for concrete words.)

Context and Encoding Specificity

We conclude this section on storage with a discussion that also previews several important ideas for the topic of retrieval. What generalizations can we draw from research on rehearsal, organization, and imagery? How are we to understand the

TABLE 6-5 Lists of Paired Associates

List 1 (A–B)	List 2 (C–D)	List 3 (A–B$_r$)
tall–bone	safe–fable	plan–bone
plan–leaf	bench–idea	mess–hand
nose–fight	pencil–owe	smoke–leaf
park–flea	wait–blouse	pear–kiss
grew–cook	student–duck	rabbit–fight
rabbit–few	window–cat	tall–crowd
pear–rain	house–news	nose–cook
mess–crowd	card–nest	park–few
print–kiss	color–just	grew–flea
smoke–hand	flower–jump	print–rain

List 4 (A–B')	List 5 (A–C)	List 6 (A–D)
smoke–arm	tall–bench	smoke–fable
mess–people	plan–pencil	print–idea
rabbit–several	nose–wait	mess–owe
park–ant	park–student	pear–blouse
plan–tree	grew–window	rabbit–news
tall–skeleton	rabbit–house	grew–duck
nose–battle	pear–card	park–cat
grew–chef	mess–color	nose–nest
pear–storm	print–flower	plan–just
print–lips	smoke–safe	tall–jump

phenomenon of storage into episodic memory? The best way to understand storage is to consider it in light of retrieval.

In Tulving and Thompson's (1973; Unsworth Spillers, & Brewer, 2012) view, an important influence on memory is **encoding specificity**. This phrase means that information is encoded into memory *not* as a set of isolated, individual items. Instead, *each item is encoded into a richer memory representation that includes the context it was in during encoding*. So, when you read *cat* in a list of words, you are likely to store not only the word *cat* but also information about the context you read it in. In a classic study of encoding specificity, Godden and Baddeley (1975) had people learn a list of words. Half of these people learned the list on land, and the other learned the list under water (all of these people were scuba divers). They were then given a recall test for the list. The important twist is the context in which they tried to recall the information. Half of the people recalled the items in the same context they experienced during learning. However, the other half recalled the information in the other context. The interesting finding, as shown in Figure 6-7, was that memory was better when the encoding and retrieval contexts were the same, relative to when they were different.

A more everyday example of encoding specificity is the experience of going to a room in your home to do something, but when you arrive, you can't remember why you are there. However, when you go back to where you started, you remember. So, reinstating the original context helped you remember. This is also why witnesses may return to the scene of a crime. Being there again reinstates the context, helping them remember details that might otherwise be forgotten.

More generally, when your memory is tested, with free recall for instance, you attempt to retrieve the trace left by your original encoding. Encoding the context along with the item allows the context to serve as an excellent **retrieval cue**—*a useful prompt or reminder for the information*. The original context cues give you the best access to the information during retrieval, and these cues can be verbal, visual, or something else (Schab, 1990, for instance, has found that odors are effective contextual cues).

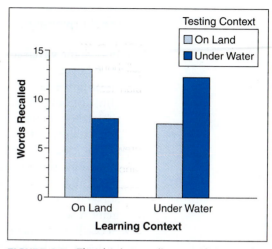

FIGURE 6-7 The classic encoding specificity result reported by Godden and Baddeley (1975), showing better performance when the encoding context matched the retrieval context. That is, memory for things learned on land was better when tested on land as opposed to underwater, whereas things learned underwater were better remembered when the people were tested underwater as opposed to on land.

The processing of content (what it is you are to remember), context, and their binding together is more complex than it initially may seem. As noted in Chapters 2, 3, and 4, the brain has separate processing streams for what something is and where it is. For context effects on memory, particularly spatial contexts, information about *what* something was is processed in the perirhinal cortex (B.A. 35), which part of the temporal lobe. In comparison, information about *where* something was, it's context, is processed in the parahippocampal cortex (B.A. 36), the part of the temporal lobe around the hippocampus. This information is then integrated, or bound, into a coherent memory in the hippocampus, thereby uniting content and context, along with contributions from controlled coordination on the part of the prefrontal cortex (Ranganath, 2010).

Another variant of the encoding specificity effect is *state-dependent learning*, which is the finding that people are more likely to remember things when their physiological state at retrieval matches that at encoding. For example, a study by Goodwin, Powell, Bremeer, Hoine, and Stern (1969) found that people made fewer errors on a memory test when they recalled information when they were drunk (a particular physiological state) if they had learned that information inebriated, than if they tried to recall it when they were sober!

In summary, the storage of information into episodic long-term memory is affected by a number of factors that can lead to better memory. Moreover, the congruence between study and test contexts can be vital. Relevant rehearsal, including organizational and imaginal elements, improves performance.

Section Summary

- Important variables in storage are rehearsal and organization, regardless of whether the information is verbal or perceptual. Maintenance and elaborative rehearsal have different functions, the former for mere recycling of information, the latter for more semantically based rehearsal, which was claimed to process the information more deeply into memory. Difficulties in this depth of processing framework involved specification of the idea of depth.
- Generally, the amount of rehearsal is positively related to recall accuracy for the primacy portion of a list. Organization, especially by category but also by subjectively defined chunks, improves memory because it stores the information securely and provides a useful structure for retrieval.
- According to encoding specificity, contextual information that was encoded along with the studied information can serve as an effective retrieval cue. The degree to which the context at learning can be reinstated at retrieval will improve performance.

RETRIEVING EPISODIC INFORMATION

We turn now to the other side of the coin, retrieving information from episodic memory. As we do, we reencounter the two theories of forgetting that have preoccupied cognitive psychology from the very beginning: decay and interference.

Decay

It's a bit unusual for the name of a theory to imply its content as clearly as does the term *decay*. Nonetheless, that is what decay theory was all about: The older a memory trace is, the more likely that it has been forgotten, just as the print on an old newspaper fades into illegibility. The principle dates back to Thorndike (1914), who called it the *law of disuse*: Habits, and by extension memories, are strengthened when they are used repeatedly, and those that are not are weakened through disuse. Thorndike's idea was a beautiful theory, easily understood and straightforward in its predictions. Unfortunately, it's wrong, at least as far as long-term memory is concerned.

The problem with the decay theory of forgetting is that it claims that the passage of time causes forgetting. The definitive attack on this claim was given by McGeoch (1932), who argued that it is the *activities* that occur during a period of time that cause forgetting, not time itself. In other words, time doesn't cause forgetting—it's what happens during that time that does. Although there are still some arguments for some, at least partial, influence of decay (Schacter, 1999), it is difficult to imagine a study that would provide a clean, uncontaminated demonstration of it. As time passes, there can be any number of opportunities for interference, even if by the momentary thoughts you have while your mind wanders. The time interval also gives opportunities for selective remembering and rehearsal, which would boost remembering old information.

Interference

Interference theory was a staple in the experimental diet of verbal learners. There were at least two reasons for this. First, the arguments against decay theory and for interference theory were convincing, on both theoretical and empirical grounds. Demonstrations such as the often-cited Jenkins and Dallenbach (1924) study made sense within an interference framework: After identical time delays, people who had remained awake after learning recalled less than those who slept (Figure 6-8). The everyday activities encountered by awake people interfered with memory. Fewer interfering activities occurred for sleeping people, so their memory was better.

This effect was replicated by Drosopoulos, Schulze, Fischer, and Born (2007), who further concluded that the memory benefit of sleep serves to mitigate the effects of interference. However, this was primarily for information that was not

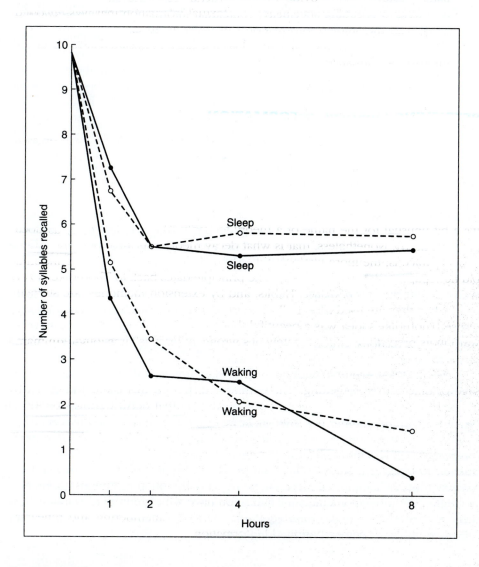

FIGURE 6-8 The classic Jenkins and Dallenbach (1924) result, showing higher recall of nonsense syllables for two people who slept after acquisition versus remaining awake after acquisition.

strongly encoded (that is, not well learned) to begin with. Although how much interference is experienced is linked to how related the material is (as seen in Chapter 5), there are other reasons for long-term memory forgetting that are influenced by whether you get some sleep.

Specifically, when you create and store new long-term memories, they don't instantly appear in your brain in a well-established form. Instead, there is a period of time during which memories go through a process of **consolidation**, *the more permanent establishment of memories in the neural architecture.* Later we see about the consequences of a dramatic disruption in consolidation that can result in amnesia. For now, it is important to note that the disruption when people are awake (and not asleep) is interference of the memory consolidation process (Wixted, 2005). New information is encoded into memory that uses the same neural parts (such as the hippocampus) that were used by the older information. This reuse of same neural networks interferes with memories for the older information, thereby disrupting consolidation and causing forgetting.

This interference is somewhat like writing messages in clay. Imagine writing a message in a bit of clay, then writing even more messages on the clay. Sometimes you'll write over messages that you had previously written, making the earlier ones harder to recover. This is the type of interference we are talking about. Still, sometimes a message doesn't get written over, and eventually the clay hardens. In this case, the message consolidates into the clay, making it harder to disrupt. Ultimately, these older memories are more robust, and less prone to the disruption.

A second reason for the popularity of interference studies is that these effects were easily obtained with a task already in wide use, the paired-associate learning task. This task was a natural for studying interference—and, it conformed to the behaviorist *Zeitgeist* or "spirit of the times" before the cognitive revolution. Unlike consolidation-disrupting interference, the interference explored using paired-associate tasks was due to *cue-overload*. In these cases, there are many memories that are related to a specific cue, and they compete with one another during retrieval.

PAIRED-ASSOCIATE LEARNING   A few moments studying the paired-associate learning task will help you understand interference theory. The basic paired-associate learning task is as follows (see also Table 6-3): *A list of stimulus terms is paired, item by item, with a list of response terms. After learning, the stimulus terms should prompt the recall of the proper response terms.*

Table 6-5 presents several paired-associate lists as a demonstration. Imagine learning List 1 to a criterion of one perfect trial (try it to get a good idea of what the task is like). After that, you switch to the second half of the study, which involves learning another list. The similarity of the first and second lists is critical. If you were switched to List 2, you would experience little or no interference because List 2 has terms that are dissimilar to List 1. In the lingo of interference theory, this was the *A–B, C–D* condition, where the letters *A* through *D* refer to different lists of stimulus or response terms. This condition represented a baseline condition because there is no similarity between the *A–B* and the *C–D* terms (however, you may need fewer trials on the second list because of "general transfer" effects from List 1, warmup or learning to learn).

TABLE 6-6   Designs to Study Two Different Kinds of Interference

	Proactive Interference (PI)			
	Learn	**Learn**	**Test**	**Interference Effect**
PI group	A–B	A–C	A–C	A–B list interferes with A–C; e.g., an A–B word intrudes into A–C
Control group	—	A–C	A–C	

	Retroactive Interference (RI)			
	Learn	**Learn**	**Test**	**Interference Effect**
RI group	A–B	A–C	A–B	A–C list interferes with A–B; e.g., an A–C word intrudes into A–B
Control group	A–B	—	A–B	

If you shifted to List 3, however, there would have been "massive" negative transfer; it would have taken you more trials to reach criterion on the second list. This is because the same stimulus and response terms were used again but in new pairings. Thus, your memory of List 1 interfered with the learning of List 3. The term for this was *A–B, A–B$_r$* where the subscript *r* stood for "randomized" or "re-paired" items. Finally, if you switched to List 4 (the *A–B, A–B'* condition), there would have been a great deal of positive transfer; you would need fewer trials to reach criterion on the second list because List 4 (designated *B'*) is related to the earlier one (*B*). For instance, in List 1 you learned "plan–leaf"; in List 4, "plan" went with "tree."

These are all *proactive* interference effects, showing the effects a prior task has on current learning. We discussed proactive interference (PI) and release from PI in Chapter 5. Table 6-6 is the general experimental design for a proactive interference study as well as for a retroactive interference (RI) study. As a reminder, retroactive interference occurs when a learning experience interferes with recall of an *earlier* experience; the newer memory interferes backward in time ("retro").

Both proactive and retroactive interference have been examined extensively, with complex theories based on the results. Although the literature is extensive, no attempt is made to cover it in depth here (but see standard works, e.g., Postman & Underwood, 1973; Underwood, 1957; Underwood & Schultz, 1960; and Klatzky, 1980, Chapter 11, for a very readable summary).

Simulate *Forgetting* in **MyPsychLab**

Retrieval Failure

Beginning in the mid-1960s, a different theory came to dominate cognitive psychology's view of forgetting. Both the decay and interference theories suggest that information in long-term memory can be lost from memory. This definition of **forgetting**, *loss from memory*, was implicit in the mechanisms thought to account for it. Forgetting is now used without the idea of complete loss from memory, however, to refer to situations in which there is difficulty remembering.

For example, one line of research looks at "retrieval-induced forgetting," the temporary forgetting of information because of having recently retrieved related information (e.g., Anderson, Bjork, & Bjork, 2000; MacLeod & Macrae, 2001). Similarly, Anderson (2003; Storm, 2011) has suggested that forgetting is an active inhibition process, designed to override mistaken retrieval of related information ("activated competitors" in Anderson's terms). Note that even here, the unwanted information that is causing interference is still in memory—if it weren't, there'd be no need to override it. That said, it should be noted that the memories that are more likely to be inhibited are the ones that have recently been processed, whereas older memories are more likely to be facilitated by recently retrieved, related information (Bäuml & Samenieh, 2010).

So, there may be no *complete* forgetting from long-term memory, aside from loss due to organic or physical factors, such as stroke or diseases like Alzheimer's dementia. Instead, forgetting may be due to retrieval failure or a process of retrieval inhibition, a deliberate (though only partially successful) attempt to forget (e.g., when you try to forget an unpleasant memory or an incorrect fact; Bjork & Bjork, 2003).

AN EVERYDAY EXAMPLE   Everyone is familiar with retrieval failure. Students often claim that they knew the information but that they "blocked" on it during the exam; *sometimes* this is an example of retrieval failure. A straightforward experience of this is the classic **tip-of-the-tongue (TOT)** phenomenon.[1] People are in the TOT state when they are *momentarily unable to recall a word, often a person's name, that they know is in long-term memory.* Interestingly, although you may be unable to retrieve a word or name during a TOT state, you usually have access to partial information about it, such as the sound it starts with, its approximate length, and the stress or emphasis pattern in pronunciation. (See Brown & McNeill, 1966; Jones, 1989; Koriat, Levy-Sadot, Edry, & de Marcus, 2003; and Meyer & Bock, 1992; Burke, MacKay, Worthley, & Wade, 1991, provide a list of questions that can be used to trigger the TOT state, if you want to try it out.)

However, retrieval failure, like the TOT phenomenon, is not limited to lapses in remembering names or words. As Tulving and his associates found, it is a fundamental aspect of memory.

RESEARCH ON RETRIEVAL FAILURE   An early demonstration of retrieval failure is a study by Tulving and Pearlstone (1966) in which two groups of people studied the same list of 48 items, four words from each of 12 categories (e.g., animals, fruits, sports). The items were preceded by the appropriate category name, such as "crimes—treason, theft; professions—engineer, lawyer," and people were told that they had to remember only the items. At retrieval, one group was asked for standard free recall. The other group was given the names of the categories as retrieval cues, that is, a **cued recall** condition.

The results were both predictable and profound. The free recall group remembered 40% of the items, whereas the cued recall group named 62%. One

---

[1]TOT is pronounced "*tee-oh-tee,*" not like the word *tot.* Furthermore, it is often used as a verb: "The subject TOTed ("*tee-oh-teed*") seven times on the list of 20 names." For another regrettable example of "cognitive verbs," see Chapters 9 and 10, on "garden pathing."

conclusion we can draw confirms intuitions dating back to Ebbinghaus: Recall often underestimates how much information was learned. Recognition scores, not to mention savings scores, usually show higher retention. More importantly, unsuccessful retrieval, say in the absence of cues, might be a critical, possibly major, cause of forgetting. On this view, *information stored in long-term memory remains there permanently,* and so is **available**, just as a book on the library shelf is available. Successful performance depends also on **accessibility**, *the degree to which information can be retrieved from memory.* Items that are not accessible are not immediately retrievable, just as the misshelved book in the library is difficult to locate or retrieve. This suggests that information is not lost *from* memory but is lost *in* memory, so to speak. This persists until an effective retrieval cue is presented that locates the memory that cannot be retrieved.

Retrieval Cues

We've already discussed how access can be increased by reinstating the original learning context. More generally, this can be thought of as providing effective retrieval cues. So, let's look at retrieval cues more generally. Any cue that was encoded along with the learned information should increase accessibility. This is why the category cues helped the people in Tulving and Pearlstone's study recall more than they otherwise would have. Similarly, this is why recognition usually reveals higher performance than recall. In a recognition test, you merely have to pick out which of several alternatives is the correct choice. What better retrieval cue could there be than the very information you are trying to retrieve? Subsequent research has shown the power of retrieval cues in dramatic fashion. (A convincing demonstration is presented in Tables 6-7 and 6-8, taken from Bransford & Stein, 1984; do that demonstration now, before reading further.)

Thomson and Tulving (1970) asked people to learn a list of words for later recall. Some of the words were accompanied by cue words printed in lowercase letters; people were told they need not recall the cue words but that the cues might be helpful in learning. Some of the cue words were high associates of the list items, such as "hot–COLD," and some were low associates, such as "wind–COLD." During recall, people were tested for their memory of the list in one of three conditions: low- or high-associate cues or no cues.

The results were that high associates used as retrieval cues benefited recall both when they had been presented during study and when no cue word had been given. When no cue word was given, people spontaneously retrieved the high associate during input and encoded it along with the list item. In contrast, when low associates had been given, only low associates functioned as effective retrieval cues. High-associate

You haven't really forgotten all seven names. If you need a big hint, try searching the Internet for "The Seven Dwarfs."

TABLE 6-7

This demonstration experiment illustrates the importance of retrieval cues. You need a blank sheet of paper and a pencil. Please follow the instructions exactly.

Instructions: Spend 3 to 5 seconds reading each of the following sentences, and read through the list only once. As soon as you are finished, cover the list and write down as many of the sentences as you can remember (you need not write "can be used" each time). Please begin now.

A brick can be used as a doorstop.
A ladder can be used as a bookshelf.
A wine bottle can be used as a candleholder.
A pan can be used as a drum.
A record can be used to serve potato chips.
A guitar can be used as a canoe paddle.
A leaf can be used as a bookmark.
An orange can be used to play catch.
A newspaper can be used to swat flies.
A TV antenna can be used as a clothes rack.
A sheet can be used as a sail.
A boat can be used as a shelter.
A bathtub can be used as a punch bowl.
A flashlight can be used to hold water.
A rock can be used as a paperweight.
A knife can be used to stir paint.
A pen can be used as an arrow.
A barrel can be used as a chair.
A rug can be used as a bedspread.
A telephone can be used as an alarm clock.
A scissors can be used to cut grass.
A board can be used as a ruler.
A balloon can be used as a pillow.
A shoe can be used to pound nails.
A dime can be used as a screwdriver.
A lampshade can be used as a hat.

Now that you have recalled as many sentences as you can, turn to Table 6-8.

---

retrieval cues were no better than no cues at all. In other words, if you had studied "wind–COLD," receiving "hot" as a cue for "COLD" was of no value. Retrieval cues thus can override existing associations during recall.

Demonstrations of the effectiveness of retrieval cues are common: For instance, you hear a "golden oldie" on the radio, and it reminds you of a particular episode (a special high school dance, with particular classmates, and so forth).

This even extends to general context effects: Marian and Neisser's (2000) bilingual participants remembered more experiences from the Russian-speaking period of their lives when they were interviewed in Russian, and more from the English-speaking period when interviewed in English (see also Schrauf & Rubin, 2000); actors remember their lines better when enacting their stage movements of a performance, even three months later (and with intervening acting roles; Noice & Noice, 1999).

TESTING IS LEARNING It is pretty clear that when you are listening to a lecture, reading a book, or studying in some other way, you are learning new information. Moreover, when you take a test, such as an essay exam, a fill-in-the-blank, or a multiple-choice test, the contents of your memory are being assessed. An interesting point is that you are learning even when you are being tested. Every time you encounter information, whether you are studying it or being tested on it, counts as a learning trial (e.g., Gates, 1917; Roediger & Karpicke, 2006). Essentially, the **testing effect** is the finding that the additional experience that you get from tests actually helps you remember the information better—better even than studying, especially if you take a recall test (McDaniel, Roediger, & McDermott, 2007). This testing benefit applies to recognition (multiple-choice)

Even simple mnemonics, such as string around your finger, can serve as a memory cue to remind you of something important.

tests (Marsh, Roediger, Bjork, & Bjork, 2007) and to nonverbal material such as maps (Carpenter & Pashler, 2007), and it transfers to new items that were neither studied nor tested (Butler, 2010). So, an effective tool to help you study and learn the material for this or any other class you may take is for you to take practice tests if they are available. If they are not available, your study group could make up practice tests and give them to each other. It may sound like a lot of work, but your memory for the material will be much better than if you had just spent the same amount of time studying by yourself.

ALL THAT GLITTERS IS NOT GOLD There is no question that, for the most part, retrieval cues help memory. However, there are some notable exceptions. One is the **part-set cuing** effect (Slamecka, 1968), which is the finding that *if you cue people with a subset of a list, they will have more difficulty recalling the rest of the set than if they had not been cued at all.* In other words, cuing people with part of the information impairs memory compared to doing nothing. For example, if someone asked you to name the seven dwarves (from Disney's movie *Snow White*), you would have a harder time with the last three if you were told the names of four of them than if you were simply asked to name all seven of them by yourself. One cause of the part-set cuing effect is that when people are provided with part-set cues, these items disrupt the retrieval plan that a person would normally use by imposing a different organization of the material. Also, part-set cuing involves the

---

TABLE 6-8

Do *not* look back at the list of sentences in Table 6-7. Instead, use the following list as retrieval cues and write as many sentences as you can. Be sure to keep track of how many you can write down, so you can compare this with your earlier recall performance. Begin now.

flashlight	lampshade
sheet	shoe
rock	guitar
telephone	scissors
boat	leaf
dime	brick
wine bottle	knife
TV antenna	pen
bathtub	pan
record	board
orange	newspaper
ladder	barrel
rug	balloon

---

use of an active inhibitory mechanism (Aslan, Bäuml, & Grundgeiger, 2007), much like what would be occurring in retrieval practice. In short, when a person is given a part-set cue, this causes an implicit retrieval of those items. At that time, the related memory traces serve as competitors and are actively inhibited.

PROVE IT
Part-Set Cuing

It seems surprising that giving people part of a set of information makes their performance worse as compared to giving them nothing. And yet, this is exactly what the part-set cuing effect says will happen. Make several lists of words. Each list should be 48 words long from 4 categories (e.g., tools, birds, countries, etc.), with 12 words from each category. Then get two groups of your friends. For both groups, read the lists of words to them, with the words in a random order (not grouped by category). Do this at a pace of about 1 word per second. Then after reading the list, have one group try to recall the entire list of 48 words. For the other group, read to them a subset of 24 words (6 from each category), and then have them try to recall the remaining 24.

When scoring their recalls, for both groups, do not count the ones that were read to the second group (the part-set cue group), but only the other 24. This is because what you are trying to test is how well people do on those particular items as a function of whether they got the part-set cues or not. If everything goes well, you should find that the people to whom you read half of the list will have a harder time than the people who simply tried to recall the entire list.

Section Summary

- Decay and interference are proposed causes of forgetting from long-term memory. Retrieval failure is forgetting caused by information that is available in long-term memory, but which is, possibly temporarily, inaccessible. Effective retrieval cues provide access to otherwise irretrievable information. Part-set cuing is a rare exception to this rule.
- Tip-of-the-tongue states illustrate that even when information cannot be successfully retrieved, partial information may be available. This partial retrieval may be so strong that retrieval seems imminent.
- Taking a test on material not only serves to assess what is and is not known, it also provides an opportunity to reinforce what is learned.

AMNESIA AND IMPLICIT MEMORY

We study dysfunctions caused by brain damage, such as the agnosias you read about in Chapter 3, to understand cognition and its organization. Sometimes the patterns of disruptions and preserved abilities can tell us a great deal about how cognition works. This has been especially fruitful for understanding long-term memory in cases of amnesia.

Amnesia is *the catastrophic loss of memories or memory abilities caused by brain damage or disease.* Amnesia is one of the oldest and most thoroughly studied mental disruptions caused by brain disorders, as well as a common result of brain injury and damage. Although some amnesias are temporary, due to a blow to the head or even acute emotional or physical stress (e.g., transient global amnesia; Brown, 1998), the amnesias we are interested in here are relatively permanent, caused by enduring changes in the brain.

Many kinds of amnesias have been studied, and we have space to discuss only a few. A few bits of terminology will help you understand the material and alert you to the distinctions in memory that are particularly relevant. First, the loss of memory in amnesia is always considered in relation to the time of the injury. If a person suffers *loss of memory for events before the brain injury,* this is **retrograde amnesia**. Interestingly, retrograde amnesia commonly shows a temporal gradient—memories that are more distant in time from the injury are less impaired (e.g., Brown, 2002; Wixted, 2004). This temporal gradient is referred to as **Ribot's Law**. The other form of amnesia is **anterograde amnesia**, *disruption in acquiring new memories for events occurring after the brain injury.* A person can show both forms of amnesia, although the extent of the memory loss usually is different for events before and after the damage—for example, anterograde amnesia often seems more extensive, simply because it disrupts learning from the time of the brain damage on to the present. The cases we talk about here are extreme in that the memory disruption is so extensive. Most cases of amnesia are not as extensive.

Second, we are trying to understand the architecture of memory, how its components are interrelated, whether some are independent of others, and so on. This is an analysis of dissociations, where the term **dissociation** refers to *a disruption in one component of cognition, but no impairment of another.* If two mental

Watch
Memory in
MyPsychLab

processes—A and B—are dissociated, then A might be disrupted by brain damage while B remains normal; patient K. C., described later, displays this kind of pattern. Sometimes another patient is found who has the reverse pattern: B is disrupted by the brain damage, but A is intact. When two such complementary patients are found, with *reciprocal patterns of cognitive disruption*, then the abilities A and B are **doubly dissociated** (a simple example would be seeing and hearing, either of which can be damaged without affecting the other).

Importantly, a double dissociation implies not only that A and B are functionally independent, but also that A and B involve different regions of the brain. A simple dissociation is not as strong. If process A is damaged while B remains normal, it could be that research has not yet found a patient with the reciprocal pattern. Or it could be that process A can be selectively damaged without affecting B but that damage to B would always disrupt A. The opposite of a dissociation is an association, that is, a situation in which A and B are so completely connected that damage to one would always disrupt the other (e.g., recognizing objects and recognizing pictures of objects).

Finally, the most useful cases are those of focal brain lesions, in which the damage is to a small, restricted area of the brain. Cases such as that of patient K. C. illuminate the underlying mental processes more clearly because many of his mental processes are intact despite the dysfunction caused by the focal lesion. Unfortunately, the widespread damage and neural deterioration of some injuries or diseases, such as Alzheimer's disease, makes it difficult to pin down the neuro-generator of the cognitive functions that are disrupted: So many regions are damaged that no single one can be pinpointed as the region responsible for a particular ability.

Dissociation of Episodic and Semantic Memory

PATIENT K. C.   We begin with a case history. Tulving (1989) described patient K. C. (you read a brief account of this in Chapter 2), who experienced serious brain injury, especially in the frontal regions, in a motorcycle accident. As a result of this injury, K. C. shows a seemingly complete loss of episodic memory: He is completely amnesic for his own autobiographical knowledge. K. C. has profound retrograde and anterograde amnesia. He shows great difficulty in both storing and retrieving personal experiences in long-term memory.

Interestingly, although K. C.'s episodic memory no longer works, his semantic memory does. He is adept at answering questions about his past by relying on general, semantic knowledge; when asked about his brother's funeral, he responded that the funeral was very sad, not because he remembers attending the funeral (he did not even remember that he had a brother) but because he knows that funerals are sad events.

K. C.'s memory disruption, intact semantic memory yet damaged episodic retrieval, is evidence of a dissociation between episodic and semantic memory. This suggests that episodic and semantic memories are separate systems, enough so that one can be damaged while the other stays intact. In Squire's (1987) taxonomy (look back to Figure 6-1), K. C. has lost one of the two major components of declarative knowledge, his episodic memory.

FUNCTIONAL IMAGING EVIDENCE   There are limitations on what can be learned about normal cognition from data from brain-damaged patients. Brain-damaged patients may be unique. Because we might worry about the generality of such results—K. C. could have been atypical before his accident—Tulving presented further support for his conclusions, studies of brain functioning among normal individuals (Nyberg, McIntosh, & Tulving, 1998).

Turn to the color illustration in the endpapers of this textbook, and you will see a set of photographs. In these pictures, the blood flow to the brain is being measured; you read about this technique in Chapter 2. The logic behind such a procedure is that mental activity—say, retrieving a memory—involves an increase in neural activity. This increase shows up as an increase in cerebral blood flow to those brain regions that are more activated. Thus, by injecting a small dose of radioactive material into the bloodstream, the apparatus detects regions of the brain that have higher concentrations of radioactivity on a short time scale (e.g., 12 separate intervals of 0.2 seconds each across an 80-second period).

The red areas in the pictures show regions where the blood flow was above the baseline level, and the green regions show where blood flow was lower than average.

Tulving and his colleagues took research such as this and other work to develop what they called the **Hemispheric Encoding/Retrieval Asymmetry (HERA) model** (Habib, Nyberg, & Tulving, 2003; Nyberg, Cabeza, & Tulving, 1996). Data from PET studies, such as the Nyberg et al. (1998) study discussed earlier, show that the left frontal lobe is more likely to be involved in the retrieval of semantic memories and the encoding of episodic memories. This makes sense, because when you encounter a new event, in order to create a new episodic memory you need to understand the event using your semantic knowledge. In comparison, the right frontal lobe is more likely to be involved in the retrieval of episodic memories. So, according to the HERA model, different parts of the brain are involved in different types of memory processing (see also Buckner, 1996; Shallice, Fletcher, & Dolan, 1998). Note that it is not the case that the HERA model is making the claim that episodic memories are stored in the right hemisphere and semantic memories in the left. Instead, it is just that those brain regions are more involved in those kinds of activities. Even researchers who do not agree with the HERA model do agree that the brain processes semantic and episodic memories differently (e.g., Ranganath & Pallar, 1999; Wiggs, Wiesberg, & Martin, 1999).

Anterograde Amnesia

The story of anterograde amnesia begins with a classic case history. A popular theoretical stance in 1950 was that memories are represented throughout the cortex, rather than concentrated in one place. This position was articulated by Karl Lashley in his famous 1950 paper "In Search of the Engram." Three years later, an accidental discovery was made by the neurosurgeon William Scoville. Scoville performed radical surgery on a patient, Henry Molaison, more commonly known as H. M., sectioning (lesioning) H. M.'s hippocampus in both the left and right hemispheres in an attempt to gain control over his severe epilepsy. To Scoville's surprise, the outcome of this surgery was pervasive anterograde amnesia; H. M. was unable to learn and recall anything new. Although his memory of events before the surgery remained intact, as did his overall IQ (118, well above average), he lost the ability to store new information in long-term memory.

Across the years, H. M. served as a participant in hundreds of tasks (e.g., Milner, Corkin, & Teuber, 1968), documenting the many facets of his anterograde amnesia. His memory of events prior to the surgery, including his childhood and school days, was quite good, with some gaps. His language comprehension was normal, and his vocabulary was above average. Yet any task that required him to retain information across a delay showed severe impairment, especially if the delay was filled with an interfering task. These impairments applied equally to nonverbal and verbal materials. For instance, after a 2-minute interference task of repeating digits, he was unable to recognize photographs of faces. He was unable to learn sequences of digits that went beyond the typical short-term memory span of seven. In a conversation reported by Cohen (in Banich, 1997), he told about some rifles he had (it was a childhood memory). This reminded him of some guns he had also had, so he told about them. Telling about the guns took long enough, however, that he forgot he had already talked about the rifles, so he launched into the rifle story again, which then reminded him of the guns—and so on until his attention was diverted to some other topic.

H. M.'S IMPLICIT MEMORY   Interestingly, the evidence also suggests that H. M.'s memory was normal when it involved implicit memory. That is, he was able to learn a motor skill, mirror-drawing; this task requires a person to trace between the lines of a pattern while looking at it and the pencil only in a mirror (Figure 6-9). H. M.'s performance (the bottom part of the figure) showed a normal learning curve, with very few errors on the third day of practice. Note, though, that on days 2 and 3 he did not remember having done the task before; he had no explicit memory of ever having done it, despite his normal performance based on implicit memory.

Likewise, H. M. showed systematic learning and improvement on the Tower of Hanoi problem (see Chapter 12). Although he did not remember the task itself, his performance nonetheless improved across repeated days of practice. Such empirical demonstrations confirm what clinicians working with amnesia patients have known or suspected for a long time: Despite profound difficulties in what we normally think of as memory, aspects of the patients' behavior do demonstrate a kind of memory—in other words, implicit memory (see Schacter, 1996). Referring back to Figure 6-1, all of the subtypes underneath "nondeclarative (implicit)" memory—skill learning, priming, and so forth—represent different aspects of implicit memory, that is, different forms and types of performance in which implicit memories can be displayed (Squire, 1993; see Gupta & Cohen, 2002, and Roediger, Marsh, & Lee, 2002, for reviews).

IMPLICATIONS FOR MEMORY   What do we know about human memory as a function of H. M.'s disrupted and preserved mental capacities? How much has this person's misfortune told us about memory and cognition?

The most apparent source of H. M.'s amnesia was a disruption in the transfer of information to long-term memory. That is, H. M.'s retrieval of information learned before surgery was intact, indicating that his long-term memory *per se,*

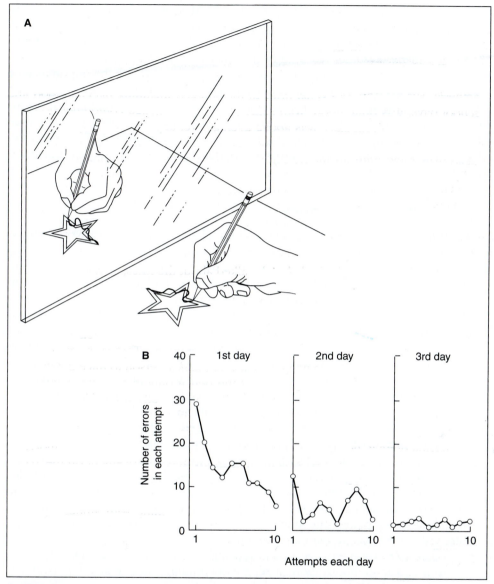

FIGURE 6-9 **A.** In this test the task is to trace between the two outlines of the star while viewing his or her hand in a mirror. The reversing effect of the mirror makes this a difficult task initially. Crossing a line constitutes an error. **B.** Patient H. M. shows clear improvement in the motor learning star task, an instance of implicit learning and memory. After Blakemore (1977).

including retrieval, was unaffected. Likewise, his ability to answer questions and do other simple short-term memory tasks indicates that his attention, awareness, and working memory functions also were largely intact. But he had a widespread disability in transferring new declarative information into long-term memory. This disability affected most or all of H. M.'s explicit storage of information in long-term memory (Milner, Corkin, & Teuber, 1968), including real-world episodic material.

It is a mistake to conclude from this that H. M.'s memory disruption—say, the process of explicit rehearsal—takes place in the hippocampus. Instead, it seems more likely that the hippocampus is on a critical *pathway* for successful transfer to long-term memory. Other research on patients with similar lesions (e.g., Penfield & Milner, 1958; Zola-Morgan, Squire, & Amalral, 1986) confirms the importance of the hippocampus to this process of storing new information in long-term, explicit memory. In some sense, then, the hippocampus is a gateway into long-term memory. Thus, the hippocampus is essential for declarative or explicit memory (see Eichenbaum & Fortin, 2003, for an introduction to the relationship between the hippocampus and episodic memory, and Barnier, 2002, for an extension of these effects to posthypnotic amnesia).

Implicit and Explicit Memory

To repeat a point made at the beginning of this chapter, the operative word in these definitions is *conscious*. Explicit memories, whether episodic or semantic, come to us with conscious awareness and therefore have an explicit effect on performance, an effect that could be verbalized. For example, name the third letter of the word meaning "unmarried man." The very fact that you can say *c* and name the word *bachelor* attests to the fact that this is an explicit memory. In contrast, fill in the following word stems: "gre__, lic__, fl__." Even without any involvement of conscious awareness, you may have filled these in with the words "green, license, flag" with greater likelihood than would have been expected by chance. The words *green, license,* and *flag* occurred in this chapter; we even made a point, early on, that you were reading *license* more rapidly after encountering it in an earlier paragraph, an effect called repetition priming. Importantly, we all demonstrate such implicit effects as repetition priming, amnesic or not (Graf & Schacter, 1987; Kolers & Roediger, 1984).

Repetition priming is a general form of implicit memory in which *a previous encounter with information facilitates later processing on the same information, even unconsciously.* Repetition priming has been established in a number of tasks, such as word identification and lexical decision (Morton, 1979), word and picture naming (Brown, Neblett, Jones, & Mitchell, 1991), and rereading fluency (Masson, 1984). In all these, a prior encounter with the stimulus yields faster performance on a later task, even though you may not consciously remember having seen it before (see Logan, 1990, for the connection of repetition priming to automaticity).

In a classic demonstration of repetition priming, Jacoby and Dallas (1981) had people study a list of familiar words, answering a question about each as they went through the list. Sometimes the question asked about the physical form of the word, as in, "Does it contain the letter *I*?" Sometimes it asked about the word's sound, as in, "Does it rhyme with *train*?" And sometimes, the question asked about a semantic characteristic, as in, "Is it the center of the nervous system?" This was a direct manipulation of *depth of processing*. Asking about the physical form of the word should induce shallow processing, leading to poor memory. Asking about rhymes demands somewhat deeper processing, and asking about semantic characteristics should demand full, elaborative processing on the list words.

At test, explicit memory was assessed by a yes/no recognition task ("Did this word occur in the study phase?"). Here, recognition accuracy was affected by the type of question answered during study. When a question related to the physical form, recognition was at chance, 51%. When it had asked about the sound of the word, performance improved. And when semantic processing had been elicited, recognition accuracy was high, 95%. This a test of explicit memory because people had to say "yes" or "no" based on whether they had seen the word earlier. As expected, more elaborative processing led to better explicit memory performance.

The other test given, the implicit memory test, was a perceptual test. Here, words were shown one at a time for only 35 ms, followed by a row of asterisks as a mask. People had to report the word they saw. In other words, the perceptual test did not require the people to remember which words they had seen earlier. They just had to identify the briefly presented words. For this test, word identification averaged about 80%, regardless of how they had been studied, in comparison to only 65% of control words that had not appeared earlier.

This is a typical implicit memory result. Even without conscious recollection of the original event, there is facilitation for a repeated stimulus. Explicit measures of memory, such as recall or recognition, show strong influences of how information was studied. However, implicit measures, such as a perceptual or word stem completion task, show clear priming regardless of how information was studied (see also Roediger, Stadler, Weldon, & Riegler, 1992; Thapar & Greene, 1994); for work on forgetting and interference in implicit memory, see Goshen-Gottstein & Kempinsky, 2001, and Lustig & Hasher, 2001, as well as Kinder & Shanks, 2003, for a counterargument).

Implicit memory is also involved in motor tasks, such as knowing how to ride a bicycle, play a musical instrument, play a sport, and so on. Here, implicit memory is often called *procedural memory*. Like other implicit memories, procedural memories are very durable, and, once acquired, show a very shallow forgetting curve. Remember the saying that once you learn to ride a bike, you never forget? This is also seen in cases of profound amnesia. These people may lose a great deal of declarative knowledge, but their procedural knowledge, or skills, remain largely intact. They can even acquire new skills, as shown by H. M.'s performance on the mirror drawing task.

Note that just because a memory is implicit does not mean it has no influence on conscious experience. For example, implicit memory may be involved in causing the *déjà vu* experience (Brown, 2004; Cleary, 2008). A new place may seem familiar to you, even though you've never been there before—not because of some psychic connection, but because the place is similar enough to other places you've been to. As a result, the new place elicits a feeling of familiarity. However, you are not consciously aware of being reminded of these other places. The end result is this eerie feeling of familiarity when you enter a place you know you've never been to before.

In addition, cognitive science learned an important lesson from patients such as H. M. and K. C. If we had stuck to laboratory-based experiments alone, and never paid attention to patients with amnesia, we would failed to realize the importance of that second, less obvious kind of long-term memory, the kind not dependent on conscious recollection. We would have missed implicit memory.

Section Summary

- Studies of people with amnesia caused by brain damage have taught us a great deal about long-term memory. Patient K. C. shows total amnesia for episodic information, although his semantic memory is unimpaired, suggesting a dissociation between episodic and semantic memories. Patients like H. M., a person with anterograde amnesia, typically are unable to acquire new explicit memories, but have intact implicit memory. The medial temporal area and especially the hippocampus are very important for the formation of new explicit memories, but different brain structures underlie implicit learning.

Key Terms

accessibility (p. *199*)
amnesia (p. *203*)
anterograde amnesia (p. *203*)
available (p. *199*)
consolidation (p. *196*)
cued recall (p. *198*)
declarative memory (p. *174*)
depth of processing (p. *184*)
dissociation (p. *203*)
distributed practice (p. *179*)
doubly dissociated (p. *204*)
dual coding hypothesis (p. *191*)
elaborative rehearsal (p. *184*)
enactment effect (p. *187*)

encoding specificity (p. *192*)
episodic memory (p. *174*)
explicit memory (p. *174*)
forgetting (p. *197*)
free recall (p. *188*)
generation effect (p. *187*)
Hemispheric Encoding/Retrieval Asymmetry (HERA) model (p. *205*)
implicit memory (p. *174*)
isolation effect (p. *181*)
levels of processing (p. *184*)
maintenance rehearsal (p. *184*)

massed practice (p. *179*)
metacognition (p. *175*)
metamemory (p. *175*)
method of loci (p. *175*)
mnemonic (p. *175*)
nondeclarative memory (p. *174*)
organization (p. *188*)
paired-associate learning (p. *191*)
part-set cuing (p. *201*)
peg word mnemonic (p. *176*)
recognition (p. *185*)
rehearsal (p. *182*)
relearning task (p. *178*)
repetition priming (p. *208*)

retrieval cue (p. *193*)
retrograde amnesia (p. *203*)
Ribot's Law (p. *203*)
savings score (p. *178*)
self-reference effect (p. *187*)
semantic memory (p. *174*)
serial recall (p. *186*)
subjective organization (p. *191*)
testing effect (p. *201*)
tip-of-the-tongue (TOT) (p. *198*)
visual imagery (p. *191*)
von Restorff effect (p. *181*)

- **Semantic Memory**
  Semantic Networks
  Feature Comparison Models
  Tests of Semantic Memory Models
  Semantic Relatedness
- **Connectionism and the Brain**
  Connectionism
  Connectionism and the Brain
- **Semantic Priming**
  Nuts and Bolts of Priming Tasks
  Empirical Demonstrations of Priming

Automatic and Controlled Priming
Priming Is Implicit
- **Schemata and Scripts**
  Bartlett's Research
  Schemata
  Scripts
  Evidence of Scripts
- **Concepts and Categorization**
  Theories of Categorization

Semantic memory is the memory necessary for the use of language. It is a mental thesaurus, organized knowledge a person possesses about words and other verbal symbols, their meaning and referents, about relations among them, and about rules, formulas, and algorithms for the manipulation of these symbols, concepts, and relations.

(TULVING, 1972, P. 386)

This chapter is about a different kind of long-term memory from that discussed in Chapter 6, namely **semantic memory** (literally "memory for meaning"), our *permanent memory store of general world knowledge,* much like an encyclopedia. Semantic memory is your conceptual knowledge. In fact, *generic memory* (Hintzman, 1978) might be a better name (although way too boring). That is, whereas your episodic memory differs substantially from mine, our semantic memories are largely similar—not in exact content, depending on our cultural backgrounds, but certainly similar in terms of structure and processes (see Medin & Atran, 2004, and Nisbett, Peng, Choi, & Norenzayan, 2001, on some cultural differences). So, although you have no idea what specific things happened during *my* driver's license test, we do share similar semantic concepts of what a driver's license test is.

The distinction between episodic and semantic memory is not simply one of convenience but does reflect different kinds of mental and neurological processes. For example, Prince, Tsukiura, and Cabeza (2007) showed that episodic memory depends more heavily on some different (but related) brain regions (e.g., hippocampus and anterior prefrontal cortex) as compared to semantic memory (e.g., lateral temporal lobe and posterior prefrontal cortex). This is also evident in the amnesia patients discussed in Chapter 6 who lost personal, episodic memories, but not general semantic memories.

The first use of the term *semantic memory* appears to have been in M. Ross Quillian's doctoral dissertation in 1966. Quillian set himself the task of programming a computer to understand language. Machine translation has been a longstanding goal in computer science. The overly confident predictions of the 1950s had failed to take into account a subtle yet important fact: Even the simplest acts of human comprehension require vast amounts of knowledge. Thus for computers to understand, answer questions, or paraphrase, they needed this kind of knowledge base. This was Quillian's goal: to provide that extensive knowledge base, to see whether the AI system could then "understand." The implicit point, of course, would be that humans also need this vast storehouse of knowledge—a semantic memory. This chapter covers the basics of semantic memory, including how concepts are stored and retrieved.

SEMANTIC MEMORY

A study on leading questions, also discussed in Chapter 8, provides a convenient entry into the topic of semantic memory. Loftus and Palmer (1974) showed people several short traffic safety films of car accidents. People were asked to describe each accident and then were asked a series of questions. One question asked for an estimate of the cars' speeds (which people are notoriously poor at estimating). One group of people was asked, "About how fast were the cars going when they hit each other?" The other groups were asked almost the same question, except that the verb *hit* was replaced with either *smashed, collided, bumped,* or *contacted.* As you might expect, people who got the stronger verbs such as *smashed* gave higher estimates of speed. The question led them to a biased answer.

Hold it. *Why* would we expect this? Why are we not surprised that people estimated higher speeds when the question said *smashed* instead of *bumped* or *hit?* Our intuitive answer is that *smashed* implies a *more severe* accident than *bumped.* But consider this intuitive answer again. How did those people know that *smashed* implies a more severe accident? It is not enough merely to say that *smashed* implies more severe. We are asking a more basic question than that. We want to know what is stored in memory that tells you what *smash* and *bump* mean. How does memory represent the fact that *smashed* implies a severe accident, that moving cars have drivers, that robins have wings, or that bananas, canaries, and daisies are all yellow? In short, what is the structure and content of semantic memory *per se,* and how do we access that knowledge?

As you just read, one of the earliest systematic attempts to answer such questions (aside from philosophical and linguistic analyses) was Quillian's (1968, 1969) work in artificial intelligence. His model of semantic memory was not a psychological model of memory but a computer program for understanding language. Shortly, however, Quillian collaborated with Allan Collins, and their psychological model was the first attempt in cognitive psychology to explain the structure and processes of semantic memory.

Semantic Networks

The Collins and Quillian model of semantic memory (1969, 1970, 1972; Collins & Loftus, 1975) was based on a network metaphor of memory. At the heart of the model were fundamental assumptions about the *structure* and *retrieval processes* of semantic memory. Collins and Quillian viewed the concepts of semantic memory as being nodes in a network. In other words, the structure of semantic memory was a **network**, *an interrelated set of concepts.* Each concept is represented as a **node**, *a point or location in the semantic space.*

Furthermore, concept nodes are linked by **pathways**, *labeled, directional, associations between concepts.* This entire collection—nodes linked via pathways—is the network. Note that every concept is related to every other concept, in that some combination of links, however indirect and long, can be traced between any two nodes.

The major process that operates on the network is **spreading activation**, *the retrieval of information from this network.* Concepts usually are at baseline, in a quiet, unactivated state. For example, as you read this sentence, one of the concepts in your semantic memory that is probably not activated is "ROMANCE." But when you read the word, its mental representation is activated. "ROMANCE" is no longer quiet; it was activated. (Here, words are italicized, and concept names are printed in capital letters.)

A key point is that activation spreads throughout a network along the links to other concepts, activating nodes it encounters along the way. Look at Figure 7-1A, a simple diagram of a few concepts and links. Even such a simple network represents a great deal of information. For instance, some of the facts in this network are that "ROBIN" is a member of the category "BIRD," that a "ROBIN" has a "RED BREAST," that a "CANARY" is "YELLOW," and so on. Each of the links records a simple fact or **proposition**, *a relation between two concepts.*

Note further that each link specifies a relationship. Thus "ROBIN *is a* BIRD," *is a member of the category* "BIRD," and "BIRD has the *property* FEATHERS." (The latter statement is called a **property statement**. The *isa* relationship was a bit of jargon from Rumelhart, Lindsay, & Norman [1972] meaning "is a," as in "is a member of the category.") Direction is important because the reversed direction is not true, that is "*All BIRDS are ROBINS." (Sentences that are intentionally wrong are marked with an asterisk.) Figure 7-1 shows what happens to this part of a semantic network when the word *robin* is presented. First, the node for *robin* is activated,

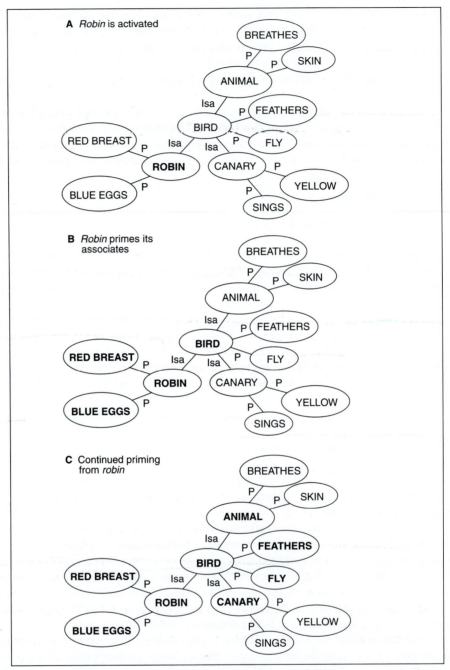

FIGURE 7-1 A portion of the semantic network is illustrated. **A.** The concept "ROBIN" has been activated and is shown in boldface. **B.** The spreading activation from "ROBIN" has activated concepts linked to "ROBIN," such as the boldface "BIRD," "RED BREAST," and "BLUE EGGS." **C.** The continued spread of activation that originated from "ROBIN" is depicted.

illustrated by boldface in Figure 7-1A. Then, activation spreads to the concepts it is linked to, like "BIRD," "RED BREAST," and "BLUE EGGS" in Figure 7-1B. *Those* concepts continue the spread of activation to their associated nodes, as depicted in Figure 7-1C.

The spread of activation is triggered each time a concept is activated. If *two* concepts are activated, then there are *two* spreads of activation, one from each node. As an exercise, study Figure 7-1A and mark which concept nodes are activated by a sentence like "A robin can breathe." To keep track of the spread, write a *1* next to links and nodes that are activated by "ROBIN" and a *2* next to those activated by "BREATHE." Take this through at least two cycles. (In a sense, you are "hand simulating" a memory search.)

What did you discover? You should have found two characteristics of spreading activation. First, activating "ROBIN" eventually primed a node that was *also* activated by "BREATHE." This explains how information is retrieved from semantic memory. The spreads of activation intersect, and a decision is made to be sure that the retrieved link represents the idea in the sentence. In other words, although a pathway would be found between "ANIMAL" and "RED BREAST," a decision would be made that the idea "all animals have red breasts" is invalid.

RELATED CONCEPTS   A second characteristic of semantic search is that other concepts also become activated or *primed*. In our example, many other concepts were primed; there should also be a *1* next to "RED BREAST" and "BLUE EGGS" from the first cycle, a *1* next to "FLY, FEATHERS, and CANARY" after the second cycle, and so on. Thus, spreading activation activates related concepts. Note that more and more distant concepts, connected by longer pathways, do not receive as much activation. Moreover, these related concepts are not activated forever, but activation decays after some amount of time.

Feature Comparison Models

Semantic networks are not the only way semantic memory has been conceived. Another is as a collection of features, as with the feature comparison model of Smith and his colleagues. In Smith's model (Rips, Shoben, & Smith, 1973; Smith, Rips, & Shoben, 1974), semantic memories were captured as **feature lists**, so semantic memory is a collection of sets of **semantic features**, *simple, one-element properties of the concept.* Thus the concept "ROBIN" is a list of its features, such as animate, red-breasted, and feathered. Furthermore, these features vary in terms of their *definingness*, with defining features being emphasized more than less defining features. Thus an essential feature is a **defining feature**, such as *animate* for "BIRD." Conversely, other features (e.g., "ROBIN" *perches in trees*) would be less so, but are **characteristic features**, *features that are common but not essential.* Thus, characteristic features do not define "ROBIN": Robins may or may not perch in trees. But defining features are essential: If it is a robin, it has to be animate.

FEATURE COMPARISON   The retrieval process in the Smith model was feature comparison; follow along with the sequence in Figure 7-2 as you read. Suppose you are given the sentence "A robin is a bird" and have to make a true/

Typical birds?

false judgment. For this model, you would access the concepts "ROBIN" and "BIRD" in semantic memory and then compare the two feature sets. Stage I involves a rapid, global comparison of features, to "compute" the similarity between the two concepts. For illustration, assume that these similarity scores range from 1 to 10.

For "A robin is a bird," the feature sets overlap a great deal; there are very few "ROBIN" features that are not also "BIRD" features, leading to a high overlap score (e.g., 8 or 9), so high that you confidently respond "yes" immediately. Conversely, for "A robin is a bulldozer," there is so little feature overlap (e.g., 1 or 2) that you can respond "no" immediately. These are "fast yes" and "fast no" Stage I responses.

What about when the relationship is not so obvious? First, consider "A chicken is a bird." For most people, chickens are less representative of the bird category: They do not perch, make nests in trees, fly, and so on. So, the Stage I comparison would find only an intermediate degree of overlap, and a second comparison is needed, called Stage II comparison. Unlike fast Stage I comparison, a Stage II comparison is slower, emphasizing more defining features. Thus, because it is true that chickens are birds, there is a match on all the features in this stage, yielding a "slow yes" response. Similarly, for "A bat is a bird," the overlap score is intermediate, triggering a Stage II. Here, however, there are important mismatches: The characteristic features that make bats similar to birds are outweighed by the defining features (mammal, furry, teeth, etc.) mismatch. Thus, the Stage II comparison gives evidence that the sentence is false.

FIGURE 7-2 The comparison and decision process in the Smith et al. model, with sample sentences.

Tests of Semantic Memory Models

Some tests of semantic memory used the **sentence verification task**, in which *simple sentences are presented for the yes/ no decisions*. Accuracy for such decisions does not tell us much; people seldom make mistakes for such simple facts. Instead, response time (RT) measures are primarily used. Table 7-1 lists the characteristics of such yes/no recognition tasks.

What a typical car used to look like.

Collins and Quillian (1969) tested a basic prediction of their model: Two concepts that are closer in the network should take less time to verify than two that are farther apart. Refer again to Figure 7-1 and your "hand simulation." If we assume that this part of semantic memory is accurately represented here, then some predictions can be made. For example, you should be quicker to verify "A robin is a bird" than "A robin is an animal," because it should take less time for activation to spread across one link rather than two. Likewise, it should take less time to verify that canaries are yellow than that they can fly or breathe, for the same reason.

Simulate
The Mind's Organization of Conceptual Knowledge in **MyPsychLab**

TABLE 7-1   Recognition Tasks in Semantic Memory

In Table 6-3 the recognition task consisted of two basic steps: The person first learned a set of words on a list and then made yes/no decisions on a test list ("yes" if the test word was on the studied list, "no" if it was not). The two important features that make a recognition test are as follows:

People make yes/no or forced-choice decisions.

The decisions are based on information stored in memory.

For semantic memory research, this task includes information already in long-term memory before the beginning of the experiment.

Generalized recognition task (semantic)

Information to be tested is already in long-term memory, such as knowledge of categories ("A robin is a bird") or words.

People make yes/no decisions to items, presented one at a time. Unlike episodic recognition, here the "yes" response usually means the item is true. For example, in a sentence verification task, people say "yes" to "A robin is a bird," that is, to any sentence that is true. In a lexical decision task, people respond "yes" if the letter string is a word (e.g., "MOTOR") and "no" if it is not (e.g., "MANTY").

Dependent variables: Typically, the primary dependent variable is response time (RT), although accuracy is also important. Occasionally, people are given a response deadline; that is, they are given a signal after some interval, say 300 ms, and must respond immediately after the signal. In such a task, error rate becomes the major dependent variable. Different electroencephalographic (EEG) patterns have also been used (see Kounios & Holcomb, 1992).

Independent variables: An enormous range of independent variables can be tested, such as the semantic relatedness between concepts, and word length, frequency, concreteness, and the like in a lexical decision task.

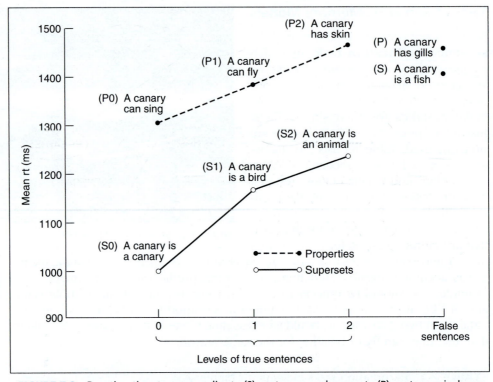

FIGURE 7-3 Reaction time to superordinate (S) sentences and property (P) sentences is shown as a function of levels within the hierarchy. An S2 sentence involves a superordinate connection two levels up the hierarchy; S1 means one level up in the hierarchy; a 0 level sentence had the predicate stored at the same hierarchical level.

From Collins and Quillian (1969).

Figure 7-3 shows the results of Collins and Quillian's (1969) study. Here, S indicates a superordinate statement, and P indicates a property statement. Tagged onto the S or P is a digit from 0 to 2, which indicates how many levels in the hierarchy the search proceeded through. As you can see, response time increased as the distance between the two concepts increased.[1] However, subsequent work by researchers, such as Rips et al. (1973), showed that human semantic memory is not structured as nicely as the Collins and Quillian model implies. For example, people verify the statement "A pig is an animal" faster than they verify "A pig is a mammal," although the Collins and Quillian model predicts the opposite result.

Semantic Relatedness

Figure 7-4 is a modified network of the *bird* category that incorporates semantic relatedness (Collins & Loftus, 1975). For example, a strict hierarchy is incorrect. Instead, these links are of different lengths, reflecting different strengths of association, with

---

[1]Collins and Quillian tested many more concepts than just canaries and robins, although the tradition in this area of research is to illustrate the models using these words.

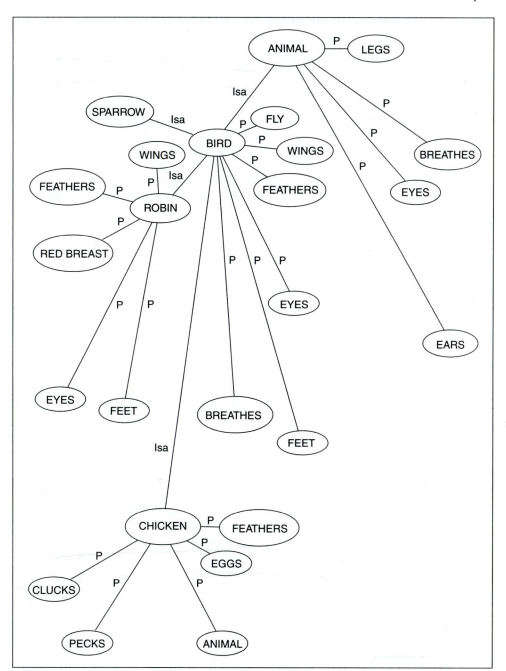

FIGURE 7-4 A portion of the semantic network is illustrated, taking into account three empirical effects: There is no strict cognitive economy in the hierarchy, so redundant information is stored at several different concepts; typical members of the category are stored more closely to the category name or prototype member; and properties that are more important are stored more closely to the concept than those of lesser importance.

stronger associations being verified faster than weaker ones. Moreover, for the feature of typicality (elaborated on later), more typical examples of a concept are linked by shorter pathways. This is why the link between *robin* and *bird* is shorter than that between *chicken* and *bird.* It is difficult in a two-dimensional figure to completely capture the associative and strength complexity of semantic memory. Thinking of semantic memory in space with three or more dimensions makes this easier to imagine, but harder to illustrate.

Regardless, the idea that performance varies directly as a function of the strength of associations is readily understood. The stronger the relation between concepts, the faster you can retrieve the idea. This is the **semantic relatedness effect**: *Concepts that are more highly interrelated are retrieved faster.* To demonstrate this, time yourself as you name the 12 months of the year; it takes only about 5 seconds. Now time yourself as you name the 12 months again, but this time in alphabetical order. How long did that take—at least half a minute, if not more, right? It should be obvious that how this information is organized in memory—based on chronological order. Thus, retrieving the information in a way that is incongruent with the storage organization makes it difficult.

Some additional evidence on semantic relatedness was reported by Kounios and Holcomb (1992; Kounios, 1996), who used event-related potential (ERP) recordings in addition to response times. In this study, pairs of words varied in relatedness, either high ("rubies–gems") or low ("spruces–gems"). Half of the time, a category member came before the category name ("rubies–gems"), and half the time the reverse ("gems–rubies"). Sentences were presented with one of three quantifiers, *all, some,* or *no,* thus altering the meaning (e.g., "All rubies are gems" and "Some gems are rubies" are true, but "No rubies are gems" is false). The results are shown in Figure 7-5. You can see the same increasing function as before, for example, when typicality varied from high to low in Figure 7-6.

FIGURE 7-5 Mean N400 amplitude recorded from three midline sites as a function of semantic relatedness and prime–target order.

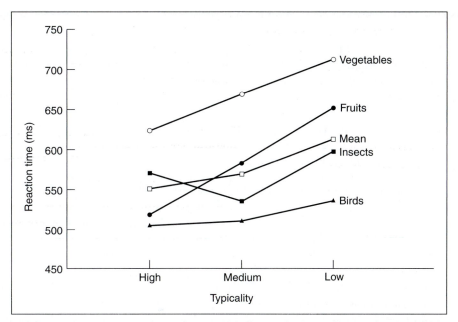

FIGURE 7-6 Mean RTs to members of categories that are high, medium, or low in typicality. The RTs are much shorter than in comparable studies because the category names were given at the beginning of a block of trials and did not change within the block. Thus each trial consisted of only the target word, and people judged whether it belonged to the given category name.

Positive P600 or P 600

We can also observe changes in electrical potential as a result of cognitive processing. In the Kounios and Holcomb study, the ERP component of interest was the N400 component, a *negative* change occurring about 400 ms after the item. Figure 7-7 shows the pattern of N400s, taken from one midline electrode site. The solid curve for "Exemplar–category, related" stimuli (e.g., "All rubies are gems")

PROVE IT
Category Retrieval and Episodic Influences

To illustrate that semantic memory is organized according to the principle of semantic relatedness, time some people as they generate lists of words for you (e.g., see how long it takes them to generate 20 words); or give people a fixed amount of time (say, 30 seconds) and tabulate how many words they generate in that period. You should test several well-known semantic categories, such as trees, flowers, vegetables, fruits, insects, or mammals. Now contrast those results with some different categories, such as red things, things that are soft, or things beginning with the letter *m*. You will see some evidence of semantic relatedness even in the latter examples; for instance, in the *red things* category, people are more likely to name *apple* and *tomato* together than *apple* and *fire engine*.

As an added episodic memory twist, at the end of the category retrieval exercise, have your participants take a new sheet of paper and list as many of the words they generated as they can remember, cautioning them to name *only* words they produced. Do you find more intrusions from the semantic categories?

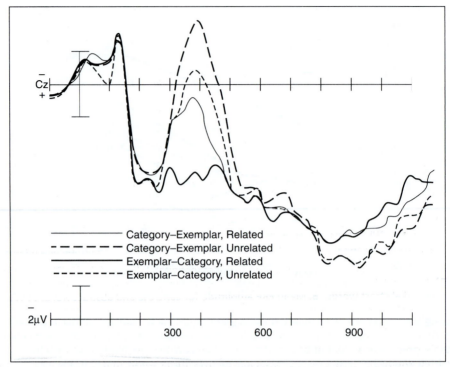

FIGURE 7-7 The event-related potentials at one midline site (*Cz*) for four types of trials; "Exemplar–category" and "Category–exemplar" refer to the order of the words. The onset of the target is shown by the vertical bar at the beginning of the time lines.

continued its negative drift across time. For all three other types, however, there was a negative peak around 400 ms, especially when the subject and predicate were unrelated. In other words, the N400 is sensitive to the relatedness of the two concepts in the sentence or, more accurately, to their *un*relatedness. Kounios and Holcomb concluded that the N400 reflects retrieval in semantic memory, and coherence and integration processes in language comprehension (see also Holcomb, 1993). When two words were related, there was a substantial difference in the ERP pattern compared to when they were unrelated.

One semantic-based result addressed in Kounios (1996) makes sense given what we know about cerebral lateralization. Most research suggests that the left hemisphere is dominant for verbal and language-based tasks, whereas the right hemisphere is dominant for visual and spatial information. Kounios describes a match between ERP results and Paivio's (1990) dual-coding theory. Recall the Paivio work from Chapter 6, that concrete words are learned and recalled better than abstract words because they can be represented in both verbally and by a mental image (Paivio, 1971). Paivio's (1990) idea was that the word-based knowledge is located in the left hemisphere and image-based in the right. Thus, concrete words enjoy an advantage because they recruit processes in both hemispheres.

Kounios and Holcomb (1994) used a lexical decision task, showing both concrete (e.g., *table*) and abstract (e.g., *justice*) words. Their ERPs provided support for

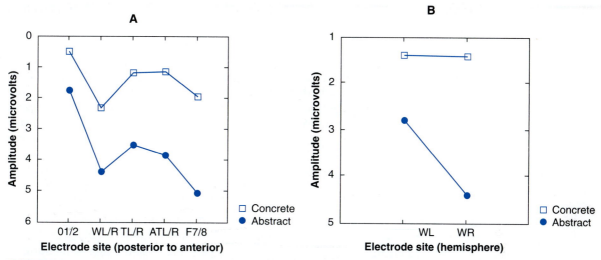

FIGURE 7-8 **A.** Mean amplitude of ERPs at five sites (occipital, left and right [01/2]; Wernicke's area, left and right [WL/R], temporal, left and right [TL/R], anterior temporal, left and right [ATL/R], and frontal, left and right [F7/8]), for concrete and abstract words. **B.** Mean ERP amplitude for concrete and abstract words at Wernicke's area in the left (WL) and right (WR) hemispheres.

Paivio's predictions. As shown in Figure 7-8, ERPs for concrete words were equal and high for both hemispheres. In contrast, the ERPs were markedly lower in the right than in the left hemisphere for abstract words, and both of these amplitudes were lower than those for concrete words. This is line with the discussion of the HERA model in Chapter 2.

EMBODIED SEMANTICS The complexity and organization of semantic memory is still being explored. Semantic memory also takes into account how we interact with the world through our senses and our actions, and so reflects embodied influences. As one illustration of this principle, it has been found that semantic distance effects that were just discussed are even found when people retrieve knowledge of body parts, with close body parts (e.g., hand and elbow) priming each other more than distant body parts (e.g., hand and knee) (van Elk & Blanke, 2011; Struiksma, Noordzij, & Postma, 2011). One such view is Barsalou's (1999) theory of **perceptual symbols**, which states that *semantic memory is built up of sensory and motor elements derived from experience.*

For example, Kalénine and Bonthoux (2008) gave people sets of three pictures (e.g., either a coat, a jacket, and a stove or a coat, a hanger, and a stove), asking them to identify which of two choice pictures went with a first. Two factors were manipulated. One was the relationship of the correct answer to the first picture. The objects were either *conceptually* related (e.g., coat-jacket) or *functionally* related (e.g., coat-hanger). The other factor was whether the objects could be interacted with and manipulated by people or not (e.g., coat can be but a castle cannot). They found that people were faster to respond to conceptually related items for objects that you can't manipulate, but were faster to respond to functionally related items for objects that you can (e.g., coat-hanger). Thus, the efficiency of using your semantic memory depends on both *how* you are using it as well as how you *interact* with the world.

Another example that involves more perceptual than motor embodiment can be seen in a study by Pecher, Zeelenberg, and Barsalou (2003), in which people were given a series of concept–property word pairs, such as "LEAVES–rustling." The task was to indicate whether the property was true of that concept. The critical comparison was the influence of one pair of items on another pair. Suppose that the second pair was "LEAVES–rustling." For *same modality* trials, the first pair would have referred to a property in same modality (hearing in this case). For example, a same modality pair here might be "BLENDER–loud." In comparison, for the *different modality* trials, the property of the object in the first pair involved some other sensory modality, such as "CRANBERRIES–tart," which involves the sense of taste. Pecher et al. found that people were slower to respond to the second pair when it involved a different modality, presumably because people needed to switch the type of semantic processing they were doing. Similar results are observed when the concepts share hand shapes (e.g., for holding something or not; Klatzky, Pellegrino, McCloskey, & Doherty, 1989). Thus, semantic memory appears to capture information in an embodied manner that takes into account our perceptual and motor interactions with the world.

Thus, our understanding of the world reflects how we each interact with the world; as our interactions differ, so will our processing of semantic information. As one example of such individual differences, in a study by Casasanto (2009), right-handed people associated positive words such as "honesty" and "intelligence" with their right side, and negative words such as "sadness" and "evil" with the left side. However, left-handed people showed the opposite pattern. So, how people interact with the world influences how they organize semantic knowledge even of abstract concepts. This embodied influence even extends to how people respond in that people find it easier to make semantic decisions if they press keys on a keyboard that are far apart compared to those that are close together (Lakens, Schneider, Jostmann, & Schubert, 2011).

AMOUNT OF KNOWLEDGE   The amount of knowledge we have makes a difference during memory search and retrieval—more knowledge and greater semantic relatedness go together. For example, Pexman, Holyk, and Monfils (2003) found that reading times were faster for concepts with more features than those with fewer features. Also, Yates, Locker, and Simpson (2003) found comparable effects in a lexical decision task, contrasting words with large versus "sparse" semantic neighborhoods; a large-neighborhood word like *bear* has many associates in memory, compared to a sparse-neighborhood word like *suds,* and is therefore judged more rapidly.

The influence of amount of knowledge extends to many settings and tasks. For example, Hambrick (2003) had people learn new information (about basketball) and found that the strongest influence on learning was the amount of domain knowledge they already had—in other words, the more you know about something, the easier it is to learn new things about that topic. Moreover, Westmacott and Moscovitch (2003) found that performance on a variety of tasks (they used recall, recognition, fame judgment, and speeded reading) was enhanced when there was some "autobiographical significance" to the knowledge being acquired. Presumably, the more you know about a topic, the more highly integrated and related that knowledge is in memory. This leads to more activation in memory and enhanced retrieval.

Section Summary

- Semantic memory contains our long-term memory knowledge of the world. Early studies of the structure and processes of semantic memory generated two kinds of models, network approaches and feature list approaches.
- In network models, concepts are represented as nodes in a semantic network, with connecting pathways between concepts. Memory retrieval involved the process of spreading activation: Activation spreads from the originating node to all the nodes connected to it by links.
- Feature comparison models assume that semantic concepts are sets of semantic features. Verification consists of accessing the feature sets and comparing these features.
- An important effect is semantic relatedness, in that concepts that are highly related are more easily processed. Also, the amount of knowledge stored in memory affects performance, possibly because more knowledge leads to higher semantic relatedness.
- Neurological measures, such as the N400 component of an ERP, provides some insight into semantic processing. For example, the N400 is larger when a person encounters semantically unrelated or anomalous information.
- Recent theories of perceptual symbols assume that semantic memories are created out of our experience with the world through perception and interaction.

CONNECTIONISM AND THE BRAIN

Connectionism

A more complex way to model human memory rather than a semantic network is to use the approach of **connectionism**. You have had small doses of this already, such as with word recognition in Chapter 3. At the most fundamental level, **connectionist models** (also known as **PDP models** and **neural net models**) contain a massive network of interconnected nodes. Depending on the model, the nodes can represent almost any kind of information, from simple line segments and patterns in letter recognition to more complex features and characteristics in semantic memory. What makes connectionist models attractive is that, in principle, they capture the essence of the neurological processes involved in semantic memory.

Examine Figure 7-9, a connectionist network for part of the "FURNISHING" category (Martindale, 1991). First, notice that each concept is connected to other nodes. The difference here is that each path has a number next to it. This is its weighting or strength. The weightings indicate how strongly or weakly connected two nodes are; generally, the weighting scale goes from +1.0 to −1.0, with positive

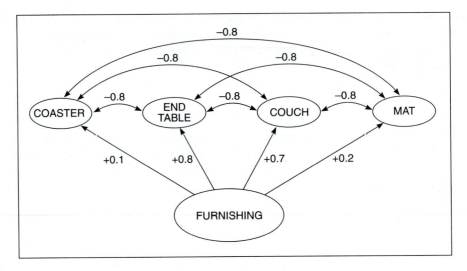

FIGURE 7-9 A small portion of a connectionist network. Note that the nodes at the same level exert an inhibitory influence on each other and receive different amounts of facilitation from the category name.

Based on Martindale (1991).

and negative numbers indicating facilitate and inhibition connections, respectively. So, for example, the weighting between "FURNISHING" and "END TABLE" is +0.8, indicating that "END TABLE" is a central member of the category; "COASTER," however, with its +0.1, is only weakly associated with "FURNISHING." In the area of semantic memory, there are many models of semantic priming (Masson, 1995) and a connectionist model of word meaning (McRae, de Sa, & Seidenberg, 1997).

The glimpse at connectionism here is very simplified. In many respects connectionist models are different from the older spreading activation models. An important distinction is that in a connectionist mode, a concept is defined as a pattern of activation across units in the network. Priming is explained by the similarity of activation patterns between a prime and a target: The "FURNISHING" concept has a similar pattern of activation to the pattern for "END TABLE," so the one serves as an effective prime for the other.

Connectionism and the Brain

What is exciting about connectionist models is that they gives us a tool for understanding the richness of cognition, a working "machine" that lets us see what happens when multiple layers of knowledge influence even the simplest acts of thought. Particularly compelling (Seidenberg, 1993) are four advantages of connectionist models. First, they are more similar to the network of neurons in the brain. The brain is a massive set of interconnected neurons, just as a connectionist network is a massive set of interconnected units. Second, the units are similar to those in the brain. In the nervous system, a neuron either fires or not; when it does fire, it affects the neurons it synapses on. This parallels to the fire/no-fire nature of connectionist units. Third, the positive and negative weights between units in connectionist models parallel excitatory and inhibitory neural synapses. Fourth, the activity of a connectionist model is massively parallel: Multiple processes are co-occurring in a model at various levels, much as there is parallel processing in the brain (McClelland, Rumelhart, & Hinton, 1986; Rumelhart, 1989).

A CONNECTIONIST MODEL OF SEMANTIC MEMORY IMPAIRMENT A puzzling disorder in semantic memory is a **category-specific deficit**. This is *a disruption in which the person loses access to one semantic category of words or concepts while not losing others*. Warrington and McCarthy (1983; also Warrington & Shallice, 1984) reported the case histories of four brain-damaged patients who showed this strange dissociation. The patients they described had difficulties identifying living things but not nonliving things (including artifacts—things that people make). For instance, patient J. B. R. could identify only 6% of pictures of living things, such as *parrot* and *daffodil,* and could define only 8% of the words that named living things. But when shown pictures of nonliving things, such as *tent* and *briefcase,* J. B. R. successfully named them 90% of the time and defined them 79% of the time.

How could semantic memory be splintered so that a person's categories of animate things is disrupted while categories of nonliving things is preserved? Or, more to the point, could semantic memory be structured to reveal these two very broad categories, living and nonliving things? Why this distinction, and not some other, such as concrete versus abstract, high versus low frequency, or something else?

Warrington and Shallice (1984) suggested a plausible explanation. Suppose that the bulk of your knowledge about living things is coded in semantic memory in terms of sensory properties: A parrot is a brightly colored animal that makes a distinctive sound. Likewise, most of what you know about nonliving things involves their function: A briefcase is for carrying around papers and books. Warrington and Shallice suggested that a reason for this dissociation could be a selective disruption to sensory knowledge in semantic memory. If so, that might explain the patients' impairments for living things.

Going a step further, Farah and McClelland (1991) built a connectionist model to evaluate the Warrington and Shallice hypothesis. In their model, semantic memory had two types of features about concepts—visual features (sensory) and functional features—with this knowledge being acquired by visual or verbal input. After constructing and training the model (establishing its memory, in a sense), Farah and McClelland "lesioned" it. That is, they "damaged" the visual units in semantic memory by altering the connection weights or disconnecting the visual units. The outcome was strikingly similar to the patients' dissociations. When the visual units were lesioned, the network had poor accuracy in associating names and pictures of living things; this is shown in the left panel of Figure 7-10, as is the modest decline in accuracy for the *nonliving things*. Conversely, when the network's functional units were lesioned instead, it was the *nonliving* category that suffered (right panel, Figure 7-10; for updates, see Cree & McRae, 2003, and Rogers et al., 2004).

Does this demonstration prove that impairment of patient J. B. R.'s visual semantic knowledge accounts for the dissociation? No; the model makes the correct prediction, a point in its favor, but this is not a proof that the model is correct. Instead, the demonstration asked, in essence, "Is it possible that impairment of sensory knowledge could produce the dissociation between living and nonliving things?" An answer is: "Yes, it is possible, because a dissociation is simulated in a connectionist model." In other words, the model provides a degree of assurance (probably a large degree) that the Warrington and Shallice hypothesis is reasonable and should be pursued further.

FIGURE 7-10 Performance of the basic model, as measured by probability of correctly associating names and pictures for living and nonliving things, after different amounts of damage to visual and functional semantic units.

SEMANTIC MEMORY LOSS There are other brain disorders that affect the part of semantic memory known as **lexical memory**, *the mental lexicon or dictionary where our word knowledge (as distinct from conceptual knowledge) is stored*. One is *a deficit in word finding*, known as **anomia** (or sometimes **anomic aphasia**). At a superficial level, anomia is like a tip-of-the-tongue (TOT) state in which you are unable to name the word even though you are certain you know it. However, whereas people in a TOT state generally have partial knowledge about the unrecallable word, such as the number of syllables or the first sound, anomic patients have no such partial knowledge. Instead, there is an inability to name a semantic concept that is otherwise successfully retrieved (Ashcraft, 1993; for work on everyday forgetting—temporary inhibition—in semantic memory, see Johnson & Anderson, 2004). That is, these people know and can use the concept—they just can't name it. For example, Kay and Ellis's (1987) anomic patient was unable to name the word *president* but, in attempting to find the word, blurted out "Government . . . leader . . . John Kennedy was one." Cases such as these suggest that the semantic memory of a concept is distinct from the memory its name, such that the concept can be retrieved but the name cannot.

Section Summary

- Connectionist approaches to memory allow one to simulate these processes in a way that is more analogous to how the brain does this.
- Connectionist approaches even furnish persuasive analyses of semantic disruptions caused by brain damage, so-called category-specific deficits.

SEMANTIC PRIMING

An important principle that has been touched on, and can be expanded on here, is the idea of the broad activation of concepts in semantic memory, namely **semantic priming**. This priming follows some basic principles, namely that (a) the priming process takes time, (b) the activation of primed concepts is smaller the more removed concepts are from the origin, and (c) the priming effect decays across time. Priming is a fundamental consequence of retrieval from semantic memory. It is one of the most frequently tested—and discussed (e.g., McNamara, 1992; Ratcliff & McKoon, 1988)—effects in long-term memory. It is *key* to understanding semantic memory. We return to it repeatedly throughout the book, so you need to understand priming, how it affects semantic memory, and how it has been studied.

Nuts and Bolts of Priming Tasks

Simulate
Ambiguous Figures in
MyPsychLab

In Chapter 2, priming was defined as the activation of concepts and their meanings. It is part of the automatic process observed in the Stroop task (name the color the word is printed in, not the color word itself), discussed in Chapter 4. Priming activates all kinds of concepts that express a joint meaning of several concepts together (e.g., Mathis, 2002; Peretz, Radeau, & Arguin, 2004).

Let's now go over how to set up a priming task. Figure 7-11 gives an illustration, and Table 7-2 gives an explanation. To begin with, we have the **prime**,

FIGURE 7-11   A depiction of two types of priming tasks.

TABLE 7-2	**Priming Tasks**

Essential Terminology

Prime: The stimulus or part of the stimulus that may have some effect; the prime can either be related to the target (e.g., "bird–robin"), unrelated (e.g., "truck–robin"), or neutral (e.g., "XXXXX–robin.")

Target: The stimulus or part of the stimulus expected to be affected by the prime.

Lag: The spacing between the prime and target in an across-trials priming task; for example, lag 2 means two trials came between the prime and target.

SOA: Stimulus onset asynchrony, the time interval between the prime and the target in a within-trial priming task, usually measured in milliseconds.

Priming Across Trials

Almost any recognition task (see Table 7-1) can be adapted to a priming task. Here, people respond to both the prime and the target. This critical measure is the influence of the processing of the prime on the processing of the target. Care must be taken so that an equal number of related targets are true and false so people are not biased to respond "yes." In some cases, the prime and target are separated by various intervals of time called the **stimulus onset asynchrony (SOA)**, which is *the length of time between the onset of the prime and the onset of the target.* If you think of the prime and target as two halves of a complete set, then the onset or beginning of the two halves occurs asynchronously, at different times. Thus, we might present a prime and 500 ms later present the target. This would be a 500-ms SOA.

Priming Within Trials

Some priming studies do not have the person respond to both the prime and the target, but only to the target after a prime has been presented. Thus, each trial has both a prime and a target. The prime is presented briefly and is followed by the target after some interval of time (SOA). In some studies, the prime is followed by a blank or unfilled (short) interval, and in some the prime is masked before the target is shown.

For both types of priming tasks, we have the following:

Dependent variables: The dependent variable generally is response time, assuming that the error rates for the different conditions are approximately equal. If accuracy is the primary dependent variable, then the hit rate and the false alarm rate are of interest. The hit rate is the proportion of true trials responded to correctly (saying "yes" to "yes trials") and the false alarm rate is the proportion of false trials responded to incorrectly (saying "yes" to "no trials").

Independent variables: Aside from different SOA intervals, major independent variables are the types and degrees of relationships between primes and targets. For instance, the prime could be a category name, and the targets would be either high or low typical category members.

which is *any item that is presented first,* to see whether it influences a later processing. The term is also used as a verb, as when we say that an item *primes* later information. Next is the **target**, *the item that follows the prime;* the target *is* that later information. It is the concept may be affected by the prime. So primes precede the targets, and targets are primed (i.e., are influenced by the primes).

When this influence is beneficial, for instance when the target is easier or faster to process, this *positive influence* is called **facilitation** or a **benefit**. Often, facilitation is a faster response time compared to performance in a baseline condition (when the prime and target are unrelated). Occasionally, the influence is negative, as when a prime is antagonistic to the target and so is irrelevant or misleading. When the prime impedes performance to the target, the *negative influence on processing* is called **inhibition** or a **cost**.

If we are interested the influence of priming over time and/or across trials, we need to keep track of the interval between the prime and the target. This is the **lag** between the prime and target, usually indexed as the *number of intervening stimuli.* For example, *lag 2* would mean that two trials came in between the prime and the target.

Empirical Demonstrations of Priming

Semantic priming generally reflects a temporary heightening of related concepts. Although most studies look at this decay of the influence of priming over a few seconds (e.g., Freedman & Loftus, 1971; Loftus & Loftus, 1974), there is evidence that prior exposure can facilitate performance even 17 years later (Mitchell, 2006), although the precise cause of this very, very long-term priming is not well known. Most priming tasks in cognitive psychology involve a lexical decision task, as described later, although some other tasks are used as well. For example, priming has been reported using sentence verification (Ashcraft, 1976). A sentence such as "A sparrow has feathers" facilitates another sentence about the same category, such as "A robin can fly" (see also Anaki & Henik, 2003).

As you read in Chapter 1, a workhorse task in cognitive science is **lexical decision**, in which *people judge whether a string of letters is a word* (remember MOTOR and MANTY?). Customarily, RT is the primary dependent variable. The name of the task comes from the word *lexicon,* meaning a dictionary or a list of words. So in a sense, the lexical decision task asks you whether the string of letters is an entry in your mental lexicon, your mental dictionary.

A huge range of topics has been investigated using lexical decision. The groundbreaking work was done by Meyer and Schvaneveldt (1971; also Meyer, Schvaneveldt, & Ruddy, 1975). What they did was present two letter strings at a time and told people to respond "yes" only if both were words. In addition to trials with unrelated words such as "TRUCK PAPER," they had trials with related pairs (there were an equal number of "yes" trials and "no" trials, the latter of which involved letter strings that were not a word, such as "CHAIR ZOOPLE"). Meyer and Schvaneveldt found that two related words such as "BREAD BUTTER" are judged more quickly as words than two unrelated words such as "NURSE BUTTER." Table 7-3 shows Meyer and Schvaneveldt's results and shows the priming effect clearly. Related words were judged in 855 ms, compared to 940 ms for unrelated words.

One interesting aspect of these results is that it is not logically necessary for people to access the meanings of words. Technically, they need only "look up" the words in the mental lexicon. Yet the results repeatedly show that it is the *meaningful* connection between "BREAD" and "BUTTER" that facilitates this decision, not some lexical connection (you might think because both begin with *B* that there is a lexical basis for the facilitation, but the same benefits are found for word pairs with dissimilar spellings, such as "NURSE DOCTOR").

TABLE 7-3 Priming in the Lexical Decision Task

Type of Stimulus Pair					
Top String	**Bottom String**	**Correct Response**	**Sample Stimuli**	**Mean RT (ms)**	**Mean % Errors**
Word	Related word	Yes	Nurse–doctor	855	6.3
Word	Unrelated word	Yes	Bread–doctor	940	8.7
Word	Nonword	No	Book–marb	1,087	27.6
Nonword	Word	No	Valt–butter	904	7.8
Nonword	Nonword	No	Cabe–manty	884	2.6

Source: From Meyer and Schvaneveldt (1971).

Automatic and Controlled Priming

This facilitation in priming appears to be automatic; that is, it happens rapidly and without intention (e.g., Smith, Bentin, & Spalek, 2001). When you see a word, you access its meaning automatically, even though you are not required to by the task, although semantic activation later may be redirected by conscious, deliberate efforts. But some priming may be more effortful and controlled. Here's an example. In a study by Neely (1977), people saw a letter string preceded either by a neutral prime (the letter X) in a baseline condition, or by a category name prime that was either related or unrelated to the target. For all trials, people had to judge whether the target string, the second member of a pair, was a word (lexical decision). Table 7-4 summarizes the study and shows sample stimuli. Because the results are a bit complicated, we'll take them in stages.

First, Neely found standard semantic priming. For prime–target trials such as "BIRD–robin," there was facilitation, as shown in the left panel of Figure 7-12 (notice that any point above the dashed line at 0 ms indicates facilitation, and any point below indicates inhibition). Because this speedup was found even at short

TABLE 7-4 Conditions and Stimuli for Neely's (1977) Study

Condition	Sample Stimulus[a]
No Category Shift Expected	
No shift	BIRD–robin
Shift	BIRD–arm
Category Shift Expected from "Building" to "Body Part"; from "Body" to "Part of a Building"	
No shift	BODY–heart, BUILDING–window
Shift to expected category	BODY–door, BUILDING–leg
Shift to unexpected category	BODY–sparrow

[a]Prime is in capital letters.

FIGURE 7-12 Reaction time to lexical decision targets. In the left half, people saw a prime and did not expect a shift in category; sample stimuli are "BIRD–robin" for a relevant prime and "BIRD–arm" for an irrelevant prime. In the right half, people expected the target to come from the building category if they saw "BODY" as a prime and from the body part category if they saw "BUILDING" as a prime. When the shift in category occurred as expected, RT was facilitated at longer SOAs. When the expected shift did not occur, there was facilitation at the short SOA when the prime was relevant ("BODY–heart"). Inhibition occurred when the shift was completely unexpected ("BODY–sparrow").

From Neely (1977).

SOAs, this suggests that normal semantic priming is automatic. Notice also that there is more facilitation as the SOA got longer. So, with more time to prepare, priming grew stronger.

Second, he found inhibition, a slow-down in RT, when the prime was unrelated to the target. If you had seen "BIRD" as a prime, you were then slower to decide that *arm* was a word. Not surprisingly, this inhibition effect grew stronger at longer SOAs: Again, the preparation for a member of the *bird* category worked against you when you saw *arm* as the target.

The impressive (and complicated) part of Neely's study comes next. He told people that when they saw one particular prime, such as the category name "BODY," they should expect a target from a *different* category, such as a part of a building (e.g., *door*). Likewise, if they saw "BUILDING" as a prime, they should expect to see a body part, such as *arm*, as the target. What happened then? When the switch from one category ("BODY") to a different one (*door*) happened, there was priming only at the long SOAs, as shown in the top right of Figure 7-12. This makes good sense; you see "BODY," and it takes you a bit of time to remember that you should see an item from the building category next. When you are given that bit of time, you are ready for *door, window,* and so on. But notice that at the shortest SOA, there was no facilitation. Clearly, at short SOAs there was not enough time to prepare for the category shift.

Finally, on a small proportion of trials, a category switch was expected but did not occur—that is, when you saw "BODY" but then saw *arm* or *heart* as the target. The clever thing about this is that it should tap into normal semantic priming because arm and heart are in the "BODY" category. This was what Neely found, but only at short SOAs. With longer SOAs, people prepared for the category to switch. Then, when that *didn't* happen, they were slowed, as shown in the bottom right panel of the figure.

Priming Is Implicit

Accessing a word's meaning is automatic (e.g., Friedrich, Henik, & Tzelgov, 1991). It occurs without conscious awareness of even having seen a word. Marcel (1980, 1983) presented primes immediately followed by a scrambled visual pattern, a visual mask. The purpose was to present the mask so soon after the prime that people were not consciously aware it at all, a form of backward masking (remember the circle marker study on visual sensory memory in Chapter 3?).

The manipulation worked. There was no conscious awareness of the prime. Yet related primes such as "CHILD" facilitated lexical decisions about words such as *infant*. Substantial work indicates that the effect is genuine (Hirshman & Durante, 1992; McRae & Boisvert, 1998). Semantic priming can occur automatically, without conscious identification of the prime. Thus, such effects are implicit and can occur without any involvement of conscious awareness. Indeed, (implicit) priming effects can be observed in ERP patterns from cortical recordings (e.g., Heil, Rolke, & Pecchinenda, 2004), or even when the people have lost the (explicit) ability to recall information consciously (i.e., in cases of amnesia, as in Levy, Stark, & Squire, 2004; see Schacter & Badgaiyan, 2001, for a readable introduction to neuroimaging results on priming).

Section Summary

- In a priming task, a prime is presented first, and RT to the target is measured. When the prime is related, RT to the target usually is faster, even at short time intervals (SOAs). This is evidence that semantic priming is automatic.
- Priming is an implicit memory process, although conscious processes can alter it later on.

SCHEMATA AND SCRIPTS

Now that we've set out some basics of semantic memory, let's move on to a more specific way of using general knowledge. We often use world knowledge to understand the events and circumstances that we encounter. We start out by looking at memory for a story. Table 7-5 contains a story called "The War of the Ghosts." The story is important both because of the psychological points it raises, but also for historical reasons: Bartlett (1932) used it in one of the earliest studies

TABLE 7-5 Bartlett's (1932) "The War of the Ghosts"

Read the following, then attempt to reproduce the story by writing it down from memory.

One night two young men from Egulac went down to the river to hunt seals, and while they were there it became foggy and calm. Then they heard war-cries, and they thought: "Maybe this is a war-party." They escaped to the shore, and hid behind a log. Now canoes came up, and they heard the noise of paddles, and saw one canoe coming up to them. There were five men in the canoe, and they said:

"What do you think? We wish to take you along. We are going up the river to make war on the people."

One of the young men said: "I have no arrows."

"Arrows are in the canoe," they said.

"I will not go along. I might be killed. My relatives do not know where I have gone. But you," he said turning to the other, "may go with them."

So one of the young men went, but the other returned home.

And the warriors went on up the river to a town on the other side of Kalama. The people came down to the water, and they began to fight, and many were killed. But presently the young man heard one of the warriors say: "Quick, let us go home: that Indian has been hit." Now he thought: "Oh, they are ghosts." He did not feel sick, but they said he had been shot.

So the canoes went back to Egulac, and the young man went ashore to his house and made a fire. And he told everybody and said: "Behold I accompanied the ghosts, and we went to fight. Many of our fellows were killed, and many of those who attacked us were killed. They said I was hit, and I did not feel sick."

He told it all, and then he became quiet. When the sun rose he fell down. Something black came out of his mouth. His face became contorted. The people jumped up and cried.

He was dead.

---

of remembering meaningful material. Do the demonstration in the table now, before reading further.

Now that you have read and recalled the story, spend a moment jotting down some of the thoughts that occurred to you as you read and then tried to recall it. For example, if you remembered some specific details, comment on what made those details memorable. Did you get most of the story line correct, or did you do some guessing? What was your sense of the story as you read it? You no doubt reflected on how peculiar the story was, with unfamiliar names and characters, vague and hard-to-understand twists of the story line, and unexplainable events. The story is a North Pacific Indian (Eskimo) folktale, so it is not surprising that it differs so much from other stories with which you are familiar.

Now, look at Table 7-6 and compare your recalled version with those retellings. Although your version may be closer to the original, because so little time passed between reading and recalling, you should be able to see points of similarity to the tabled retellings.

Bartlett's Research

Bartlett (1932), like Ebbinghaus, wanted to study memory experimentally. Very much unlike Ebbinghaus, however, he wanted to study memory for *meaningful* material, so he used folktales, ordinary prose, and pictures. His typical method

TABLE 7-6   Two Retellings of Bartlett's (1932) "The War of the Ghosts"

First recall, attempted about 15 min after hearing the story:

Two young men from Egulac went out to hunt seals. They thought they heard war-cries, and a little later they heard the noise of the paddling of canoes. One of these canoes, in which there were five natives, came forward towards them. One of the natives shouted out: "Come with us: we are going to make war on some natives up the river." The two young men answered: "We have no arrows." "There are arrows in our canoes," came the reply. One of the young men then said: "My folk will not know where I have gone"; but, turning to the other, he said: "But you could go." So the one returned whilst the other joined the natives.

The party went up the river as far as a town opposite Kalama, where they got on land. The natives of that part came down to the river to meet them. There was some severe fighting, and many on both sides were slain. Then one of the natives that had made the expedition up the river shouted: "Let us return: the Indian has fallen." Then they endeavored to persuade the young man to return, telling him that he was sick, but he did not feel as if he were. Then he thought he saw ghosts all round him.

When they returned, the young man told all his friends of what had happened. He described how many had been slain on both sides.

It was nearly dawn when the young man became very ill; and at sunrise a black substance rushed out of his mouth, and the natives said one to another: "He is dead."

Second recall, attempted about 4 months later:

There were two men in a boat, sailing towards an island. When they approached the island, some natives came running towards them, and informed them that there was fighting going on on the island, and invited them to join. One said to the other: "You had better go. I cannot very well, because I have relatives expecting me, and they will not know what has become of me. But you have no one to expect you." So one accompanied the natives, but the other returned.

Here there is a part I can't remember. What I don't know is how the man got to the fight. However, anyhow the man was in the midst of the fighting, and was wounded. The natives endeavored to persuade the man to return, but he assured them that he had not been wounded.

I have an idea that his fighting won the admiration of the natives.

The wounded man ultimately fell unconscious. He was taken from the fighting by the natives.

Then, I think it is, the natives describe what happened, and they seem to have imagined seeing a ghost coming out of his mouth. Really it was kind of materialisation of his breath. I know this phrase was not in the story, but that is the idea I have. Ultimately the man died at dawn the next day.

had people study material for a period of time, then recall it several times, once shortly after study and again at later intervals. By comparing successive recalls, Bartlett examined the progressive changes in what people remembered.

Using these methods, Bartlett found that memory for meaningful material is not especially reproductive, that is, it does not strictly reproduce the original passage. Instead, Bartlett characterized this remembering as "an effort after meaning." The modern term for this is **reconstructive memory**, in which *we construct a memory by combining elements from the original together with existing knowledge.*

Two notable aspects of Bartlett's results led him to this conclusion. The first concerns omissions, information people failed to recall. For the most part, people did not recall many story details, either specific names (e.g., Egulac) or events (e.g., the phrase "His face became contorted"). The level of recall for the main plot and sequence of events was not too bad, but minor events often were omitted. As a result, the retellings are shorter than the original.

A second aspect was a tendency for the successive recalls to normalize and rationalize the story. That is, people added to and altered it by adding material that was not in the original (the island mentioned after four months, for example). These changes often made the story more "normal." Because the story was strange to Bartlett's readers, his friends and colleagues in Great Britain, their retellings modernized and demystified the original. For example, note how the ghost theme becomes less prominent in the two retellings in Table 7-6, even though *ghosts* is in the title of the story. What is fascinating is the *source* of the additional material. Where did it come from, if not from the story? It came from the people's semantic memories.

Schemata

Bartlett borrowed the idea of a **schema** to explain these adjustments and additions (although he complained about the vagueness of the term). A schema is *a mental framework or body of knowledge about some topic.* Bartlett claimed that when we encounter new material, such as the "Ghosts" story, we try to relate it to something we already know, to existing schemata (the plural of "schema"). If the material does not match an existing schema, then we tend to alter the memory to make it fit. So, recall is not an exact reproduction of the original material, but a reconstruction based on elements from the original story and on existing schemata.

The use of semantic knowledge, such as schemata, to fill in our knowledge with more expected information can sometimes lead to errors. When unusual bits of information are encountered, a person's schema may dominate cognitive processing, leading a person to make errors that, when caught, reveals this powerful influence. Questions such as 19 and 20,

(19) How many animals of each kind did Moses take onto the ark?

(20) What is the nationality of Thomas Edison, inventor of the telephone?

show the semantic errors that can crop up. Read sentences 19 and 20 again, if you didn't notice the semantic illusion (Erickson & Mattson, 1981; Reder & Kusbit, 1991). The reason we fall for the illusion, and not immediately notice what is wrong with the sentence, should be clear: It's another illustration of the power of schemata on cognition and conceptually driven processing.

Subsequent research fleshed out our understanding of schemata. For example, knowledge of the theme or topic of a passage improves people's memory of the passage (Bransford & Johnson, 1972; Dooling & Lachman, 1971). On the other hand, providing a theme, say by attaching a title to a story, can also distort recall or recognition in the direction of the theme.

A demonstration of this distortion was provided by Sulin and Dooling (1974). One group of people read a paragraph about a fictitious character: "Gerald Martin's seizure of power. Gerald Martin strove to undermine the existing government to satisfy his political ambitions. Many of the people of his country supported his efforts" (P. 256). A second group read the same paragraph, but the name *Adolf*

Simulate
Schemata in
MyPsychLab

Hitler was substituted for *Gerald Martin*. After a five-minute waiting period, people were shown a list of sentences and had to indicate whether each was from the original story or not. Pre-experimental knowledge led to significant distortions in memory. People who read the Hitler paragraph rated sentences as "the same" more frequently when they matched their existing knowledge, even though the original passage did not contain such items (e.g., "Hitler was obsessed by the desire to conquer the world," P. 259). Furthermore, these thematic distortions grew stronger one week after reading the story.

This effect was particularly striking in a second experiment. One group read an account of Carol Harris: "Carol Harris was a problem child from birth. She was wild, stubborn, and violent." Only 5% of the people said "yes" when asked if the sentence "She was deaf, dumb, and blind" was part of the passage. In a contrasting group, the same paragraph was given, but the name *Helen Keller* was used. Fully 50% of these people said "yes" to the same critical question.

In general, the more expertise a person has, the more elaborate their schemata are. Although schemata can be helpful at encoding, by directing attention to what is and is not relevant, helping organize that knowledge, and so on, there are also some pitfalls. For example, experts have a greater tendency to classify individual experiences in terms of their schemata. As a result, they are less likely to actually remember individual events (Castel, McCabe, Roediger, & Heitman, 2007).

Note that schemata are not just for linguistic information, but for any commonly experienced aspects of one's culture. As just one illustration of this, a study by Curtis and Bharucha (2009) looked at memory for music. They had people listen to melodies in a familiar (Western) or unfamiliar (Indian) mode, and then had people indicate whether a test tone was in the just-heard melody. What they found was that people's memory for the melody was biased based on their cultural schemata for different kinds of music that they had been exposed to.

Scripts

One specific type of schema captures the order in which events occur. These are called **scripts**, *the semantic knowledge that guides our understanding of ordered events*. For example, consider the knowledge you have that guides your comprehension of even a simple story:

> *Billy was excited about the invitation to his friend's birthday party. But when he went to his room and shook his piggy bank, it didn't make a sound. "Hmm," he thought to himself, "maybe I can borrow some from Mom."*

SCRIPTS IN MEMORY Think for a moment about the common meaning of the word *script*: the dialogue and actions that are performed by actors and actresses in a play. The script for a play details what is supposed to happen on stage. Similarly, a mental script is a general knowledge about ordinary events and situations. In

PROVE IT
Schematic Distortion

This aim of this prove it section is to give an opportunity to observe how schemata can distort memory for a text, and how to overcome that distortion. This demonstration is based on a study reported by Hasher and Griffin (1978). Essentially, what we are looking for here are things that people recall from a text, but which were never actually mentioned—that is, information that would be in a person's schema, but not what they actually read. What you should do is get two groups of people. Have them all read the story below. Tell each group that this story is called "The Escaped Convict." After some period of time has elapsed (at least 10 minutes), ask your groups to recall the story. For one group, remind them that the title of the story was "The Escaped Convict." However, for the other group of people, act all flustered and tell them that you screwed up, and that the actual title of the story was "The Deer Hunter."

After people are done, look at what they have recalled. One thing you should find is that people in the repeated title group should recall details about an escaped convict that weren't actually in the story. This illustrates how a schema can distort memory to make it more schema consistent. The other thing is that people in the title switch group should have fewer intrusions of new information having to do with either the escaped convict or deer hunter themes. If so, then what you've done is make memory more accurate by discrediting the schema in semantic memory, and leading people to rely more on their episodic memory of what they actually read.

The Escaped Convict/The Deer Hunter

The man walked carefully through the forest. Several times he looked over his shoulder and scrutinized the woods behind him. He trod carefully trying to avoid snapping twigs and small branches that lay in his path, for he did not want to create excess noise. The chirping of the birds in the trees almost annoyed him, their loud calls serving to distract him. He did not want to confuse those sounds with the type he was listening for.

Source: Hasher & Griffin (1978).

other words, a script mentally represents what is supposed to happen in a particular circumstance. Are you going to a restaurant? Your script tells you what to expect, the order of events, who the central characters are, and what you and they are supposed to do. Are you invited to a birthday party, taking an airplane flight, or sitting in a class on human memory and cognition? Your general knowledge of what happens in these settings guides your comprehension as the events unfold, and leads to certain expectations.

The theory behind scripts is straightforward. People have a generalized memory of experienced events, and this is invoked, or retrieved, when a new experience matches an old script. One function of a script is to provide a kind of shorthand for the whole event; you need not describe every element of the event but can refer to the whole by invoking the script. More important, the script provides a framework within which new experiences are understood and within which a variety of inferences can be drawn to complete your understanding (Abbot, Black, & Smith, 1985; Reiser, Black, & Abelson, 1985; Seifert, Robertson, & Black, 1985).

Let's develop this idea of scripts with a few examples. Consider the following abbreviated stories (taken or adapted from Schank & Abelson, 1977, PP. 38–40):

> *(9) John went to a restaurant. He asked for a hamburger. He paid the check and left.*

> *(10) John went to a restaurant. He asked the waiter for a hamburger. He paid the check and left.*

> *(11) John went into the restaurant. He ordered a Big Mac. He paid for it and then ate it while driving to work.*

For Schank and Abelson (1977), understanding stories 9 and 10 is guided by scripted knowledge of a particular situation: going to restaurants. Story 11 is understood by a particular variant or track. Schank and Abelson claimed that we have a large number of scripts in memory. The average adult, having experienced many different instances of eating in restaurants, has a script of this situation. Whenever we encounter a story like 9, elements of the story trigger or activate the appropriate script. As a consequence, all subsequent events in the story (or in a real-world experience) are interpreted with reference to the script in memory.

Consider another longer story (from Abelson, 1981):

> *(12) John was feeling very hungry as he entered the restaurant. He settled himself at a table and noticed that the waiter was nearby. Suddenly, however, he realized that he'd forgotten his reading glasses.*

Although this story does not necessarily call up any particular track of the restaurant script, it does illustrate some of the interpretive power of scripts. Almost all readers (or listeners) understand John's problem as "unable to read the menu." It matters little that "the menu" or even "a menu" was never mentioned. The restaurant script is activated, which in turn activates a whole set of **frames**, *details about events within the script*. This prepares you to receive specific information about those frames. When a detail comes along, such as "the waiter," that detail is stored in the appropriate frame. If it does not come along (e.g., "the menu"), it is inferred from the script. Your comprehension then proceeds normally after "forgotten his reading glasses" because the unmentioned "thing you read in a restaurant" is supplied by the script.

In script terminology, the menu is a **default value**, *the common, typical value or concept that occurs in the script*. In the restaurant script, the default value "MENU" is the ordinary way that people find out what is available to eat. Thus unmentioned details in the story are filled in by the default values. So, a storyteller does not need to mention every little detail. We can assume that the missing details will be supplied from the stored script.

PREDICTIONS Figure 7-13 presents a generic restaurant script. If you have such a script, this enables you to understand and predict the various events in the sequence. A person with different experiences, however, may have difficulties understanding what is going on—for example, a small child who has only been to fast food restaurants. Thus, comprehension should suffer to the degree that your current experience mismatches your script.

Sample Restaurant Script

- Open door
- Wait to be seated
- Go to table
- Be seated
- Look at menu
- Order meal
- Meal arrives
- Eat food
- Finish meal
- Order dessert
- Ask for bill
- Bill arrives
- Pay bill
- Leave tip
- Get coat
- Leave

FIGURE 7-13 A depiction of a standard restaurant script. Based on Schank and Abelson (1977). A small portion of a connectionist network. Note that the nodes at the same level exert an inhibitory influence on each other and receive different amounts of facilitation from the category name.

Adapted from Martindale (1991).

A well-known example of processing difficulties is shown in the story in Table 7-7 (Bransford, 1979); be sure to try to understand the story before you read the explanation at the bottom of the table. As this passage shows, a story may activate a script but mismatch the expected events in it, producing difficulties in comprehension and recall.

So, recall of a story is influenced not just by the details that were mentioned, but also by the details that were inferred based on a script. For example, in the story about Billy and the birthday party, didn't you read "Maybe I can borrow some money from Mom"? (Answer: No, you didn't.) Likewise, if we developed a longer restaurant story, you might "recall" that the customer left a tip, even though no tip was ever mentioned. Where do the "money from Mom" and the "tip" come

TABLE 7-7   Restaurant Episode with Explanation

Jim went into the restaurant and asked to be seated in the gallery. He was told that there would be a one-half hour wait. Forty minutes later, the applause for his song indicated that he could proceed with the preparation. Twenty guests had ordered his favorite, a cheese soufflé.

Jim enjoyed the customers in the main dining room. After two hours, he ordered the house specialty—roast pheasant under glass. It was incredible to enjoy such exquisite cuisine and yet still have fifteen dollars. He would surely come back soon.

Assume, therefore, that Jim went to a special type of restaurant. The owner allows people who can cook at least one special meal to compete for the honor of preparing their specialty for other customers. Those who wish to compete sit in the gallery rather than the main dining room (although a central stage is accessible to both).

The competition centers on the competitor's entertaining the crowd, by singing, for example, or dancing or playing an instrument. The approval of the crowd is a prerequisite for allowing the person to announce his or her cooking specialty. The rest of the crowd then has the option of ordering it, and the person receives a certain amount of money for each meal prepared. After cooking and serving the meal, the person can then order from the regular restaurant menu and pay for it out of the money received for cooking. In general, this arrangement benefits the manager as well as the person. The manager obtains relatively inexpensive entertainment, and the person is usually able to make more than enough money to pay for an excellent meal.

Source: From Bransford (1979).

from? They come from your script, from your long-term semantic knowledge. And, importantly, such "recall" reflects reconstructive memory.

Evidence of Scripts

Evidence for people's use of scripts has been reported by a variety of researchers (Bower, Black, & Turner, 1979; Graesser, 1981; Graesser & Nakamura, 1982; Long, Golding, Graesser, & Clark, 1990; Maki, 1989). The work by Smith and Graesser (1981) is a good representative of such data. Smith and Graesser were studying the role of typicality or relevance of events and actions in people's memory for script-based passages: Do we remember predictable events and actions better than unpredictable ones, or is it the other way around? They gave 10 passages to people, each one related to a different scripted activity (e.g., taking the dog to the vet, washing a car, cleaning an apartment), and tested them with a recall or recognition task. Tests were done 30 minutes after people heard the passages, then again after 2 days, 1 week, and 3 weeks.

What made Smith and Graesser's study so compelling was the care they took in constructing their passages. Stories mentioned both script typical and atypical actions; Smith and Graesser collected norms to know what is typical and what is not. In their standard analyses of recall and recognition, typical information was remembered better than atypical information. These scores, however, were then corrected for guessing because the high accuracy on typical information probably included both events that were genuinely remembered as well as events that were reconstructed from the script knowledge.

When the scores were corrected, recall and recognition were higher for atypical than typical events. In other words, in a story about taking the dog to the vet, people had more accurate memory for the unusual, atypical events (e.g., "While waiting for the vet, Jack dropped his car keys"). Typical events, those anticipated by the script (e.g., "Jack led the dog into the waiting room"), were recalled more poorly. Thus memory conformed to a schema-copy-plus-tag hypothesis: You store a copy of the generic script as your main memory for the story and tag onto that generic script the specific, atypical details that occurred (Graesser, 1981; Schutzwohl, 1998).

Hannigan and Reinitz (2001) studied a somewhat different script effect—cause and effect. They introduced manipulations into the scripted stories that corresponded either to a cause of an event or to an effect of some event. For example, in a slide sequence that depicted going grocery shopping, some people saw a woman taking an orange from the bottom of a pile of oranges—but they didn't see the pile of oranges rolling to the floor. In a different condition, people saw the oranges on the floor, but not the slide showing the woman taking the orange from the pile. In other words, some people saw the cause (pull an orange from the bottom), and some saw only the effect (oranges on the floor). Their script-guided comprehension, however, made up for causes they didn't see. That is, when they saw the effect, they mistakenly judged new cause scenes (i.e., never seen before) as "old"—if you've seen the oranges on the floor, you're more likely to remember later on that you saw the woman pulling an orange from the bottom of the pile. In terms of script knowledge, and what we generally know to be true about cause and effect, remembering the woman pulling an orange from the bottom of the pile is understandable—after all, *something* had to cause the oranges to fall to the floor. (See Hannigan & Reinitz, 2003, for evidence that an object from one scripted scene, say a vase of flowers in a restaurant, can "migrate" to a different restaurant memory.)

Section Summary

- Through his early work with materials such as "The War of the Ghosts," Bartlett developed a schema theory. From this view, schemata are generalized knowledge structures, as are semantic memories, that people use as guides for common experiences. Schemata can help organize information to facilitate learning, but can also cause people to misremember information in a more schema-consistent fashion.
- Scripts are representations of ordered events, such as going to a restaurant or attending a birthday party.
- Script theories make predictions about comprehension and retrieval and provide a useful way to explain how people understand and interact with the real world, including how people can "remember" events because they are consistent with a stored script.

CONCEPTS AND CATEGORIZATION

Let's look at another area of study that addresses semantic relatedness, namely the structure of concepts and categories in semantic memory.

Theories of Categorization

As you move about the world, you interact with a wide range of entities—objects, people, events, and so on. In many cases, the particular entities you are dealing with may be novel to you. For example, when walking down the street, you may come across a particular squirrel you've never encountered before. Will it attack you? Is it food? Will it run away? Will this squirrel make a good pet? What does it eat? How does it reproduce and raise its young? Can it vote in an election? You know what it is likely to do, and how you should interact with it, by using your categorical knowledge of what a squirrel is. Categories are aspects of semantic memory that allow us to predict what is likely to happen in new encounters. Essentially, when you use categories you treat individual members as if they were more or less the same (all squirrels are pretty much alike, after all). This allows you to save a lot of time and mental effort. While this is a benefit in most situations, categorization can have a few draw-backs, such as when we overextend our categories, for example using stereotypes (which are a kind of category) to draw conclusions about people we hardly even know.

CLASSIC VIEW OF CATEGORIZATION There are three general classes of theories of categorization that we cover. These are the classic view, probabilistic theories, and explanation-based theories. Note that each of these has strong points for how people create and use their categories, and they all also have weaknesses.

The **classic view of categorization** (e.g., Bruner, Goodnow, & Austin, 1956) takes the view that *people create and use categories based on a system of rules*. That is, if something satisfies a set of rules, then it is a member of a category, but if it does not, then it isn't. Of critical importance is that the rules identify *necessary* and *sufficient* features for something to be in a category. For example, the category BACHELOR can be defined as an unmarried adult male. These features are necessary in that if they are not present, the person is not a bachelor. A person who is a married adult male would not qualify, nor would an unmarried male child, or an unmarried adult female (although she could be a bachelorette). These features are also sufficient in that nothing more is needed to identify a bachelor. For example, a person's occupation, the kind of car they drive, how tall they are, how many legs they have—are all features that may be present, but do not contribute to identifying the category beyond the sufficient ones.

The classic view of categorization follows on scientific taxonomies, such as the definition of what makes an animal a member of a species. This is the type of classification that allows us to identify a bat as a mammal rather than a bird, a penguin as a bird rather than an amphibian, and a chimpanzee as an ape rather than a monkey. It is quite clear that people can create and use categories defined by necessary and sufficient rules. When given novel stimuli, people can readily derive the features that define a category. The more important question is whether this is how semantic memory derives and uses categories. That is, is this a psychologically real way of describing human categorization? There is a great deal of evidence to suggest that it is not. Before turning to other theories, let's cover some important aspects of human categorization.

CHARACTERISTICS OF HUMAN CATEGORIES So, if semantic memory doesn't typically use necessary and sufficient rules or features to create categories, what are human categories like? One of the clearest things is that the categories in semantic memory are loose and fuzzy. That is, members vary in how good examples of that category are. This is called *graded membership*. For example, take the category BIRD. The zoological taxonomy of what makes a creature a bird is fairly clear. But if you stop to think about it, some birds are "better" birds than others. Most people agree that robins, sparrows, hawks, and cardinals are better examples of the BIRD category than penguins, chickens, ostriches, and flamingos. Thus, there is some variability in the degree to which members belong to a category. We can even say things like "*loosely speaking*, a bat is a bird, although *technically* it is a mammal." The use of these linguistic hedges indicates that the boundaries of a category are not fixed. As another example, for the category FRUIT, apples, peaches, oranges, and pears are good examples, whereas coconuts, tomatoes, cucumbers, and walnuts are not such good members. So, loosely speaking, tomatoes are vegetables, but technically, they are fruits. Also, technically coconuts aren't nuts, they're seeds.

The amazing thing about graded category membership is that people show evidence of this principle even for categories that are clearly defined by necessary and sufficient rules. In a study by Armstrong, Gleitman, and Gleitman (1983), people showed evidence of graded category membership for the categories EVEN NUMBER and ODD NUMBER. People said that 4 is a better member of the category

EVEN NUMBER than 28! Thus, graded category membership is a fundamental principle of human categorization in semantic memory.

There are some other principles of categorization related to graded membership. The first is the idea that categories have a **central tendency**. That is, *there is some mental core or center to the category where the best members are found.* This is related to the idea of **typicality effects**, presented in the Smith et al. model of semantic memory discussed earlier. So, categories reflect **typicality**, *the degree to which items are viewed as typical, central members of a category.* In general, the time to make category judgments depends on how typical or central an item is in a category. The typicality of category members is reflected in *category norms*, originally developed by Battig and Montague (1969) and more recently updated by Van Overschelde, Rawson, and Dunlosky (2004), in which people listed members of various categories. The norms showed that some items are listed as members of a category more frequently than others, such as listing *robin* more frequently as a member of the bird category (85%) than *chicken* (9%).

One clever study of typicality was reported by Rips (1975). In this study, people read a story about an island inhabited by only eight species: sparrows, robins, eagles, hawks, ducks, geese, ostriches, and bats. Some people read that a highly contagious disease had been discovered among all the sparrows; others read that the robins had the disease, others that eagles were affected, and so on. People were then asked to estimate the percentages of the other animals that would also contract the disease. Importantly, people's estimates yielded evidence of typicality. Species that are rated as more typical, such as sparrows, were judged very likely to infect almost all the other species. Atypical members, such as geese, were judged likely to infect only other atypical members—ducks, for instance—and this to a lesser degree. The underlying issue is typicality. People assumed that if a typical instance had a property, then that was sufficient to predict that all instances, typical and atypical, would share the property. However, if the property was true of an atypical instance, people doubted that it would be shared throughout the category.

The typicality or centrality of a category member depends in part on the number of attributes it shares with other members, with more central members having a greater number of typical features (Rosch, 1978; Rosch & Mervis, 1975). Thus, although different members of a category may or may not have certain features, they all share a **family resemblance**. That is, there is a set of features that many or most of the category members have, although all features may not be present in all members. Think of your own family—various members have different combinations of the features that are found across the different individuals.

Finally, related to the family resemblance principle is the idea that real-world features do not occur independently of one another. Instead, they come in bundles: for example, the things in the real world that have wings often have beaks, too. We structure our mental categories in terms of these **correlated attributes**. These factors, correlated features and typicality, play a major role in the organization of semantic memory (McRae et al., 1997).

So, in short, there are a number of aspects of how people create and use categories that are inconsistent with the classic view of categorization. Qualities such as typicality, family resemblance, and correlated attributes are inconsistent with the idea that categories are defined by necessary and sufficient features. In the next few sections, we look at some other theories of human categorization that are more flexible and allow for categories that have these characteristics.

PROBABILISTIC THEORIES OF CATEGORIZATION Some of the theories that have been developed beyond the classic view are **probabilistic theories**. These assume that categories in semantic memory take into account various probabilities and likelihoods across a person's experience.

One way of making categories probabilistically is by using a **prototype**, which is essentially the *central, core instance of a category*. A prototype is an average of all of your experiences with members of a category. Imagine taking many pictures of many types of dogs, and then morphing all of those images together. That average would be a prototype. Note that the prototype is an idealized representation that probably does not correspond to any individual member. For a prototype view, our mental categories are represented with reference to the prototype, with typical members stored close to the prototype and peripheral members stored farther away. Again, when you think of a *dog*, your prototype is less likely to be like a Chihuahua but instead is more like a German shepherd, a golden retriever, or some other more "doggy dog." Similarly, for your *bird* category, the prototype is a rather ordinary, typical, nondescript bird, and the *flower* category would be a generic flower.

Although the idea that people use prototypes is appealing, there are some aspects of human categories that are not captured by a prototype, such as category size variability, correlated attributes, and anything else about the category that requires a person to consider the category as a whole. A prototype cannot do this because it is a mental representation of the average of the category members, not the variation among them. Another idea for how people use probabilistic information to create and use categories is **exemplar theory**, which assumes that when people think about categories, they *mentally take into account each experience, instance or example, of the encounters they have had with members of that category* (e.g., Medin, Goldstone, & Gentner, 1993; Murphy & Medin, 1985; Nosofsky, 1986; Rips, 1989; Rips & Collins, 1993). Thus, an "exemplar" is, basically, an example—robin is an exemplar of the bird category. Exemplar theory, in contrast to prototype theory, suggests that we store exemplars in memory, then make category judgments by comparing the object to be classified to the stored exemplars.

Notice that both approaches make the same or similar predictions—prototype theory predicts that a typical example is judged rapidly because it is highly similar to the prototype, and exemplar theory says it's because the typical example resembles so many of the stored exemplars. Because of this similarity, it is difficult to distinguish between these two views, although there have been attempts to do so (e.g., Feldman, 2003; Rehder, 2003). Chin-Parker and Ross (2004) have shown how multiple classification schemes are possible, either prototype- or exemplar-based, depending on how people are mentally oriented and process information. They oriented people to either "diagnostic" features (necessary features) or "prototypical" features (typical, but not necessary features) in a learning task. The results showed that a category could be learned in either way, but people showed sensitivity only to the kind of feature they used during learning. In other words, if they learned via the diagnostic features, they did not show sensitivity to the prototype, and likewise for the other group—learning via prototypes, then showing no sensitivity to diagnostic features (for work on slower reasoning and decision making in this type of task, see Ross & Murphy, 1999, and Yamauchi & Markman, 2000).

So, probabilistic theories move beyond the classic view by assuming people average across their experiences, and with the need to derive hard and fast rules about what is and is not in a category. Moreover, there is fMRI imaging evidence to suggest that different brain regions are involved depending on whether people are deriving categories using rules (consistent with the classic view) or based on the similarity of the items (consistent with the probabilistic views). For example, rule-based categorization appears to involve brain regions implicated in cognitive control, such as regions of the frontal lobes, whereas similarity-based categorization appears to involve regions implicated in the configural processing of perceptual images (e.g., Grossman et al., 2002). Apart from the neuroimaging evidence, the prototype and exemplar probabilistic views capture the flexibility of semantic memory to understand and appropriately interact with all kinds of new instances or category members that we encounter in our experiences in the world.

EXPLANATION-BASED THEORIES   There is no question that probabilistic theories do a good job at capturing human categorization. However, there are also a few issues that they have trouble with. For one, there is a circularity problem. Specifically, how does memory know which experiences to average across to form a category without knowing what the category is ahead of time?

Another issue is the high degree of flexibility of semantic categories. For example, think of the category "Things to take out of a burning building." You can generate a category on the fly, so to speak, that has all of the qualities of more traditional categories, such as birds, tools, or fruits. These **ad hoc categories** are created based on situational circumstances and have characteristics of regular categories (Barsalou, 1983). Ad hoc categories have a graded structure (e.g., a baby is a better member of this category than a television set), have a prototype (e.g., a highly valued, irreplaceable thing that can be damaged by fire), exhibit typicality effects (e.g., the family dog would be highly typical, but a visiting neighbor is something that most people are unlikely to list), and so on.

These points have led to a theory of semantic classification called **explanation-based theories**. For these views semantic categories are essentially theories of the world we create to explain why things are the way they are. This highlights the important aspect of categories that they are structures we impose on the world, structures that may or may not reflect how the world actually is. For example, *shoe* is in the same category as *brick*, but in a different category than *sock*, if your category is "Things to pound a nail with if you don't have a hammer." This is because we have a theory about what makes something good to hammer a nail with, and can then apply this to the world around us. People can use their understanding of the causal relations among category members to make inferences about the internal structure and functioning of other members of a category (Rehder & Burnett, 2005).

Explanation-based theories are also reflected in findings that show the influence of embodied cognition on the use of semantic concepts. A study by Borghi, Glenberg, and Kaschak (2004) clearly makes this point. In this study, people indicated whether words corresponded to parts of an object, such as a car. Importantly, before this people read a sentence that encouraged them to take a particular perspective, such as either "You are driving a car" (inside) or "You are washing a car" (outside). The results showed that response times to names of parts were faster when they conformed to the person's perspective. So, people who were told to imagine they were driving a car responded faster to parts that were in the interior of the car (e.g., speedometer) than the parts on the exterior (e.g., trunk), whereas the reverse was true for the other perspective. Thus, people can take an embodied perspective during semantic memory retrieval, and this can influence the ease with which they retrieve information.

Another explanation-based categorization idea is that people treat categories by following the principle of **psychological essentialism** (Medin, 1989), in which they *treat members of a category as if they have the same underlying, perhaps invisible, property or essence.* In some cases, this corresponds to something real, such as the chemical composition of a liquid, the DNA of an animal, or the water content of different cloud formations. Other times, these essences are strictly psychologically imposed. For example, there is no underlying essence that makes an object a member of the category TOOL. Tools vary widely in their shape, size, components, and so forth. Yet, they all seem to have a certain "tool-ness" that we "recognize." The basic point of psychological essentialism is that people are making decisions about how to categorize things not just on how they look or how they use them, but also based on their beliefs, right or wrong, about the members of a category. This is related to why you may view people who are members of one particular social group as being distinct from another (e.g., if you think to yourself "There is just something about the girls in my sorority that sets them apart").

The nature of these psychological essences also explains why people view some things as possible in the world, but not others. Take the distinction between natural kinds and artifacts (things people make). With natural kinds, such as animals, plants, or natural substances, it is hard to imagine transforming one thing into another. For example, people are unwilling to accept the idea that painting stripes on a donkey can transform it into a zebra. The psychological essence of donkey-ness is impervious to changing the appearance of the animal. However, with artifacts, the things that people make, it is easier to imagine transforming one thing into another. For example, people are more willing to accept that idea that by painting numbers on a plate and putting hands on it, one can turn it into a clock. The psychological essence of plate-ness was exchanged for the essence of clock-ness rather easily (Frisson & Wakefield, 2012). So, not only does psychological essentialism influences how we treat things, and how we categorize them, but also is influence by the nature of that underlying psychological essence and our ability to change it.

So, explanation-based theories capture some of the conscious and unconscious reasoning that we go through to try to make sense of the world. We use these mini-theories for what makes a category—we don't need the hard and fast rules of the classic view and don't have to mentally average or abstract across our experiences to derive a category, as with the probabilistic views. Instead, we bring our power of reasoning to bear on the causal structure of the world—that is why things are the way they are—to understand how it can be organized and classified.

Overall, these various theories of categorization demonstrate that people have a number of ways to mentally characterize their world, a number of ways to draw on their old experiences to help them act and think in a way that increases their success and performance in new situations.

Section Summary

- The classic view of categorization is that people use necessary and sufficient rules. Although people *can* make classifications in this way, they typically do not in most situations.
- For probabilistic views, categories take into account regularities, such as typicality and correlated attributes, to produce categories with graded structures.
- For the prototype view, categories are based on an averaged representation, the prototype, against which all other members of the category are compared.
- Exemplar theories suggest that we store multiple examples or exemplars in memory, then make judgments by comparing an item to the stored exemplars.
- Explanation-based theories suggest that people are problem solving when they create categories. People develop (largely implicit) theories of why something is in a category. This is how people create ad hoc categories on the fly and exhibit psychological essentialism—the intuitive belief that members of a category share an underlying essence.

Key Terms

ad hoc categories (p. *247*)
anomia (p. *228*)
anomic aphasia (p. *228*)
benefit (p. *230*)
category-specific deficit (p. *227*)
central tendency (p. *245*)
characteristic features (p. *215*)
classic view of categorization (p. *244*)
connectionism (p. *225*)
connectionist models (p. *225*)
correlated attributes (p. *245*)

cost (p. *231*)
default value (p. *240*)
defining feature (p. *215*)
exemplar theory (p. *248*)
explanation-based theories (p. *247*)
facilitation (p. *230*)
family resemblance (p. *215*)
feature lists (p. *215*)
frames (p. *240*)
inhibition (p. *231*)
lag (p. *231*)
lexical decision (p. *231*)
lexical memory (p. *228*)

network (p. *213*)
neural net models (p. *225*)
node (p. *213*)
pathways (p. *213*)
PDP models (p. *225*)
perceptual symbols (p. *223*)
prime (p. *229*)
probabilistic theories (p. *246*)
proposition (p. *213*)
prototype (p. *246*)
psychological essentialism (p. *248*)
reconstructive memory (p. *236*)
schema (p. *237*)
scripts (p. *238*)

semantic features (p. *215*)
semantic memory (p. *211*)
semantic priming (p. *229*)
semantic relatedness effect (p. *220*)
sentence verification task (p. *217*)
spreading activation (p. *213*)
stimulus onset asynchrony (SOA) (p. *230*)
target (p. *230*)
typicality (p. *245*)
typicality effects (p. *245*)

Using Knowledge in the Real World

Sometimes we forget the past and at other times we distort it; some disturbing memories haunt us for years. Yet we also rely on memory to perform an astonishing variety of tasks in our everyday lives. Recalling conversations with friends or recollecting family vacations, remembering appointments and errands we need to run, calling up words that allow us to speak and understand others, remembering food we like and dislike, acquiring knowledge needed for a new job—all depend, in one way or another, on memory.

(SCHACTER, 1996, P. 1)

H aving studied episodic and semantic memory separately in the previous two chapters, we now put them back together. You read about the evidence of a dissociation between episodic and semantic memories, showing how they are separate in several important respects; after all, patient K. C. seems to have lost his episodic memory, suffering brain damage that nonetheless preserved his semantic memory. Be that as it may, we also need to understand the normal, everyday operation of long-term memory, the continual, coordinated, cooperative processes of interaction between episodic and semantic memory that let us understand and remember our experiences. Thus, this chapter is about these interactions, about using our knowledge in real-world settings.

In Chapter 7, you read that in semantic memory research, we test people on the knowledge they already have. Episodic tasks, in contrast, present to-be-learned material to people, then test their memory for it. Although most of the research presented in this chapter also presents specific materials to people, there are at least two major differences from standard episodic memory situations. First, the material to be learned is more meaningful than random lists of words. We are interested in people's memory for passages of text they read or hear, memory for natural events that happen to them, and so on. As you will see, what we remember from our everyday experiences is influenced by semantic knowledge, our knowledge of concepts, relationships, and general information about the world. The term for this, when already-known information influences our memory of new events, is conceptually driven processing.

A second difference in this chapter is that there is a greater emphasis on accuracy rather than speed (response time, RT); in fact, in many cases the emphasis is on *inaccuracy*. A stunning aspect of many of the results is inaccurate, error-prone memory, such as eyewitness recollection of the details of an event that are just plain wrong. Schacter (1996) writes eloquently of the "fragile power" of memory, the paradoxical situation in which we are capable of remembering amazing quantities of information yet have a strong tendency to misremember under a variety of circumstances. We focus on the fragile part of this description here.

THE SEVEN SINS OF MEMORY

In a very approachable work, Schacter (1999) provides some specifics about the fragile nature of memory by enumerating Seven Sins of Memory, seven ways in which long-term memory lets us down (see Table 8-1). Material about the first three of the Seven Sins was covered in Chapter 6. First, there is a transience to long-term memory, a tendency to lose access to information over time. Although we attributed that to interference and retrieval failure in Chapter 6, Schacter asserts that there may also be genuine forgetting from long-term memory, especially when a memory is neither used nor rehearsed. Second, we tend to be absent-minded, losing track of information, details, intended activities, and so on. The absent-mindedness can be both for information from the past and also for future activities; when studying *remembering to do something in the future*, we're studying **prospective memory**. In Schacter's view, absent-mindedness is largely a failure of attention during encoding, especially because we may have been relying on automatic processing, thus failing to encode information at a deeper, more elaborate level (for attention-based

TABLE 8-1   The Seven Sins of Memory

Sin	Description
Transience	The tendency to lose access to information across time, whether through forgetting, interference, or retrieval failure
Absent-mindedness	Everyday memory failures in remembering information and intended activities, probably caused by insufficient attention or superficial, automatic processing during encoding
Blocking	Temporary retrieval failure or loss of access, such as the tip-of-the-tongue state, in either episodic or semantic memory
Misattribution	Remembering a fact correctly from past experience but attributing it to an incorrect source or context
Suggestibility	The tendency to incorporate information provided by others into your own recollection and memory representation
Bias	The tendency for knowledge, beliefs, and feelings to distort recollection of previous experiences and to affect current and future judgments and memory
Persistence	The tendency to remember facts or events, including traumatic memories, that one would rather forget, that is, failure to forget because of intrusive recollections and rumination

From Schacter (1999).

explanations of prospective memory, see Marsh & Hicks, 1998; R. E. Smith, 2003; Smith & Bayen, 2004). Third, we sometimes experience blocking, a temporary loss of access to information, say in a stressful situation such as an exam. The most common example of such blocking is the tip-of-the-tongue (TOT) phenomenon.

Schacter describes the first three as sins of omission: Just when you need to remember something, you can't. The next three are described as sins of commission—situations in which you remember something, but the memory involves an error, such as an incorrect time or person, or a detail you picked up from a different source. These three sins are misattribution, suggestibility, and bias. Misattribution is remembering something but being mistaken about the correct source of the information. Suggestibility is related to this and involves incorporating information supplied by other sources into your own memory. Finally, bias is a version of top-down processing; it involves "the distorting influences of present knowledge, beliefs, and feelings on recollection of previous experiences" (Schacter, 1999, p. 193). (Schacter's seventh Sin of Memory is persistence, by which he means the intrusive recollection of past events, especially traumatic ones—quite literally, failures to forget. We run into this in the section on repressed and recovered memories.)

FACTS ABOUT THE WORLD

In many memory studies, we intentionally lure people into making mistakes. That is, we present meaningful material such as a story or a set of related sentences, then do something that invites mistakes of one sort or another. This is unlike most of the episodic and semantic memory studies, where people are simply asked to learn and remember material in a straightforward way.

This is not to say that such research on reconstructive memory is unrepresentative, biased, or unfair. There are many situations in everyday life in which related information lures us into remembering something that was not in the original. Furthermore, it is important to understand how human memory can be influenced by such factors. Alternatively, there is a more general kind of research in which semantic and episodic factors are combined, but people are not deliberately misled.

The Nature of Propositions

In this section we discuss the idea that what people remember from meaningful material is the idea or gist—in other words, we don't usually remember superficial aspects of a passage, exact words or exact phrasings, but we do remember the basic idea. However, psychology needs ways to represent those ideas, needs a scientific way to quantify what the vague term *meaning* means. Also, to do research on content accuracy, we need a way to score recall to see how well people remembered meaningful content. The unit that codes meaning is called a **proposition**. A proposition represents the meaning of a single, simple idea, the smallest unit of knowledge about which you can make true/false judgments.

ELABORATED PROPOSITIONS   Just as some semantic theories try to capture memory in terms of a network structure, propositional theories can do the same—as networks of interconnected propositions. To illustrate, consider a sentence and its propositional representation, as presented in Figure 8-1 (sentence from Anderson & Bower, 1973). The sentence,

> *(1) The hippie touched the debutante in the park,* is represented here as a set of interrelated concepts, one for each main word in the sentence. The relationships among the words are specified by the types of pathways that connect

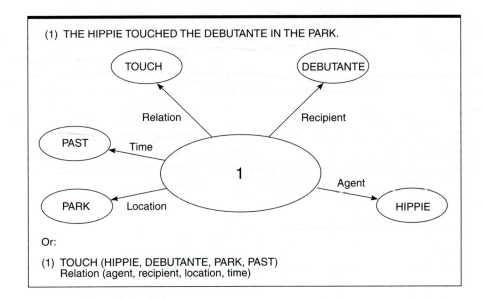

FIGURE 8-1 A propositional representation, in "node-plus-pathway" notation and in written form, of the sentence "The hippie touched the debutante in the park." Network notation after Anderson (1980) and Anderson and Bower (1973); written proposition after Kintsch (1974).

(1) THE HIPPIE TOUCHED THE DEBUTANTE IN THE PARK.

Or:

(1) TOUCH (HIPPIE, DEBUTANTE, PARK, PAST)
     Relation (agent, recipient, location, time)

the nodes (e.g., agent, recipient or patient, location). Sentence 1 is composed of five *relationships or connections of meaning,* five **semantic cases**:

"TOUCH" is the **relation** in the sentence, the *topic or major event* in the sentence.

"HIPPIE" is the **agent** for this event, the *actor or person* who did the touching.

"DEBUTANTE" is the **patient** (or **recipient**) of the event, the *one who received the action* of touching.

"PARK" is the **location** of the event, and the

"PAST" is the **time** at which the touching occurred.

REMEMBERING PROPOSITIONS Let's begin with a classic study by Sachs (1967). She was testing the idea that people tend to remember meaning rather than verbatim information. Her participants heard passages of connected text and were then tested on one critical sentence in the passage 0, 80, or 160 syllables after it had been heard. (See Table 8-2 for an example; why not read it now and confirm Sachs's results for yourself?)

The test was a simple recognition test among four alternatives. One alternative was a verbatim repetition, another represented a change both in surface form and in meaning, and the other two represented changes only in surface form. When recognition was tested immediately, people were very good at recognizing the exact repetition; in other words, they rejected changes in superficial structure

---

TABLE 8-2   Sample Passage from Sachs (1967) Including Multiple-Choice Recognition Test for Critical Sentence

Read the passage below at a comfortable pace but without looking back. After you have finished reading, your memory of one of the sentences in the paragraph will be tested.

While most gardeners enjoy tulips, it is unlikely that they would be valued as highly today as they were in Holland during the seventeenth century. For some reason, the tulip became very popular at this time. The tulip was first brought into Europe from Turkey. In 1551, the Viennese ambassador to Turkey wrote of seeing these plants. Years later, in 1562, a cargo of tulip bulbs was sent to Antwerp. The flower then spread through Holland from there. At first, only the rich collected and traded tulips. Eventually, most of Holland was involved in the matter. Almost everyone tried to outdo their neighbors, both in the growing of tulips with rare colors and also in the high prices that were paid for them. A price of 6000 florins was paid for one bulb of the variety Semper Augustus in 1636. At this time, 6000 florins was the price of a house and grounds. Soon, everyone in Holland was working in the tulip trade, and ordinary business was being neglected. People who had been away from Holland and then returned during the craze sometimes made mistakes. A sailor is said to have mistaken a tulip bulb worth several thousand florins for an onion, and cut it up to eat with his herring.

Now, without looking back, decide which of the following sentences occurred in the paragraph.

a. The Viennese ambassador to Turkey wrote of seeing these plants in 1551.
b. A sighting of these plants was written about in 1551 by the Viennese ambassador in Turkey.
c. The ambassador to Turkey from Vienna, in 1551, wrote of seeing these plants.
d. In 1551, the Viennese ambassador to Turkey wrote of seeing these plants.

Check to see whether your answer was correct by referring back to the paragraph.

and changes in meaning. After comprehending the next 80 syllables in the passage, however, performance was accurate only in rejecting the alternative that changed the meaning. In other words, after the 80 syllable delay, people showed no preference for the repetition (*d*, the correct answer) over the paraphrases (*a* and *c* in the table).

Sachs's concluded that we quickly lose information about the actual, verbatim words that we hear (or read), but we do retain the meaning. We reconstruct what must have been said based on the meaning that is stored in a propositional representation. Only when there is something "special" about the verbatim words, say in recalling a joke, do we retain surface form as part of our ordinary memory for meaningful discourse (but see Masson, 1984).

Confirmation of this was offered by Kintsch and Bates (1977), who gave a surprise recognition test to students either two or five days after a classroom lecture. Some evidence of verbatim memory was present after two days, but very little persisted five days afterward. As expected, verbatim memory for details and extraneous comments was better than verbatim memory for general lecture statements (see also Bates, Masling, & Kintsch, 1978). Even here, however, reconstructive memory seemed to play a role; students were better at rejecting items such as jokes that had not been presented than they were at recognizing jokes and announcements that had been heard (see also Schmidt, 1994, on the effects of humor on sentence memory). For jokes, the wording can be important, so there was better surface form memory because the nature of the information constrains the wording. Similarly, people can have better memory for verbatim information if people are reading poetry, where wording is important, rather than prose (Tillman & Dowling, 2007).

PROPOSITIONS AND INTERFERENCE Taking the idea that people are storing propositions in memory and that these are organized in a network, we can make some predictions about how this affects performance. First, as noted earlier, a given concept can have multiple associations with it. That is, a node in a network can have multiple links to multiple concepts. Furthermore, we can assume that there is a limit to people's cognitive resources—that is, how much of a network a person can search at once. We've already covered a number of these sorts of mental limits in our discussions of attention and working memory, and we're just extending that logic here. Given these two simple assumptions, we can make some predictions about memory.

In a classic study, Anderson (1974) had people memorize a list of sentences about people in locations, such as "The hippie is in the park." The important part of the study was that, across the list, he varied the number of associations with the person and location concepts. That is, a given person in the study list could be described as being in 1, 2, or 3 different locations, and each location could have 1, 2, or 3 different people in it. When we graph a network representation of this type of information, we can see various number of links "fanning" off of a given concept node.

Now, Anderson (1974) further assumed that the amount of activation that could spread along the links of the network was limited. As such, the more links there were fanning off of a concept node in memory, the more widely the activation was distributed, and longer that the processing of the activation along any one

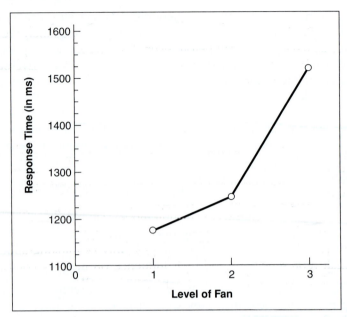

FIGURE 8-2 An example of data showing a fan effect, with an increase in response time (RT) with an increase in the number of newly learned associations with a concept (fan).

of those pathways took. The end result is the prediction that the more links there are off a given concept—the more links fanning off of a concept node—the slower the retrieval process would be. This, of course, would yield a longer response time, which, as can be seen in Figure 8-2, is exactly what happened in Anderson's (1974) study. After people memorized the list of sentences, they were given a recognition test in which they had to indicate whether the test sentences were studied on the list or not. The **fan effect** that was found was that *when more words associated with a concept, response times were longer.*

The fan effect is a retrieval interference effect—the more words associated with a concept, the slower people were to retrieve any one of them. In an interesting extension of this finding, Bunting, Conway, and Heitz (2004; see also Radvansky & Copeland, 2006a) looked at the fan effect in terms of the working memory capacity of their participants. They found that people with lower working memory capacity exhibited greater interference—a larger fan effect—than people with a higher working memory capacity. That is, people with less working memory capacity were further disrupted when their capacity was divided up among many words (larger "fans"). They were working with fewer working memory resources to begin with, so a cognitive task that places a greater burden on them has a more disruptive effect because they have less extra capacity to compensate for that disruption.

Section Summary

- Comprehending and remembering ideas can involve constructing propositional representations in which meaningful elements are represented as nodes connected by various pathways (e.g., agent, recipient).

- We tend to remember the gist or general meaning of a passage but not the more superficial aspects such as exact wording. We routinely "recognize" a sentence as having occurred before even if the sentence is a paraphrase.
- Network theories of how we store and retrieve propositions have been able to make accurate predictions of future memory performance, such as the fan effect.

SITUATION MODELS AND EMBODIED COGNITION

There is a great deal of evidence that basic idea units can influence memory. However, there is more to life than simple ideas. One of the themes of this text is embodied cognition, the idea that how we think is influenced by how we act or are otherwise involved with the world. One way that embodied cognition manifests itself is the idea that people are creating models (Johnson-Laird, 1983; Zwaan & Radvansky, 1998) of the situations described, and do not just create memories of the simple propositional idea in sentences. One way of thinking about different types of mental representations and their influence on memory comes from van Dijk and Kintsch's (1983) work on language comprehension.

Levels of Representation

According to van Dijk and Kintsch, there are three levels of representation when we comprehend. These are the surface form, the textbase, and the situation model. The surface form corresponds to a verbatim mental representation of the exact words used, as well as the syntax of the sentences read or heard. At the intermediate level is the textbase. These are the basic idea units actually present in a text you might read. The textbase level corresponds to the propositional representations you read about in the previous section. At the third level is the situation model. This is a representation of the state of affairs described by a text, rather than a representation of the text itself. So, the idea is not only that you can create different kinds of mental representations and memories of what you may be reading, but that you're creating all of them in parallel.

This division of different kinds of mental representation can be seen in how well people remember information at the different levels over time. This is illustrated in a study by Kintsch, Welsch, Schmalhofer, and Zimny (1987). In this study, people read a text and then took a later memory test. For the test, people were shown sentences and indicated whether they had been read before or not. Four types of memory probes were used on the recognition test: (a) verbatim probes, which were exact sentences that had been read earlier, (b) paraphrases, which captured the same ideas as those in the text, but with a different wording, (c) inferences, which were ideas that were likely to be true, but not actually mentioned, and (d) "wrongs," incorrect probes that were thematically consistent with the passage but were incorrect if one had read and understood the passage. Kintsch et al. compared performance on these various types of memory probes to assess the strength of the representations at the various levels. For example, by comparing performance on the verbatim probes and paraphrases, one can estimate memory for the exact wording. This is because both of these probe types refer to ideas that were actually in the text, but only one uses the exact wording. So, the degree to

FIGURE 8-3
Retention of
knowledge at the
surface form,
textbase, and
situation model
levels.

Adapted from Kintsch
et al. (1987).

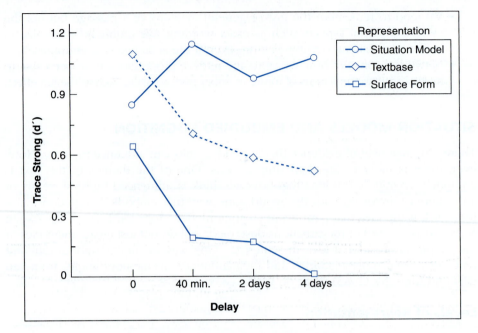

FIGURE 8-3
Retention of knowledge at the surface form, textbase, and situation model levels.

Adapted from Kintsch et al. (1987).

which memory is better in the verbatim condition compared to the paraphrase condition is a measure of surface form memory.

The results of Kintsch et al.'s (1987) study are shown in Figure 8-3. Although memory for all three levels is reasonably good immediately after reading, there are big differences later on, depending on what is being assessed. First, for the surface form, verbatim information is lost quickly from memory and reaches chance performance by the end of the four days. Second, memory was better for the textbase level than for the surface form. So, although people may forget the exact words they read before, they are better at remembering the ideas that were presented (cf. the work described by Sachs earlier in the chapter). However, even memory at this level declines over time. However, for the third level, the situation model, performance starts out high and then stays high, with little evidence of forgetting over the four-day retention interval. Thus, there is something psychologically real about looking at mental representations in this way.

A more everyday example of this would be your memory for a newspaper article you might read. Soon after reading the article, your ability to remember verbatim sentences from the article is pretty poor. Furthermore, over time, you start to forget what specific ideas were actually read in the article, and what ideas are inferences you may have created when you were trying to understand it. However, you have a relatively good memory over time for the events described in the article, and this memory stays with you for a much longer period of time.

Remembering Facts

So, now that we've seen that situation models are remembered better over the long term, are there any other benefits? Yes, there are. Think back a few sections to our discussion of the fan effect. As you remember, a fan effect is an increase in retrieval time that accompanies an increase in the number of associations with a concept. However, this can shift around somewhat when we start thinking about how the studied information might be organized into situation models. For example, in one study Radvansky and Zacks (1991) had people memorize sentences about objects in locations, such as the following:

The potted palm is in the hotel.

The potted palm is in the museum.

The potted palm is in the barber shop.

The pay phone is in the library.

The welcome mat is in the library.

The waste basket is in the library.

Under these circumstances, how people think about the situations described by the learned sentences influences the ease with which they remember this information later. In the first three sentences, there is a fan of 3 off of the object concept because the potted palm is described as being in three places. According to propositional network theories, the division of the spreading activation causes retrieval to proceed more slowly. Similarly, according to a situation model view, because these three sentences are interpreted as referring to different events (that is, different potted palms), people would create a separate situation model for each one. Then during retrieval, these three situation models would each contain a potted palm and would interfere with one another, thereby producing a fan effect.

In comparison, for the last three sentences, there is again a fan of 3, this time off of the location concept, because there are three objects in the library. However, in this case, it is not difficult for people to think of these three sentences as referring to a common event (it's the same library). As such, people can integrate this information into a single situation model and store one representation in memory (e.g., one library, with a pay phone, welcome mat, and waste basket in it). Then, during memory retrieval, because everything is stored together in a single situation model, there should be no retrieval interference, and no fan effect. This is exactly what was observed. As you can see in Figure 8-4, Radvansky and Zacks (1991) found a fan effect when there was a single object in multiple locations, but not when there was a single location with multiple objects.

This mental organization is based on how people think about interaction with the world. In a study by Radvansky, Spieler, and Zacks (1993), students learned sentences about people in small locations that typically contain only a single person, such as witness stand, tire swing, or store dressing room. Here, a situation in which multiple people are in one of these locations is unlikely. But, because people can move from place to place, a person-based organization is plausible—and this is what is observed with a fan effect when a single location was associated with multiple people, but not when a single person was associated with multiple locations.

This applies not only to information that people learn from sentences, but also to how we interact with the world. Specifically, if a given object is encountered in more than one location, the memory for that object will be worse. For

FIGURE 8-4 Response times to sentence memory probes as a function of the level of fan (number of associated with a sentence concept). Data are divided based on whether the shared concept is a single location with multiple objects or a single object in multiple locations.

Derived from Radvansky and Zacks (1991).

example, in a study by Radvansky and Copeland (2006b; Radvansky, Krawietz, & Tamplin, 2011; Radvansky, Tamplin, & Krawietz, 2010), people navigated a virtual environment in which people picked up objects and moved them either across a room or from one room to another. What they found was that, compared to moving objects across a room, when objects were moved from one room to another, people had a harder time remembering. That is, walking through doorways caused forgetting. This occurred because people had memories of the object being in more than one event, more than one room. Therefore, when they needed to remember something about these objects, these different memories interfered with one another, and memory was worse. This is much like a fan effect, only with objects and the places where you interact with them.

Explore
What Do You Remember? in
MyPsychLab

METAMEMORY

Much of what we have been discussing regarding memory is the ability to remember some sort of content information, such as a word on a list, a picture, a face, or a story. In this section, we take a different tack. Instead of looking at what we remember, we look at how good we are at assessing how accurate our memories are. Overall, although we do have some awareness into our memories, there are many aspects of memory that people are not aware of. For example, many college students are unaware that their memories can be improved by various strategies that have already been discussed in the text, including dual coding, testing, distributed practice, and the generation effect (McCabe, 2011). That is, metamemory concerns your ability to assess when you've learned something, your realization that you need to remember something in the future, and even the basics of what you do and do not know. This captures the idea that memory is not primarily for recollecting about the past, but preparing a person to act in the now and the near future (e.g., Klein, Robertson, & Delton, 2010).

Source Monitoring

First, let's consider your ability to remember where information came from. **Source monitoring** (Johnson, Hashtroudi, & Lindsay, 1993) is *the ability to accurately remember the source of a memory, be it something you encountered in the world or something that you imagined.* Failures of source monitoring can sometimes occur in which a person remembers the content of the information, but cannot accurately attribute it to a particular source. Source monitoring is a complex process that involves many parts of the brain. The hippocampus seems to be important for integrating content and source information, the prefrontal cortex is important for searching and using source information, particularly the right dorsolateral (B.A. 10), ventrolateral (B.A. 45), and medial regions (B.A. 11), as well as the temporal lobes, are important for remembering content itself (Burgess, Scott, & Frith, 2003; Davachi, Mitchell, & Wagner, 2003; Senkfor & Van Petten, 1998). In extreme cases, such as schizophrenia, people experiencing hallucinations may be having trouble source monitoring—that is, distinguishing between what is real and what is only imagined (Ditman & Kuperberg, 2005).

An example of a source monitoring might be if you have a memory of a fact about a historical figure, and it is important to know whether this is a fact that came from a history textbook or an inaccurate fictionalization that came from a novel. So, to know how reliable this fact is, you need to know where you learned it. If you misremember the source of an idea as being a textbook when it actually came from a movie, then you mistakenly think that fiction is fact, a source monitoring failure. This can be important, as you will see later, in situations such as trying to determine whether something was witnessed during an accident or crime. A more everyday example of source monitoring is trying to remember which of your friends told you a secret. If you get this wrong, then you could be in big trouble with one (or more) of your friends.

Source monitoring involves not only trying to distinguish between things that may have come to you from various external sources, but also things that you thought of yourself. For example, did you really turn off the oven, or did you just think about it? Source monitoring for your own internal thoughts and actions is important. Source monitoring failures of this type typically occur for those activities that you do routinely. Every time you do something, you store a memory of that experience. Things you do quite a lot have a large number of memory traces stored. What happens when you have a source monitoring failure is that you confuse a memory of having done something in the past with having actually done it today, even though you didn't. This may help explain some work accidents; somebody forgot to do some simple task that's done every day, several times a day, but instead just remembered having done it, and confused the memory with what they actually did (or didn't do).

Source monitoring can sometimes have serious consequences in academic and artistic domains. When you take another person's ideas and present them as your own, this is plagiarism, and it is wrong. You should know this well by now. However, sometimes plagiarism occurs without the plagiarist consciously trying to do something known to be wrong. This is known as **cryptomnesia** (Brown & Murphy, 1989), in which *a person unconsciously plagiarizes something they have heard or read before, but because they have forgotten the source, mistakenly think that it is a new idea that they thought of.* Essentially, a person remembers the idea, melody, or whatever, but has forgotten the source of the information. As a consequence, the person thinks that the idea is a novel one and is not aware of the plagiarism unless it is discovered and pointed out by another person. Factors that increase the likelihood of experiencing cryptomnesia are those that make memory of the original source less likely. For example, if people elaborate on an idea, they are less likely to remember the original source and are more likely to only remember their own thoughts on the idea (Stark & Perfect, 2008). A similar thing happens when we observe other people. We sometimes see other people do things, and then later misremember having done that activity ourselves (Linder, Echterhoff, Davidson, & Brand, 2010).

Cryptomnesia is more likely to occur when people have their attention and working memory resources directed elsewhere. For example, in one study (Brown & Murphy, 1989), people were asked to sit in a circle, generating members of a category one person after the other (e.g., for the category TOOL, one person might say "hammer," the next "screwdriver," the next "pliers," etc.) without repeating anything that had been said earlier. The results showed that a person was more likely to repeat a previously said item—that is, to plagiarize someone else in the group—if it had been said by the person just before that particular participant. This actually makes good sense, from the standpoint of attention and working memory. Imagine yourself in this situation. As your turn is approaching, you start racking your brains for something to say. When the person just before you is talking, you are likely to have some of your attention drawn away, and are focusing more on your own thoughts, trying to come up with something to say. As a consequence of this divided attention, you may store a memory for the word that person said, but are less likely to store the source information as well. Then, because that word was primed by having heard it, you retrieve it from memory, but you do not retrieve the source. So you say it, unaware that it had just been mentioned.

Prospective Memory

Another interesting aspect of memory in the real world focuses not on dredging up information from the past, but rather on knowing how to use your memory to do things in the future. This is **prospective memory** (Loftus, 1971), *the ability to remember to do something in the future.* This is in contrast to retrospective memory, memory for things that happened in the past.

In general, there are two basic kinds of prospective memory (Einstein & McDaniel, 1990). The first is *time-based prospective memory* in which a person needs to remember to do something based on the passage of time. This can be after a certain amount of time has passed, such as needing to remember to take the pizza out of the oven in 10 minutes, remembering to take your medication at 3:00, or remembering to call your mother on Mother's Day. In general, time-based

PROVE IT
Cryptomnesia

For this demonstration you will need at least three volunteers (although you can use more). It is a variation of a study by Brown and Halliday (1991) that can result in people reporting answers that they present as their own, but which, in fact, other people gave. This is cryptomnesia. Have your three volunteers sit in a circle. Tell them that you will first read the name of a category, such as "Countries," "Flowers," "Insects," and so on (prepare a list of 10 or so category names ahead of time). Then, going around in a circle, people will need to name members of that category aloud, without using names that were said previously. What is likely to happen is that at various times people will say things that someone else had already said. Furthermore, these should be more likely to be things that the person just before them in the circle had said as compared to the person just after him or her. To make this a bit more likely, give people a time limit of 5 seconds to say their answer. You will need to record what people say, so an audio recoding might be better than trying to write things down. You should also limit the number of times you go around the circle before the task becomes very hard. Limiting the number of responses to 25 should do this.

After the first part of the task is completed, write down, in random order, the responses people gave. Then ask people to pick out which ones they themselves said. Simply having them circle the ones they remember saying. This can be done an hour after the first part, or a day later, or a week later. If you want to get fancy, you could have several groups of volunteers and see how the amount of time that passed influences your results. What you may find is that people will pick answers that they did not actually say. Again, these are more likely to be things that were said by the person just before them in the circle.

---

prospective memory is more difficult because it requires people to keep track of time, which we are generally not very good at.

The other basic kind of prospective memory is *event-based prospective memory*. Here a person needs to remember to do something when a certain event occurs—for example, giving your roommate a message when you see her, remembering to stop at the hardware store next time you drive by, or remembering how to give CPR when you see someone in distress. In general, event-based prospective memory is easier than time-based prospective memory. This is because a person does not need to monitor the passage of time, but is reminded of the intended action when the relevant event occurs. Under these circumstances, people either are actively monitoring the environment for the event cue or have previously formed a mental association with that cue and the intended action, so they are spontaneously reminded when the reminder presents itself (Einstein & McDaniel, 2005; Marsh, Hicks, & Cook, 2005)—basically, the event cue acts as a retrieval cue. A good strategy, by the way, is to take advantage of your superior event-based memory performance by turning a time-based prospective memory task into an event-based one. For example, set a timer rather than trying to remember to notice the time on a clock yourself, or mark a date on a calendar rather than trying to remember an appointment in your head (of course, you'll still have to remember to look at your calendar).

To improve your daily prospective memory, a study by Trawley, Law, and Logie (2011) found, using a virtual environment, that prospective memory to do a number of tasks was best if people made a plan ahead of time and then stuck to it. When this plan is interrupted and deviated from, this caused people to be more likely to forget something that they were supposed to do. It has been found, as with other types of memory, that sleeping after encoding a prospective memory goal can also help performance (Scullin & McDaniel, 2010).

Knowing What You Know

Strategies like that—turning a time-based prospective memory task into an event-based task—involve **metamemory**, people's knowledge about their own memory and its functioning. In this section we look at three ways that researchers examined what people know, and what they think they know. The first of these should seem familiar to you; it's the assessment that you, as a student, often make when you study. These are called **judgments of learning** (Arbuckle & Cuddy, 1969), in which *a person makes a prediction, after studying some material, whether it will be remembered on a later memory test (was it learned?).* This is important because of how we use that kind of self-assessment. If your judgment of learning is that some body of knowledge has been learned sufficiently, that suggests to you that it requires less additional study time (say for an upcoming test), whereas if you decide that the information or knowledge has not been learned, it requires more study time.

So, how good are people at judging whether they've learned something? The answer is "it depends." Generally, when a person is asked to make a judgment of learning immediately after studying some material, the estimates of future performance are poor predictors of what will, and will not, be remembered (e.g., Zaromb, Karpicke, & Roediger, 2010). However, if there is a meaningful delay between studying and being asked to predict future performance, estimates become much better (Dunlosky & Nelson, 1994). This is because the delay allows information to be removed from working memory, and the person has a more accurate estimate of what it will be like to try to retrieve it from long-term memory later. Otherwise, if the information is currently active in working memory, there is a bias to mistakenly assume that it will be easier to remember it later because it is easy to think about it at the moment.

Another way to assess metamemory is to look at when people fail to remember something. When this occurs, the person might be asked to make a **feeling of knowing** judgment (Hart, 1965) in which *an estimate is provided of how likely it is that that item will be recognized on a later memory test.* An everyday example of this is when you see someone you know in a mall, and you start up a conversation even though you can't remember the person's name. A likely reason for the retrieval failure is that you are seeing the person out of the normal context in which you interact with him or her (Gruppuso, Lindsay, & Masson, 2007). In this situation, you might provide a high feeling of knowing estimate for the name—you feel that you would recognize the name if you heard it or saw it. In comparison, if the person you were talking to was someone you did not feel that you knew, your feeling of knowing judgment would be low because you would feel that the person's name would not be in your memory. Essentially, a feeling of knowing rating provides a measure of how familiar something is. That is, it is an estimate that there has been an increase in activation of some memories, with some partial knowledge possibly being retrieved, but not enough to recall the needed information (Koriat, 1993, 1995).

An experience that is related to feeling of knowing is the **tip of the tongue (TOT)** state (R. Brown & McNeill, 1966), where you feel like the word or name you can't remember is on the verge of being remembered. This is the primary difference between a tip of the tongue state and feeling of knowing. In feeling of knowing, despite a strong feeling that you could recognize something later, you cannot say much more about the inaccessible information. In comparison, when a person is in a tip of the tongue state, *there is a feeling that retrieval is imminent* (A. S. Brown, 1991). Often a person can provide a great deal of additional information, or partial retrieval, about the word that may be on the tip of the tongue. For example, the person may know what letter the word begins with, how many syllables it has, and even words that rhyme with it, and still not be able to recall it (Hanley & Chapman, 2008). There are a number of ideas about what may be causing the tip of the tongue experience. For example, when people are in this state they tend to recall related words, which then become more active in memory, causing interference and blocking the retrieval of the desired memory. Alternatively, the various, similar memories may be actively inhibiting the needed memory because they are in competition. These ideas would explain why a word that is on the tip of your tongue may suddenly be remembered several minutes later when the retrieval competition has had time to diminish, and the memory can be readily retrieved.

An interesting corollary to this is the question of how well do people judge the ability of another person to remember something. In general, the more effort a person puts into learning something at the time of encoding, the better it will be remembered later. However, if a person did not know that an event will be important later, the amount of effort a person later puts into trying to remember it does not help much. When people are trying to remember something themselves, they are well-aware of the futility of "trying harder" to remember. But, sadly, when dealing with other people, we are not so sympathetic, and often feel that if a person tried harder to remember they would, even though that is just not the case (Kassam et al., 2009).

FALSE MEMORIES, EYEWITNESS MEMORY, AND "FORGOTTEN MEMORIES"

Schacter (1996) spoke of the fragile nature of memory and the Seven Sins of Memory, discussing how our memories can fail us in certain situations. Indeed, we've been discussing a variety of things that show different memory weaknesses in this chapter—the fan effect that can lead to retrieval interference, source monitoring failures, cryptomnesia, poor predictions based on judgments of learning, and the like. Is this what Schacter meant when he talked about the "sins" of memory, the weaknesses in our memory systems? What is the weakness that Schacter pinpointed—what situations did he have in mind? A straightforward answer is that memory fails us in exactly those situations that call for absolutely accurate recall, completely correct recollection of real-world events exactly as they happened. The weakness of memory seems to be that we are often unable to distinguish between what really happened and what our existing knowledge and comprehension processes might have contributed to recollection. We discuss two research programs that show incorrect or distorted memory, then tackle the issues raised by these results.

In eyewitness memory and testimony, any new information about an event is integrated with relevant existing knowledge. Thus, we are less than accurate when we attempt to retrieve such knowledge because we are often unable to discriminate between new and original information.

False Memories

A simple yet powerful laboratory demonstration of **false memory**, *memory of something that did not happen,* was reported by Roediger and McDermott (1995), based on a demonstration by Deese (1959; see Roediger & McDermott, 2000, for an introduction to this work and the DRM—Deese–Roediger–McDermott—task, as it's often called; see Gallo, 2010 for a review of this work). Roediger and McDermott had people study 12-item lists made up of words such as *bed, rest, awake,* and *pillow,* words highly associated with the word *sleep.* Importantly, *sleep* was never presented. Instead, it was the *critical lure* word, a word that was highly related to the other words in the list but which never actually appeared. In immediate free recall, 40% of the people recalled *sleep* from the list and later recognized it with a high degree of confidence. This is a false memory.

In a second study, people studied similar lists, recalling the list either immediately or after a distractor task (arithmetic). Then, everyone was given a recognition task. During free recall, 55% of the people recalled the lure. The recognition results, shown in Figure 8-5, were even more dramatic. Of course, a few people "recognized" nonstudied words that were unrelated to the study list words (e.g., *thief* for the *sleep* list). More importantly, correct recognition for studied words increased to well above chance for the study/arithmetic lists and even higher for study/recall lists. However, false recognition of the critical lure was higher than correct recognition of words actually shown on the list, showing the same pattern of increases across conditions. There was an 81% false alarm rate for critical lures when the lists had been studied and recalled. In other words, falsely remembering the lure during recall strengthened memories of the lure word, leading to a higher false recognition rate. When questioned further, most people claimed to "remember" the critical lure word rather than merely "know" it had been on the list.

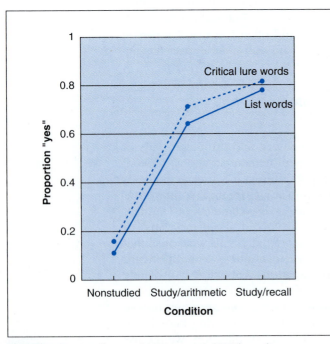

FIGURE 8-5   Roediger and McDermott's (1995) results.

PROVE IT
False Memory

Simulate
Creating False Memories in
MyPsychLab

This is a fairly easy demonstration to perform if you have several volunteers and about 15 minutes available. It is an adaptation of the Deese/Roediger and McDermott (1995) method, shorter than the original experiment while demonstrating the same effect; see Stadler, Roediger, and McDermott (1999) for additional word lists that can be used. Prepare enough copies of your distractor task (e.g., a page full of simple arithmetic problems) to have one for each volunteer.

1. Tell your volunteers they will hear three lists and afterward will be asked to recall as many of the words as they can; order of recall is not important.
2. Read the three lists to your volunteers at an "easy" speaking rate, about one word per 2 seconds. Pause only briefly between lists.
3. After finishing the third list, have your volunteers do 2 minutes of arithmetic, finishing as many problems as they can.
4. Ask your volunteers to write down as many words as they can remember from the three lists. Give ample time (approximately 3 minutes) so they can get as many words as possible.
5. When everyone is done, have them all turn over their sheets of paper and make recognition decisions, one by one, to the 20-word recognition test. For each word, they should say "no" if the word was not on the list and "yes" if it was on the list. When they say "yes," also have them note whether they remember the word specifically or whether they just "know" it was on the list.
6. Look especially for recall of the words sleep, thief, and chair, because these are the nonpresented, critical lures. On recognition, look for false alarms (saying "yes") to the critical lures in positions 5, 13, and 16.

Word Lists

1. bed, rest, awake, tired, dream, wake, snooze, blanket, doze, slumber, snore, nap, peace, yawn, drowsy
2. steal, robber, crook, burglar, money, cop, bad, rob, jail, gun, villain, crime, bank, bandit, criminal
3. table, sit, legs, seat, couch, desk, recliner, sofa, wood, cushion, swivel, stool, sitting, rocking, bench

Recognition List

1-dream, 2-fork, 3-weather, 4-bracelet, 5-chair, 6-robber, 7-stool, 8-traffic, 9-snooze, 10-couch, 11-radio, 12-jail, 13-sleep, 14-sand, 15-blanket, 16-thief, 17-bed, 18-boy, 19-skin, 20-cushion

Scoring Key

"Yes" words	1, 6, 7, 9, 10, 12, 15, 17, 20
"No" words	2, 3, 4, 8, 11, 14, 18, 19
Critical lures	5, 13, 16

In terms of content accuracy—memory for the ideas—performance is good, exactly what we would expect; you see a list of words such as *bed, rest, awake,* and *pillow,* and, because the list is "about" sleep, you then recall *sleep.* But in terms of technical accuracy, memory for the exact experience, performance is poor because people came up with the word *sleep* based on their understanding of the list and then could not distinguish between what had really been there and what was supplied from memory. These sorts of meaning-based false memories are formed quickly, in as little as 4 seconds (Atkins & Reuter-Lorenz, 2008). It appears that the critical process is not the automatic spread of activation, such as that observed in lexical decision priming, but the use of the thematic information in the study lists during efforts to remember what had been heard earlier (Meade, Watson, Balota, & Roediger, 2007). Roediger and McDermott's (1995, p. 812) conclusion about this compelling memory illusion summarized the situation aptly:

> *All remembering is constructive in nature. . . . The illusion of remembering events that never happened can occur quite readily. Therefore, as others have also pointed out, the fact that people may say they vividly remember details surrounding an event cannot, by itself, be taken as convincing evidence that the event actually occurred.*

Integration

False memories can also be created by inappropriately combining information from different sources or events, where the combined information becomes linked or fused in memory. To illustrate this, let's look at a classic set of studies by Bransford and Franks (1971, 1972). This set of results will make more sense to you if you begin with the demonstration in Table 8-3.

Bransford and Franks (1971) were interested in the general topic of how people acquire and remember ideas, not merely individual sentences but integrated wholes. They asked people to listen to sentences like those in Table 8-3 one by one, and then (after a short distractor task) answer a simple question about each sentence. After going through this procedure for all 24 sentences and taking a five-minute break, people were given another test. During this second test, people had to make yes/no recognition judgments, saying "yes" if they remembered reading the sentence in the original set and "no" otherwise. They also had to indicate, on a 10-point scale, how confident they were about their judgments: Positive ratings (from 1 to 5) meant they were sure they had seen the sentence, negative ratings (from −1 to −5) meant they were sure they had not. *Without* looking back at the original sentences, take a moment now to make these judgments about the sentences in Table 8-4; "OLD" means "Yes, I've seen it before" and "NEW" means "No, I didn't see it before."

All 28 sentences in this recognition test are related to the original ideas in the first set of sentences. The clever aspect of the recognition test is that only 4 of the 28 sentences had in fact appeared on the original list; the other 24 are new. As you no doubt noticed, the separate sentences were all derived from four basic idea

TABLE 8-3	Sample Experiment of Bransford and Franks (1971)

Instructions: Read each sentence in the table individually. As soon as you have read each one, close your eyes and count to five. Then look at and answer the question that follows each sentence. Begin now.

Sentence	Question
The girl broke the window on the porch.	Broke what?
The tree in the front yard shaded the man smoking his pipe.	Where?
The hill was steep.	What was?
The sweet jelly was on the kitchen table.	On what?
The tree was tall.	Was what?
The old car climbed the hill.	What did?
The ants in the kitchen ate the jelly.	Where?
The girl who lives next door broke the window on the porch.	Lives where?
The car pulled the trailer.	Did what?
The ants ate the sweet jelly that was on the table.	What did?
The girl lives next door.	Who does?
The tree shaded the man who was smoking his pipe.	What did?
The sweet jelly was on the table.	Where?
The girl who lives next door broke the large window.	Broke what?
The man was smoking his pipe.	Who was?
The old car climbed the steep hill.	The what?
The large window was on the porch.	Where?
The tall tree was in the front yard.	Was what?
The car pulling the trailer climbed the steep hill.	Did what?
The jelly was on the table.	What was?
The tall tree in the front yard shaded the man.	Did what?
The car pulling the trailer climbed the hill.	Which car?
The ants ate the jelly.	Ate what?
The window was large.	What was?

groupings, such as "The ants in the kitchen ate the sweet jelly that was on the table." Each of the complete idea groupings consisted of four separate simple propositions; for example,

The ants were in the kitchen.

The ants ate the jelly.

The jelly was sweet.

The jelly was on the table.

The original set of sentences (Table 8-4) presented six sentences from each idea grouping. Two of the six were called "ones," simple, one-idea propositions such as "The jelly was on the table." Another two sentences were "twos," where two simple propositions were merged, as in "The ants in the kitchen ate the jelly." Finally, the last two were "threes," as in "The ants ate the sweet jelly that

TABLE 8-4   Sample Experiment by Bransford and Franks (1971)

Instructions: Check "OLD" or "NEW" for each sentence, then indicate how confident you are on a scale from 1 to 5 (5 is "very high confidence").

	OLD/NEW	Confidence (−5 to +5)
1. The car climbed the hill.	O	
2. The girl who lives next door broke the window.	N	
3. The old man who was smoking his pipe climbed the steep hill.	N	
4. The tree was in the front yard.	N	
5. The ants ate the sweet jelly that was in the kitchen.	N	
6. The window was on the porch.	O	
7. The barking dog jumped on the old car in the front yard.	N	
8. The tree in the front yard shaded the man.	O	
9. The ants were in the kitchen.	O	
10. The old car pulled the trailer.	O	
11. The tree shaded the man who was smoking his pipe.	N	
12. The tall tree shaded the man who was smoking his pipe.	O	
13. The ants ate the jelly on the kitchen table.	N	
14. The old car, pulling the trailer, climbed the hill.	N	
15. The girl who lives next door broke the large window on the porch.	O	
16. The tall tree shaded the man.	O	
17. The ants in the kitchen ate the jelly.	N	
18. The car was old.	N	
19. The girl broke the large window.	O	
20. The ants ate the sweet jelly that was on the kitchen table.	N	
21. The ants were on the table in the kitchen.	N	
22. The old car pulling the trailer climbed the steep hill.	O	
23. The girl broke the window on the porch.	O	
24. The scared cat that broke the window on the porch climbed the tree.	N	
25. The tree shaded the man.	O	
26. The old car climbed the steep hill.	O	
27. The girl broke the window.	O	
28. The man who lives next door broke the large window on the porch.	N	

STOP. Count the number of sentences judged OLD.

was on the table." In Bransford and Franks' experiments, the final recognition test (Table 8-4) presented ones, twos, threes, and the overall four for each idea grouping.

So what did they find? Just as your performance probably indicated, people overwhelmingly judged threes and fours as having been on the study list (just as you probably judged question 20, the four, as old). Furthermore, they were confident in their ratings, as shown in Figure 8-6. That is, people were recognizing the sentences that expressed the overall idea most thoroughly, even when they had not seen exactly those sentences during study. Such responses are called *false alarms,* saying "OLD" when the correct response is "NEW."

Moreover, people were not confident about having seen old sentences (e.g., sentences 11, 17, 23, and 26 in Table 8-4); the only sentences they were sure about

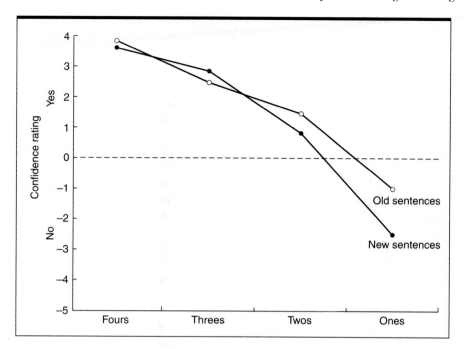

FIGURE 8-6
Confidence ratings for peoples' judgments of new and old sentences.

From Bransford and Franks (1971).

were sentences in which ideas from different groupings had been combined (e.g., sentences 3, 7, 24, and 28 in Table 8-4). Furthermore, they were fairly confident that they had not seen ones, as shown by the strong negative ratings in the figure (between 21 and 23), even though they had seen several sentences that were that short (e.g., sentence 9 in Table 8-4). Because the shorter sentences did not express the whole idea, people believed that they had not seen them before.

These results (Bransford & Franks, 1971, 1972) suggest that people had acquired a more general idea than any of the individual study sentences had expressed. In essence, people were reporting a *composite* memory, in which related ideas were fused together, forming one memory of the whole idea. Therefore, later recognition performance was entirely reasonable: They were matching the combined ideas in the recognition sentences to their composite memory. Rather than verbatim memory, Bransford and Franks found "memory for meaning," memory based on the **integration** of related material.

Leading Questions and Memory Distortions

Another line of research provides a simple yet powerful demonstration of how inaccurate memories can be. This was begun by Elizabeth Loftus and her colleagues on the topic of leading questions and memory distortion (see Loftus, 2003, 2004, for highly readable introductions to this area). Loftus started by examining the effects of leading questions, that is, questions that tend to suggest to a person what answer is appropriate. She wondered whether there were long-term consequences of leading questions in terms of what people remember about events they witnessed (you read about this in Chapter 7).

Simulate
Closer Look:
Memory in
MyPsychLab

FIGURE 8-7 Loftus and Palmer's (1974) results.

In one study, Loftus and Palmer (1974) showed several short traffic safety films, depicting car accidents, to college classes. The students were asked to describe each accident after seeing the film and then answer a series of questions about what they had seen. As you read in Chapter 7, one of the questions asked for an estimate of the car's speed, something people are notoriously poor at. The longer-term importance of this effect gets to the heart of issues about eyewitness testimony and memory distortion. Loftus and Palmer wondered whether the question about speed altered the people's memories of the filmed scene. In other words, if participants are exposed to the implication that the cars had "smashed" together, would they remember a more severe accident than they had actually seen? This is called a **memory impairment**: *a genuine change or alteration in memory of an experienced event as a function of some later event.*

This is exactly what Loftus and Palmer found. A week after the original film and questions, people were given *another* set of questions (but they did not see the film again). One of the questions asked, "Did you see any broken glass?" Many of the participants in the "smashed" group said "yes," even though there had been none in the film. In fact, 34% of the "smashed" group said "yes," compared with only 14% of the group who got *hit.* Furthermore, the likelihood of saying "yes" grew stronger as the speed estimates went up, as shown in Figure 8-7. At each point in the graph, "remembering" broken glass was more common for people who had got "smashed."

Think about that again. Although there was no broken glass in the film, they remembered it, partly as a function of their own speed estimate and the verb they had been questioned with earlier. What happened *after* the memory was formed altered its nature. The question about "smashed" was not just a leading question; it was a source of misleading information.

The Misinformation Effect

Investigators have developed several tasks to test for the effects of misleading information (e.g., Zaragoza, McCloskey, & Jamis, 1987). In a typical study, people see the original event in a film or set of pictures (e.g., pictures depicting a car accident, with one showing a stop sign). Later, they are exposed to additional information, such as a narrative about the accident. Some people receive only neutral information, whereas others are given a bit of misinformation (the narrative mentions "the yield sign," for instance). Finally, there is a memory test, often a yes/no recognition task that asks about the critical piece of information: Was there a stop sign or a yield sign?

A common result is that some *people incorrectly claim to remember the misinformation,* the yield sign here; this is the **misinformation effect**. Belli (1989), for instance, found that misled people had more than 20% lower accuracy than did control groups who were not exposed to the misinformation. Furthermore, Loftus, Donders, Hoffman, and Schooler (1989) found that misled groups were faster in their incorrect judgments—picking the yield sign, for example—than in their correct decisions. This suggests a high degree of misplaced confidence on the part of the misled people. What is particularly troubling is that misinformation effects can persist even if the information is later corrected. For example, a study by Lewandowsky, Stritzka, Oberauer, and Morales (2005) looked at misinformation about the Iraq war that was reported by the press, and then later retracted. However, people continued to inappropriately remember the misinformation as true. This was particularly true for Americans who had more support for the war than for Australians or Germans, who had less support. These later groups better remembered that the misinformation was false and had been retracted.

Source Misattribution and Misinformation Acceptance

Several reviews and summaries (Ayers & Reder, 1998; Loftus, 1991; Loftus & Hoffman, 1989; Roediger, 1996) outline the overall message of this research. As Loftus (1991) noted, alteration of the original memory may be only one part of memory distortion. There seem to be three important memory distortion effects: source misattribution, misinformation acceptance, and overconfidence in the accuracy of memory.

SOURCE MISATTRIBUTION   Sometimes people come to believe that they remember something that never happened. This is **source misattribution**, *the inability to distinguish whether the original event or some later event was the true source of the information*. Source misattribution suggests a confusion in which we cannot clearly remember the true origin of a piece of knowledge (Zaragoza & Lane, 1994). Using the stop sign/yield sign example, source misattribution occurs when we cannot correctly distinguish whether memory of the yield sign came from the original film or from another source, maybe the mistaken narrative that was read later or maybe from prior knowledge and memory (Lindsay, Allen, Chan, & Dahl, 2004).

Another example of source misattribution can be seen in studies of the false fame effect. In these studies, people read a list of nonfamous names, which increases the familiarity of those names. Later, people are more likely to judge the names as famous, essentially confusing familiarity with fame (Jacoby, Woloshyn, & Kelly, 1989). That is, they have lost memory for the source of the feeling of familiarity (that it had been read on a list of explicitly labeled as nonfamous names), so they make their decisions solely on the basis of how familiar the names were. This confusion is particularly likely when people did not remember reading the original list of names, suggesting that the effect occurred at an implicit level (Kelley & Jacoby, 1996; see also Busey, Tunnicliff, Loftus, & Loftus, 2000).

MISINFORMATION ACCEPTANCE For Loftus (1991), a second, possibly larger component of memory distortion is **misinformation acceptance**, in which people *accept additional information as having been part of an earlier experience without actually remembering that information.* For example, a person in a misinformation experiment may not remember seeing a stop sign but is willing to accept that there was a yield sign when the narrative mentions it. Later on, the person reports having seen the yield sign. In short, people accept information presented after the fact and often become certain about these "secondhand" memories. These tendencies probably grow stronger as more time elapses after the event and the original memory becomes less accessible (Payne, Toglia, & Anastasi, 1994).

Part of the reason for misinformation acceptance may be related to reconsolidation. Essentially, **reconsolidation** is the idea that *when a memory is retrieved, this puts it in a plastic, malleable state where it can be changed before it is stored in memory again* (e.g., Sara, 2000). It may be that reminding people of the event before the presentation of misleading post-event information makes the memories pliable again, making it more likely that the incorrect information will be incorporated into the memory trace. In fact, consistent with this, it has been found that having a person recall an eyewitnessed event before hearing misleading information actually makes it more likely that a person will misremember the event later (Chan, Thomas, & Bulevich, 2009).

IMPLANTED MEMORIES Yet another way to examine the acceptance of misinformation is by creating **implanted memories** of events that never happened. Early use of this approach (e.g., Hyman, Husband, & Billings, 1995; Loftus & Hoffman, 1989) involved telling people childhood stories about themselves that their parents had supplied to the researchers, then questioning them about their memory for the episode. Unknown to the person, one of the stories was a fictional, although plausible, event (called a *pseudo-event;* for instance, "when you were six, you knocked over a punch bowl at a wedding reception"). A large number of people came to accept the bogus story as true and claimed to "remember" it. For example, none of Hyman et al.'s participants claimed to remember the pseudo-event when they were first told about it, but 25% "recalled" it by their third session of questioning.

More recently, several studies have looked at other ways of conveying misinformation or pseudo-events. Wade, Garry, Read, and Lindsay (2002), for example, showed people a photo of themselves as children, riding in a hot-air balloon. There had never been a hot-air balloon ride, however; the photos were digitally altered to include an actual picture of the person as a child. Fully 50% of the (now adult) people later reported memories of the ride in the hot-air balloon.

Note, however, that this may be *too* persuasive—if you saw a picture of yourself riding in a hot-air balloon at age six, wouldn't you just decide that it must have happened, and that your memory was faulty? As a follow-up, Lindsay, Hagen, Read, Wade, and Garry (2004) implanted a memory of a pseudo-event with the aid of a more conventional photograph—they got participants' grade-school class photos from their families and showed those photos as "memory cues." The pseudo-event was a prank the person was told he/she and a friend had pulled in grade school, sneaking some Slime (that brightly colored gelatinous toy, made by Mattel) into the teacher's desk. Three childhood stories, two true events and one

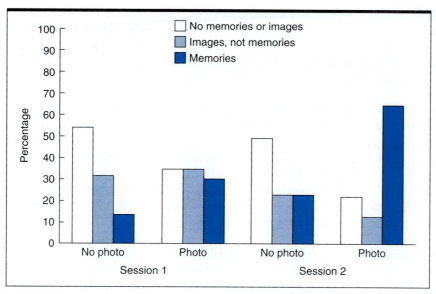

FIGURE 8-8 The percentages of people in the no-photo and photo groups who claimed to have no memories of the pseudo-event, claimed to have images but not memories, and claimed to have genuine memories. The left panel shows performance in the original session, and the right panel shows Session 2 results, collected one week later.

From Lindsay, Hagen, et al., 2004, p. 152. American Psychological Society.

pseudo-event, were read to everyone, and half of them were also shown their grade-school class picture. People were asked to recall whatever they could about the three stories, then to come back in a week for further testing. They were encouraged to spend some time every day "working at remembering more about that event" during the week.

Figure 8-8 presents the results for the pseudo-event, tabulating in each condition the percentage of people having no memory of the event, the percentage having images but not memories of the event, and the percentage that reported having genuine memories of the pseudo-event. Look first at the left half of the figure, showing the results from Session 1. Here, well over 50% of the people who merely heard the story said they had no memory of the event, a correct memory, and roughly 15% claimed they *did* remember it, an incorrect memory. Surprisingly, only about 33% of the group who saw the class photo was correct ("no memory") in Session 1, but 30% in the photo group were wrong when they claimed they did remember the event.

The most stunning result involved how the photo group changed from Session 1 to 2. The percentage of people who incorrectly claimed to remember the event climbed from 30% to nearly 70% in the photo group. Apparently, having a photo that "took them back" to grade-school years boosted the acceptance of misinformation and seemed to implant the bogus memory more thoroughly and convincingly. Indeed, the authors reported that after they told the people that the Slime event had never happened, they often expressed surprise (e.g., "You mean that didn't happen to me?"). It is important to note that not only can implanted memories come from other people, they can also come from ourselves. People who are asked to invent eyewitnessed events sometimes later remember them as being actual events, even though they made them up themselves (e.g., Chrobak & Zaragoza, 2008). That said, it should also be noted that, conversely, people who feign amnesia then find it harder to remember accurately later when they are not trying to fake it (Sun, Punjabi, Greenberg, & Seamon, 2009).

OVERCONFIDENCE IN MEMORY   Despite our feeling that we remember events accurately ("I saw it with my own eyes!"), we often misremember experiences. And, as you've just read, we can be induced to form memories for events that never happened on the basis of suggestion, evidence, or even just related information (e.g., the class photos).

As if this weren't bad enough, we often become overly confident in the accuracy of our memories (see Wells, Olson, & Charman, 2002, for an overview) and surprisingly unaware of how unreliable memory can be (a classic illustration is shown in Figure 8-9). As you read a moment ago, Roediger and McDermott's (1995) participants not only (falsely) recalled and recognized the critical lure, the majority of them claimed that they genuinely remembered it, claiming to have explicit, "vivid memory" of hearing the word in the list. The reason for this overconfidence, aside from a basic belief in ourselves, seems to involve two factors. The first is **source memory**, *our memory of the exact source of information*. A second reason may have something to do with **processing fluency**, *the ease with which something is processed or comes to mind,* as if you thought to yourself, "I remembered 'sleep' too easily to have just imagined that it was on the list, so it must have been on the list" (see Kelley & Lindsay, 1993).

Stronger Memory Distortion Effects

Can something as simple as this in the laboratory explain real-world inaccuracies in memory? Probably. Consider just a sampling of influences on false memories

FIGURE 8-9
Which penny drawing is accurate?

From Nickerson and Adams (1979).

and memory distortions. First, repeated exposure to information can distort memories. Repeated exposure to misinformation increases memory reports of the misinformation (Mitchell & Zaragoza, 1996) and, at least when the information was read in story format, increases the tendency to believe that the information was known before being in the experiment (Marsh, Meade, & Roediger, 2003). There has been some suggestion that the retrieval of misinformation may actually suppress the availability of accurate information, thereby increasing the impact of misinformation (MacLeod & Saunders, 2008). Moreover, repetition increases confidence in the misinformation (Roediger, Jacoby, & McDermott, 1996; Schreiber & Sergent, 1998), as do repeated attempts to remember (Henkel, 2004), or any efforts that involve the person actually generating information (Lane & Zaragoza, 2007). Finally, repeated questioning can enhance recall of some details and induce forgetting of others, even when no misinformation was present (Shaw, 1996; Shaw, Bjork, & Handal, 1995). Repeated questioning also increases confidence in one's memories, whether they are correct or not (Heaps & Nash, 2001; Shaw, 1996).

In addition to the influences of repetition, *imagining that something happened increases later memory reports that it actually did happen*—a situation called **imagination inflation** (Garry, Manning, Loftus, & Sherman, 1996; Garry & Polaschek, 2000; Hyman & Pentland, 1996; Libby, 2003; Mazzoni & Memon, 2003; Seamon, Philbin, & Harrison, 2006; Thomas, Bulevich, & Loftus, 2003), as can instructions to accept consistent information as having happened (Brainerd & Reyna, 1998).

Misinformation effects are often found even when people are told to be careful about mistakes or warned that misleading information might be presented (Belli, Lindsay, Gales, & McCarthy, 1994; Chambers & Zaragoza, 2001; Eakin, Schreiber, & Sergent-Marshall, 2003; Neuschatz, Benoit, & Payne, 2003; Watson, McDermott, & Balota, 2004), which might normally be expected to make people more cautious. Misinformation effects are not limited to situations when memory is explicitly being tested; for example, Dodd and MacLeod (2004) found the effect even when people believed they were merely doing a typical Stroop color naming task.

Finally, there is a social aspect to false memory. Suggestions from others can make you more certain that an event happened or that you remember it (e.g., Meade & Roediger, 2002; Roediger, Meade, & Bergman, 2001; Zaragoza, Payment, Ackil, Drivdahl, & Beck, 2001) or lead you to forget even emotional experiences (Coman, Manier, & Hirst, 2009).

It doesn't take much to realize the implications of this work: Memory is pliable. Memories of events can be altered and influenced, both by the knowledge people have when the event happens and by what they encounter afterward. People report that they remember events that did not happen. And in many cases, they become confident about their accuracy for those events. Unfortunately, at this point, because true and false memories overlap so much on so many dimensions, there is no reliable way to assess whether any given memory is true or false without other corroborating evidence (Bernstein & Loftus, 2009).

Repressed and Recovered Memories

There are broad, disturbing implications of these findings, for when people are trying to remember real-world events (Mitchell & Zaragoza, 2001). If we can "remember" things with a high degree of confidence and conviction, even though they never happened, then how seriously should eyewitness testimony be weighed in court proceedings? Juries usually are heavily influenced by eyewitnesses. Is this justified? Should a person be convicted of a crime based solely on someone's memory of a criminal act? The controversy over recovered memories is an obvious and worrisome arena in which our understanding of human memory is critical.

Here is a summary of a recovered memory case. A person "recovers" a memory, possibly a horrible childhood memory of abuse. The absence of that memory for many years is said to indicate that the experience was repressed or intentionally forgotten. Although the recovery sometimes is spontaneous, it can also be an outcome of efforts by (not very good) therapists trying to bring a memory into awareness. Now that the awful memory is "recovered," the person may seek restitution, such as having the "perpetrator" brought to trial. There is often no objective way to determine whether the recovered memory is real, no sure way to determine whether the remembered event actually happened. Therefore, these cases often simply become one person's word against another's, both people claiming the truth.

There have been court cases involving recovered memories, and several people have been convicted of crimes based on someone's recovered memory (Loftus, 1993; Loftus & Ketcham, 1991). Cognitive science has become involved in this controversy for the obvious reason, our understanding of how memory works. As the research has developed, certain aspects of the recovered memory situation have fallen under greater scrutiny.

Of these, two are especially important. First is the idea of **repression**, *intentional forgetting of painful or traumatic experiences* (Freud, 1953/1905). There is little hard, empirical evidence on the nature of this type of forgetting, however, often not even reliable estimates on how often it occurs. Also, some data suggest that the opposite reaction may occur in cases of trauma: painfully clear and explicit memory of the trauma (Schacter's seventh sin, persistence).

Some disreputable therapeutic techniques for "helping" a client recover a memory are similar to variables shown to increase false memories, including imagery, suggestive questioning, and repetition. In fact, essentially these techniques were used in a case that documents how a completely false, fabricated memory can be "implanted" in a susceptible person (Ofshe, 1992). In addition, as several studies have shown, it is not necessary to go to extreme lengths to implant a memory (Loftus & Coan, 1994; Wade et al., 2002).

No one doubts that child abuse and other personal traumas occur, and no one questions the need for genuine victims to overcome such tragedy. However, it is equally important that cognitive science provide its expertise on issues that hinge so critically on memory. We should be especially mindful that memories are (sadly) prone to distortion and error, perhaps especially so for genuine victims of abuse (Bremner, Shobe, & Kihlstrom, 2000) as well as those who report recovered memories (Clancy, Schacter, McNally, & Pittman, 2000). The very reconstructive processes that bestow power on long-term memory bring with them a degree of fragility.

This sort of work is difficult because there are no reliable indicators of true versus false memories, although there are some overall patterns that distinguish them. For example, overall, people show less confidence in false than true memories, tend to recall them later, and provide less detail about false than true memories (Frost, 2000; Heaps & Nash, 2001). Moreover, there is some evidence of different physiological processing for true versus false memories. As one example, it has been shown that true memories are more likely to produce distinct patterns of gamma oscillations in certain regions of the brain (Sederberg et al., 2007). (EEG recordings show regular oscillations at different frequencies, and gamma oscillations occur in the 28–100 Hz range. You may remember studying these different oscillations when you learned about the different stages of sleep in other psychology classes.)

Section Summary

- Several paradigms give clear evidence of false memories, such as the Roediger and McDermott (1995) list presentation studies and eyewitness memory research by Loftus and others. "Remembering" in such situations is affected by source misattribution, the acceptance of misinformation, and bias. People tend to be overconfident about their memories, regardless of the distortions that might be involved.
- Cases of "forgotten" and "recovered" memories are particularly difficult to assess because of the fragile, reconstructive nature of memories. It is a concern, however, that therapeutic techniques used to assist in "recovering" memory of trauma are so similar to variables such as repetition and repeated questioning, variables that increase the false memory effect.

AUTOBIOGRAPHICAL MEMORIES

We conclude this chapter on a less controversial topic: *the study of one's lifetime collection or narrative of memories,* or **autobiographical memory**. These are memories for more natural experiences and information—a self-memory system (Conway & Pleydell-Pearce, 2000). A set of impressive investigations by Bahrick and his colleagues illustrates the nature of real-world memory for personal events.

The Bahrick Work

Bahrick, Bahrick, and Wittlinger (1975) reported a fascinating study of "Fifty Years of Memory for Names and Faces." Nearly 400 people, ranging in age from 17 to 74, were tested for their retention of the names and faces about members of their own high school graduating classes. For the youngest people, this represented a retention

Recognition memory for information acquired across an extended period is remarkably accurate across many years, whereas recall performance begins to decline within months.

interval of only two weeks; for the oldest, the retention interval was 57 years. Pictures and names were taken from high school yearbooks and were used in a variety of tests. People were first asked for free recall of names and then were given five other tests: name recognition, picture recognition, picture-to-name matching, name-to-picture matching, and cued recall of names using pictures as cues.

Figure 8-10 shows the performance on these six tests across the time since graduation. The free recall curves on the right show an average of just under 50 names accessible a mere 3 months after graduation. Because the average size of graduating classes was 294 (and no one had fewer than 90), this level is quite low: It works out to only about 15% of classmates' names. This number then dwindles further, so that the oldest group recalled only about 18 names, something like 6% recall. Cued recall, with pictures as cues, was largely the same as free recall. In contrast, all four recognition tests showed impressive levels of retention. Simple recognition of names and faces was 90% at the 3-month retention interval. Name recognition did not begin to decline noticeably until about 15 years later, and picture recognition remained in the 80% to 90% range until about 35 years later.

What leads to such impressive levels of memory, particularly as compared with the lower performance levels in laboratory studies? As Bahrick et al. note, typically people have learned the names and faces of their classmates across a

FIGURE 8-10

Results from the Bahrick et al. (1975) study of memory of faces and names across 50 years.

From Bahrick, Bahrick, and Wittlinger (1975).

four-year (or longer) period. This is prolonged acquisition. According to the authors, this principle has two important components, overlearning and distributed practice. First, the information tested in the Bahrick et al. study was overlearned to a higher degree than laboratory studies have examined (even Ebbinghaus didn't test the effects of a four-year learning phase). The result of such overlearning is much-improved retention.

Second, prolonged acquisition represents learning that was distributed across a long period of time, in contrast to typical memory experiments in which learning opportunities are massed over a short period. This neatly confirmed the standard laboratory finding that distributed practice leads to better retention than massed practice (Underwood, Keppel, & Schulz, 1962). Bahrick's work, including memory of foreign language (1984; Bahrick, Bahrick, Bahrick, & Bahrick, 1993), memory of math learned in school (Bahrick & Hall, 1991), and memory of a city's streets and locations 50 years later (Bahrick, 1983), shows this to be one of the soundest bits of advice cognitive psychology gives to students. Distribute your practice and learning rather than massing it together (a.k.a., cramming). Indeed, the Bahrick results suggest that the laboratory-based effect not only is general to more naturalistic settings, but is magnified when naturalistic, everyday memories are tested (see Burt, 1992, and Burt, Kemp, & Conway, 2001, for similar work on diarists' autobiographical memories).

PSYCHOLOGISTS AS SUBJECTS   Several modern-day Ebbinghauses have also tested their own memories in carefully controlled, long-term studies. One major difference from Ebbinghaus's procedure was that Linton (1975, 1978), Wagenaar (1986), and Sehulster (1989) tested their memories for naturally occurring events, not artificial laboratory stimuli. For instance, Wagenaar recorded daily events in his own life for more than six years, some 2,400 separate events, and tested his recall with combinations of four different cue types: what the event was, who was involved, and where and when it happened. Although he found that pleasant events were recalled better than unpleasant ones at shorter retention intervals, his evidence also showed that none of the events could truly be said to have been forgotten (but contrast this with the Bahrick, Hall, & Berger, 1996, evidence that bias toward pleasant things affects our memories of high school grades).

Phenomena of Autobiographical Memory

The research on autobiographical memory has revealed a number of phenomena that characterize it. In this section, we present three of them to give you a feel for why it is important to consider autobiographical memory beyond what is known about episodic and semantic memory. More specifically, we consider infantile amnesia, or why you have trouble remembering events from when you were a young child, the reminiscence bump, and spontaneous memories.

INFANTILE AMNESIA   Think about the first thing you can remember. The very first thing. What is your earliest memory? Where were you? What was going on? Who were you with? How old were you? For most people, this memory is from the ages of 2 to 4 years old. But, wait a minute! What about all of the things that came before that? Why can't we remember anything earlier than that? Furthermore, if you think about it, your memory for your childhood is quite spotty, getting better only as you got older. **Infantile amnesia** is *the inability to remember early life events and very poor memory for your life at a very young age.* One of the first people to discuss this phenomenon was Sigmund Freud (1899/1938). He thought that this was a true amnesia in which there was a catastrophic forgetting of early life events. For him, this was done to protect the ego from threatening psycho-sexual content. However, there has been little empirical support for this idea across the years, so we don't consider it further.

Instead, it appears more likely that infantile amnesia is not an amnesia at all. That is, it is not a massive forgetting of things that would otherwise be remembered. Instead, this reveals how memory is developing. Keep in mind that humans are born neurologically immature and quite helpless. It takes some time for the nervous system to develop to the point that we can have autobiographical memories. Clearly there is some memory, even before birth. Newborns prefer the sound of their own mother's voice, which they heard *in utero*. Moreover, implicit, procedural learning begins almost immediately as a person learns to do things such as control his or her head, arms, and legs, then more complex tasks such as sitting up, using a spoon, and dumping cereal on the floor. Children also are developing semantic memories as they learn what things are and what they are called. They also have episodic memories in that they are clearly influenced by context. However, young children have a difficult time remembering specific events from their lives, especially as they move away from them.

Infantile amnesia resolves itself as one develops a sense of self and can start organizing information around this self concept (Howe & Courage, 1993). There are even neurological correlates that indicate the use of self-referential memories as opposed to more general knowledge (Magno & Allan, 2007). As we have noted earlier, information that you can relate to yourself is often remembered best. In a sense, then, the offset of infantile amnesia marks the beginning of autobiographical memory. A number of things contribute to the development of the self concept. For example, this is also the time when there is a tremendous increase in the child's use of expressive language (K. Nelson, 1993). If you think about your own autobiographical memories, they are heavily influenced by language in terms of their content, their structure, and how you think about them. Also, this period of time is when the hippocampus is maturing, allowing more complex memories to be formed (Nadel & Zola-Morgan, 1984). Finally, at this age, a child has started to develop schemas and scripts that are complex enough to begin making sense of the world in a more adult-like fashion, thereby facilitating memory for individual life experiences (K. Nelson, 1993).

REMINISCENCE BUMP When you talk to people older than the typical college student, you might find that they have a bias to remember events from when they were in college. Why is that? Are they trying to make a social connection with you? Was that the best time of their lives? Although we can't answer most of these questions, we can tell you that your observation is correct, and that we can provide some insight into the first question. The **reminiscence bump** is *superior memory than would otherwise be expected for life events around the age of 20, between the* *ages of 15 and 25.* This is illustrated in Figure 8-11 (Rubin, Rahhal, & Poon, 1998). What this figure shows is the rate of remembering events as a function of how old the person was at the time (older adults are used here to make the reminiscence bump clearer). These studies often use what is known as the Galton-Crovitz technique (Crovitz & Shiffman, 1974; Galton, 1879), in which people are given lists of words and asked to respond with the first autobiographical memory that comes to mind. The first thing to notice is that most of the reported memories come from the recent past, and that the further away in time the event is (the older the event is, hence the younger a person was at the time), the less likely it will be recalled. However, note that around the age of 20 there is a tendency to remember more events than would be expected if this were a normal forgetting curve. So, why does this happen?

There are a number of ideas about what causes the reminiscence bump. One is that memory tends to be better for things that happen for the first time. For example, it is easier to remember your first kiss than your

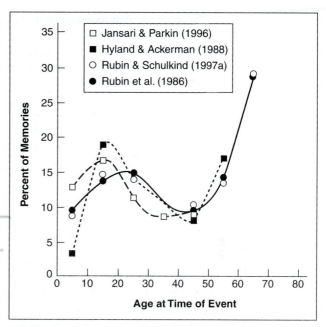

FIGURE 8-11 Illustration of the reminiscence bump (note that data from the most recent decade have been excluded to make the bump clearer). Note that memory performance is better around the age of 20.

Adapted from Rubin, Rahhal, and Poon (1998).

27th, although you may have just as much fun during each. The early 20s is a period in a person's life when a number of things are happening for the first time—the first time a person lives alone, drives, votes, gets a real job, gets a speeding ticket, pays taxes, and so on. Because there are so many "firsts," it is easier to remember events from this period of life. This idea is supported by the fact that people who move from one country to another, where another language is spoken, show a reminiscence bump for the time of their immigration, regardless of how old they were at the time (Schrauf & Rubin, 1998). Presumably this move brought on a number of new experiences, a number of "firsts" that made that time in their life more memorable.

Another idea is that we remember so much more from this period of our lives because we expect to. That is, we all carry out cultural life scripts (Berntsen & Rubin, 2004; Rubin & Berntsen, 2003) about when the exciting times in our lives are supposed to be, such as graduating from school, getting married, buying your first home, having your first child, and so on. This reflects the idea that many aspects of how we think about our lives and structure our autobiographical memories are influenced by our culture (Ross & Wang, 2010). There is also a "life stories" account that is based on the story of our lives that we create over time and as we develop (Glück & Bluck, 2007). So, part of what is driving the reminiscence bump is the expectation that people are supposed to remember more from these important points in their lives. In fact, when people recall events from their lives, the intensity that they report for those events, particularly positive events (e.g., weddings, birth of children, or graduations), corresponds with the cultural expectation (Collins, Pillemer, Ivcevic, & Gooze, 2007). Another source of support for this idea is the fact that people show a reminiscence bump for a character they read about in a novel (Copeland, Radvansky, & Goodwin, 2009). That is, people remember events about a character better when the character was around 20, or when the character went through major life change (for instance, a character's long-time husband dies and she goes out into the working world), as compared to earlier events in the novel (when she was younger), or chapters that were read more recently (when she was older). This seems more likely to occur if people are using life scripts about what should be more memorable to actually guide their memory retrieval.

SPONTANEOUS MEMORY   Autobiographical memories are recalled not only when we actively try to remember, but they also occur spontaneously, without any clear effort to do so. These types of memories often occur (Berntsen, 2010), and they often refer to single events, rather than general periods of time (Berntsen & Hall, 2004). An example of a **spontaneous memory** would be remembering a specific event that happened during a specific chemistry class when you were in high school, compared to just remembering that you took a chemistry class. These spontaneous memories are often triggered by some cue—literally a retrieval cue—in the environment. For example, a person may see a highly valued object (an old toy) that then has the power to elicit a strong autobiographical memory (Jones & Martin, 2006). In general, emotionally intensity is commonly a critical aspect of such triggered autobiographical memories (Talarico, LaBar, & Rubin, 2004).

Some of the strongest cues to spontaneously bring about autobiographical recollections are odors. Memories elicited by odors produce a strong feeling of being back in time (what it was like to experience the event long ago) (Herz & Schooler, 2002; Willander & Larsson, 2006, 2007). Moreover, odors elicit stronger emotions in the person experiencing the memory.

The Irony of Memory

We conclude on the topic of the irony of memory: the question of how this powerful, flexible system can also be so fragile, so prone to errors.

IS HUMAN MEMORY SO AWFUL?   We complain about how poor our memories are, how forgetful we are, how hard it is to learn and remember information. We deal with difficulties of the transience of our memories, our absent-mindedness, the occasionally embarrassing blocking we experience when trying to remember. Are these accurate assessments of our memories (e.g., Roediger & McDermott, 2000)?

Well, they're probably exaggerated. First, as Anderson and Schooler (1991) note, when we complain about memory failures, we neglect the huge stockpile of facts and information that we expect memory to store and to provide immediate access to. We underestimate the complexities, not to mention the sheer volume, of information stored in memory (e.g., some have estimated that the typical adult has at least a half-million–word vocabulary, and it is almost impossible to estimate how many people we have known across the years).

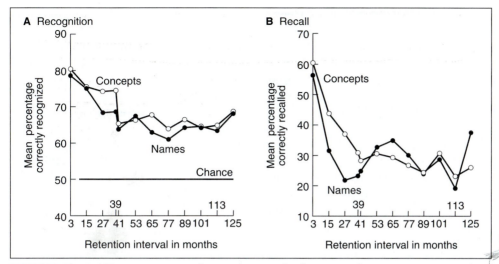

FIGURE 8-12   A. Mean percentages of correctly recognized names and concepts across retention intervals. **B.** Mean percentages of correctly recalled names and concepts across retention intervals. From Conway, Cohen, and Stanhope (1991).

Second, we fall into the trap of equating remembering with recall. When we say we have forgotten something, we probably mean we are unable to recall it right now. As you have read, however, recall is only one way of testing memory. Recognition and relearning are far more forgiving in terms of showing that information has indeed been retained in memory. (And third, we focus on the failures of retrieval, without giving credit for the countless times we remember accurately; see also Chapter 11, on our tendency to search for confirming evidence.)

How much cognitive psychology will you remember in a dozen years? A study by Conway, Cohen, and Stanhope (1991) examined exactly that: students' memory of the concepts, specific facts, names, and so on from a cognitive psychology course taken up to 12 years earlier. Figure 8-12 shows their results. Recall of material dwindled quite a bit across the 12 years, from 60% to 25% for concepts, for example. But recognition for the same material dropped only a bit, from 80% to around 65% to 70%. Correct recognition for all categories of information remained significantly above chance across all 12 years. Your honest estimate—your meta-cognitive awareness of having information in storage—can be quite inaccurate.

Section Summary

- Studies of autobiographical memory, or memory in real world settings, show the same kinds of effects as laboratory studies but sometimes more strongly. Recognition memory for information acquired across an extended period is remarkably accurate across many years, whereas recall begins to decline within months.

Key Terms

autobiographical memory (p. *279*)
cryptomnesia (p. *262*)
false memory (p. *266*)
fan effect (p. *256*)
feeling of knowing (p. *264*)
imagination inflation (p. *277*)
implanted memories (p. *274*)

infantile amnesia (p. *282*)
integration (p. *271*)
judgments of learning (p. *264*)
memory impairment (p. *272*)
metamemory (p. *264*)
misinformation acceptance (p. *274*)
misinformation effect (p. *273*)

processing fluency (p. *276*)
proposition (p. *253*)
prospective memory (p. *262*)
reconsolidation (p. *274*)
reminiscence bump (p. *282*)
repression (p. *278*)
semantic cases (p. *254*)
source memory (p. *276*)

source misattribution (p. *273*)
source monitoring (p. *261*)
spontaneous memory (p. *284*)
tip of the tongue (TOT) (p. *265*)

9 Language

The beginning of wisdom is learning the names of things. (Confucius)
Language is a system of signs, different from the things signified, but
able to suggest them.

(JAMES, 1890, P. 980)

L anguage, along with music, is one of the most common and universal features of human
   society. Language pervades every facet of our lives, from our most public behavior to
   our most private thoughts. We might imagine a society that has no interest in biology, or
even one with no formal system of numbers and arithmetic. But a society without language is
inconceivable. Every culture, no matter how primitive or isolated, has language; every person,

unless deprived by nature or accident, develops skill in the use of language. The human use of language is astounding, with people typically being able to process around three words per second, drawing on a vocabulary of around 75,000 words.

This is a chapter on the basics of language, its characteristics, functions, structure, and form. **Linguistics** is *the discipline that takes language as its topic.* As you learned in Chapter 1, linguistics had a profound influence on cognitive psychology. It was a major turning point when Chomsky rejected behaviorism's explanation of language. Because approaches such as Chomsky's seemed likely to yield new insights and understanding, psychology renewed its interest in language in the late 1950s and early 1960s, borrowing heavily from linguistic theory.

And yet, as psychologists began to apply and test linguistic theory, they discovered an important limitation. Language is a purposeful activity. It's there to *do* something: to communicate, to express thoughts and ideas, to make things happen. Linguistics, however, focused on language itself as a formal, almost disembodied system. In such an approach, the *use* of language by humans was seen as less interesting, tangential, or even irrelevant. On reflection, this view denied a fundamental interest of psychology—behavior. Thus a branch of cognitive psychology evolved, called **psycholinguistics**, *the study of language as it is learned and used by people*.

We present only a brief survey of psycholinguistics here. This chapter and the next focus on the nature and structure of language and cover two of the three traditional concerns in psycholinguistics, language comprehension and production. The third concern, language acquisition, is covered in the chapter on development.

LINGUISTIC UNIVERSALS AND FUNCTIONS

Defining Language

One might define language as "the use of words and how they are spoken in various combinations so that the message can be understood by other people who also speak that language." That's not a bad start. For example, one critical idea in the definition is that meaning and understanding is *attributed* to the words and their pronunciation, rather than being part of those words. As an illustration, the difference in sound between the words *car* and *cars* is the *s* sound, denoting plural in English. But this meaning is not inherent in the *s* sound, any more than the word *chalk* necessarily refers to the white stuff used on blackboards. This is an important idea: Language is based on arbitrary connections between linguistic elements, such as sounds (pronunciations), and the meanings denoted by them.

The definition is a bit confining, however. For instance, it restricts language to human speech. By this rule, writing would not be language, nor would sign language for the deaf. It is true that writing is a recent development, dating back only about 5,000 years, compared to the development of articulate speech, thought to have occurred some 100,000 years ago (e.g., Corballis, 2004). It is equally true that the development of writing depends critically on a spoken language. Thus the spoken, auditory form of a language is more basic than the written version; is there any doubt that children would fail to acquire language if they were exposed only to books instead of to speech? Nonetheless, we include written language for the reason that reading and writing are major forms of communication.

Let's offer a definition that is more suitable here. **Language** is *a shared symbolic system for communication*. First, language is symbolic. It consists of units (e.g., sounds that form words) that symbolize or stand for the referent of the word; the referent, the thing referred to by the final *s,* is the meaning *plural*. Second, the symbol system is shared by all users of a language culture. Language users all learned the same set of arbitrary connections between symbols and meaning, and they also share a common rule system that translates the symbols-to-meaning connections. Third, the system enables communication. The user translates from the thought into a public message, according to the shared rule system. This enables the receiver to retranslate the message back into the underlying thought or meaning.

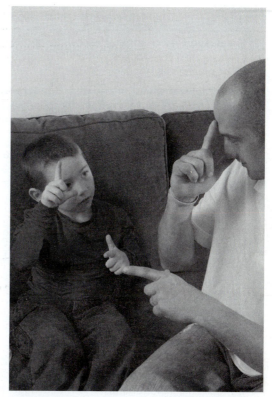

A language does not have to be spoken to be a true language, as sign language for the deaf and symbolic computer languages show.

Language Universals

There are a large number of differences between languages. Take word order, for example. English is largely subject-verb-object (SVO) language in which the sentence subject comes first, followed by the verb and then the object of the sentence. Other languages have other structures. Japanese, for instance, is an SOV language in which the verb typically comes at the end. Despite the many differences among languages, there are some universal properties that they all share as human languages.

Hockett (1960a, b, 1966) proposed a list of 13 **linguistic universals**, *features or characteristics that are common to all languages.* To distinguish human language from animal communication, Hockett proposed that only human language contains all 13 features. Several of the universals he identified, such as the vocal–auditory requirement, are not essential characteristics of human language, although they were likely essential to its evolution. Other features are critically important to our analysis here. Hockett's full list is presented in Table 9-1, along with short explanations. We limit our discussion to four of these, plus two others implied, but absent from the list.

SEMANTICITY   As you already know, the term *semantic* means "meaning." It is an important point that language exhibits **semanticity**—that *language conveys meaning.* For example, the sounds of human language carry meaning, whereas other sounds that we make, say coughing or whistling, are not part of our language because they do not usually convey meaning in the normal sense. (I'm ignoring here the example of a roomful of students coughing in unison at, say, a professor's boastful

TABLE 9-1 Hockett's Linguistic Universals

- **Vocal–auditory channel.** The channel or means of transmission for all linguistic communication is vocal–auditory. Hockett excluded written language by this universal because it is a recent invention and because it is not found in all language cultures.

- **Broadcast transmission and directional reception.** Linguistic transmissions are broadcast, that is, transmitted in all directions from the source, and can be received by any hearer within range; therefore, the transmission is public. By virtue of binaural hearing, the direction or location of the transmission is conveyed by the transmission itself.

- **Transitoriness: rapid fading.** The linguistic transmission is of a transitory nature; it has to be received at exactly the right time, or it will fade (as contrasted with, say, a message transmitted to a recording device, which preserves the information). This implies that the hearer must perform the message preservation task by recording the message on paper or storing information in memory.

- **Interchangeability.** "Any speaker of a human language is capable, in theory, of saying anything he can understand when someone else says it. For language, humans are what engineers call 'transceivers': units freely usable for either transmission or reception" (Hockett, 1960a). In other words, because I can understand a sentence you say to me, I can therefore say that sentence back to you: I can both receive and transmit any message. Contrast this with certain animal systems in which males and females produce different calls or messages that cannot be interchanged.

- **Total feedback.** The human speaker has total auditory feedback for the transmitted message, simultaneous with the listener's reception of the message. This feedback is used for moment-to-moment adjustments to the production of sound.

- **Specialization.** The sounds of language are specialized to convey meaning, that is, linguistic intent, as opposed to nonlanguage sounds. Consider a jogger saying, "I'm exhausted," when the speech act conveys a specific meaning. Contrast this with a jogger panting loudly at the end of a run, when the sounds being produced have no necessary linguistic function (although a hearer might infer that the jogger is exhausted).

- **Semanticity.** Linguistic utterances, whether simple phrases or complete sentences, convey meaning by means of the symbols we use to form the utterance.

- **Arbitrariness.** There is no inherent connection between a symbol and the concept or object to which it refers; there is only an arbitrary connection between sound and meaning. Contrast this with iconic communication systems, such as the bee's waggle dance.

- **Discreteness.** Although sound patterns can vary continuously across several dimensions (e.g., duration of sound, loudness of sound), language uses only a small number of discrete ranges on those dimensions to convey meaning. Thus languages do not rely on continuous variation of vowel duration, for instance, to signal changes in meaning.

- **Displacement.** Linguistic messages are not tied in time or space to the topic of the communication; this implicates an elaborate memory system within the speaker or hearer to recall the past and anticipate the future.

- **Productivity.** Language is novel, consisting of utterances that have never been uttered or comprehended before; new messages, including words, can be coined freely by means of rules and agreement among the members of the language culture.

- **Duality of patterning (duality of structure).** A small set of sounds, or phonemes, can be combined and recombined into an infinitely large set of sentences, or meanings. The sounds have no inherent meaning; the combinations do have meaning.

- **Cultural or traditional transmission.** Language is acquired by exposure to the culture, to the language of the surrounding people. Contrast this with various courtship and mating communications of animals, in which the specific messages are genetically governed.

remark, to indicate a collective opinion. In this situation, the coughing sound is *paralinguistic* and functions much the way rising vocal pitch indicates anger. Then again, it could just be a roomful of coughing students.)

ARBITRARINESS   The feature of arbitrariness was encountered in the definition of language. **Arbitrariness** means that *there is no inherent connection between the units (sounds, words) used in a language and their meanings*. There are a few exceptions, such as onomatopoeias like *buzz, hum,* and *zoom* (but as Pinker, 1994, notes, some units we think of as onomatopoetic, such as a pig's oink, aren't; that sound is "boo-boo" in Japanese). But far more commonly, the language symbol bears no relationship to the thing itself. The word *dog* has no inherent correspondence to the four-legged furry creature, just as the spoken symbol *silence* does not resemble its referent, true silence. Hockett's example drives the point home; *whale* is a small symbol for a very big thing, and *microorganism* is a big symbol for an extremely small thing.

Because there are no built-in connections between symbols and their referents, knowledge of language must involve learning and remembering the arbitrary connections. It is in this sense that we speak of language as being a shared system. We all have learned essentially the same connections, the same set of word-to-referent associations, and stored them in memory as part of our knowledge of language. Thus, by convention—by agreement with the language culture—we all know that *dog* refers to one particular kind of physical object. Obviously, we have to know what word goes with what referent because there's no way to look at an object and decide what its name must be.

Two important consequences of the arbitrariness of language deserve special attention, partly because they help to distinguish human language from animal communication and partly because they tell us about the human language user. These two consequences concern flexibility and the principle of naming. Neither of these was listed by Hockett, although they are derived from his point about arbitrariness.

FLEXIBILITY OF SYMBOLS   Note that arbitrariness makes language symbolic. *Desk* and *pupitre* are the English and French symbols for a particular object. Were it not for the history of our language, we might call it a *zoople* or a *manty*. A consequence of this symbolic aspect of language is that the system demonstrates tremendous **flexibility**. That is, *because the connection between symbol and meaning is arbitrary, we can change those connections and invent new ones*. We routinely shift our terms for the things around us, however slowly such change takes place.

Contrast this flexibility with the opposite of a symbolic system, called an iconic system. In an iconic system, each unit has a physical resemblance to its referent, just as a map is physically similar to the terrain

Although our names for things, such as "dog" seem so strongly tied to the object, the word is actually arbitrary and can vary from language to language. For example, instead of "dog," the same things would be called "chien," "gǒu," or "canis," in French, Chinese, and Latin.

it depicts. In such a system there is no flexibility because changing the symbol for a referent would make the connection arbitrary.

NAMING A corollary to arbitrariness and flexibility involves **naming** (Glass & Holyoak, 1986). *We assign names to all the objects in our environment, to all the feelings and emotions we experience, to all the ideas and concepts we conceive of.* Obviously, wherever it is you are sitting right now as you read this text, each object in the room has a name. Of course, in an unfamiliar or unusual place (an airport control tower or a car repair shop) you may not know the name of something, but it never occurs to you that the thing might have no name.

Furthermore, we don't stop by naming just the physical objects around us. We have a vocabulary for referring to unseen characteristics, privately experienced feelings, and other intangibles and abstractions. Terms such as *perception, mental process, spreading activation,* and *knowledge* have no necessary physical referent, nor do words such as *justice, cause, truth, likewise,* and *however* refer to concrete objects. Indeed, we even have words such as *abstractions* and *intangibles* that refer to the *idea* of being abstract. Going one step further, we generate or invent names for new objects, ideas, activities, and so forth. Think of the new vocabulary that had to be invented and mastered to describe the various actions and operations for using the internet and modern technology, for instance. Because we need and want to talk about new things, new ideas, and new concepts, we invent new terms. (See Kaschak & Glenberg, 2000, on how we invent new verbs from already known words; e.g., "to crutch" or "to google.")

DISPLACEMENT One of the most powerful tools of language is *the ability to talk about something other than the present moment,* a feature called **displacement**. By conjugating verbs to form past tense, future tense, and so on, we can communicate about objects, events, and ideas that are not present but are remembered or anticipated. When we use constructions such as "If I go to the library tomorrow, then I'll be able to . . .," we demonstrate a particularly powerful aspect of displacement: We can communicate about something that has never happened, and indeed might never happen, while anticipating future consequences of that never-performed action. To illustrate the power and importance of displacement, try speaking only in the present tense for about five minutes. You'll discover how incredibly limiting it would be if we were "stuck in the present."

PRODUCTIVITY By most accounts, the principle of productivity (also called generativity) is important because it gives language a notable characteristic—novelty. Indeed, the novelty of language, and the productivity that novelty implies, formed the basis of Chomsky's (1959) critique of Skinner's book (see Chapter 1) and the foundation for Chomsky's own theory of language (1957, 1965). It is an absolute article of faith in both linguistics and psycholinguistics that the key to understanding language and language behavior lies in an understanding of novelty, an understanding of the productive nature of language.

Consider the following: Aside from trite phrases, customary greetings, and so on, hardly any of our routine language is standardized or repetitive. Instead, the bulk of what we say is novel. Our utterances are not memorized, are not repeated, but are new. This is the principle of **productivity**, that *language is a productive and inherently novel activity, that we generate utterances rather than repeat them*. We (your textbook authors) lecture on the principle of productivity every time we teach our memory and cognition classes, each time uttering a stream of sounds, a sequence of words and sentences, that is novel, new, literally invented on the spot—the ideas we talk about may be the same semester after semester, but the sentences are new each time. Even in somewhat stylized situations, as in telling a joke, the language is largely new. Only if the punchline requires a specific wording, do we try to remember the exact wording of a previously used sentence.

What does this mean? It means that language is *creative*, not just repetitive. We do not recycle sentences. Instead, we create them on the spur of the moment, now in the active voice, now in the passive, with a prepositional phrase sometimes at the beginning, sometimes at the end, and so on. In a very real sense then, applying our productive rules of language to the words in our vocabulary permits us to generate an infinite number of utterances.

How can we understand any and all of the infinite set of sentences? What does it mean for a theory of language that speakers and listeners can generate and comprehend any one of this numberless set? In brief, it means that language users must have some flexible basis for generating novel utterances, for coming up with the different sequences of symbols that can be comprehended. And, likewise, comprehenders must have the same flexible basis to hear the sequence of words and recover from them what the intended meaning is. By most accounts, the basis for such productivity is a set of rules. To anticipate later sections of the chapter, rules form the basis for each level of language we discuss, from our phonological system up through the highest level of analysis, the conceptual and belief systems we hold as we comprehend language.

Animal Communication

In contrast to flexible and productive human language, animal communication is neither. Animal communication is seen in a wide range of circumstances, from insects to primates. For example, bees communicate the location of honey through a waggle dance (Dyer, 2002; Sherman & Visscher, 2002; von Frisch, 1967). Essentially, they orient themselves within the hive to the relative position of the sun, and then act out a dance that conveys how the flight will progress to get to the source of the nectar. This is even more impressive given that it is fairly dark in a beehive, and the dance is performed on a vertical surface.

Closer to humans, consider the signaling system of vervet monkeys (Marler, 1967). This consists of several distress and warning calls, alerting an entire troupe to imminent danger. These monkeys produce a guttural "rraup" sound to warn of an eagle, one of the monkey's natural predators; they "chutter" to warn of snakes and "chirp" to warn of leopards. The system thus exhibits semanticity, an important characteristic of language. That is, each signal in the system has a different, specific referent (eagle, snake, and leopard). Furthermore, these seem to be arbitrary connections; "Rraup" doesn't resemble eagles in any physical way.

But as Glass and Holyoak (1986) note, the troupe of monkeys cannot get together and decide to change the meaning of "rraup" from *eagle* to *snake*. The arbitrary connections to meaning are completely inflexible. (This inflexibility results at least in part from genetic influence; compare this with Hockett's last universal, cultural transmission.) Furthermore, there is a vast difference between naming in human languages and in animal communication. There seem to be no words in the monkey system for other important objects and concepts in their environment, such as "tree." And as for displacement and productivity, consider the following quotation from Glass and Holyoak (1986, p. 448): "The monkey has no way of saying 'I don't see an eagle,' or 'Thank heavens that wasn't an eagle,' or 'That was some huge eagle I saw yesterday.'" Even human infants can use displacement by pointing to refer to things that are not immediately present, whereas chimpanzees do not (Liszkowski, Schäfer, Carpenter, & Tomasello, 2009), suggesting that nonhuman animals lack even the basic cognitive abilities required by language.

Although there are no true languages among the animal communication systems, this is not to say that nothing can be learned about language from studying animals. As one illustration, work by Hopkins, Russell, and Cantalupo (2007) used magnetic resonance imaging (MRI) with chimpanzees to show that there was a lateralization of function as a consequence of tool use. Moreover, those regions of the brain that were more affected corresponded to Broca's and Wernicke's areas in humans, which correspond to critical areas of human language production and comprehension (as you will see later in the chapter). This suggests that our development of language may be tied, to some extent, to the development of tool use by our ancestors.

In short, beyond a level of arbitrariness, animal communication does not exhibit the characteristics that appear to be universally true of human language. There are no genuine languages in animals, although there may be genuine precursors to human language among various apes. In human cultures, genuine language is the rule. (For a more up-to-date discussion of animal cognition, see Bekoff, Allen, & Burghardt, 2002.)

Levels of Analysis, a Critical Distinction, and the Sapir-Whorf Hypothesis

We conclude this introduction with three points. The first concerns the five levels of analysis for an exploration of language. The second is a traditional distinction between language performance and competence. And finally, we talk briefly about the relationship between language and cognition, specifically the question of how strongly our language influences our thinking, known as the Sapir-Whorf linguistic relativity hypothesis (Whorf, 1956).

LEVELS OF ANALYSIS The traditional view of language from linguistics is that it is the set of all acceptable, well-formed utterances. In this scheme, the set of rules used to generate the utterances is called a **grammar**. In other words, the grammar of a language is *the complete set of rules that will generate all the acceptable utterances and will not generate any unacceptable, ill-formed ones.* According to most linguists (e.g., Chomsky, 1965), such a grammar operates at three levels: Phonology of language deals with the sounds of language; syntax deals with word order and grammaticality; and semantics deals with accessing and combining the separate word meanings into a sensible, meaningful whole.

TABLE 9-2 Miller's (1973) Five Levels of Language Analysis

Level	Explanation
1. Phonology	Analysis of the sounds of language as they are articulated and comprehended in speech
2. Syntax	Analysis of word order and grammaticality (e.g., rules for forming past tense and plurals, rules for determining word ordering in phrases and sentences)
3. Lexical or semantic	Analysis of word meaning and the integration of word meanings within phrases and sentences
4. Conceptual	Analysis of phrase and sentence meaning with reference to knowledge in semantic memory
5. Belief	Analysis of sentence and discourse meaning with reference to one's own beliefs and one's beliefs about a speaker's intent and motivations

Miller (1973) proposed that language is organized on five levels (Table 9-2). In addition to the three traditional levels of phonology, syntax, and lexical or semantic knowledge, Miller suggested two higher levels as well. He called these the conceptual knowledge and belief levels. For organizational purposes, we focus primarily on the first three of the levels in this chapter. The last two levels are addressed in Chapter 10.

A CRITICAL DISTINCTION Chomsky (1957, 1965) insisted that there is an important distinction in any investigation of language, the distinction between **competence** and **performance**. Competence is *the internalized knowledge of language and its rules that fully fluent speakers of a language have.* It is an ideal knowledge, to an extent, in that it represents a person's complete knowledge of how to generate and comprehend language. Performance is *the actual language behavior a speaker generates, the string of sounds and words that the speaker utters.*

When we produce language, we are not only revealing our internalized knowledge of language, our competence, but we are also passing that knowledge through the cognitive system. So, it is not surprising that our performance sometimes reveals errors. Speakers may lose the train of thought as they proceed through a sentence, and so may be forced to stop and begin again. We pause, repeat ourselves, stall by saying "ummm," and so on. All these **dysfluencies**, these *irregularities or errors in otherwise fluent speech,* can be attributed to the language user. Lapses of memory, momentary distractions, intrusions of new thoughts, "hiccups" in the linguistic system—all of these are imperfections in the language user rather than in the user's basic competence or knowledge of the language. These were performance-related aspects that Chomsky was not particularly interested in, as a linguist. Psychology, on the other hand, views them as rich sources of evidence for understanding language and language users.

THE SAPIR-WHORF HYPOTHESIS We tend to think of mental processes, including those related to language, as universal, as being equally true of all languages. Even

Dani tribe member from New Guinea.

slight familiarity with another language, however, reveals at least some of our beliefs to be misconceptions.

An organizing issue in studies of cultural influences on language and thought is how one's language affects one's thinking. This topic is called the Sapir-Whorf hypothesis, or more formally the **linguistic relativity hypothesis** by Whorf (1956). This idea comes out of work by Edward Sapir, a linguist and anthropologist, and his student Benjamin Whorf. The basic idea was that *the language you know shapes the way you think about events in the world around you.* In its strongest version, the hypothesis claims that language *controls* both thought and perception to a large degree; that is, you cannot think about ideas or concepts that your language does not name. In its weaker version, the hypothesis claims that your language *influences* and shapes your thought, for instance making it merely more difficult, rather than impossible, to think about ideas without having a name for them.

In a series of studies testing the Sapir-Whorf hypothesis, Eleanor Rosch tested members of the Dani tribe in New Guinea on a perceptual and memory test (Rosch-Heider, 1972). She administered both short- and long-term memory tasks, using chips of different colors as the stimuli. She found that the Dani learned and remembered more accurately when the chips were "focal" colors rather than "nonfocal" colors—for example, when the learning trial presented a "really red red" as opposed to a "sort-of-red red." In other words, the central, perceptually salient, "good" red was a better aid to accuracy than the nonfocal "off-red." The compelling aspect of the study that tested the Sapir-Whorf hypothesis involved the language of the Dani people; their language contains only two color terms, one for "dark" and one for "light." Nothing in their language expresses meanings such as "true red" or "off-red," and yet their performance was influenced by the centrality of focal versus nonfocal colors. Thus, this is an example where a person's language could have affected cognition (the language had very few color terms), and yet did not. There is other work showing that different ways of referring to objects, such as the distinction between count and mass nouns in English, which does not occur in Japanese and Chinese, does not influence object perception (Barner, Li, & Snedeker, 2010). Results such as these seem to disconfirm the strong Sapir-Whorf hypothesis.

Current research is finding more and more support for the weaker form of the Sapir-Whorf hypothesis, the hypothesis that language does influence our thoughts, sometimes to a surprising degree (e.g., Boroditsky, 2001, but see Chen, 2007; January & Kako, 2007). Here are two examples, the first involving number, the second involving intentionality. For the first, "English speakers have no difficulty expressing the idea that, if there are 49 men and 37 pairs of shoes, some men will have to go without shoes. There are non-literate societies where this would be a difficult situation to describe, because the language may have number terms only for 'one-two-many' (Greenberg, 1978)" (Hunt & Agnoli, 1991, p. 385; see also Roberson, Davies, & Davidoff, 2000; Malt, Sloman, & Gennari, 2003, discuss how one's linguistic and cultural history influence perception and naming). In other words, one person's language and culture would make it very difficult to think and talk about this situation—12 men going barefoot—whereas another person's language and culture supports that kind of thinking and expression.

Second, consider intentionality, whether someone did something on purpose or by accident. In English, we would say "Sue broke the vase" in both cases, both when she intended to break the vase and when she knocked the vase over by accident. But in Spanish and Japanese, the agent is less likely to be mentioned in the case of an accident; the appropriate sentence is much more like "the vase broke." In a test of this language effect, Fausey and Boroditsky (2011) showed English and Spanish speakers several videos of the two kinds of scenarios, intentional and accidental acts, and then gave them a surprise memory test. Both groups remembered the agent (Sue) well when the act was intentional, but the Spanish speakers tended not to remember the agent as well when the act was accidental; after all, their language-based way of thinking about the accident deemphasizes the agent and focuses on the breaking itself. Thus, there was a clear effect of the participants' language on their interpretation of the event, and their later memory for the event (see Boroditsky, 2011, for a highly readable summary of similar language effects).

Section Summary

- Language is our shared system of symbolic communication, unlike naturally occurring animal communication. True language involves a set of characteristics, linguistic universals, that emphasize the arbitrary connections between symbols and referents, the meaningfulness of the symbols, and our reliance on rules for generating and comprehending language.
- Three traditional levels of analysis—phonology, syntax, and semantics—are joined by two others in psycholinguistics, the levels of conceptual knowledge and beliefs. Linguists focus on an idealized language competence as they study language, but psycholinguists are also concerned with language performance. Therefore, the final two levels of analysis take on greater importance as we investigate language users and their behavior.
- To some degree, we can use people's linguistic intuitions, their linguistic competence, to discover what is known about language; language performance, on the other hand, is also affected by memory lapses and the like.
- The Sapir-Whorf linguistic relativity hypothesis made a claim that language controls or determines thought, making it impossible to think of an idea if there was no word for it in the language. The weak version of this hypothesis is generally accepted now; language exerts an influence on thought, by making it more difficult to think of an idea without having a word to name or express it.

PHONOLOGY: THE SOUNDS OF LANGUAGE

In any language interaction, the task of a speaker is to communicate an idea by translating that idea into spoken sounds. The hearer goes in the opposite direction, translating from sound to intended meaning. In essence, a person is transferring the contents of his or her mind to another person (a lot like ESP, only in a plausible—spoken!—way). Among the many sources of information available in the spoken message, the most obvious and concrete one is the sound of the language itself, the stream of speech signals that must be decoded. Other sources, say the gestures and facial expressions of the speaker, are also available, but we focus on the speech sounds here. Thus our study of the grammar of language begins at this basic level of **phonology**, *the sounds of language and the rule system for combining them.*

TABLE 9-3 English Consonants and Vowels

English Consonants

Manner of Articulation		Bilabial	Labio-dental	Dental	Alveolar	Palatal	Velar	Glottal
(oral) Stops	Voiceless	P (*put*)			t (*tuck*)		k (*cap*)	
	Voiced	b (*but*)			d (*dug*)		g (*got*)	
Nasal (stop)		m (*map*)			n (*nap*)		ŋ (*song*)	
Affricatives	Voiceless					č (*churn*)		
	Voiced					ǰ (*jump*)		
Fricatives	Voiceless		f (*fit*)	Q(*think*)	s (*sad*)	š (*fish*)		h (*had*)
	Voiced		v (*vote*)	∂ (*them*)	z (*zip*)	ž (*azure*)		
Glides		w (*won*)				y (*yes*)		
Liquids					l (*lame*)	r (*rage*)		

English Vowels

	Front	Center	Back
High	i (*beef*)		u (*boom*)
			U (*book*)
	i (*bit*)		
Middle		I (*bird*)	o (*bowl*)
		(*sofa*)	
	e (*babe*)		
	ε (*bed*)		(*bought*)
	æ (*bad*)	(*bus*)	
Low			
			a (*palm*)

Based on Glucksberg and Danks (1975).

Sounds in Isolation

To state an obvious point, different languages sound different: They are composed of different sets of sounds. *The basic sounds that compose a language* are called **phonemes**. If we were to conduct a survey, we would find around 200 different phonemes across all known spoken languages. No single language uses even half that many, however. English, for instance, uses about 46 phonemes (experts disagree on whether some sounds are separate phonemes or blends of two phonemes; the disagreement centers on diphthong vowel sounds, as in *few,* seemingly a combination of "ee" and "oo"). Hawaiian, however, uses only about 15 phonemes (Palermo, 1978). Note here that there is little significance to the total tally of phonemes in a language; no language is superior to another because it has more (or fewer) phonemes.

Table 9-3 shows the typology of the phonemes of English, based on the characteristics of their pronunciation. For consonants, three variables are relevant: place of articulation, manner of articulation, and voicing. *Place of articulation* is the place in the vocal tract where the disruption of airflow occurs; as shown in Figure 9-1, a bilabial consonant such as /b/ disrupts the airflow at the lips, whereas

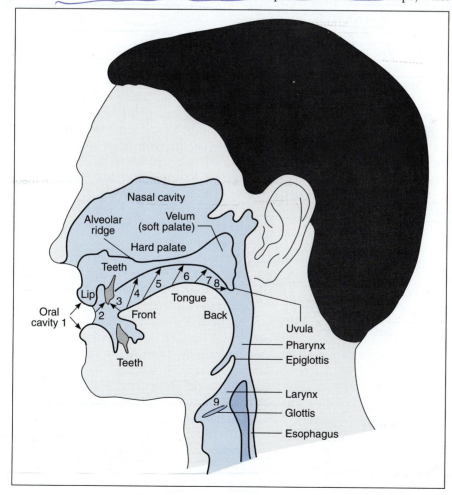

FIGURE 9-1 The vocal tract, illustrating places of articulation: 1, bilabial; 2, labiodental; 3, dental; 4, alveolar; 5, palatoalveolar; 7, velar; 8, uvular; 9, glottal.

Based on Fromkin & Rodman (1974).

/h/ disrupts the column of air at the rear of the vocal tract, at the glottis. Second, *manner of articulation* is how the airflow coming up from the lungs is disrupted. If the column of air is completely stopped and then released, it's called a stop consonant, such as the consonant sounds in *bat* and *tub*. A fricative consonant, such as the /f/ in *fine*, involves only a partial blockage of airflow. Finally, *voicing* refers to whether the vocal cords begin to vibrate immediately with the obstruction of airflow (for example, the /b/ in *bat*) or whether the vibration is delayed until after the release of air (the /p/ in *pat*).

Vowels, by contrast, involve no airflow disruption. Instead, they differ on two dimensions, placement in the mouth (front, center, or back) and tongue position in the mouth (high, middle, or low). Scan Table 9-3, pronouncing the sample words, and try to be aware of the characteristics that you (if you're a native or fluent English speaker) know so thoroughly at an unconscious, automatic level.

Let's develop a few more conscious intuitions about phonemes. Stop for a moment and put your hand in front of your mouth. Say the word *pot* and then *spot*. Did you notice a difference between the two /p/ sounds? Most speakers produce a puff of air with the /p/ sound as they say *pot;* we puff very little (if at all) for the /p/ in *spot* if it's spoken normally. Given this, you would have to agree that these two /p/ sounds are different at a purely physical level. And yet you hear them as the same sound in those two words. Figure 9-2 shows hypothetical spectrograph patterns for two families of syllables, the /b/ family on the left and the /d/ family on the right. Note how remarkably different "the same" phoneme can be.

For psycholinguistics, the two /p/ sounds, despite of their physical differences, are both instances of the same phoneme, the same basic sound group. That is, the fact that these two sounds are treated as if they were the same in English means that they represent one phoneme. So, let's redefine the term phoneme as *the category or group of language sounds that are treated as the same, despite physical differences among the sounds.* In other words, the English word *spot* does not change its meaning when pronounced with the /p/ sound in *pot.*

A classic illustration of phoneme boundaries is shown in Figure 9-3, from a study by Liberman, Harris, Hoffman, and Griffith (1957). When the presented sound crossed a boundary, that is, between stimulus values 3 and 5 and between 9 and 10, identifications of the sound switched rapidly from /b/ to /d/ and then from /d/ to /g/. Variations within the boundaries did not lead to different identifications; despite the variations, all the sounds from values 5 to 8 were identified as /d/.

There are two critical ideas here. First *all the sounds falling within a set of boundaries are perceived as the same, despite physical differences among them.* This is called **categorical**

FIGURE 9-2 Illustrations of changes in vocal formant frequencies for different consonant-vowel pairings.

FIGURE 9-3 One person's labeling data for synthesized consonants ranging from /b/to /g/. Note that small changes in the stimulus value (e.g., from values 3 to 4) can result in a complete change in labeling, whereas larger changes (e.g., from values 4 to 8) that do not cross the phoneme boundary do not lead to a change in labeling.

From Liberman et al. (1957).

perception. Because English speakers discern no real difference between the hard /k/ sounds in *cool* and *keep,* they are perceived categorically, that is, perceived as belonging to the same category, the /k/ phoneme. Second, different phonemes are the sounds that are perceived as different by speakers of the language. The physical differences between /s/ and /z/ are important in English; changing from one to the other gives you different words, such as *ice* and *eyes.* Thus, the /s/ and /z/ sounds in English are different phonemes.

An interesting side effect of such phonemic differences is that you can be insensitive to differences of other languages if your own language doesn't make that distinction. Spanish does not use the /s/ versus /z/ contrast, so native speakers of Spanish have difficulty distinguishing or pronouncing *ice* and *eyes* in English. Conversely, the hard /k/ sounds at the beginning of *cool* and *keep* are interchangeable in English; they are the same phoneme. But, this difference is phonemic in Arabic; the Arabic words for *heart* and *dog* differ only in their initial sounds, exactly the two different hard /k/ sounds in *cool* and *keep.*

Combining Phonemes into Morphemes

From a stock of about 46 phonemes, English generates all its words, however many thousands that might be. This fact, that a small number of units can be combined so flexibly into so many words, is the linguistic universal of productivity at the level of phonology. So, from a small set of phonemes we can generate a functionally infinite number of words. Recall further that the essential ingredient of productivity is rules. We turn now to the rules of combining phonemes into words.

PHONEME COMBINATIONS Let's work with a simple example here. There are three phonemes in the word *bat:* the voiced stop consonant /b/, the short vowel sound /ae/, and the final voiceless /t/. Substitute the voiceless /p/ for /b/, and you get *pat*. Now rearrange the phonemes in these words, and you'll discover that some of the arrangements don't yield English words, such as *abt, *tba,* and *atp.* Why? What makes *abt or *atp* illegal strings in English?

Although it's tempting to say is that syllables like *abt cannot be pronounced, a moment's reflection suggests that this is false. After all, many such "unpronounceable" strings are pronounced in other languages; for example, the initial *pn-* in the French word for *pneumonia* is pronounced, whereas English makes the *p* silent. Instead, the rule is more specific. English usually does not use a "voiced–voiceless" sequence of two consonants within the same syllable; in fact, it only seldom uses any two-consonant sequence when both are in the same "manner of articulation" category. (Of course, if the two consonants are in different syllables, then the rule doesn't apply.)

PHONEMIC COMPETENCE AND RULES Why does this seem to be an unusual explanation? The reason is that our knowledge of English phonology and pronunciation is not particularly verbalizable. You can look at Table 9-3, try to think of words that combine consonants, and come up with tentative pronunciation rules. But this is different from knowing the rules in an easily accessed and expressible fashion. And yet you are a true expert at deciding what phoneme sequences can and cannot be used in English. Your implicit knowledge of how sounds are combined tells you that *abt is illegal because it violates a rule of English pronunciation. This *extensive knowledge of the rules of permissible English sound combinations* is your **phonemic competence**. These rules tell you what is and isn't permissible; *bat* is, but *abt isn't. No one ever explicitly taught you these rules; you abstracted them from your experience as you acquired language. This competence tells you that a string of letters like "pnart" is legal only when the *p* is silent but that "snart" is a legal string—not a word, of course, but a legal combination of sounds. Speakers of the language have this phonemic competence as part of their knowledge of language, an implicit, largely unverbalizable part to be sure, but a part nonetheless.

Speech Perception and Context

We are now ready to approach the question of how people produce and perceive speech. Do we hear a word and segment it in some fashion into its separate phonemes? When we speak, do we string phonemes together, one after another, like stringing beads on a necklace?

CATEGORICAL PERCEPTION AND THE PROBLEM OF INVARIANCE The answer to both questions is "No." Even when the "same" sound is being pronounced, it is not physically identical to other instances of that "same" sound. The sounds change—they change from speaker to speaker and from one time to the next

FIGURE 9-4
Coarticulation is illustrated for the three phonemes in the word *bag;* solid diagonals indicate the influence of the /b/ phoneme and dotted diagonals, the influence of /g/.

From Liberman (1957).

within the same speaker. Most prominently, they change or vary from one word to another, depending on what sounds precede and follow.

This *variability in sounds* is the **problem of invariance**. This term is somewhat peculiar because the problem in speech perception is that the sounds *are not* invariant; they change all the time. You saw an illustration of this in Figure 9-2, where the initial /b/ and /d/ sounds looked very different in the spectrographic patterns depending on the vowel that followed. A second illustration of the problem of invariance is in Figure 9-4, which shows the influence of each of the three phonemes in the word *bag*. To pronounce *bag*, do you simply articulate the /b/, then /ae/, then /g/? No! As the figure shows, the /ae/ sound influences both /b /and /g/, the /g/ phoneme (dotted lines) exerts an influence well back into the /b/ sound, and so on.

The term for this is **coarticulation**: *More than one sound is articulated at the same time.* As you type the word *the* on a keyboard, your right index finger starts moving toward *h* before your left index finger has struck the *t*. In like fashion, your vocal tract begins to move toward the /ae/ before you have articulated /b/ and toward /g/ before even finishing the /b/. This is another illustration of the problem of invariance: Each phoneme changes the articulation of each other phoneme and does so depending on what the other phonemes are. The problem of invariance is made clearer by considering what we do when we whisper. Whispering changes some of the vocal characteristics of the phonemes. For example, voiced phonemes become voiceless. Yet, we typically have little trouble understanding what is being whispered to us.

In short, the sounds of language, the phonemes, vary widely as we speak them. Yet we tolerate a fair degree of variability for the sounds within a phoneme category, both when listening and decoding from sound to meaning and also when speaking, converting meaning into spoken sound. This categorical perception of phonemes in spoken language is a decision-making process that requires some cognitive control to take into account a variety of factors to make this categorization decision. Studies using fMRI scans have found that the left inferior frontal sulcus (B.A. 44) is critically involved in this process (Myers, Blumstein, Walsh, & Eliassen, 2009), supporting the idea that some mental control is need to make these decisions.

THE EFFECT OF CONTEXT   But how do we do this? How do we tolerate the degree of variability—how do we make these decisions? The answer is *context and conceptually driven processing*. If we had to rely entirely on the spoken signal to figure out what was being said, then we would be processing speech in an entirely data-driven, bottom-up fashion. We would need some basis for figuring out what every sound in the word was and then retrieve it from memory. This is almost impossible, given the variability of phonemes. Instead, context—in this case the words, phrases, and ideas already identified—leads us to correct identification of new, incoming sounds.

A clever demonstration of this was done by Pollack and Pickett (1964). They recorded several spontaneous conversations, spliced out single words, then played them to people. When the words were isolated, people identified them correctly only 47% of the time. But performance improved when longer and longer segments of speech were played, because more and more supportive syntactic and semantic context was then available.

In a related study, Miller and Isard (1963) presented three kinds of sentences: fully grammatical sentences such as "Accidents kill motorists on the highways," semantically anomalous sentences such as "Accidents carry honey between the house," and ungrammatical strings such as "Around accidents country honey the shoot." They also varied the loudness of the background noise, from the difficult –5 ratio, when the noise was louder than speech, to the easy ratio of +15, when the speech was much louder than the noise. People shadowed the strings they heard, and correct performance was the percentage of their shadowing that was accurate. As shown in Figure 9-5, accuracy improved going from the difficult to easy levels of speech-to-noise ratios. More interestingly, the improvement was especially dramatic for grammatical sentences, as if grammaticality helped counteract the background noise. For instance, at the ratio labeled 0 in the figure, 63% of the grammatical sentences were shadowed accurately, compared with only 3% of the ungrammatical strings. Indeed, even at the easiest ratio of +15, fewer than 60% of the ungrammatical strings could be repeated correctly.

People use their linguistic knowledge even to the point of hearing things that are not there. In a study by Richard Warren (1970), people heard sentences in

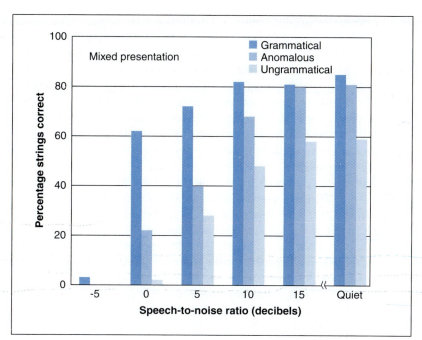

FIGURE 9-5
Percentage of
strings shadowed
correctly.

From Miller & Isard
(1963).

which part of the sentence was removed from the recording and replaced with a cough. For example, in the sentence "The state governors met with their respective legislatures convening in the capital city," the "s" sound was replaced with a cough at the point indicated by the asterisk. The vast majority of people did not report that any speech sounds were missing and could not report the location of the cough when asked to do so on a printed version of the sentence later on. A similar finding has been reported with music (DeWitt & Samuel, 1990), with people reporting hearing music notes or tones that were obscured by noise. So, when people are listening, they are actively using their knowledge to interpret what they hear.

TOP-DOWN AND BOTTOM-UP PROCESSES   More recent evidence is largely consistent with these early findings. That is, there is a combination of data-driven and conceptually driven processing in speech-recognition, a position called the integrative or interactive approach (Rapp & Goldrick, 2000). At a general level, a variety of conceptually distinct language processes, from the perception of the sounds up through integration of word meanings, operate simultaneously, each having the possibility of influencing the ongoing activity of other processes. While features of the speech signal are analyzed perceptually, a listener's other linguistic knowledge is also called into play at the same time. These higher levels of knowledge and analysis operate in parallel with the phonemic analysis and help to identify the sounds and words (Dahan, 2010; Dell & Newman, 1980; Pitt & Samuel, 1995; Samuel, 2001). Moreover, to overcome the relative dearth of invariant information in the speech signal, it also appears that language perception relies heavily on characteristic knowledge of the speaker, such as whether the person speaks with a lisp (Kraljik, Samuel, & Brennan, 2008).

As a concrete example, imagine a sentence that begins "The grocery bag was. . . ." You are processing the *bag* segment of this speech signal. Having already processed the previous word to at least some level of semantic interpretation, you have developed a useful context for the sentence. To be simple about it, *grocery* limits the number of possibilities that can be mentioned in the sentence. Similar evidence of the role of context was reported by Marslen-Wilson and Welsh (1978) in a task that asked people to detect mispronunciations, and by Dell and Newman (1980) in a task that asked people to monitor spoken speech for the occurrence of a particular phoneme (recall also the demonstrations of context effects in Treisman's shadowing experiments, e.g., 1960, 1964).

Such results are so powerful that theories of speech recognition must account for both aspects of performance, the data driven and the conceptually driven. A specific connectionist model that does exactly that was proposed by McClelland and Elman (1986). In their TRACE model, information is continually being passed among the several levels of analysis. Lexical or semantic knowledge, if activated, can alter the ongoing analysis at the perceptual level by "telling" it what words are likely to appear next; the model's predictions of what words are likely to appear are based on semantic knowledge. At the same time, phonemic information is passed to higher levels, altering the patterns of activation there (see Dell, 1986, for a spreading activation network theory of sentence production, and Tyler, Voice, & Moss, 2000, for a useful review).

Embodiment in Speech Perception

The perception of speech is critical for language. Intuitively this may seem like an odd place for aspects of embodied cognition to show up. However, speech perception is actually where one of the first embodied theories of cognition came from (although it was not labeled as such at the time). This is the **motor theory of speech perception** (see, e.g., Liberman, Cooper, Shankwiler, & Studdert-Kennedy, 1967; Liberman & Mattingly, 1985).

According to the motor theory of speech perception, people perceive language, at least in part, by comparing the sounds that they are hearing with how they themselves would move their own vocal apparatus to make those sounds. That is, we create embodied representations of how those sounds might be spoken to help us perceive speech. There are several lines of evidence for this idea (for an excellent review, see Galantucci, Fowler, & Turvey, 2006). According to Galatucci et al., as some examples, people find it much easier to understand synthesized speech if it takes issues of coarticulation into account, rather than simply presenting a string of phonemes. Also, the parts of the cortex that are more active during speech perception overlap substantially with those involved in speech production. This is similar to the idea of mirror neurons that fire when primates observe actions of others. Finally, people find it easier to comprehend speech if they can see the person talking, which gives them more information about how the sounds are being made. It is also true that people can better understand song lyrics if they can see a person singing (Jesse & Massaro, 2010). This theory does not explain all aspects of speech perception, such as how people who could never speak can understand spoken language. However, it does illustrate how the structure of our bodies, and how we use them in the environment (in this case moving the air around with our vocal apparatus), influences cognition.

Related to the idea that motor programs are involved in speech perception, there is also some evidence that people activate mental motor programs just by thinking about words to themselves. Take the example of tongue twisters, which involve difficult movements of the vocal apparatus when they are spoken aloud. What is interesting is that people are likely to show evidence of articulation difficulty, such as reading times, when they are simply asked to read tongue twisters. That is, even when the people were only "saying" (inner speech) the twisters silently to themselves in their minds, the language processing system takes into account and simulates the muscle movements that would be involved if the person were actually speaking, and these simulated movements produce the normal tongue twister difficulty (Corley, Brocklehurst, & Moat, 2011; but see Oppenheim & Dell, 2010).

A Final Puzzle

As if the preceding sections weren't enough to convince you of the need for conceptually driven processing, consider one final feature of the stream of spoken speech. Despite coarticulation, categorical perception, and the problem of invariance, we naively believe that words are somehow separate from each other in the spoken signal—that there is a physical pause or gap between spoken words, just as there is a blank space between printed words.

This is not true. Our intuition is entirely wrong. Analysis of the speech signal shows that there is almost no consistent relationship between pauses and the ends of words. If anything, the pauses we produce while speaking are longer *within* words than between words. As evidence of this, see Figure 9-6, a spectrograph

FIGURE 9-6   A spectrogram from the sentence "John said that the dog snapped at him," taken from fluent spoken speech. Note that the pauses or breaks do not occur regularly at the ends of words; if anything, they occur more frequently *within* the individual words (e.g., between the /s/ and /n/ sounds, between the /p/ and /t/ sounds; compare with the end of *the* and the beginning of *dog*).

From Foss & Hakes (1978).

recording of a spoken sentence. Inspection of the patterns in correspondence to the words listed at the bottom illustrates the point: The pauses in the spectrograph bear no particular relationship to the ends of words. There must be other kinds of information that human cognition uses to decode spoken language.

How can our intuitions about our own language, that words are articulated as separate units, be so wrong? (Note that our intuitions about foreign languages—they sound like a continuous stream of speech—are more accurate.) How do we segment the speech stream and come to know what the words and phrases are? Part of the answer is our knowledge of words in the language and the fact that some phoneme combinations simply cannot or do not form words (Norris, McQueen, Cutler, & Butterfield, 1997). Another part of the answer to these questions is syntax, the second level of language analysis and the topic we address next.

Section Summary

- Phonology is the study of the sounds of language. Spoken words consist of phonemes, the smallest units of sound that speakers of a language can distinguish. Surprisingly, a range of physically different sounds are classified as the same phoneme; we tolerate some variation in the sounds we categorize as "the same," called categorical perception.
- Categorical perception is particularly important in the study of speech recognition because the phonemes in a word exhibit coarticulation, overlapping effects among successive phonemes, such that an initial sound is influenced by the sounds that follow and the later sounds are influenced by what came before.
- Speech recognition relies heavily on conceptually driven processes. This includes our knowledge of the sentence and word context, our estimates of how we would produce the sounds ourselves, and our knowledge of what the words in our language are.
- As an illustration of embodied cognition, according to the motor theory of speech perception, part of the way that people go about understanding spoken language may be to try to mentally simulate those sounds as if they were actually being spoken.

SYNTAX: THE ORDERING OF WORDS AND PHRASES

At the second level of analysis we have **syntax**, *the arrangement of words as elements in a sentence to show their relationship to one another.* We've already studied how sounds combine to form meaningful words. At this level of analysis, we are interested in how the words are sequenced to form meaningful strings, the study of syntax. Just as with phonology, where the rules for combining sounds might be called a phonological grammar, our syntactic grammar is a set of rules for ordering words into acceptable, well-formed sentences.

If you have a connotation associated with the word *syntax,* it probably is not the psycholinguistic sense of *grammar* but the "school grammar" sense instead. In school, if you said "He ain't my friend no more," your teacher might have responded, "Watch your grammar." To an extent, this kind of school grammar is irrelevant to the psycholinguistic study of syntax. Your teacher was being *prescriptive* by teaching you what is proper or prestigious according to a set of cultural values. In another way, though, school grammar does relate to the psycholinguistic study of language; language is for expressing ideas, and anything that clarifies this expression, even arbitrary rules about "ain't" and double negatives, improves communication. (And finally, your teacher was sensitive to another level of language: People do judge others on the quality of their speech.)

WORD ORDER   Unlike the school grammar idea, the psycholinguistic study of syntax is *descriptive*; that is, it takes as its goal a description of the rules of how words are arranged to form sentences. Let's take a simple example, one that taps into your syntactic competence. Which is better, sentence 3 or 4?

(3) *Beth asked the man about his headaches.*

(4) **About the Beth headaches man asked his.*

Your "school grammar" taught you that every sentence must have a subject and a verb. According to that rule, sentence 4 is just as much a sentence as 3. Your syntactic competence, on the other hand, tells you that sentence 4 is ill-formed, unacceptable. You can even specify some of the rules that are being violated; for example, definite articles such as *the* do not usually precede a person's name, and two nouns usually don't follow one another in the same phrase or clause.

The point here is that the meaning of a sentence is far more than the meanings of the words. The "far more" here is the arrangement or sequencing of the words. We're speaking of syntactic word order rules for English (Gershkoff-Stowe & Goldin-Medow, 2002, argue that word order is more than just syntax, and that it reflects a more general property of human thought). More than some languages (e.g., Latin), English relies heavily on word order. Consider "red fire engine" versus "fire engine red" (or even "red engine fire"). Despite the fact that *red* and *fire engine* can be nouns, our word-order knowledge tells us that the first word in these phrases is to be treated as an adjective, modifying the following noun. Thus by varying word order alone, "red fire engine" is a fire engine of the usual color, and "fire engine red" is a particular shade of red.

PHRASE ORDER   There's more to it than just word order, however. We also rely on the ordering of larger units such as phrases or clauses to convey meaning. Consider the following sentences:

(5) *Bill told the men to deliver the piano on Monday.*

(6) *Bill told the men on Monday to deliver the piano.*

In these examples, the positioning of the phrase "on Monday" helps us determine the intended meaning, whether the piano was to be delivered on Monday or whether Bill had told the men something on Monday. Thus, the sequence of words and phrases contains clues to meaning, clues that speakers use to express meaning and clues that listeners use to decipher meaning.

NUMBER AGREEMENT Yet another part of syntax involves the adjustments we make depending on other words in the sentence. In particular, a part of every sentence is a subject and a verb. It's required, furthermore, that the subject and verb agree in number—if the subject of the sentence is singular, you must use a singular verb, as in "The car has a flat tire" (obviously, pronouns have to be coordinated in terms of number, too). As Bock (1995, p. 56) noted, agreement helps listeners know what the topic of a sentence is going to be about. For example, consider "The mother of the girls who was . . ." versus "The mother of the girls who were. . . ." You're pretty sure that the first sentence is going to be about the mother, and the second one about the girls just because of the number agreement of "was" versus "were." So number agreement, like word and phrase order, is a clue to meaning, part of the spoken and written language that we rely on when we comprehend. (See Bock & Miller, 1991, and Hartsuiker, Anton-Mendez, & van Zee, 2001, for experimental work on number agreement errors, e.g., when you make the verb agree in number with the nearest noun rather than the subject noun, as in "*The difficulty with all of these issues are that. . . .")

In general, we need to understand what these syntactic clues are and how they are used. We need to explore the syntactic rules that influence comprehension. We begin by looking at the underlying syntactic structure of sentences, taking a piece-by-piece approach to Chomsky's important work.

Chomsky's Transformational Grammar

At a general level, Chomsky intended to "describe the universal aspects of syntactic knowledge" (Whitney, 1998), that is, to capture the syntactic structures of language. He noted that language has a hierarchical phrase structure: The words do not simply occur one after the other. Instead, they come in groupings, such as "on Monday," "the men," and "deliver the piano." Furthermore, these groupings can be altered, either by moving them from one spot to another in the structure or by modifying them to express different meanings (e.g., by changing the statement into a question). These two ideas—words come in phrase structure groupings, and the groupings can be modified or transformed—correspond to the two major syntactic rule systems in Chomsky's theory.

PHRASE STRUCTURE GRAMMAR Let's start with the phrase structure grammar that generates the overall structure of sentences. An important point in Chomsky's system is that the **phrase structure** grammar accounts for *the constituents of the sentence, the word groupings and phrases that make up the whole utterance, and the relationships among those constituents*. To illustrate this consider an example from Lachman, Lachman, and Butterfield (1979):

(7) The patio resembles a junkyard.

In a phrase structure grammar, the entire sentence is symbolized by an *S*. In this grammar, the sentence *S* can be broken down into two major components, a noun phrase *(NP)* and a verb phrase *(VP)*. Thus the first line of the grammar illustrated in Figure 9-7A shows $S \rightarrow NP + VP$, to be read, "The sentence can be rewritten as a noun phrase plus a verb phrase." In the second rule, the *NP* can be

FIGURE 9-7 A depiction of a phrase structure grammar: **A.** The rewrite rules of the grammar; **B.** Sentence generation by the rules; **C.** A tree diagram or hierarchical representation; **D.** A "bracket equivalent" diagram of the sentence.

From Lachman, Lachman, & Butterfield (1979).

rewritten as a determiner *(D)*, an article such as *the* or *a,* plus a noun *(N): NP →* *D + N*; in other words, a noun phrase can be rewritten as a determiner and a noun. In rule 3 we see the structure of a verb phrase; a *VP* is rewritten as a verb *(V)* plus an *NP: VP → V + NP.*

As Figure 9-7B shows, six rewrite rules are necessary for generating the sentence. A different but equivalent depiction of the grammar is shown in Figure 9-7C, in which a tree diagram shows the most general components at the top and the specific words at the bottom. An advantage of the tree diagram is that it reveals the hierarchical structure of the sentence as well as the internal structure and interrelations. Finally, a bracket equivalent is shown in Figure 9-7D.

THE INADEQUACY OF PHRASE STRUCTURE GRAMMAR ALONE Chomsky's theory relied heavily on a phrase structure approach because it captures an important aspect of language—its productivity. That is, this kind of grammar is generative; by means of such phrase structure rules, an entire family of sentences can be generated.

Furthermore, the phrase structure grammar is joined with two other components, the lexical entries (the words of a sentence) and the lexical insertion rules (the rules for putting the words into their slots). These components, as shown in Figure 9-7, generated the first representation of the sentence, the **deep structure** representation. In Chomsky's view the deep structure is *an abstract syntactic representation of the sentence* being constructed, with only bare-bones lexical entries (words).

The deep structure is critical for two reasons. First, it is the representation passed to the transformational "fix-it" rules to yield the surface structure of the sentence; we deal with those in a moment. Second, the deep structure is also submitted to a semantic component that "computes" meaning. This takes the deep structure and produces a semantic representation that reflects the underlying meaning. Notice that, because of the separate treatment of the semantic component, a sentence's true meaning might not be reflected accurately in the **surface structure**; a surface structure might be **ambiguous**, or *have more than one meaning*. For instance, consider two classic examples of ambiguous sentences:

(8) Visiting relatives can be a nuisance.

(9) The shooting of the hunters was terrible.

A moment's reflection reveals the ambiguities. These alternative meanings are revealed when we **parse** the sentences, when we *divide the sentence into phrases and groupings,* much the way the phrase structure grammar does. The two meanings of sentence 8—that is, the two deep structures—correspond to two different phrase structures. For sentence 8, the ambiguity boils down to the grammatical function of *visiting,* whether it is used as an adjective or a verb. These two grammatical functions translate into two different phrase structures (*verb+noun* versus *adjective+noun*).

Sentence 9, however, has only one phrase structure; there is only one way to parse it: {[*the shooting of the hunters*] [*was terrible*]}. Thus sentence 9 is ambiguous at the level of surface structure. Because phrase structure rules can generate such ambiguous sentences, Chomsky felt that this illustrated a limitation of the pure phrase structure approach: There must be something missing in the grammar. If it were complete, it wouldn't generate ambiguous sentences.

A second difficulty Chomsky pointed out involves examples such as the following:

(10a) Pierre bought a fine French wine.

(10b) A fine French wine was bought by Pierre.

According to phrase structure rules, there is almost no structural similarity between these two sentences. And yet they mean nearly the same thing. People's intuitions, that active and passive paraphrases are more or less identical at the level of meaning, are not captured by the phrase structure approach.

TRANSFORMATIONAL RULES Chomsky's solution to such problems was to postulate a second component to the grammar, a set of **transformational rules** that handle the many specific surface forms that can express an underlying idea. These transformational rules *convert the deep structure into a surface structure, a sentence* *ready to be spoken.* By applying different transformations, we can form an active declarative sentence, a passive voice sentence, a question, a negative, a future or past tense, and so on. With still other transformations, phrases can exchange places, and words can be inserted and deleted. In this view, sentences 10a and 10b differ only in their surface structures; one deep structure (the core meaning) is transformed in two different fashions. Likewise, for a simple deep structure idea such as {(boy kisses girl)}, the **transformational grammar** could generate any of the following, depending on which particular grammatical transformations were selected:

(11a) The boy kissed the girl.

(11b) The girl was kissed by the boy.

(11c) Was the girl kissed by the boy?

More elaborate rules are also applied by this transformational component, including rules that allow us to combine ideas, such as the idea that {(boy kisses girl)} and the idea that {(girl is pretty)}:

(12a) The boy kissed the pretty girl.

(12b) The boy kissed the girl who was pretty.

(12c) The girl whom the boy kissed was pretty.

(12d) Will the girl who is pretty be kissed by the boy?

Thus one surface structure for the {(girl) (is) (pretty)} idea is merely "the pretty girl"; an equivalent structure, in terms of meaning, is "the girl who is pretty." On the other hand, sentences 12c and 12d are the most difficult to comprehend, largely because of the passive voice and the embedded relative "who" clauses.

Limitations of Transformational Grammar

A great deal of early psycholinguistic research was devoted to structural aspects of language. For example, there was a lot of focus on testing the derivational complexity hypothesis. This hypothesis suggests that the difficulty of comprehending a sentence is directly related to the number of grammatical transformations applied. So, if a deep structure has two transformations applied to it, it is more difficult to comprehend than if only one transformation is applied. Early results tended to support the theory (e.g., Palermo, 1978). However, over time, psychology became dissatisfied with this approach. Work by Fodor and Garrett (1966) was especially instrumental in dimming the enthusiasm. They noted that much of the support for the derivational complexity hypothesis failed to control potentially important factors. For instance, a derivationally more complex sentence generally has more words in it than a simpler one (contrast sentences 12a and 12c).

Moreover, there was a metatheoretical point of view. To oversimplify a bit, the major components were said to be the syntactic rules for generating first a deep then a surface structure.

Noam Chomsky, developer of Transformational Grammar Theory.

Meaning was literally off to the side. This depicts the difficulty psychology had with linguistic theory: It seemed that meaning was secondary to syntax. It's almost as if the theory, as it was applied to language *use,* suggested that we first make up our minds what phrase constituents we're going to use and only then decide what we're going to talk about. To psychologists concerned with how we use language to express meaning, this seemed wrong.

Note that this is an oversimplification, making it seem as if Chomsky encouraged linguists to avoid meaning. It was not that extreme. In fact, Chomsky repeatedly emphasized the importance of both syntax and semantics. He pointed out that even a perfectly grammatical, syntactically acceptable sentence may be semantically anomalous. His most famous example is "Colorless green ideas sleep furiously." The sentence is grammatically acceptable—consider a sentence with completely parallel syntax, such as "Tired young children sleep soundly." But, Chomsky's sentence has no meaning in any ordinary sense.

Still, Chomsky's work never dealt satisfactorily with meaning, in the view of psychologists. Furthermore, trying to apply his theory to the actual use of language—that is, turning his competence-based theory into a performance theory of language production and comprehension—only made it more apparent that a different approach was needed.

We turn to the major focus of this research, the semantic level of analysis, in a moment. But first, we must conclude this section on syntax with a psycholinguistic view of syntax.

The Cognitive Role of Syntax

From a psychological perspective, what is the purpose of syntax? Why follow syntactic rules? Essentially, we use syntax to help figure out meaning. If an infinite number of sentences are possible, then the one sentence being said to us right now could be about *anything.* Syntax helps listeners extract meaning and helps speakers convey it.

Bock's (1982) article on a cognitive psychology of syntax discusses several important issues that psycholinguistics must explain. She notes that the syntactic burden falls more heavily on the speaker than the listener. That is, when you have to produce a sentence rather than comprehend it, you must create a surface structure, a string of words and phrases to communicate your idea as well as possible. Thus, syntax is a feature of language that is related to the speaker's mental effort.

AUTOMATIC PROCESSING   Two points Bock raises should illustrate some issues in the psycholinguistic study of syntax. First, consider the issues of automatic and conscious processes as they apply to language production. As we know, automatic processes are the product of a high degree of practice or overlearning. Bock noted that several aspects of syntactic structure are consistent with the idea of automaticity. For instance, children rely heavily on regular word orders, even if the native language they are learning has irregular word order. The purpose is that by relying over and over on the same syntactic frames, they can be generated and used more automatically. Similarly, adults tend to use only a few syntactic structures with regularity, suggesting that they can be called into service rapidly and automatically.

Interestingly, the syntax you use can be influenced by a previous sentence, quite literally syntactic priming (Bock, 1986; West & Stanovich, 1986). Bock's later work (Bock & Griffin, 2000) found evidence that a particular syntactic construction can prime later ones up to lag 10 (i.e., with 10 intervening sentences), even in written language (Branigan, Pickering, & Cleland, 1999; Branigan, Pickering, Stewart, & McLean, 2000).

PLANNING   In Bock's second point, she reviewed evidence of an important interaction between syntax and meaning. In general, we tailor the syntax of our sentences to the accessibility of the lexical or semantic information being conveyed. This is known as the **given-new strategy** (Clark & Clark, 1977). Phrases that contain more accessible information, or given information, tend to occur earlier in sentences. This is information that is either well known or recently discussed in a discourse (and so more available). In comparison, less accessible, newer concepts tend to come later, possibly to give ourselves extra time for retrieval (but see Clifton & Frazier, 2004, for an alternative account). Ferreira and Swets (2002) demonstrated this in a clever experiment, by asking people to state the answer to easy and hard addition problems, in sentence frames like "The answer is __." They found that people delayed nearly a half a second more before they started talking when the problem was hard (e.g., 23 + 68) than when it was easy (e.g., 21 + 22). Clearly speech production is sensitive to the ease of memory retrieval.

Our planning and execution of speech is also sensitive to grammatical complexity and presumably to the possibility that a listener (or a speaker, for that matter) might lose track of information if too much time passes. As an example, Stallings, MacDonald, and O'Seaghdha (1998) showed a particular kind of syntactic adjustment used for complex noun phrases, "heavy NPs" in their words ("heavy" because they're long). Specifically, we tend to shift heavy NPs to the end of a sentence, and insert other material in between the subject and NP, but not when the noun phrase is short. Consider the simple sentence "The boy found the textbook in his car." The noun phrase (the textbook) is short, so doesn't need to be shifted. But, if there's more to say about the textbook, you might say "The boy found in his car the textbook that had been lost for so long," shifting the textbook phrase to the end and putting "in his car" in the middle. But you probably wouldn't shift the short noun phrase to the end, as in "The boy found in his car the textbook." Moving "the textbook" to the end isn't needed here because the listener's working memory isn't being over-taxed. But the heavy NP "the textbook that had been lost for so long" is sufficiently long that working memory might lose essential information, the connections between the boy, the car, and finding the book, if the phrase separated those ideas by too many intervening ideas. More generally, as syntactic complexity increases, this increasingly taxes working memory (e.g., Fedorenko, Gibson, & Rohde, 2006).

These effects tell us something interesting about the cognitive mechanisms that create sentences. Earlier theories of sentence planning, such as Fromkin's (1971; see Table 9-4), described planning as sequential: First you identify the meaning to be conveyed, then you select the syntactic frame, and so on. Recent research, however, shows how interactive and flexible the planning process is (Ferreira, 1996; Griffin & Bock, 2000). Difficulties in one component, for instance

TABLE 9-4	**Fromkin's (1971) Model for the Planning and Production of Speech**
Stage	**Process**
1	Identify meaning; generate the meaning to be expressed.
2	Select syntactic structure; construct a syntactic outline of the sentence, specifying word slots.
3	Generate intonation contour; assign stress values to different word slots.
4	Insert content words; retrieve appropriate nouns, verbs, adjectives, and so on from the lexicon and insert into word slots.
5	Add function words and affixes; fill out the syntax with function words (articles, prepositions, etc.), prefixes, suffixes.
6	Specify phonetic segments; express the sentence in terms of phonetic segments according to phonological (pronunciation) rules.

word retrieval, can prompt a return to an earlier planning component, say to rework the syntax (Ferreira & Firato, 2002), or can prompt you to delay the sentence. By selecting an alternative syntax, the speaker buys more time for retrieving the intended word (see also Kempen & Hoehkamp, 1987). Needless to say, such a highly interactive system runs counter to strictly hierarchical or sequential approaches, such as Chomsky's.

In general, we begin our utterances when the first part of the sentence has been planned but before the syntax and semantics of the final portion have been worked out (see Bachoud-Levi, Dupoux, Cohen, & Mehler, 1998, and Griffin, 2003, for comparable effects). The time it takes to begin speaking (e.g., Bock, Irwin, Davidseon, & Levelt, 2003) and hesitations in our spoken speech are clues to the nature of planning and memory retrieval, as are the effects of momentary changes in priming, lexical access, and working memory load (Bock & Miller, 1991; Lindsley, 1975). In fact, several reports detail how the false starts, hesitations, and restarts in speaking often reflect both the complexity of the intended sentence and a genuine online planning process that unfolds as the sentence is developed (Clark & Wasow, 1998; Ferreira, 1996; Ferreira & Dell, 2000; see Bock, 1996, for a review of methods of studying language production).

More recent work has taken Chomsky to task even further. In a connectionist model of language processing, Chang, Dell, and Bock (2006) have challenged Chomsky's idea that language has a strong genetic component, as compared to the strong learning stance taken by the behaviorists. That is, Chomsky suggested that although you may need to learn your own language, all humans have a strong genetic bias to learn some language, and that aspects of transformational grammar were somehow part of that genetic process. The Chang et al. model assumes, in contrast, that language processing has a strongly learned component, similar to other memory processes. Part of how the model learns a language is by comparing its predictions for what will be said next to what is actually said, and then adjusting the connection weights based on any discrepancy (see also Griffiths, Steyvers, & Tenebaum, 2007, for a predictive model of word meaning in the context of sentences).

Another interesting aspect of the Chang et al. connectionist model is the idea that language may operate in a parallel fashion to vision. That is, there are two routes in visual processing, one for processing *what* something is, and one for processing *where* it is (Ungerleider & Haxby, 1994), with the *what* system taking the ventral visual pathway toward the temporal lobe, and the *where* system taking the dorsal pathway toward the parietal lobe. An idea in the Chang et al. model is that there is a network for processing the meaning aspect of language, and a separate system for the sequencing of the words. Together, these two systems converge to predict what type of word will come next, allowing the system to learn and adjust to new input, such as new words, or new ways of using words (e.g., I *googled* you the other day and was surprised by how many hits there were).

Section Summary

- Syntax involves the ordering of words and phrases in sentence structure and features such as active versus passive voice. Chomsky's theory of language was a heavily syntactic scheme with two sets of syntactic rules. Phrase structure rules were used to generate a deep structure representation of a sentence, and then transformational rules converted the deep structure into the surface structure, the string of words that makes up the sentence.
- There are a variety of syntactic clues to the meaning of a sentence, so an understanding of syntax is necessary to psycholinguists. On the other hand, psycholinguistics has developed its own theories of language, at least in part because of linguists' relative neglect of semantic and performance characteristics.
- Studies of how we plan and execute sentences reveal a highly interactive set of processes, rather than a strictly sequential sequence. We pause, delay, and rearrange sentences as a function of planning and memory-related factors like accessibility and working memory load.

LEXICAL AND SEMANTIC FACTORS: THE MEANING IN LANGUAGE

We now turn to lexical and semantic factors. This is the level of meaning in language. In particular, we refer to retrieval from the **mental lexicon**, *the mental dictionary of words and their meanings*. After rapid perceptual and pattern recognition processes, the encoded word provides access to the word's entry in the lexicon and also to the semantic representation of the concept. The evidence you've read about throughout this book, such as results from the Stroop and the lexical decision tasks, attests to the close relationship between a word and its meaning and the seemingly automatic accessing of one from the other. Recall in the Stroop task that seeing the word *red* printed in green ink triggers an interference process with naming the ink color, clear evidence that *red* is processed to the level of meaning (MacLeod, 1992). Likewise, the lexical decision task does not

Simulate
*Lexical Bias
in Slips of the
Tongue* in
MyPsychLab

PROVE IT
Speech Errors

Work by Fromkin (1971), Garrett (1975), and others (e.g., Ferreira & Humphreys, 2001; for work on error monitoring, see Hartsuiker & Kolk, 2001) has tabulated and made sense of speech errors that occur when we substitute or change sounds, syllables, words, and so on. Speech errors are not random but are quite lawful. For instance, when we make an exchange error, the exchange is between elements at the same linguistic level; initial sounds exchange places with other initial sounds, syllables with syllables, words with words (e.g., "to cake a bake"). If a prefix switches places, its new location will be in front of another word, not at the end.

Collect a sample of speech errors, say, from radio news broadcasters or your professors' lectures, then analyze them in terms of the linguistic level of the elements involved and the types of errors such as (intended phrase in parentheses):

Shift	She decide to hits it. (decides to hit it)
Exchange	Your model renosed. (your nose remodeled)
Perseveration	He pulled a pantrum. (tantrum)
Blend	To explain clarefully. (clearly/carefully)

require that you access the word's meaning but only that you identify a letter string as a genuine word. Nonetheless, identifying *doctor* as a word primes your decision to *nurse* (e.g., Table 7-3).

Morphemes

A **morpheme** is *the smallest unit of language that has meaning.* To return to the example early in the chapter, the word *cars* is composed of two morphemes: *Car* refers to a concept and a physical object, and *-s* is a meaningful suffix, denoting "more than one of." Likewise, the word *unhappiness* is composed of three morphemes: *happy* as the base concept, the prefix *un-* meaning "not," and the suffix *-ness* meaning "state or quality of being." In general, morphemes that can stand on their own and serve as words are called *free morphemes*, such as *happy, car,* and *legal,* whereas morphemes that need to be linked onto a free morpheme are called *bound morphemes,* such as *un-, -ness,* and *-s.* Although the concept of a morpheme is important, note that there is some debate as to whether the meaning of more common words such as *unhappiness* may be stored directly in memory or "computed" from the three morphemes (see Carroll, 1986; Whitney, 1998).

Lexical Representation

Think about the word *chase* as an example of how free morphemes might be represented in the mental lexicon. The representation of *chase* must specify its meaning—indicate that it means "to run after or pursue, in hopes of catching." Like other semantic concepts, *chase* can be represented in reference to related information, like *run, pursue,* the idea of *speed.* Given this, along with what you know about events in the real world from schemas and scripts, you can easily understand a sentence like

(13) The policeman chased the burglar through the park.

From a more psycholinguistic perspective, however, you know more about *chase* than just its basic meaning. For one thing, you know it's a verb, specifying a kind of physical action. Related to that, you have a clear idea of how *chase* can be used in sentences, the kinds of things that can do the chasing, and the kinds of things that can be chased (e.g., McKoon & Macfarland, 2002). Imagine, then, that your lexical representation of *chase* also includes this knowledge; *chase* requires some animate thing to do the chasing, some other kind of thing to be chased, and a location where the chasing takes place.

Lexical knowledge can include information that can capture embodied characteristics of cognition. For example, in a study by Willems, Hagoort, and Casasanto (2010), people did a lexical decision task while in a functional MRI (fMRI) scanner. What they observed was that when people responded to action verbs, the appropriate motor areas of the cortex became more active. Moreover, for right-handers, this was more on the left hemisphere motor areas (which control the right side of the body), whereas for the left-handers, the opposite was true. So, when a word strongly implied using a specific part of the body, the lexical information associated with that word involved information about how to move that part of the body. In another study, Willems, Labruna, D'Espisito, Ivry, and Casasanto (2011) again had people do a lexical decision task, but this time in conjunction with TMS treatment in which the hand portion of the brain was stimulated. What they found was that when people are given verbs that involved using the hand, such as *throw* or *write*, people responded faster under stimulation, compared to verbs that did not involve using the hands, such as *earn* or *wander*. Thus, activating the part of the brain that controls that part of the body made it easier to identify and respond to words that also strongly involve that part of the body. This suggests that our mental lexicon contains motor information about how we do things.

POLYSEMY: ONE WORD, MULTIPLE MEANINGS Whereas our understanding of words like *chase* is very clear, it's not too long before you run into cases of **polysemy**, the fact that *many words in a language may have multiple meanings*. The task of the language processing system is to figure out which meaning is the intended one. While a word may be polysemous, not all meanings are equal. Generally, there is one primary meaning that people typically would think of first when they hear the word, or would likely be listed first in a dictionary. This is the *dominant* meaning of a word. Other meanings then would be the *subordinate* meanings. So, take a simple word like *run*. The dominant meaning has something to do with using your legs to move fast. However, there are many subordinate meanings, too, such as having a run in your stockings, a movie having a run at the theater, having your nose run, to cut and run (retreat), to run your engine, watching paint colors run, and so on. The way you distinguish which specific meaning to use from the mental lexicon would depend on the context a word is in.

POLYSEMY AND PRIMING Let's consider two examples of how context can resolve polysemy to determine the intended meaning. As one example, the word *count* is ambiguous by itself. Putting the word in a sentence may not help: "We had trouble keeping track of the count." You still can't tell the intended meaning. What's missing is context, some conceptual framework to guide the interpretation of the polysemous word. With an adequate context, you can determine which sense of the word *count* is intended in these two contexts:

My dog wasn't included in the final count.

The vampire was disguised as a handsome count.

These sentences, taken from Simpson's (1981, 1984) work on polysemy, point out the importance of context: Context can help determine the intended meaning. With neutral contexts, such as the "We had trouble" sentence, word meanings are activated as a function of their dominance: The number sense of *count* is dominant, so that meaning is more activated. But a context that biases the interpretation one way or the other results in a stronger activation for the biased meaning. With *vampire* you activated the meaning of *count* related to nobility and Count Dracula (see also Balota & Paul, 1996; Klein & Murphy, 2002; Piercey & Joordens, 2000; but cf. Binder, 2003; Binder & Rayner, 1998).

The resolution of lexical ambiguity with polysemous words is important for successful comprehension. If you don't get the intended meaning of a word, then you won't get the intended message. It appears that ambiguity resolution works, in part, in a two-stage process. When people encounter an ambiguous word, what they do is activate all of the meanings, at least to some degree. Then in the second stage, they deactivate the inappropriate ones, based on the information from the rest of the discourse context. However, not everyone does this equally well. Work by Gernsbacher and Faust (1991) shows that good readers suppress inappropriate meanings faster. In comparison, poor readers maintained multiple meanings for a much longer period of time, which may be contributing to the problems they are having.

Watch the video *Bilingual Education* in **MyPsychLab**

BILINGUALISM What happens if you know more than one language? How does cognition deal with that? Generally, when people are multilingual, cognition needs to keep the words, syntax, idioms, and such for languages separate enough that they do not intrude on one another and end up intermixing in the person's speech. At the same time, the words and phrases in one language need to map onto the same underlying ideas in the other languages. In general, human cognition is able to handle this task quite well. People who learn a second language early on even show semantic priming effects across languages (Perea, Duñabeitia, & Carreiras, 2008), suggesting that the different words tap into the same underlying semantic knowledge base.

The need to keep two or more languages separate, but still be fluent in both of them, requires increased attention and cognitive control to mentally keep the languages from interfering with one another. This need for bilinguals to engage in such cognitive control spills over to other cognitive abilities that require cognitive control, such as showing larger negative priming effects (see Chapter 4), because bilinguals are more effective at suppressing salient but incorrect information (Treccani, Argyri, Sorace, & Della Salla, 2009). Thus, there seems to be an overall cognitive benefit to knowing more than one language; bilinguals show superior performance on intelligence tests compared to otherwise similar monolinguals (Lambert, 1990) and even do better on tests of their primary language (Bialystok, 1988; van Hell & Dijkstra, 2002).

Although bilingualism has advantages for cognition, learning a second language as an adult is more difficult and requires more cognitive attention and effort. For example, there is some evidence to suggest that when people are immersed in a second language that was learned as a adult, the person's first language is actively suppressed (Linek, Kroll, & Sunderman, 2010), which is not what is observed with people who grew up speaking more than one language.

CONTEXT AND ERPS   Let's consider a second example, an offshoot of the Kounios and Holcomb work with event-related potentials (ERPs) that you read about earlier. In one study, Holcomb, Kounios, Anderson, and West (1999; see also Laszlo & Federmeier, 2009; Lee & Federmeier, 2009; Sereno, Brewer, & O'Donnell, 2003) recorded ERPs in a simple sentence comprehension task. People saw sentences one word at a time and were asked to respond after seeing the last word, with "yes" if the sentence made sense and "no" if it did not. The experimental sentences varied along two dimensions, whether the last word was concrete or abstract and whether it was congruent with the sentence meaning or anomalous (i.e., made no sense). As an example, "Armed robbery implies that the thief used a weapon" was a concrete–congruent sentence; substituting *rose* for *weapon* made it concrete but anomalous. Likewise, "Lisa argued that this had not been the case in one single instance" was abstract–congruent sentence, and substituting *fun* for *instance* made it abstract–anomalous.

Figure 9-8 shows some of the ERP patterns obtained. In the left panel, you see the "normal" ERP patterns for the congruent, sensible sentences; the three profiles, from top to bottom, came from the three midline electrode sites shown in the schematic drawing (frontal, central, and parietal). In the right panel are the ERP patterns when the sentences ended in an anomalous word. Notice first in the left panel that the solid and dotted functions, for concrete and abstract sentences, tracked each other very closely: Whatever neural mechanisms operated during comprehension, they generated similar ERP patterns. But now make a left-to-right comparison of the patterns, seeing the differences in the right panel when the sentences ended in a nonsensical, anomalous word (*rose* in the armed robbery sentence, for example). Here, there were marked changes in the ERP profiles. At the central location, for example, there was a steadily downward trend (in the positive direction, in terms of electrical potentials) for sensible sentences but a dramatic reversal of direction for anomalous words.

In short, the neural mechanisms involved in comprehension generated dramatically different patterns when an anomalous word was encountered. The mismatch between the context, the already-processed meaning of the sentence, and the final word yielded not only an overt response (the response indicating "no, that sentence makes no sense"), but also a neural response, signifying the brain-related activity that detected the anomalous ending of the sentence. (Don't get confused about directions here. The functions underneath the gridline are electrically positive, so deflection upward in these graphs is a deflection toward the

FIGURE 9-8 ERP profiles at three midline sites (frontal [F_z], central [C_z], parietal [P_z]) for sentences ending with a congruent (left panel) or contextually anomalous (right panel) word.

Adapted from Figures 3 and 4 in Holcomb et al. (1999).

negative, a deflection going in a negative direction; this is what the *N* in *N400* signifies, a "negative going" pattern.) Even at the level of neural functioning then, there is a rapid response to nonsensical ideas that follow sensible context, a kind of "something's wrong here" response that the brain makes some 400 ms after the nonsensical event.

Case Grammar

In this section we consider issues of how the language processing system knows what role a word or concept is playing in a sentence. This approach is called **case grammar**. The ideas came originally from Fillmore (1968). The basic idea is that *the semantic analysis of sentences involves figuring out what semantic role is being played by each word or concept in the sentence and computing sentence meaning based on those semantic roles*. Two sample sentences illustrate this:

(14) The key will open the door.

(15) The janitor will open the door with the key.

Fillmore pointed out that syntactic aspects of sentences—which words serve as the subject, direct object, and so on—often are irrelevant to sentence meaning. For example, in sentences 14 and 15 the word *key* plays different grammatical roles; subject of the sentence in 14 but object of the preposition in 15. For Fillmore, focusing on this difference misses a critical point for language. Regardless of its different grammatical roles, the key is doing exactly the same thing in both cases, playing the same semantic role of *instrument*. A purely syntactic analysis misses this, but a semantic analysis captures it perfectly.

Fillmore's theory was called case grammar. Fillmore proposed that sentence processing involves a semantic parsing that focuses on the semantic *roles played by the content words in the sentences*. These semantic roles are called **semantic cases**, or simply **case roles**. Thus, *door* is the recipient or patient of the action of *open* in sentences 14 and 15; *janitor* is the agent of *open; key* is the instrument; and so on. Stated simply, each content word plays a semantic role in the meaning of the sentence. That role is the word's *semantic case*. The significant—indeed, critical—point about such a semantic parsing is that it relies on people's existing semantic and lexical knowledge, their knowledge of what kinds of things will open, who can perform the opening, and so on.

Reconsider the *chase* sentence 13, "The policeman chased the burglar through the park," and three variations, thinking of the content words in terms of their semantic roles:

(16) The mouse chased the cat through the house.

(17) His insecurities chased him even in his sleep.

(18) *The book chased the flower.

Your lexical and semantic knowledge of *chase* is that some animate being does the chasing, the agent case. Some other thing is the recipient of the chasing, the patient, but that thing need not be animate, just capable of moving rapidly (e.g., you can chase a piece of paper being blown by the wind). On this analysis, it is clear that sentence 13 conforms to the normal situation stored in memory, so it is easy to comprehend. Sentence 16, however, mismatches the typical state of affairs between mice and cats. Nonetheless, either of these creatures can serve as the required animate agent of the relation *chase,* so sentence 16 is sensible. Because of other semantic knowledge, you know that sentence 17 violates the literal meaning of *chase* but could still have a nonliteral, metaphorical meaning. But your semantic case analysis provides the reason sentence 18 is unacceptable. A book is inanimate, so it mismatches the required animate agent role for *chase; book* cannot play the role of agent for *chase*. Likewise, *flower* seems to violate the movable restriction on the patient case for *chase*.

Work by Bresnan (1978; Bresnan & Kaplan, 1982) and Jackendoff (1992) has amplified and extended work on case grammars. For example, in Jackendoff's theory of a cognitive grammar (1992; see Figure 9-9), the goal is to build a conceptual structure, an understanding of the sentence. We use language and language rules to get from the spoken or written sentence to a meaningful mental structure or understanding. Each lexical entry includes the meaning of the word and, for verbs, a list of the arguments or semantic cases that go along with it. Thus, the lexical entry *chase* would state that *chase* requires an animate agent, some recipient or patient, and so on. Likewise, for *give,* the case arguments would state that an animate agent and recipient are needed for the *give* relation, and some *object* is the thing being given (for an excellent summary of these positions, see Whitney, 1998).

Accordingly, when we perceive words, we look up the concepts in the lexicon. This look-up process accesses not only the word's meaning, but also its syntactic and semantic case roles and any other restrictions. Each word in the sentence is processed as it is encountered, with content words being assigned to their

FIGURE 9-9 In Jackendoff's (1992) conceptual semantics approach, comprehension of meaning is the process of arriving at a conceptual structure for the sentence. To accomplish this, we use both the syntactic structure of the sentence and a set of correspondence rules; the correspondence rules translate from syntactic roles (e.g., noun and verb) into semantic roles (agent, patient, and so forth).

Adapted from Whitney (1998).

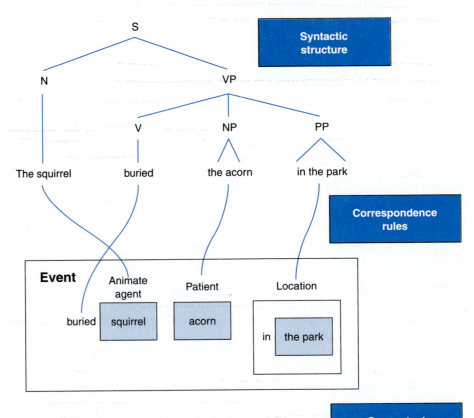

semantic roles. If all goes well, the sentence conveys an exact, specified meaning that is captured accurately by the analysis of the cognitive grammar.

Interaction of Syntax and Semantics

Note that semantic factors do not stand alone in language, just as syntactic factors are not independent of semantics. Syntax is more than just word and phrase order rules; it's a clue to how to understand sentences. For example, O'Seaghdha's (1997) evidence shows separable effects of syntactic assignment and semantic integration of word meanings, with syntactic processes occurring before semantic integration. His results, based on RTs, are largely consistent with those in other studies (e.g., Peterson, Burgess, Dell, & Eberhard, 2001, on how we process idioms), including ERP studies of syntactic and semantic processing (Ainsworth-Darnell, Shulman, & Boland, 1998; Friederici, Hahne, & Mecklinger, 1996; Osterhout, Allen, McLaughlin, & Inoue, 2002). And, as you just read, syntax in speech production is sensitive to a word's accessibility; words that can be easily retrieved right now tend to appear earlier in a sentence.

SEMANTIC FOCUS   Likewise, semantic factors refer to more than just word and phrase meanings, because different syntactic devices can be clues to meaning. To anticipate just a bit, note how syntactic differences in the following sentences influence the semantic interpretation:

> *(19a) I'm going downtown with my sister at four o'clock.*
>
> *(19b) It's at four o'clock that I'm going downtown with my sister.*
>
> *(19c) It's my sister I'm going downtown with at four o'clock.*

Sentences 19b and 19c differ subtly from 19a in the focus of the utterance. The focus of each sentence is different, so each means something slightly different. Imagine how inappropriate sentence 19c would be, for instance, as a response to the question "Did you say you're going downtown with your sister at three o'clock?" Our judgments about appropriateness make an important point: Our theories of language performance must be as sophisticated as our own knowledge of language is. We are sensitive to the focus or highlighted aspects of sentences and subtleties of the ordering of clauses, so a theory of language must reflect this in a psychologically relevant way.

SEMANTICS CAN OVERPOWER SYNTAX   Semantic features can do more than alter the syntax of sentences. Occasionally semantics can overpower syntax. Let's focus on a classic study by Fillenbaum (1974). As you read, note how current terminology would label this an effect of top-down processing.

Fillenbaum presented several kinds of sentences and asked people to write paraphrases that preserved the original meaning. Ordinary "threat" sentences such as "Don't print that or I'll sue you" were then reordered into "perverse" threats, such as "Don't print that or I won't sue you." Regular "conjunctive" sentences such as "John got off the bus and went into the store" were then changed into "disordered" sentences, such as "John went into the store and got off the bus." When Fillenbaum scored paraphrases of reordered sentences, he found remarkably high

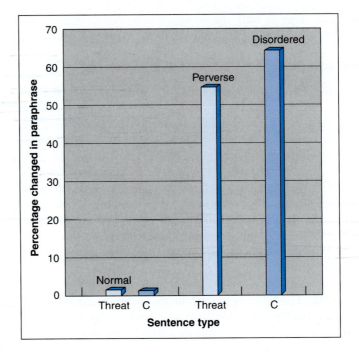

percentages of changes, as shown in Figure 9-10. More than 50% of people "normalized" the perverse threatening sentences, making them conform to the more typical state of affairs, and more than 60% normalized the "disordered" conjunctive sentences. He then asked people to reread their paraphrases to see whether there was even a "shred of difference" from the originals. More than half the time, people saw no discrepancies. Apparently, their general knowledge was influential enough that it overpowered the syntactic and lexical aspects of the sentences. (Try these examples: "Nice we're having weather, isn't it?" and "Ignorance is no excuse for the law.")

Sometimes, the information that guides language processing can also come from the context and the environment as well as what a person already knows. Essentially, according to such *interactionist* views of language processing, people are simultaneously, in parallel, deriving alternative interpretations of language they hear or read. Over (a very short period of) time, cognition uses the constraints derived from the preceding context and the environment to help determine which interpretation is preferred, and which to let go (Altmann, 1998; Altmann & Steedman, 1988).

This is most clearly illustrated in studies of eye movements as people listen to spoken instructions. Imagine a person is faced with the arrangement of objects in Figure 9-11. If people hear the sentence "Put the apple on the towel in the box" after hearing "put the apple" there is an equal probability that a person will look at either apple, but as soon as "on the towel" is heard, eye fixations converge on the apple on the bottom. This happens online during the comprehension of the sentence even though this sentence is technically ambiguous because the sentence could refer to a box that has a towel in it. However, because there is no such box

FIGURE 9-11
Picture of two
apples and a box.
Participants would
have their eye
movements tracked
as they heard a
sentence such as
"Put the apple on
the towel in the
box."

in the environment, people don't experience any ambiguity and are unlikely to notice it. In short, the psycholinguistic approach to lexical and semantic factors in language relies on conceptually driven processing.

Evidence for the Semantic Grammar Approaches

A major prediction of semantic grammar theory can be stated in two parts. First, comprehenders begin to analyze a sentence immediately, as soon as the words are encountered. Second, this analysis assigns each word to a particular semantic case role, with each assignment contributing its part to overall sentence comprehension. As an example, read sentence 20:

> (20) After the musician had bowed the piano was quickly taken off the stage.

Your analysis of this sentence proceeds easily and without disruption; it's a fairly straightforward sentence. Now read sentence 21:

> (21) After the musician had played the piano was quickly taken off the stage.

What's different about sentence 21? The verb *played* suggests that the *piano* is the semantic recipient of *play*. When you read *played*, your semantic role assignment for piano was *recipient*. But then you read *was quickly* and realized you had made a mistake in interpretation. Sentences such as 21 are called **garden path sentences**: *the early part of the sentence sets you up so that the later phrases in the sentence don't make sense given the way you assigned case roles in the first part.* Figuratively speaking, the sentence leads you down the garden path; when you realize your mistake, you have to retrace your steps back up the path to reassign earlier words to different cases. Additional examples (from Singer, 1990) of this effect are shown in sentences 22 and 23:

> (22) The groundsman chased the girl waving a stick in her hand.

> (23) The old train the young.

Many research reports have studied how people comprehend garden path sentences as a way of evaluating case grammar theory (Frazier & Rayner, 1982; Mitchell & Holmes, 1985; but see McKoon & Ratcliff, 2007, for an account based on semantic plausibility). For the most part, the results have been supportive. For example, when people read such sentences, their eyes tend to fixate longer on the later phrases, signaling their error in comprehension (e.g., on "was quickly taken off" in sentence 21). As shown in Figure 9-12, people spent 40 to 50 ms longer when they encountered their error (at point D in the figure; D stands for the disambiguating part of the sentence that reveals the earlier misinterpretation). This is a recovery time effect; it takes additional time to recover from the initial role assignment when that turns out to be incorrect (see Christianson, Hollingworth, Halliwell, & Ferreira, 2001; and Ferreira, Henderson, Anes, Weeks, & McFarlane, 1996, for comparable results with spoken language). Interestingly, the more committed you are to an initial interpretation, that is, the more you "dig in," the harder it becomes to change your interpretation (Tabor & Hutchins, 2004).

There is also important work, also using the eye fixations and fMRI, on how we *parse*—figure out—the syntax of a sentence and the degree to which parsing can be overridden or at least affected by semantic context and other factors (see Clifton et al., 2003; Mason, Just, Keller, & Carpenter, 2003; Rayner & Clifton, 2002; Tannenhaus & Trueswell, 1995).

FIGURE 9-12 A depiction of the effect of garden path sentences on reading time. The curves show eye fixations on phrases before and after D, the point in the sentence where the ambiguity is noticed and disambiguated. The top curve shows the data from garden path sentences; eye fixation time grows noticeably longer for these curves at D, when the ambiguity is noticed (the D phrase is underlined in the sample sentences). The bottom curve shows data from the control sentences and no increase in reading time at point D.

Data from Rayner, Carlson, & Frazier (1983).

A final point to note is that the case restrictions sometimes can be violated intentionally, although there are still constraints on that violation. For instance, consider sentence 17 again: "His insecurities chased him even in his sleep." Such a sentence is understood as a technical but permissible violation of the animate restriction for the agent role of *chase*. In a metaphorical sense, we can "compute" how insecurities might behave like an animate agent; thoughts can behave as if they were animate and can take on the properties of pursuing relentlessly, catching, and so on. A particularly fascinating aspect of language involves such figurative uses of words and how case grammar accommodates such usage (see Glucksberg & Keysar, 1990; Keysar, Shen, Glucksberg, & Horton, 2000; Tourangeau & Rips, 1991).

Section Summary

- Semantic factors in language can sometimes override syntactic and phonological effects. The study of semantics breaks words down into morphemes, the smallest meaningful units in language; *cars* contains the free morpheme *car* and the bound morpheme *-s* signifying a "plural."
- Speech errors that people make can be used to help reveal the processes by which language is produced. These speech errors follow regularities that are likely to be produced by otherwise consistent and stable cognitive processes.
- As the study of language comprehension has matured, the dominant approach to semantics claims that we perform a semantic parsing of sentences, assigning words to their appropriate semantic case roles as we hear or read.
- Garden path sentences, where later phrases indicate an error in interpretation, have provided rich information about how syntax and semantics are processed online during comprehension and how we recover from comprehension errors.

BRAIN AND LANGUAGE

Although we have covered a number of ways that cognition is related to underlying cortical structure and function, perhaps one of the most fruitful areas of research on the brain-cognition relation is work on language processing. In this section we discuss aspects of language processing that have strong neural components. This includes a consideration of people with intact brains, as well as how language processing has been disrupted in people who have had the misfortune to suffer some sort of brain damage.

Language in the Intact Brain

With the advent of modern imaging methods, we have begun to learn an extraordinary amount about how the brain processes language from neurologically intact people. Consider a representative study, looking at people's sensitivity to the syntactic structure of sentences. Osterhout and Holcomb (1992) presented sentences to people and recorded the changes in their brain wave patterns (ERPs) as they comprehended. In particular, they examined ERP patterns for sentences that violated syntactic or semantic expectations, comparing these with the patterns obtained with control sentences. When sentences ended in a semantically anomalous fashion ("The woman buttered her bread with socks"), a significant N400 ERP pattern was observed, much as reported in Kounios and Holcomb's (1992) study of semantic relatedness (see Figure 9-8). But when the sentence ended in a syntactically anomalous fashion ("The woman persuaded to catch up"), a strong P600 pattern occurred (a positive electrical potential) 600 ms after the anomalous word "to" was seen; see Figure 9-13. This is confirms the important and seemingly separate role of syntactic processing during language comprehension.

A wealth of evidence illustrates the importance to cognitive science of such imaging and neuropsychological techniques and strongly suggests that the research on language processing will increasingly feature techniques such as imaging and ERP methods. Here are four examples.

LEARNING LANGUAGE McCandliss, Posner, and Givon (1997) taught people a new, miniature artificial language and recorded ERPs during learning. Early in training, words in the new language showed ERP patterns typical of nonsense material. But, after five weeks of training, the ERP patterns looked like those obtained with English words. Furthermore, left hemisphere frontal areas reacted to semantic aspects of the language, whereas posterior areas were sensitive to the visual characteristics of the words, the orthography.

SYNTACTIC PROCESSING Rosler, Pechmann, Streb, Roder, and Hennighausen (1998) did an ambitious study on syntactic processing, using ERPs. Sentences were

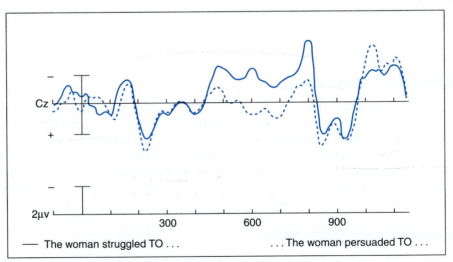

FIGURE 9-13 Mean ERPs to syntactically acceptable sentences (solid curve) and syntactically anomalous sentences (dotted curve). The P600 component, illustrated as a downward dip in the dotted curve, shows the effect of detecting the syntactic anomaly. Note that, in this figure, positive changes go in the downward direction.

presented word by word; to make sure people were comprehending, they had to answer a question about the sentence five seconds after they saw the last word. The sentences were all grammatical, but some of them differed from normal, canonical word order. The ERP patterns demonstrated a variety of effects; for example, the patterns differed appreciably when the sentences violated canonical word order and when elements in the sentence cued people that an unusual word order would follow. The especially compelling aspect of these results is that the ERP patterns tapped into purely mental processes that are not revealed by outward, behavioral measures such as RT or accuracy.

RIGHT HEMISPHERE LANGUAGE   Although the left hemisphere is typically credited with being the primary source of language processing, the right hemisphere has important work to do as well. A general characterization of the role of the right hemisphere in the cortex is that it serves to process information in a more wholistic way, rather than in the more analytic manner characteristic of the left hemisphere. In other words, the right hemisphere is more adept at processing information in a coarse-grained fashion, whereas the left hemisphere is more adept at processing information at a fine-grained level (Beeman, 1998). One role of the right hemisphere is in making more distant, remote semantic connections between words. For example, the connection between *tiger* and *stripe* is relatively direct and close, but the connection between *tiger* and *beach* is more remote and requires some creativity to see a connection. An illustration of this differential operation of the left and right hemispheres was shown in a study by Coulson, Federmeier, Van Petten, and Kutas (2005). In this study, ERP patterns were recorded in the left and right hemispheres as people read sentences. What Coulson et al. found was that the left hemisphere was more involved in integrating lexical information with sentence-level information, such as whether a word is sensible in the context of a given sentence (e.g., responses to the word *tire* after reading the sentence "They were truly stuck, since she didn't have a spare"), but not so much the lexical relations of the words to each other. In comparison, the right hemisphere was more involved in this sort of word-to-word associative processing (e.g., the fact that *spare* and *tire* are more associated than *spare* and *pencil*).

INDIVIDUAL DIFFERENCES   Reichle, Carpenter, and Just (2000) used fMRI to look at brain activity while people verified sentence–picture stimuli (e.g., "The star is above the plus," followed by a picture that did or did not match the sentence). When people used a verbal strategy to make their decisions, brain regions associated with language processing (especially Broca's area) were active; when people used a visual imagery strategy, regions in the parietal lobe were active, the same regions that are active when visual–spatial reasoning tasks are given. Interestingly, the language area activity was lower when high-verbal people were tested and likewise for visual areas in people high in visual–spatial abilities, as if high verbal or spatial ability reduced the amount of brain work needed to do the task.

Aphasia

A large literature exists on brain-related disorders of language, based on people who through the misfortune of illness or brain injury have lost the ability to use

TABLE 9-5 Brain-Related Disruptions of Language and Cognition

Disorder	Disruption of
Language Related	
Broca's aphasia	Speech production, syntactic features
Wernicke's aphasia	Comprehension, semantic features
Conduction aphasia	Repetition of words and sentences
Anomia (anomic aphasia)	Word finding, either lexical or semantic
Pure word deafness	Perceptual or semantic processing of auditory word comprehension
Alexia	Reading, recognition of printed letters or words
Agraphia	Writing
Other Symbolic Related	
Acalculia	Mathematical abilities, retrieval or rule-based procedures
Perception, Movement Related	
Agnosia	Visual object recognition
Prosopagnosia	(Visual) face recognition
Apraxia	Voluntary action or skilled motor movement

language. Formal studies of such disorders date back to the mid-1800s, although records dating back to 3500 BC mention language loss caused by brain injury (see McCarthy & Warrington, 1990). Table 9-5 provides a list and short explanation of these disruptions and some others you've already encountered.

The disruption of language caused by a brain-related disorder is called **aphasia**. Aphasia is always the product of some physical injury to the brain sustained either in an accident or a blow to the head or in diseases and medical syndromes such as stroke. A major goal in neurology is to understand the aphasic syndromes more completely so that people who suffer from aphasia may be helped more effectively. From the standpoint of cognitive neuroscience, the language disruptions of aphasic patients can also help us understand language and its neurological basis.

Although there are many different kinds of aphasias, with great variety in their effects and severity, three basic forms are the most common: *Broca's aphasia, Wernicke's aphasia,* and *conduction aphasia*.

Simulate
Broca's Area and Wernicke's Area in **MyPsychLab**

BROCA'S APHASIA   As described by Kertesz (1982), **Broca's aphasia** is characterized by *severe difficulties in producing speech;* it is also called expressive or production aphasia. Patients with Broca's aphasia show speech that is hesitant, effortful, and phonemically distorted. Aside from stock phrases such as "I don't know," such patients generally respond to questions with one-word answers. If words are strung together, there are few if any grammatical markers, such as bound morphemes like *-ing, -ed,* and *-ly.* In less severe cases, the aphasia may be limited to more complex aspects of language production, such as the production of verb inflections (Faroqi-Shah & Thompson, 2007). Interestingly, such patients typically show less (or even no) impairment of comprehension for both spoken and written language.

This syndrome was first described in the 1860s by French neurosurgeon Pierre Broca, who also identified the damaged area responsible for the disorder. The site of the brain damage, an area toward the rear of the left frontal lobe, is therefore called Broca's area. Broca's area lies adjacent to a major motor control center in the brain.

WERNICKE'S APHASIA   Loosely speaking, the impairments in **Wernicke's aphasia** are the opposite of those in Broca's aphasia; see Table 9-6 for a listing of the typical impairments in both aphasias, including speech samples. In patients affected by Wernicke's aphasia, *comprehension is impaired, as are repetition, naming, reading, and writing, but the syntactic aspects of speech are preserved*; it is sometimes called receptive or comprehension aphasia. In this syndrome there may be unrecognizable content words; recognizable but often inappropriate semantic substitutions; or neologisms, invented nonsense words. What is striking is that victims of this disorder are sometimes unaware of the aphasia.

German investigator Carl Wernicke identified this disorder, and the left-hemisphere region that is damaged, in 1874. This region is thus known as Wernicke's area. Note that the area, toward the rear of the left temporal lobe, is adjacent to the

---

TABLE 9-6   Classic Impairments in Broca's and Wernicke's Aphasias

Broca's Aphasia	Wernicke's Aphasia
Quality of Speech	
Severely impaired; marked by extreme effort to generate speech, hesitant utterances, short (one-word) responses.	Little if any impairment; fluent speech productions, clear articulation, no hesitations.
Nature of Speech	
Agrammatical; marked by loss of syntactic markers and inflections and use of simple noun and verb categories.	Neologistic; marked by invented words (neologisms) or semantically inappropriate substitutions; long strings of neologistic jargon.
Comprehension	
Unimpaired compared with speech production. Word-finding difficulty caused by production difficulties.	Severely impaired; marked by lack of awareness that speech is incomprehensible; comprehension impaired also in nonverbal tasks (e.g., pointing).

Speech Samples

Broca's aphasia. Experimenter asks the patient's address.

"Oh dear. Um. Aah. O! O dear. Very-there-were-ave. avedeversher avenyer." (Correct address was Devonshire.)

Wernicke's aphasia. Experimenter asks about the patient's work before hospitalization. "I wanna tell you this happened when happened when he rent. His-his kell come down here and is—he got ren something. It happened. In these ropliers were with him for hi-is friend—like was. And he roden all of these arranjen from the pedis on from iss pescid."

auditory cortex, in the left temporal lobe, a very different area with very different abilities than Broca's area in the frontal lobe. Note also that this demonstrates a double dissociation, a basic distinction at the level of brain organization between syntax and semantics (see Breedin & Saffran, 1999, for a case study showing loss of semantic knowledge but preserved syntactic performance).

CONDUCTION APHASIA   Much less common than Broca's and Wernicke's aphasias, **conduction aphasia** is a more narrow disruption of language ability. Both Broca's and Wernicke's areas seem to be intact in conduction aphasia, and people with conduction aphasia can understand and produce speech quite well. Their language impairment is that they are *unable to repeat what they have just heard*. In intuitive terms, the intact comprehension and production systems seem to have lost their normal connection or linkage. Indeed, the site of the brain lesion in conduction aphasia appears to be the primary pathway between Broca's and Wernicke's areas, called the *arcuate fasciculus* (Geschwind, 1970). Quite literally, the pathway between the comprehension and production areas is no longer able to conduct the linguistic message.

ANOMIA   Another type of aphasia deserves brief mention here because it relates to the separation of the semantic and lexical systems discussed earlier. **Anomia** or **anomic aphasia** is a disruption of word finding, an *impairment in the normal ability to retrieve a semantic concept and say its name*, you encountered this briefly back in Chapter 7. In anomia, some aspect of the normally automatic semantic or lexical components of retrieval has been damaged. Although moderate word-finding difficulty can result from damage almost anywhere in the left hemisphere, full-fledged anomia seems to involve damage especially in the left temporal lobe (Coughlan & Warrington, 1978; see McCarthy & Warrington, 1990, for details). Although there is a similarity between anomia and the tip-of-the-tongue (TOT) phenomenon, the similarity is superficial. Several researchers (e.g., Geschwind, 1967; Goodglass, Kaplan, Weintraub, & Ackerman, 1976) have found no evidence among anomic patients of the partial knowledge that characterizes a TOT state. Evidence also indicates that anomia can involve retrieval blockage only for the lexical component of retrieval, leaving semantic retrieval of the concept intact (e.g., the patient described in Chapter 7; Kay & Ellis, 1987). This, along with other cases (e.g., Ashcraft, 1993), suggests preserved semantic retrieval but a blockage in finding the lexical representation that corresponds to the already retrieved semantic concept.

OTHER APHASIAS   As Table 9-5 shows, a variety of highly specific aphasias are also possible. Although most of these are quite rare, they nonetheless give evidence of the separability of several aspects of language performance. For instance, in *alexia* (or dyslexia), there is a disruption of reading without any necessary disruption of spoken language or aural comprehension. In *agraphia,* conversely, the patient is unable to write. Amazingly, a few reports describe patients with alexia but without agraphia—in other words, patients who can write but cannot read what they have just written (Benson & Geschwind, 1969). In *pure word deafness,* a patient cannot comprehend spoken language, although he or she is still able to read and produce written and spoken language.

There is documentation for even more specific forms of aphasia than those—for instance, difficulties in retrieval of verbs in written but not spoken language (Berndt & Haendiges, 2000) and difficulties in naming just visual stimuli, without either generalized visual agnosia or generalized anomia (Sitton, Mozer, & Farah, 2000).

RIGHT HEMISPHERE DAMAGE   Despite the fact that most of the aphasias discussed here involve processing in the left hemisphere of the cortex, there is also evidence of the right hemisphere's contribution to language comprehension and production (see Beeman & Chiarello, 1998, for a useful overview of the complementary right- and left-hemisphere language processes).

Work by Beeman (1993, 1998) suggests that a problem right-hemisphere–damaged people have is an inability to activate an appropriately diverse set of information from long-term memory from which inferences can be derived. In one study, after reading a text, people were given a lexical decision task. Some of the words in the task were related to inferences that needed to be drawn for comprehension. For example, read the following short text: "Then he went into the bathroom and discovered that he had left the bathtub water running. He had forgotten about it while watching the news. The mess took him a long time to mop up." After reading, you are then given a lexical decision probe word like "overflow." Because the tub overflowing was not mentioned in the text, responding to "overflow" faster than baseline would be evidence of having inferred it based on reading the text itself. The results showed that normal controls responded 49 ms faster relative to neutral control words—they drew the appropriate inference. However, the right-hemisphere–damaged patients responded 148 ms more *slowly* to these words.

Generalizing from Cases of Brain Damage

Although it is a mistake to believe that our eventual understanding of language will be reducible to a catalog of biological and neurological processes (e.g., Mehler, Morton, & Jusczyk, 1984), knowledge of the neurological aspects of language is useful for something beyond the rehabilitation and treatment of aphasia. What do studies of such abnormal brain processes tell us about normal cerebral functioning and language?

Well, for one, the different patterns of behavioral impairments in Broca's and Wernicke's aphasias, stemming from different physical structures in the brain, implies that these two physical structures are responsible for different aspects of linguistic skill. Furthermore, these selective impairments reinforce the notion that syntax and semantics are two separable but interactive aspects of normal language (e.g., O'Seaghdha, 1997; Osterhout & Holcomb, 1992). That is, the double dissociations indicate that different, independent modules govern comprehension and speech production. Other dissociations indicate yet more independent modules of processing, such as separate modules corresponding to reading and writing.

An intriguing inference from such studies is that the specialized regions signal an innate, biological basis for language; that is, the human nervous system is specifically adapted to learn and use language, as opposed to simply being able to do so. Several theorists have gone so far as to discuss possible evolutionary mechanisms responsible for lateralization, hemispheric specialization, the dissociation of syntax and semantics revealed by Broca's and Wernicke's aphasias, and even cognition in general (Corballis, 1989; Geary, 1992; Lewontin, 1990). These are fascinating lines of reasoning on the nature of language and cognition as represented in the brain.

Section Summary

- Extensive evidence from studies with brain-damaged people and more modern work using imaging and ERP methods reveals several functional and anatomical dissociations in language ability.
- The syntactic and articulatory aspects of language seem centered in Broca's area, in the left frontal lobe, whereas comprehension aspects are focused more on Wernicke's area, in the posterior left hemisphere junction of the temporal and parietal lobes.
- The study of these and other deficits, such as anomia and right hemispheric damage, converges with evidence from imaging and ERP studies to illustrate how various aspects of language performance act as separable, distinct components within the overall broad ability to produce and comprehend language.

Key Terms

ambiguous (p. *312*)
anomia (p. *334*)
anomic aphasia (p. *334*)
aphasia (p. *332*)
arbitrariness (p. *291*)
Broca's aphasia (p. *332*)
case grammar (p. *323*)
case roles (p. *323*)
categorical perception (p. *300*)
coarticulation (p. *303*)
competence (p. *295*)
conduction aphasia (p. *334*)
deep structure (p. *312*)

displacement (p. *292*)
dysfluencies (p. *295*)
flexibility (p. *291*)
garden path sentences (p. *327*)
given-new strategy (p. *315*)
grammar (p. *323*)
language (p. *289*)
linguistic relativity hypothesis (p. *296*)
linguistic universals (p. *289*)
linguistics (p. *288*)
mental lexicon (p. *317*)

morpheme (p. *318*)
motor theory of speech perception (p. *306*)
naming (p. *292*)
parse (p. *312*)
performance (p. *295*)
phonemes (p. *298*)
phonemic competence (p. *302*)
phonology (p. *298*)
phrase structure (p. *310*)
polysemy (p. *319*)
problem of invariance (p. *303*)

productivity (p. *293*)
psycholinguistics (p. *288*)
semantic cases (p. *323*)
semanticity (p. *289*)
surface structure (p. *312*)
syntax (p. *308*)
transformational grammar (p. *313*)
transformational rules (p. *312*)
Wernicke's aphasia (p. *333*)

10 Comprehension: Written and Spoken Language

*Language simply does not work in isolation. . . . Understanding
what one has heard is a complex process that . . . cannot be
reasonably isolated into [separate] linguistic and memory
components but must be a combined effort of both.*

(SCHANK, 1972, PP. 626–628)

Comprehension—even the title of this chapter must be explained a bit, if only because much of Chapter 9 dealt with language, too. What does the word *comprehension* mean here? Basically, the expanded meaning here includes not only the fundamental language processes we studied in Chapter 9, but also the additional processes we use when comprehending realistic samples of language, say a passage in a book or a connected, coherent conversation, or even a perceived event. How do we comprehend? What do we *do* when we read, understand,

and remember connected sentences? By taking a larger unit of analysis than isolated sentences, we confront a host of issues that are central to communication and to cognitive psychology. And by confronting Miller's (1973) highest two levels of analysis, conceptual knowledge and beliefs, we address the important issues Miller (1977) described as the "distant bridge that may someday need to be crossed." In short, it's time to cross the bridge.

GETTING STARTED: AN OVERVIEW

Conceptual and Rule Knowledge

You read about the first three levels of language analysis—the phonological, syntactic, and lexical and semantic levels—in Chapter 9. Let's start digging into Miller's (1977) fourth and fifth levels, the conceptual and belief levels. Here's the sentence Miller uses to illustrate these:

> *(1) Mary and John saw the mountains while they were flying to California.*

If this sentence were spoken aloud, your comprehension would begin with phonological processes, translating the stream of sounds into words. Your syntactic knowledge would parse the sentence into phrases and would assist the semantic level of analysis as you determined the case roles for each important word: Mary and John are the agents of *see*, the word *mountains* is assigned the patient or recipient role, *they* is the agent of *fly* in the second main clause, and so on.

So far so good. But this sentence is more challenging than that. It's ambiguous, has more than one meaning. There's the obvious one, that Mary and John looked out the plane window and saw mountains during a flight to California. But there's also the possibility that *they* refers to the mountains. *They* merely denotes something plural, after all, so syntactically, the *they* could refer to the mountains.

Those of you who noticed this ambiguity probably rejected it immediately for the obvious reason: Mountains don't fly. We're getting close to the Miller's point. Knowing that mountains don't fly is part of your semantic, **conceptual knowledge**. Look in as many dictionaries as you'd like, and you won't find "mountains don't fly" in any of them. Accordingly, your comprehension of sentence 1 must also have included a conceptual level of analysis, in which you compared your interpretation with semantic knowledge.

Miller also argues that **beliefs** are important for comprehension. I could tell you "No, I'm not saying that Mary and John were flying to California. I'm saying that it was the *mountains* that were flying." Although you can understand that I might think mountains can fly, you wouldn't change your mind about the issue; your belief in your own knowledge and your feeling that I'm lying or playing some kind

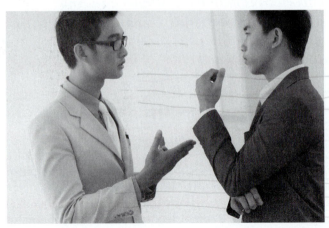

Language comprehension involves a complex set of processes that need to occur in real time.

of trick (or just plain crazy) are an important for comprehension. A purely linguistic analysis of language misses this critical aspect of comprehension as well: Think how prominent your beliefs are, and how important they are to comprehension and memory, when you hear advertisements or speeches in political campaigns.

Rules are yet another part of the knowledge that must be taken into account. In Chapter 9 we discussed tacit knowledge at the phonological and syntactic levels, and the semantic knowledge of case rules. But additional rules are operating when we deal with more complex passages of text or with connected conversation. Some rules have the flavor of strategies; for example, we tend to interpret sentence 2 as focusing on Tina, largely because she is mentioned first in the sentence (Gernsbacher, 1990):

(2) Tina gathered the kindling as Lisa set up the tent.

Several lines of evidence speak to this idea, that we provide a focus to our sentences by using mechanisms such as first mention and certain kinds of reference (e.g., "There was this guy who . . ." instead of "A guy . . .").

Other rules have to do with reference, building bridges between words referring to the same thing. For example, after reading sentence 2, how do you know that the phrase "After she got the fire started" refers to Tina? Still more rules parade under the name **pragmatics** and refer to a variety of extralinguistic factors. As an example, indirect speech acts such as "Do you have the time?" or "Can you open the window?" mean something different from what a literal reading would suggest. And finally, high-level rules operate in conversational interactions, rules that specify how people in a conversation structure their remarks and how they understand the remarks of others. As always, simply because you can't state the rule or were never explicitly taught it doesn't mean that it isn't there. It simply means that the rules are part of your implicit, tacit knowledge.

Comprehension Research

Much of the traditional evidence about comprehension relied on people's linguistic intuitions, their (leisurely) judgments about the acceptability of sentences, or simple measures of recall and accuracy. The Sachs (1967) study you read about in Chapter 8 was a classic example of early comprehension research, with a straightforward conclusion. Recall that as people were reading a passage, they were interrupted and tested on a target sentence, either 0, 80, or 160 syllables after the end of the target. Their recognition of the sentence was very accurate at the immediate interval. But beyond that, they were accurate only at rejecting the choice that changed the sentence meaning. That is,

The difficulty of language comprehension when working memory is overloaded.

people could not accurately discriminate between a verbatim target sentence and a paraphrase: If the choice preserved the original meaning, then people mistakenly "recognized" it. Clearly, these results showed that memory for meaningful passages does not retain verbatim sentences for long but does retain meaning quite well.

Online Comprehension Tasks

As work on comprehension developed, researchers needed *a task that measures comprehension as it happens*, or an **online comprehension** task. Such tasks involve the same approach you've been reading about throughout this book: Find a dynamic, time- or action-based task that yields measurements of the underlying mental processes as they occur. Contrast performance in a variety of conditions, pitting factors against each other to see how they affect comprehension speed or difficulty. Then draw conclusions about the underlying mental processes, based on the performance measures.

WRITTEN LANGUAGE A common assessment of cognition during comprehension involves reading times. These can be gathered by using eye movement data, or having people control the presentation of text by pressing a button to advance to the next word, clause, or sentence. Reading times for these individual components can then be analyzed, and inferences about online comprehension can be drawn. In general, language that a person is prepared for is read faster, whereas those aspects that require a large involvement of mental resources result in longer reading times.

In one commonly used method to assess what a person is thinking about while reading, a text appears on a computer screen and is immediately followed by a probe word. Sometimes a person must make a "yes" or "no" response, indicating whether the word was in the just-read sentence. Sometimes the person must simply name the word or perform a lexical decision task on it. Look at Table 10-1 to see some sample stimuli and test words for these tasks. Response times would lead us to inferences about the nature and operation of cognition. For example, if the ambiguous word *boxer* activates both the dog and the fighter meanings, then we might expect RT to dog and fight to be about the same, but faster than to the neutral word *plate*. But if *boxer* is interpreted only in one of its two senses, then dog would be faster than fight (or the other way around, depending on which meaning is dominant).

TABLE 10-1 Sample Stimuli and Test Words for Online Comprehension Tasks

Task	Sentence	Yes	Related	Unrelated	No
Was this word in the sentence?	Ken really liked the boxer.	Ken			Bill
Naming	Ken really liked the boxer.		Dog/fight	Plate	
Lexical decision	Ken really liked the boxer.		Dog/fight	Plate	Lamt

Another way to assess online comprehension is the think-aloud verbal protocol method (e.g., Magliano, Trabasso, & Graesser, 1999). In this method, people are asked to verbalize their thoughts as they read a passage of text. The verbal protocols can then be analyzed later to assess what conscious thoughts people were having as they read. For example, how do they link up a current portion of text with events that occurred earlier, were they making predictions about what would happen next, did they notice an inconsistency in the text, and so on? The data generated from think-aloud protocols can provide insight into what aspects of a text might be fruitful candidates for further research. For example, this information can be used to focus investigation of which aspects of a text will yield interesting reading time data, or what kind of information to test using a probe task.

Finally, as in many other areas of cognitive psychology, there has been an increase in the use of neural imaging to aid our investigations. For online comprehension, these measures often require the temporal resolution necessary to capture understanding across relatively brief periods of time, as would be done with event-related potential (ERP) and functional magnetic resonance imaging (fMRI) recordings. Using these methods, we can reveal aspects of comprehension that might be difficult to uncover otherwise.

Metacomprehension

Explore
What Learning Techniques Do You Use? in **MyPsychLab**

Reading a passage, and having some understanding of what you've read, doesn't mean you've actually learned something or will remember it later. Yet, we need to use our **metacomprehension** abilities (e.g., Dunlosky & Lipko, 2007) to *monitor how well we are understanding and will remember information later*. Metacomprehension is important because it can influence how much we may study information later, and just what information we devote our time to.

A popular measure of metacomprehension is **judgments of learning (JOLs)** (Arbuckle & Cuddy, 1969). These are *estimates people are asked to make of how well they feel they have learned some material they have just read* (recall that we talked about judgments of learning in Chapter 9, too). Research on JOLs typically compares people's estimates of how well they have learned information with how they actually do. Unfortunately, in many cases, the relationship between JOLs and actual performance is quite low—in other words, people are typically not very good at estimating whether they've learned something or not. As a consequence, when you plan your studying, say for an upcoming exam, you may not spend the time you need on some material because you think you know it better than you really do. Your test performance would be better if you could better monitor what you have and have not learned.

In addition to difficulty in judging whether something was learned, people also have metacomprehension problems when it comes to choosing how to plan or distribute their study time. Here's an example: Although you learned in Chapter 8 that memory is worse when people study using massed practice (cramming), rather than distributed practice, many people are unaware that massed practice is a poor learning strategy. Another metacomprehension error that people make is to spend their study time focusing on very difficult material. The problem with this is that it is an inefficient strategy (Nelson & Leonesio, 1988). This **labor-in-vain effect** occurs when *people spend large amounts of time trying to learn information that is too far beyond their current level of knowledge, but end up with little to no new learning.*

A better strategy is to spend time learning information that falls within the **region of proximal learning** (e.g., Metcalfe, 2002). This is *information that is just beyond a person's current level of understanding.* So, what we have here a bit like the Goldilocks and the Three Bears story. Obviously it is a waste of time to study information that one knows well (this material is too soft). Also, as the labor-in-vain effect shows, trying to study information that is far too difficult will not help either (this material is too hard). However, learning that occurs in the region of proximal learning is just beyond what a person currently knows, so they can draw on their existing knowledge as a scaffolding to integrate new information (this material is just right).

Some classroom settings are set up to take advantage of the region of proximal learning, provided you've had the prerequisites, and you keep up with the material in the class. In addition to this, what are some other ways to improve your metacomprehension? Here are three (cf. Dunlosky & Lipko, 2007; Griffin, Wiley, & Thiede, 2008). First, before making a judgment about whether you've learned something, wait a few minutes (Dunlosky & Nelson, 1991). Often, when people are making judgments of learning, they are assessing whether they can retrieve the information from long-term memory into working memory. But when you make these judgments right after reading material, there is still a lot of information *in* working memory, and so you are overconfident in your ability to remember the information. Second, rereading the material can also be very helpful. Reading the material before lecture, then going to lecture can give you the same benefit and will save you time and effort later. Finally, generating summaries, or even lists of key words, can boost the accuracy of your JOLs. In this way, you help reveal to yourself what you do and do not yet know.

Comprehension as Mental Structure Building

A convenient way to organize thinking about comprehension is to use Gernsbacher's (1990) **structure-building** framework. The theory is summarized in Table 10-2. The basic theme is that comprehension is a process of building mental structures.

TABLE 10-2 Summary of Gernsbacher's Structure-Building Framework

Process	Explanation
1. Laying a foundation	Initiate a structure for representing clause or sentence meaning.
2. Mapping information	Map or store congruent information into the current structure.
3. Shifting	Initiate a new structure to represent a new or different idea.

Control Mechanisms	Function
1. Enhancement	Increase the activation of coherent, related information.
2. Suppression	Dampen the activation of information no longer relevant to current structure.

Laying a foundation, mapping information onto the structure, and shifting to new structures are the three principal components.

LAYING A FOUNDATION   As we read we begin to build a mental structure that captures the meaning of a sentence. A foundation is initiated as the sentence begins and typically is built around the first mentioned character or idea. This is equivalent to saying that sentence 6 is about Dave and studying:

> *(6) Dave was studying hard for his statistics midterm.*

MAPPING INFORMATION   As more elements appear, they are added to the structure, by the process called **mapping**. Mapping here simply means that additional word and concept meanings are added to the "DAVE" structure by specifying Dave's activities. For instance, the prepositional phrase "for his statistics midterm" is processed. Because the concept "MIDTERM" is coherent in the context of studying, these concepts are added to the structure. Also, any inferences that you draw would be added to the structure. For instance, when your knowledge about "MIDTERM" was activated, you drew the inference that Dave probably was enrolled in a statistics course.

SHIFTING TO A NEW STRUCTURE   We continue trying to map incoming words to the current structure on the assumption that those words belong to the structure under construction right now. But at some point, a different idea is encountered that signals a change in focus or topic shift. As an example, consider this continuation of the Dave story:

> *(7) Because the professor had a reputation for giving difficult exams, the students knew they'd have to be well prepared.*

When you read "Because the professor," a coherence process detects the change in topic or focus. One clue is the word *because* or other connectives (e.g., *later*, *although*, *meanwhile*). Another clue involves the introduction of a new character and the inferences you need to draw to figure out who the professor is; you inferred that Dave must be enrolled in a statistics class, and because midterms are exams given in college classes that are taught by professors, the professor must be the one who teaches that statistics class. At such moments, you close off or finish the "Dave structure" and begin a new one, one about the professor. Although the "Dave structure" still retains its prominence in memory, you are now working on a new current structure, mapping the incoming ideas (e.g., reputation, difficult exams) onto it. And at the end of that phrase, you will have constructed two related structures, one for each meaning (the phrase beginning "the students" will trigger yet another structure to be built, yielding three substructures).

ENHANCEMENT AND SUPPRESSION   Finally, let's consider the two control mechanisms. Let's add one more sentence to the Dave story:

> *(6) Dave was studying hard for his statistics midterm.*
>
> *(7) Because the professor had a reputation for giving difficult exams, the students knew they'd have to be well prepared.*
>
> *(8) Dave wanted an A on that test.*

As noted earlier, reading sentence 7 results in a new substructure and a change in focus. Still, the new substructure is related to the first one. That is, two ideas in sentence 7 map onto those from sentence 6: *Exams* refers to the same concept as *midterms*, and the *professor* maps onto the statistics course implied by sentence 6. Such mappings reflect the activation of related concepts, especially those mapped into the foundation of the first structure (Millis & Just, 1994). This activation combines with the activation from *midterm* and *statistics course* because of their semantic relatedness. This is the process of **enhancement**, that the many related *concepts are now boosted or enhanced in their level of activation*. This enhancement process is the priming process in semantic memory. It is the degree of enhancement and activation among concepts that predicts which ones will be remembered better or responded to more rapidly. The more frequently the same set of concepts is enhanced across a sentence, the more coherent the passage is.

Note, however, that the enhancement of some concepts implies that others lose activation. That is, while sentence 7 enhances the activation of concepts related to "PROFESSOR," "EXAM," and so on, there is also **suppression** of concepts that are now out of the main discourse focus. In other words, *activated concepts that become unrelated to the focus decrease in activation* by the process of suppression. Figure 10-1 is an illustration of these competing tendencies. Note that as the professor clause is processed (ideas 3 and 4), the activation level for "DAVE" is suppressed because it's no longer the main discourse focus. Then, as the story unfolds further (ideas 5 to 7), the concept "DAVE" regains its enhancement, and

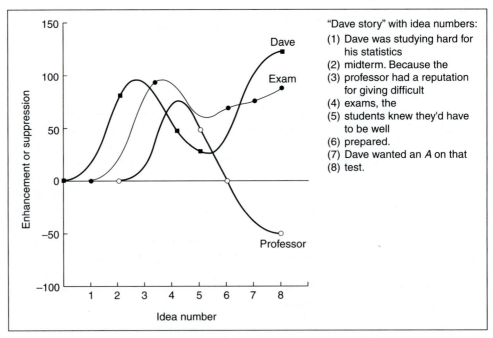

FIGURE 10-1 Hypothetical activation curves for the concepts *Dave, exam,* and *professor* from the "Dave story" in the text. As concepts are introduced or mentioned again (*Dave, exam*), their activation becomes enhanced. When the focus shifts, old concepts (*professor*) become suppressed; that is, their activation dwindles.

the "PROFESSOR" dwindles. Thus the original Dave structure from sentence 6 receives renewed enhancement when you read in sentence 8 that Dave wanted an *A* on the test (O'Brien et al., 1995; for an extension of enhancement and suppression to the topic of metaphor comprehension, see Gernsbacher, Keysar, Robertson, & Werner, 2001, and Kintsch, 2000). And, in the meantime, less important concepts are suppressed (e.g., McNamara & McDaniel, 2004).

Levels of Comprehension

As you read earlier, comprehension is a complex process, involving a number of different levels. One of the ways of characterizing these different levels was already discussed in Chapter 8, namely van Dijk and Kintsch's (1983) levels of representation theory. As a reminder, at one level is the **surface form**. This is our verbatim mental representation of the exact words and syntax used. At an intermediate level is the **propositional textbase**, which captures the basic idea units present in a text. Finally, there is the level of the **situation model** (Johnson-Laird, 1983; Van Dijk & Kintsch, 1983; Zwaan & Radvansky, 1998), which is *a mental representation that serves as a simulation of a real or possible world as described by a text.* These different levels of comprehension involve different cognitive processes that operate at different time scales, with surface-level cognitive processing occurring more rapidly than situation-model–level processing (Huang & Gordon, 2011).

As you read, try to keep in mind and understand how comprehension may depend on these different levels. For example, research on order of mention in establishing discourse reference will depend on the surface form. Work on bridging inferences requires processing at the textbase level. And finally, work showing how people monitor various aspects of experience involves the situation model.

Section Summary

- A variety of online tasks have been devised to investigate comprehension, such as tasks involving reading times, the use of probes, think-aloud protocols, and neuroimaging evidence.
- Successful comprehension is best achieved when people can self-monitor what they are and are not learning, though judgments of learning. However, these judgments are often poor estimates of how much has actually been learned. Estimates can be improved by delaying these judgments, rereading, and providing summaries of the material.
- Comprehension involves processing at many levels, including the surface form, textbase, and situation model levels. Evidence of processing at each of these levels can be derived across many different aspects of understanding.

READING

For years, the standard way to study reading was to have people read a passage of text, then take a memory test, such as a multiple choice or recall test. Such tasks certainly have face validity; they test memory for the text, because much of our reading is for the purpose of learning and remembering what we read.

But this approach suffers from the fact that it doesn't gather online measures of comprehension, only what people remember after reading (not that this isn't important, there's just more to what's going on). In Figure 10-1, you saw a graph of the hypothetical activation levels for concepts in a set of sentences. We would like to know *directly* how concepts vary in their activation levels across a passage because that tells us a great deal about online reading comprehension. A multiple-choice test is too blunt to give us such answers.

Gaze Duration

At the end of Chapter 9, you saw a figure of eye gaze fixation times, where those times went up when the ambiguity of a sentence became apparent (see Figure 9-12). This methodology reveals mental processing at the level of eye gazes, levels of activation, and so on. You'll read about it in this section.

In reading research that assesses gaze duration, the equipment used is an **eye tracker**, a camera- and computer-based apparatus that records eye movements and the exact words that are fixated on during reading; one is depicted in Figure 10-2. In this system, continuous recording of at least one eye, while keeping track of head position, enables the system to determine exactly what you're looking at on the computer screen. As such, the machine records the duration of the eyes' gaze as they scan across lines of text (this system has other purposes in addition to reading, such as evaluating the usefulness of web pages). Typically, people simply see a passage of text on the screen, and the eye tracker records the eye movements and durations as the words in the passage are read. In this task, the researcher knows which word is being processed on a moment-by-moment basis and *how long the eyes dwell*

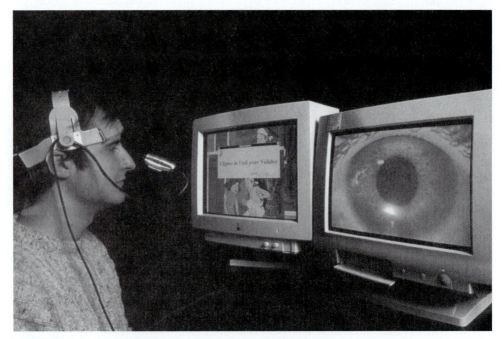

FIGURE 10-2   Researcher uses eye access interactive computer.

on each word, so **gaze duration** is a prime measure of what's going on when people read (see Kambe, Duffy, Clifton, & Rayner, 2003, and Rayner, 1998, for thorough discussions of alternatives). Time-based eye movement data provide a window on the process of comprehension and reading.

Recall from Chapter 3 that the eyes move in rapid sweeps—*saccades*—and then stop to focus on a word—**fixations**. Fixations in reading (English) last about 200 to 250 ms, and the average saccade size is from seven to nine letter spaces, although as Figure 10-3 shows, there is considerable variability in these measures (Rayner, 1998). Eye tracking gives us gaze durations on a word-by-word basis, as shown in Figure 10-4. Notice in the left panel of the figure, a good reader moves fairly rapidly through the text (fixation durations in milliseconds are in the circles above the words) and in a forward direction, at least on this passage. In contrast, the poor reader shown in the right panel moves more slowly through the text and makes many regressive eye movements—that is, returns to an already fixated word. Even at this level of detail, we can draw two conclusions. First, poor readers spend more time going back to reread what they've already processed and can spend considerably more time on some words than good readers do (e.g., 2,065 ms versus 267 ms on "topography"). Second, even good readers spend variable amounts of time on different words, for example as little as 100 ms on "such" but 566 ms on "a knowledge." This second point is important because characteristics of the words and passages exert a tremendous influence on how we read.

Two assumptions that have guided much of the work using eye movements were the immediacy and the eye-mind assumptions (Just & Carpenter, 1980, 1987, 1992). The **immediacy assumption** states that *readers try to interpret each content word of a text as that word is encountered*. In other words, we do not wait until we take in a group of words, say in a phrase, before we start to process them. Instead, we begin interpreting and comprehending immediately, as soon as we encounter a word. The **eye–mind assumption** is the idea that *the pattern of eye movements directly reflects the complexity of the underlying cognitive processes*.

Although these assumptions are fairly robust, they do have some limitations. For example, eye gazes often take in more than one word, depending on the length of the words, the size of the text fonts, and the span of the perceptual beam. So, there is not always a direct one-to-one relationship between an eye fixation and the words being

FIGURE 10-3 Frequency distributions for fixation durations (top) in ms, and saccade length (bottom) in number of character spaces.
From Rayner (1998).

Good Reader **Poor Reader**

makes the short wave enthusiast resort to the   makes the short wave enthusiast resort to the

study of such seemingly unrelated subjects as   study of such seemingly unrelated subjects as

geography, chronology, topography and even   geography, chronology, topography and even

meteorology. A knowledge of these factors is   meteorology. A knowledge of these factors is

decidedly helpful in logging foreign stations.   decidedly helpful in logging foreign stations.

FIGURE 10-4 The pattern of fixations of a good (left panel) and poor (right panel) reader, showing where the fixations occurred in the sentences and the duration of the fixations (in the circles above the fixation points, measured in milliseconds). Arrows indicate regressive eye movements to earlier words; otherwise the fixations went from left to right.

From Just, M. A., & Carpenter, P. A. (1987), *The psychology of reading and language comprehension.* Boston: Allyn & Bacon. Figure 2.1 (p. 27). Credited source: Buswell, G. T. (1937). *How adults read.* Chicago: Chicago University Press, Plates II and IV, pp. 6–7.

processed. Moreover, eye gazes do not reflect only the processing of the current word; they can also reflect some spillover processing of previous words and some anticipatory processing of upcoming words (Kliegl, Nuthmann, & Engbert, 2006). Despite these limits, eye tracking is still a powerful tool for the reading researcher.

Also, keep in mind that outside of reading, eye gaze can be used to understand other aspects of comprehension, such as the understanding of spoken language. For example, if you listen to and follow a set of directions, say to pick up and move an object from one place to another, your eye movements track the spoken instructions very closely—as you hear, "Put the apple in the box," your eyes fixate immediately on those objects in the visual scene (Spivey, Tanenhaus, Eberhard, & Sedivy, 2002; see Crosby, Monin, & Richardson, 2008, for an application of eye tracking to social cognition).

Basic Online Reading Effects

An example of online reading research examined regressive eye movements back to a portion of text that had been read earlier. Just (1976) was interested in such eye movements when the referents in the sentence could not be immediately determined: If an initial assignment of a character to a case role was wrong, then what happened? Was there a regressive eye movement back to the correct referent? People read sentences such as 17 and 18, and eye movements were monitored:

> *(17) The tenant complained to his landlord about the leaky roof. The next day, he went to the attic to get his luggage.*

> *(18) The tenant complained to his landlord about the leaky roof. The next day, he went to the attic to repair the damage.*

In sentence 17, when *luggage* was encountered, eye movements bounced up immediately to the word *tenant*. In sentence 18, they bounced up to *landlord*. These eye movements provided evidence of the underlying mental processes of finding antecedents and determining case roles.

Another study provides a demonstration of the detail afforded by eye trackers. Look at Figure 10-5, taken from Just and Carpenter (1987; see also Just & Carpenter, 1980). You see two sentences taken from a larger passage. Above the words are two numbers. The top number indicates the order in which people fixated on the elements in the sentence; 1 to 9 in the first sentence and 1 to 21 in the second. The number below is the gaze duration (in milliseconds). So, for example, the initial word in sentence 1, *Flywheels*, was fixated for 1,566 ms. The next word, *are*, was fixated only 267 ms. The fourth word, *of*, wasn't fixated at all by this person, so neither a gaze number nor time is presented there. In fact, you can raerragne the lteters in wodrs, usch as is odne in this snetence, and people have little trouble extracting the meaning. There is some disruption to reading, but not as much as if different letters are substituted for correct letters (Rayner, White, Johnson, & Liversedge, 2006). So, reading does not *require* a strict adherence to the printed form.

FIGURE 10-5 Eye fixations of a college student reading a scientific passage. Gazes within each sentence are sequentially numbered above the fixated words with the durations (in milliseconds) indicated below the sequence number.

From Just & Carpenter (1980).

In the Just and Carpenter study, these passages were technical writing, in which a new concept, such as a flywheel, is introduced, defined, and explained. The average reading rate was about 225 words per minute, slower than for simpler material, such as newspaper stories or novels. At a general level, note that every content word was fixated. According to Just and Carpenter, this is the norm for all kinds of text. In fact, about 85% of the content words are fixated. Short function words, however, like *the* or *of* often tend not to be fixated; Rayner and Duffy (1988) estimate that function words are fixated only about 35% of the time. Readers also tend to skip some content words if the passage is very simple for them (say, a children's story given to an adult), if they are skimming or speed reading, or if a word is very predictable (Rayner & Well, 1996).

As noted already, gaze durations are quite variable, and the duration of a saccade is about 100 ms, followed by a fixation of 200 to 250 ms. These estimates come from situations in which the viewer is merely gazing out on a scene. In reading studies, however, people don't move their eyes as far, averaging 2 degrees of angle versus 5 degrees in scene perception. Hence, saccades during reading are shorter—they take about 30 ms. Although word fixations may be brief, readers often make repeated fixations on the *same* word. In some studies, successive fixation times are summed together; alternatively, investigators report both the first-pass fixations and total fixation duration.

A Model of Reading

A strength of online reading measures is that they provide evidence at *two* levels of comprehension. First, there are word-level processes operating at the surface form level. These are crucial to an understanding of reading. For instance, several studies attest to the early use of syntactic features of a sentence when we comprehend not just major syntactic characteristics such as phrase boundaries but even characteristics such as subject–verb agreement (Pearlmutter, Garnsey, & Bock, 1999) and pronoun gender (McDonald & MacWhinney, 1995). Reichle, Pollatsek, Fisher, and Rayner (1998) provide an account of such word-level processes with their E-Z Reader models of eye movement control in reading.

Second, reading time measures can also be used to examine larger, macroscopic processes, such as at the textbase and situation model levels. We'll hold off a discussion of situation model processing until the next section. At the textbase level, Table 10-3 presents Just and Carpenter's (1980) analysis of the "flywheel" passage. To the left of each line is a category label; each sector was categorized as to its role in the overall paragraph structure. To the right are two columns of numbers— observed gaze durations for a group of people and estimated durations—based on the "READER" model's predictions. For example, the 1,921 ms observed for sector 1 is the sum of the separate gaze durations for that sector (averaged across people). Note that different kinds of sectors take different amounts of time; for instance, definition sectors have more difficult words and are longer than other sector types, so they show longer gaze durations. Even a casual examination of the observed and predicted scores shows that the model does a good job of predicting reading times.

So, in general, an analysis of reading times needs to take into account a number of surface form and textbase factors that are tied to the text itself. Reading time is

TABLE 10-3   Sector-by-Sector Analysis of "Flywheel" Passage

Category	Sector	Gaze Duration (ms)	
		Observed	Estimated
Topic	Flywheels are one of the oldest mechanical devices	1,921	1,999
Topic	known to man.	478	680
Expansion	Every internal-combustion engine contains a small flywheel	2,316	2,398
Expansion	that converts the jerky motion of the pistons into the smooth flow of energy	2,477	2,807
Expansion	that powers the drive shaft.	1,056	1,264
Cause	The greater the mass of a flywheel and the faster it spins,	2,143	2,304
Consequence	the more energy can be stored in it.	1,270	1,536
Subtopic	But its maximum spinning speed is limited by the strength of the material	2,400	2,553
Subtopic	it is made from.	615	780
Expansion	If it spins too fast for its mass,	1,414	1,502
Expansion	any flywheel will fly apart.	1,200	1,304
Definition	One type of flywheel consists of round sandwiches of fiberglass and rubber	2,746	3,064
Expansion	providing the maximum possible storage of energy	1,799	1,870
Expansion	when the wheel is confined in a small space	1,522	1,448
Detail	as in an automobile.	769	718
Definition	Another type, the "superflywheel," consists of a series of rimless spokes.	2,938	2,830
Expansion	This flywheel stores the maximum energy	1,416	1,596
Detail	when space is unlimited.	1,289	1,252

From Just & Carpenter (1980).

strongly influenced by word length, with words that are composed of more letters or syllables taking longer to read than shorter words. Also, word frequency plays a vital role, with infrequent words resulting in longer reading times as the reader needs to engage in extra mental effort to retrieve this lexical information from memory. Serial position is also an important factor. The further along a person is in a passage, the more of a foundation there is from which to build mental structures, thereby making comprehension easier and faster. A more complete listing of factors is shown in Table 10-4.

TABLE 10-4 **Variables that Affect Reading Times**

Variables That Increase Reading Times:

Surface form effects: sweep of the eyes to start a new line, sentence wrap-up, number of syllables, low frequency or new word, unusual spelling patterns

Textbase effects: integration of information (after clauses, sentences, sectors, etc.), topic word, new argument, other error recovery, reference and inference processes, difficulty of passage/topic

Variables That Decrease Reading Times:

Surface form effects: familiar word, higher word frequency, repetition of infrequent word

Textbase effects: appropriate title, supportive context, semantic-based expectation (if confirmed)

MODEL ARCHITECTURE AND PROCESSES Figure 10-6 illustrates the architecture and processes of the Just and Carpenter (1980, 1987, 1992) model. Note that several elements are already familiar. For instance, working memory is where different types of knowledge—visual, lexical, syntactic, semantic, and so on—are combined. Not surprisingly, working memory capacity is important in reading comprehension (e.g., Kaakinen, Hyona, & Keenan, 2003). Long-term memory contains a wide variety of knowledge used during reading. Each of these types of knowledge can match the

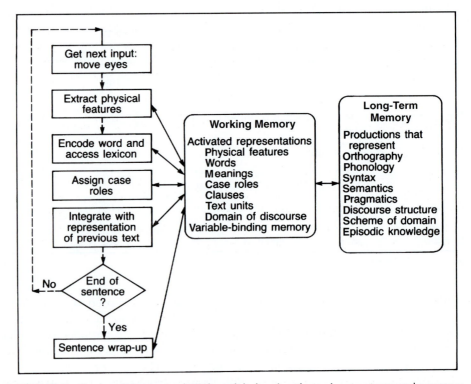

FIGURE 10-6 The Just & Carpenter (1980) model, showing the major structures and processes that operate during reading. Solid lines represent the pathways of information flow; the dashed line shows the typical sequence of processing.

current contents of working memory and update or alter those contents. In simple terms, what you know combines with what you've already read and understood, and together these permit comprehension of what you are reading. Finally, wrap-up is an integrative process that occurs at the end of a sentence or clause. During wrap-up, readers tie up any loose ends; for instance, any remaining inconsistencies or uncertainties about reference are resolved here.

Summary

An in-depth description of all of the variables that influence reading is not possible here—there are simply too many. Here is just a brief list of some of the important factors listed in Table 10-4:

- The effects of word frequency, syntactic structure, and context (Altmann, Garnham, & Dennis, 1992; Inhoff, 1984; Juhasz & Rayner, 2003; Schilling, Rayner, & Chumbley, 1998)
- The effects of sentence context on word identification (Paul, Kellas, Martin, & Clark, 1992; Schustack, Ehrlich, & Rayner, 1987; Simpson, Casteel, Peterson, & Burgess, 1989), including ERP work showing how rapidly we resolve anaphoric references (van Berkum, Brown, & Hagoort, 1999)
- The effects of ambiguity (Frazier & Rayner, 1990; Rayner & Frazier, 1989) and figurative language (Frisson & Pickering, 1999)
- The effects of topic, plausibility, and thematic structure on reading (O'Brien & Myers, 1987; Pickering & Traxler, 1998; Rayner, Warren, Juhasz, & Liversedge, 2004; Speer & Clifton, 1998; Taraban & McClelland, 1988), especially the relatedness of successive paragraphs and the presence of an informative introductory paragraph (Lorch, Lorch, & Matthews, 1985) or title (Wiley & Rayner, 2000)
- The effects of scripted knowledge on word recognition and comprehension (Sharkey & Mitchell, 1985)
- The effects of discourse structure on the understanding of reference (Malt, 1985; Murphy, 1985) and the resolution of ambiguity (Vu, Kellas, Metcalf, & Herman, 2000)

In addition, even phonology plays an important role in reading comprehension, such as research showing that phonological information is activated as rapidly as semantic knowledge in silent reading (Lee, Rayner, & Pollatsek, 1999; Rayner, Pollatsek, & Binder, 1998), especially for readers of lower skill levels who rely more on print-to-sound-to-meaning processes than a direct print-to-meaning route (Jared, Levy, & Rayner, 1999).

Section Summary

- Tremendous progress has been made in understanding the mental processes of reading, largely by using the online measures of comprehension, such as reading times and gaze durations.
- Modern models of reading make predictions about comprehension based on a variety of factors; for instance, word frequency and recency in the passage influence surface form and textbase processing, respectively.

- Online measures of language comprehension provide a unique window into human cognition. Using these sorts of measures, we can gain moment-to-moment insights into the effectiveness of processing, but also into the very contents of people's minds.

REFERENCE, SITUATION MODELS, AND EVENTS

Although the cognitive mechanisms and processes involved in comprehension at the surface form and textbase levels are critically important, they are not the goal of comprehension. A person who has successfully comprehended something that's been read has not only derived an adequate representation of the text itself. This person also has an understanding of the circumstances being described—the reference of the text. In this section, we address this process of reference, the creation of the mental representations of a described state of affairs, the situation model, and explore how research on comprehension has moved on beyond language to capture event comprehension more generally.

Reference

Reference involves finding the connections between elements in a passage of text, finding the words that refer to other concepts in the sentence. In sentence 6 from earlier, "Dave was studying hard for his statistics midterm," the word *his* refers back to *Dave*. In this situation *Dave* is the **antecedent** of *his*, because *Dave* comes before the pronoun. And *the act of using a pronoun or possessive later on* is **anaphoric reference**. So, **reference** is the *linguistic process of alluding to a concept by using another name*. Commonly we use pronouns or synonyms to refer to the antecedent, although there are other types of reference. For example, using a person's name would be a form of identity reference in that it refers back to a previous instance of using their name.

Reference is as common in language as any other feature we can identify. Part of reference is that it reduces redundancy and repetition. Contrast a normal passage such as 9a with 9b to see how boring and repetitive language would be without synonyms, pronouns, and so on.

> *(9a) Mike went to the pool to swim some laps. After his workout, he went to his psychology class. The professor asked him to summarize the chapter that he'd assigned the class to read.*

> *(9b) Mike went to the pool to swim some laps. After Mike swam some laps, Mike went to Mike's psychology class. The professor of Mike's psychology class asked Mike to summarize the chapter that Mike's psychology professor had assigned Mike's psychology class to read.*

This repetition of identity reference can actually be detrimental to comprehension. Research has shown a **repeated name penalty**, *an increase in reading times when a direct reference is used again (e.g., the person's name) compared to when a pronoun is used* (e.g., Almor, 1999; Gordon & Chan, 1995; Gordon & Scearce, 1995). That said, when we produce language, if there is more than one character being discussed or present in a situation, people are less likely to use indirect references, such as pronouns, and are more likely to use a direct reference, such as a person's name (Arnold & Griffin, 2007). This may be more acceptable under these circumstances because there may be some ambiguity as to who is being referenced.

SIMPLE REFERENCE   In natural discourse, different kinds of reference can occur; Clark's (1977) useful list is shown in Table 10-5. Consider three simple forms of reference:

(10) I saw a convertible yesterday. The convertible was red.

(11) I saw a convertible yesterday. The car was red.

(12) I saw a convertible yesterday. It was red.

In sentence 10 the reference is so direct that it requires no inference on the part of the listener; this is identity reference, using the definite article *the* to refer back to a previously introduced concept, *a convertible*. Synonym reference requires that you consider whether the second word is an adequate synonym for the first, as in sentence 11; can a convertible also be referred to as "the car"? Pronoun reference requires similar reference and inference steps. In sentence 12 *it* can refer only to the *convertible*, because it is the only concept in the earlier phrase that can be equated with "it." That is, in English, the word *it* must refer to an ungendered

TABLE 10-5   Types of Reference and Implication

Direct Reference

Identity. Michelle bought a computer. The computer was on sale.

Synonym. Michelle bought a computer. The machine was on sale.

Pronoun. Michelle bought a computer. It was on sale for 20% off.

Set membership. I talked to two people today. Michelle said she had just bought a computer.

Epithet. Michelle bought a computer. The stupid thing doesn't work.

Indirect Reference by Association

Necessary parts. Eric bought a used car. The tires were badly worn.

Probable parts. Eric bought a used car. The radio doesn't work.

Inducible parts. Eric bought a used car. The salesperson gave him a good price.

Indirect Reference by Characterization

Necessary roles. I taught my class yesterday. The time I started was 1:30.

Optional roles. I taught my class yesterday. The chalk tray was empty.

Other

Reasons. Rick asked a question in class. He hoped to impress the professor.

Causes. Rick answered a question in class. The professor had called on him.

Consequences. Rick asked a question in class. The professor was impressed.

Concurrences. Rick asked a question in class. Vicki tried to impress the professor too.

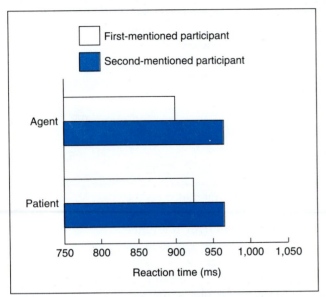

FIGURE 10-7 Mean response time to names that had appeared in the studied sentences when the name was the first- or second-mentioned participant and when the name played the agent or patient case role in the sentence.

Data from Gernsbacher & Hargreaves (1988).

concept, just as *he* must refer to a male, and so on. In some languages the nouns have gender and pronouns must agree with the gender of the noun; translated literally from French, we get, "Here is the Eiffel Tower. She is beautiful."

Another important idea is that there is some evidence that the order in which antecedents are encountered influences the likelihood that they will be linked to later reference. Two effects of this type are the **advantage of first mention** and the **advantage of clause recency**. In the advantage of first mention, *characters and ideas that were mentioned first have a special significance.* For example, in a study by Gernsbacher and Hargreaves (1988), after reading a sentence such as "Tina gathered the kindling as Lisa set up the tent," people responded faster to *Tina* than *Lisa* (see Figure 10-7).

Conversely, there is also a period of time, at the end of the sentence, when the most recent character has an advantage—this is the *advantage of clause recency*. Again, for the sentence "Tina gathered the kindling as Lisa set up the tent," if you are probed immediately after it, Lisa has a slight advantage due to recency, but this advantage is short-lived, showing an advantage at about 50 to 60 ms, but disappearing by 150 ms (Gernsbacher, Hargreaves, & Beeman, 1989).

In other work, it has been found that even the article (e.g., *a* or *the*) used can influence reference. Definite articles, such as *the*, convey given information and make sentences seem more coherent and sensible as compared to when indefinite articles (e.g., *a, an,* and *some*) are used (Robertson et al., 2000; see Table 10-6 for sample sentences), and sentences with definite articles are remembered better later (Haviland & Clark, 1974). For Gernsbacher (1997), *the* is a cue for discourse coherence, enabling us to map information more efficiently and accurately. In one study (Robertson et al., 2000), people read sentences, followed by a recognition test (to make sure people actually tried to comprehend the sentences). Overall, sentences using *the* showed

TABLE 10-6   Sample Sentences with Indefinite and Definite Articles

Indefinite	Definite
A grandmother sat at a table.	The grandmother sat at the table.
A child played in a backyard.	The child played in the backyard.
Some rain began to pour down.	The rain began to pour down.
An elderly woman led some others outside.	The elderly woman led the others outside.

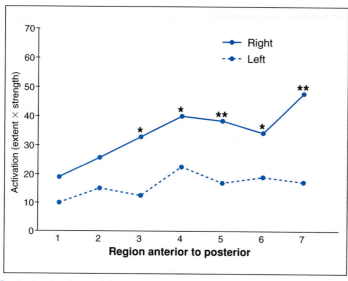

FIGURE 10-8   Activation levels for sentences presented with definite versus indefinite articles (levels in the figure are difference scores, showing how much greater the activations for definite than indefinite article sentences were), for seven left and right hemisphere locations in the brain.

From Robertson et al. (2000).

greater evidence of coherence than those with the indefinite *a*, *an*, and *some*. Importantly, people in this study were tested using fMRI, and the levels of activity of different brain regions were measured. As Figure 10-8 shows, sentences that used the definite article showed greater activation than those with indefinite articles. Moreover, these activations were greater in the right hemisphere than the left, whereas more commonly it's the left hemisphere that's implicated in language processing (e.g., Polk & Farah, 2002), as you recall from Chapter 9. Thus, the right hemisphere is particularly involved in establishing coherence in language comprehension.

Situation Models

In constructing and using a situation model (Johnson-Laird, 1983; Van Dijk & Kintsch, 1983; Zwaan & Radvansky, 1998), a person combines information that is available from the text, along with prior semantic and episodic knowledge, to create a mental simulation of the events being described. This mental representation is a **situation model**, *a mental representation that serves as a simulation of a real or possible world as described by a text.* The important idea is that comprehension is a search after meaning (Graesser, Singer, & Trabasso, 1994). Although comprehension does use some passive activation of semantic and episodic memories (e.g., McKoon & Ratcliff, 1992), we also actively build situation models that elaborate on the causal structure of the event a person is trying to understand. In this section we cover two basic processes in the use of situation models in comprehension. The first is the use of inferences to elaborate on the information provided by a text, and the second is the updating of the situation model as shifts in the described events are encountered.

Instead of specifying everything, we rely on people to know the meanings of words, to know about syntactic devices that structure our discourse, and to share our general conceptual knowledge of the world (e.g., to know that swimming laps can be a workout, or that professors assign chapters for their students to read; you remember a similar point from the earlier chapter, in discussing scripts). In fact, as you'll read later, if you *do* specify everything exactly, you're breaking an important conversational rule, and people will be unhappy with you. Let's turn to how comprehenders flesh out some missing information: implication and inference.

In **implication** there is *an intended reference in a sentence or utterance, but it is not mentioned explicitly.* The intention here is on the part of the speaker (or writer), who implies but does not state some conclusion or connection; in a sense, implication is in the mind of the speaker. If the listener (reader) draws the appropriate conclusion or connection during comprehension, then we say that the listener has drawn an inference. Thus, **inference** is *the process by which the comprehender draws connections between concepts, determines the referents of words and ideas, and derives conclusions from a message.* Implication is something that language producers do, and drawing inferences is something comprehenders do. If your professor says in class, "The next exam is on Wednesday, and it covers a lot of material," he or she is implying something about the difficulty of the exam, but is leaving it up to the students to draw that inference.

PROVE IT

People spontaneously draw inferences as they comprehend language. These inferences are then incorporated into the situation models of what was being heard or read. As a result, people frequently misremember information as having been heard or read, when in fact it was not. For this prove it section, a list of sentences follows. Along with each sentence is an inference that people are likely to make (in parentheses). What you should do is read these sentences to a group of volunteers. Then, after all of the sentences have been read, give your volunteers some distractor task, such as having them solve math problems for 3 to 5 minutes. When the distractor period is over, have your volunteers try to recall the sentences. What you should find is that people will likely report the inferences that they made while they were comprehending. That is, they will "recall" more information that you actually read to them. These inferences—false memories, in a sense—are now part of their memory.

1. The housewife spoke to the manager about the increased meat prices (complained)
2. The paratrooper leaped out of the door (jump out of a plane/helicopter)
3. The cute girl told her mother she wanted a drink (asked)
4. The weatherman told the people of the approaching tornado (warned)
5. The karate champion hit the cement block (broke)
6. The absent-minded professor didn't have his car keys (lost or forgot)
7. The safecracker put the match to the fuse (lit)
8. The hungry python caught the mouse (ate)
9. The man dropped the delicate glass pitcher (broke)
10. The clumsy chemist had acid on his coat (spilled)
11. The barnacle clung to the sides (ship)
12. Dennis sat in Santa's chair and asked for an elephant (lap)

Source: Adapted from Harris & Monaco (1978).

INFERENCE MAKING AND SITUATION MODEL CREATION   A simple type of inference making is what Clark (1977) termed a **bridging inference**, which is *a process of constructing a connection between concepts*. A bridging inference binds two units of language together. For example, determining that a reference like the epithet *the stupid thing* refers to the same entity as *a computer* is a bridging inference—it builds a connection between these two forms of reference, indicating that they refer to the same discourse entity. In bridging inference, the language producer uses reference to indicate the intended kinds of implications. For their part, comprehenders interpret the statement in the same fashion, computing the references and drawing the inferences needed. When the implication and inferences are intended, we call it **authorized**. Alternatively, unintended implications and inferences are called **unauthorized**, as when I say, "Your hair looks pretty today," and you respond, "So you think it was ugly yesterday?" (see also McKoon & Ratcliff, 1986).

The examples in Table 10-6 make it clear that the bridges we need to build for comprehension vary in their complexity, from simple and direct to difficult and remote. Even on intuitive grounds, consider how the following sentences differ in the ease of comprehension:

(13) *Marge went into her office. It was very dirty.*

(14) *Marge went into her office. The floor was very dirty.*

(15) *Marge went into her office. The African violet had bloomed.*

Whereas sentence 13 is a simple case of pronoun reference, sentence 14 refers back to *office* with the word *floor*. Because an office necessarily has a floor, it is clear that the implication in sentence 14 is that it was Marge's office floor that was dirty. One property you retrieve from semantic memory is that an office has a floor. Thus, if you comprehend that the office floor was dirty, you draw this inference. But it's an even longer chain of inference to draw the inference in sentence 15 that Marge has an African violet in her office; a floor is necessary, but an African violet isn't. Overall, the integration of this semantic knowledge with the information in the text is part and parcel of creating a situation model.

Think back to the discussion of semantic memory and the typicality of category instances and properties. It seems likely that the structure of concepts in semantic memory activation influences the ease with which information is inferred during situation model construction (e.g., Cook & Myers, 2004). So, more predictable pieces of information are processed faster (McKoon & Ratcliff, 1989; O'Brien, Plewes, & Albrecht, 1990). Marge's office necessarily has a floor as well as a desk, a chair, some shelves, and so on. It's conceivable that it has some plants, but that is optional enough that sentence 15 would take more time to comprehend.

Further evidence that people are drawing on their semantic knowledge, and that this knowledge has an embodied character, was given in a study by Zwaan, Stanfield, and Yaxley (2002). People read short descriptions of situations and then were shown pictures of objects. The task was to indicate whether the pictured object had been in the description they read. The critical manipulation was whether the picture either matched or mismatched the perceptual characteristics of the object in the description. For example, the critical sentence could be either *The ranger saw the eagle in the sky* or *The ranger saw the eagle in its nest* followed by a picture of either an eagle with its wings outstretched or perched (see Figure 10-9). Zwaan et al. found that people responded faster when the picture matched the described state. That is, even though they saw an eagle in both pictures, the eagle with its wings outstretched "matched" the "eagle in the sky" description better, so people responded faster (see also Connell & Lynott, 2009, for the activation of perceptual color information). Thus, people seemed to be activating perceptual qualities of objects during comprehension. Conversely, if people view a picture before reading, they are faster if the sentence matches the picture than if it doesn't (Wassenburg & Zwaan, 2010).

People are also aware of the intended consequence of someone saying something, called a **speech act** (Searle, 1969). For example, if you ask your roommate to turn down the stereo, the *speech* itself is the set of words you say, but the *speech act* is your intention, getting your roommate to let you study for an upcoming exam. Not only do people spontaneously derive the implied speech acts of what other people say, but they may misremember what was said in terms of the speech act itself. For instance, in a study by Holtgraves (2008b), people read a series of short vignettes, some of which conveyed speech acts. For example, suppose people read the following story: "Gloria showed up at the office wearing a new coat. When her coworker Heather saw it she said to her, 'Gloria, I like your new coat.'" The last sentence conveys the speech act of complimenting Gloria. What Holtgraves found was that people were more likely to mistakenly remember that they had read "I'd like to compliment you on your new coat," an utterance

FIGURE 10-9
Examples of pictures of an eagle in flight or on a perch.

that actually describes the speech act. However, a different group of people read a different version of the story, in which the last two sentences were: "When her coworker Heather saw it, she said to *her friend Stacy*: 'I like *her* new coat.'" In this condition, people were less likely to misremember having read "I'd like to compliment her on her new coat." Because there was no actual complimenting speech act to Gloria, people did not store this information in memory and so did not make the memory error.

It should be noted that we do not automatically and spontaneously draw all possible inferences while we read. Although some inferences are directly and typically drawn, such as simple and straightforward references, others are more complex and may not be drawn, and possibly shouldn't be drawn. If we did, our cognitive resources would be quickly overwhelmed (Singer, Graesser, & Trabasso, 1994). For example, when you read a sentence like 13 or 14, you are likely not to draw an inference that Marge decided to clean her office, although if the next sentence in the story said that, you'd certainly understand it. Most of the inferences people make are *backward* inferences. That is people are trying to understand what has already been described, and how it all goes together. *Forward* inferences— that is, trying to predict what will happen next—are made under much rarer circumstances (Millis & Graesser, 1994).

Moreover, the creation of the situation model needs to take into account constraints of embodiment. For example, in a study by de Vega, Robertson, Glenberg, Kaschak, and Rinck (2004; see also Radvansky, Zwaan, Federico, & Franklin, 1998), people were asked to read a series of passages. Embedded in those passages were critical sentences that described two actions that a character was doing, either at the same time or in sequence. If a person is described as doing two things that require the same parts of the body, such as *While chopping wood with his large axe, he painted the fence white*, reading times were slower, as if readers were trying to figure out how this could be done. However, reading times were faster when either different parts of the body were being used, such as *While whistling a lively folk melody, he painted the fence white*, or were done in sequence, such as *After chopping wood with his large axe, he painted the fence white*. Thus, people take into account the limits of our human bodies, and the way actions happen in time, to help them comprehend what they are reading.

INDIVIDUAL DIFFERENCES Interestingly, reference and inference processes depend significantly on individual characteristics of the reader, particularly on the reader's skill. For instance, Long and De Ley (2000) found that less skilled readers resolve ambiguous pronouns just as well as more skilled readers, but they do so only when they are integrating meanings together; the more skilled readers resolve the pronouns earlier, probably when they first encounter a pronoun.

Several studies have also examined inferences as a function of working memory capacity (e.g., Fletcher & Bloom, 1988). One study by Singer, Andrusiak, Reisdorf, and Black (1992) explored individual differences in bridging as a function of working memory capacity and vocabulary knowledge. The gist of this work is that the greater your working memory capacity and vocabulary size, the greater the likelihood that information necessary for an inference will still be in working memory and can be used (see also Long, Oppy, & Seely, 1997; Miyake, Just, & Carpenter, 1994).

Evidence for individual differences in comprehension has also revealed itself in neurological measures. In a study by Virtue, van den Broek, and Linderholm (2006), people read sentences that had causal constraints that were either weak (e.g., *As he arrived at the bus stop, he saw his bus was already five blocks away.*) or strong (*As he arrived at the bus stop, he saw his bus was just pulling away.*). During reading, the researchers presented lexical decision probes that corresponded to likely inference that the readers might make (e.g., *run* in this case). Importantly, this presentation was done to the left and right hemispheres by presenting the words on either the right or left half (respectively) of the computer screen. The data showed that the right hemisphere was more involved in generating remote associations (that is, associated concepts that are not closely semantically related to the concepts in the sentences). Moreover, people with high working memory capacity activated fewer remote associations than low-span people. Essentially, people with a high working memory span were more focused in the amount of knowledge they activated during comprehension.

UPDATING   Situations that we experience or read about are often in a state of flux. Things are always changing, and the events may differ from one moment to the next. Thus, the cognitive processes involved in comprehension must be able to shift the current understanding to adapt to these ongoing changes. There are a number of **updating** processes that *alter a person's situation model in the face of information about how the situation has changed.* To provide a framework for understanding how these changes can occur, we'll use Rolf Zwaan's Event Indexing Model (Zwaan, Langston, & Graesser, 1995; Zwaan, Magliano, & Graesser, 1995; Zwaan & Radvansky, 1998). According to this theory, people actively monitor multiple event dimensions during reading to assess whether there has been a meaningful change along any of them.

In the original version of the theory, five dimensions were proposed: space, time, entity, intentionality (goals), and causality. When there is a disruption along any one of these dimensions, people update their situation models, and this updating process takes time. For example, a break along the space and time dimensions could happen if a story protagonist moves to a new location, or there is a jump in time (e.g., a week later . . .). Similarly if a new character is introduced into a story, the person would need to update the entity dimension, and so on. Further research has shown that people actually monitor more than just these five dimensions. For example, people also track emotional information (e.g., Komeda & Kusumi, 2006).

To give you a better idea of what goes on in situation model updating, let's look at a classic paradigm that explores updating along the spatial dimension. In a seminal paper by Morrow, Greenspan, and Bower (1987), people memorized a diagram of a research lab, where each room had four objects in it (see Figure 10-10). They then read narratives about people moving about in that space. During reading, people were occasionally probed with pairs of object names, such as *sink-furnace.* The task was to indicate whether the two

FIGURE 10-10 Example of the map of the research center memorized by people in Morrow, Greenspan, & Bower's (1987) study of spatial updating during language comprehension.

objects were in the same room or not (in this case, they were not). The critical factor was the distance on the map between the story protagonist's current location, and the location of the probe objects. Moreover, these memory probes came after motion sentences in which the person moved from one room to another, such as "He walked from the laboratory into the wash room." Based on this, four conditions were defined. The Location Room was the room that the person just moved to—the wash room in this case. The Path Room was the (unmentioned) room that the person walked through to get to the Location room—the storage room here. The Source Room was the room the person was in just before moving to the Location Room—the laboratory here. Finally, there was an Other Room condition, which corresponded to probes from any other room in the building.

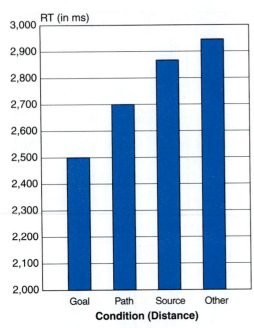

FIGURE 10-11 Response time data from a study by Morrow, Greenspan, & Bower (1987). While reading a passage about a character moving about the building in Figure 10-10, people were interrupted with memory probes. In this case, the probes were two objects, and the person's task was to indicate whether they were in the same room or not. In this task, the Goal room is the room the story character had just moved to (the goal of the movement), the Path room is a room along the character's path of travel, the Source room is the room that the movement started from (the source from which the movement began), and the Other room is just some other room in the building.

The results from one study, shown in Figure 10-11, reveal that response times to the memory probes increased with an increase in distance between the protagonist and the objects. It is as if people were mentally scanning their situation models from the protagonist's current place in the building to another room. The further away that other room was, the longer it took people to scan. People actively updated their situation models as there were changes in spatial locations in the texts. When a person reads that a story character has moved from one room to another, they update their situation model so that the spatial framework that is at the focus of comprehension is now different. What is particularly compelling here are the response times to the probes from the Path Room condition—this room was not even mentioned, yet people are scanning their situation model in a way that activates that information. If people were simply activating knowledge of the rooms that the protagonist was in, then this would not have occurred. But, because people are mentally simulating the environment as they read, this activation of an intermediate location emerges.

Similar influences of situation model updating can be seen for other situation model dimensions, including shifts in time (Gennari, 2004; Zwaan, 1996), monitoring characteristics of story characters (Albrecht & O'Brien, 1995), the processing of character goal information (Lutz & Radvansky, 1997; Suh & Trabasso, 1993), and so on.

Tracking these changes along various dimensions is part of an attempt to create an analog to the world. Work with fMRI recordings have shown that there are increases in brain activity when event shifts are encountered and people need to update their situation models (Speer, Zacks, & Reynolds, 2007). For example, looking at the dimension of time in a story, memory access to events earlier in a sequence is more difficult if the described intervening events are longer in duration (e.g., a year) than if they are shorter (e.g., a day), even if the event is presented as a flashback (that is later in the text than the intervening events) (Claus & Kelter, 2006).

Events

ON BEYOND LANGUAGE Our discussion of comprehension up to now has largely focused on language comprehension of either written or spoken language, and this reflects the thrust of research in this area. However, this is not the only type of comprehension that people can engage in. We also comprehend events that we see or are involved in. As an example of the first type, work by Magliano (Magliano, Miller, & Zwaan, 2001; Magliano, Taylor, & Kim, 2005) and Zacks (Zacks et al., 2001; Zacks, Speer, Swallow, Braver, & Reynolds, 2007) show that people are actively comprehending events viewed on video or film. For example, in a study by Magliano et al. (2001), rather than having people read texts, people watched narrative films such as *Star Trek 2: The Wrath of Khan*. As people watched these movies, they indicated when they thought the situation depicted by the film changed. The results showed that people made these indications at the same points as situation model theory suggested they would update their understanding. For example, people indicated that there was a change in the film if a new character entered a scene, if there was a change in spatial location, if something unexpected happened, and so on, exactly as the theory predicts.

There have also been extensions of the study of comprehension to how people understand interactive events that they find themselves in. The development of virtual reality technologies has been helpful here because the experimenter has a great deal of control in creating environments that a person can interact with, which allows the experimenter to make precise, controlled measurements. An example of this is a study by Tamplin, Krawietz, Copeland, and Radvansky (in press) that was modeled after the Morrow et al. (1987) studies described earlier. In these experiments, people memorized the map of a research center, as was done in the earlier text comprehension work. Then, rather than reading a story, people navigated through a virtual representation of the environment. As they moved about, their primary task was to respond to memory probes that consisted of object names at critical points, similar to what had been done in the text comprehension work. However, the pattern of data that was obtained was very different, as shown in Figure 10-12.

As can be seen, rather than having information about objects become less available as one moves farther and farther away from them, this information is similarly available in memory, except for objects in the Path Room. Response times to probes in this condition were much slower, suggesting that people suppressed this information. So, there is something different about how people comprehend events that they are involved in compared to ones that they just read about. Now why would people want to suppress this knowledge? Why isn't it more available since the person had just been in that room? Well, when people passed through the Path Room, this information was salient because they were actually in that (virtual) context. However, because this was not their destination, this information was irrelevant. As such, knowledge about objects in the Path Room was interfering knowledge in memory. Similar to other examples of interference in cognition that you have studied, this interference can disrupt cognitive processing. So, this is a similar cognitive process (in this case, retrieval interference) that has been observed with simpler materials (e.g., lists of words) showing up in a more real-to-life situation, with similar consequences (i.e., interfering knowledge hinders memory).

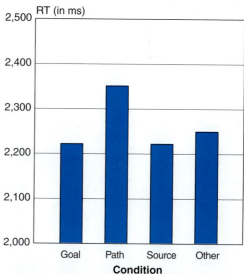

FIGURE 10-12 Response time data from a study by Tamplin, Krawietz, Copeland, & Radvansky (in press). Rather than reading a text, people navigated a virtual environment after memorizing the map of the research center in Figure 10-10. Note the different pattern of data compared to the reading comprehension task illustrated in Figure 10-11.

Section Summary

- Reference in language involves the idea of bridging together different elements of a statement. The source of knowledge that permits speakers to include reference in their messages and listeners to infer the basis for those bridges is not just our knowledge of syntax and word meanings, but the entirety of semantic memory and much top-down processing.
- Situation models are created by combining information from the language itself as well as inferences people draw based on their prior semantic and episodic knowledge.
- The capacity and operation of working memory are known to be important factors in understanding individual differences in reading comprehension.
- Situation model updating occurs when people detect a meaningful change in an event dimension. This updating process is cognitively effortful, resulting in increases in reading times and brain activity.
- Comprehension occurs not only for language that people hear or read, but also for other aspects of experience, including narrative films, videos, and interactive experiences.

CONVERSATION AND GESTURE

We turn now to the comprehension of conversation and gesture. We focus on conversation, normal, everyday language interactions, such as an ordinary talk among friends. The issues we consider, however, apply to all kinds of linguistic interactions: how professors lecture and students comprehend, how people converse on the telephone, how an interviewer and a job applicant talk, how we reason and argue with one another (Rips, 1998), and so on. Furthermore, we look at how we expand on what we say by moving our hands about, making gestures, and by examining the cognitive role of these gestures.

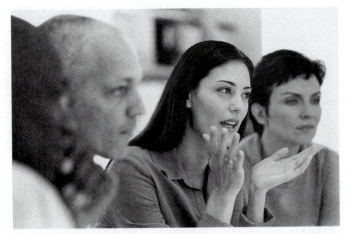

During a conversation, speakers develop a rhythm as each person takes successive turns speaking. Nonverbal interaction can occur during a turn, such as when a listener nods to indicate attention or agreement.

The Structure of Conversations

Let's examine two characteristics of conversations, the issues of turn taking and social roles, to get started and introduce some of the more cognitive effects we're interested in.

TAKING TURNS Conversations are structured by a variety of cognitive and social variables and rules governing the what and how of our contributions. To begin with, we take turns. Typically, there is little overlap between participants' utterances.

Generally, two people speak simultaneously only at the change of turns, when one speaker is finishing and the other is beginning. In fact, interchanges in conversation often come in an adjacency pair, a pair of turns that sets the stage for another part of the conversation. For instance, if Ann wants to ask Betty a question, there can be an adjacency pair of utterances in which Ann sets the stage for the actual question:

Ann: Oh there's one thing I wanted to ask you.

Betty: mhm

Ann: in the village, they've got some of those . . . rings. . . . Would you like one? (From Svartvik & Quirk, 1980, cited in Clark, 1994.)

The neutral "mhm" is both an indication of attention and a signal that Ann can go ahead and ask the question (Duncan, 1972).

The rules we follow for turn taking are straightforward (Sacks, Schegloff, & Jefferson, 1974). First, the current speaker is in charge of selecting the next speaker. This is often done by directing a comment or question toward another participant ("What do you think about that, Fred?"). The second rule is that if the first rule isn't used, then anyone can become the current speaker. Third, if no one else takes the turn, the current speaker may continue but is not obliged to.

Speakers use a variety of signals to indicate whether they are finished with their turn. For example, a long pause at the end of a sentence is a turn-yielding signal, as are a comment directed at another participant, a drop in the pitch or loudness of the utterance, and establishing direct eye contact with another person; the last is often merely a nonverbal way of selecting the next speaker. If the current speaker is not relinquishing the conversational turn, however, these signals are withheld. Other "failure to yield" signals include trailing off in midsentence without completing the grammatical clause or the thought, withholding such endings as "you know," or even looking away from other participants during a pause (Cook, 1977).

In addition to overt signals of when turn taking may occur, there are neurological underpinnings. Margaret and Thomas Wilson (Wilson & Wilson, 2005) have suggested that conversational turn taking may be tied to neurological oscillators that help us keep track of time. The idea is that these oscillators become synchronized to one another on the basis of the rate at which people are producing syllables. These oscillators give us a neurologically based intuition about the pace of the conversation, and when it would be appropriate to step in and take our turn.

SOCIAL ROLES AND SETTINGS The social roles of conversational partners, along with conversational setting, influence the contributions made by participants (Kemper & Thissen, 1981). Formal settings among strangers or mere acquaintances lead to more structured, rule-governed conversations than informal settings among friends (Blom & Gumperz, 1972). Conversations with a "superior"—for instance, your boss or a police officer—are more formal and rule-governed than those with peers (e.g., Brown & Ford, 1961; Edwards & Potter, 1993, and Holtgraves, 1994, discuss the social and interpersonal aspects of such situations). More generally, when involved in conversation, people take into account a wide variety of information, not just the words and syntax, but the context and who is speaking (Van Berkum, 2008).

Cognitive Conversational Characteristics

Conversations are structured by cognitive factors. We focus on three: the conversational rules we follow, the issue of topic maintenance, and the online theories of conversational partners.

CONVERSATIONAL RULES   Grice (1975; see also Norman & Rumelhart, 1975) suggested four **conversational rules** or maxims, *rules that govern our conversational interactions with others*, all derived from the **cooperative principle**, *the idea that each participant in a conversation implicitly assumes that all speakers are following the rules and that each contribution to the conversation is a sincere, appropriate contribution.* In a sense, we enter into a pact with our conversational partner, pledging to abide by certain rules and adopting certain conventions to make our conversations manageable and understandable (Brennan & Clark, 1996; Wilkes-Gibbs & Clark, 1992). This includes issues of syntax, where we choose syntactic structures that mention important discourse focus information early in our sentences (Ferreira & Dell, 2000) and use syntactic structures that are less ambiguous (Haywood, Pickering, & Branigan, 2005); we use intonation and prosody that helps disambiguate an otherwise ambiguous syntactic form (Clifton, Carlson, & Frazier, 2006); we decide on word choice, as in situations when two conversational partners settle on a mutually acceptable term for referring to some object (Metzing & Brennan, 2003; Shintel & Keysar, 2007); and we often use gestures to amplify or disambiguate our speech (Goldin-Meadow, 1997; Kelly, Barr, Church, & Lynch, 1999; Özyürek, 2002). As Table 10-7 shows, the four maxims specify in detail how to follow the cooperative principle. (Two further rules have been added to the list for purposes that will become clear in a moment.)

TABLE 10-7   Grice's (1975) Conversational Maxims, with Two Additional Rules

The Cooperative Principle

Be honest, reasonable, and germane

- **Relevance:** Your utterances should be relevant to the discourse (e.g., stay on topic; don't make statements on things that others aren't interested in).

- **Quantity:** As needed, provide as much information as is necessary (e.g., don't give too much information; don't go beyond or give short shrift to what you know; don't give too much information).

- **Quality:** Have what you say be truthful (e.g., don't give misleading information; don't lie; don't exaggerate).

- **Manner and tone:** Aim for clarity (e.g., avoid saying things that are unnecessarily ambiguous or obscure); keep it brief, but polite, and don't interrupt someone else.

Two Additional Rules

- **Relations with conversational partner:** Infer and respond to partner's knowledge and beliefs (e.g., tailor contributions to partner's level; correct misunderstandings).

- **Rule violations:** Signal or mark intentional violations of rules (e.g., use linguistic or pragmatic markers [stress, gestures]; use blatant violations; signal the reason for the violation). From Grice (1975); see also Norman and Rumelhart (1975).

A simple example or two should help you understand the point of these maxims. When a speaker violates or seems to violate a maxim, the listener assumes there is a reason for this and may not detect a violation (Engelhardt, Bailey, & Ferreira, 2006). That is, the listener assumes that the speaker is following the overarching cooperative principle and so must have intended the remark as something else, maybe sarcasm, or maybe a nonliteral meaning (Kumon-Nakamura, Glucksberg, & Brown, 1995). As an example, imagine studying in the library when your friend asks:

(21) Can I borrow a pencil?

This is a straightforward speech act, a simple request you could respond to directly. But if you had just lent a pencil to your friend, and he said,

(22) Can I borrow a pencil with lead in it?

the question means something different. Assuming that your friend was being cooperative, you now have to figure out why he broke the quantity maxim about overspecifying; all pencils have lead in them, and mentioning the lead is a violation of a rule. You infer that it was a deliberate violation, where the friend's authorized implication can be expressed as "The pencil you lent me doesn't have any lead in it, so would you please lend me one I *can* use?" In general, people are fairly adept at decoding speech acts and knowing what a person is trying to achieve by what they say (Holtgraves, 2008a).

TOPIC MAINTENANCE We also follow the conversational rules in terms of **topic maintenance**, *making our contributions relevant to the topic and sticking to it.* Topic maintenance depends on two processes, comprehension of the speaker's remark and expansion, contributing something new to the topic.

Schank (1977; see also Litman & Allen, 1987) provides an analysis of topic maintenance and topic shift, including a consideration of what is and is not a permissible response, called simply a move, after one speaker's turn is over. The basic idea is that the listener comprehends the speaker's comment and stores it in memory. As in reading, the listener must infer what the speaker's main point was or what the discourse focus was. If the speaker, Ben, says,

(23) I bought a new car in Baltimore yesterday,

then Ed, his conversational partner, needs to infer Ben's main point and expand on that in his reply. Thus, sentence (24) is legal because it apparently responds to the speaker's authorized implication, whereas sentence *(25#) is probably not a legal move (denoted by the # sign)*:

(24) Ed: Really? I thought you said you couldn't afford a car.

(25#) Ed: I bought a new shirt yesterday.

Sentence 24 intersects with two main elements for sentence 23, "BUY" and "CAR," so it is probably an acceptable expansion. Sentence 25# intersects with "BUY," but the other common concept seems to be the time case role "YESTERDAY," an insufficient basis for most expansions. Thus, in general a participant's responsibility is to infer the speaker's focus and expand on it in an appropriate way. That's the relevance maxim: Sticking to the topic means you have to infer it correctly. Ed seems to have failed to draw the correct inference.

On the other hand, maybe Ed *did* comprehend Ben's statement correctly. If so, then he deliberately violated the relevance maxim in sentence 25#. But it's such a blatant violation that it suggests some other motive; Ed may be expressing disinterest in what Ben did or may be saying indirectly that he thinks Ben is bragging. And if Ed suspects Ben is telling a lie, then he makes his remark even more blatant, as in 26:

(26) *Yeah, and I had lunch with the Queen of England.*

ONLINE THEORIES DURING CONVERSATION   A final point involves the theories we develop of our conversational partners, something called **theory of mind**. The most obvious one is a **direct theory.** This is the mental model of *what the conversational partner knows and is interested in, what the partner is like.* We tailor our speech so that we're not being too complex or too simplistic, so we're not talking about something of no interest to the listener. Some clear examples of this involve adult–child speech, where a child's smaller vocabulary and knowledge prompt adults to modify and simplify their utterances in a number of ways (DePaulo & Bonvillian, 1978; Snow, 1972; Snow & Ferguson, 1977). But sensitivity to the partner's knowledge and interests is present to some degree in all conversations—although not perfectly, of course. We don't talk to our college classes the way we would to a group of second graders, nor do we launch into conversations with bank tellers about our research. Horton and Gerrig (2002) call this "audience design," that is, being aware of the need to design your speech to the characteristics of your audience (e.g., Lockridge & Brennan, 2002). Alternatively, if we don't know much about you, we may make an assumption that you know what we know (Nickerson, 2001) and then revise our direct theory as we observe how well you follow our remarks (Clark & Krych, 2004).

Audience design has implications beyond conversations. When we tell stories, we modify what we tell our listeners based on who they are and our social relationship to them. This retelling is not the same as recall. We modify the information we report to fit the social situation. In retelling stories, people often exaggerate some parts, minimize others, add information that was not there originally, and leave some bits out, all to suit our audience and the broader message we are trying to convey (Marsh, 2007).

There is another layer of theories during a conversation, an interpersonal level related to "face management," or public image (Holtgraves, 1994, 1998). Let's call this the **second-order theory**. This second-order theory is *an evaluation of the other participant's direct theory: what you think the other participant believes about you.* Let's develop an example of these two theories to illustrate their importance. Imagine that you're registering for classes next semester and say to your friend Frank that you've decided to take Psychology of Personality. What would your reaction be if Frank responded to you with these statements?

(27) *Why would you want to take that? It's just a bunch of experiments with rats, isn't it?*

(28) Yeah, I'm taking Wilson's class next term too. John told me he's going to assign some books he thinks I'll really like.

(29) Maybe you shouldn't take Wilson's class next term. Don't you have to be pretty smart to do all that reading?

In sentence 27, you assume that your friend has made the remark in sincerity, that it was intended to mean what it says. Because you know that research on laboratory animals had little to do with the field of personality, you conclude that your friend knows a lot less about personality theory than you do. This becomes part of your direct theory, as shown in Table 10-8. For sentence 28, you probably interpret Frank's remark as boastful, intended to show that he's on a first-name basis with the professor. Frank has authorized that inference by using a more familiar term of address. You update both your direct theory of Frank and your second-order theory. You update your direct and second-order theories after sentence 29, too, but the nature of the updates is different: You've been insulted by the implication in Frank's response, something like "He thinks I'm not smart enough to take the class."

Empirical Effects in Conversation

INDIRECT REQUESTS   Let's conclude with some evidence about the conversational effects we've been discussing. One of the most commonly investigated aspects of conversation involves **indirect requests**, such as when *we ask someone to do something* ("Close the window"; "Tell me what time it is") *by an indirect and presumably more polite statement* ("It's drafty in here"; "Excuse me, but do you have the correct time?").

TABLE 10-8   Examples of Direct and Second-Order Theories

Setting: For all three conversations, Chris's first sentence and direct theory are the same.

Chris: "I think I'll take Personality with Dr. Wilson next term."

Chris's direct theory: Frank is interested in the courses I'm taking.

Conversation 1

Frank replies: "Personality? Ah, that's just a bunch of experiments with rats, isn't it?"

Chris's updated direct theory: Frank doesn't know much about personality research.

Conversation 2

Frank replies: "Yeah, I am too. John told me he's going to assign some books he thinks I'll really like."

Chris's updated direct theory: Frank knows the professor on a first-name basis, and he's bragging about it by calling him John.

Chris's second-order theory: Frank thinks I'll be impressed that he calls the professor John.

Conversation 3

Frank replies: "Hmm, maybe you shouldn't take that class. Don't you have to be pretty smart to do all that reading?"

Chris's updated direct theory: Frank is a jerk, he just insulted me.

Chris's second-order theory: Frank thinks I'm not smart.

One of the best student demonstration projects we've ever graded was a test of the politeness ethic in conversational requests. On five randomly selected days, the student sat next to a stranger on the bus, turned, and asked, "Excuse me, but do you have the correct time?" All five strangers answered her. On five other randomly selected days, she said to the stranger, "Tell me what time it is," not in an unpleasant tone, but merely in a direct fashion; none of the strangers answered. Devise other situations in which you violate the politeness ethic or other conversational rules and note people's reactions. If you do it properly, you'll learn about the rules of conversation; but be careful that it doesn't turn into a demonstration project on aggression. Do the same thing again, but this time with a close friend or family member. You'll see how necessary some polite forms are with strangers and how inappropriate they are with people you know well.

An impressive investigation of indirect requests was reported by Clark (1979). The study involved telephone calls to some 950 merchants in the San Francisco area in which the caller asked a question that the merchant normally would be expected to deal with on the phone (e.g., "What time do you close?" "Do you take credit cards?" "How much does something cost?"). The caller would immediately write down a verbatim record of the call immediately after hanging up. A typical conversational interaction was as follows:

(30) Merchant: "Hello, Scoma's Restaurant."

Caller: "Hello. Do you accept any credit cards?"

Merchant: "Yes we do; we even accept Carte Blanche."

Of course, the caller's question here was indirect: "Yes" isn't an acceptable answer to "Do you accept any credit cards?" because the authorized implication of the question was, "What credit cards do you take?" Merchants almost always responded to the authorized implication rather than merely to the literal question. Furthermore, they tailored their answers to be informative while not saying more than is necessary (obeying the second rule, on quantity), as in "We accept *only* Visa and MasterCard," or "We accept *all* major credit cards." Such responses are both informative and brief.

Such research has been extended to include not just indirect requests, but a variety of indirect statements and replies to questions. For instance, Holtgraves (1994) examined comprehension speed for indirect requests as a function of whether the speaker was of higher status than the listener (e.g., boss and employee) or whether they were of equal status (two employees). People read a short scenario (e.g., getting a conference room ready for a board of directors meeting), which concluded with one of two kinds of indirect statements. Conventional statements were normal indirect requests, such as, "Could you go fill the water glasses?" Negative state remarks were more indirect, merely stating a negative situation and only indirectly implying that the listener should do something (e.g., "The water glasses seem to be empty."). People showed no effects of status when comprehending regular indirect requests; it didn't matter whether it was a peer or the boss who said, "Could you go fill the water glasses?" But comprehension time increased significantly with negative state remarks made by peers. In other words, when the boss says, "The water glasses seem to be empty," we comprehend the conventional indirect request easily. But when a peer says it, we need additional time to comprehend.

INDIRECT REPLIES Holtgraves (1998) also focused on indirect replies, especially the idea of making a "face saving" reply. His participants read a description of a situation, such as:

> *(31) Nick and Paul are taking the same history class. Students in this class have to give a 20-minute presentation to the class on some topic.*

They then read a sentence that gave positive (32) or negative (33) information about Nick's presentation or a sentence that was neutral (34):

> *(32) Nick gave his presentation and it was excellent. He decides to ask Paul what he thought of it: "What did you think of my presentation?"*

> *(33) Nick gave his presentation and it was truly terrible. He decides to ask Paul what he thought of it: "What did you think of my presentation?"*

> *(34) Nick gave his presentation and then decided to ask Paul what he thought of it: "What did you think of my presentation?"*

If you were Paul and faced the prospect of telling Nick that his presentation was awful, wouldn't you look for some face-saving response? This is exactly how people responded when they comprehended Paul's responses. In the excuse condition, Paul says,

> *(35) It's hard to give a good presentation,*

in effect giving Nick a face-saving excuse for his poor performance. Another possible move is to change the topic, to avoid embarrassing Nick, as in

> *(36) I hope I win the lottery tonight.*

Holtgraves (1998) collected several measures of comprehension, including overall comprehension time for the critical sentences 35 or 36. The comprehension times, shown in Figure 10-13 (from Experiment 2), were very clear. When people had heard positive information—the talk was excellent— it took them a long time to comprehend either the excuse (35) or topic change (36) responses. But having heard negative information—the talk was terrible—was nearly the same as having heard nothing about the

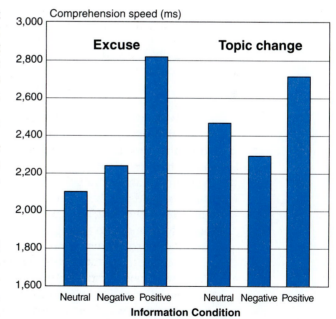

FIGURE 10-13 Comprehension times from Holtgraves's (1998) study. Participants read settings in which negative information, positive information, or neutral information was offered about a character, followed by a conversational move in which the speaker made an excuse for the character or changed the topic. In both cases it took longer to comprehend the remark when positive information about the character had just been encountered.

talk; people comprehended the excuse or topic change responses more rapidly, and there was no major difference between no information and negative information. People interpreted the violations of the relevance maxim as attempts to save face and avoid embarrassment.

Another role of indirect speech is to provide some element of *plausible deniability* (Lee & Pinker, 2010). Indirect requests and responses may carry implicit requests and replies that would be inappropriate otherwise. For example, suppose you are told by a not-so-savory relative of the defendant of a trial "I hear you're the foreman of the jury. It's an important responsibility. You have a wife and kids. We know you'll do the right thing." Thus, while the literal wording is acceptable, the implied meaning (a threat) is not. Thus, indirect speech can play many roles in human communication.

Watch *The Role of Gesture in Thinking: Susan Goldwin-Meadow* in **MyPsychLab**

Gesture

When we speak, we not only move our lips, tongues, throats and so on, we may also move our arms and hands. This movement, or **gesture**, is *done to facilitate communication to listeners, and excludes sign language and noncommunicative mannerisms, such as touching one's hands to one's face* (McNeill, 1992). That is, if they are not *beat gestures* that mark out important words or ideas, the movements we make with our hands communicates information to augment the words we are using. For example, when describing the route you took to get to school, you may make gestures to convey information about turns to made, obstructions you encountered, speeders that you saw, and so on. Although gesturing may serve a more holistic function when we use it while speaking, when people gesture in the absence of spoken speech, it takes on more linguistic characteristics, much as sign languages do (Goldin-Meadow, 2006).

Work by researchers such as Bavelas, Gerwing, Sutton, and Prevost (2008) shows that people even gesture when they are talking on the telephone, and they know the person on the other end cannot see them (although they gesture less than when they can see the other person). So, there must be something cognitively important about gesturing that facilitates language production in conversation. It should also be noted that people gesture less when they are speaking into a tape recorder (Bavelas et al., 2008) or when listeners do not appear to be attending to what they are saying (Jacobs & Garnham, 2007), so this impact of gesture has a strong social component and is not purely psycholinguistic.

Gesture may even help learning and thinking (for a review, see Goldin-Meadow & Beilock, 2010). The gestures a person produces when trying to solve a problem may reveal knowledge that the person has that is in a nascent, implicit stage. In some way, the gestures reveal to the person that knowledge is present, but not fully developed in a way that can be used consciously. So, if people are encouraged to gesture, they may make the knowledge conscious faster and facilitate learning. In a study by Broaders, Cook, Mitchell, and Goldin-Meadow (2007), third- and fourth-grade children were told to gesture while they solved math problems. They then showed an increased ability to develop new strategies and solve those types of math problems and were faster than children who did not gesture. Moreover, when two people are solving problems together, such as assembling a piece of furniture, they can solve the problems more effectively when the person communicating gestures, and the person assembling can use the gestures (Lozano & Tversky, 2006). In essence, gestures communicate embodied information that cognition is able to more directly process than linguistic information alone (Hostetter & Alibali, 2008; Kelly, Özyürek, & Maris, 2010).

Section Summary

- Conversations follow a largely implicit set of conversational rules. Some of these involve turn taking and social status and conventions, but many more govern the nature or topic of participants' contributions. Topic shifts involve selecting some part of a person's utterance to form the basis for a new contribution but then adding some new information. Schank's work on topic shift is a particularly important analysis of this process of topic shifting.
- Participants in a conversation develop theories of mind of the other speakers, called direct theories, as well as theories of what the other speakers think of them, called second-order theories. When we converse, we tailor our contributions to these theories and also follow a set of conversational rules, the unspoken contract between conversational partners. When a rule is violated intentionally, usually to make some other point (e.g., sarcasm), we mark our violation so that its apparent illegality as a conversational move is noticed and understood.
- Empirical work on conversational interaction often tests general notions about direct theories, the politeness rule, or indirect requests. Although we sometimes attempt to manipulate another person's direct theory of us, research also shows that the initially planned utterance usually is from a very egocentric perspective, whereas later adjustments may take the other person's perspective into account.
- Gestures made during conversation are a way that simulated spatial and action information can be communicated. Making gestures is part of the social act of conversation, although it may sometimes occur when our partner cannot see us, as when we are talking on the telephone. Gesture even has the ability to serve as a working memory aid and help people solve problems.

Key Terms

advantage of clause recency (p. *356*)

advantage of first mention (p. *356*)

anaphoric reference (p. *354*)

antecedent (p. *354*)

authorized (p. *358*)

beliefs (p. *338*)

bridging inference (p. *358*)

conceptual knowledge (p. *338*)

conversational rules (p. *368*)

cooperative principle (p. *368*)

direct theory (p. *370*)

enhancement (p. *344*)

eye–mind assumption (p. *347*)

eye tracker (p. *346*)

fixations (p. *347*)

gaze duration (p. *347*)

gesture (p. *374*)

immediacy assumption (p. *347*)

implication (p. *358*)

indirect requests (p. *371*)

inference (p. *358*)

judgments of learning (JOLs) (p. *341*)

labor-in-vain effect (p. *341*)

mapping (p. *343*)

CHAPTER

11

Decisions, Judgments, and Reasoning

From the psychologist's point of view, thinking must not be confused with logic because human thinking frequently is not rigorous or correct, does not follow the path of step-by-step deduction—in short, is not usually "logical."

(Newell & Simon, 1972, p. 876)

Although it's important for you to appreciate the material on cognitive psychology that we've already covered, the picture wouldn't be complete without the slower, more deliberate kinds of thinking that we cover in this chapter. How do we reason? How do we make decisions under conditions of uncertainty? These are the topics we turn to now. A general thread that runs through much of the decision-making and reasoning research is that we are often overly influenced by our general world knowledge. The influence of stored information is pervasive; it affects how we perform in the classic forms of reasoning as well as less well-defined judgment and decision-making situations. A second pervasive and important thread is: Far more than is logical, we tend to search for evidence that confirms our decisions, beliefs, and hypotheses. In general, we are much less skeptical than we ought to be.

Let's begin by examining two classic kinds of reasoning problems and then switch to a seemingly simple kind of decision making and reasoning, mental comparisons between concepts or objects. We then proceed to the study of a somewhat different kind of situation, reasoning about the likelihood of events for which relevant information in memory is generally lacking or insufficient. The strategies people use to make these judgments are interesting because they reveal a variety of rules of thumb or shortcuts on which people rely. These methods work well sometimes, but sometimes they lead to distortions and biases in reasoning. Overall, this research provides convincing examples of the uncertainty of human reasoning and the often surprising inaccuracies in our stored knowledge.

FORMAL LOGIC AND REASONING

At some point during their college careers, many students are exposed to the classic forms of reasoning, often in a course on logic. For our purposes, two of these forms, *syllogistic* and *conditional reasoning*, are important (although there others, such as relational reasoning [e.g., Goodwin & Johnson-Laird, 2005]). Overall, people are not particularly good at solving such problems correctly when they are presented in an abstract form. Solutions often are better when problems are presented in terms of concrete, real-world concepts. If we generate our own examples, however, solution accuracy depends on how critically or skeptically we generated the examples. In some situations, our world knowledge almost prevents us from seeing the "pure" (i.e., logical) answer to logic problems (e.g., Markovits & Potvin, 2001).

Syllogisms

A **syllogism**, or categorical syllogism, is *a three-statement logical form, with the first two parts stating the premises taken to be true, and the third part stating a conclusion based on those premises.* The goal of syllogistic reasoning is to understand how different premises can be combined to yield logically true conclusions and to understand what combinations of premises lead to invalid or incorrect conclusions. Often, syllogisms are presented in an abstract form, such as

(1a) *All A are B.*

All B are C.

Therefore, all A are C.

In this example, the two premises state a relation between the abstract elements *A*, *B*, and *C*, basically a class inclusion or subset-superset relation. "*All A are B*" says that the set *A* is a subset of the group *B*, that *A* is included in the set *B*. The third statement is the conclusion. By applying the rules of syllogistic reasoning, it can be determined that the conclusion "*All A are C*" is true in this example; that is, the conclusion follows logically from the premises. Inserting words into the syllogism will verify the truth of the conclusion: for instance,

(1b) *All poodles are dogs.*

All dogs are animals.

Therefore, all poodles are animals.

One difficulty or confusion that people have is illustrated by the following example:

(1c) *All poodles are animals.*

All animals are wild.

Therefore, all poodles are wild.

The difficulty here is that the conclusion is logically true; because the conclusion follows from the premises, the syllogism is valid. Of course, it's easy to think of counterexamples, situations in which the conclusion is not true in the real world of poodles; hardly any poodles are wild, after all (Feldman, 1992). The proneness of people to ignore the logical form of an argument and focus on their prior world knowledge is called the **belief bias** (Evans, Barston, & Pollard, 1983; see also Copeland, Gunawan, & Bies-Hernandez, 2011, for a similar source credibility effect). Yet the rules of syllogistic reasoning are that the truth of the premises is *separate* from the validity of the syllogistic argument. What matters is that the conclusion does or does not follow from the premises. In the case of example (1c), the conclusion is valid even though the second premise is empirically false. Thus applying syllogistic reasoning to real-world problems is at least a two-step process. First, determine whether the syllogism itself is valid; second, if the syllogism is valid, determine the empirical truth of the premises.

Now consider another example:

(2a*) *All A are B.*

Some B are C.

Therefore, some A are C.

(In formal logic, *some* means "at least one and possibly all," although research shows that some people have trouble understanding this [Schmidt & Thompson, 2008].) Try inserting words into this example to see whether the conclusion is correct. For example,

(2b*) *All polar bears are animals.*

Some animals are white.

Therefore, some polar bears are white.

Despite the fact that words can be substituted that lead to an empirically correct statement, this second syllogism is *false*. Because the two premises do not invariably lead to a correct conclusion, the entire form of the syllogism is invalid (the reason for the asterisk). The incorrectness of the conclusion in (2a) stems from the qualifier *some*. Although the conclusion may be empirically true when you use one or another concrete example, this isn't necessarily the case for *all* examples, as shown by the following:

(2c*) All polar bears are animals.

    Some animals are brown.

    Therefore, some polar bears are brown.

As shown in Figure 11-1, Euler circles can help in determining whether a syllogism is true. For instance, in the first illustration, the "All–All" form shows that it is necessarily true that "All *A* are *C*." The circles, which represent the class of things known as *A*, *B*, and *C*, are nested such that *A* is a subset of *B* and *B* is a subset of *C*. There is no other way to represent the premises except by concentric circles (when *A* and *B* are identical, their boundaries overlap completely, and the diagram merely shows one circle labeled both *A* and *B*).

FIGURE 11-1 Euler circle illustrations for three categorical syllogisms. If a diagram can be constructed that shows the conclusion doesn't hold for all cases, then the conclusion is false. The first diagram in 2* shows why 2* is incorrect; it is not necessarily true that some *A* are *C*. The second diagram in 2* shows that an arrangement can be found that seems to support the argument. Likewise, the first diagram in 3* shows why 3* is incorrect; it is not necessarily true that no *A* are *C*. The second diagram in 3* shows an arrangement that does seem to support the conclusion.

In the second entry in the figure, the *incorrectness* of syllogism 2 is illustrated by the first diagram. In that illustration, a portion of *B* that does not contain *A* is exactly the portion that overlaps with *C*. Thus it isn't necessarily true that some *A* are *C*. The second diagram for this problem, however, illustrates the "Some polar bears are white" conclusion, one that is true of the real world even though the syllogism is not true. (The third syllogism is similar to the second; that is, it's false, but the second diagram seems to show that it's true.)

In general, performance on syllogisms improves when people are shown how to use diagrams or generate specific examples (Helsabeck, 1975). This will work only if you try to find ways to show the syllogism to be false. That is, it is easy to come up with examples or diagrams that mistakenly confirm an incorrect conclusion. Adopting a skeptical attitude about the conclusion and trying to diagram the situation to show how the conclusion is false are more likely to be helpful strategies. As an exercise, try generating diagrams for the final three syllogisms in the figure. As you work, bear in mind that the best strategy is to search for negative evidence. In other words, try to diagram the problem so that the syllogism is shown to be false (see work by Chater & Oaksford, 1999, on a probability-based explanation of such reasoning, and Sloman, 1998, on situations when people fail to draw appropriate category inclusion inferences; e.g., "All stereos are electronic equipment, all electronic equipment has parts made of germanium, therefore all stereos have parts made of germanium").

Conditional Reasoning: If *P* Then *Q*

Conditional reasoning is a second kind of logical reasoning. Conditional reasoning problems always contain two parts, a *conditional clause,* a statement that expresses some relationship (*if P then Q*), followed by some *evidence* pertaining to the conditional clause (*p*, for example). **Conditional reasoning** involves *a logical determination of whether the evidence supports, refutes, or is irrelevant to the stated if–then relationship.*

The conditional in these problems is the *if–then* statement. Respectively, the *if* clause and the *then* clause are known as the **antecedent** and the **consequent** of the conditional clause (for clarity, we'll just refer to "the *if*" or "the antecedent," and "the *then*" or "the consequent"). The *if* states the possible cause, and the *then* states the effect of that possible cause. So the conditional *if P then Q* means "if *P* is true, then *Q* is true"; for example, if it rains (*P*) then the streets will be wet (*Q*). So far so good.

After the *if–then*, you are given a second statement, some evidence about the truth or falsity of one of the propositions in the *if–then* relationship. The goal of such reasoning is to take this evidence and decide what follows logically from it. In other words, is the conditional *if–then* statement true or false given this observed evidence, or is the evidence irrelevant to the *if–then*?

The general form of the conditional is *If P, then Q.* The conditional is then followed by the evidence, any one of the four possible outcomes. For "If it rains, the streets will be wet," the four possibilities are

P: In other words, P is true, it's raining.

not P: In other words, P is not true, it's not raining.

Q: In other words, Q is true, the streets are wet.

not Q: In other words, Q is not true, the streets are not wet.

Putting all of this together yields four possibilities:

Conditional	If *P*, then *Q*.	If *P*, then *Q*.	If *P*, then *Q*.	If *P*, then *Q*.
Evidence	*P*.	Not *P*.	*Q*.	Not *Q*.
Conclusion	Therefore, *Q*.	(No conclusion)	(No conclusion)	Not *P*.

According to the conditional *if–then* statement, if some antecedent condition *P* is true, then its consequence (the *consequent*) *Q* is true. If we then obtain evidence showing that *P* is indeed true, it follows logically that *Q* must be true. As an expanded example, consider the following example (adapted from Matlin, 1983), completely worked out for all four possibilities in Table 11-1:

If I am a freshman, then I must register for next semester's classes today.

VALID ARGUMENTS   As the table shows, only two of the four possibilities lead to a true conclusion according to the rules of logic. In the first one, when given the evidence that *P* is true, "I am a freshman," then the consequent *Q* must be true, "I do have to register today." This is *affirming the antecedent*, in other words, saying that the antecedent is true. The classic name for this is *modus ponens*. Likewise, if the evidence is that *Q* is not true, "I do not have to register today," it must therefore be that *P* is not true, "*I am not a freshman.*" This is *denying the consequent*, saying that the consequent is not true, is *modus tollens*.

INVALID ARGUMENTS   Whereas both of these arguments lead to a correct conclusion, the other two possibilities are not valid. That is, denying the antecedent does not permit the conclusion that the consequent is false; likewise, affirming the consequent

TABLE 11-1   Conditional Reasoning

Form	Name	Example
If *P*, then *Q*. Evidence: *P*. Therefore, *Q*.	*Modus ponens:* affirming the antecedent (valid inference)	If I am a freshman, I have to register today. Evidence: I am a freshman. Therefore, I have to register today.
If *P*, then *Q*. Evidence: not *P*. *Therefore, not *Q*.	Denying the antecedent (invalid inference)	If I am a freshman, I have to register today. Evidence: I am not a freshman. *Therefore, I do not have to register today.
If *P*, then *Q*. Evidence: *Q*. *Therefore, *P*.	Affirming the consequent (invalid inference)	If I am a freshman, I have to register today. Evidence: I have to register today. *Therefore, I am a freshman.
If *P*, then *Q*. Evidence: not *Q*. Therefore, not *P*.	*Modus tollens:* denying the consequent (valid inference)	If I am a freshman, I have to register today. Evidence: I do not have to register today. Therefore, I am not a freshman.

does not permit the conclusion that the antecedent is true. Let's continue with the college registration example, "If I am a freshman, then I must register today." If we deny the antecedent by offering the evidence "I am not a freshman," this does not lead to the conclusion that "I do not have to register today." It could be that two groups of students must register today; (a) all freshmen and (b) all sophomores in the first half of the alphabet. Thus, just because you're not a freshman doesn't necessarily mean you don't have to register today. Likewise, if we affirm the consequent, we assert that "I must register today." This does not permit the conclusion that "I'm a freshman," however; you might be a sophomore in the first half of the alphabet.

EVIDENCE ON CONDITIONAL REASONING Generally, people are good at inferring the truth of the consequent given evidence that the antecedent is true (affirming the antecedent, *modus ponens*). When given the conditional *if P, then Q* and the evidence that *P* is true, people usually infer correctly that *Q* is true. For instance, Rips and Marcus (1977) found that 100% of their sample drew this correct conclusion. The other valid inference, denying the consequent (*modus tollens*), is more difficult. Only 57% of Rips and Marcus's participants drew this conclusion (in a simpler version of the problem, 77% concluded correctly that *P* could never be true given the evidence *not Q*). Wason and Johnson-Laird (1972) found similar results in their investigation of conditional reasoning, in which problems were stated in either concrete or abstract form.

Errors in conditional reasoning fall into three broad categories, involving the form of the reasoning problem, the search for evidence, and memory-related phenomena.

FORM ERRORS First, people sometimes draw incorrect conclusions simply by using one of the two invalid forms, either denying the antecedent or affirming the consequent. In fact, they commonly do so when comprehending discourse, according to Rader and Sloutsky (2002). These researchers gave people short scenarios that contained an *if–then* conditional, then tested their recognition of either words from the stories or ideas in the stories (i.e., was this information in the story?). Table 11-2 gives examples of the stories and their results. About 60% of the people (incorrectly) "recognized" the affirm-the-consequent conclusion as having been in the story, not different from the 61% who (correctly) recognized the *modus ponens* conclusion. The response time (RT) data on recognizing words from the stories showed the same pattern, no difference between "recognizing" the *modus ponens* and affirm-the-consequent conclusions. So, both kinds of conclusions are routinely drawn when we read, even though one of them is logically incorrect (see Bonnefon & Hilton, 2004, for a demonstration of how the desirability of the consequent influences our predictions about the truth of the antecedent).

Another form error is more subtle. People have a tendency to reverse the propositions in the *if* and *then*. They then proceed to evaluate the given evidence against the now-reversed conditional. This kind of error is an *illicit conversion*. As an example, with a conditional of *If P, then Q* and evidence *Q*, people tend to switch the conditional to *If Q, then P*. They then decide that the evidence *Q* implies that *P* is true. This is incorrect because the order of *P* and *Q* in the conditional is meaningful. The *if* often specifies some possible cause, and the *then*

TABLE 11-2   Sample Stories and Tests from Rader and Sloutsky (2002)

Participants read four sentences. Sentence 1 was the same for both groups, but Sentence 2 differed between Version A and Version B. Sentence 3 was the same for both groups, but Sentence 4 differed for the two groups, containing either an inference or no inference. In other words, one-quarter of the participants saw Version A and an Inference, one-quarter saw Version A and No Inference, one-quarter saw Version B and an Inference, and one-quarter saw Version B and No Inference.

1. Frank woke up on his couch after taking a long nap and realized that he didn't know what time it was.
2. (Version A) He thought that if it was cold outside, then it was night.

OR

(Version B) He thought that if it was night, then it was cold outside.
3. Still feeling sleepy, Frank arose to open a window.
4. (Inference condition) He discovered that it was cold outside.

OR

(No Inference condition) He wondered whether it was cold outside.

Inference Test: Yes/No—Was this information in the story?

The time of day was night.

Argument Form	Percentage saying "yes" to the Inference Test	
	Inference	**No Inference**
Modus Ponens (Version A) If it's cold, then it's night. Yes/No—The time of day was night.	61%	24%
Affirm—the Consequent (Version B) If it's night, then it's cold. Yes/No—The time of day was night.	59%	21%

From: Rader & Sloutsky (2002), Tables 2 and 4 (pp. 61, 65).

---

specifies a possible effect. So, we cannot draw correct conclusions if we reverse the roles of the cause (*P*) for some outcome and the result (*Q*) of some cause.

SEARCH ERRORS   The second kind of error involves a search for evidence. People often don't search for evidence but instead rely on a first impression or on the first example—the first mental model—that comes to mind (Evans, Handley, Harper, & Johnson-Laird, 1999). Another flaw is *searching for positive evidence*, also called the **confirmation bias**. Despite the rules of logic, we often seek only the information that confirms a conclusion, information that is consistent with a conclusion we have already drawn or a belief we already have. In fact, knowing an outcome and the conditions that might lead to it causes people to overestimate how likely that outcome is as a result of those prior conditions. That is, because people are more likely to draw backwards causal inferences (as noted in Chapter 10), they mistakenly think that the prior events are more likely to lead to the actual outcome (Koriat, Fiedler, & Bjork, 2006).

As a demonstration, consider the now-classic study of conditional reasoning (reported in Wason & Johnson-Laird, 1972) illustrated at the top of Figure 11-2, the Wason card problem. Four cards are visible to you, as shown in the figure, and each

Watch
Confirmation
Bias in
MyPsychLab

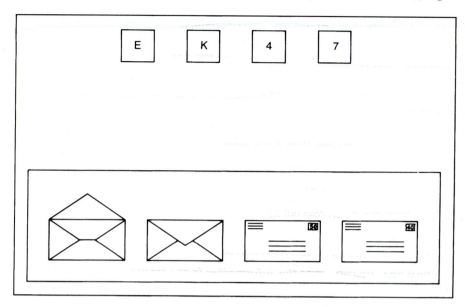

FIGURE 11-2 At the top of the illustration are the four cards in the Wason card problem. Which card or cards would you turn over to obtain conclusive evidence about the following rule: A card with a vowel on it will have an even number on the other side? At the bottom of the illustration are four envelopes. Which envelopes would you turn over to detect postal cheaters, under the rule that an unsealed envelope can be stamped with the less expensive stamp?

card has a letter on one side and a number on the other. The task is to pick the card or cards you would turn over to gather conclusive evidence on the following rule:

If a card has a vowel on one side, then it has an even number on the other side.

Give this statement some thought and decide how you'd test that rule before you continue reading.

Of the people Wason tested, 33% turned over only the *E* card, a correct choice conforming to *modus ponens* (affirming the antecedent). A thorough test of the rule's validity, however, requires that another card be turned over (in other words, the rule might be rephrased "Only if a card has a vowel on one side will it have an even number on the other side"). Only 4% of the people turned over the correct combination to check on this possibility, the *E* card *(modus ponens)* and the 7 card *(modus tollens)*. That is, turning over the 7, which might yield negative evidence (*not Q*), was rarely considered. Instead, people preferred turning over the *E* and the 4 card: 46% of the people did this. Note two points. First, turning over the 4 is an instance of the invalid process of affirming the consequent (in other words, the rule doesn't say anything about what will be on the other side of a consonant; it could be an odd or an even number). Second, turning over the *E* represents a search for positive evidence about the rule, the (tentative) "yes" conclusion that *P* is true. Our general tendency is either to stop the search after turning over the *E* (positive evidence) or to continue searching for additional positive evidence (turning over the 4). This pattern of poor performance on this task has spawned a great deal of effort to understand the cognitive processes that give rise to this. Part of this effort includes computational models (Klauer, Stahl, & Erdfelder, 2007) that reveal that people are not considering the cards one by one when reasoning, but, rather, looking at the configuration of cards before them.

In a different situation, however, Johnson-Laird, Legrenzi, and Legrenzi (1972) found that 21 of 24 people made both of the correct choices. The difference had to do with the concreteness of the situation. In the Johnson-Laird et al. study, people were trying to find cheaters on the postal regulations, where unsealed envelopes could be mailed with a less expensive stamp than sealed envelopes.

Think about this situation. What *if–then* rule is being tested? Because either a sealed or an unsealed envelope could be mailed with a more expensive stamp, the rule must be:

If the envelope is sealed, then it must carry the expensive stamp.

When asked to detect cheaters, people turned over not only the sealed envelope (*modus ponens*) but also the envelope stamped with the less expensive stamp, that is, the *modus tollens* choice corresponding to the 7 card. Because the people were not postal workers, it seems clear that it was the concreteness of the situation that oriented the people toward the skeptical attitude mentioned earlier. Their skepticism led them to search actively for negative evidence; in the process, they demonstrated logical conditional reasoning.

While making the information in the premises more concrete can improve performance, other ways of making the information more "naturalistic" can impede reasoning. Specifically, people are more likely to make reasoning errors if more intense emotions are involved (Blanchette & Richards, 2004). For example, if people are given the premise "If there is danger, then one feels nervous," they will be more likely to affirm the consequent "There is danger" if told that "Betty feels nervous" as compared to if they are given more emotionally neutral information, such as the letter problem.

PROVE IT
Conditional Reasoning

As you have noticed from reading the chapter, some things can come into play to affect how well people reason, such as whether the problem is naturalistic or abstract. What you can do is set up a version of the Wason card task, and then come up with some interesting variations. You will need four index cards for each version of the task. Set up your task so that each of the four cards corresponds to each of the four response alternatives, namely Modus Ponens (Affirming the Antecedent), Modus Tollens (Denying the Consequent), Affirming the Consequent, and Denying the Antecedent. You might try having an abstract version, such as the original card layout used by Wason or something similar (e.g., if the card is red on one side, it will be green on the other side), and then some more naturalistic version that you come up with (e.g., the "freshmen registering for class" example from earlier, or one testing the rule "If a person is drinking alcohol, then he/she is at least 21 years old").

What you should do, after you've made your cards, is lay them down in front of your volunteers, tell them the rule they are verifying, and then have them tell you which card(s) they would choose to turn over.

You might also want to try some variations based on other things you've learned about memory and cognition. For example, what would happen if people were put in a dual-task, divided-attention situation? What would happen if you made the memory load a verbal load versus a visual/spatial load? Does emotional salience play a role? What if you prime different aspects of a person's semantic memory? The possibilities are endless.

MEMORY-RELATED ERRORS   The third category of errors involves limitations in memory. A major proponent of this type of explanation is Johnson-Laird, who suggested that we do reasoning tasks not by some formal logic but by constructing **mental models**, *mental representations of meanings of the terms in reasoning problems* (Johnson-Laird & Byrne, 2002; Johnson-Laird, Byrne, & Schaeken, 1992). It's difficult to flesh out a set of meanings in conditional reasoning problems of the "If *P* then *Q*" variety. But because of our semantic knowledge, it's far easier in concrete, meaningful problems such as:

> *If it was foggy, then the match was canceled.*
>
> *It was foggy.*
>
> *Therefore, the match was canceled.*

Furthermore, if additional terms appear in the problem, additional mental models must be derived, two additional ones in the following case:

> *If it was foggy, then the match was canceled.*
>
> *The match was not canceled.*
>
> *Therefore, it was not foggy.*

When additional models are needed, the load on working memory mounts and can begin to interfere with reasoning; the same is true when the phrasing of the problem places a greater load on comprehension (e.g., Thompson & Byrne, 2002). And finally, as noted earlier, Evans et al. (1999) point out that if a conclusion matches the first mental model derived from the problem, it is particularly easy to accept the conclusion, leading to fallacies or errors in reasoning.

Hypothesis Testing

Part of the importance of conditional reasoning derives from its connection to scientific hypothesis testing. Consider a typical experimental hypothesis:

> *If theory* A *is true, then data resembling* X *should be obtained in the experiment.*

If data resembling *X* are indeed obtained, there is a strong tendency to conclude that theory *A* must be true. That is, if the evidence is that data resembling *X* were obtained, this affirms the consequent. We then feel as if this evidence lets us conclude that *P* is true, that theory *A* is correct. What's wrong with this? It's a simple error of affirming the consequent and concluding mistakenly that this is evidence that the antecedent is true. Note how seductive this error is. Of course, it might be true that theory *A* is correct. But it's also possible that theory *A* is incorrect and that some other (correct) theory would also predict data *X*.

Because of the illogic of affirming the consequent, and because we want to test hypotheses, our experiments test a *different* hypothesis than "Theory *A* is correct." As you learned (or will learn) in statistics, we test the null hypothesis in hopes that our evidence will be inconsistent with the predicted null outcome. Note the form of such a test:

> *If the null hypothesis is true (if* P *), then there will be no effect of the variable (then* Q *).*

If we obtain evidence that there *is* an effect of the variable, then we have evidence that the consequent is not true. We can then conclude that the antecedent is not true—in other words, we reject the null hypothesis, deciding that it is false. This is the essence of hypothesis testing, to conclude that the *if* portion (the null hypothesis) is false based on an outcome that denies the consequent of the null hypothesis. Although people make a variety of errors in such situations, especially when the *if–then* relationship becomes more complex (Cummins, Lubart, Alksnis, & Rist, 1991), the typical mistake is simply to search for positive, confirming evidence (Klayman & Ha, 1989). In a similar vein, another strategy is simply to make a judgment as to the relevance or strength of the arguments and base a decision on that (e.g., Medin, Coley, Storms, & Hayes, 2003; Rips, 2001).

Section Summary

- Human reasoning is not especially logical, as shown in formal syllogistic and conditional reasoning problems. In syllogism tasks, conditional reasoning *if–then* problems, and hypothesis testing, people often fail to search for negative evidence. Instead, they often look for positive evidence, called confirmation bias, and are often influenced, both positively and negatively, by semantic knowledge. When a more skeptical attitude is adopted, and when the reasoning involves more concrete concepts, reasoning accuracy improves.

DECISIONS

How do we make decisions? How do we choose among several alternatives, say, on a multiple-choice test, or decide which of several options is best? What role does the information stored in memory play, and how certain are the decisions we make based on that information?

In a sense we've been studying decision making all along in this book, although the decisions often were fairly simple—for example, deciding "yes" or "no" in semantic or lexical decision tasks. At base, decision making can be viewed as a search for evidence, where the ultimate decision depends on some criterion or rule for evaluating the evidence. A search may turn up either positive or negative evidence. How we make decisions as a function of such evidence and how the evidence itself is evaluated are at the heart of decision making and reasoning.

Let's turn to a very simple setting, in which we compare two objects or symbols, to see how the information stored in memory can influence comparison. We then turn to more complex decision-making and reasoning situations, again looking for the influence of knowledge and the evaluation of that information.

Decisions about Physical Differences

One of the very earliest areas of research in psychology was **psychophysics**; indeed, a great deal of research on psychophysics was done well before psychology per se came into existence (Fechner, 1860). The topic of interest in psychophysics was the *psycho*logical experience of *physical* stimulation, that is, *how* *perceptual experience differs from the physical stimulation being perceived.* In particular, research on psychophysics investigated the relationships between the physical dimensions of stimuli and the subjective, psychological experience of perceiving them.

In general, what was discovered was that the subjective experience of magnitude, regardless of the particular dimension involved (brightness, loudness, or the like), was not identical to the physical magnitude. Instead, there is a psychological dimension of magnitude that forms the basis of our perceptions.

For instance, the perceived brightness of a light is not a linear function of the light's physical brightness. Instead, perceived brightness depends on several factors, such as the absolute level of brightness, the brightness of the background, and the duration of the stimulus. Likewise, the amount by which brightness must be changed to perceive the change depends on more than just the amount of physical change in brightness. Perceived change depends critically on the initial level of the light's brightness. A dim light needs only a small boost in brightness for people to detect a difference, whereas a very bright light needs a larger boost for the change to be noticed. *The amount of change needed for people to detect the change is called a* **just noticeable difference (jnd)** (as in Weber's law; see Haber & Hershenson, 1973, for example). The point is that the size of the jnd increases as the physical stimulus becomes more intense. If only one jnd separates two dim lights, the same physical difference in brightness between two bright lights may not be detectable. Our perceptual mechanism is affected by the psychological dimension of brightness, a different dimension than physical brightness. Thus psychological processing of a stimulus does not accurately mirror the physical stimulus properties. Instead, distortions and alterations of the stimulus are introduced during perception, and these distortions and alterations can be attributed to the human perceiver.

Of particular relevance to our discussion is the **distance effect** or **discriminability effect**: *The greater the distance or difference between the two stimuli, the faster the decision that they differ* (Woodworth & Schlosberg, 1954). In other words, it's easier to discriminate between two stimuli that are very different (a finger snap versus a gunshot) than two that are very similar (shots from two different guns).

Decisions about Symbolic Differences

Investigators have found that a variety of similar effects in tasks involving **symbolic comparisons**, that is, comparisons not between two physical objects or stimuli but between two mental symbols. The connection with the earlier work is that the distance effect still holds. But because the effect is now based on symbolic rather than physical differences, it is called the **symbolic distance effect**. Just as in psychophysical judgments, the source of the symbolic distance effect is the person making the mental comparison. The big difference is that semantic and other long-term memory knowledge, rather than perceptual information, is influencing decision making. Briefly,

Decisions about size differences are psychophysical judgments, which are speeded up when stimuli differ by a great amount.

the symbolic distance effect is that *we judge differences between symbols more rapidly when they differ considerably on some symbolic dimension, such as value.*

Consider the stimuli in panels A and B of Figure 11-3. Which dot is higher? Despite the simple nature of this decision, it takes some amount of time to make the decision. To begin with, the time to decide which dot is higher depends on the separation of the dots; the greater the separation, the faster the decision. This is the simple physical distance effect again: Two stimuli can be discriminated more quickly when they differ more (Moyer & Bayer, 1976).

Now consider the bottom two illustrations. For panel C in Figure 11-3, which balloon is higher? For panel D, which yo-yo is lower? It is probably not obvious to you at a conscious level, but when people are asked, "Which balloon is higher?" their judgments are affected not only by the discriminability of the two heights, but also by the

FIGURE 11-3

Stimuli used by Banks, Fujii, & Kayra-Stuart (1975) in a study of physical and symbolic comparisons. In the top two panels, people were asked which dot is higher or lower. In the bottom two panels, people were asked which balloon is higher/lower and which yo-yo is higher/lower.

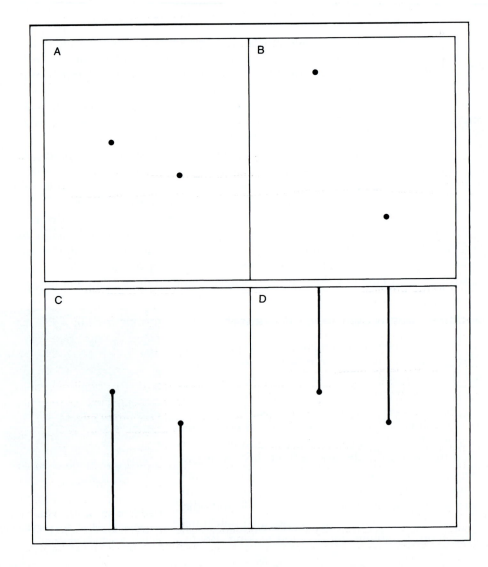

semantic dimension needed for the judgments (Banks, Clark, & Lucy, 1975). In other words, the semantic knowledge that balloons are held at the bottom by strings, float up in the air, and are therefore oriented in terms of highness was a significant influence on the participants' decision times; describing the illustrations as balloons led people to treat the pictures symbolically rather than as mere physically different stimuli. When the same pictured display was accompanied by the question "Which balloon is lower?" judgments were much slower. And as you would expect, the situation was reversed when people judged stimuli such as those in panel D, the yo-yos. "Which yo-yo is lower?" yielded faster decisions than "Which yo-yo is higher?" because semantic knowledge about yo-yos is that they hang down from their strings.

The name for this is the **semantic congruity effect** (Banks, 1977; Banks et al., 1975) in which a person's *decision is faster when the dimension being judged matches or is congruent with the implied semantic dimension.* In other words, the implied dimension in the balloon illustration is height because balloons float up. When asked to judge "how high" some "high" object is, the judgment is faster because "height" is semantically congruent with "high." Likewise, "lowness" is implied in the yo-yo display, so judging which of two "low things" is lower is also a congruent decision. Figure 11-4 displays the general form of the symbolic distance effect and the semantic congruity effect (Banks, 1977).

NUMBER MAGNITUDE Some of the clearest research supporting these idealized diagrams comes from Banks's work on judgments of numerical magnitude. In this research, people are shown a pair of digits, say, 1 and 2 or 7 and 8. In one condition, the instructions are to pick the smaller of the two values; in another, people are asked to pick the larger value. Of course, in all conditions, the RT to make the judgments is the dependent variable of major interest.

Can you predict what the results of such comparisons are, based on the distance and congruity effects? First, the larger the difference between the digits, the faster the judgments are made. In other words, picking the smaller of the pair 1 and 3 is faster than picking the smaller of 2 and 3. This is the symbolic distance effect, similar to the physical distance effect but now based purely on the symbolic meanings of the digits and the magnitudes to which they refer; panels B and C in Figure 11-5 show this clearly. Second, judgment time is affected by semantic congruity. Picking the smaller of two small digits is faster than picking the larger of two small digits, and the difference is more pronounced when picking the larger instead of the smaller of two large digits; for instance, the 8 and 9 pair in Figure 11-5. When the instructions ask for a judgment of smallness, symbols referring to small quantities are faster; when the instructions ask for a judgment of largeness, symbols referring to large quantities are faster to judge. This is the semantic congruity effect.

A variety of fascinating conclusions are supported by such results. First, when people make mental comparisons of purely symbolic quantities, there is a pronounced semantic distance effect. Just as in psychophysics, the psychological difference is not the same as the physical difference; the mental differences between digits do not perfectly mirror the numerical differences between digits. Banks's research (Banks, Fujii, & Kayra-Stuart, 1976) suggests that our mental representation of number and numerical magnitude is nonlinear, one in which the psychological distances between larger numbers are *compressed*, relative to the distances between

FIGURE 11-4
Idealized curves:
A. the symbolic
distance effect;
B. the semantic
congruity effect.

From Banks (1977).

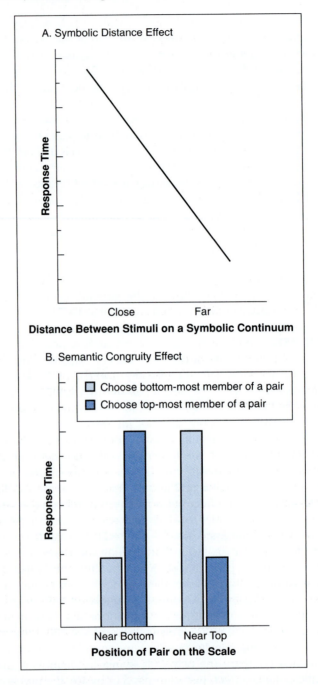

smaller numbers. Thus, just as two bright lights are perceived as being more similar than two dim lights, two large numbers are psychologically closer together than two small numbers; 1 and 2 are more different psychologically than 8 and 9 are.

Second, when we judge magnitudes, the dimension of judgment must match the implied semantic dimension for the comparison to be made quickly. A mismatch between the psychological dimension and the one specified by instructions

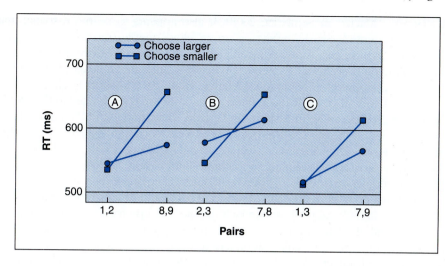

FIGURE 11-5
Response time
performance
(in ms) on number
comparisons.

From Banks et al.
(1976), Figure 1.

(e.g., "choose the larger one" when the two things are small) slows down the comparison, even when the same quantities are being compared (see also Marschark & Paivio, 1979; Shoben, Sailor, & Wang, 1989).

At a more global level, the research also attests to another important idea: The particular *form* of a concept's representation in memory exerts an influence on the judgments we make. We are asking people to compare two concepts in memory on some dimension of magnitude. By timing their judgments, we can understand how those concepts are represented in memory. This kind of task, timed mental comparisons, can be applied widely to all sorts of symbolic concepts, even cases where the underlying magnitude dimension is arbitrary and learned only by trial and error (Tzelgov, Yehene, Kotler, & Alon, 2000).

The influence of embodied cognition can be seen in decision making, even for simple number judgments. In a seminal study, Dehaene, Bossini, and Giraux (1993) had people make judgments about a series of numbers, such as whether they were odd or even. What they found was that *judgments about smaller numbers were made more quickly with the left hand and judgments about larger numbers were made more quickly with the right hand*. This pattern of performance is known as the **SNARC effect** (for Spatial-Numerical Association of Response Codes). This occurrence of the SNARC effect is consistent with the idea that many people have a mental number line going from left to right with small numbers on the left and larger numbers occurring as one moves to the right (although there are other accounts, e.g., Santens & Gevers, 2008).

This is an embodied effect because most people (two-thirds of people according to Fischer, 2008) typically start counting on their fingers using their left hand. Moreover, left-hand counters show a much stronger SNARC effect than people who start counting with their right hand. This mental arrangement then appears to have a direct influence on how people make decisions and respond based on those decisions. This decision process clearly involves the visuo-spatial sketchpad of working memory more than the phonological loop, because the effect is more disrupted when people are in a visuo-spatial dual-task situation as compared to a verbal one (e.g., Herrera, Macizo, & Semenza, 2008). It also appears to be more spatial than visual, as an identical SNARC effect occurs in blind people (Castronovo & Seron, 2007). Note that this effect shows some influence of linguistic relativity (remember the Sapir-Whorf hypothesis from Chapter 9?), in that it is larger for languages that are read left to right as opposed to right to left (Dehaene et al., 1993; Shaki & Fischer, 2008).

The influence of embodied cognition on number use is not limited to the SNARC effect per se. For example, in a study by Eerland, Guadalupe, and Zwaan (2011), if people were asked to estimate the height of objects, such as the Eiffel Tower, their estimates were smaller if they were leaning slightly (unconsciously) to the left, and greater if they were leaning slightly to the right. Furthermore, it does not appear that the basic phenomenon underlying the SNARC effect is unique to our mental representation of numbers. A study by Lidji, Kolinsky, Lochy, and Morais (2007) produced a similar effect with musical pitches, in which people had a preference of responding to lower tones with the left and higher tones with the right hand, similar to the arrangement of notes on a piano or guitar string (see also Gevers, Reynvoet, & Fias, 2004, for a day-of-the-week effect). Also, Prado, Van der Henst, and Noveck (2008) report a SNARC-like effect for symbolic distances (as described earlier).

IMAGERY   Which is larger, a squirrel or a rabbit? Which is smaller, a mouse or a dog? Several investigators, notably Moyer (1973), have documented the symbolic distance and semantic congruity effects when people make judgments of this sort. Here, the judgments are made on the basis of the visual image of the object. That is, when people make these larger/smaller judgments about real-world objects, they retrieve mental images of them, then mentally scan the images to determine which one is larger or smaller. Moyer had people estimate the absolute sizes of animals and make timed comparisons between different pairs. His results showed that RT decreased as the differences in size between the animals increased—the symbolic distance effect. Furthermore, the relationship between image size and RT was logarithmic; in other words, the size differences are smaller at the larger end of the scale than at the smaller end, exactly what Banks (1977) found about the mental number line.

A final important aspect of these results relates to mental imagery. As Moyer (1973) and others (Kosslyn & Pomerantz, 1977) argue, results such as these imply strongly that the semantic information being retrieved from memory is perceptual. That is, the retrieved information is in the form of visual images that have been stored in long-term memory, not simply verbal or abstract propositions (see also Anderson, 1983). As confirmation of this, do the following demonstration (inspired by Matlin, 2002): Imagine two clock faces, set at the times listed below. Compare the two clock faces to decide which one's hands make the smaller angle, *A* or *B*.

	A	**B**
	3:20	7:25
	2:15	9:20

In keeping with the symbolic distance effect, your decision times here were probably much faster for the second pair of times. Why? Because 2:15 on a clock face yields a very small angle, but 9:20 yields a large one—and it's easier to discriminate between two things that are very different from each other.

SEMANTIC ORDERINGS   Consider some results by Holyoak and Walker (1976). They had people make comparisons along the semantic orderings of time, quality, and temperature; for example, compare "minute versus hour," "average versus poor," "cool versus cold." The instructions said either to choose the longer, better, or warmer or the shorter, worse, or colder of the two concepts. Just as with numerical judgment, performance demonstrated both the symbolic distance and the semantic congruity effects. Judgments were faster when the pair of terms differed a great deal (e.g., perfect versus poor) than when they differed by less (perfect versus excellent). Also, judgments were faster if the dimension was congruent with the stimulus values; for example, choosing the longer of "century versus decade" was easier than choosing the shorter of those two. Furthermore, in a study by Friedman (1978), the same kind of symbolic distance and semantic congruity effects were found when the concepts had no physical or quantitative dimension at all; for example, choose the better or worse of pairs such as "lose versus peace" or "hate versus pressure."

The important extension of this is that the distance and congruity effects influenced decisions even when the underlying representations were not quantitative. The implication here is that more abstract orderings must be similarly mentally represented to number and other quantity-based orderings because they all "behave" in a similar way. Our mental representations of such terms influence our judgments in much the same way as more quantitative representations do. The nature of the mental representation, furthermore, can introduce distortions that are analogous to those found in perceptual tasks. We make simple comparisons and decisions based on our stored knowledge. The form of that knowledge can distort our judgments to a surprising degree.

Decisions about Geographical Distances

Perhaps not surprisingly, judgments of geographical distance seem to follow the same principles (Baum & Jonides, 1979; Holyoak & Mah, 1982). The point in this research is to have people make distance or location comparisons, then determine what their mental maps are like. In one study, Holyoak and Mah (1982) tested people at the University of Michigan, asking them to rate the distances between American cities on a 1 to 9 scale. When no particular geographical reference point was given—the neutral condition—people based their judgments on their own local viewpoint. As Figure 11-6 shows, they overestimated distances for nearby Midwestern cities; they rated Kansas City, a fairly nearby city, as much farther away than it really is, but Denver and Salt Lake City, more distant cities from Ann Arbor, as much closer together. This is the symbolic distance effect: The farther away the cities were, the closer together they were in the mental representation. They also confirmed a certain egocentrism in adult thought; in a sense, the distorted "New Yorker's view of the world" can be transplanted anywhere (but cf. Friedman, Kerkman, & Brown, 2002, who suggest that one's categories of locations—"that's a northern city," for example—are the important determinant of biased judgments).

In an investigation of people's reasoning about geography, Friedman and Brown (2000; Friedman, Brown, & McGaffey, 2002) asked people to estimate the latitude of 34 North American cities (from Edmonton to Miami) and 34 European and North African cities (from Oslo to Cairo). People's estimates fit a *plausible-reasoning*

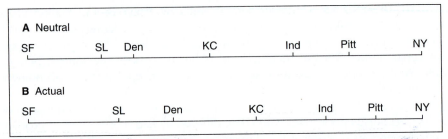

FIGURE 11-6 Results of Holyoak & Mah's (1982) study of the relative locations of cities along an east–west line. Estimates in the neutral perspective were made from a person's current location, Ann Arbor, Michigan, roughly halfway between Indianapolis and Pittsburgh on the east–west line. People overestimated the distances to Denver, Kansas City, and Indianapolis, as shown by the actual distances at the bottom.

process, where knowledge from a variety of sources is factored into a decision. In particular, people may have some specific knowledge of the location of certain cities. For others, they may only know the city's general region but do not know enough about the region's location. Among other things, the Friedman and Brown studies replicated evidence of the so-called Chicago–Rome illusion, the illusion that Chicago is farther north than Rome (in fact, they have the same latitude). People maintain the illusion because they view Chicago (correctly) as being in "northern North America," whereas Rome is viewed (also correctly) as southern European or Mediterranean; of course, all of this is based on the misconception that North America and Europe are aligned in latitude (they aren't) and that "northern" and "southern" refer to approximately the same latitudes in both (they don't). Just as found in reasoning based on magnitude, imagery, and semantic ordering, reasoning about geography is influenced by conceptual knowledge retrieved to help solve the reasoning problem, however faulty or incomplete that knowledge is (see Friedman & Montello, 2006, for similar results with relative city judgments instead of absolute latitude judgments).

Section Summary

- Deciding which of two physical stimuli is louder, brighter, and so on is a psychophysical judgment. These decisions are speeded up when the two stimuli differ by a great amount.
- When symbolic stimuli are compared, the same effect is obtained, called the symbolic distance effect. Additionally, judgments are faster when the evaluated dimension (e.g., choose the larger) matches the stimuli being compared (e.g., two "large" digits); this is called the semantic congruity effect. Both of these results are obtained in simple comparisons of numbers and in comparisons of qualities such as "hot/cold."
- The existence of the SNARC effect with responding to numbers using the left and right hands suggests an embodied component to at least some types of decisions.
- In all symbolic and reasoning situations, including those about geographical location, our mental representation and knowledge influence our judgments.

DECISIONS AND REASONING UNDER UNCERTAINTY

Some of the decisions we've been discussing, such as judging which of two numbers is smaller, are rapid and fairly automatic. Typically we are aware only of the outcome of those processes: We know consciously that we responded "7" to the question "Which is larger, 4 or 7?" If asked why we responded that way, we tend to give intellectualized answers that likely have little if anything to do with the actual mental basis for the decision (Ericsson & Simon, 1993). Furthermore, we are unaware of the exact nature of the mental representation that leads us to the judgment; to be blunt, nobody has conscious awareness of the compressed mental number line, although this is how numerical magnitude is mentally represented from young children up through adults (Banks, 1977; Duncan & McFarland, 1980).

In contrast to such relatively automatic decision making, the bulk of the research on reasoning and decision making investigates processes that are slower and more deliberate. In fact, in many ways the research on such decisions is similar to the area of problem solving, in which there is a clear connotation of slow, deliberate processing. One aspect of this similarity relates to familiarity: The domains of reasoning and problem solving we investigate are not well known or understood by the person, or they involve material that is not highly familiar. Another similarity involves the idea of uncertainty: There is often no certain answer to the problems or at least no good way of deciding whether a particular type of solution is the correct approach. Despite this, taking a principled and careful look at how people make decisions under uncertainty can provide enormous benefits and guide further research. For example, there are emerging findings that people who are convicted of crimes and sentenced to jail show principled differences in how they make decisions, and possibly that parts of their brains are working less effectively, thereby leading to these decision-making differences (Yechiam et al., 2008).

Finally, the major conclusions of this kind of research are similar to the conclusions you'll read about in Chapter 12, on problem solving. People make decisions and base their reasoning on a variety of strategies, some good and some not so good. This is also a characteristic of much problem solving. Because of these similarities, investigations of such strategies often are impossible to categorize clearly as reasoning on the one hand or problem solving on the other.

Algorithms and Heuristics

A basic distinction is necessary at the outset to understand the nature of the research you'll be reading about. In many reasoning and problem-solving settings, two general approaches can be taken, an algorithmic approach and a heuristic approach.

An **algorithm** is *a specific solution procedure, often detailed and complex, that is guaranteed to furnish the correct answer if it is followed correctly; for example, a formula.*

A rich source of evidence about human reasoning is gambling.

We are familiar with algorithms largely through our schoolwork in arithmetic and mathematics. For example, we all learned an algorithmic approach to complex multiplication, a set of rules for applying operations in certain orders to arrive at the correct answer. If the rules are applied correctly, the algorithm provides the correct answer.

In contrast, a **heuristic** is an informal method or guideline rather than a formal, specified rule. It's a "seat of the pants" *strategy that works most of the time,* for some of the time, but *is not guaranteed to yield the correct answer.* (The word *heuristic* comes from the Greek stem meaning "to invent or discover." The same word stem leads to the word *eureka,* the classic exclamation, supposedly uttered by Archimedes in his bathtub, meaning roughly "Aha, I've found it!") Heuristic rules of thumb aren't foolproof or guaranteed—but they're often right.

Answer these questions:

1. *If you toss a fair coin, what is the probability of getting heads?*
2. *If you toss a fair coin, what is the probability of getting heads two times in a row?*

Most people know that the probability of tossing heads is .50—that's a simple 50/50 situation. But you may be hazy about the correct algorithm to apply to the second problem, two heads in a row. It's actually fairly simple and requires two basic probability statements.

First, the chance of getting heads once is 50/50, or stated as a probability, .50.

Second, the probability of any particular sequence of independent events (like coin tosses) is the basic probability of the event (.50) multiplied by itself once for each event in the sequence, that is .50 × .50 for two heads in a row. More formally, the formula is $p(e)^2$, the basic probability of the event $p(e)$ raised to the nth power, where n is the number of events in the sequence. So the answer here is .25 for two heads, $.50^2$ or simply .50 × .50.

People tend to be poor at probability questions. In a survey of an undergraduate class that used those questions, 89% got question 1 correct, but only 42% got the second question right; 37% said that the correct answer was .50, the same as in Question 1 (Ashcraft, 1989). It is clear that these people didn't know the formula.

Likewise, people generally don't know the algorithm for answering this kind of question:

3. *If each of 10 people at a business meeting shakes hands (once) with each other person, then how many handshakes are exchanged?*

If you don't know how to compute this, then make an estimate—and then introspect for a moment on how you came up with that estimate. If you guessed, then what guided your guess? The algorithm for this problem is also fairly easy. If N is the number of people, then the number of handshakes is $N \times (N-1)/2$; for 10 people, that's $10 \times 9/2 = 45$ handshakes. "Without repetitions" simply means that after person A shakes B's hand, B doesn't then also shake A's hand.

Notice that the algorithm provides a systematic and orderly procedure that is guaranteed to yield the correct result (assuming you do the math correctly). Algorithmic methods, in all these settings, follow the *normative model,* the method provided by mathematics and probability. Heuristics, in contrast, seem very human;

they are not necessarily systematic or orderly, and they rely heavily on educated guessing. This is referred to as the *descriptive model,* just a description of how the question was answered. A large part of the research on reasoning and decision making looks at how different the normative and descriptive models are, meaning how people diverge from the normative method. Under certain circumstances, or for particular kinds of questions, heuristics seem prone to distortions, inaccuracies, and omissions—the descriptive model diverges from what's normative or "right."

One reason people use heuristics, rather than algorithms, to make decisions is because heuristics can be used more quickly and easily, which is an advantage when decisions need to be made rapidly. Generally, people do not exert the effort to do more deliberate reasoning when quick and dirty processes suffice, unless they encounter a difficulty in using their more intuitive judgments (Alter, Oppenheimer, Epley, & Eyre, 2007).

Heuristics, Biases, and Fallacies

By far the most influential work done on decision making and heuristics has been that of Tversky and Kahneman (1973, 1974, 1980; Kahneman, Slovic, & Tversky, 1982; Kahneman & Tversky, 1972, 1973; Shafir & Tversky, 1992). This is one of the areas of cognitive psychology to have a clear influence on other disciplines and fields. Tversky and Kahneman's work on heuristics and fallacies has had an impact in such diverse areas as law, medicine, and business. Most prominently, it has affected the field of economics, and Daniel Kahneman received the Nobel Prize in Economics in 2002 (see Kahneman, 2003a, for a first-person account of that work, and 2003b for his personal history of the collaboration with the late Amos Tversky; see Kahneman & Tversky, 2000, for a compendium of chapters on this approach). In a way, it isn't surprising that this topic is of interest to many different fields—after all, think of how many situations and settings involve reasoning and making decisions. The Nobel Prize signifies more than just the relevance of the topic; it signifies noteworthy achievement in tackling and explaining a large and important set of idea, how humans reason and make decisions.

Kahneman and Tversky's research focused extensively on a set of heuristics and biases that appear to characterize everyday reasoning about uncertain events, an area now called behavioral decision research (Medin & Bazerman, 1999). Their interest was in how people predict the likelihood of future events, how people categorize events, and how various biases and errors in such judgments can be accounted for by understanding the reasoning process.

In some of the situations they studied, an algorithm can be applied to arrive at a correct answer. Many of these situations involve probabilistic reasoning, the sort of judgments students often are asked to make in the probability chapter of an undergraduate statistics book. Knowledge of the algorithms doesn't necessarily mean that the person understands them, can use them spontaneously, or can recognize when they should be applied. Indeed, Kahneman and Tversky found that a sample of graduate students in psychology, all of whom had been exposed to the relevant statistical algorithms, did well on simple problems but still relied on a heuristic rather than an algorithm when given more complex situations. However, several studies have shown more positive effects—good transfer and improved reasoning—when some relevant training is given (Agnoli, 1991; Agnoli & Krantz, 1989; Fong & Nisbett, 1991; Lehman, Lempert, & Nisbett, 1988). (Incidentally, reading Tversky and Kahneman's work, such as the 1973 article, often is helpful to students as they *study* probability in a statistics class. See Nisbett, Krantz, Jepson, & Kunda, 1983, on statistical heuristics that people use in everyday reasoning.)

Other situations that have been studied involve estimates of likelihood when precise probabilities cannot be assigned or have not been supplied, although elements of statistical and probabilistic reasoning are still appropriate, and in situations contrasting verbal and numerical descriptions (for instance, "rain is likely" versus "there's a 70% chance of rain;" Windschitl & Weber, 1999). Finally, some of the settings that have been studied involve very uncertain or even impossible situations, such as asking people to predict the outcome of a hypothetical event. For instance, how would the outcome of World War II have changed if Germany had developed the atomic bomb before the United States?

We begin with the more heavily researched heuristics, the representativeness and availability heuristics, then devote some attention to others. We'll then cover a newer approach that has challenged some of the assumptions in Kahneman and Tversky's work. As you read, try to develop your own examples of situations that are similar to the stated examples. You'll be surprised at how often we use heuristics in everyday decision making and reasoning. A table at the end of the section lists the heuristics and biases in a convenient summary form.

The Representativeness Heuristic

Back to coin tosses for a moment. If you toss a coin six times in a row, which of the following two outcomes is more likely: HHHTTT or HHTHTT? Most of us would say—and quite rapidly at that—that the second alternative is a more likely outcome than the runs of three heads and three tails. But if you stop and think about it, you realize that each of these is *exactly* as likely as the other, because each is one of the possible ways six coin tosses can occur (the total number of outcomes is 2^6, i.e., 64 sequences of heads and tails).

Part of what fools us is that we think of the alternating pattern HHTHTT as a representative of a whole class of outcomes, in which most of the outcomes have alternations between heads and tails. This is incorrect because the problem asked about the likelihood of exactly the two given sequences, not the general class of sequences. But the mistake we make is an important indicator of how we reason in similar situations (the math for this problem is explained in the Appendix, at the end of this chapter).

According to Kahneman and Tversky (1972), when we judge the likelihood of uncertain events, we do so on the basis of the event's representativeness. The **representativeness heuristic** is a judgment rule in which *an estimate of the probability of an event is determined by one of two features, how similar the event is to the population of events it came from or whether the event seems similar to the process that produced it.* In other words, we judge whether event *A* belongs to class *B* based on the extent to which *A* is representative of *B,* the degree to which it resembles *B,* or the degree to which it resembles the kind of process that *B* is known to be.

RANDOM PROCESSES   In our coin toss example, we know that getting heads or tails is a random process. Given that tossing coins is random, we judge the sequence HHTHTT as more likely than HHHTTT because the sequence HHTHTT resembles the outcome of a random process more than HHHTTT. The thinking here, illogical but understandable, is that a random process ought to look random (e.g., Burns & Corpus, 2004). The sequence of three heads then three tails looks nonrandom and so seems less likely. Likewise, because the likelihood for six tosses is three heads and three tails (in the long run), almost any sequence with three of each will appear more representative than sequences with more of one outcome than the other. (See Pollatsek, Konold, Well, & Lima, 1984, and Nickerson, 2002, for evidence on people's beliefs about random sampling processes, and the ability to produce and perceive randomness.)

REPRESENTATIVENESS OF THE PARENT POPULATION   Consider a situation more like Kahneman and Tversky's first criterion, where the event is similar in essential characteristics to its parent population (i.e., to the population of events from which the event of interest is drawn). These authors' example of this situation goes as follows:

> *In a certain town there are two hospitals. In one, about 45 babies are born each day, in the other only about 15. As you know, about 50% of all babies are boys, although on any day, of course, this percentage may be higher or lower. Across one year, the hospitals recorded the number of days on which 60% or more of the babies were male. Which hospital do you think had more such days?*

(After Kahneman & Tversky, 1972, p. 443. Decide on your answer before reading further.)

The majority of people in Kahneman and Tversky's study (28 out of 50) claimed that the number of days with 60% or more male babies would be about the same for the two hospitals. Twelve of the 50 said the larger hospital, and only 10 said the smaller hospital. Overall, most people believed that both hospitals would have about the same number of days on which 60% or more (or fewer) of the babies would be male.

Let's explain this. Consider the conclusion that people drew, that both hospitals will have about the same number of "extreme" days. People know that there will be variations around the expected percentage of 50% boy/50% girl and that 60% is somewhat extreme. Because "somewhat extreme" events occasionally happen, a small and a large hospital both having 60% or more male babies is viewed as representative of a larger population. Note the implicit and incorrect assumption here that "extreme" means the same thing for the two hospitals.

In fact, the correct answer is that the smaller hospital will have more days on which 60% or more of the babies are male. This is because of an elementary notion in statistics. Extreme or unlikely outcomes are more likely with small sample sizes. That is, with fewer events, the likelihood is greater for variations from the expected proportion. Thus, it is more likely that the small hospital will have more extreme days than the large hospital. The reason is that the 60% proportion is being computed on an average of 15 births instead of 45. Another way of saying this is that, given the fifty-fifty odds, 60% is not as extreme an occurrence out of 15 opportunities as it is out of 45; 60% or more male babies is not as extreme for the small hospital as it is for the large one. (On statistical grounds, this is precisely the same reason that all heads is a more likely outcome for two coin tosses than it is for six coin tosses. See the Appendix for the algorithmic and statistical explanations.)

The representativeness heuristic embodies a bias called *insensitivity to sample size* (see Table 11-3 for several of the biases that stem from representativeness). It means that when people reason, they fail to take into account the size of the sample or group on which the event is based. They seem to believe that both small and large samples should be equally similar to the population they were drawn from. Another way of expressing this is that people believe in the *law of small numbers*. Now the *law of large numbers*—that a large sample is more representative of its population—is true. But people erroneously believe that there is also a law of small

---

TABLE 11-3   Biases in the Representativeness Heuristic

Ignoring base rates (ignoring prior odds) (Based on Johnson & Finke, 1985)

Questions:

(a) Why are more fighter pilots first-born than second-born sons?

(b) Why do more apartment building fires occur on the first three floors than the second three floors?

(c) In football, do more interceptions occur on first down or second down?

The bias: In all three questions, people tend to ignore base rates. To answer the questions correctly, we should consider:

(a) How many first-born versus second-born sons are there?

(b) How many apartment buildings even have more than three floors?

(c) How many times do teams make first downs and compared to second downs?

Base rates and stereotypes

Question:

Frank is a meek and quiet person whose only hobby is playing chess. He was near the top of his college class and majored in philosophy. Is Frank a librarian or a businessman?

The bias: The personality description seems to match a librarian stereotype, whether the stereotype is true or not. Second, we fail to consider base rates, that is, the relative frequencies of the two professions. In other words, there are far more businessmen than librarians, a base rate that tends to be ignored because of the stereotype "match."

Gambler's fallacy

Question:

You've watched a (fair) coin toss come up heads five times in a row. If you bet $10 on the next toss, would you choose heads or tails?

The bias: The gambler's fallacy is that the next toss is more likely to be tails, because "it's time for tails to show up." Of course, the five previous tosses have no bearing at all on the sixth toss, assuming a fair coin. The bias is related to the law of small numbers, in particular, that we expect randomness even on the "local" or short-run outcomes. Thus getting tails after five heads seems more representative of the random process that produces the outcomes, so we mistakenly prefer to bet $10 on tails.

numbers—believe that a small sample is just as representative of its parent population as a large sample (see also Bar-Hillel, 1980)—but that isn't the case.

STEREOTYPES   Another bias, also resulting from the representativeness heuristic, is of particular importance because it probably affects our reasoning about other people (see Table 11-3 for additional examples and explanations). Kahneman and Tversky (1973) reported evidence on estimations based on personality descriptions. They read various personality descriptions to people, then had them estimate the probability that the described person was a member of one or another profession. They found that people's estimations are influenced by the similarity of a description to a widely held **stereotype**.

Consider first the situation: 100 people are in a room, 70 of them lawyers, 30 of them engineers. Given this situation, answer the following question:

1. *A person named Bill was randomly selected from this roomful of 100 people. What is the likelihood that Bill is a lawyer?*

Simple probability tells us that the chances of selecting a lawyer are .70. People generally reason correctly in a "bare bones" situation. The technical term for these "bare bones," the 70:30 proportion, is *prior odds, prior probabilities,* or simply *base rates.*

Consider two slightly different situations. There are still the same 70 lawyers and 30 engineers. But now you are given a description of two randomly selected people and are asked "What is the likelihood that this person is an engineer?" (adapted from Kahneman & Tversky, 1973, pp. 241–242):

2. *"Dick is a 30-year-old man. He is married with no children. A man of high ability and high motivation, he promises to be quite successful in his field. He is well liked by his colleagues."*

3. *"Jack is a 45-year-old man. He is married and has four children. He is generally conservative, careful, and ambitious. He shows no interest in political and social issues and spends most of his free time on his many hobbies, which include home carpentry, sailing, and mathematical puzzles."*

Here, people did *not* judge the probabilities to be the same as the prior odds. Instead, they assumed that the personality descriptions contained relevant information and adjusted their estimates accordingly. In particular, for both descriptions 2 and 3, people responded that the probability was close to .50, that is, about a fifty-fifty chance that Dick and Jack were engineers.

Description 3 resembles the stereotype many people have of engineers. It mentions such factors as "careful" and "mathematical puzzles." Here, people de-emphasized the prior odds (.30) and based their judgments on the description. Because the description seemed representative of engineers, people adjusted their estimates upward from the .30 level, allowing an influence of the stereotype.

But description 2 was intentionally written to be uninformative about Dick's profession—it offers no relevant information at all. And yet, people still changed their estimates. In fact, people tend to view *any evidence* as a basis for changing and, they hope, improving their prediction (Fischhoff & Bar-Hillel, 1984; Griffin & Tversky, 1992).

The correct way to deal with these problems—the normative model—is to assess the usefulness or relevance of the additional information to decide how much weight to give it; usefulness is called "diagnosticity"—whether it "diagnoses" engineers correctly, in a sense. Then the estimate is adjusted by the appropriate weighting. This is *Bayes's theorem,* which states that estimates should be based on two kinds of information, the base rate of the event and the "likelihood ratio," which is an assessment of the usefulness of the new information. In description 2, the information should have no impact—the description is uninformative, it's not diagnostic. Nonetheless, people still adjusted their estimates.

BELIEFS Our beliefs can also introduce bias, certainly in situations that rely on Bayes's theorem (e.g., Evans, Handley, Over, & Perham, 2002). For instance, it's easy to see how a belief—say in our stereotype about lawyers (or other groups)— could influence your judgments. If the evidence is consistent with your beliefs, then you give weight to the evidence and adjust your estimates accordingly; if the additional evidence is inconsistent with your belief, you could just ignore it. This is consistent with what you read earlier about confirmation bias—pay attention to evidence that confirms your belief, but pay little attention to evidence that does not.

The effects that beliefs can have on reasoning are pervasive. For example, Kim and Ahn (2002) showed how clinical psychologists' diagnoses are affected by their individual "theories" of mental disorders. In particular, if a clinician views symptom *X* as a central cause for disorder *Y*, then hypothetical patients who present symptom *X* are diagnosed as having disorder *Y;* another clinician views symptom *X* as being peripheral, so diagnoses a different disorder. In both cases, the belief guides the diagnosis, rather than the "supposedly" atheoretical symptom lists in the *DSM (Diagnostic and Statistical Manual)* that clinicians are taught to use. Moshinsky and Bar-Hillel (2002) have documented how beliefs can even affect judgments of when different world events happened. Israeli students often are surprised to learn that an event in U.S. history happened at about the same time as another event in Europe. The source of the surprise is that the United States is representative of the "New" World, so events that happened there are interpreted as being more recent than events in Europe, the "Old" World. In a sense, the United States is more representative of the recent or "not long ago" category. Hence events in the New World were judged as being more recent than those in the Old World.

The Availability Heuristic

What proportion of medical doctors are women? What proportion of U.S. households own a wireless router, a flat screen TV, or an iPad? How much safer are you in a commercial airliner than in a private car, or vice versa? Questions such as these ask you to estimate the frequency or probability of real-world events, even though you are unlikely to have more than a few shreds of relevant information stored in memory. Short of doing the fact finding necessary to know the real answers, how do we make such estimates?

The simplest way of making estimates is to try to recall relevant information from memory. Event frequency is coded in memory (Brown & Siegler, 1992;

Simulate
Heuristics in
MyPsychLab

Hasher & Zacks, 1984), perhaps automatically. If the retrieval of examples is easy—if examples come to mind easily—we infer that the event must be fairly frequent or common. If retrieval is difficult, then we estimate that it must not be frequent. Interestingly, frequency estimates affect your eventual judgments about the information: If it's repeated often enough, even false statements becomes "truer" (Brown & Nix, 1996).

Frequency is closely related to the second heuristic that Tversky and Kahneman (1973) discussed, the **availability heuristic**. In this heuristic, we estimate the likelihood of events based on how easily examples come to mind. "Ease of retrieval" is what the term *availability* means here.[1] In short, when people have to make estimates of likelihood, their *estimates are influenced by the ease with which relevant examples can be remembered.*

BIASES WITHIN THE AVAILABILITY HEURISTIC

Although the availability heuristic often is reliable (indeed, it is often the only way we have of making estimates), some distortions and biases may stem from it. Because our judgments are based on what we can remember easily, any factor that leads to storing information in memory can influence our reasoning. If reasonably accurate and undistorted information is in memory, then the availability heuristic does a good job. But if memory contains information that is inaccurate, incomplete, or influenced by factors other than objective frequency, there may be biases and distortions in our reasoning. As a simple example, if your friend's Volvo needs repeated trips to the mechanic, you may develop a biased view that Volvos are unreliable. If your only source of knowledge is the friend's opinion, the availability heuristic has biased your judgment. More generally, our biases result from other kinds of knowledge.

GENERAL WORLD KNOWLEDGE

As an illustration of the availability heuristic, estimate the ratio of the number of Chevrolets sold to the number of Cadillacs sold. According to the availability heuristic, you base your estimate on whatever frequency-based knowledge you may have. If you have no personal reason to notice one kind of car more than another, your estimate may be a reasonably fair guess. Apart from personal biases, however, your general world knowledge tells you that Cadillacs are more expensive than Chevrolets. Given this, you might estimate that fewer Cadillacs are sold than Chevrolets. Alternatively, the cost might cause you to adjust your initial guess, altering your estimate; this is called the *anchoring and adjusting heuristic* (Carlson, 1990). Most people estimated that Chevrolets are about 10 or 15 times more numerous than Cadillacs. According to recent General Motors data, however, the ratio was almost exactly 5:1.

FAMILIARITY BIASES

Another example shows clearly how the availability bias is related to ease of recall. Tversky and Kahneman constructed lists of names,

Simulate
Anchoring and Adjustment in
MyPsychLab

---

[1]In Chapter 6, "availability" meant whether some information was stored in memory, and "accessibility" referred to whether the information could be retrieved. Clearly, "availability" in the Kahneman and Tversky sense is referring to "accessibility" in the memory retrieval sense. Kahneman (2003a) has acknowledged that his original choice of terms was confusing in this sense and now refers to this as the accessibility heuristic. We continue to use the original term, however, to be consistent with the 50-year history of its usage in the decision-making literature.

39 names per list, with 19 women's and 20 men's names per list. One group of people heard the lists and then had to recall as many names as they could remember. Another group heard the lists, then estimated whether the list contained more names of men or women. In two of the four lists that were tested, the women's names were famous (e.g., Elizabeth Taylor), and the men's names were not; in the other two lists, the men's names were famous (e.g., Richard Nixon), and the women's names were not. In the recall groups, people remembered an average of 12 of the 19 famous names but only 8 of the 20 less famous names. This shows that familiar or famous names were more easily recalled.

The important connection between ease of recall and estimation bias came from the groups that had to estimate the proportion of male versus female names. Here, too, the fame of the names influenced the judgments. People who heard the "famous female" lists estimated that there had been more women's names, and those who heard the "famous male" lists said there had been more men's names. Thus, there was clear evidence, first, that the famous names were more easily recalled and, second, that this greater availability influenced the estimates of frequency. So the **familiarity bias** is just that, *judging events as more frequent or important because they are more familiar*. Note that familiarity can influence decision making beyond just how frequent something is. For example, food additives with unfamiliar, low-frequency, hard-to-pronounce names are rated as being riskier than additives whose names are more familiarly structured and easier to pronounce (Song & Schwarz, 2009).

SALIENCE AND VIVIDNESS BIASES   Examples of the availability heuristic in everyday life are not difficult to imagine. Consider people's feelings about traveling by airplane. Statistically, one is far safer traveling by commercial airliner than by private car (by one estimate, some 25 times safer, based on normalized passenger-miles traveled). People who have no particularly relevant information in memory, that is, those whose only information comes from casual attention to news media and the like, judge that one is much safer when traveling by car (e.g., Hertwig, Barron, Weber, & Erev, 2004).

This bias can be attributed to the factor of **salience or vividness**. News accounts of an airline accident are far more vivid and given far more attention than car accidents. Also, even though airplane crashes are rare, the number of victims involved often is dramatic enough that the event makes a much stronger impression. Thus, when you estimate air versus car safety, the vividness of the recalled information tends to bias your judgment. In a revealing demonstration, Gigerenzer (2004) examined U.S. highway traffic fatality data for the three months following the 9/11 terrorist attack, on the hypothesis that people's "dread fear" of flying after the attack might have led them to drive instead. As predicted, traffic fatalities were higher in those months than they had been for those months during the previous five years. (Ironically and sadly, approximately 350 additional lives were lost because of increased driving during that three-month period.)

The Simulation Heuristic

A variation on the availability heuristic is the **simulation heuristic**. Here people make a prediction of future events or are asked to imagine a different outcome of an event or action. The simulation involves *a mental construction or imagining of outcomes, a forecasting of how some event will turn out or how it might have turned out under another set of circumstances.* The ease with which these outcomes can be imagined is the basis for this heuristic. To the extent that a sequence of events can easily be imagined, the events are available. Alternatively, if it is difficult to construct a plausible scenario, the hypothetical outcome is viewed as unlikely or might not even be constructed or imagined at all. In short, the ease of imagining an outcome is the operative factor in the simulation heuristic.

An example of this was given earlier, when you were asked to imagine possible outcomes if Germany had developed the atomic bomb before the United States. Given the role the atomic bomb played in ending World War II, people would give that far more weight than if they were asked about the development of some other device, say a long-range bomber or submarine.

Alternatively, imagining a different outcome may be difficult. This should also affect how the simulation heuristic guides our thinking. Consider an example by Kahneman and Tversky (1982, p. 203):

> *Mr. Crane and Mr. Tees were scheduled to leave the airport on different flights, at the same time. They traveled from town in the same limousine, were caught in a traffic jam, and arrived at the airport 30 minutes after the scheduled departure time of their flights. Mr. Crane is told that his flight left on time. Mr. Tees is told that his flight was delayed, and just left five minutes ago. Who is more upset, Mr. Crane or Mr. Tees?*

As you would expect, almost everyone decides that Mr. Tees is more upset; in Kahneman and Tversky's study, 96% of the people made this judgment. The unusual aspect of this is that from an objective standpoint, Mr. Crane and Mr. Tees are in identical positions: Both missed their planes, and because of the traffic jam, both *expected* to miss their planes. The reason Mr. Tees might be more upset is that it was more "possible," in some sense, for him to have caught his flight. That is, it's easier to imagine an outcome in which the limousine arrives a few minutes earlier than it is to imagine one in which it arrives a half hour earlier. As such, we feel that the traveler who "nearly caught his flight" will be more upset.

The Undoing Heuristic: Counterfactual Reasoning

A more complete example of the simulation heuristic, including Kahneman and Tversky's (1982) data, is shown in Table 11-4. This illustrates a version of the simulation heuristic, the undoing of an outcome by changing what led up to it. This is called **counterfactual reasoning**, *when a line of reasoning deliberately contradicts the facts in a "what if" kind of way* (e.g., "what would have happened if Germany had developed the bomb first?"; see Mandel & Lehman, 1996; Roese, 1997, 1999; Spellman & Mandel, 1999). This is the process of judging that some event "nearly happened," "could have occurred," "might have happened if only," and so on. Read the story now and decide how you would complete the "if only" phrase before continuing.

The results are shown at the bottom of Table 11-4. A surprisingly large number of people—51%—chose to change the unusual event in the Mr. Jones story,

TABLE 11-4	Stories for the Simulation Heuristic

Route Version

1.	Mr. Jones was 47 years old, the father of three, and a successful banking executive. His wife had been ill at home for several months.
2a.	On the day of the accident, Mr. Jones left his office at the regular time. He sometimes left early to take care of home chores at his wife's request, but this was not necessary on that day. Mr. Jones did not drive home by his regular route. The day was exceptionally clear, and Mr. Jones told his friends at the office that he would drive along the shore to enjoy the view.
3.	The accident occurred at a major intersection. The light turned amber as Mr. Jones approached. Witnesses noted that he braked hard to stop at the crossing, although he could easily have gone through. His family recognized this as a common occurrence in Mr. Jones's driving. As he began to cross after the light changed, a light truck charged into the intersection at top speed and rammed Mr. Jones's car from the left. Mr. Jones was killed instantly.
4a.	It was later ascertained that the truck was driven by a teenage boy, who was under the influence of drugs.
5.	As commonly happens in such situations, the Jones family and their friends often thought and often said, "If only . . .," during the days that followed the accident. How did they continue this thought? Please write one or more likely completions.

Time Version (substitute 2b for 2a)

2b.	On the day of the accident, Mr. Jones left the office earlier than usual to attend to some household chores at his wife's request. He drove home along his regular route. Mr. Jones occasionally chose to drive along the shore, to enjoy the view on exceptionally clear days, but that day was just average.

"Boy" Focus Version (substitute 4b for 4a)

4b.	It was later ascertained that the truck was driven by a teenage boy named Tom Searler. Tom's father had just found him at home under the influence of drugs. This was a common occurrence, as Tom used drugs heavily. There had been a quarrel, during which Tom grabbed the keys that were lying on the living room table and drove off blindly. He was severely injured in the accident.

Percentage of People Responding to the "If Only" Stem in the Five Different Response Categories

"If Only" Completion Focuses On:	Route Version	Time Version
Route	51%	13%
Time	3%	26%
Crossing	22%	31%
Boy	20%	29%
Other	4%	1%
	$n = 65$	$n = 62$

From Kahneman & Tversky (1982).

that he took a different route home than normal; in the participants' responses, they basically said, "If only he had taken his normal route home, the accident could have been avoided." This is a **downhill change**, when *we alter an unusual story element, substituting a more typical or normal element in its place.* In general, such changes focus on an unusual event. The change substitutes something more ordinary and thus "normalizes" the story. Other kinds of changes, for instance inserting an unusual event (after he left work, Mr. Jones had a flat tire), were rarely supplied. (By the way, the term "downhill" came from an analogy with cross-country skiing, where the easiest thing to do is ski downhill.)

Other studies have confirmed this tendency to alter or undo unusual events but not the more common, usual events. That is, while any change to the Mr. Jones story might have undone the accident, people confine themselves largely to downhill or "normalizing" changes. We are biased toward that kind of change for at least three reasons. First, downhill changes are more easily imagined—the ease of retrieval factor again (e.g., Koehler & Macchi, 2004). Second, downhill changes seem more plausible; it's more plausible that Mr. Jones left on time than it is that he left early and then had a flat tire. And third, we have a tendency to judge unusual events as being the cause for an unanticipated outcome (e.g., Roese, 1997; see Reyna, 2004, and Trabasso & Bartolone, 2003, for gist- or comprehension-based explanations of reasoning).

Other factors have also been implicated in counterfactual reasoning. Byrne and McEleney (2000) have suggested that people focus on actions, not failures to act, when they undo events. They had people read a story about Joe and Paul. Joe got an offer to trade his stock in Company *B* for stock in Company *A,* which he did, although he ultimately lost money on Company *A.* Paul got a comparable offer, to trade his stock in Company *A,* but he decided not to take the offer. Staying with Company *A,* he ultimately lost the same amount of money as Joe, even though they both started with the same amount.

Despite the equal loss by both, however, 87.5% of the people claimed that Joe, the one who acted, would feel worse about his decision ("If only I hadn't traded my stock"); only 12.5% felt it would be Paul who felt worse. In a companion article, McCloy and Byrne (2000) developed a scenario in which a character is late for an appointment, because of either controllable or uncontrollable factors—the character stopped to buy a hamburger or was delayed because a tree had fallen in the street. The people undid the controllable factors far more frequently, although they distinguished among delaying factors in terms of interpersonal and social norms of how acceptable or polite the factor was; stopping to visit his parents on the way to the appointment was viewed less negatively than stopping for the hamburger.

BLAMING THE VICTIM   A puzzle in the Mr. Jones story—and often in other counterfactual reasoning scenarios—was that people seldom focused on the actual cause of the accident, the teenage boy. That is, they seldom altered anything concerning the boy's behavior, even though it was his actions, not Mr. Jones's, that caused the accident. Kahneman and Tversky speculate that this tendency is caused by a focus rule: We tend to maintain properties of the main object or focus of the story unless a different focus is provided. In support of this, when people read a version of the story that focused more on the boy, they were more likely to undo the boy's actions as a way of preventing the accident.

However, undoing Mr. Jones's behavior—having him take his normal route home—essentially claims that Mr. Jones was responsible for the accident, because it was his behavior that people altered. It's a case of "blaming the victim"—a situation in which the victim rather than the person who caused the accident is held responsible. This is especially common when there was an unusual event in the story that could have been altered via a downhill change. For instance, Goldinger, Kleider, Azuma, and Beike (2003) offer clear examples:

> *Paul normally leaves work at 5:30 and drives directly home. One day, while following this routine, Paul is broadsided by a driver who violated a stop sign and receives serious injuries.* (p. 81)

When people consider how much compensation Paul should receive for his injuries and how much punishment is appropriate for the other driver, they examine Paul's behavior closely. In this scenario, however, Paul tends not to be blamed for the accident. But if the scenario is changed to:

> *Paul, feeling restless at work, leaves early to see a movie. . . . Paul is broadsided by a driver. . . .*

and so forth, then we tend to view him as somehow less deserving of compensation. In addition, in an echo of the social norms result of McCloy and Byrne (2000), Goldinger et al. pointed out the following: If *Paul receives an emergency call to return home,* and then is broadsided, "the accident now appears exceptionally tragic, and compensation awarded to him increases" (p. 81). This kind of reversal, observed by Miller and McFarland (1986), depends on how free Paul was to choose what to do and how socially acceptable his choices were.

HINDSIGHT Note, that the simulation heuristic provides a nice explanation of the **hindsight bias** (Fischhoff, 1975), *the after-the-fact judgment that some event was very predictable, even though it wasn't.* This is the "I knew it all along" effect. In thinking about the now-finished event, the scenario under which that event could have happened is easy to imagine—after all, it just happened (Sanna & Schwartz, 2006). The connection between the initial situation and the final outcome is very available after the fact, and this availability makes other possible connections seem less plausible than they otherwise would (e.g., Hell, Gigerenzer, Gauggel, Mall, & Muller, 1988, and Hoch & Loewenstein, 1989). The hindsight bias can even distort our perceptual memories. For example, Gray, Beilock, and Carr (2007) report that batters misremember how well they thought they would hit a baseball when they have been hitting well as compared to when they have struggled. That is, the current success with batting causes the player to experience the hindsight bias by misremembering the batting as being better than it actually was.

Interestingly, the hindsight bias even influences our memory for events. People routinely "remember" their original position to be more consistent with their final decision than it really was (Erdfelder & Buchner, 1998; Holyoak & Simon, 1999) and even reconstruct story elements so that they are more consistent with the final outcome. As a demonstration of this, Carli (1999) had two groups of people read a story (about Pam and Peter in Experiment 1, and Barbara and Jack in Experiment 2) with no ending (control group), a happy ending (Jack proposes marriage to Barbara), or a tragic ending (Peter/Jack rapes Pam/Barbara). The stories had information that was consistent with both scenarios; e.g., "Barbara met many men at parties" and "Pam wanted a family very much"). After finishing the stories, people were questioned about the story events. The groups that heard either one of the stories with an ending agreed far more than the control group that they would have predicted that ending all along—but of course the endings were completely different. As a follow-up, in a later memory test, both groups mistakenly "remembered" information that had not been in the story but was consistent with the ending they had read. (See Harley, Carlsen, & Loftus, 2004, and Mather, Shafir, & Johnson, 2000, for an extension of the hindsight bias to identifying pictures, important for eyewitness testimony situations and remembering blind dates, respectively.)

APPLICATIONS OF THE SIMULATION HEURISTIC   In many ways the simulation heuristic may come closer to what people mean by such terms as thinking and contemplating than anything else we've covered so far. That is, it is easy to recognize less dramatic examples of undoing and other kinds of forecasting or simulating in our everyday thinking, and the influence of factors such as salience and hindsight bias. For example:

> *If I stop for a cup of coffee, I might miss my bus.*
>
> *If I hadn't been so busy yesterday, I would have remembered to go to the ATM for money.*
>
> *In looking back, I guess I could have predicted that waiting until senior year to take statistics was a bad idea.*

Presumably, such thinking often is the reason we decide to do one thing versus another; we think through the possible outcomes of different actions, then base our decision on the most favorable of the forecasted outcomes. Thus the mental simulation process, taking certain input conditions then forecasting possible outcomes, could be an important way to understand cognitive processes related to planning. A general warning is important to bear in mind, based on studies of how people generate possible outcomes of future events (e.g., Hoch, 1984, 1985). If you begin planning by thinking only of the desirable, favorable outcomes, you tend to blind yourself to possible undesirable outcomes—people generate fewer possible negative outcomes if they begin by thinking of positive ones. By starting with positives, you also become more confident that the plan you select will have a positive outcome. In other words, overly optimistic predictions at the outset bias our ability to imagine negative outcomes and inflate our view of the likelihood of a positive outcome. ("Hey, what could go wrong if I wait until next week to start my term paper?"; see Petrusic & Baranski, 2003, on how confidence affects decision making.)

Adaptive Thinking and "Fast, Frugal" Heuristics

Another way of thinking about heuristics is as *adaptive thinking*. The biggest proponent of this adaptive thinking view is Gigerenzer (e.g., 1996). For Gigerenzer, it is a mistake to assume that the correct answer to any decision-making problem must be the normative answer supplied by classic probability theory (e.g., Bayesian probability). Instead, it's important to assess how well people's heuristics actually do in guiding behavior. That is, people use heuristics not just because of memory limitations, incomplete algorithm knowledge, and so forth. They also use them because they work—because they're adaptive in the sense of leading to successful behavior.[2] That is, people use heuristics because they are tractable and robust (Gigerenzer, 2008). Saying that they are *tractable* means that people can mentally keep track of everything they need to use the heuristic, in contrast to algorithms that require people to track (often) much larger amounts of information. Saying that they are *robust* means that they provide reasonable answers under a wide range of circumstances.

Gigerenzer (2008) provides some compelling illustrations of the value of heuristics. He notes that the 1990 Nobel Prize winner in economics, Harry Markowitz, derived an algorithm for maximizing the allocation of funds into various financial assets. However, even Markowitz did not use this principle for his own retirement savings, but instead used a simple $1/N$ heuristic (where N is the number of possible funds that the investments could go into). According to this heuristic, your retirement funds are equally distributed across the number of available funds. Pretty simple, huh? This is the heuristic used by about half of the people in the real world. Although many financial wizards sneer at this strategy, when it was pitted against 12 different optimal return strategies, the $1/N$ heuristic beat them all. Bravo, heuristics!

Another example Gigerenzer (2008) gives has to do with organ donation. He notes that the rate of organ donation is only 28% in the United States but is 99% in France. His explanation has to do with a *go-with-the-default* heuristic. In the United States, the default is not to have your organs donated if you die. That is, people in the United States need to make an effort to be an organ donor (so that other people may live), for example by filling out a form or having the option checked on a driver's license. In the absence of this, the default is "not an organ donor." In contrast, the default in France is to be an organ donor.

Part of the appeal of Gigerenzer's approach is that it is "positive"—that is, it doesn't emphasize errors or deviations from some norm, but searches for the usefulness of heuristics. A second appealing feature is that the "fast and frugal" heuristics are simple. Third, the approach seems more open to input from general cognitive principles. For example, it acknowledges and takes into account memory limitations, incomplete knowledge, time limitations, and so on, as well as the general cognitive processes you've been studying. There is also the idea that human cognition is tuned to environmental statistics, and there is often a need to make assumptions based on small numbers of experiences (Hahn & Warren, 2009). So, if six coin flips in a row end in heads, although this is a completely acceptable outcome from a random process, it may also reflect some causal systematicity in the environment, such as a weighted coin.

[2] This is "adaptive" in an evolutionary sense, an explicit argument in Gigerenzer's approach. If a biological factor is adaptive, in evolutionary terms, it leads to greater success of the individual, hence greater spread of the feature into succeeding generations. In similar fashion, an adaptive heuristic will be successful, so it will be used more widely. Gigerenzer also advocates devoting more attention to the reasoning processes that are used, as opposed to the heavy focus on how answers deviate from the normative model.

TABLE 11-5   Fast and Frugal Heuistics

Heuristic	Description
Recognition	If one of two alternatives is recognized, go with it.
Fluency	If one of two alternatives is recognized faster than the other, go with it.
Take the Best	Given two alternatives, go with the one that is preferred by (a) searching through cues in order of validity, (b) stopping the search as soon as a cue discriminates, and (c) choosing the one this cue favors.
Tallying	Count the number of favoring cues and go with the option that satisfies the most.
Satisficing	Take the first choice that exceeds your aspiration level.
1/N (Equality)	Allocate resources equally to each of N alternatives.
Default	If there is a default, do nothing about it.
Tit-for-Tat	Cooperate at first, and then imitate your partner's last behavior.
Imitate the Majority	Look at a majority of people in your peer group, and imitate their behavior.
Imitate the Successful	Look for the most successful person, and imitate his or her behavior.

Adapted from Gigerenzer (2008).

This approach has generated a number of heuristics that differ in some ways from those outlined by Kahneman and Tversky and others. A listing of heuristics provided by Gigerenzer (2008) is given in Table 11-5. We'll look at some of them in more detail in the following sections—namely *satisficing, recognition,* and *take-the-best*—to better illustrate this approach. It should also be noted that although these heuristics can be useful, people can sometimes become overly dependent on one, such as persisting with one when it has become clear that it is no longer optimal and that a switch in strategies would be better (Bröder & Schiffer, 2006).

SATISFICING   An important adaptive thinking heuristic that has been on the scene for some time is Simon's (1979) **satisficing** heuristic. This principle is that *we make a decision by taking the first solution that satisfies some criterion we may have—it's the "good enough" heuristic.* For example, if you are looking for a place to eat dinner while travelling, rather than checking out every single eatery in town, you simply pick the first one that satisfies your criterion, such as "cheap fast food place." People can use this heuristic to make reasonably optimal decisions.

THE RECOGNITION HEURISTIC   One of Gigerenzer's simplest heuristics is the **recognition heuristic,** where you *base a decision on whether you recognize the thing to be judged.* For instance, if I ask you, "Which city is larger, Kansas City or Junction City?" you might choose Kansas City because you've never heard of the alternative. Of course, it is illogical in some sense to base a decision on ignorance or missing knowledge—"I've never heard of it, so it must be smaller" doesn't come across as a sound, ironclad basis for deciding. On the other hand, to the extent that we notice things and store information in memory about them, the fact that we don't know about something could be informative. This is Gigerenzer's point—when having heard of something correlates with the decision criterion, here the population of the city, then *not* having heard of something is useful.

"TAKE THE BEST" HEURISTIC Another heuristic is the **"take the best" heuristic** (Gigerenzer & Goldstein, 1996), *where you decide between alternatives based on the first useful information you find.* Essentially, you search the alternatives for some characteristic—Gigerenzer calls this a "cue"—that is relevant and that you might know about, and check to see if one option or the other has a positive value for that cue. For example, if I ask which is larger, Kansas City or Oklahoma City, simple recognition won't work, because you've probably heard of both. You then try to retrieve a cue to help you decide, a cue that correlates with city populations—maybe something like, "Does the city have a major league sports team?" If you know that Kansas City does but Oklahoma City doesn't, you decide Kansas City is larger based on that bit of positive evidence. Of course if I asked you about two cities that both had sports teams, then you'd have to search for yet another cue and continue doing so until one of the cities differed—or until you finally ran out of cues and merely guessed. Figure 11-7 shows a flow diagram of the "take the best" heuristic. The heuristic is simple—you search for some evidence favoring one over the other alternative, and you make your decision as soon as you find such evidence.

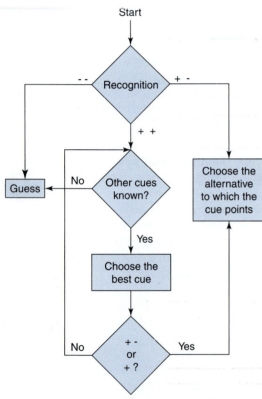

FIGURE 11-7 Flow chart of the "take the best" heuristic. Processing starts with a comparison of two objects, *A* and *B*. If neither is recognized (− −), guess. If one is recognized and one is not (+ −), choose the recognized alternative. If both are recognized (+ +), search for a cue that might discriminate. If one cue is positive and the other is negative or null (+ −) and (+ ?), choose the alternative with the positive cue. If both are positive or both are negative, return to search for another cue.

From Goldstein & Gigerenzer (2002).

The Ongoing Debate

Gigerenzer and Goldstein (1996; also Gigerenzer, 1996, and Goldstein & Gigerenzer, 2002) present considerable modeling and survey data to show how these heuristics do a good job of making decisions. Other supportive work has begun to appear as well (for instance Burns, 2004, in a challenge to the well-known Gilovich, Vallone, & Tversky, 1985, paper on the "hot hand" in basketball). A final example will illustrate. Take a moment now to read the question in Table 11-6 and do the rankings of the alternatives about Linda.

LINDA AND THE CONJUNCTION FALLACY Tversky and Kahneman (1983) had people read the Linda question and then complete the rankings of the eight alternatives. They found that people endorse the compound alternative "bank teller and active in the feminist movement" as more likely than either "bank teller" or "active in the feminist movement." Such a judgment, from

TABLE 11-6   The Linda Problem

Linda is 31 years old, single, outspoken, and very bright. She majored in philosophy. As a student, she was deeply concerned with issues of discrimination and social justice and also participated in antinuclear demonstrations.

Now rank the following options in terms of the probability of their describing Linda. Give a ranking of 1 to the most likely option and a ranking of 8 to the least likely option.

_____ Linda is a teacher at an elementary school.
_____ Linda works in a bookstore and takes yoga classes.
_____ Linda is active in the feminist movement.
_____ Linda is a psychiatric social worker.
_____ Linda is a member of the League of Women Voters.
_____ Linda is a bank teller.
_____ Linda is an insurance salesperson.
_____ Linda is a bank teller and is active in the feminist movement.

Adapted from Tversky & Kahneman (1983).

purely probabilistic standpoints, is odd. In particular, it illustrates the **conjunction fallacy**, *the mistaken belief that a compound outcome of two characteristics is more likely than either one of the characteristics by itself.* According to strict probability, this is impossible—making up some numbers to illustrate, if the chances are .20 that Linda is a bank teller, and .30 that she is active in the feminist movement, then the conjunction of those two characteristics should never be larger than .20. In fact, in stripped down form, the probability ought to be .06; that is,

> *In a room with 100 people, 20 are bank tellers, 80 are something else. Furthermore, 30 of the people are feminists, and 70 are not. What is the probability of randomly selecting someone who is both a bank teller and a feminist?*

And yet people routinely say that the compound "bank teller and feminist" is more likely (has a higher rank) than the simpler probability that she's a bank teller. Considerable significance has attached to this fallacy in Kahneman and Tversky's work—it comes close to epitomizing the errors, the departures from the normative model, found in human reasoning.

OTHER EXPLANATIONS   Considering humans from a broader perspective than simply "lousy probabilists," however, reveals other reasonable interpretations of these rankings and judgments. Indeed, Moldoveanu and Langer (2002) supply a whole variety of explanations to justify this choice. For instance, many people treat the statement "Linda is a bank teller and is active in the feminist movement" not as a conjunction of two characteristics but as a conditional probability—in other words, as if it said, "*Given* that Linda is a bank teller, what is the likelihood that she is active in the feminist movement?" The probabilities for a conditional probability are very different than those for a conjunction.

A second reason involves the idea of how consistent personality tends to be—in other words, whatever job a person may end up in, there still should be some consistency in the person's personality, something like "once an activist, always an activist." Such a comment also exemplifies an idea you studied in the last chapter, on conversational rules and the cooperative principle. If you were supposed to judge the Linda problem solely on the basis of the probabilities of being a bank teller and being active in the feminist movement, then there is no communicative need to supply all of the background information on the character—in other words, "Why did you tell me about Linda's activism as a college student if I was supposed to ignore it?" The fact that personality information *was* supplied tells people that it is important and should be factored into the answer. So people rather naturally take that into account and come up with a plausible scenario—"OK, maybe she ended up as a bank teller, but she can still be a social activist by being active in the feminist movement." In short, they may be developing a personality-based model of Linda.

The adaptive thinking approach does have its detractors. For instance, Newell and Shanks (2004) have questioned whether the simple recognition heuristic is as powerful as Goldstein and Gigerenzer (2002) claimed, showing how recognition is discounted when other cues of higher validity are presented. Similarly, Newell and Shanks (2003) showed that the "take the best" heuristic is used especially when the mental "cost" (e.g., in terms of time) of information is high. When the cost is low, however, for instance when it takes very little time to retrieve additional information, people seem to rely on that heuristic less frequently. (Table 11-7 presents a review list of the heuristics, biases, and fallacies discussed so far.)

More recently, there have been some attempts to address how reasoning and decision making take into account people's understanding of the causal structures of situations when making decisions (e.g., Garcia-Retamero, Wallin, & Dieckmann, 2007; Hagmayer & Sloman, 2009; Kim, Yopchick, & Kwaadsteniet, 2008; Kynski & Tenebaum, 2007), as opposed to the more statistical approach of Kahneman and

TABLE 11-7 Review List of Heuristics, Biases, and Fallacies

Heuristic	Biases and Fallacies
Representativeness	Insensitivity to sample size
	Belief in the law of small numbers
	Stereotype bias, belief bias, confirmation bias
Availability	Familiarity bias, salience and vividness bias
Anchoring and adjustment	Order bias
Simulation	Overly optimistic predictions inflate our confidence and prevent thinking of possible negative outcomes
Undoing/counterfactual reasoning	Bias to undo unusual event, bias to focus on action, bias to focus on controllable events, hindsight bias
	Blaming the victim
Recognition	Familiarity bias
"Take the best"	Reliance on ignorance or lack of knowledge

Tversky, and Gigerenzer's adaptive thinking approach. For example (see Kynski & Tenebaum, 2007), using standard base rate information, there is the finding that people who use sunscreen are more likely to develop skin cancer than those who do not, which runs counter to most people's intuitive judgments. This is because most people who don't use sunscreen are not out in the sun to begin with. It is important to note that using sunscreen does not cause skin cancer; rather, sunbathing does. When the problem is recast with this additional information, we see that among those people who sunbathe (a smaller group), those who use sunscreen are less likely to get skin cancer. Thus, when people are provided with the appropriate causal structure, their decisions processes can be very good.

This approach can also explain why people make some of the errors that they do. For example, Figure 11-8 illustrates the causal model that many people have of personality and career choice, and how it relates to the lawyer-engineer problem. When statistical principles are applied to this model, then the results are similar to the estimates provided by people. That is, people take into account the causes that produce various outcomes, as well as their combined influence, then make their decisions.

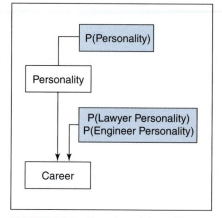

FIGURE 11-8 Causal model used by Kynski & Tenebaum (2007) to illustrate the concept that people use ideas of causal information and relations to help make them decisions. In this case, people are assuming that there is a causal relationship between a person's personality and their career choice.

Section Summary

- Algorithms are systematic rules that generate correct answers to problems, whereas heuristics are quick, informal rules that are often useful but are not guaranteed to yield the correct solution. Kahneman and Tversky investigated three important heuristics used in circumstances when people reason about uncertain events.
- The representativeness heuristic guides people to judge outcomes as likely if they seem representative of the type of event being evaluated; for instance, a random-looking sequence of coin tosses is judged more representative of coin toss outcomes almost regardless of the true probabilities involved. Included among the reasoning effects predicted by this heuristic are various stereotyping results.
- In the availability heuristic, people judge the likelihood of events by how easily they can remember examples or instances. These judgments therefore can be biased by any other factor that affects memory, such as salience or vividness.
- In the simulation heuristic, people forecast or predict how some outcome could have been different. These forecasts are influenced by how easily the alternative outcomes can be imagined. Interestingly, when people complete "if only" statements, the changes they include tend to normalize the original situation by removing an unusual event and substituting a more common one. Such normalizations can be affected by the *focus* of the situation.
- Work on "fast and frugal" heuristics reveals that simple one-reason decision-making heuristics often do a very good job. These heuristics come from the

adaptive thinking approach to decision making, the source of a current debate about the basis for reasoning under uncertainty.

- Recent work on causal reasoning suggests that people use more normative reasoning than has otherwise been suspected if it is assumed that people have a reasonably correct causal model of the situation they are trying to make decisions about.

LIMITATIONS IN REASONING

A central fact in studies of decision making and reasoning bears repeating. We use heuristics because of limitations. There are limitations in our knowledge, both of relevant facts and also of relevant algorithms. You had to estimate the latitudes of Chicago and Rome because you (probably) didn't know them; you simply didn't have those facts stored in memory. Likewise, you probably estimated the number of handshakes in the earlier question because you didn't know the relevant algorithm. In addition, there are also limitations in the reasoner that are important, sometimes as ordinary as unwillingness to make the effort needed, but sometimes more central than that.

Limited Domain Knowledge

Everyday examples of how limited knowledge affects decision making and reasoning are abundant. Kempton (1986), for example, looked at reasoning based on

analogies, particularly how we develop analogies based on known events and situations to reason about unknown or poorly understood domains. Focusing on a mechanical device, Kempton studied people's understanding of home heating, particularly their understanding of a furnace thermostat. The results indicated that some people's (incorrect) mental model is that a thermostat works like a water faucet: Turn it up higher to get a faster flow of heat. Likewise, many people's behavior suggests that they believe that the call button on an elevator works like a doorbell: If the elevator doesn't arrive reasonably soon, press the button again (see Shafir & Tversky, 1992).

It should be obvious that our mental models—our cognitive representations of the reasoning or decision-making situation—can vary from true and complete knowledge (expertise, in other words) all the way down to no knowledge or information at all, ignorance. (People's awareness that they do not know something is actually quite interesting itself; see Gentner & Collins, 1981, and Glucksberg & McCloskey, 1981.) The most interesting situation to study is when knowledge is incomplete or inaccurate. Indeed, the fact that we are so concerned with how people estimate under uncertainty, and with their errors in reasoning, implies that complete and certain knowledge usually is not available to people.

We often are asked to make decisions, sometimes explicitly, about things that we may not have complete knowledge about.

A MENTAL MODEL OF THE PHYSICAL WORLD: NAIVE PHYSICS Some of the most intriguing research has been in the area of **naive physics**, *people's conceptions of the physical world, in particular, their understanding of the principles of motion.* Figure 11-9 presents several of the problems. The remaining section will be more meaningful to you if you spend a few moments working through the problems before reading further.

By asking people to complete such diagrams and then explain their answers, McCloskey (1983) provided examples of the misconceptions people often have. For instance, in one study (McCloskey, Caramazza, & Green, 1980; see also Freyd & Jones, 1994), 51% of the people believed that a marble would follow a curved path after leaving the tube depicted in Figure 11-9A. Likewise, some 30% responded that the ball in Figure 11-9B would continue on a curved path after the string broke, often adding that this curved path eventually would straighten out. In the airplane question (Figure 11-9C), only 40% gave the correct answer; the most common incorrect answer (36% of the people) was that the ball would fall straight down. Figure 11-10 shows both the correct and incorrect answers people gave to these problems, along with the percentage of people who gave the answers.

A compelling aspect of these results is that the motion of physical objects is not a rarefied, unusual kind of knowledge. We have countless opportunities in our everyday experience to witness the behavior of objects in motion and to derive an

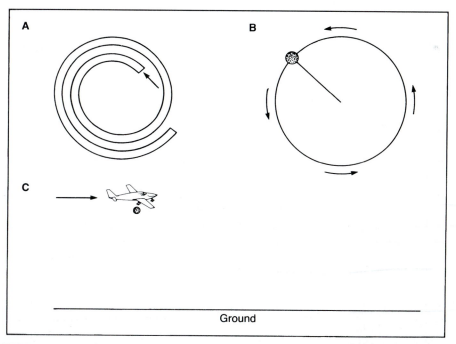

FIGURE 11-9 Stimuli used by McCloskey. **A.** Imagine that the curved tube is on a tabletop, and a ball or marble is tossed in (see arrow). Draw the path of the ball when it exits the tube. For **B,** imagine that the ball is being twirled around and that the string breaks. Draw the path the ball will take once the string breaks. **C.** Imagine an airplane is traveling at a constant speed, and a ball is dropped from the airplane. Draw the path of the ball as it falls to the ground.

FIGURE 11-10
Stimuli and responses to McCloskey's problems in Figure 11-9, with the percentages of people making that response.

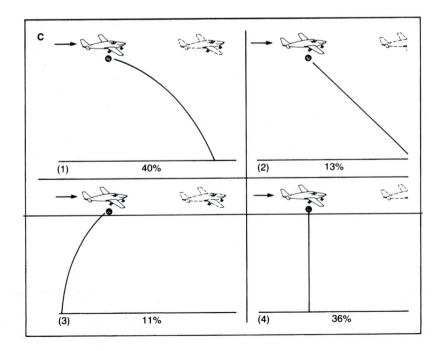

understanding of the principles of motion. Anyone who has ever thrown a ball has had such opportunities. And yet the mental model we derive from that experience is flawed and is different from the perceptual–motor model that actually governs throwing a ball (Krist, Fieberg, & Wilkening, 1993; Schwartz & Black, 1999).

A second compelling aspect to the research concerns the nature of the mental model itself. People's erroneous understanding of bodies in motion is amazingly similar to the so-called impetus theory, which states that setting an object in motion puts some impetus or "movement force" into the object, with the impetus slowly dissipating across time (e.g., Catrambone, Jones, Jonides, & Seifert, 1995; see Cooke & Breedin, 1994, and Hubbard, 1996, on the notion of impetus). The punchline here is that the impetus theory was the accepted explanation of motion during the 13th and 14th centuries, a view that was abandoned by physics when Newton's laws of gravity and motion were advanced some 300 years ago. The correct mental model, basically, is that a body in motion continues in a straight line unless some other force, such as gravity, is applied. If some other force is applied,

PROVE IT
Naive Physics

Having people complete the diagrams on the naive physics beliefs is an almost failsafe project. Be sure you interview your participants on their reasons for drawing the pathways they drew (be sure you understand the correct pathways before you try explaining the principles behind them). Also, come up with some new diagrams or problems to test other aspects of people's intuitive understanding of motion and gravity, for instance the puzzling "water-level" problem (when a glass of fluid is tilted sideways, people—even those with presumed expertise—draw the line representing the water as perpendicular to the glass, rather than parallel to the horizon; e.g., Hecht & Proffitt, 1995; Vasta & Liben, 1996).

It would be interesting to know how other groups of people respond. For example, in Donley and Ashcraft's (1992) article, the professors in the physics department performed essentially perfectly, whereas professors in other departments were no more accurate than students in the undergraduate physics sequence. It's not clear whether children would perform less accurately than adults; after all, adults do pretty badly. On the other hand, perhaps children will report more interesting reasons for their beliefs. Some adults complete the cliff-and-ball problem below with a "straight out, then straight down" pathway, a pathway called the Road Runner effect, from the cartoon character. It would be interesting to know whether children (or adults) appeal to that in justifying their answers.

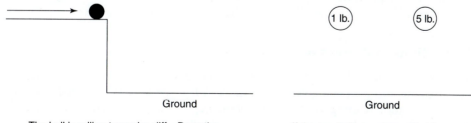

The ball is rolling toward a cliff. Draw the path of the ball as it goes over the edge.

If the two balls are dropped at the same time, do they hit the ground at the same time or at different times?

then that force combines with the continuing straight-line movement. Thus when the ball leaves the tube, or when the string breaks, the ball moves in a straight line; no "curved force" continues to act on it because no such thing as "impetus" has been given to it. Likewise, the horizontal movement of the ball dropped from the airplane continues until the ball hits the ground. This movement is augmented by a downward movement caused by gravity; the ball accelerates vertically as it continues its previous horizontal motion. (If you demonstrated a naive belief in impetus, you might take some consolation in the fact that, across recorded history, people have believed in impetus theory longer than they have in Newton's laws.)

EXPERIENCE AND KNOWLEDGE Only a little research addresses the nature of our experience and the kind of information we derive from it. In some of the naive physics problems, especially the plane problem, an optical illusion seems partly responsible for the "straight down belief" (McCloskey, 1983; Rohrer, 2003). Beyond that, some inattentiveness on the reasoner's part, or perhaps difficulty in profiting from real-world feedback, may also account for some of the inaccuracy. To be sure, some of the difficulties we experience involve the difficulty of the problems themselves (Proffitt, Kaiser, & Whelan, 1990). For example, Medin and Edelson (1988) found that, depending on the structure and complexity of the problem, people may use base rate information appropriately, may use it inappropriately, or may ignore it entirely. We do know that instruction and training influence reasoning. Taking a physics class improves your knowledge of the rules of motion, but it doesn't completely eliminate the misbeliefs (Donley & Ashcraft, 1992; Kozhevnikov & Hegarty, 2001). Likewise, instruction in statistics, probability, and hypothesis testing improves your ability to reason accurately in those domains (Agnoli & Krantz, 1989; Fong & Nisbett, 1991; Lehman et al., 1988). In short, acquiring a fuller knowledge of the domain is an important part of making more accurate decisions.

The types of reasoning errors we've been encountering here don't just apply to physics and statistics problems, but even extend to everyday objects. Lawson (2006) gave people partial drawings of bicycles, such as those shown in Figure 11-11, and asked people to select the drawing from a set of options that correctly depict the proper position of the bicycle frame, pedals, and chain. What she found was that, although bicycles are very familiar objects to most people, an average of 39% errors were made in their selections. Performance was better for expert cyclists, although even they made 15% errors. So, what we can learn from this is that even when people have a great deal of familiarity with a common object, they may still have trouble reasoning about the structure of that object and how it works.

Limitations in Processing Resources

Likewise, several studies attest to the role of processing resources in adequate decision making and problem solving. Cherniak (1984; see also Tversky & Kahneman, 1983) has studied the *prototypicality heuristic*, a strategy in which we generate examples to reason out an answer rather than follow the correct, logical procedures of deductive reasoning. The heuristic is useful in the sense that it reduces people's errors when they are working under time constraints. However, it depends on a limitation, possibly of working memory, possibly of time in which to perform the

FIGURE 11-11
Response choices
for a study by
Lawson (2006) in
which people
needed to select
the correct location
of a bicycle's frame,
pedals, and chain.

task, or possibly in the willingness to do the slow, effortful work of following the algorithmic procedure. As an example, what is the answer to the following?

$$8 \times 7 \times 6 \times 5 \times 4 \times 3 \times 2 \times 1$$

Be honest—even though you know how to multiply, you didn't really multiply out all those values, did you? You probably estimated; you used a heuristic. One way we know this is by comparing your estimate to a different problem,

$$1 \times 2 \times 3 \times 4 \times 5 \times 6 \times 7 \times 8$$

In Tversky and Kahneman's (1983) data, people's estimates for the first problem averaged 2,250, but for the second problem, estimates averaged 512. Heuristic processing was clearly involved, because the estimates depended on whether the arithmetically identical sequences began with a large or small number and because both estimates were wildly inaccurate: The correct answer to 8! is 40,320.

Although it's tempting to say the limitation was in your lack of willingness to solve the problem (a nice way of saying laziness), note that a full solution would take considerable working memory resources if you attempted to solve the problem mentally. Even if you were only approximating in your calculations, a sequence of problem-solving and keeping-track steps would tax working memory. Surely such a limited system as working memory would interfere with this type of processing.

An intriguing study demonstrates an entirely compatible result—that limited working memory resources compromise the ability to reason and make decisions in difficult situations. The study, by Waltz et al. (1999), tested normal people, six patients with brain damage in the prefrontal cortex, and five with damage to the anterior temporal lobes. People were given two reasoning tasks. In the first, people read transitive inference problems such as "Beth is taller than Tina. Tina is taller than Amy," where anywhere from two to four propositions were included (the "Beth" example has two propositions), and had to arrange the sentences in order of height (so the "Beth" sentence would be at the top). Problems presented in this order were at Level 1 complexity, and performance was contrasted with Level 2 complexity, in which the propositions were in scrambled order (e.g., for a four-proposition problem, "Beth is taller than Tina. Sally is taller than Laura. Tina is taller than Joyce. Laura is taller than Beth."). The critical difference between conditions was that Level 1 problems, because they were in correct transitive order, never required more than one relation ("Beth is taller than Tina") to be held in mind at one time, whereas the Level 2 sentences required simultaneous consideration and integration of two relations (and that happened two to four times per trial, depending on how many propositions were shown).

In the other half of the experiment, people solved a set of matrix problems from the Raven's Standard Progressive Matrices test (Raven, 1941). Figure 11-12 illustrates three such problems. The problem in Figure 11-12A was a "nonrelational" Level 0 problem; the correct answer merely involved finding the matching pattern among the six choices at the bottom. Figure 11-12B shows a one-relation, Level 1 problem (technically, the relation is "reflect the pattern across the x-axis," that is, flip the pattern from bottom to top; the answer is choice 3), and Figure 11-12C, a two-relation, Level 2 problem (the two relations are from solid to checked, and remove the upper-right quarter; the correct answer is choice 1).

Waltz et al.'s (1999) results for transitive inference are shown in the left half of Figure 11-13. Normal control participants (dashed line) showed only a modest decline in the Level 2 condition and did only slightly better than the patients with temporal lobe damage (the dotted line). However, patients with frontal lobe damage (solid line) dropped from more than 80% correct on Level 1 problems to

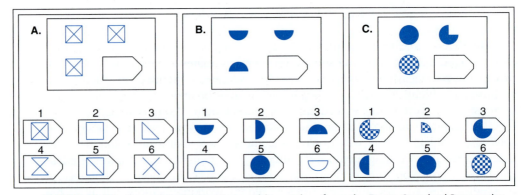

FIGURE 11-12 Examples of reasoning problems taken from the Raven Standard Progressive Matrices test. The task asks people to pick the one correct choice out of six possibilities at the bottom to complete the pattern at the top. **A.** Level 0 problem (nonrelational). **B.** Level 1 problem (one-relation problem). **C.** Level 2 problem (two-relation problem). Correct answers are choice 1 in A, choice 3 in B, and choice 1 in C. Figure 2 from Waltz et al. (1999).

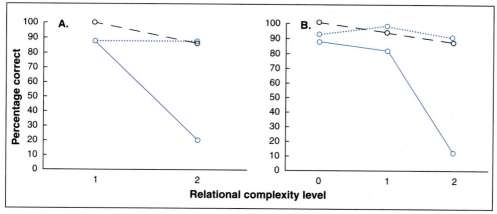

FIGURE 11-13 Percentage correct in the transitive inference **(A)** and Raven's Matrices **(B)** problems, as a function of relational complexity (Levels 0, 1, and 2), for normals (dashed lines), temporal lobe patients (dotted lines), and prefrontal lobe patients (solid lines).

around 20% correct on Level 2 problems, seemingly unable to consider and integrate multiple propositions at the same time. In the right half of the results, it's clear that the frontal lobe patients were unable to maintain two relational changes at the same time, their performance dropping from about 80% down to around 10% at Level 2. The temporal lobe patients were again very close in performance to the normal controls. Despite this very poor performance by the prefrontal patients, their accuracy on memory tests (for instance, "Which of these names did you read about, Amy or Susan?") was very high, about 96% correct, actually about 10% higher than the normal controls. Here, consistent with material in Chapter 6, it was the temporal lobe patients whose declarative memory for the tasks was poor; their name recognition performance was at 56%, not appreciably different from chance. Thus declarative memory for the tasks was damaged selectively for the temporal lobe patients, but reasoning performance was selectively damaged for the prefrontal patients (see also, Wagar & Thagard, 2004).

The results are compatible with the idea that the frontal lobes are important for reasoning and in particular for maintaining relational information in working memory while the reasoning task is being done. The connection between the dorsolateral prefrontal cortex (DLPFC) and executive control in working memory was discussed in Chapter 5. The Waltz et al. results extend that research: "In other words, relational integration may be the 'work' done by working memory. We thus view our results as being consistent with the idea that the DLPFC, which was severely damaged in all our prefrontal patients, is critical for working memory" (1999, p. 123; see also Hinson, Jameson, & Whitney, 2003).

Section Summary

- In everyday reasoning, we rely on mental models of the device or event to make our judgments. These mental models sometimes are quite inaccurate. In the best-known research, people's mental models of physical motion lead them to incorrect predictions (e.g., the trajectory of a ball dropped from an airplane).

- Ongoing research is focused on the kinds of limitations that lead to incorrect reasoning and decision making, including limited domain knowledge and limitations in working memory processes.

Key Terms

algorithm (p. *397*)
antecedent (p. *381*)
availability heuristic (p. *405*)
belief bias (p. *379*)
conditional reasoning (p. *381*)
confirmation bias (p. *384*)
conjunction fallacy (p. *415*)
consequent (p. *381*)

counterfactual reasoning (p. *407*)
discriminability effect (p. *389*)
distance effect (p. *389*)
downhill change (p. *409*)
familiarity bias (p. *406*)
heuristic (p. *398*)
hindsight bias (p. *410*)
just noticeable difference (jnd) (p. *389*)

mental models (p. *387*)
naive physics (p. *419*)
psychophysics (p. *388*)
recognition heuristic (p. *413*)
representativeness heuristic (p. *400*)
salience or vividness (p. *406*)
satisficing (p. *413*)
semantic congruity effect (p. *391*)

simulation heuristic (p. *406*)
SNARC effect (p. *393*)
stereotype (p. *403*)
syllogism (p. *378*)
symbolic comparisons (p. *389*)
symbolic distance effect (p. *389*)
"take the best" heuristic (p. *414*)

APPENDIX: ALGORITHMS FOR COIN TOSSES AND HOSPITAL BIRTHS

Coin Tosses

To begin with the obvious, the probability of a head on one coin toss is .50. Flipping a coin twice and keeping track of the possible sequences yields a .25 probability for each of the four possibilities HH, HT, TH, TT. In general, when the simple event has a probability of .50, the number of possibilities for a sequence of n events is 2 raised to the nth power. Thus the number of distinct sequences for six coin tosses is 2^6, a total of 64 possibilities.

Two of the 64 possibilities are pure sequences, HHHHHH and TTTTTT. Two more are double sequences, HHHTTT and TTTHHH. All the remaining 60 possibilities involve either or both of the following characteristics: more of one outcome (e.g., heads) than the other and at least one alternation between the two outcomes at a position *other than* halfway through the sequence. Thus the probability of a pure sequence is 2/64, as is the probability of a double sequence. Getting any one of the other 60 possibilities has a likelihood of 1/64. However, getting a "randomlike" outcome, that is, any outcome other than straight or double, has a probability of 60/64.

Hospital Births

Many statistics texts contain tables of the binomial distribution, the best way to understand the hospital births example. Because most of these tables go up only to a sample size of 20, we'll use a revised hospital example, comparing hospitals with three versus nine births per day (note that the 1:3 ratio is the same as the original example, 15:45). The probabilities for the original example are more extreme than these, but they'll be in the same direction.

Just as with coin tosses, we are dealing with an event whose basic probability is .50, the likelihood that a newborn infant is male (ignoring the fact that male births are actually slightly more common than 50%). What is the probability that, in three births, all three will be boys? According to the binomial tables (Table 11-A), this probability is .1250. This is the probability that on any randomly selected day, the three-birth hospital will have all boys, $p = .1250$. Across the 365 days in a year, we expect an average of 45.625 such days (365 × .1250).

The temptation now is to consider the likelihood of exactly three boys in the nine-birth hospital. But this is not the relevant comparison. The relevant comparison to the all boys probability in the three-birth hospital would be all boys in the nine-birth hospital. This puts the comparison on the same footing as the original problem, 60% as the "extreme" cutoff.

The probability of exactly nine boys out of nine births is .0020, two chances in a thousand. For a whole year, we expect only 0.73 such days (365 × .0020). Now it should be clearer. The criterion of "extreme," all boys, is much more likely in the smaller sample than in the larger one, $p = .1250$ versus .0020. Multiplied out, the prediction is 45 days for the small hospital and .70 days for the large one.

By extension, and using the appropriate binomial values, the 15-birth hospital should have about 111 days per year with 60% or more boys, contrasted with 42 such days per year for the 45-birth hospital.

TABLE 11-A   Binomial Probabilities for Exact Number of Relevant Outcomes, Where the Simple Probability of the Outcome is .50

$n = 3$		$n = 9$		$n = 15$		$n = 45$	
Exact Number of Relevant Outcomes:							
0	.1250	0	.0020	9	.1527	27	.0488
1	.3750	1	.0176	10	.0916	28	.0314
2	.3750	2	.0703	11	.0417	29	.0184
3	.1250	3	.1641	12	.0139	30	.0098
		4	.2461	13	.0032	31	.0047
		5	.2461	14	.0005	32	.0021
		6	.1641	15	.0000	33	.0008
		7	.0703	etc.		34	.0003
		8	.0176	.		35	.0001
		9	.0020	.		36	.0000

The Newell and Simon approach to problem-solving did not produce a flurry of related experiments by other cognitive psychologists, and problem solving never became a central research area in information-processing cognition. . . . Newell and Simon's conceptual work, however, formed a cornerstone of the information-processing approach.

(LACHMAN, LACHMAN, AND BUTTERFIELD, 1979, P. 99)

A favorite example of "problem solving in action" is the following true story. When I (M.H.A.) was a graduate student, I attended a departmental colloquium at which a candidate for a faculty position was to present his research. As he started his talk, he realized that his first slide was projected too low on the screen. A flurry of activity around the projector ensued, one professor asking out loud, "Does anyone have a book or something?" Someone volunteered a book, the professor tried it, but it was too thick; the slide image was now too high. "No, this one's too big. Anyone got a thinner one?" he continued. After several more seconds of hurried searching for something thinner, another professor finally exclaimed, "Well, for Pete's sake, I don't believe this!" He marched over to the projector, grabbed the book, opened it halfway, and put it under the projector. He looked around the lecture hall and shook his head, saying, "I can't believe it. A roomful of PhDs, and no one knows how to open a book!"

This chapter examines the slow and deliberate cognitive processing called problem solving. As with decision making and reasoning, problem solving studies a person who is confronted with a difficult, time-consuming task: A problem has been presented, the solution is not immediately obvious, and the person often is uncertain what to do next. We are interested in all aspects of the person's activities, from initial understanding of the problem to the steps that lead to a final solution, and, in some cases, how a person decides that a problem has been solved. Our interest needs no further justification than this: We confront countless problems in our daily lives, problems that are important for us to figure out and solve. We rely on our wits in these situations. We attempt to solve problems by mentally analyzing the situation, devising a plan of action, then carrying out that plan. Therefore, the mental processing involved in problem solving is, by definition, part of cognitive psychology.

Let's start with a simple "recreational" problem (Anderson, 1993). It will take you a minute or two at most to solve it, even if you lose patience with brain teasers very quickly; VanLehn's (1989) nine-year-old child seemed to understand it completely in about 20 seconds and solved it out loud in about two minutes:

> *Three men want to cross a river. They find a boat, but it is a very small boat. It will only hold 200 pounds. The men are named Large, Medium, and Small. Large weighs 200 pounds, Medium weighs 120 pounds, and Small weighs 80 pounds. How can they all get across? They might have to make several trips in the boat.* (VanLehn, 1989, p. 532)

Why should we be interested in such recreational problems? The answer is straightforward. As is typical of all scientific disciplines, cognitive science studies the simple before the complex, searching simpler settings to find basic principles that generalize to more complex settings. After all, not all everyday problems are tremendously complex; figuring out how to prop up a slide projector is not of earthshaking significance (well, it probably was to the fellow interviewing for the job). In either case, the reasoning is that we often see large-scale issues and important processes more clearly when they are embedded in simple situations. Indeed, one aspect of problem solving you'll read about, functional fixedness, accounts for why a roomful of PhDs didn't think about opening the book to make it thinner. Functional fixedness was discovered with a simple, recreational problem.

STUDYING PROBLEM SOLVING

Unlike many areas of cognitive psychology, the study of significant problem solving requires us to examine a lengthy sample of behavior, often up to 20 or 30 minutes of activity. A major kind of data in problem solving is the **verbal protocol**, *the transcription and analysis of people's verbalizations as they solve the problem*. Without a doubt, the use of verbal protocols influenced many opinions about problem solving. In fact, the status of verbal reports as data is still a topic of some debate (see Dunlosky & Hertzog (2001); Ericsson & Simon (1980, 1993); Fleck & Weisberg (2004); and Russo, Johnson, & Stephens (1989) for a range of views).

Let's begin with a description of the classic problem-solving research of the Gestalt psychologists. As you read in Chapter 1, the Gestalt movement coexisted with behaviorism early in the 20th century but never achieved the central status that behaviorism did. In retrospect, however, it was an important influence on cognitive psychology.

By the way, possibly more than in any material you've read so far, it's important in this chapter for you to spend some time working through the examples and problems. Hints usually accompany the problems, and the solutions are presented in the text or, for numbered problems, at the end of the chapter. Many of the insights of the problem-solving literature pertain to conscious, strategic activities you'll discover on your own as you work through the sample problems. Furthermore, simply by working the examples, you'll probably improve your own problem-solving skills.

GESTALT PSYCHOLOGY AND PROBLEM SOLVING

Gestalt is a German word that translates poorly into English; the one-word translations "whole," "shape," or "field" fail to capture what the term means. Roughly speaking, a **Gestalt** is *a whole pattern, a form, or a configuration*. It is a cohesive grouping, a perspective from which the entire field can be seen. A variety of translations have been used, but none ever caught on, which prompted Boring (1950) to remark that Gestalt psychology "suffered from its name." So, we use the German term *Gestalt*, rather than an inadequate translation. Chapter 4 covered perceptual patterns that demonstrate various Gestalt principles (e.g., closure, good continuation). They show that humans tend to perceive and deal with integrated, cohesive wholes.

Early Gestalt Research

The connection between *Gestalt* psychologists and problem solving is best explained by anecdote (see Boring, 1950, pp. 595–597). In 1913, Wolfgang Köhler, a German psychologist, went to the Spanish island of Tenerife to study "the psychology of anthropoid apes" (p. 596). Trapped there by the outbreak of World War I, Köhler experimented with visual discrimination among several animal species. In the course of this research, he began to apply Gestalt principles to animal perception. His ultimate conclusion was that animals do not perceive individual elements in a stimulus, but that they perceive relations among stimuli. Furthermore, "Köhler also observed that the perception of relations is a mark of intelligence, and he called the sudden perception of useful or proper relations *insight*" (p. 596).

Still stranded on the island, Köhler continued to examine "insight learning." He presented problems to chimpanzees and searched for evidence of genuine problem solving in their behavior. By far, the most famous of his subjects was a chimpanzee named Sultan (Köhler, 1927). In a simple demonstration, Sultan was able to use a long pole to reach through the bars of his cage and get a bunch of bananas. Köhler made the situation more difficult by giving Sultan two shorter poles, neither of which was long enough to reach the bananas. After failing to get the bananas, and sulking in his cage for a while, Sultan (as the story goes) suddenly went over to the poles and put one inside the end of the other, thus creating one pole that was long enough to reach the bananas.

Köhler found this to be an apt demonstration of insight, a sudden solution to a problem by means of an insightful discovery. In another situation, Sultan discovered how to stand on a box to reach a banana that was otherwise too high to reach. In yet another, he discovered how to get a banana that was just out of reach through the cage bars: He walked *away* from the banana, out a distant door, and around the cage. All these problem solutions seemed to illustrate Sultan's perception of relations and the importance of insight in problem solving.

Difficulties in Problem Solving

Other Gestalt psychologists, most notably Duncker and Luchins, pursued research with humans. Two major contributions of this work are essentially the two sides of the problem-solving coin. One involved a set of negative effects related to rigidity or difficulty in problem solving; the other, insight and creativity during problem solving.

Grande builds a three-box structure to reach the bananas, while Sultan watches from the ground. *Insight*, sometimes referred to as an "Ah-ha" experience, was the term Kohler used for the sudden perception of useful relations among objects during problem solving.

FUNCTIONAL FIXEDNESS   Two articles on functional fixedness, one by Maier (1931) and one by Duncker (1945), identify and define this difficulty. **Functional fixedness** is *a tendency to use objects and concepts in the problem environment in only their customary and usual way.* Maier (1931), for instance, had people work on the two-string problem. Two strings are suspended from the ceiling, and the goal is to tie them together. The problem is that the strings are too far apart for a person to hold one, reach the other, then tie them together. Also available are several other objects, including a chair, some paper, and a pair of pliers. Even standing on the chair does not get the person close enough to the two strings.

Simulate
Obstacles to Problem Solving in **MyPsychLab**

In Maier's results only 39% of the people came up with the correct solution during a 10-minute period. The solution (if you haven't tried solving the problem, do so now) involves using an object in the room in a novel way. A correct solution is to tie the pliers to one string, swing it like a pendulum, then catch it while holding the other string. Thus the functional fixedness in this situation was failing to think of the pliers in any but their customary function; people were fixed on the normal use for pliers and failed to appreciate how they could be used as a weight for a pendulum.

A similar demonstration is shown in Figure 12-1, the candle problem from Duncker (1945). The task is to find a way to mount the candle on a wall using just the objects illustrated. Can you solve the problem? If you haven't come up with a solution after a minute or two, here's a hint: Can you think of another use for a box besides using it as a container? In other words, the idea of functional fixedness is that we generally think only of the customary uses for objects, whereas successful problem solving may involve finding novel uses. By thinking of the box as a platform or means of support, you can then solve the problem (empty the box, thumbtack it to the door or wall, then mount the candle in it).

It's probably not surprising that problem solvers experience functional fixedness. After all, we comprehend the problem situation by means of our world knowledge, along with whatever procedural knowledge we have that might be relevant. When you find "PLIERS" in semantic memory, the most accessible properties involve the normal use for pliers. Far down on your list would be characteristics related to their weight or aspects of their shape that would enable you to tie a string to them. Likewise, "BOX" probably is stored in semantic memory in terms of "container" meanings—that a box can hold things, that you put things into a

FIGURE 12-1 The candle problem used by Duncker. Using only the pictured objects, figure out how to mount the candle to the wall.

box—and not in terms of "platform or support" meanings (see Greenspan, 1986, for evidence on retrieval of central and peripheral properties). Simply from the standpoint of routine retrieval from memory, then, we can understand why people experience functional fixedness.

NEGATIVE SET A related difficulty in problem solving is **negative set** (or simply *set effects*). This is *a bias or tendency to solve problems in a particular way, using a single specific approach, even when a different approach might be more productive*. The term *set* is a rough translation of the original German term **Einstellung**, which means something like "approach" or "orientation."

A classic demonstration of set effects comes from the water jug problem, studied by Luchins (1942). In this problem, you are given three jugs, each of a different capacity, and are to measure out a quantity of water using just the three jugs. As a simple illustration, consider the first problem in Table 12-1. You need to measure out 28 cups of water and can use containers that hold 5, 40, and 18 cups (jugs *A, B,* and *C*). The solution is to fill *A* twice, then fill *C* once, each time pouring the contents into a destination jug. This approach is an addition solution because you add the quantities together. For the second problem, a subtraction solution is appropriate: Fill *B* (127), subtract jug *C* from it twice (−3, −3), then subtract jug *A* (−21), yielding 100.

Luchins's (1942) demonstration of negative set involved sequencing the problems so that people developed a particular set or approach for measuring out the quantities. The second group of problems in Table 12-1 illustrates such a sequence. Go ahead and work the problems now before you read any further.

TABLE 12-1 Water-Jug Problems

Problem	Capacity of Jug *A*	Capacity of Jug *B*	Capacity of Jug *C*	Desired Quantity
1	5 cups	40 cups	18 cups	28 cups
2	21 cups	127 cups	3 cups	100 cups

		Luchins's Water-Jug Problems		
Problem	Capacity of Jug *A*	Capacity of Jug *B*	Capacity of Jug *C*	Desired Quantity
1	21	127	3	100
2	14	163	25	99
3	18	43	10	5
4	9	42	6	21
5	20	59	4	31
6	23	49	3	20
7	15	39	3	18
8	28	76	3	25
9	18	48	4	22
10	14	36	8	6

Note. All volumes are in cups.

If you were like most people, your experience on Problems 1 through 7 led you to develop a particular approach or set: specifically, $B - 2C - A$: Fill jug B, subtract C from it twice, then subtract A from it to yield the necessary amount (subtracting A can be done before subtracting $2C$, of course). People with such a set or *Einstellung* generally failed to notice the simpler solution possible for Problems 6 and 10, simply $A - C$. That is, about 80% of the people who saw all 10 problems used the lengthy $B - 2C - A$ method for these problems. Compare this with the control participants, who saw only Problems 6 through 10: Only 1% of people used the longer method. Clearly, the control people had not developed a set for using the lengthy method, so they were better able to find the simpler solution.

Consider Problem 8 now. Only 5% of Luchins's control people failed to solve Problem 8. This was a remarkable because 64% of the "negative set" people, those who saw all 10 problems, failed to solve it correctly. These people had such a bias to use the method they had already developed that they were unable to generate a method that would solve Problem 8 ($B - 2C - A$ does not work on this problem). Greeno's (1978) description here is useful: By repeatedly solving the first seven problems with the same formula, people learned an integrated algorithm. This algorithm was strong enough to bias their later solution attempts and prevent them from seeing the simple solution, $28 - 3 = 25$. Consistent with this idea—that if people develop a routine way of solving problems then they are more likely to experience *Einstellung*— there is evidence that experts at a task are more prone to this than others (Bilalić, McLeod, & Gobet, 2008) because they are more likely to have developed a set of routines for solving certain kinds of problems. Also, people are less likely to show mental set effects if they are given actual water jugs as compared to just paper and pencil problems (Vallée-Tourangeau, Euden, & Hearn, 2011). Moreover, if more varied initial problems are given, then people can more easily generalize their solution to a variety of other problems (e.g., Chen & Mo, 2004).

Several problems that often yield such negative set effects are presented in Table 12-2; hints to help overcome negative set, if you experience it, are at the bottom of the table. These problems lack the precision of Luchins's demonstration, of course: We cannot point to the exact equation or method that is the negative set in these problems but only to the general approach or incorrect representation people often adopt. However, they are useful in that they resemble real-world problems more closely than the rather arbitrary water jugs do.

As the slide projector problem in the introduction suggests, functional fixedness and negative set are common occurrences. The occurrence of mental set in problem solving can result from people focusing their attention on information that is consistent with an initial solution attempt for a problem, at the expensive of other possible solutions. For example, eye tracking data reveal that people look more often at information consistent with their first solution attempt than at other information (Bilalić, McLeod, & Gobet, 2010). Possibly because we eventually find an adequate solution to our everyday problems despite the negative set or without overcoming our functional fixedness (e.g., eventually locating a thinner book), we are less aware of these difficulties in our problem-solving behavior. The classic demonstrations, however, illustrate dramatically how rigid such behavior can be and how barriers to successful problem solving can arise.

TABLE 12-2 Sample Negative Set Problems

Buddhist Monk

One morning, exactly at sunrise, a Buddhist monk began to climb a tall mountain. The narrow path, no more than a foot or two wide, spiraled around the mountain to a glittering temple at the summit. The monk ascended the path at varying rates of speed, stopping many times along the way to rest and to eat the dried fruit carried with him. He reached the temple shortly before sunset. After several days of fasting and meditation, he began his journey back along the same path, starting at sunrise and again walking at variable speeds with many pauses along the way. His average descending speed was, of course, greater than his average climbing speed.

Show that there is a spot along the path that the monk will occupy on both trips at precisely the same time of day.

Drinking Glasses

Six drinking glasses are lined up in a row. The first three are full of water, the last three are empty. By handling and moving only one glass, change the arrangement so that no full glass is next to another full one, and no empty glass is next to another empty one.

Six Pennies

Show how to move only two pennies in the left diagram to yield the pattern at the right.

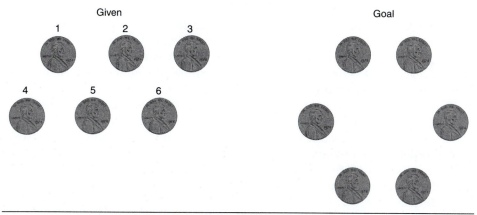

Hints

Buddhist Monk. Although the problem seems to ask for a quantitative solution, think of a way of representing the problem using visual imagery.

Drinking Glasses. How else can you handle a glass of water besides moving it to another location?

Six Pennies. From a different perspective, some of the pennies might already be in position.

Section Summary

- Cognitive psychology often studies how people solve "recreational" problems, simple brain teasers, as a way of understanding problem solving. A common kind of data collected is the verbal protocol, a transcription of the person's verbalizations as the problem is being solved.

- The early Gestalt psychologists studied problem solving and discovered two major barriers to successful performance: functional fixedness and negative set. Kohler also studied chimpanzees and found evidence for insight during problem solving.

INSIGHT AND ANALOGY

Insight

On a more positive side of problem solving are the topics of insight and problem solving by analogy. **Insight** is *a deep, useful understanding of the nature of something, especially a difficult problem.* We often include the idea that insight occurs suddenly—the "Aha!" reaction—possibly because a novel approach to the problem is taken, or a novel interpretation is made (Sternberg, 1996), or even just because you've overcome an impasse (for research on the various sources of difficulty in insight problems, see Chronicle, MacGregor, & Ormerod, 2004, and Kershaw & Ohlsson, 2004). Puzzle over the insight problems in Table 12-3 for a moment to see whether you have a sudden "Aha!" experience when you realize how to solve the problems.

Sometimes, the necessary insight for solving a problem comes from an analogy: An already-solved problem is similar to a current one, so the old solution can be adapted to the new situation. The historical example of this is the story of Archimedes, the Greek scientist who had to determine whether the king's crown was solid gold or whether some silver had been mixed with the gold. Archimedes knew the weights of both gold and silver per unit of volume but could not imagine how to measure the volume of the crown. As the anecdote goes, he stepped into his bath one day and noticed how the water level rose as he sank into the water. He then realized the solution to his problem. The volume of the crown could be determined by immersing it in water and measuring how much water it displaced. Excited by his insight, he then jumped from the bath and ran naked through the streets, shouting "Eureka! I have found it!"

Metcalfe and Wiebe (1987; also Metcalfe, 1986) studied how people solved such problems and compared that with how they solved algebra and other routine problems. They found two interesting results. First, people were rather accurate in predicting whether they'd be successful in solving routine problems but not in predicting success with insight problems. Second, solutions to the insight problems seemed to come suddenly, almost without warning. This result is shown in Figure 12-2. That is, as they worked through them, people were interrupted and asked to indicate how "warm" they were, that is, how close they felt they were to finding the solution. For routine algebra problems, "warmth" ratings grew steadily as people worked through the problems, reflecting their feeling of getting closer and closer to the solution. But there was little or no such increase for the insight problems even 15 seconds before the solution was found.

Although these results support the idea that insight arrives suddenly, insight problems can be thought of in simpler terms, say overcoming functional fixedness or negative set (as in prisoner's escape and nine-dot), taking a different perspective

TABLE 12-3 Insight Problems

Chain Links

A woman has four pieces of chain. Each piece is made up of three links. She wants to join the pieces into a single closed ring of chain. To open a link costs 2 cents and to close a link costs 3 cents. She has only 15 cents. How does she do it?

Four Trees

A landscape gardener is given instructions to plant four special trees so that each one is exactly the same distance from each of the others. How would you arrange the trees?

Prisoner's Escape

A prisoner was attempting to escape from a tower. He found in his cell a rope which was half long enough to permit him to reach the ground safely. He divided the rope in half and tied the two parts together and escaped. How could he have done this?

Bronze Coin

A stranger approached a museum curator and offered him an ancient bronze coin. The coin had an authentic appearance and was marked with the date 544 B.C. The curator had happily made acquisitions from suspicious sources before, but this time he promptly called the police and had the stranger arrested. Why?

Nine Dots

Connect the nine dots with four connected straight lines without lifting your pencil from the page as you draw.

● ● ●

● ● ●

● ● ●

Bowling Pins

The ten bowling pins below are pointing toward the top of the page. Move any three of them to make the arrangement point down toward the bottom of the page.

①

② ③

④ ⑤ ⑥

⑦ ⑧ ⑨ ⑩

Hints

Chain links. You don't have to open a link on each piece of chain.
Four trees. We don't always plant trees on flat lawns.
Prisoner's escape. Is there only one way to divide a rope in half?
Bronze coin. Imagine that you lived in 544 B.C. What did it say on your coins?
Nine dots. How long a line does the problem permit you to draw?
Bowling pins. Pins 1, 2, 3, and 5 form a diamond at the top of the drawing. Consider where the diamond might be for the arrangement that points down.

Adapted from Metcalfe (1986) and Metcalfe & Wiebe (1987).

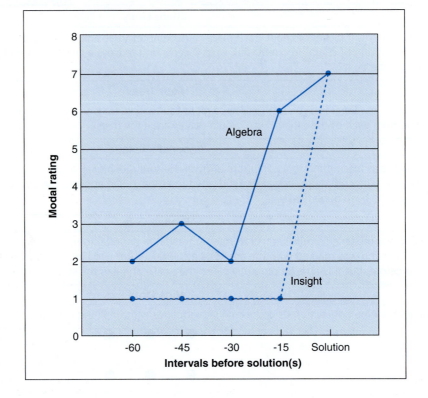

(bronze coin), and the like (Smith, 1995). A neuroimaging study by Kounios et al. (2006) provides some support for this idea. Using both electroencephalographic and functional magnetic resonance imaging recordings, they found increased cortical activity centered on the frontal lobes (particularly the anterior cingulate cortex) when people produced insight solutions as compared to normal problem solving. Kounios et al.'s theory is that this part of the frontal lobe suppresses the irrelevant information (an attentional process; see Chapter 4) that tends to dominate a person's thinking up to that point. When these dominant thoughts become suppressed, this allows more weakly activated ideas, such as those remote associations drawn by the right hemisphere, to come to the fore, possibly providing the solution to a problem. In other words, part of a person's thought processes are working on the problem along with the steps that are being worked on at the forefront of consciousness (which are going nowhere). When these dead-end thoughts are moved aside, alternative solutions can then present themselves.

This release from irrelevant modes of thinking, seen in the neuroimaging data, can be extended to a process called *incubation*. With incubation, when people have difficulty solving a problem, they may stop working on it for a while. Then at some point, the solution or key to a solution may present itself to them. Although this can work at times, it appears that incubation is most useful when people have originally been provided with misleading information, either by others or themselves, that steers them away from the correct solution. What happens during incubation is that the representations for these misleading ideas lose strength, so that later on the more successful alternatives can then present themselves (Vul & Pashler, 2007).

In some circumstances, *insight* may mean that we've drawn a critical inference that leads to a solution; for example, there's more than one way to divide a rope in half (Wickelgren, 1974). Weisberg (1995) reports that some people solve insight problems like those in the table without any of the sudden restructuring or understanding that supposedly accompanies insight.

Other evidence, however, suggests that verbalization can interfere with insight, can disrupt "nonreportable processes that are critical to achieving insight solutions" (Schooler, Ohlsson, & Brooks, 1993, p. 166). Furthermore, being unable to report the restructuring that accompanies insight, or the actual insight itself, may be more common in insight situations than we realize. For instance, Siegler and Stern (1998; see also Siegler, 2000) reported a study of second-graders solving arithmetic problems, then reporting verbally on their solutions. There was the regular computational, noninsightful way to solve the problems, which the second-graders followed, but also a shortcut way that represented an insight (e.g., for a problem like $18 + 24 - 24$, simply state 18). Almost 90% of the sample discovered the insight for solving such problems, as shown by the dramatic decrease in their solution times from around 12 seconds for the computational method to a mean of 2.7 seconds with the shortcut. However, the children were unaware of their discovery when questioned about how they solved the problems. Within another five trials, however, 80% of the children's verbal reports indicated that they were aware of their discovery.

Sometimes we can take a long time to figure out a problem, but with effort, the passage of time, and insight, we can reach sometimes stunning and novel conclusions.

Analogy

In general, an **analogy** is *a relationship between two similar situations, problems, or concepts.* Understanding an analogy means putting the two situations into some kind of alignment so that the similarities and differences are made apparent (Gentner & Markman, 1997). Take a simple example, the analogy "MERCHANT : SELL :: CUSTOMER : _____." Here, you must figure out the structure for the first pair of terms and then project or *map* that structure onto the second part of the analogy. Because "SELL" is the critical activity of "MERCHANT," the critical activity relationship is then mapped onto "CUSTOMER," and retrieval from memory yields "BUY."

Researchers argue that analogies provide excellent, widely applicable methods for solving problems. That is, if you're confronted with a difficult problem, a useful heuristic is to find a similar or related situation and build an analogy from it to the current problem. Such reasoning and problem solving may help us understand a variety of situations, such as how students should be taught in school, how people adopt professional role models, and how we empathize with others (Holyoak & Thagard, 1997; Kolodner, 1997). Furthermore, it's long been held that important scientific ideas, breakthroughs, and explanations have often depended on finding analogies—for instance, that neurotransmitters fit into the receptor sites of a neuron much the way a key fits into a lock (see Gentner & Markman, 1997, for a description of reasoning by analogy in Kepler's discovery of the laws of planetary motion). Curiously, analogical problem solving is better when people receive the information by hearing about it rather than reading it (Markman, Taylor, & Gentner, 2007), perhaps reflecting the more natural use of spoken over written language.

ANALOGY PROBLEMS To gain some feeling for analogies, read the parade story at the top of Table 12-4, a story used by Gick and Holyoak (1980). Try to solve the problem now, before reading the solution at the bottom of the table.

Gick and Holyoak had people read the parade problem, a somewhat different army fortress story, or no story at all. They then asked them to read and solve a second problem, the classic Duncker (1945) radiation problem, shown in Table 12-5 (which you should read and try to solve now).

The radiation problem is interesting for a variety of reasons, including the fact that it is rather ill defined and thus comparable to many problems in the real world. Duncker's participants produced two general approaches that led to dead

---

TABLE 12-4   The Parade Problem

A dictator ruled over a small country. He ruled from a strong fortress. The fortress was located in the center of the country, surrounded by numerous towns, villages, and farms. Like spokes on a wheel, many roads radiated out from the fortress. As part of a celebration of his glorious grab of power, this dictator demanded from one of his generals a large, over-the-top parade of his military might. The general's troops were assembled for the march in the morning, the day of the anniversary, at the end of one of these roads that led up to the dictator's fortress. At that time, the general was given a report by one of his captains that brought him up short. As commanded by the dictator, this parade needed to be far more spectacular and impressive than any other parade that had ever been seen in the land (or else). The dictator demanded that everyone in every region of the country see and hear his army at the same time. Given this demand, it seemed nearly impossible for the general to have the whole country see the parade as requested.

The Solution

The general, however, knew just what to do. He divided his army up into small groups and dispatched each group to the head of a different road. When all was ready he gave the signal, and each group marched down a different road. Each group continued down its road to the fortress, so that the entire army finally arrived together at the fortress at the same time. In this way, the general was able to have the parade seen and heard through the entire country at once, and thus please the dictator.

TABLE 12-5 Radiation and Attack Dispersion Problems

Radiation Problem

Suppose you are a doctor faced with a patient who has a malignant tumor in his stomach. It is impossible to operate on the patient, but unless the tumor is destroyed the patient will die. There is a kind of ray that can be used to destroy the tumor. If the rays reach the tumor all at once at a sufficiently high intensity, the tumor will be destroyed. Unfortunately, at this intensity the healthy tissue that the rays pass through on the way to the tumor will also be destroyed. At lower intensities the rays are harmless to healthy tissue, but they will not affect the tumor either. What type of procedure might be used to destroy the tumor with the rays without destroying the healthy tissue?

Attack Dispersion Story

A small country was controlled by a dictator. The dictator ruled the country from a strong fortress. The fortress was situated in the middle of the country, surrounded by farms and villages. Many roads radiated outward from the fortress like spokes on a wheel. A general arose who raised a large army and vowed to capture the fortress and free the country of the dictator. The general knew that if his entire army could attack the fortress at once, it could be captured. The general's troops were gathered at the head of one of the roads leading to the fortress, ready to attack. However, a spy brought the general a disturbing report. The ruthless dictator had planted mines on each of the roads. The mines were set so that small bodies of men could pass over them safely because the dictator needed to be able to move troops and workers to and from the fortress. However, any large force would detonate the mines. Not only would this blow up the road and render it impassable, but the dictator would then destroy many villages in retaliation. It therefore seemed impossible to mount a full-scale direct attack on the fortress.

Solution to the Radiation Problem

The ray can be divided into several low-intensity rays, no one of which will destroy the healthy tissue. If these several rays are positioned at different locations around the body and focused on the tumor, their effect will combine, thus being strong enough to destroy the tumor.

Solution to the Attack Dispersion Story

The general, however, knew just what to do. He divided his army up into small groups and dispatched each group to the head of a different road. When all was ready he gave the signal, and each group marched down a different road. Each group continued down its road to the fortress, so that the entire army finally arrived together at the fortress at the same time. In this way, the general was able to capture the fortress and thus overthrow the dictator.

---

ends: trying to avoid contact between the ray and nearby tissue, and trying to change the sensitivity of surrounding tissue to the effects of the ray. But the third approach, reducing the intensity of the rays, was more productive, especially if an analogy from some other, better understood situation was available.

Gick and Holyoak (1980) used this problem to study analogy. In fact, we've just simulated one of their experiments here by having you read the parade story first and then the radiation problem. In case you didn't notice, there are strong similarities between the problems, suggesting that the parade story can be used to develop an analogy for the radiation problem.

Gick and Holyoak found that 49% of people who first solved the parade problem realized it could be used as an analogy for the radiation problem. A different initial story, in which armies are attacking a fortress, provided a stronger hint about the radiation problem. Fully 76% of these participants used the attack analogy in solving the radiation problem. In contrast, only 8% of the control group, which merely attempted to solve the radiation problem, came up with the dispersion solution (i.e., multiple pathways) described at the bottom of Table 12-5.

When Gick and Holyoak provided a strong hint, telling people that the attack solution might be helpful as they worked on the radiation problem, 92% of them used the analogy, and most found it "very helpful." In contrast, only 20% of the people in the no-hint group produced the dispersion solution, even though they too had read the attack dispersion story. In short, only 20% spontaneously noticed and used the analogous relationship between the problems. Table 12-6 summarizes Gick and Holyoak's results.

MULTICONSTRAINT THEORY   Holyoak and Thagard (1997) proposed a theory of analogical reasoning and problem solving, based on such results. The theory, called the multiconstraint theory, predicts how people use analogies in problem solving and what factors govern the analogies people construct. In particular, the theory says that people are constrained by three factors when they try to use or develop analogies.

The first factor is problem similarity. There must be some degree of similarity between the already-understood situation, the *source* domain, and the current

---

TABLE 12-6   **Summary of Gick and Holyoak's (1980) Results**

Study 1 (Experiment II originally; after Gick & Holyoak, Table 10)

People in groups *A* and *B* are given a general hint that their solution to one of the earlier stories may be useful in solving the radiation problem.

Group	Order of Stories	Percentage of People Who Used the Analogy on the Radiation Problem
Group *A*	Parade, radiation	49%
Group *B*	Attack dispersion, radiation	76%
Group *C*	No story, radiation	8%

Study 2 (Experiment IV originally)

People in group *A* are given the general hint (as above). People in group *B* are given no hint whatsoever.

Group	Order of Stories	Percentage of People Who Used the Analogy on the Radiation Problem
Group *A* (hint)	Attack dispersion, radiation	92%
Group *B* (no hint)	Attack dispersion, radiation	20%

problem, the *target* domain. In the parade story, for example, the fortress and troops are similar to the tumor and the rays. Similarity between source and target has been shown to be important. Chen, Mo, and Honomichl (2004), for example, found that similarities from well-known folk tales to new problems were especially important for finding problem solutions, even if participants did not report remembering the folk tale. Alternatively, Novick (1988) found that novices focus especially on similarities, even when they are only superficial, which can interfere with performance.

The second factor is problem structure. People must find a parallel structure between the source and target problems to map elements from the source to elements in the target. Figuring out these correspondences or mappings is important because it corresponds to working out the relationships of the analogy. In the parade–radiation analogy, you have to map troops onto rays so that the important relationship of different converging roads can serve as the basis for the solution. The most prominent mappings from parade to radiation are shown in Figure 12-3. It turns out that mapping the relations is hard; for instance, in a dual-task setting, Waltz, Lau, Grewal, and Holyoak (2000) found that holding on to a working memory load seriously reduced the ability to find correct mappings between two problems. Also, Bassok, Pedigo, and Oskarsson (2008) found that the semantic memory can interfere with drawing analogies. For example, when people are doing addition-based word problems, making the analogy between the word problem and addition was easier when items are semantically similar, such as *tulips* and *daisies* (which are separate things that can easily be added together), but not when there is an inconsistency, such as *records* and *songs*. In this case, the knowledge that songs are parts of records implies a hierarchical, part-whole relationship, so it is more difficult to make the additional analogy where is it easier to think of things that can be treated on more equal footing.

The third factor that constrains people is the purpose of the analogy. The person's goals, and the goal stated in the problem, are important. This is deeper

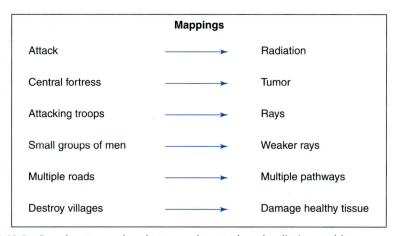

FIGURE 12-3 Prominent mappings between the attack and radiation problems.

than merely the general purpose of trying to solve the problem. Notice that the goals in the attack and radiation stories match, whereas the goals do not match for parade and radiation (parade involves sending troops *out* from the central fortress, for display purposes, but radiation involves sending rays *in* toward the tumor). This mismatch may have been responsible for the low use of parade as a source for the analogy to radiation. Likewise, Spellman and Holyoak (1996) report a study in which college students drew analogies between two soap opera plots. When different purposes or goals were given in the instructions, the students developed different analogies; that is, their problem solving by analogy was sensitive to purposes and overall goals. Kurtz and Loewenstein (2007) reported that people are more likely to draw on analogies from previous problems when they are comparing two other problems than if they are working on a single problem alone. This suggests that the processing goals and tactics, in this case direct comparison, in use can influence whether people actually use analogies or not.

A final point is that most of the work on analogy, like many studies of problem solving, has focused on the conscious, explicit use of analogies. However, there is some evidence to suggest that people may use analogies in a more unconscious, implicit manner as well. In a study by Day and Gentner (2007), people were given pairs of texts to read. When the events described by the second text were analogous to those described in the first (in terms of their relational structure), people read the second text faster. That is, people were able to use their unconscious knowledge of the event structure from the first text to help them understand the second text. When asked, people showed no awareness of this relationship between the two texts. So, in some sense, by having people read the first text, the relational structure of the event was primed, and this made the processing of the second text easier.

Neurocognition in Analogy and Insight

Some exciting work has been reported on the cognitive neuropsychology of analogical reasoning and insight. Wharton et al. (2000) identified brain regions that are associated with the mapping process in analogical reasoning. In their study, people saw a source picture of geometric shapes, followed by a target picture. They had to judge whether the target picture was an analog pattern—whether it had the same system of relations as the source picture. In the control condition, they judged whether the target was literally the same as the source. See Figure 12-4 for sample stimuli. In the top stimulus, the correct target preserves both the spatial relations in the source (a shape in all four quadrants) and the object relations (the patterned figures on the main diagonal are the same shape, and the shapes on the minor diagonal are different). Response times to analogy trials were in the 1,400 to 1,500 ms range and approximately 900 to 1,000 ms in the literal condition; accuracy was at or above 90% in both kinds of trials.

But the stunning result came from positron emission tomography (PET) scan images that were taken. Wharton et al. found significant activation in the medial frontal cortex, left prefrontal cortex, and left inferior parietal cortex.

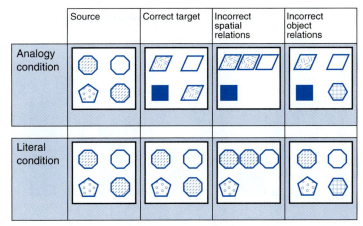

FIGURE 12-4 A depiction of analogy condition and literal condition trials. The first column shows the source stimuli, the second shows the correct choice, and the third and fourth show incorrect choices for the stated reasons.

From Wharton et al. (2000), Figure 2, p. 179.

Explore *Intuition and Discovery in Problem Solving* in **MyPsychLab**

In contrast, Bowden and Beeman (1998; Beeman & Bowden, 2000) found a significant role for *right* hemisphere processing in solving insight problems. Before reading further, try this demonstration:

> *What one word can form a compound word or phrase with each of the following? Palm Shoe House*

> *What one word can form a compound word or phrase with each of the following? Pie Luck Belly?*

People were given such word triples—called "compound remote associates"—and had to think of a fourth word that combines with each of the three initial words to yield a familiar word pair. On many trials, people fail to find an immediate solution and end up spending considerable time working on the problem. They also report that when they finally solve the problems, the solution came to them as an insight—an "Aha!" type of solution.

In the Bowden and Beeman (1998) study, people saw the problems and then after 15 seconds were asked to name a new word that appeared on the screen (if they solved the problem before the 15-second period was up, they were given the word immediately). When the target word was unrelated to the three words seen before (e.g., "planet"), there was the typical effect—that targets presented to the right visual field, hence the left hemisphere of the brain, were named faster than those presented to the left visual field–right hemisphere. But when the target was the word that solved the insight problem (*tree* in the first problem, *pot* in the second one), there was a significant priming effect. As shown in Figure 12-5, naming time was shorter for the solution words than for the unrelated words. And the priming effect—the drop-off from "unrelated" to "solution"—was greater for targets presented to the right hemisphere than to the left (in other words, presented to the left visual field so going first to the right hemisphere).

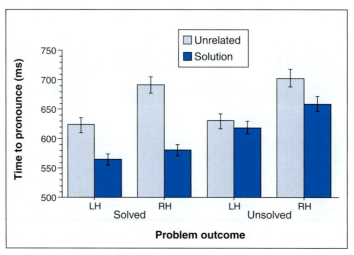

FIGURE 12-5 Mean naming time (time to pronounce) the target word for solved and unsolved trials. Bars labeled LH refer to target words presented to the right visual field, left hemisphere of the brain; RH means left visual field, right hemisphere. The figure shows priming effects for solution words, especially in the right hemisphere.

From Bowden & Beeman (1998).

Putting it differently, semantic priming in the right hemisphere was more prominent than in the left hemisphere for these problems: People were faster to name *pot* when it was presented to the right hemisphere, presumably because it had been primed by the initial three words. As the authors noted, these results fit nicely with other results concerning the role in language comprehension that the right hemisphere plays (you read about this in Chapter 10), especially the part having to do with drawing inferences (Bowden, Beeman, & Gernsbacher, 1995).

Section Summary

- Insight is a deep understanding of a situation or problem, often thought to occur suddenly and without warning. Although there is some debate on the nature of insight, insights may be discovered and used unconsciously and only later be available to consciousness.
- Reasoning by analogy is a complex kind of problem solving in which relationships in one situation are mapped onto another. People are better at developing analogies if given a useful source problem and an explicit hint that the problem might be used in solving a target problem. Holyoak and Thagard's multiconstraint theory of analogical problem solving claims that we work under three constraints as we develop analogies: constraints related to the similarity of the source and target domains, the structure of the problems, and our purposes or goals in developing the analogies.
- Some new evidence suggests a particularly important role for the left frontal and parietal lobes in solving problems by analogy and a right hemisphere role in insight problems involving semantic priming.

BASICS OF PROBLEM SOLVING

Compared to the Gestalt tradition, modern cognitive psychology has adopted a more reductionistic approach to the study of problem solving. For instance, Newell and Simon's analysis of a cryptarithmetic problem (1972, Chapter 6) is a microscopic analysis and interpretation of every statement made by one person as he solved a problem, all 2,186 words and 20 or so minutes of problem-solving activity. In Newell and Simon's (1972) description, "A person is confronted with a *problem* when he wants something and does not know immediately what series of actions he can perform to get it" (p. 72). The "something" can be renamed for more general use as a **goal**, *the desired end-point of the problem-solving activity*. Problem solving consists of goal-directed activity, moving from some initial configuration or state through a series of intermediate steps until finally the overall goal has been reached: an adequate or correct solution. The difficulty is determining which intermediate states are on a correct pathway ("Will step *A* get me to step *B* or not?") and in devising operations or moves that achieve those intermediate states ("How do I get to step *B* from here?").

Characteristics of Problem Solving

Let's start by listing several characteristics that define what is and is not a genuine instance of problem solving. Anderson (1980, 1985), for example, lists the following:

- **Goal directedness.** The overall activity we're examining is directed toward achieving some goal or purpose. As such, we exclude daydreaming, for instance; it's mental, but it's not goal directed. Alternatively, if you've locked your keys in your car, both physical and mental activity are going on. The goal-directed nature of those activities, your repeated attempts to get into the locked car, makes this an instance of true problem solving.
- **Sequence of operations.** An activity must have a sequence of operations or steps to be problem solving. A simple retrieval from memory, say, remembering that 2×3 is 6, is not problem solving because it is not a slow, discernible sequence of separate operations. Alternatively, doing a long-division problem or solving the locked-car problem definitely involves a sequence of mental operations, so these are instances of problem solving.
- **Cognitive operations.** Solving the problem involves the application of various cognitive operations. Various operators can be applied to different problems, where each operator is a distinct cognitive act, a permissible step or move in the problem space. For long division, retrieving an answer would be an operator, as would be subtracting or multiplying two numbers at some other stage in problem solution. Often, the cognitive operations have a behavioral counterpart, some physical act that completes the mental operation, such as writing down a number during long division.
- **Subgoal decomposition.** As implied by the third characteristic, each step in the sequence of operations is itself a kind of goal, a **subgoal**. A subgoal is *an intermediate goal along the route to eventual solution of the problem*. Subgoals represent the decomposition, or breaking apart, of the overall goal into separate components. In many instances, subgoals themselves must be

further decomposed into smaller subgoals. Thus solving a problem involves breaking the overall goal into subgoals, then pursuing the subgoals, and *their* subgoals, one after another until the final solution is achieved. This yields a hierarchical or nested structure to the problem-solving attempt.

An intuitive illustration of such a nested solution structure is presented in Figure 12-6, a possible solution route to the locked-car problem. Note that during the solution, the first two plans led to barriers or blocks, thus requiring that another plan be devised (much like the radiation problem). The problem solver finally decided on another plan, breaking a window to get into the locked car. This decision is followed by a sequence of related acts: the search for some heavy object that will break a window, the decision as to which window to break, and so forth. Each of these decisions is a subgoal nested within the larger subgoal of breaking into the car, itself a subgoal in the overall solution structure.

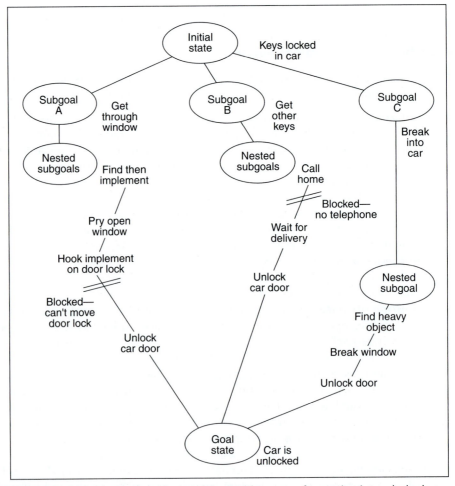

FIGURE 12-6 A representation of part of the problem space for getting into a locked car. Note the barriers encountered under plans *A* and *B*.

A Vocabulary of Problem Solving

These four characteristics define what qualifies as problem solving. Many important ideas are embedded in these four points, however. Let's reexamine some of these points, looking now toward an expanded vocabulary of problem solving, a set of terms we use to describe and understand how people solve problems.

THE PROBLEM SPACE   The term *problem space* is critical. Anderson (1985) defines it as the various states or conditions that are possible. More concretely, the **problem space** includes *the initial, intermediate, and goal states of the problem. It also includes the problem solver's knowledge at each of these steps,* both knowledge that is currently being applied and knowledge that could be retrieved from memory and applied. Any external devices, objects, or resources that are available can also be included in the description of the problem space. Thus, a difficult arithmetic problem that must be completed mentally has a different problem space than the same problem as completed with pencil and paper.

To illustrate, VanLehn (1989) describes one man's error in the "three men and a rowboat" problem. The man focused only on the arithmetic of the problem and said essentially "400 pounds of people, 200 pounds per trip, it'll take two trips of the boat." When he was reminded that the boat couldn't row itself back to the original side, he adopted a different problem space.

In some problem contexts, we can speak of problem solving as a search of the problem space or, metaphorically, a search of the solution tree, in which each branch and twig represents a possible pathway from the initial state of the problem. For problems that are "wide open," that is, those with many possibilities that must be checked, there may be no alternative but to start searching the problem space, node by node, until some barrier or block is reached. As often as not, however, there is information in the problem that permits us to restrict the search space to a manageable size. Metaphorically, this information permits us to *prune* the search tree.

A general depiction of this is in Figure 12-7. The initial state of the problem is the top node, and the goal state is some terminal node at the bottom. For "wide open" problems, each branch may need to be searched until a dead end is encountered. For other problems, information may be inferred that permits a restriction in the branches that are searched (the shaded area of the figure). Clearly, if the search space can be restricted by pruning off the dead-end branches, then problem-solving efficiency is increased.

THE OPERATORS   **Operators** are *the set of legal moves that can be done during problem solution.* The term *legal* means permissible in the rules of the problem. For example, an illegal operator in the six-penny problem of Table 12-2 would be to move more than two pennies. In "three men and a rowboat," an illegal operator is having the men swim across the river or loading the boat with too heavy a load.

For transformation problems (Greeno, 1978), applying an operator transforms the problem into a new or revised state from which further work can be done. In general, a legal operator moves you from one node to the next along

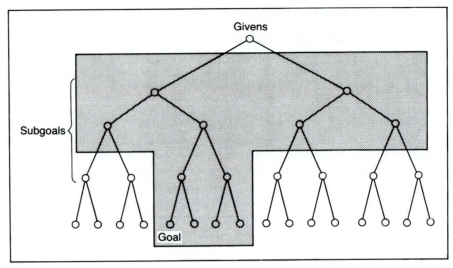

FIGURE 12-7 A general diagram of a problem space, with various branches of the space illustrated. Often a hint or an inference can prune the search tree, restricting the search to just one portion; this idea is represented by the shaded area of the figure. Note that, in most problems, the problem space tree is much larger, so the beneficial effect of pruning is far greater.

Adapted from Wickelgren (1974).

some connecting pathway in the search space. For instance, in solving algebraic equations, one transformation operator is "move the unknowns to the left." Thus for the equation $2X + 7 = X + 10$, applying the operator would move the single X to the left of the equal sign by subtracting X from both sides of the equation.

Often, constraints within the problem prevent us from applying certain operators. In a vague way, the destruction of healthy tissue was such a constraint in the radiation problem. That constraint prevented the simple solution of applying the ray directly, where direct application would be a simple operator. In algebra, by contrast, constraints are imposed by the rules of algebra; for example, you can't subtract X from one side of the equation without subtracting it from the other side, too.

THE GOAL The goal is the ultimate destination or solution to the problem. For recreational problems in particular, the goal is typically stated explicitly in the problem. Given that recreational problems usually present *an explicit and complete specification of the initial and goal states,* we call them as **well-defined problems**. Solutions involve progressing through the legal intermediate states, by means of known operators, until the goal is reached. In contrast, in **ill-defined problems,** *the states, operators, or both may be only vaguely specified.* For instance, the Buddhist monk problem in Table 12-2 states a vague goal ("Show that there is a spot . . ."). Likewise, problems with more real-world character often are distressingly vague in their specification of the goal ("write a term paper that will earn you an *A,*" "write a computer program that does *X* in as economical and elegant a fashion as possible," and so on).

AN EXAMPLE: DONALD + GERALD Let's consider one recreational problem, to pin down some of these terms and ideas. The problem is a cryptarithmetic problem, in which letters of the alphabet have been substituted for the digits in an addition problem. Your task is to reverse the substitutions—to figure out which digits go with which letters to yield a correct addition problem. The restriction is that the digits and letters must be in one-to-one correspondence (only one digit per letter and vice versa). Plan on spending 15 minutes or so, about the amount of time it takes people on their first attempt. Make notes on paper as you work so you can go back later to retrace and analyze your attempt to solve the problem. (Incidentally, this is the cryptarithmetic problem Newell and Simon's single person worked on.)

$$DONALD \quad \quad (Hint: D = 5)$$
$$+ \; GERALD$$
$$\overline{ROBERT}$$

Now that you've worked on the problem and have found (or come close to) the solution, we can use the insights you developed to fill in our definitions of terms. To begin with, the initial state consists of the statement of the problem, including the rules, restrictions, and hint you are given. These, along with your own knowledge of arithmetic (and pencil and paper), are your problem-solving tools. Each conceivable assignment of letters to digits makes up the problem space, and each substitution operator you might apply constitutes a branch or pathway on the search tree (a substitution operator here is an operator that substitutes a digit for a letter). Like the shaded area of Figure 12-7, the hint $D = 5$ prunes the search tree by a tremendous amount. Without the hint, you can only start working on the problem by trying arbitrary assignments, then working until an error shows up, then returning to an earlier node and reassigning the letters to different digits. (Even without the hint, however, there is only one solution.)

You no doubt started working on the problem by replacing the Ds in the 1s column with 5s, then immediately replacing the T with a 0. You also probably wrote a 1 above the 10s column, for the carry operation from $5 + 5$. A quick scan revealed one more D that could be rewritten. Note that the position you were in at this point, with three Ds and a T converted to digits, is a distinct step in the solution, an intermediate state in the problem, a node in the problem space. Furthermore, each substitution you made reflected the application of an operator, a cognitive operation that transforms the problem to a different intermediate state.

As you continued to work, you were forced to infer information as a way of making progress. For instance, in working on the 10s column, $L + L +$ the carried 1, you can infer that R is an odd number because any number added to itself and augmented by 1 yields an odd number. Likewise, you can infer from the $D + G$ column that R must be in the range 5 to 9 and that $5 + G$ can't produce a carried 1. Putting these together, R must be a large odd number, and G must be 4 or less. Each of these separate inferences, each mental conclusion you draw, is also an instance of a cognitive operation, a simple mental process or operator

TABLE 12-7 Intermediate

State	Known Values	Reasons and Statements from Protocol
1 5ONAL5 <u>GERAL5</u> ROBERØ	Ø123456789 T D R is odd	Because D is 5, then T = Ø, and carry a 1 to the next column. So the first column is 5 + something = odd because L + L + 1 = R will make R odd
	G is less than 5 R is odd and greater than 5	R must be bigger than 5 because less than 5 would yield a two-digit sum in the D + G column and there would be an extra column in the answer. G is less than 5.
1 1 5ONAL5 <u>G9RA15</u> ROB9RØ	Ø123456789 T D E G is less than 5 R is odd, greater than 5	O + E is next. If E were Ø, it would be fine, but T is already Ø So this column must have a carry brought to it. This means that E must be 9, so that the O + 9 + the carried 1 = O.
1 11 5ONAL5 <u>G9RAL5</u> ROB9RØ		If E = 9, then A + A must have a carry brought to it, so then the A + A + the carried 1 = 9. 4 would work for A and so would 9, but 9 is already taken
1 11 5ON4L5 <u>G9R4L5</u> ROB9RØ	Ø123456789 T AD E R is odd, greater than 5 G is less than 5 L is greater than 5	So A has to be 4. So L + L + the carried 1 has to produce a carry, so L is greater than 5. 5 and 9 are taken.
1 11 5ON4L5 <u>G974L5</u> 7OB97Ø	Ø123456789 T AD R E G is less than 5, L is greater than 5	So the odd R must be 7. Because L + L yields a carry, L isn't 3.
11 11 5ON485 <u>G97485</u> 7OB97Ø	Ø123456789 T AD RLE N is greater than or equal to 3 G is less than 5	L must be 8 because 8 + 8 + 1 = 17. That only leaves O, N, G, and B. Because O + 9 needs a carry, N + 7 has to yield a carry. So N has to be at least 3.
11 11 5ON485 <u>197485</u> 7OB97Ø	Ø123456789 TG AD RLE N is greater than or equal to 3	So G looks like 1. That leaves O, N, and B, for 2, 3, and 6. N can't be 3 because B can't be the Ø in 3 + 7 = 1Ø And it can't be 2 because 2 + 7 = 9 and the 9 is taken.
11 11 5O6485 <u>197485</u> 7O397Ø	Ø123456789 TGBADNRLE	That leaves N to be 6, so that makes B = 3.
11 11 526485 <u>197485</u> 723970	Ø123456789 TGOBADNRLE	So O has to be 2. Check the addition.

A sample solution of the DONALD problem, showing intermediate states, known values, and an edited protocol. (Zero is drawn with the slash, Ø, to distinguish it from the letter O.)

TABLE 12-8 Additional Cryptarithmetic Problems

6.	CROSS	7.	LETS	8.	SEND
	+ ROADS		+ WAVE		+ MORE
	DANGER		LATER		MONEY
Hint: $R = 6$					

that composes a step in the problem-solving sequence. Each of these, further-more, accomplishes progress toward the immediate subgoal, find out about *L*.

Greeno (1978) calls this process a constructive search. Rather than blindly assigning digits and trying them out, people usually draw inferences from the other columns and use those to limit the possible values the letters can take. This approach is typical in arrangement problems, the third of Greeno's categories, in which some combination of the given components must be found that satisfies the constraints in the problem. In other kinds of arrangement problems, say anagrams, a constructive search heuristic would be to look for spelling patterns and form candidate words from those familiar units. The opposite approach, sometimes known as generate and test, merely uses some scheme to generate all possible arrangements, then tests those one by one to determine whether the problem solution has been found.

A related aspect of problem solving here (it can be postponed, but your solution will be more organized if it's done now) is quite general and almost con-stitutes good advice rather than an essential feature of performance. Some mecha-nism or system for keeping track of the information you know about the letters is needed, if only to prevent you from forgetting inferences you've already drawn. Indeed, such an external memory aid can go a long way toward making your problem solving more efficient. In some instances it may even help you generalize from one problem variant to another (as in the next example, the Tower of Hanoi problem). Table 12-7 presents a compressed verbal protocol of the solution to the DONALD problem, which you might want to compare with your own solution pathway. The table also shows intermediate steps and a notational system for keeping track of known values. Table 12-8 presents more cryptarithmetic prob-lems that you might want to solve.

Section Summary

- We are solving a problem when our behavior is goal directed and involves a sequence of cognitive steps or stages. The sequence involves separate cognitive operations, where each goal or subgoal can be decomposed into separate, smaller subgoals. The overall problem, including our knowledge, is called the problem space, within which we apply operators, draw infer-ences, and conduct a constructive search for moves that bring us closer to the goal.

MEANS–END ANALYSIS: A FUNDAMENTAL HEURISTIC

Several problem solving heuristics have been discovered and investigated. You've already read about analogy, and the final section of the chapter illustrates several others. But in terms of overall significance, no other heuristic comes close to means–end analysis. This formed the basis for Newell and Simon's groundbreaking work (1972), including their very first presentation of the information-processing framework in 1956 (on the "day cognitive psychology was born"; see footnote 2 in Chapter 1). Because it shaped the entire area and the theories devised to account for problem solving, it deserves special attention.

The Basics of Means–End Analysis

In this **means–end analysis** approach, *the problem is solved by repeatedly determining the difference between the current state and the goal or subgoal state, then finding and applying an operator that reduces this difference.* Means–end analysis nearly always implies the use of subgoals because achieving the goal state usually involves the intermediate steps of achieving several subgoals along the way.

The basic notions of a means–end analysis can be summarized in a sequence of five steps:

1. *Set up a goal or subgoal.*
2. *Look for a difference between the current state and the goal or subgoal state.*
3. *Look for an operator that will reduce or eliminate this difference. One such operator is the setting of a new subgoal.*
4. *Apply the operator.*
5. *Apply steps 2 through 4 repeatedly until all subgoals and the final goal are achieved.*

At an intuitive level, means–end analysis and subgoals are familiar and represent "normal" problem solving. If you have to write a term paper for class, you break the overall goal down into a series of subgoals: Select a topic, find relevant material, read and understand the material, and so on. Each of these may contain its own subgoals.

The Tower of Hanoi

The most thoroughly investigated problems are the missionary–cannibals problem in Table 12-9 (it's also known as the Hobbits–Orcs problem) and the Tower of

---

TABLE 12-9   The Missionary–Cannibal Problem

Three missionaries and three cannibals are on one side of a river and need to cross to the other side. The only means of crossing is a boat, and the boat can hold only two people at a time. Devise a set of moves that will transport all six people across the river, bearing in mind the following constraint: The number of cannibals can never exceed the number of missionaries in any location, for the obvious reason. Remember that someone will have to row the boat back across each time.

Hint: At one point in your solution, you will have to send more people back to the original side than you just sent over to the destination.

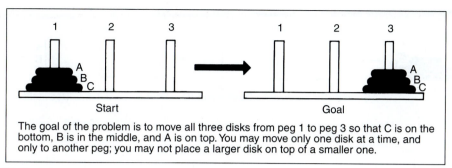

The goal of the problem is to move all three disks from peg 1 to peg 3 so that C is on the bottom, B is in the middle, and A is on top. You may move only one disk at a time, and only to another peg; you may not place a larger disk on top of a smaller one.

FIGURE 12-8   The Tower of Hanoi problem.

Hanoi problem in Figure 12-8. These problems show clearly the strengths and limitations of the means–end approach.

THE THREE-DISK VERSION   Work on the Tower of Hanoi problem carefully, using the three-disk version in the figure. Try to keep track of your solution so you'll understand how it demonstrates the usefulness of a means–end analysis. So that you'll be familiar with the problem and be able to reflect on your solution, do it several times again after you've solved it. See whether you can become skilled at solving the three-disk problem by remembering your solution and being able to generate it repeatedly. (By the way, an excellent heuristic for this problem is to solve it physically; draw the pegs on a piece of paper and move three coins of different sizes around to find the solution.)

Having done that, consider your solution in terms of subgoals and means–end analysis. Your goal, as stated in the problem, is to move the *ABC* stack of disks from peg 1 to peg 3. Applying the means–end analysis, your first step sets up this goal. The second step reveals a difficulty: There is a difference between your current state and the goal, simply the difference between the starting and ending configurations. You look for a method or operator that reduces this difference and then apply it. As you no doubt learned from your solution, your first major subgoal is "Clear off disk *C.*" This entails getting *B* off *C,* which entails another subgoal, getting *A* off *B.*

The next step involves a simple operator that satisfies the most immediate subgoal, "Move *A* to 3," which permits satisfying the next subgoal, "getting *B* off *C.*" So the next operator is "move *B* to 2"; it can't go on top of *A* (rule violation), and it can't stay on top of *C* because that prevents achieving a subgoal. Now peg 3 can be cleared by moving *A* to 2. This allows the major subgoal to be accomplished, putting *C* on 3.

From here, it's easy to see the final route to solution: "unpack" *A* from 2, putting it temporarily on 1, move *B* to 3, then move *A* to 3. The seven moves that solve the problem are shown in Figure 12-9.

THE FOUR-DISK VERSION   After you've done the problem several times, solving it becomes easy. You come to see how each disk must move to get *C* on 3, then *B,* and finally *A.* Spend some time now on the same problem but use four disks

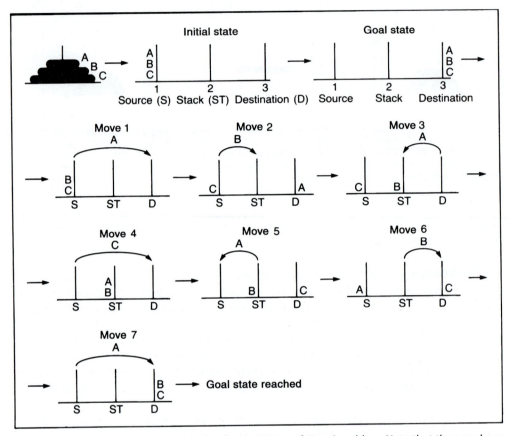

FIGURE 12-9 The seven-step solution for the Tower of Hanoi problem. Note that the pegs have been renamed as "Source," "Stack," and "Destination." Moving the three disks takes seven moves. Consider these seven moves as one unit, called "moving a pyramid of three disks."

instead of three. Don't work on this version blindly, however. Think of it as a variation on the three-disk problem, where parts of the new solution are "old." As a hint, try renaming the pegs as the source peg, the stack peg, and the destination peg. Furthermore, think of the seven moves not as seven discrete steps but as a single chunk, "moving a pyramid of three disks," which should help you see the relationships between the problems more clearly (Simon, 1975). According to Catrambone (1996), almost any label attached to a sequence of moves probably will help you remember the sequence better.

What did you discover as you solved the four-disk problem? Most people come to realize that the four-disk problem has two three-disk problems embedded in it, separated by the bridging move of *D* to 3. That is, to free *D* so it can move to peg 3 you must first move the top three disks out of the way, moving a "pyramid of three disks," getting *D* to peg 3 on the eighth move. Then the *ABC* pyramid has to move again to get them on top of *D*—another seven moves. Moving the disks entails the same order of moves as in the simpler problem, although the pegs take on different functions: For the four-disk problem, peg 2 serves as the destination for the first half of the solution, then as the source for the last half. The entire

FIGURE 12-10 The four-disk Tower of Hanoi problem, with solution. The variation from the three-disk version is that the pegs must switch roles. In the beginning, the subgoal is to move a pyramid of three disks so that *D* can move to peg 3. After that, the subgoal again is to move a three-disk pyramid. In both the first and second halves, the pegs must switch roles for the problem to be solved.

scheme of 15 moves is illustrated in Figure 12-10. Because the three-disk solution is embedded in the four-disk problem—and, likewise, the four-disk solution is embedded in the five-disk problem—this is known as a recursive problem, where *recursive* simply means that simpler components are embedded in the more difficult versions.

General Problem Solver

Means–end analysis was an early focus of research on problem solving, largely because of early work by Newell, Shaw, and Simon (1958; Ernst & Newell, 1969; Newell & Simon, 1972). Their computer simulation was called **general problem solver (GPS)**. This program was *the first genuine computer simulation of problem-solving behavior.* It was a general-purpose, problem-solving program, not limited to just one kind of problem but widely applicable to a large class of problems in which means–end analysis was appropriate. Newell and Simon ran their simulation on various logical proofs, on the missionary–cannibal problem, on the Tower of Hanoi, and on many other problems to demonstrate its generality. (Notice the critical analogy here. Newell and Simon drew an analogy between the way computer programs solve problems and the way humans do: Human mental processes are of a symbolic nature, so the computer's manipulation of symbols is a fruitful analogy to those processes. This was a stunningly provocative and useful analogy for the science of cognition.)

PRODUCTION SYSTEMS An important characteristic of GPS was its formulation as a production system model, essentially the first such model proposed in psychology. A **production** is a pair of statements, called either *a condition–action pair or an if–then pair.* In such a scheme, if the production's conditions are satisfied, the action part of the pair takes place. In the GPS application to the Tower of Hanoi, three sample productions might be

1. *If the destination peg is clear and the largest disk is free, then move the largest disk to the destination peg.*
2. *If the largest disk is not free, then set up a subgoal to free it.*
3. *If a subgoal to free the largest disk is set up and a smaller disk is on it, then move the smaller disk to the stack peg.*

Such an analysis suggests a very "planful" solution by GPS: Setting up a goal and subgoals that achieve the goal sounds exactly like what we call planning. And indeed, such planning characterizes both people's and GPS's solutions to problems, not just the Tower of Hanoi but all kinds of transformation problems. GPS had what amounted to a planning mechanism, a mechanism that abstracted the essential features of situations and goals then devised a plan that would produce a problem-solving sequence

PROVE IT

The problems you've been solving throughout the chapter can be used without change to demonstrate the principles of problem solving. Here are some interesting contrasts and effects you might want to test.

Compare either the time or number of moves people make in learning and mastering the Tower of Hanoi problem when the pegs are labeled *1*, *2*, and *3* and when they are labeled *source*, *stack*, and *destination*. Try drawing the pegs in a triangular pattern rather than in a left-to-right display to see whether that makes the "stack" peg idea more salient. Compare how long it takes to master the problem when your participants learn to do it by moving three coins around on paper and when they keep track of their moves mentally.

of moves. Provided with such a mechanism and the particular representational system necessary to encode the problem and the legal operators, GPS yielded an output that resembles the solution pathways taken by human problem solvers.

LIMITATIONS OF GPS Later investigators working with the general principles of GPS found some cases when the model did not do a good job of characterizing human problem solving. Consider the missionary–cannibal problem in Table 12-9; the solution pathway is presented in Figure 12-11. The problem is difficult, most people find, at step 6, where the only legal move is to return one missionary and one cannibal back to the original side of the river. Having just brought two missionaries over, this return trip seems to be moving away from the overall goal. That is, returning one missionary and one cannibal seems to be incorrect because it appears to increase the distance to the goal: It's the only return trip that moves two characters back to the original side. Despite the fact that this is the only available move (other than returning the same two missionaries who just came over), people have difficulty in selecting this move (Thomas, 1974).

GPS did not have this difficulty because sending one missionary and one cannibal back was consistent with its immediate subgoal. On the other hand, at step 10, GPS is trying to fulfill its subgoal of getting the last cannibal to the destination side and seemingly can't let go of this subgoal. People, however, realize that this subgoal should be abandoned: Anyone can row back over to bring the last cannibal across and in the process finish the problem (Greeno, 1974). GPS was simply too rigid in its application of the means–end heuristic, however: It tried to bring the last cannibal across and then send the boat back again.

BEYOND GPS Newell and Simon's GPS model, and models based on it, often provided a good description of human problem-solving performance (Atwood &

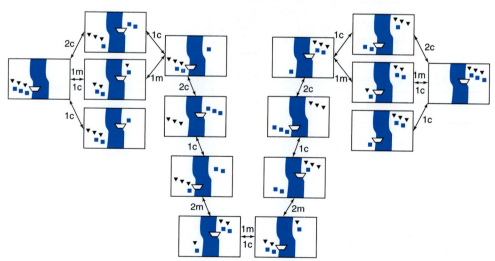

FIGURE 12-11 An illustration of the steps needed to solve the missionary–cannibal problem. The left half of each box is the "start side" of the river, and the right half is the "destination side." The numbers and letters next to the arrows represent who is traveling on the boat.

Based on Glass & Holyoak (1986).

Polson, 1976) and provided a set of predictions against which new experimental results could be compared (Greeno, 1974). Despite some limitations (Hayes & Simon, 1974), the model demonstrated the importance of means–end analysis for an understanding of human problem solving.

Section Summary

- The best-known heuristic for problem solving is means–end analysis, in which the problem solver cycles between determining the difference between the current and goal states and applying legal operators to reduce that difference. The importance of subgoals is revealed most clearly in problems such as the Tower of Hanoi.
- Newell and Simon's general problem solver (GPS) was the earliest cognitive theory of problem solving, implemented as a computer simulation. Studying GPS and comparing its performance with human problem solving showed the importance of means–end analysis.

IMPROVING YOUR PROBLEM SOLVING

Sprinkled through the chapter have been hints and suggestions about how to improve your problem solving. Some of these were based on empirical research and some on intuitions that people have had about problem solving. Let's close the chapter by pulling these hints and suggestions together and offering a few new ones. Table 12-10 provides a list of these suggestions.

Increase Your Domain Knowledge

In thinking about what makes problems difficult, Simon suggests that the likeliest factor is **domain knowledge,** what one knows about the topic. Not surprisingly,

---

TABLE 12-10 Suggestions for Improving Problem Solving

Increase your domain knowledge.

Automate some components of the problem-solving solution.

Follow a systematic plan.

Draw inferences.

Develop subgoals.

Work backward.

Search for contradictions.

Search for relations between problems.

Find a different problem representation.

Stay calm.

If all else fails, try practice.

---

a person who has only limited knowledge or familiarity with a topic is less able to solve problems efficiently in that domain (but see Wiley, 1998, on some disadvantages of too much domain knowledge). In contrast, extensive domain knowledge leads to expertise, a fascinating topic in its own right (see Ericsson & Charness, 1994, and Medin, Lynch, Coley, & Atran, 1997, for example).

Much of the research supporting this comes from Simon's work with chess (Chase & Simon, 1973; Gobet & Simon, 1996; see also Reeves & Weisberg, 1993). In several studies of chess masters, an important but not surprising result was obtained: Chess masters need only a glimpse of the arrangement of chess pieces to remember the arrangement, far beyond what novices or players of moderate skill can do. This advantage holds, however, only when the pieces are in legal locations (i.e., sensible within the context of a real game of chess). When the locations of the pieces are random, then there is no advantage for the skilled players. This advantage of expertise in remembering legal board positions is attributed to experts' more skilled perceptual encoding of the board, literally more efficient eye movements and fixations while looking at the board (Reingold, Charness, Pomplun, & Stampe, 2001).

Automate Some Components of the Problem-Solving Solution

A second connection also exists between the question, "What makes problems difficult?" and the topics you've already studied. Kotovsky, Hayes, and Simon (1985) tested adults on various forms of the Tower of Hanoi problem and also on problem isomorphs, problems with the same form but different details. Their results showed that a heavy working memory load was a serious impediment to successful problem solving: If the person had to hold three or four nested subgoals in working memory all at once, performance deteriorated.

Thus, a solution to this memory load problem was to automate the rules that govern moves, just as you were supposed to master and automate the seven-step sequence in the Tower of Hanoi. This frees working memory to be used for higher-level subgoals (Carlson, Khoo, Yaure, & Schneider, 1990). This is the same reasoning you encountered early in the book, where automatic processing uses few if any of the limited conscious resources of working memory.

Follow a Systematic Plan

Especially in long, multistep problems, it's important to follow a systematic plan (Bransford & Stein, 1993; Polya, 1957). Although this seems straight-forward, people do not always generate plans when solving problems, although doing so can dramatically improve performance (Delany, Ericsson, & Knowles, 2004). A plan helps you keep track of what you've done or tried and also keep you focused on the overall goal or subgoals you're working on. For example, on DONALD + GERALD, you need to devise a way to keep track of which digits you've used, which letters remain, and what you know about them. If nothing else, developing and following a plan helps you avoid redoing what you've already done. Keep in mind that people often make errors when planning how long a task will take, but can plan their time better if they break the task down into the problem subgoals, estimate the time needed for each of those, and then add those times together (Forsyth & Burt, 2008).

Draw Inferences

Wickelgren's (1974) advice is to draw inferences from the givens, the terms, and the expressions in a problem before working on the problem itself. If you do this appropriately, it can often save you from wasting time on blind alleys, as in the two trains problem in Table 12-11. It can also help you abandon a misleading representation of the problem and find one that's more suitable to solving the problem (Simon, 1995). Here's a hint: Don't think about how far the bird is flying; think of how far the trains will travel and how long that will take.

Beware of unwarranted inferences, the kinds of restrictions we place on ourselves that may lead to dead ends. For instance, for the nine-dot problem in Table 12-3, an unwarranted inference is that you must stay within the boundaries of the nine dots.

Develop Subgoals

Wickelgren also recommends a subgoal heuristic for problem solving, that is, breaking a large problem into separate subgoals. This is the heart of the means–end approach. There is a different slant to the subgoal approach, however, that bears mention. Sometimes in our real-world problem solving, there is only a vaguely specified goal and, as often as not, even more vaguely specified subgoals. How do you know when you've achieved a subgoal, say when the subgoal is "find enough articles on a particular topic to write a term paper that will earn an *A*"?

Simon's (1979) *satisficing* heuristic is important here; recall from Chapter 11 that satisficing is a heuristic in which we find a solution to a goal or subgoal that is satisfactory although not necessarily the best possible one. For some problems, the term paper problem included, an initial satisfactory solution to subgoals may

---

TABLE 12-11 Two Trains and Fifteen Pennies Problems

Two Trains

Two train stations are 50 miles apart. At 2 P.M. one Saturday afternoon, the trains start toward each other, one from each station. Just as the trains pull out of the stations, a bird springs into the air in front of the first train and flies ahead to the front of the second train. When the bird reaches the second train it turns back and flies toward the first train. The bird continues to do this until the trains meet.

If both trains travel at the rate of 25 miles per hour and the bird flies at 100 miles per hour, how many miles will the bird fly before the trains meet?

Fifteen Pennies

Fifteen pennies are placed on a table in front of two players. Players must remove at least one but not more than five pennies on their turns. The players alternate turns of removing pennies until the last penny is removed. The player who removes the last penny from the table is the winner. Is there a method of play that will guarantee victory?

Hints

Fifteen pennies. What do you want to force your opponent to do to leave you with the winning move? What will the table look like when your opponent makes that move?

give you additional insight for further refinement of your solution. For instance, as you begin to write your rough draft, you realize there are gaps in your information. What seems originally to be a satisfactory solution to the subgoal of finding references turns out to be insufficient, so you can recycle back to that subgoal to improve your solution. You might only discover this deficiency by going ahead and working on that next subgoal, the rough draft.

Work Backward

Another heuristic is working backward, in which a well-specified goal may permit a tracing of the solution pathway in reverse order, thus working back to the givens. The fifteen pennies problem in Table 12-11 is an illustration, a problem that is best solved by working backward. Many math and algebra proofs can also be worked backward or in a combination of forward and backward methods.

Search for Contradictions

In problems that ask "Is it possible to?" or "Is there a way that?" you should search for contradictions in the givens or goal state. Wickelgren uses the following illustration: Is there an integer x that satisfies the equation $x^2 + 1 = 0$? A simple algebraic operation, subtracting 1 from both sides, yields $x^2 = -1$, which contradicts the known property that any squared number is positive. This heuristic can also be

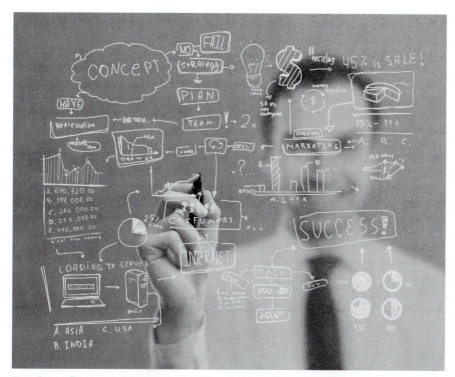

Drawing a diagram to represent a problem helps to improve problem-solving abilities.

helpful in multiple-choice exams. That is, maybe some of the alternatives contradict some idea or fact in the question or some fact you learned in the course. Either will enable you to rule those choices out immediately.

Search for Relations among Problems

In searching for relations among problems, you actively consider how the current problem may resemble one you've already solved or know about. The four- and more-disk Tower of Hanoi problems are examples of this, as are situations in which you search for an analogy (Bassok & Holyoak, 1989; Ross, 1987). Don't become impatient. Bowden (1985) found that people often found and used information from related problems, but only if sufficient time was allowed for them to do so. Try it on the problem in Figure 12-12.

Find a Different Problem Representation

Another heuristic involves the more general issue of the problem representation, or how you choose to represent and think about the problem you're working on. Often, when you get stuck on a problem, it is useful to go back to the beginning and reformulate or reconceptualize it. For instance, as you discovered in the Buddhist monk problem, a quantitative representation of the situation is unproductive. Return to the beginning and try to think of other ways to think about the situation, such as a visual imagery approach, especially a mental movie that includes action. In the Buddhist monk problem, superimposing two such mental movies permits you to see him walking up and down at the same time, thus yielding the solution. Likewise, animated diagrams, with arrows moving in toward a point of convergence, helped participants solve the radiation problem in Pedone, Hummel, and Holyoak's (2001) study, as compared to either static diagrams or a series of diagrams showing intermediate points in problem solution (see also Reed & Hoffman, 2004).

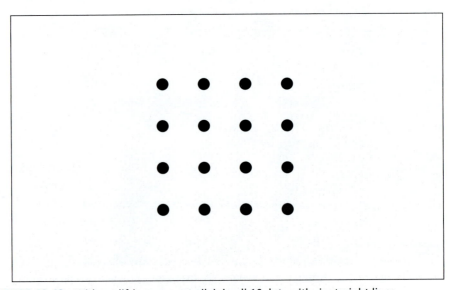

FIGURE 12-12   Without lifting your pencil, join all 16 dots with six straight lines.

For other kinds of problems, try a numerical representation, including working the problem out with some examples, or a physical representation, using objects, scratch paper, and so forth. Simon (1995) makes a compelling point that one representation of a problem may highlight a particular feature of a problem while masking or obscuring a different, possibly important feature. According to Ahlum-Heath and DiVesta (1986), verbalizing your thinking also helps in the initial stages of problem solving.

Earlier, it was suggested that you can master the Tower of Hanoi problem more easily if you used three coins of different sizes. This is more than just good advice. Recall from Chapter 6 where you read about patient H. M., who had profound anterograde amnesia. H. M. was unable to form new explicit long-term memories but was normal when implicit learning was tested. The major result you read about was the mirror tracing study: In a mirror tracing study, H. M. showed normal learning curves on this task, despite not remembering the task from day to day. Interestingly, H. M. was also tested on the Tower of Hanoi task, and he learned it as well as anyone (although he had no explicit memory of ever having done it before). The important ingredient here is the motor aspect of the tower problem: Learning a set of motor responses, even a complex sequence, relies on implicit memory. Thus, working the Tower of Hanoi manually by moving real disks or coins around should enable you to learn how to solve the problem from both an explicit and an implicit basis.

If All Else Fails, Try Practice

Finally, for problems we encounter in classroom settings, from algebra or physics problems up through such vague problems as writing a term paper and studying

Becoming an effective problem solver requires practice to strengthen certain knowledge, as these chess players exhibit.

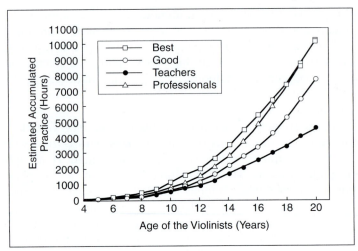

FIGURE 12-13   Illustration of the relationship between amount of practice over the course of years and the level of expertise.

From Ericsson, Krampe, & Tesch-Römer (1993).

effectively for an exam, a final heuristic should help. It's well known in psychology; even Ebbinghaus recommended it. If you want to be good at problem solving, *practice* problem solving. Practice within a particular knowledge domain strengthens that knowledge, pushes the problem-solving components closer to an automatic basis, and gives you a deeper understanding of the domain. Although it isn't flashy, practice is a major component of skilled problem solving and of gaining expertise in any area (Ericsson & Charness, 1994).

In Ericsson and Charness's (1994) review, people routinely believe that stunning talent and amazing accomplishments result from inherited, genetic, or "interior" explanations, when the explanation usually is dedicated, regular, long-term practice. This relationship between practice and performance level is seen in an analysis of practice and expertise data by Ericsson, Krampe, and Tesch-Römer (1993) shown in Figure 12-13. As can be seen, the people who had higher levels of expertise also were the ones who engaged in more practice. So, practice is important to becoming an expert. However, it is unclear whether there is also some innate characteristic such as motivation, interest, or talent that could also be driving those people to practice more. Regardless, if you want to become highly skilled at something, your elementary school clarinet teacher was right—you really do need to practice.

Section Summary

- The set of recommendations for improving your problem solving includes increasing your knowledge of the domain, automaticity of components in problem solving, developing and following a plan, and not becoming anxious. Several special-purpose heuristics are also listed, including the mundane yet important advice about practice.

Key Terms

analogy (p. *439*)

domain knowledge
(p. *460*)

Einstellung
(p. *433*)

functional fixedness
(p. *431*)

general problem
solver (GPS)
(p. *458*)

Gestalt (p. *430*)

goal (p. *447*)

ill-defined problems
(p. *450*)

insight (p. *436*)

means–end analysis
(p. *454*)

negative set (p. *433*)

operators (p. *449*)

problem space
(p. *449*)

production (p. *458*)

subgoal (p. *447*)

verbal protocol
(p. *430*)

well-defined problems
(p. *450*)

Answers to Chapter 12 Problems

Three Men and a Rowboat   Medium and Small row themselves across the river, then either one of them rows back to the start side. Large rows himself across to the destination side. The man who stayed on the destination side now rows back to the start side, and both of the lighter men row to the destination.

Buddhist Monk   Rather than thinking in terms of one monk, let a different monk walk down from the top on the same day as the other walks up. Looking at it this way, isn't it obvious that the two will meet during their journey? Thus, his walking on separate days is irrelevant to the goal, "Show that there is a spot. . . ."

Six Glasses   Numbering the glasses from left to right, pour the contents of glass 2 into glass 5.

Six Pennies   Coins 1, 2, 4, and 6 are already in place, so move coins 3 and 5.

Chains and Links   Open all three links on one chain; that's 6 cents. Put one opened link at the end of each other piece, then join the pieces by looping a closed link into an opened one. Closing the three links costs 9 cents, for a total of 15 cents.

Four Trees   Dead-end approaches try to arrange the trees on a flat, two-dimensional lawn. Instead, think in three dimensions. Put three trees around the base of a hill and the fourth one at the top of the hill. The arrangement is that of an equilateral, three-sided pyramid.

Prisoner's Escape   Divide the rope in half by cutting with the length rather than across the length, similar to unbraiding the rope. Tie the two thinner pieces together and lower yourself to the ground.

Bronze Coin   In 544 B.C., no one knew what might happen 544 years later, so coins could not have had B.C. stamped on them. The dealer is a crook.

Nine Dots

Ten Bowling Pins

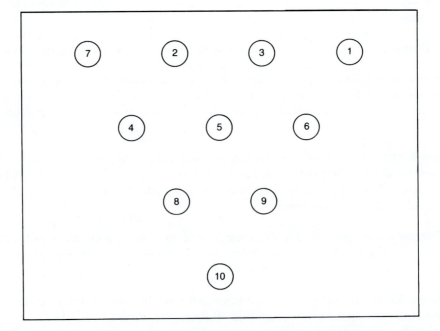

Cryptarithmetic

6. Cross + Roads	7. Lets + Wave	8. Send + More
96,233	1,567	9,567
+ 62,513	+ 9,085	+ 1,085
158,746	10,652	10,652

Two Trains   The trains are 50 miles apart and travel at 25 miles per hour. The trains will meet halfway between the cities in exactly 1 hour. The bird flies at 100 miles per hour, so it will fly 100 miles.

Fifteen Pennies   On your last move you must remove the final penny or pennies. There must be from one to five pennies on the table for you to be the winner. By working backward from this goal, on your next-to-last turn, you must force your opponent to leave you at least one penny on the table. So, leave your opponent six pennies when you finish your next-to-last turn. To guarantee victory, make sure that your opponent leaves you from one to five pennies, so remove only as many pennies as you must to leave your opponent with six pennies on the table.

Sixteen Dots

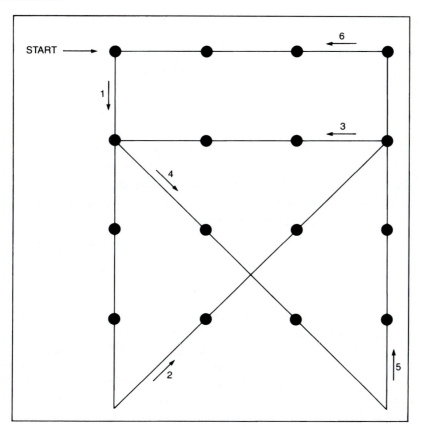

> *Affect is the least investigated aspect of human problem solving,*
> *yet it is probably the aspect most often mentioned as deserving*
> *future investigation. . . . If cognitive psychology aspires to an*
> *understanding of human thought and action, it can ill afford*
> *to leave out their emotional aspects.*

> (MANDLER, 1989, PP. 3–4)

Although the computer metaphor has been a dominant guide for years in cognitive psychology, people are much more than computational machines. One of the big differences between us and our silicon-based creations is in the realm of emotions. We've got them, and they don't. Although much of the research in cognitive psychology might be described by some as "cold cognition," because it does not take people's emotions into account, there is more and more new research doing just that (see Mather & Sutherland, 2011, for a nice overview of major issues). What has been found is that emotion can influence cognition in a variety of complex but systematic ways.

This chapter presents an overview of various ways that cognition is affected by emotion. In a sense, this chapter serves to recapitulate many of the topics already covered in the book. We start with a consideration of how emotion can influence seemingly basic perceptual and attention processes. We then consider how emotion influences memory, making it better in some cases and worse in others. After this we consider roles of emotion in language, followed by some coverage of how emotion can influence our ability to make decisions and solve problems.

WHAT IS EMOTION?

Although we all have an intuitive sense about what emotions are, we need to go beyond that here and offer a formal definition to work with. Consider **emotion** to be *both the state of mind a person is in at a particular moment, as well as the physiological response a person is experiencing at that time* (in terms of heart rate, pupillary dilation, neurotransmitter release, and so on). There are other, similar, related terms that mean somewhat different things, such as affect, mood, and arousal, but we leave these aside for now. Our purpose here is to look at some basic ideas about how emotion can influence and interact with other aspects of cognition, such as perception, attention, and memory.

Types of Emotion

There are a number of ways of dividing up and classifying different types of emotion. Also, it certainly is the case that we all have a lot of variety and subtlety in the different types of emotions that we experience. However, for our purposes, we use a simple approach of looking at two dimensions of emotion and use these to guide our coverage of how emotion influences cognition. The first of these dimensions is the **valence** of an emotion. This is simply *whether an emotion is positive, like happiness, joy, and ecstasy, or negative, such as sadness, anger, or disgust.* The second dimension is the **intensity** of the emotion. This is basically *how strongly an emotion is experienced.* For example, dislike would be less emotionally intense than hatred. We use these two dimensions because many of the cognitive phenomena that we discuss can be understood in terms of where an emotion is along the two dimensions—that is, closer to the positive or negative end of the valence dimension, or closer to the low or high end of the intensity dimension.

Neurological Underpinnings

Emotion has both physical and mental components. It is certainly a visceral experience. We feel it in our bodies—our hearts race, our breathing speeds up. It also triggers a different kind of mental experience than basic kinds of thought. As a mental experience, it has the power to influence brain and cognition in meaningful ways. In the brain, emotional experience is associated with a number of structures and areas, but we focus on two here that are most relevant for understanding how cognition and emotion interact. These structures are the amygdala and the prefrontal cortex.

Explore
Do You Fly or Flight? in
MyPsychLab

Watch *Brain Stem and the Limbic System* in **MyPsychLab**

As noted in Chapter 2, the **amygdala** is an almond-shaped structure located next to the hippocampus. The amygdala is critically involved in more instinctual emotions that are important for survival, such as the experience of fear (e.g., Davis, 1997; LeDoux, 2000) and is more active when a person is in an emotional state. The amygdala receives sensory information from various parts of the brain, allowing for a fast emotional response to environmental conditions. This is particularly true for biologically related emotions related to fear (e.g., seeing a snake), as compared with socially related emotions (e.g., seeing a happy family) (Sakaki, Niki, & Mather, 2012).

One interesting aspect of the amygdala is that there are very few neural synapses in the chain between the olfactory receptors of your sense of smell and the amygdala, which is why odors can be strongly associated with emotions (Herz & Engen, 1996). The amygdala in turn sends its signals to the hypothalamus and brainstem, which helps regulate the body's arousal state, as well as to areas tied to cognitive processes, such as the prefrontal cortex (attention) and the hippocampus (memory). Thus, emotional responses have the potential to directly influence the context and processing of thoughts in ways that differ from when we are not in an emotionally aroused state.

In addition to the amygdala, another region of the brain that is important in emotional processing is the **ventro-medial prefrontal cortex** (B.A. 10). This part of the brain is involved in the identification and interpretation of emotional stimuli and responses, and the integration of that emotional interpretation with the surrounding context (Roy, Shohamy, & Wager, 2012), as well as the regulation and control of those experiences.

The famous case of Phineas Gage illustrates the important role of the prefrontal cortex in emotion regulation. Specifically, Gage suffered a massive trauma that destroyed a large portion of his frontal lobe. This occurred in 1848 Vermont when Gage was working on a blasting crew for a railroad. He was using a tamping rod to press some blasting power into a hole that had been drilled into a rock formation. The powder accidentally ignited, shooting the rod through Gage's skull, destroying part of his brain. Miraculously, Gage survived. After the accident, however, people claimed that Gage was no longer Gage. One of the biggest changes was that he was less able to control his emotions and would impulsively act and express himself in ways that were inconsistent with who he was before the accident. This was because the part of his brain in the frontal lobe that was responsible for controlling and regulating emotional responses and behaviors was seriously damaged in the accident.

Section Summary

- Emotion is a characteristic of human thought that varies in valence and intensity. Emotional experiences have meaningful influences on cognition.
- Two important neurological structures important for emotion processing are the amygdala and the prefrontal cortex. The amygdala is important for the experience of emotion, and the prefrontal lobes are important for the control of emotional responses.

EMOTION, PERCEPTION, AND ATTENTION

We turn now to the question of how emotion can influence cognition. We start with perception and attention, just as we started out this text. After this, we move on to topics in memory, language, and decision making and problem solving.

Perception

Our first question seems very simple—Can emotion influence even basic perceptual processes? There is some evidence to suggest that the answer is "yes," emotions *can* meaningfully influence perception, making some things easier to perceive than others. For instance, people generally recognize things faster if they are emotionally meaningful (such as identifying briefly flashed words like "death" and "love") than if they are not (Zeelenberg, Wagenmakers, & Rotteveel, 2006). This can be seen in Figure 13-1. Thus, the emotional content of an item can influence the accuracy with which it is processed. Looking more deeply, we can see that emotion appears to actually increase the amount of neural activity in perceptual brain areas, such as the occipital and occipital-parietal cortex areas (Taylor, Liberzon, & Koeppe, 2000).

However, it is not the case that there is a uniform boost in the ability to perceive emotional items. Instead, what appears to be happening is that there is an increase in the ability to process broad, global, or general characteristics of the threating item, but a decline in the ability to perceive details (Bocanegra & Zeelenberg, 2011). That is,

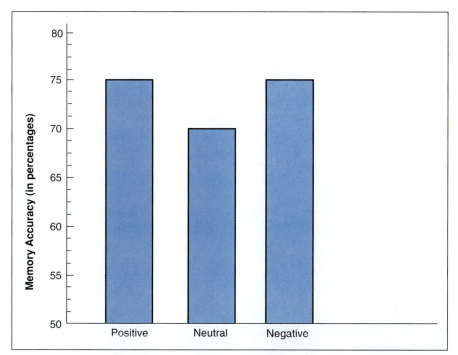

FIGURE 13-1 Memory accuracy for previously seen words as a function of whether they were emotionally positive, neutral, or emotionally negative. Memory is better for emotionally charged items.

Data from Zeelenberg, Wagenmakers, & Rotteveel (2006).

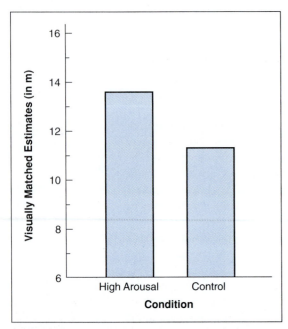

FIGURE 13-2 Estimated height of a balcony as a function of whether a person was emotionally aroused (by viewing pictures) or not. Emotional arousal results in greater height estimations.

Data from Stefanucci & Storbeck (2009).

when are emotions are aroused by a threating stimulus, the perceptual processes in our cognitive system direct processing efforts to knowing generally what and where that emotional something is, so that we can be safe from it. In doing so, the cognition system is, in some sense, making sure that it does not waste its limited energies and resources on details that are probably trivial, thereby increasing the probability of survival.

In addition to influencing the ease with which different objects and entities in the world are recognized, emotion can alter the subjective perception of the world when the situation has characteristics that are emotionally arousing in a person. Take the example of the height of a balcony on a building. When you are standing on the balcony looking down, how high off the ground do you perceive yourself to be? A study by Stefanucci and Storbeck (2009) found that people who were more emotionally aroused (by viewing a series of emotionally arousing pictures), either positively or negatively, experienced the height of the balcony as greater (see Figure 13-2). What may have been happening here is that the emotional arousal a person was experiencing, although it was different from any emotions elicited by the height itself, was interpreted cognitively as being part of the experience of looking down from the balcony. In a sense, the perceptual processes were saying, "Hmmm . . . if I am feeling aroused, then the balcony must be pretty high." And so, people who were already emotionally aroused rated the balcony as being higher than those people who were not so aroused.

Emotional stimuli have a way of capturing our attention.

Emotional Guidance of Attention

In addition to these effects on perceptual processes, there is some evidence that emotion can influence attention as well. A moment's reflection will reveal that this basic idea is not all that surprising. If there is something that elicits our emotions, we are more likely to pay attention to it, whatever that thing is. What the work on emotion and attention has shown is that this influence can be more extensive and unconscious than a casual moment's reflection might reveal. Let's start by looking at a very basic form of attention, namely the orienting reflex that was discussed in Chapter 4.

Cowan (1995) noted that the kinds of stimuli that can trigger the orienting reflex boil down to two basic categories: (a) stimuli that are significant for the organism (the rock thrown toward your head) and (b) stimuli that are novel or unexpected. The important point here is that what is significant to you often has some relation to emotions, either positive or negative. What is important to keep in mind is that emotion and attention use some of the same neural components. These include structures such as the amygdala, portions of the frontal lobes, and the anterior cingulate cortex (B. A.s 24, 32, & 33). Thus, emotion can affect the direction of attention (Vuilleumeir, 2005). For example, people are more likely to direct their attention to emotionally arousing stimuli, such as a seeing a snake in the grass. Attention can also influence how you feel about things. For example, people can develop a negative emotional response toward things that they try to ignore (Fenske & Raymond, 2006).

Visual Search

One of the tasks in cognitive psychology that has been used extensively for the study of the operation of attention is visual search—trying to find an object in a display of irrelevant distractors. Research using this task has found that emotions, particularly negative emotions such as fear, can influence the visual search processes (e.g., Öhman, Flykt, & Esteves, 2001). The inclusion of emotion-eliciting stimuli in a display, such as spiders or fearful faces, facilitates the direction of attention to such objects during visual search. In some sense this seems like a form of attention capture, with attention being preferentially moved to more fearful stimuli. This shifting of attention to emotional items seems to be directed more by the amygdala than by emotional control processes in the frontal lobe (Vuilleumeir & Huang, 2009). Also, it may have more to do with an increase in attentional resources because even the processing of non-emotional targets in a visual search task is facilitated when emotions are triggered (Becker, 2009).

During visual search, it is easier to direct our attention to emotionally charged items, such as a spider.

Looking more deeply at emotion and the processing of visual stimuli, several investigators have tested the effects of emotional stimuli on the attentional blink phenomenon you read about earlier; as a reminder, if two stimuli are presented very rapidly in sequence, we sometimes miss the second one, as if our attentional mechanism had "blinked" for a brief moment while the second one was present. Researchers have now found that the length of this attentional blink is attenuated if the stimulus that occurs during that critical "moment" is emotionally loaded. As an example, there is a reduced or absent attentional blink for an emotion-eliciting word, such as "whore," compared to emotionally neutral words, such as "veiled" (Anderson, 2005). Thus, emotional relevance and intensity can override other, standard operating features of the cognitive system, such as the normal attentional blink phenomenon.

Emotional Stroop

Emotional processing can even influence attention and cognition in ways where it might at first seem irrelevant. An example of this is the **emotional Stroop task** (see Williams, Matthews, & MacLeod, 1996, for a review). As a reminder, in the standard form of the Stroop task, people are given a series of color words printed in a color that may be inconsistent with the word names; you see the word "red" printed in blue ink, but you need to name the ink color, that is, need to say "blue." The standard Stroop effect is that people are slower to name the color a word is printed in if the word and ink color are inconsistent (see Chapter 4).

In the emotional Stroop task, words are still presented in different colors, and the people are asked to name those colors. However, rather than having color words on the list, the critical comparison has to do with words that elicit an emotional response in a person, such as "spider," as compared to more neutral words, such as "spade." What is typically found with this task is that people name the color of the word more slowly if the word is emotional for them. For example, a person who has a deathly fear of spiders would be slower to say "green" if "spider" were printed in green ink, whereas a person without this fear would not show this effect. The explanation is actually very straightforward. Even though the person is supposed to focus on the color of ink, reading the word and accessing its meaning happens automatically. If the word is related to an emotional stressor for the person, it intrudes on the person's cognitive processing, and thus takes away resources from the other cognitive processes necessary for focusing on and naming the ink color. Thus color naming is slowed down for the emotional word condition, but not for the neutral word condition. This emotional Stroop task has been used to study a number of psychopathologies, including depression (e.g., Mitterschiffthaler et al., 2008), anxiety (e.g., Dresler, Mériau, Heekeren, & van der Meer, 2009), and post-traumatic stress disorder (e.g., Cisler et al., 2011).

Emotion and Self-Control

An important function for attention is to guide thoughts and behavior. To some degree this is automatic, but to some degree it is under conscious control. What role does emotion play in this self-control? One would intuitively think that expressing emotions would lead to less self-control; however, there is some evidence that *suppression* of your emotions can lead to attentional control problems. An example of this is a study by Inzlicht and Gutsell (2007) in which people watched an emotional movie and were either asked to simply watch the movie (the control condition) or were asked to suppress their emotions while viewing the film (experimental suppression condition). After this they were asked to do a traditional color-word Stroop task. What was found, as can be seen in Figure 13-3, was that people who had suppressed their emotions had a harder time doing the Stroop task.

The explanation was that suppressing one's emotions drained resources from the error monitoring aspect of attentional control, which is

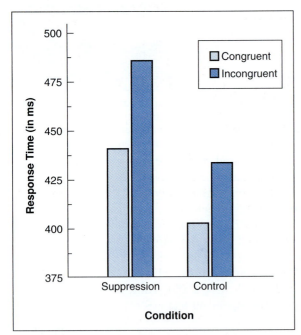

FIGURE 13-3 Response times to Stroop color words (when both the word and printed color were either congruent or incongruent) when people had either just spent time suppressing their emotions while watching an emotional movie or not. As can be clearly seen, previously suppressing one's emotions made the task harder.

Data from Inzlicht & Gutsell (2007).

guided by the anterior cingulate cortex (B.A.s 24, 25, & 32). When these attentional resources were drained by the effort to control one's emotions over a long period of time, there were fewer resources available for doing other tasks.

So, overall, there is clear evidence that emotional content and responses can influence even basic perceptual and attention processes. This suggests that emotion serves as a primary and fundamental force in guiding and influencing cognition.

Section Summary

- Emotion can influence perceptual processing by channeling cognitive processing resources toward those stimuli in the environment that are more emotional.
- The estimation of some perceptual qualities, such as size or height, can be influenced by whether an emotional state is aroused.
- Emotional responses can guide where attention is directed, even to the extent of sending attention to nominally irrelevant information in the environment, which can produce a processing cost, as in the emotional Stroop effect.
- The experience of intense emotions can consume cognitive resources, such as attention, to the point that that there is less available for other tasks and performance shows a deficit.

EMOTION AND MEMORY

One of the aspects of cognition where emotion has its largest effects is with memory. The influence of emotion on memory is somewhat complicated. In some ways and under certain circumstances, emotion can make memories more pleasant, but in other ways or under different circumstances, emotion can make have the opposite effect on memory. Let's take a systematic look at these different influences and try to make clear to you when your emotions help and hinder what you remember from an event.

The influence of emotion on memory is not a simple and direct process. Again, as a reminder, two primary brain areas for the processing of emotional information are the amygdala and the prefrontal cortex. In general, the amygdala is more involved in more implicit aspects of memory, whereas the prefrontal cortex is more involved in explicit memory processes. This differential influence of these areas on memory can be seen in patients with brain damage. For example, Bechera et al. (1995) reported three case studies of patients, one with bilateral damage to the amygdala, one with bilateral damage to the hippocampus, and one with bilateral damage to both. These patients were exposed to stimuli, either a tone or a visual image, that were paired with an aversive stimulus (i.e., a loud boat horn), a standard classical conditioning study. The results were fascinating. For the patients with damage to the amygdala, there was no evidence of classical conditioning when the tone or image were shown again; they had not learned the pairing with the loud boat horn. The results were very different when the damage was to the hippocampus, a structure that the prefrontal lobe relies on for conscious memories. In this case, the patients showed normal classical conditioning of the

The influence of emotion on memory is a powerful one. This can easily be demonstrated by giving people lists of words and asking them to remember them later. Below is a sample list of words. This list is 20 words long to make sure that it exceeds your participants' working memory capacity and that they are using long-term memory to retrieve the items. What you should do is read the list of words, in a random order to your participants. Read these words aloud at a rate of about 1 per second, using a metronome or a watch to help your pacing. After you have read all of the words, give people a distractor task, such as solving three-digit math problems (e.g., 284 + 923 = ?) for two minutes. This will displace any memory for the words in the list that still may be in working memory. After the two minutes are up, give your participants a sheet of paper and have them recall as many words from the original list of 20 as they can remember. What you should find is that people will remember more of the emotional words than the non-emotional words. If you want, try mixing things up by creating word lists of your own that compare emotionality to other things that can influence memory, such as word frequency, generation effects, or von Restorff effects.

Emotional words: hate, happy, joy, anger, disgust, fear, thrill, love, sad, pleased
Non-emotional words: date, caddy, boy, ranger, digest, near, drill, live, had, pleated

tone (image)-to-horn pairing—but they had no conscious memory for either the tone or the visual image. In other words, with damage to the amygdala, there was no implicit learning, and with damage to the hippocampus, there was no explicit learning. Thus, the different aspects of emotion processing in the brain directly influence different types of learning and memory.

In terms of the role of emotion in memory, a study by Kissler, Herbert, Peyk, and Junghofer (2007) asked people to read a series of words while event-related potential (ERP) recordings were made (they were given a free recall test at the end to make sure they were actually reading). The results showed a difference in cortical processing as a function of the emotional intensity of the words that were read. Specifically, in the occipito-temporal area (around where there occipital and temporal lobes meet), about 250 ms after the presentation of the word, there was an increase in cortical activity for more emotionally intense words relative to emotionally neutral words. Thus, when people access information in semantic memory, any emotional content becomes available as well. Emotion is part of semantic memory.

Making Memory Better

If you think about your own life, and the things you remember, one of the things you quickly notice is that your emotional experiences are often the most memorable. This can include negative memories such as losing a close family member or friend, an emotional breakup, or being in a serious car accident, as well as positive memories, such as a new birth in the family, a marriage, or landing a greatly desired job. Thus, emotion can have clear benefits for memory. Emotional information is generally remembered better than more neutral information (see Kensinger, 2009, for a review), even when the emotional words, such as "happy," "disgust," or "sad," are compared to more neutral words, such as "hammer," "digest," or "fad." The quality of emotion that seems to be influencing memory the most is not the *valence* of the emotion (such as whether it is positive or negative), but how intense the emotional experience is (Talarico, LaBar, & Rubin, 2004). In other words, what is important about the influence of emotion on memory is how strong the emotion is, not whether you feel good or bad about the event.

The idea that people remember emotional information better than neutral information has also been demonstrated in laboratory work. For example, people remember emotionally arousing pictures better than neutral ones (Bradley, Greenwald, Petry, & Lang, 1992), particularly the details of negative images (Kensinger, Garoff-Eaton, & Schacter, 2006). People also remember emotional utterances better than neutral ones (Armony, Chochol, Fecteau, & Belin, 2007). Work using functional magnetic resonance imaging (fMRI) scanning, such as that by Dolcos, Labar, and Cabeza (2005) and Kensinger and Corkin (2004; see also Kensinger, 2007), has shown that the superior memory for emotional memories appears to reflect the involvement of the amygdala and medial temporal-lobe structures, such as the hippocampus, with the amygdala-hippocampus network being more important for emotional intensity, and a hippocampal–frontal lobe network being more important for emotional valence (whether the emotion is positive or negative, happy or sad).

It is important to note that the emotional benefit of memory does not need to be present at the time the event is originally learned. In a fascinating study that exploits the phenomenon of reconsolidation (see Chapter 8), Finn and Roediger (2011) had people learn a set of English–Swahili vocabulary pairs (essentially the English translations of Swahili words). What was so interesting about this study is that after the initial learning phase was over, people were asked to recall the word pairs. As they recalled each pair, they were shown either a blank screen, or a neutral or an emotional picture. Then, after another period of time, they were asked to recall the word pairs again. On this final test, memory was better for words that had been followed by the emotional pictures, as can be seen in Figure 13-4. It seemed that when the word pairs were retrieved the first time, they were in a labile and fluid state, not yet firmly in memory. If an emotional picture was shown with the pairs, the person's emotional

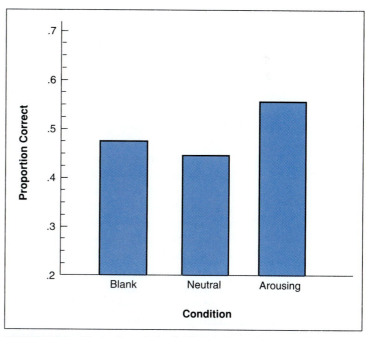

FIGURE 13-4 Illustration of the finding that recall memory for English–Swahili word pairs was better when people were looking at an emotional picture compared to looking at either a blank screen or a neutral picture.

Data from Finn & Roediger (2011).

response to the picture was incorporated into the memory trace and stored with it during the reconsolidation process. Thus, emotional responses can be incorporated into memory traces after the event has occurred if we experience an emotion when we are remembering the event. Note that Finn and Roediger did not find this benefit when people merely restudied the information, but only when they actively retrieved, as would be expected in a reconsolidation process.

So, why does emotion help memory so much? There are probably a number of reasons that, together, help make emotional memories easier to remember. First, emotional events are likely to be things that are important to us. As a consequence, people are likely to devote more attention to processing that information relative to something that is more emotionally neutral. Part of this is driven by the recruitment of the amygdala, which is a critical brain structure for processing emotions. There is also some evidence that emotionally charged memories appear to benefit more from the process of memory consolidation offered by sleep compared to emotionally neutral memories (Hu, Stylos-Allan, & Walker, 2006).

Another reason why emotion may help memory is that emotional information is more distinctive. Much of what we encounter in our day-to-day lives does not elicit much in the way of a strong emotional reaction. Thus truly emotional information is more likely to be distinctive, resulting in a kind of a von Restorff effect, which orients an increase in attention toward the emotion-eliciting stimulus (e.g., Talmi & Garry, 2012; Talmi, Schimmack, Paterson, & Moscovitch, 2007).

EMOTIONAL CONTEXT Emotions influence memory beyond just the fact than emotional memories are better. Another way that your emotions influence memory involves the kind of information that becomes activated or primed in long-term memory. With **mood-congruent memories**, your emotional state at the time makes knowledge in long-term memory that is more consistent with that mood more available. So, when you are in a happy mood, you tend to think more about things that make you happy, such as rainbows, butterflies, and home, but when you are sad, you are more likely to think of things that make you sad, such as death, taxes, and arguments. Most of what is going on with mood-congruent memories happens below consciousness, where you are not aware of it. It is a kind of priming. This can be seen in the fact that mood-congruent priming can be observed when people are doing a lexical decision task and are unaware that the influence of their emotional state on their performance is being tested (Olafson & Ferraro, 2001).

As noted earlier, emotions are visceral experiences. They reflect and influence the internal physiological state of your body. If you remember from Chapter 6, the internal state of your body can be a kind of contextual information that is stored in memory. In other words, emotions can be contexts as well. As a consequence, we should see encoding specificity effects for emotions, just as we do for external environments and physiological states. As it turns out, that is exactly what happens. People have **mood-dependent memories**, in which they find it easier to remember things when they are in the same mood at retrieval as they were during encoding (Bower, 1981). Thus, it is easier to remember happy times when you are happy than when you are sad, depressed, angry, or in some other emotional state.

Distinctiveness or rated memorability is an important determinant of how accurately we remember an event, such as the attack on the World Trade Center.

FLASHBULB MEMORIES   We often seem to have—or believe we have—extremely accurate and very detailed memories of particular events, especially when the events were surprising and highly emotional. These are often called **flashbulb memories**. For example, Brown and Kulik (1977) examined the flashbulb memories of college students for the assassination of President Kennedy in 1963. People were asked to recall their own particular circumstances when they heard news of the event, not whether they remembered the event itself. The data showed an increase in the amount of recallable detailed information (see also Mahmood, Manier, & Hirst, 2004; and Winograd & Killinger, 1983; for flashbulb memories of emotional but not surprising events, such as good friends dying of AIDS, President Nixon's resignation, and the Apollo moon landings). Emotional experience is critical to the formation of flashbulb memories. Although no one has been able to measure brain activity when a person learns of news that would produce a false memory, fMRI scans of people remembering a flashbulb memory event, such as the terrorist attacks of September 11, 2001, show increased amygdala activity during retrieval (Sharot, Martorella, Delgado, & Phelps, 2007), highlighting the involvement of emotional experience in these memories.

Although distinctiveness of the event is important (Dodson & Schacter, 2002; Hunt & Lamb, 2001; Schmidt, 1985), reminiscent of the von Restorff effect you encountered earlier, as well as surprise (Hirshman, Whelley, & Palij, 1989), it's also important for a person to be emotionally involved in the event. Kensinger and Schacter (2006) reported people's memories of the 2004 Red Sox–Yankees World Series games. Not surprisingly, it made a difference if they were Red Sox fans (winners, positive affect), Yankees fans (losers, negative affect), or not a fan of either team (neutral). People who had either positive or negative emotions about the outcome had more detailed memories. People who had positive memories, however, showed less consistency (their memory reports changed over time) and more over-confidence (they were more inappropriately confident than the Yankees fans), but remembered more about the game overall (see also work by Breslin & Safer, 2011).

Several studies suggest that flashbulb memories share many qualities with ordinary types of memories (McCloskey, Wible, & Cohen, 1988). For instance, Christianson (1989) tested Swedes' memories for the assassination of their prime minister in 1986, once barely six weeks after the assassination and again a year later. He found that only general information about the assassination was recalled with accuracy. Details that were recalled, in contrast, seemed to be a creative mixture of a few specifics plus more general knowledge, exactly the kind of memory first identified by Bartlett (1932; see also Neisser, 1982; Weaver, 1993). In a similar vein, Talarico and Rubin (2003) tested undergraduates the day after the 9/11 terrorist attacks and then again either 1, 6, or 32 weeks afterward, asking them to record both their memory of when they first heard of the attack and also a recent "everyday" memory. They found that both flashbulb and everyday memories declined across time in their consistency, but that the people *believed* that their flashbulb memories remained highly accurate (see also Schmolck, Buffalo, & Squire, 2000, who tested people's recollections of the O. J. Simpson trial).

Conway et al. (1994) did a similar, extensive study and found evidence of special memory qualities. They tested people on their personal recollections at the time of British Prime Minister Margaret Thatcher's surprise resignation, first just two weeks after the event, then again nearly a year later. More than 86% of their sample from the United Kingdom had accurate, detailed recollections of the event, including specific personal details (e.g., what they had eaten for breakfast that day). Because fewer than 30% of the non-U.K. participants had such memories, the authors conclude that vivid, accurate flashbulb memories can be formed. Furthermore, you are more likely to form a flashbulb memory if you view the event as especially important to you and if it has an emotional effect on you (see also Libkuman, Nichols-Whitehead, Griffith, & Thomas, 1999, on the role of emotional arousal in remembering). Interestingly, visual imagery and emotions seem to be important in the recollection of autobiographical memories (Rubin, Schrauf, & Greenberg, 2003). And in addition to the visual images, Schmidt (2004) found that the participants' emotionality also influenced the errors made in recalling personal memories of the 9/11 attack (for a list of criteria needed to form a flashbulb memory, see Finkenhauer et al., 1998).

But here's the irony again: Is memory good, even flashbulb-quality good, or is it widely subject to the sins of misattribution, suggestibility, bias, and the rest? The circumstances Conway et al. (1994) isolated as important for forming flashbulb memories—high level of importance, high affective response to the event—should also characterize memories of traumatic events, exactly those that are in dispute in cases of repressed and recovered memories.

Making Memory Worse

When you are in an excited emotional state, there are certainly some things that you remember, really, really well. So, it is clear that there are ways in which emotions make memories better. However, when your emotions are running high, there also happen to be a lot of things that get missed, and so there are ways that emotions make memories less complete. In this section we cover some ideas about how the accuracy of memory is tied to how intense your memories are, and then discuss some ways in which memory is harmed by emotions.

INTENSITY AND MEMORY   Emotions can be described in terms of how intense they are, how much you are emotionally aroused. This level of arousal is systematically related to how much is remembered. In general sense, memory follows what is known as the **Yerkes-Dodson law**, which is shown in Figure 13-5. According to the Yerkes-Dodson law, when you are in a low arousal state, such as when you are tired and bored, your memory for information is not that good. However, as your arousal level goes up, so does your memory performance—but only up to a point. That point is an optimal level of arousal that allows the most learning to occur. Beyond that, things change. At even higher levels of arousal your memory starts to decline. You are too agitated and excited, and the amount of information you can adequately remember goes down. As you can see, at high levels of arousal, emotions can make memory worse.

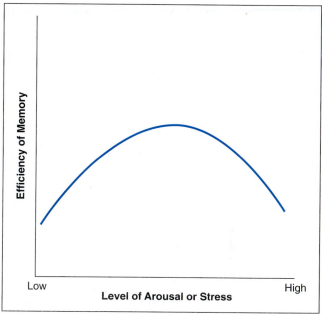

FIGURE 13-5   Illustration of the Yerkes-Dodson law, in which performance is poor at low levels of intensity, then increases as intensity grows larger, and then decreases for high levels of intensity.

Although the Yerkes-Dodson law accurately captures what is going on with emotional arousal in a general sense, the actual situation is a bit more complex. At higher levels of arousal, memory does not decline for everything—there are some things for which memory actually continues to improve. This is captured by the **Easterbrook hypothesis**, which says that at higher levels of emotional arousal there is a narrowing of attention onto whatever is eliciting the emotions in a person. *That* information can be thought of as being at the center of the event. The more irrelevant details of the event are less emotionally arousing, however, and can be thought of as the peripheral information. According to the Easterbrook hypothesis, when people are in more highly emotion arousing situations, their attention narrows in on the central information and away from the peripheral information. As a consequence, with high levels of emotional intensity, memory for the central details continues to get better, but memory for peripheral details declines. Because there are more peripheral than central details, overall memory is getting worse at high levels of emotional arousal, but things that are most important might be remembered really well.

This idea is supported by several memory studies. For example, in a study by Safer, Christiansen, Autry, and Österlund (1998), people were shown a series of pictures. Some of these depicted emotionally arousing scenes, such as a bloody body on the hood of a car, and others showed more emotionally neutral scenes, such as a picture of a woman in a park. On the later memory test, as can be seen in Figure 13-5, performance was better for central aspects of the scene in the emotionally arousing pictures compared to the more emotionally neutral pictures. Safer et al. called these **tunnel memories**—it was as if people were narrowing or tunneling their vision in on the emotional central details, causing them to be remembered better. There was no tunneling on the neutral scenes, however: Memory performance was more expansive and inclusive for the peripheral details in the emotionally neutral than the arousing scenes.

A related result is called the **weapon focus effect** (Maass & Köhnken, 1989; Steblay, 1992). This is the finding that when there are emotionally arousing elements in a scene, such as a gun or a knife, people's attention will go to the weapon. This presumably occurs because, at some level, people want to know where that weapon is directed and whether it could harm them. Note that this occurs not only in scenes depicting violence, but even when a weapon is present in nonviolent scenes (Kramer, Buckout, & Eugenio, 1990). As with other tunnel memories, when a weapon is present, memory for that weapon is better, but memory for the other details in the scene get worse.

So, as you can see, emotional information can both make memories better and make memories worse, depending on which aspect of an event is focused on. Memory for central information from an event is heightened by emotion, but memory for peripheral information is harmed by emotion. This differential influence of emotion on memory is exaggerated as time goes on during the consolidation process, particularly the consolidation that occurs during sleep (e.g., Payne & Kensinger, 2010). The neural processing that occurs during rapid–eye-movement (REM) sleep seems to be particularly important for the consolidation of emotional information in memory because of the increase in cortisol levels during this time, which reinstates the emotional experience.

Section Summary

- There is a general benefit for remembering emotional over neutral information. However, people who have suffered brain damage to areas critical for emotion processing, such as the amygdala, do not exhibit such a benefit.
- The memory benefit for emotional information comes from a number of sources, including its importance, its distinctiveness, the amount of attention and rehearsal it is given, and the superior benefit it seems to derive from neural consolidation processes.
- Emotion can serve as a form of contextual information that can facilitate some memory processes, as with mood-congruent and mood-dependent memories.
- The highly detailed memories we have for very emotional events, and for the contexts in which we learn about such events, are called flashbulb memories. Flashbulb memories, although not perfect and prone to some forgetting, appear to be more durable than normal everyday memories.
- Although emotion can improve some types of memories, it can also impose a cost on later memory. Specifically, at high levels of emotional intensity, attention is captured by central information at the cost of processing of

peripheral information. As a consequence, memory for more peripheral information is worse under conditions of higher emotional intensity. The weapon focus effect is an example of the kind of memory impairment that can occur with high levels of emotion.

EMOTION AND LANGUAGE

Emotion can also influence language processes in cognition and is a quality that is communicated by language. In this section we cover the transmission and impact of emotional information. This includes emotional tone that is carried by the speech signal, as well as the tracking of emotional information in a situation model and how that influences the cognitive processing of other event dimensions.

Prosody

Language is typically not delivered in a monotone, but involves *a moving up and down in pitch, somewhat like a melody;* this is called **prosody**. Prosody conveys meaning in language, although a different kind of meaning than the semantic meanings of the words themselves. For example, the sentences "Those are my shoes." and "Those are my shoes?" contain exactly the same words but are spoken with different prosodies. One conveys a statement and the other a question, often with a rise in pitch at the end of the sentence. One other aspect of meaning that prosody can convey is the emotional tone of the speaker. For example, imagine the sentence "Those are my shoes." spoken in happy, sad, and angry tones of voice, and notice the different prosodies that are used to convey this emotional meaning.

As you should recall from our earlier discussions of language, in most people, most language-processing components are lateralized in the left hemisphere. For example, this is the location of Broca's and Wernicke's areas. However, not all language processing is strongly left lateralized, and the processing of emotional prosody is one example of this. A number of studies, including research involving fMRI imaging, have found that the brain is right lateralized for the processing of emotional prosody (e.g., Buchanan et al., 2000). This is further supported by evidence from people with damage to the right hemispheres. Patients with right hemisphere damage often have difficulty deriving emotional information from linguistic prosody (e.g., Pell, 1999).

Note that although damage to the right hemisphere can impede the processing of linguistic prosody, damage to other brain structures involved in emotion processing, such as the amygdala, does not (Adolphs & Tranel, 1999). In other words, the processing of emotional prosody by the right hemisphere does not depend of emotional input from the amygdala, but involves a determination of emotional content from the pitch information in speech that is heard. Overall, although prosody is a deeply linguistic characteristic, this meaning is processed more by the right hemisphere than the left.

Hearing language that conveys characteristics of emotion does not mean that a listener will be convinced that the person speaking is experiencing that particular emotion. Sometimes, we know that people are only play-acting and that the emotion expressed is not one that he person is actually feeling. What people need to do is take the emotional information conveyed by the prosody, along with other characteristics of the language, to determine whether the emotion is genuinely being experienced or not. There is some evidence that people have some success at doing this and that different regions of the brain are involved in such detection (e.g., Drolet, Schubotz, & Fischer, 2012). For example, if vocal expressions of emotion are taken from the radio and played to people, the detection of genuine emotion is above chance, particularly for emotions such as anger and sadness. Moreover, as measured by fMRI recordings, there is greater activity in the medial prefrontal cortex and the temporal-parietal junction. The latter is often found to be important in perspective taking. Thus people are able to use information in the language signal to determine not only the emotion that is being expressed by the prosody of the spoken words, but also the genuineness of that emotion.

Words and Situations

Let's shift our focus at this point away from *how* language is said to *what* is said, and how language is influenced by emotional processing. First, and most obviously, some words are about emotion, such as "happy," "sad," and "angry." We have specific words that aim to capture and communicate the experience of emotion, and the fact that such words are common in the language attests to the fact that such ideas are readily transmitted and received.

However, are these words the only ones that communicate emotional information? Probably not. There is some suggestion that many words in the language communicate some emotional character, even if they are abstract words. If you remember from Chapter 6, words can vary along a number of dimensions, which can then influence cognition in meaningful ways. For example, words can be classified along the concrete-abstract dimension. Concrete words—words that refer to some physical entity, such as "ball"—are often remembered better than abstract words, such as "truth," because people can generate mental images of concrete words. Because of this, people can exploit dual encoding and form mental images of the concrete words, boosting their memory performance.

The temptation at that point is to say that abstract words are more poorly remembered because they do not have any perceptual/embodied/grounded qualities. However, a closer look reveals that this is not the case. Abstract words do convey embodied information, but more in terms of emotional connotations than the more perceptual qualities of concrete words (e.g., Altarriba, Bauer, & Benvenuto, 1999). For example, words such as "courage" and "revenge" are abstract words that convey emotional qualities. If people are asked to process abstract words, those with higher emotional content are processed faster than neutral words (Kousta, Vigliocco, Vinson, Andrews, & Campo, 2010). Thus, emotional but abstract words can show an advantage in cognition, and this advantage is due to the fact that people can take advantage of the embodied nature of emotion to facilitate their processing of these words.

Emotional information is also processed and tracked at the situation model level. As was described in Chapter 10, during language comprehension people track a number of aspects of a described situation, such as spatial location, time frame, and people's goals. There is some evidence to suggest that people are actively tracking emotional reactions of story characters as they experience various events in the narrative world (de Vega, León, & Díaz, 1996; Gernsbacher, Hallada, & Robertson, 1998; Gernsbacher & Robertson, 1992; Gygax, Garnham, & Oakhill, 2004). Moreover, when there is a change in a story character's emotional state, there is an increase in cognitive effort expended, as revealed by reading time, as a reader updates the emotional information in a story (Komeda & Kusumi, 2006). Thus, emotion is important enough to people for them to want to know what even fictional characters are experiencing.

Thinking further about emotion, and how it factors into our understanding of events, there can be two ways that emotion can be experienced. One way is by the person who is feeling the emotion. This is the mental and physiological state of the person depending on the emotion they are experiencing. The second is by people other than the person experiencing the emotion. For example, some external person might see the emotion-experiencer smiling, scowling, blushing, and so on. These are external manifestations of emotion that are available to viewers. When comprehending language that involves emotion, how emotion is represented in the situation model may reflect, in part, whose perspective is emphasized by the language, the person experiencing or observing the emotion. These different ways of thinking about and processing emotional information may require different kinds of cognitive processes.

In a study by Oosterwijk et al. (2012), people read individual sentences that conveyed emotional information. A given sentence conveyed emotion either from an internal perspective of the experiencer, such as "Hot embarrassment came over her," or the external perspective that some other person would see "His nose wrinkled in disgust." People were simply asked to judge the sensibility of the sentences as fast and as accurately as possible (some non-sensible sentences were included as well). The researchers found that people showed a processing cost when they had to switch from an internal emotional focus to an external one (or vice versa) from one sentence to the next, but not when the nature of the emotional focus stayed the same across the sentences. This shows that we mentally represent emotional information in our understanding of situations and events depending on the perspective we take, and the kind of experience that needs to be captured in the situation model.

Why would it be important to track emotional information in a story, other than the additional experience one gets from reading about a story character's emotional state? It is important to keep in mind that emotions do not exist in a vacuum, but are human reactions to events that are experienced. More specifically, emotions can be seen as being strongly tied to people's goals. For example, negative emotions come from having one's goals impeded or blocked, such as not being able to buy a bicycle or not having one's parents continue to be healthy. Likewise, positive emotions come from having one's goals achieved, such as getting to go on a hot date or winning the lottery. Goals are important for language comprehension because they help provide an understanding of the motivations and causes of narrative events as the circumstances unfold.

Section Summary

- A great deal of emotional meaning is conveyed by the prosody of spoken utterances. Brain-damaged people, particularly those with damage to the right hemisphere, may be able to understand the words spoken to them but often lack the ability to process the prosody of what is being said, and so miss out on emotional cues in the speech stream.
- Emotion is infused in a lot of language processing, even beyond auditory cues such as prosody. Some words, even abstract words, carry emotional meaning in their lexical entries, thereby influencing how people process that information.
- People actively track and simulate emotional experiences in the situation models that are created during comprehension. There is evidence that people show processing costs of changes in emotional quality of a character, and in changes in the internal or external experience of an emotion.

EMOTION AND DECISION MAKING

Decision making is another area of cognition that is affected by emotion. The effectiveness and quality of the decisions a person makes in a heightened emotional state differ from those made in a more relaxed and neutral state. Note that the terms *emotion*, *stress*, and *pressure* have different meanings, but for our current purposes, we gloss over some of these.

Stress Impairs Performance

It is clear to anyone who has ever been under emotional stress, such as being anxious, that decision-making and problem-solving performance can decline under these conditions. Essentially, when people experience anxiety, they tend to crowd their working memory with irrelevant thoughts about whatever it is they are anxious about. For example, people who are math anxious (i.e., they avoid doing math problems, taking math classes, exploring careers that use a lot of math) do more poorly on math problems because their working memory capacity is consumed by off-topic irrelevant thoughts that stem from their anxiety about doing math (Ashcraft & Krause, 2007). These thoughts take away from the limited capacity they have to devote to the problem, and their performance suffers. This may also disrupt the mental representations people hold in memory, making them less precise, thereby decreasing performance (Maloney, Ansari, & Fugelsang, 2011).

People who are threatened also experience physiological changes due to the stress they are placed under (e.g., Kassam, Koslov, & Mendes, 2009). Specifically, there is a decrease in cardiovascular efficiency, reducing blood flow to the body and brain, causing the body to slow down. This makes thinking, including decision making, less effective. Part of the reason for this is that when a person is in a threatened state, it may be adaptive (under certain circumstances) to be more immobile, and for the body to be prepared for some damage. Although this may have some survival advantages in the wild, in the circumstances we are faced with

Sometimes we choke under pressure as when our performance deviates from what normally do, such as missing a shot at a critical time in a game.

in our everyday lives, this is a maladaptive response because we cannot make decisions that would be to our advantage.

CHOKING UNDER PRESSURE   We've all been there. The pressure is on. We've done well in this situation before. It comes time to step up and do it again. And we choke (rats!). When people become anxious because of external pressures, their performance can decline.

If you recall from Chapter 4, as a process becomes increasingly practiced, it becomes more and more automatized, allowing people to do it better and more quickly. Thus, as people gain expertise, they become more fluid in the task as its components become more and more unconscious. For the most part, this is a good thing. However, it can also cause problems, especially when the pressure is on. In a pressure situation, what skilled people should do is allow their unconscious cognitive processes to play themselves out. However, what can sometimes happen is that these people start to consciously think about what they are doing and how they are doing it. This is the classic case of when a person, such as a basketball player, chokes under pressure. What can happen under these circumstances is that the athlete's conscious thought processes about what he or she is doing begins to intrude on and compete with more unconscious and automatic cognitive processes.

In a classic demonstration of this, Beilock and Carr (2001) tested people in a golf-putting situation. There were two groups of people in this study—people who were expert golf players, and golf novices. At first Beilock and Carr had people just putt to gain a sense of how well they did normally. Then they placed these people under pressure, asking them to consciously focus on their putting. What happened, not surprisingly, was that novices did better when they focused on accuracy. Surprisingly, however, the golf experts did worse when they focused on their putting. This is because the conscious thoughts disrupted their normally automatic performance on this task. In fact, people who are experts actually did better if they focused on speed (Beilock, Bertenthal, McCoy, & Carr, 2004).

There are two different types of pressure that can influence performance (DeCaro, Thomas, Albert, & Beilock, 2011). One type is **outcome-based pressure** in which *a person is distracted from focusing on what he or she supposed to be doing, but instead focuses on the outcome of the task.* For example, if a person is worried about passing an exam, attention is directed toward thoughts about the outcome, depleting resources from doing the task itself. The consequence is that performance declines and the grade suffers. This type of pressure results in a decline in attentional control for the person. That is, their attention is more likely to wander away from what it is that they are supposed to be processing toward task-irrelevant thoughts.

An example of outcome-based pressure, and the cognitive distraction that can accompany it, is when people are solving math problems (e.g., Beilock, 2008; Beilock, Kulp, Holt, & Carr, 2004). People in the low-pressure groups were simply instructed to do their best. In comparison, the high-pressure groups were told that if they did well, then they could earn some money (some pressure). However, they could only earn the money if both they and a person they were partnered with did well, and the partner had already finished and had done well (increasing the pressure on the participant). Finally, people were told that their performance on the test was being video-recorded to be used as examples for other teachers and students (even more pressure). What was found was that people under high pressure did worse than those under low pressure, particularly for the more challenging problems. The explanation is that people under high pressure generate more off-task thoughts about things generating the pressure. These off-task thoughts use up working memory capacity that would otherwise be used by the primary task, solving math problems.

Interestingly, one recommendation that has been made to help keep thoughts focused on the task at hand, rather than being distracted by pressure-related irrelevant thoughts, is to talk aloud when solving a problem (DeCaro, Rotar, Kendra, & Beilock, 2010). Talking aloud is thought to keep mental resources dedicated to doing the task at hand and keep working memory from being co-opted by irrelevant thoughts. Performance can then be more like normal.

The other type of pressure situation is **monitoring pressure** in which *a person focuses too much attention on the task and how they are doing it.* For example, if a person is trying to make a free throw to win the game, he may start focusing on how he is standing, how he is holding the ball, how his arm is moving through the shot, and so on. This type of pressure is a result of conscious working memory processes disrupting more automatic processes, where any conflicts between the two disrupt performance. That is, a more automatic process that works well with largely unconscious control is disrupted when conscious thoughts in working memory jostle and conflict with those automatic processes.

STEREOTYPE THREAT The influence of emotion and stress on cognition can come from any number of different sources. Some sources that people often do not think about are the social and ethnic groups we belong to and identify with, along with the cultural stereotypes of these groups that we carry around with us. When these stereotypes convey a negative view of our abilities in a typical domain, there can be an (unconscious) mental activation of this knowledge. This activation may happen even when doing something as simple as indicating gender or ethnic group when beginning to fill out a questionnaire. **Stereotype threat** occurs when this *unconscious activation of negative stereotypes leads a person to perform worse on a task than they would otherwise.* This can come about in any way that orients a person to identify with the stereotyped group, such as indicating membership in that group on a form, or being placed in a situation in which the person feels like a minority (e.g., Murphy, Steele, & Gross, 2007). For example, asking people to indicate their gender before taking tests in science or engineering can lead women to do more poorly on such tests because of a (mistaken) cultural stereotype that women are not as good at these tasks (or lead Whites to do more poorly when exposed to the stereotype that Asians do better).

Stereotype threat can influence the types of choices and decisions a person makes (Carr & Steele, 2010). For example, people do worse at solving math problems, as a consequence of stereotype threat, if they belong to a group for which the stereotype claims that they should not be good at math (e.g., Beilock, Rydell, & McConnell, 2007). As with the research on choking under pressure, stereotype threat lowers performance because a person's thoughts, and consequently working memory capacity, are consumed to some degree by counterproductive thoughts related to the stereotype. This is the case even if that effort is oriented toward suppressing the stereotype-related thoughts (Schmader, 2010). As a result, less mental capacity is available for doing the task at hand, and performance suffers.

Note that priming can also lead to an increase in performance. For example, in a study by Lang and Lang (2010), students were asked to do a series of verbal analogy problems. Before actually doing the task, one group of students was asked to imagine a person who is successful at solving problems and write down a number of abilities such a person would have, the personality traits of such a person, and how such a person would feel just before starting to solve a problem. Compared to a control group that did not do this, people who spent time imagining what it was like to be such a successful person did better on the analogy test. Thus, it is possible to attenuate test anxiety as well as magnify it.

Stress Improves Performance

Emotion, stress, and pressure can decrease performance, but it should also be noted that there are times when they can increase performance. There is bad stress and good stress. Performance can improve when the stress being experienced is viewed as challenging rather than threatening (e.g., Kassam et al., 2009). Under these circumstances there is an increase in cardiovascular efficiency, and more blood and oxygen is delivered to the body and brain, allowing it to perform at a heightened level. So, people perform better under these conditions.

As an example, consider a study by LePine, LePine, and Jackson (2004). In this study, people were assessed for their stress level at school, along with other factors such as exhaustion and academic aptitude, and their performance as measured by their grade point average. Importantly, stress was identified as being either negative stress, where school work was viewed as negative stressor and a threat, or as positive stress, where school work was viewed as a positive stressor and a challenge. Their results showed that when there was negative stress, performance was negatively affected—grades were lower. However, when it was viewed as a challenge, performance was positively affected—students had higher grades.

In addition to physiological changes that can facilitate performance, there are also more cognitive changes where pressure can improve performance. For example, if people learned a skill in a way that involved more implicit unconscious processes, such as learning to putt under dual-task conditions where attention is divided (Masters, 1992), then most of the cognitive processes involved in the task were unconscious. People trained under more explicit conscious conditions did worse under pressure. However, placing people under pressure after divided-attention training, and more implicit learning, actually improved performance. To be sure, the implicit learning people had slower learning and had worse overall accuracy—but they experienced less disruption, compared to their baseline, when they were put under pressure. Thus, the overall effect of making a task more unconscious is to insulate it more from the disruption that can occur when a person is put in stressful situations. This is why it is valuable for some professions to constantly drill and practice their skills, in a variety of settings, to the point that they are automatic and unconscious. This way, when people need these skills for real, say in a genuine emergency, they can execute the skills without succumbing to the detrimental effects of pressure.

Section Summary

- When the source of stress is viewed as a threat, there can be declines in performance, causing people to choke under pressure.
- Choking under pressure can occur when the pressure is outcome based and the focus is on the outcome of the task, or monitoring-based and the focus is on how the task is done. These different types of pressure arise under different kinds of situations.
- Some forms of pressure may be more subtle and unconscious, such as when a person experiences stereotype threat. This occurs when people are reminded of their membership in a group that cultural stereotypes suggest will not do well, and so their performance goes down.
- Stress can also improve performance when it involves activities that are highly overpracticed, or when the stress is viewed as a challenge rather than a threat.

Key Terms

amygdala (p. 472)
Easterbrook hypothesis (p. 483)
emotion (p. 471)
emotional Stroop task (p. 475)
flashbulb memories (p. 481)

intensity (p. 471)
mood-congruent memories (p. 480)
mood-dependent memories (p. 480)
outcome-based pressure (p. 489)

monitoring pressure (p. 490)
prosody (p. 485)
stereotype threat (p. 490)
tunnel memories (p. 484)
valence (p. 471)

ventro-medial prefrontal cortex (p. 472)
weapon focus effect (p. 484)
Yerkes-Dodson law (p. 483)

REFERENCES

Abbot, V., Black, J. B., & Smith, E. E. (1985). The representation of scripts in memory. *Journal of Memory and Language, 24,* 179–199.

Abelson, R. P. (1981). Psychological status of the script concept. *American Psychologist, 36,* 715–729.

Abraham, W. C. (2006). Memory maintenance: The changing nature of neural mechanisms. *Current Directions in Psychological Science, 15,* 5–8.

Abrams, R. A., & Christ, S. E. (2003). Motion onset captures attention. *Psychological Science, 14,* 427–432.

Adams, C., Smith, M. C., Nyquist, L., & Perlmutter, M. (1997). Adult age-group differences in recall for the literal and interpretive meanings of narrative text. *Journals of Gerontology, 52B,* P187–P195.

Adler, M. J., & Van Doren, C. (1972). *How to read a book: The classic guide to intelligent reading.* New York: Simon & Schuster.

Adolphs, R., & Tranel, D. (1999). Intact recognition of emotional prosody following amygdala damage. *Neuropsychologia, 37,* 1285–1292.

Agnoli, F. (1991). Development of judgmental heuristics and logical reasoning: Training counteracts the representativeness heuristic. *Cognitive Development, 6,* 195–217.

Agnoli, F., & Krantz, D. H. (1989). Suppressing natural heuristics by formal instruction: The case of the conjunction fallacy. *Cognitive Psychology, 21,* 515–550.

Ablum-Heath, M. E., & DiVesta, F. J. (1986). The effect of conscious controlled verbalization of a cognitive strategy on transfer in problem solving. *Memory & Cognition, 14,* 281–285.

Ainsworth-Darnell, K., Shulman, H. G., & Boland, J. E. (1998). Dissociating brain responses to syntactic and semantic anomalies: Evidence from event-related potentials. *Journal of Memory and Language, 38,* 112–130.

Albert, M. S., & Kaplan, E. (1980). Organic implications of neuropsychological deficits in the elderly. In L. W. Poon, J. L. Fozard, L. S. Cermak, D. Arenberg, & L. W. Thompson (Eds.), *New directions in memory and aging* (pp. 403–432). Hillsdale, NJ: Erlbaum.

Albrecht, J. E., & O'Brien, E. J. (1995). *Goal processing and the maintenance of global coherence.* Hillsdale, NJ: Erlbaum.

Allen, P. A., & Madden, D. J. (1990). Evidence for a parallel input serial analysis (PISA) model of word processing. *Journal of Experimental Psychology: Human Perception and Performance, 16,* 48–64.

Allen, R. J., Baddeley, A. D., & Hitch, G. J. (2006). Is the binding of visual features in working memory resource-demanding? *Journal of Experimental Psychology: General, 135,* 298–313.

Allport, A. (1989). Visual attention. In M. I. Posner (Ed.), *Foundations of cognitive science* (pp. 631–682). Cambridge, MA: Bradford.

Almor, A. (1999). Noun-phrase anaphora and focus: The informational load hypothesis. *Psychological Review, 106,* 748–765.

Altarriba, J., Bauer, L. M., & Benvenuto, C. (1999). Concreteness, context availability, and imageability ratings and word associations for abstract, concrete, and emotion words. *Behavior Research Methods, 31,* 578–602.

Alter, A. L., Oppenheimer, D. M., Epley, N., & Eyre, R. N. (2007). Overcoming intuition: Metacognitive difficulty activates analytic reasoning. *Journal of Experimental Psychology: General, 136,* 569–576.

Altmann, E. M., & Gray, W. D. (2002). Forgetting to remember: The functional relationship of decay and interference. *Psychological Science, 13,* 27–33.

Altmann, E. M., & Schunn, C. D. (2012). Decay versus interference: A new look at an old interaction. *Psychological Science, 23*(11), 1435–1437.

Altmann, G. T. M. (1998). Ambiguity in sentence processing. *Trends in Cognitive Sciences, 2,* 146–157.

Altmann, G. T. M., Garnham, A., & Dennis, Y. (1992). Avoiding the garden path: Eye movements in context. *Journal of Memory and Language, 31,* 685–712.

Altmann, G. T. M., & Steedman, M. (1988). Interaction with context during human sentence processing. *Cognition, 30,* 191–238.

Ambday, N., & Bharucha, J. (2009). Culture and the brain. *Current Directions in Psychological Science, 18,* 342–345.

Anaki, D., & Henik, A. (2003). Is there a "strength effect" in automatic semantic priming? *Memory & Cognition, 31,* 262–272.

Anderson, A. K. (2005). Affective influences on the attentional dynamics supporting awareness. *Journal of Experimental Psychology: General, 134,* 258–281.

Anderson, J. R. (1974). Retrieval of propositional information from long-term memory. *Cognitive Psychology, 6,* 451–474.

Anderson, J. R. (1980). *Cognitive psychology and its implications.* San Francisco: Freeman.

Anderson, J. R. (1983). *The architecture of cognition.* Cambridge, MA: Harvard University Press.

Anderson, J. R. (1985). *Cognitive psychology and its implications* (2nd ed.). New York: Freeman.

Anderson, J. R. (1993). Problem solving and learning. *American Psychologist, 48,* 35–44.

Anderson, J. R., & Bower, G. H. (1973). *Human associative memory.* Washington, DC: Winston & Sons.

Anderson, J. R., Qin, Y., Jung, K-J., & Carter, C. S. (2007). Information-processing modules and their relative modality specificity. *Cognitive Psychology, 54,* 185–217.

Anderson, J. R., & Schooler, L. J. (1991). Reflections of the environment in memory. *Psychological Science, 2,* 396–408.

Anderson, M. C. (2003). Rethinking interference theory: Executive control and mechanisms of forgetting. *Journal of Memory and Language, 49,* 415–445.

Anderson, M. C., Bjork, E. L., & Bjork, R. A. (2000). Retrieval-induced forgetting: Evidence for a recall-specific mechanism. *Psychonomic Bulletin & Review, 7,* 522–530.

Andrade, J. (1995). Learning during anaesthesia: A review. *British Journal of Psychology, 86,* 479–506.

Arbuckle, T. Y., & Cuddy, L. L. (1969). Discrimination of item strength at time of presentation. *Journal of Experimental Psychology, 81,* 126–131.

Arbuckle, T. Y., Vanderleck, V. F., Harsany, M., & Lapidus, S. (1990). Adult age differences in memory in relation to availability and accessibility of knowledge-based schemas. *Journal of Experimental Psychology: Learning, Memory, and Cognition, 16,* 305–315.

Armony, J. L., Chochol, C., Fecteau, S., & Belin, P. (2007). Laugh (or cry) and you will be remembered. *Psychological Science, 18,* 1027–1029.

Armstrong, S. L., Gleitman, L. R., & Gleitman, H. (1983). What some concepts might not be. *Cognition, 13,* 263–308.

Arnold, J. E., & Griffin, Z. M. (2007). The effect of additional characters on choice of referring expression: Everyone counts. *Journal of Memory and Language, 56,* 521–536.

Ashcraft, M. H. (1976). Priming and property dominance effects in semantic memory. *Memory & Cognition, 4,* 490–500.

Ashcraft, M. H. (1989). *Human memory and cognition.* Glenview, IL: Scott Foresman.

Ashcraft, M. H. (1993). A personal case history of transient anomia. *Brain and Language, 44,* 47–57.

Ashcraft, M. H. (1995). Cognitive psychology and simple arithmetic: A review and summary of new directions. *Mathematical Cognition, 1,* 3–34.

Ashcraft, M. H., & Christy, K. S. (1995). The frequency of arithmetic facts in elementary texts: Addition and multiplication in grades 1–6. *Journal for Research in Mathematics Education, 26,* 396–421.

Ashcraft, M. H., Kellas, G., & Needham, S. (1975). Rehearsal and retrieval processes in free recall of categorized lists. *Memory & Cognition, 3,* 506–512.

Ashcraft, M. H., & Krause, J. A. (2007). Working memory, math performance, and math anxiety. *Psychonomic Bulletin & Review, 14,* 243–248.

Aslan, A., & Bäuml, K-H. (2011). Adaptive memory: Young children show enhanced retention of fitness-related information. *Cognition, 122,* 118–122.

Aslan, A., Bäuml, K-H., & Grundgeiger, T. (2007). The role of inhibitory processes in part-list cuing. *Journal of Experimental Psychology: Learning, Memory, and Cognition, 33,* 335–341.

Atkins, S. A., & Reuter-Lorenz, P. A. (2008). False working memories? Semantic distortion in a mere 4 seconds. *Memory & Cognition, 36,* 74–81.

Atkinson, R. C., & Shiffrin, R. M. (1968). Human memory: A proposed system and its control processes. In W. K. Spence & J. T. Spence (Eds.), *The psychology of learning and motivation: Advances in research and theory* (Vol. 2, pp. 89–195). New York: Academic Press.

Atkinson, R. C., & Shiffrin, R. M. (1971). The control of short-term memory. *Scientific American, 225,* 82–90.

Atwood, M. E., & Polson, P. (1976). A process model for water jug problems. *Cognitive Psychology, 8,* 191–216.

Averbach, E., & Coriell, A. S. (1961). Short-term memory in vision. *Bell System Technical Journal, 40,* 309–328. (Reprinted in *Readings in cognitive psychology,* by M. Coltheart, Ed., 1973, Toronto: Holt, Rinehart & Winston of Canada).

Averbach, E., & Sperling, G. (1961). Short term storage and information in vision. In C. Cherry (Ed.), *Information theory* (pp. 196–211). London: Butterworth.

Axmacher, N., Cohen, M. X., Fell, J., Haupt, S., Dümpelmann, M., Elger, C. E., et al. (2010). Intracranial EEG correlates of expectancy and memory formation in the human hippocampus and nucleus accumbens. *Neuron, 65,* 541–549.

Ayers, M. S., & Reder, L. M. (1998). A theoretical review of the misinformation effect: Predictions from an activation-based memory model. *Psychonomic Bulletin & Review, 5,* 1–21.

Ayers, T. J., Jonides, J., Reitman, J. S., Egan, J. C., & Howard, D. A. (1979). Differing suffix effects for the same physical suffix. *Journal of Experimental Psychology: Human Learning and Memory, 5,* 315–321.

Baars, B. J. (1986). *The cognitive revolution in psychology.* New York: Guilford Press.

Bachoud-Levi, A. C., Dupoux, E., Cohen, L., & Mehler, J. (1998). Where is the length effect? A cross-linguistic study of speech production. *Journal of Memory and Language, 39,* 331–346.

Baddeley, A. D. (1966). Short-term memory for word sequences as a function of acoustic, semantic, and formal similarity. *Quarterly Journal of Experimental Psychology, 18,* 302–309.

Baddeley, A. D. (1976). *The psychology of memory.* New York: Basic Books.

Baddeley, A. D. (1978). The trouble with levels: A reexamination of Craik and Lockhart's framework for memory research. *Psychological Review, 85,* 139–152.

Baddeley, A. D. (1986). *Working memory.* Oxford, England: Oxford University Press.

Baddeley, A. D. (1992a). Is working memory working? The Fifteenth Bartlett Lecture. *Quarterly Journal of Experimental Psychology, 44A,* 1–31.

Baddeley, A. D. (1992b). Working memory. *Science, 255,* 556–559.

Baddeley, A. D. (2000a). The episodic buffer: A new component of working memory? *Trends in Cognitive Sciences, 4,* 417–423.

Baddeley, A. D. (2000b). The phonological loop and the irrelevant speech effect: some comments on Neath (2000). *Psychonomic Bulletin & Review, 7,* 544–549.

Baddeley, A. D., & Hitch, G. (1974). Working memory. In G. H. Bower (Ed.), *The psychology of learning and motivation* (Vol. 8, pp. 47–89). New York: Academic Press.

Baddeley, A. D., & Lieberman, K. (1980). Spatial working memory. In R. Nickerson (Ed.), *Attention and performance VIII.* Hillsdale, NJ: Erlbaum.

Baddeley, A. D., Thomson, N., & Buchanan, M. (1975). Word length and the structure of short-term memory. *Journal of Verbal Learning and Verbal Behavior, 14,* 575–589.

Baddeley, A. D., & Wilson, B. (1988). Comprehension and working memory: A single case neuropsychological study. *Journal of Memory and Language, 27,* 479–498.

Bahrick, H. P. (1983). The cognitive map of a city: 50 years of learning and memory. In G. H. Bower (Ed.), *The psychology of learning and motivation: Advances in research and theory* (Vol. 17, pp. 125–163). New York: Academic Press.

Bahrick, H. P. (1984). Semantic memory content in permastore: Fifty years of memory for Spanish learned in school. *Journal of Experimental Psychology: General, 113,* 1–29.

Bahrick, H. P., Bahrick, L. E., Bahrick, A. S., & Bahrick, P. E. (1993). Maintenance of foreign language vocabulary and the spacing effect. *Psychological Science, 4,* 316–321.

Bahrick, H. P., Bahrick, P. C., & Wittlinger, R. P. (1975). Fifty years of memories for names and faces: A cross-sectional approach. *Journal of Experimental Psychology: General, 104,* 54–75.

Bahrick, H. P., & Hall, L. K. (1991). Lifetime maintenance of high school mathematics content. *Journal of Experimental Psychology: General, 120,* 20–33.

Bahrick, H. P., Hall, L. K., & Berger, S. A. (1996). Accuracy and distortion in memory for high school grades. *Psychological Science, 7,* 265–271.

Baillargeon, R. (1986). Representing the existence and the location of hidden objects: Object permanence in 6- and 8-month-old infants. *Cognition, 23,* 21–41.

Baillargeon, R. (1987). Object permanence in 3½- and 4½-month-old infants. *Developmental Psychology, 23,* 655–664.

Baillargeon, R., Spelke, E. S., & Wasserman, S. (1985). Object permanence in five-month-old infants. *Cognition, 20,* 191–208.

Balota, D. A, & Duchek, J. M. (1988). Age-related differences in lexical access, spreading activation, and simple pronunciation. *Psychology and Aging, 3,* 84–93.

Balota, D. A., & Paul, S. T. (1996). Summation of activation: Evidence from multiple primes that converge and diverge within semantic memory. *Journal of Experimental Psychology: Learning, Memory, and Cognition, 22,* 827–845.

Balota, D. A., & Yap, M. J. (2011). Moving beyond the mean in studies of mental chronometry: The power of response time distributional analyses. *Current Directions in Psychological Science, 20,* 160–166.

Banich, M. T. (1997). *Neuropsychology: The neural bases of mental function.* Boston: Houghton Mifflin.

Banich, M. T. (2004). *Cognitive neuroscience and neuropsychology* (2nd ed.). Boston: Houghton Mifflin.

Banich, M. T. (2009). Executive function: The search for an integrated account. *Current Directions in Psychological Science, 18,* 89–94.

Banks, W. P. (1977). Encoding and processing of symbolic information in comparative judgments. In G. H. Bower (Ed.), *The psychology of learning and motivation* (Vol. 11, pp. 101–159). New York: Academic Press.

Banks, W. P., Clark, H. H., & Lucy, P. (1975). The locus of the semantic congruity effect in comparative judgments. *Journal of Experimental Psychology: Human Perception and Performance, 1,* 35–47.

Banks, W. P., Fujii, M., & Kayra-Stuart, F. (1976). Semantic congruity effects in comparative judgments of magnitude of digits. *Journal of Experimental Psychology: Human Perception and Performance, 2,* 435–447.

Bar-Hillel, M. (1980). What features make samples seem representative? *Journal of Experimental Psychology: Human Perception and Performance, 6,* 578–589.

Barnard, P. J., Scott, S., Taylor, J., May, J., & Knightley, W. (2004). Paying attention to meaning. *Psychological Science, 15,* 179–186.

Barner, D. Li, P., & Snedeker, J. (2010). Words as windows to thought: The case of object representation. *Current Directions in Psychological Science, 19,* 195–200.

Barnier, A. J. (2002). Posthypnotic amnesia for autobiographical episodes: A laboratory model for functional amnesia? *Psychological Science, 13,* 232–237.

Barron, E., Riby, L. M., Greer, J., & Smallwood, J. (2011). Absorbed in thought: The effect of mind wandering on the processing of relevant and irrelevant events. *Psychological Science, 22,* 596–601.

Barsalou, L. W. (1983). Ad hoc categories. *Memory & Cognition, 11,* 211–227.

Barsalou, L. W. (1999). Perceptual symbol systems. *Behavioral and Brain Sciences, 22,* 577–660.

Barshi, I., & Healy, A. F. (1993). Checklist procedures and the cost of automaticity. *Memory & Cognition, 21,* 496–505.

Bartlett, F. C. (1932). *Remembering: A study in experimental and social psychology.* London: Cambridge University Press.

Bassok, M., & Holyoak, K. H. (1989). Interdomain transfer between isomorphic topics in algebra and physics. *Journal of Experimental Psychology: Learning, Memory, and Cognition, 15,* 153–166.

Bassok, M., Pedigo, S. F., & Oskarsson, A. T. (2008). Priming addition facts with semantic relations. *Journal of Experimental Psychology: Learning, Memory, and Cognition, 34,* 343–352.

Bates, E., Masling, M., & Kintsch, W. (1978). Recognition memory for aspects of dialogue. *Journal of Experimental Psychology: Human Learning and Memory, 4,* 187–197.

Battig, W. F., & Montague, W. E. (1969). Category norms for verbal items in 56 categories: A replication and extension of the Connecticut category norms. *Journal of Experimental Psychology Monograph, 80* (3, Pt. 2), 1–46.

Bauer, P. J. (2007). Recall in infancy. *Current Directions in Psychological Science, 16,* 142–146.

Baum, D. R., & Jonides, J. (1979). Cognitive maps: Analysis of comparative judgments of distance. *Memory & Cognition, 7,* 462–468.

Bäuml, K-H. T., & Samenieh, A. (2010). The two faces of memory retrieval. *Psychological Science, 21,* 793–795.

Bavelas, J., Gerwing, J., Sutton, C., & Prevost, D. (2008). Gesturing on the telephone: Independent effects of dialogue and visibility. *Journal of Memory and Language, 58,* 495–520.

Bayen, U. J., Erdfelder, E., Bearden, J. N., & Lozito, J. P. (2006). The interplay of memory and judgment processes in effects of aging on hindsight bias. *Journal of Experimental Psychology: Learning, Memory, and Cognition, 32,* 1003–1018.

Bechera, A., Tranel, D., Damasio, H., Adolphs, R., Rockland, C., & Damasio, A. R. (1995). Double dissociation of conditioning and declarative knowledge relative to the amygdala and hippocampus in humans. *Science, 269,* 1115–1118.

Becker, M. W. (2009). Panic search: Fear produces efficient visual search for nonthreatening objects. *Psychological Science, 20,* 435–437.

Beech, A., Powell, T., McWilliams, J., & Claridge, G. (1989). Evidence of reduced cognitive inhibition in schizophrenics. *British Journal of Psychology, 28,* 109–116.

Beeman, M. J. (1993). Semantic processing in the right hemisphere may contribute to drawing inferences from discourse. *Brain and Language, 44,* 80–120.

Beeman, M. J. (1998). Coarse semantic coding and discourse comprehension. In M. Beeman & C. Chiarello (Eds.), *Brain right hemisphere language comprehension: perspectives from cognitive neuroscience* (pp. 255–284). Malwah, NJ: Erlbaum.

Beeman, M. J., & Bowden, E. M. (2000). The right hemisphere maintains solution-related activation for yet-to-be-solved problems. *Memory & Cognition, 28,* 1231–1241.

Beeman, M. J., & Chiarello, C. (1998). Complementary right- and left-hemisphere language comprehension. *Current Directions in Psychological Science, 7,* 2–8.

Beilock, S. L. (2008). Math performance in stressful situations. *Current Directions in Psychological Science, 17,* 339–343.

Beilock, S. L., Bertenthal, B. I., McCoy, A. M., & Carr, T. H. (2004). Haste does not always make waste: Expertise, direction of attention, and speed versus accuracy in performing sensorimotor skills. *Psychonomic Bulletin & Review, 11,* 373–379.

Beilock, S. L., & Carr, T. H. (2001). On the fragility of skilled performance: What governs choking under pressure? *Journal of Experimental Psychology: Learning, Memory, and Cognition, 33,* 983–998.

Beilock, S. L., & DeCaro, M. S. (2007). From poor performance to success under stress: Working memory, strategy selection, and mathematical problem solving under pressure. *Journal of Experimental Psychology, 130,* 701–725.

Beilock, S. L., Kulp, C. A., Holt, L. E., & Carr, T. H. (2004). More on the fragility of performance: Choking under pressure in mathematical problem solving. *Journal of Experimental Psychology: General, 133,* 584–600.

Beilock, S. L., Rydell, R. J., & McConnell, A. R. (2007). Stereotype threat and working memory: Mechanisms, alleviation, and spillover. *Journal of Experimental Psychology: General, 136,* 256–276.

Bekoff, M., Allen, C., & Burghardt, G. (Eds.) (2002). *The cognitive animal: Empirical and theoretical perspectives on animal cognition.* Cambridge, MA: MIT Press.

Bellezza, F. S. (1992). Recall of congruent information in the self-reference task. *Bulletin of the Psychonomic Society, 30,* 275–278.

Belli, R. F. (1989). Influences of misleading postevent information: Misinformation interference and acceptance. *Journal of Experimental Psychology: General, 118,* 72–85.

Belli, R. F., Lindsay, D. S., Gales, M. S., & McCarthy, T. T. (1994). Memory impairment and source misattribution in postevent misinformation experiments with short retention intervals. *Memory & Cognition, 22,* 40–54.

Benjamin, L. T., Jr., Durkin, M., Link, M., Vestal, M., & Acord, J. (1992). Wundt's American doctoral students. *American Psychologist, 47,* 123–131.

Benson, D. J., & Geschwind, N. (1969). The alexias. In P. Vincken & G. W. Bruyn (Eds.), *Handbook of clinical neurology* (Vol. 4, pp. 112–140). Amsterdam: North-Holland.

Berger, A., Henik, A., & Rafal, R. (2005). Competition between endogenous and exogenous orienting of visual attention. *Journal of Experimental Psychology: General, 134,* 207–221.

Berman, M. G., Jonides, J., & Kaplan, S. (2008). The cognitive benefits of interacting with nature. *Psychological Science, 19,* 1207–1212.

Berndt, R. S., & Haendiges, A. N. (2000). Grammatical class in word and sentence production: Evidence from an aphasic patient. *Journal of Memory and Language, 43,* 249–273.

Bernstein, D. M., & Loftus, E. F. (2009). How to tell if a particular memory is true or false. *Perspectives on Psychological Science, 4,* 370–374.

Berntsen, D. (2010). The unbidden past: Involuntary autobiographical memories as a basic mode of remembering. *Current Directions in Psychological Science, 19,* 138–142.

Berntsen, D., & Hall, N. M. (2004). The episodic nature of involuntary autobiographical memories. *Memory & Cognition, 32,* 789–803.

Berntsen, D., & Rubin, D. C. (2004). Cultural life scripts structure recall from autobiographical memory. *Memory & Cognition, 32,* 427–442.

Bertsch, S., Pesta, B. J., Wiscott, R., & McDaniel, M. A. (2007). The generation effect: A meta-analytic review. *Memory & Cognition, 35,* 201–210.

Berntsen, D., & Rubin, D. C. (2006). Flashbulb memories and posttraumatic stress reactions across the life span: Age-related effects of the German occupation of Denmark during World War II. *Psychology and Aging, 21,* 127–139.

Besner, D., & Stolz, J. A. (1999). What kind of attention modulates the Stroop effect? *Psychonomic Bulletin & Review, 6,* 99–104.

Bialystok, E. (1988). Levels of bilingualism and levels of linguistic awareness. *Developmental Psychology, 24,* 560–567.

Biederman, I. (1987). Recognition by components: A theory of human image understanding. *Psychological Review, 94,* 115–147.

Biederman, I. (1990). Higher-level vision. In E. N. Osherson, S. M. Kosslyn, & J. M. Hollerbach (Eds.), *An invitation to cognitive science* (Vol. 2, pp. 41–72). Cambridge, MA: MIT Press.

Biederman, I., & Blickle, T. (1985). *The perception of objects with deleted contours.* Unpublished manuscript, State University of New York, Buffalo.

Biederman, I., Glass, A. L., & Stacy, E. W. (1973). Searching for objects in real world scenes. *Journal of Experimental Psychology, 97,* 22–27.

Bigler, E. D., Yeo, R. A., & Turkheimer, F. (1989). Introduction and overview. In E. D. Bigler, R. A. Yeo, & F.

Turkheimer (Eds.), *Neuropsychological function and brain imaging* (p. 10). New York: Plenum Press.

Bilalić, M., McLeod, P., & Gobet, F. (2008). Inflexibility of experts—Reality or myth? Quantifying the Einstellung effect in chess masters. *Cognitive Psychology, 56,* 73–102.

Bilalić, M., McLeod, P., & Gobet, F. (2010). The mechanism of the Einstellung (set) effect: A pervasive source of cognitive bias. *Psychological Science, 19,* 111–115.

Binder, K. S. (2003). Sentential and discourse topic effects on lexical ambiguity processing: An eye movement examination. *Memory & Cognition, 31,* 690–702.

Binder, K. S., & Rayner, K. (1998). Contextual strength does not modulate the subordinate bias effect: Evidence from eye fixations and self-paced reading. *Psychonomic Bulletin & Review, 5,* 271–276.

Bireta, T. J., Surprenant, A. M., & Neath, I. (2008). Age-related differences in the von Restorff isolation effect. *Quarterly Journal of Experimental Psychology, 61,* 345–352.

Birmingham, E., Bischof, W. F., & Kingstone, A. (2008). Social attention and real world scenes: The roles of action, competition and social content. *Quarterly Journal of Experimental Psychology, 61,* 986–998.

Bisiach, E., & Luzzatti, C. (1978). Unilateral neglect of representational space. *Cortex, 14,* 129–133.

Bjork, E. L., & Bjork, R. A. (2003). Intentional forgetting can increase, not decrease, residual influences of to-be-forgotten information. *Journal of Experimental Psychology: Learning, Memory, and Cognition, 29,* 524–531.

Bjorklund, D. F., Dukes, C., & Brown, R. D. (2009). The development of memory strategies. In M. L. Courage & N. Cowan (Eds.) *The development of memory in infancy and childhood,* pp. 145–175. New York: Psychology Press.

Blair, M., Vadaga, K. K., Shuchat, J., & Li, K. Z. H. (2011). The role of age and inhibitory efficiency in working memory processing and storage components. *Quarterly Journal of Experimental Psychology, 64,* 1157–1172.

Blakemore, C. (1977). *Mechanics of the mind.* Cambridge, England: Cambridge University Press.

Blanchette, I., & Richards, A. (2004). Reasoning about emotional and neutral materials. *Psychological Science, 15,* 745–752.

Blaser, E., & Kaldy, Z. (2010). Infants get five stars on iconic memory tests: A partial-report test of 6-month-old infant's iconic memory capacity. *Psychological Science, 21,* 1643–1645.

Bliss, T. V. P., & Collingridge, G. L. (1993). A synaptic model of memory: Long-term potentiation in the hippocampus. *Nature, 232,* 31–39.

Bliss, T. V. P., & Lomo, T. (1973). Long-lasting potentiation of synaptic transmission in the dentate area of the anaesthetized rabbit following stimulations of the preforant path. *Journal of Physiology, 232,* 331–356.

Bloesch, E. K., Davoli, C. C., Roth, N., Brockmole, J. R., & Abrams, R. A. (2012). Watch this! Observed tool use affects perceived distance. *Psychonomic Bulletin & Review, 19,* 177–183.

Blom, J. P., & Gumperz, J. J. (1972). Social meaning in linguistic structure: Code-switching in Norway. In J. J. Gumperz & D. Hymes (Eds.), *Directions in sociolinguistics: The ethnography of communication* (pp. 407–434). New York: Holt.

Bloom, F. E., & Lazerson, A. (1988). *Brain, mind, and behavior.* New York: W. H. Freeman.

Bocanegra, B. R., & Zeelenberg, R. (2011). Emotion-induced trade-offs in spatiotemporal vision. *Journal of Experimental Psychology: General, 140,* 272–282.

Bock, J. K. (1982). Toward a cognitive psychology of syntax: Information processing contributions to sentence formulation. *Psychological Review, 89,* 1–47.

Bock, J. K. (1986). Meaning, sound, and syntax: Lexical priming in sentence production. *Journal of Experimental Psychology: Learning, Memory, and Cognition, 12,* 575–586.

Bock, K. (1995). Producing agreement. *Current Directions in Psychological Science, 4,* 56–61.

Bock, K. (1996). Language production: Methods and methodologies. *Psychonomic Bulletin & Review, 3,* 395–421.

Bock, K., & Griffin, Z. M. (2000). The persistence of structural priming: Transient activation or implicit learning? *Journal of Experimental Psychology: General, 129,* 177–192.

Bock, K., Irwin, D. E., Davidson, D. J., & Levelt, W. J. M. (2003). Minding the clock. *Journal of Memory and Language, 48,* 653–685.

Bock, K., & Miller, C. A. (1991). Broken agreement. *Cognitive Psychology, 23,* 45–93.

Bohn-Gettler, C. M., Rapp, D. N., van den Broek, P., Kendeou, P., & White, M. J. (2011). Adults' and children's monitoring of story events in the service of comprehension. *Memory & Cognition, 39,* 992–1011.

Bonebakker, A. E., Bonke, B., Klein, J., Wolters, G., Stijnen, T., Passchier, J., et al. (1996). Information processing during general anesthesia: Evidence for unconscious memory. *Memory & Cognition, 24,* 766–776.

Bonnefon, J. F., & Hilton, D. J. (2004). Consequential conditionals: Invited and suppressed inferences from valued outcomes. *Journal of Experimental Psychology: Learning, Memory, and Cognition, 30,* 28–37.

Borghi, A. M., Glenberg, A. M., & Kaschak, M. P. (2004). Putting words in perspective. *Memory & Cognition, 32,* 863–873.

Boring, E. G. (1950). *A history of experimental psychology* (2nd ed.). New York: Appleton-Century-Crofts.

Boroditsky, L. (2001). Does language shape thought? Mandarin and English speakers' conceptions of time. *Cognitive Psychology, 43,* 1–22.

Boroditsky, L. (2011). How language shapes thought. *Scientific American,* 63–65.

Botvinick, M. M., & Bylsma, L. M. (2006). Distraction and action slips in an everyday task: Evidence for a dynamic representation of task context. *Psychonomic Bulletin & Review, 12,* 1011–1017.

Bousfield, W. A. (1953). The occurrence of clustering in the recall of randomly arranged associates. *Journal of General Psychology, 49,* 229–240.

Bousfield, W. A., & Sedgewick, C. H. W. (1944). An analysis of sequences of restricted associative responses. *Journal of General Psychology, 30,* 149–165.

Bowden, E. M. (1985). Accessing relevant information during problem solving: Time constraints on search in the problem space. *Memory & Cognition, 13,* 280–286.

Bowden, E. M., & Beeman, M. J. (1998). Getting the right idea: Semantic activation in the right hemisphere may help solve insight problems. *Psychological Science, 9,* 435–440.

Bowden, E. M., Beeman, M., & Gernsbacher, M. A. (1995, March). *Two hemispheres are better than one: Drawing coherence inferences during story comprehension.* Paper presented at the annual meeting of the Cognitive Neuroscience Society, San Francisco.

Bower, G. H. (1970). Analysis of a mnemonic device. *American Scientist, 58,* 496–510.

Bower, G. H. (1981). Mood and memory. *American Psychologist, 36,* 129–148.

Bower, G. H., Black, J. B., & Turner, T. J. (1979). Scripts in memory for text. *Cognitive Psychology, 11,* 177–220.

Bower, G. H., Clark, M. C., Lesgold, A. M., & Winzenz, D. (1969). Hierarchical retrieval schemes in recall of categorical word lists. *Journal of Verbal Learning and Verbal Behavior, 8,* 323–343.

Bowers, J. S., & Jones, K. W. (2008). Detecting objects is easier than categorizing them. *Quarterly Journal of Experimental Psychology, 61,* 552–557.

Bradley, M. M., Greenwald, M. K., Petry, M. C., & Lang, P. J. (1992). Remembering pictures: Pleasure and arousal in memory. *Journal of Experimental Psychology: Learning, Memory, and Cognition, 18,* 379–390.

Brainerd, C. J., & Reyna, V. F. (1998). When things that were never experienced are easier to "remember" than things that were. *Psychological Science, 9,* 484–489.

Branigan, H. P., Pickering, M. J., & Cleland, A. A. (1999). Syntactic priming in written production: Evidence for rapid decay. *Psychonomic Bulletin & Review, 6,* 635–640.

Branigan, H. P., Pickering, M. J., Stewart, A. J., & McLean, J. F. (2000). Syntactic priming in spoken production: Linguistic and temporal interference. *Memory & Cognition, 28,* 1297–1302.

Bransford, J. D. (1979). *Human cognition: Learning, understanding and remembering.* Belmont, CA: Wadsworth.

Bransford, J. D., & Franks, J. J. (1971). The abstraction of linguistic ideas. *Cognitive Psychology, 2,* 331–350.

Bransford, J. D., & Franks, J. J. (1972). The abstraction of linguistic ideas: A review. *Cognition: International Journal of Cognitive Psychology, 1,* 211–249.

Bransford, J. D., & Johnson, M. K. (1972). Contextual prerequisites for understanding: Some investigations of comprehension and recall. *Journal of Verbal Learning and Verbal Behavior, 11,* 717–726.

Bransford, J. D., & Stein, B. S. (1984). *The ideal problem solver.* New York: Freeman.

Bransford, J. D., & Stein, B. S. (1993). *The ideal problem solver* (2nd ed.). New York: Freeman.

Braver, T. S., Barch, D. M., Keys, B. A., Carter, C. S., Cohen, J. D., Kaye, J. A., et al. (2001). Context processing in older adults: Evidence for a theory relating cognitive control to neurobiology in healthy aging. *Journal of Experimental Psychology: General, 130,* 746–763.

Breedin, S. D., & Saffran, E. M. (1999). Sentence processing in the face of semantic loss: A case study. *Journal of Experimental Psychology: General, 128,* 547–562.

Bremner, J. D., Shobe, K. K., & Kihlstrom, J. F. (2000). False memories in women with self-reported childhood sexual abuse: An empirical study. *Psychological Science, 11,* 333–337.

Brennan, S. E., & Clark, H. H. (1996). Conceptual pacts and lexical choice in conversation. *Journal of Experimental Psychology: Learning, Memory, and Cognition, 22,* 1482–1493.

Breslin, C. W., & Safer, M. A. (2011). Effects of event valence on long-term memory for two baseball championship games. *Psychological Science, 22,* 1408–1412.

Bresnan, J. (1978). A realistic transformational grammar. In J. Bresnan, M. Halle, & G. Miller (Eds.), *Linguistic theory and psychological reality* (pp. 1–59). Cambridge, MA: MIT Press.

Bresnan, J., & Kaplan, R. M. (1982). Introduction: Grammars as mental representations of language. In J. Bresnan (Ed.), *The mental representation of grammatical relations* (pp. xvii–iii). Cambridge, MA: MIT Press.

Bridgeman, B. (1988). *The biology of behavior and mind.* New York: Wiley.

Broadbent, D. E. (1952). Speaking and listening simultaneously. *Journal of Experimental Psychology, 43,* 267–273.

Broadbent, D. E. (1958). *Perception and communication.* London: Pergamon.

Broaders, S. C., Cook, S. W., Mitchell, Z., & Goldin-Meadow, S. (2007). Making children gesture brings out implicit knowledge and leads to learning. *Journal of Experimental Psychology: General, 136,* 539–550.

Broaders, S. C., & Goldin-Meadow, S. (2010). Truth is at hand: How gesture adds information during investigative interviews. *Psychological Science, 21,* 623–628.

Bröder, A., & Schiffer, S. (2006). Adaptive flexibility and maladaptive routines in selecting fast and frugal decision strategies. *Journal of Experimental Psychology: Learning, Memory, and Cognition, 32,* 904–918.

Broggin, E., Savazzi, S., & Marzi, C. A. (2012). Similar effects of visual perception and imagery on simple reaction time. *Quarterly Journal of Experimental Psychology, 65,* 151–164.

Brooks, J. O. III, & Watkins, M. J. (1990). Further evidence of the intricacy of memory span. *Journal of Experimental Psychology: Learning, Memory, and Cognition, 16,* 1134–1141.

Brooks, L. R. (1968). Spatial and verbal components of the act of recall. *Canadian Journal of Experimental Psychology, 22,* 349–368.

Brosch, T., Sander, D., Pourtois, G., & Scherer, K. R. (2008). Beyond fear: Rapid spatial orienting toward positive emotional stimuli. *Psychological Science, 19,* 362–370.

Brown, A. S. (1991). A review of the tip-of-the-tongue experience. *Psychological Bulletin, 109,* 204–223.

Brown, A. S. (1998). Transient global amnesia. *Psychonomic Bulletin & Review, 5,* 401–427.

Brown, A. S. (2002). Consolidation theory and retrograde amnesia in humans. *Psychonomic Bulletin & Review, 9,* 403–425.

Brown, A. S. (2004). The déjà vu illusion. *Current Directions in Psychological Science, 13,* 256–259.

Brown, A. S., & Halliday, H. E. (1991). Cryptomnesia and source memory difficulties. *American Journal of Psychology, 104,* 475–490.

Brown, A. S., & Murphy, D. R. (1989). Cryptomnesia: Delineating inadvertent plagiarism. *Journal of Experimental Psychology: Learning, Memory, and Cognition, 15,* 432–442.

Brown, A. S., Neblett, D. R., Jones, T. C., & Mitchell, D. B. (1991). Transfer of processing in repetition priming: Some inappropriate findings. *Journal of Experimental Psychology: Learning, Memory, and Cognition, 17,* 514–525.

Brown, A. S., & Nix, L. A. (1996). Turning lies into truths: Referential validation of falsehoods. *Journal of Experimental Psychology: Learning, Memory, and Cognition, 22,* 1088–1100.

Brown, G. D. A., Neath, I., & Chater, N. (2007). A temporal ratio model of memory. *Psychological Review, 114,* 539–576.

Brown, J. A. (1958). Some tests of the decay theory of immediate memory. *Quarterly Journal of Experimental Psychology, 10,* 12–21.

Brown, N. R., & Siegler, R. S. (1992). The role of availability in the estimation of national populations. *Memory & Cognition, 20,* 406–412.

Brown, R., & Ford, M. (1961). Address in American English. *Journal of Abnormal and Social Psychology, 62,* 375–385.

Brown, R., & Kulik, J. (1977). Flashbulb memories. *Cognition, 5,* 73–99.

Brown, R., & McNeill, D. (1966). The "tip-of-the-tongue" phenomenon. *Journal of Verbal Learning and Verbal Behavior, 5,* 325–337.

Bruner, J. S., Goodnow, J. J., & Austin, G. A. (1956). *A study of thinking.* New York: Wiley.

Bryden, M. P. (1982). *Laterality: Functional asymmetry in the intact human brain.* New York: Academic Press.

Buchanan, T. W., Lutz, K., Mirzazade, S., Specht, K., Shah, N. J., Zilles, K., et al. (2000). Recognition of emotional prosody and verbal components of spoken language: An fMRI study. *Cognitive Brain Research, 9,* 227–238.

Buchner, A., & Wippich, W. (2000). On the reliability of implicit and explicit memory measures. *Cognitive Psychology, 40,* 227–259.

Buckner, R. L. (1996). Beyond HERA: Contributions of specific prefrontal brain areas to long-term memory retrieval. *Psychonomic Bulletin & Review, 3,* 149–158.

Bundesen, C. (1990). A theory of visual attention. *Psychological Review, 97,* 523–547.

Bunting, M. F., Conway, A. R. A., & Heitz, R. P. (2004). Individual differences in the fan effect and working memory capacity. *Journal of Memory and Language, 51,* 604–622.

Burgess, G. C., Gray, J. R., Conway, A. R. A., & Braver, T. S. (2011). Neural mechanisms of interference control underlie the relationship between fluid intelligence and working memory span. *Journal of Experimental Psychology: General, 140,* 674–692.

Burgess, P. W., Scott, S. K., & Frith, C. D. (2003). The role of the rostral frontal cortex (area 10) in prospective memory: a lateral versus medial dissociation. *Neuropsychologia, 41,* 906–918.

Burke, D. M., MacKay, D. G., Worthley, J. S., & Wade, E. (1991). On the tip of the tongue: What causes word finding failures in young and older adults? *Journal of Memory and Language, 30,* 542–579.

Burns, B. D. (2004). Heuristics as beliefs and as behaviors: The adaptiveness of the "hot hand." *Cognitive Psychology, 48,* 295–331.

Burns, B. D., & Corpus, B. (2004). Randomness and inductions from streaks: "Gambler's fallacy" versus "hot hand." *Psychonomic Bulletin & Review, 11,* 179–184.

Burt, C. D. B. (1992). Reconstruction of the duration of autobiographical events. *Memory & Cognition, 20,* 124–132.

Burt, C. D. B., Kemp, S., & Conway, M. (2001). What happens if you retest autobiographical memory 10 years on? *Memory & Cognition, 29,* 127–136.

Busey, T. A., & Parada, E. F. (2010). The nature of expertise in fingerprint examiners. *Psychonomic Bulletin & Review, 17,* 155–160.

Busey, T. A., Tunnicliff, J., Loftus, G. R., & Loftus, E. F. (2000). Accounts of the confidence–accuracy relation in recognition memory. *Psychonomic Bulletin & Review, 7,* 26–48.

Buswell, G. T. (1937). *How adults read.* Chicago: Chicago University Press.

Butler, A. C. (2010). Repeated testing produces superior transfer of learning relative to repeated studying. *Journal of Experimental Psychology: Learning, Memory, and Cognition, 36,* 1118–1133.

Butler, C., Muhlert, N., & Zeman, A. (2010). Accelerated long-term forgetting. In S. Della Sala (Ed.) *Forgetting* (pp. 211–238). New York: Psychology Press.

Butler, J., & Rovee-Collier, C. (1989). Contextual gating of memory retrieval. *Developmental Psychobiology, 22,* 533–552.

Byrne, R. M. J., & McEleney, A. (2000). Counterfactual thinking about actions and failures to act. *Journal of Experimental Psychology: Learning, Memory, and Cognition, 26,* 1318–1331.

Cabeza, R. (2002). Hemispheric asymmetry reduction in older adults: The HAROLD model. *Psychology and Aging, 17,* 85–100.

Campbell, J. I. D., & Graham, D. J. (1985). Mental multiplication skill: Structure, process, and acquisition. *Canadian Journal of Psychology, 39,* 338–366.

Cantor, J., & Engle, R. W. (1993). Working-memory capacity as long-term memory activation: An individual differences approach. *Journal of Experimental Psychology: Learning, Memory, and Cognition, 19,* 1101–1114.

Carli, L. L. (1999). Cognitive reconstruction, hindsight, and reactions to victims and perpetrators. *Personality and Social Psychology Bulletin, 25,* 966–979.

Carlson, B. W. (1990). Anchoring and adjustment in judgments under risk. *Journal of Experimental Psychology: Learning, Memory, and Cognition, 16,* 665–676.

Carlson, R. A., Khoo, B. H., Yaure, R. G., & Schneider, W. (1990). Acquisition of a problem-solving skill: Levels of organization and use of working memory. *Journal of Experimental Psychology: General, 119,* 193–214.

Carpenter, S. K., & Pashler, H. (2007). Testing beyond words: Using tests to enhance visuospatial map learning. *Psychonomic Bulletin & Review, 14,* 474–478.

Carr, P. B., & Steele, C. M. (2010). Stereotype threat affects financial decision making. *Psychological Science, 21,* 1411–1416.

Carr, T. H., McCauley, C., Sperber, R. D., & Parmalee, C. M. (1982). Words, pictures, and priming: On semantic activation, conscious identification, and the automaticity of information processing. *Journal of Experimental Psychology: Human Perception and Performance, 8,* 757–777.

Carriere, J. S. A., Cheyne, J. A., Solman, G. J. F., & Smilek, D. (2010). Age trends for failures of sustained attention. *Psychology and Aging, 25,* 569–574.

Carroll, D. W. (1986). *Psychology of language.* Pacific Grove, CA: Brooks/Cole.

Carstensen, L. L., & Mikels, J. A. (2005). At the intersection of emotion and cognition aging and the positivity effect. *Current Directions in Psychological Science, 14,* 117–121.

Casasanto, D. (2009). Embodiment of abstract concepts: Good and bad in right- and left-handers. *Journal of Experimental Psychology: General, 138,* 351–367.

Case, R. (1972). Validation of a neo-Piagetian mental capacity construct. *Journal of Experimental Child Psychology, 14,* 287–302.

Castel, A. D., Farb, N. A. S., & Craik, F. I. M. (2007). Memory for general and specific value information in younger and older adults: Measuring the limits of strategic control. *Memory & Cognition, 35,* 689–700.

Castel, A. D., McCabe, D. P., Roediger, H. L., & Heitman, J. L. (2007). The dark side of expertise: Domain-specific memory errors. *Psychological Science, 18,* 3–5.

Castronovo, J., & Seron, X. (2007). Semantic numerical representation in blind subjects: The role of vision in the spatial format of the mental number line. *Quarterly Journal of Experimental Psychology, 60,* 101–119.

Catrambone, R. (1996). Generalizing solution procedures learned from examples. *Journal of Experimental Psychology: Learning, Memory, and Cognition, 22,* 1020–1031.

Catrambone, R., Jones, C. M., Jonides, J., & Seifert, C. (1995). Reasoning about curvilinear motion: Using principles or analogy. *Memory & Cognition, 23,* 368–373.

Cave, K. R., & Bichot, N. P. (1999). Visuospatial attention: Beyond a spotlight model. *Psychonomic Bulletin & Review, 6,* 204–223.

Cave, K. R., & Kosslyn, S. M. (1989). Varieties of size-specific visual selection. *Journal of Experimental Psychology: General, 118,* 148–164.

Chaffin, R., & Imreh, G. (2002). Practicing perfection: Piano performance as expert memory. *Psychological Science, 13,* 342–349.

Chambers, K. L., & Zaragoza, M. S. (2001). Intended and unintended effects of explicit warnings on eyewitness suggestibility: Evidence from source identification tests. *Memory & Cognition, 29,* 1120–1129.

Chan, J. C. K., Thomas, A. K., & Bulevich, J. B. (2009). Recalling a witnessed event increases eyewitness suggestibility. *Psychological Science, 20,* 66–73.

Chang, F., Dell, G. S., & Bock, J. K. (2006). Becoming syntactic. *Psychological Review, 113,* 234–272.

Charles, S. T., Mather, M., & Carstensen, L. L. (2003). Aging and emotional memory: The forgettable nature of negative images for older adults. *Journal of Experimental Psychology: General, 132,* 310–324.

Chase, W. G., & Ericsson, K. A. (1982). Skill and working memory. In G. H. Bower (Ed.), *The psychology of learning and motivation* (Vol. 16, pp. 1–58). New York: Academic Press.

Chase, W. G., & Simon, H. A. (1973). Perception in chess. *Cognitive Psychology, 4,* 55–81.

Chasteen, A. L., Park, D. C., & Schwarz, N. (2001). Implementation intentions and facilitation of prospective memory. *Psychological Science, 12,* 457–461.

Chater, N., & Oaksford, M. (1999). The probability heuristics model of syllogistic reasoning. *Cognitive Psychology, 38,* 191–258.

Chauvel, G., Maquestiaux, F., Hartley, A. A., Joubert, S., Didierjean, A., & Masters, R. S. W. (2012). Age effects shrink when motor learning is predominantly supported by nondeclarative, automatic memory processes: Evidence from golf putting. *Quarterly Journal of Experimental Psychology, 65,* 25–38.

Chen, Y. (2007). Chinese and English speakers think about time differently? Failure of replicating Boroditsky (2001). *Cognition, 104,* 427–436.

Chen, Z., & Mo, L. (2004). Schema induction in problem solving: A multidimensional analysis. *Journal of Experimental Psychology: Learning, Memory, and Cognition, 30,* 583–600.

Chen, Z., Mo, L., & Honomichl, R. (2004). Having the memory of an elephant: Long-term retrieval and the use of analogues in problem solving. *Journal of Experimental Psychology: General, 133,* 415–433.

Cherniak, C. (1984). Prototypicality and deductive reasoning. *Journal of Verbal Learning and Verbal Behavior, 23,* 625–642.

Cherry, E. C. (1953). Some experiments on the recognition of speech, with one and with two ears. *Journal of the Acoustical Society of America, 25,* 975–979.

Cherry, E. C., & Taylor, W. K. (1954). Some further experiments on the recognition of speech with one and two ears. *Journal of the Acoustical Society of America, 26,* 554–559.

Chin-Parker, S., & Ross, B. H. (2004). Diagnosticity and prototypicality in category learning: A comparison of inference learning and classification learning. *Journal of Experimental Psychology: Learning, Memory, and Cognition, 30,* 216–226.

Chomsky, N. (1957). *Syntactic structures.* The Hague: Mouton.

Chomsky, N. (1959). A review of Skinner's *Verbal Behavior*. *Language, 35,* 26–58.

Chomsky, N. (1965). *Aspects of a theory of syntax*. Cambridge, MA: Harvard University Press.

Chomsky, N. (1968). *Language and mind*. New York: Harcourt Brace Jovanovich.

Christianson, K., Hollingworth, A., Halliwell, J. F., & Ferreira, F. (2001). Thematic roles assigned along the garden path linger. *Cognitive Psychology, 42,* 368–407.

Christianson, S. (1989). Flashbulb memories: Special, but not so special. *Memory & Cognition, 17,* 435–443.

Chrobak, Q. M., & Zaragoza, M. S. (2008). Inventing stories: Forcing witnesses to fabricate entire fictitious events leads to freely reported false memories. *Psychonomic Bulletin & Review, 15,* 1190–1195.

Chronicle, E. P., MacGregor, J. N., & Ormerod, T. C. (2004). What makes an insight problem? The roles of heuristics, goal conception, and solution recoding in knowledge-lean problems. *Journal of Experimental Psychology: Learning, Memory, and Cognition, 30,* 14–27.

Chugani, H. T., Phelps, M. E., & Mazziotta, J. C. (1986). Positron emission tomography study of human brain functional development. *Annals of Neurology, 22,* 487–497.

Cisler, J. M., Wolitzky-Taylor, K. B., Adams, T. G., Babson, K. A., Badou, C. L., & Willems, J. L. (2011). The emotional Stroop task and posttraumatic stress disorder: A meta-analysis. *Clinical Psychology Review, 31,* 817–828.

Clancy, S. A., Schacter, D. L., McNally, R. J., & Pittman, R. K. (2000). False recognition in women reporting recovered memories of sexual abuse. *Psychological Science, 11,* 26–31.

Clapp, F. L. (1924). *The number combinations: Their relative difficulty and frequency of their appearance in textbooks*. Research Bulletin No. 1. Madison, WI: Bureau of Educational Research.

Clark, H. H. (1977). Bridging. In P. N. Johnson-Laird & P. C. Wason (Eds.), *Thinking: Readings in cognitive science* (pp. 411–420). Cambridge, England: Cambridge University Press.

Clark, H. H. (1979). Responding to indirect speech acts. *Cognitive Psychology, 11,* 430–477.

Clark, H. H. (1994). Discourse in production. In M. A. Gernsbacher (Ed.), *Handbook of psycholinguistics* (pp. 985–1021). San Diego, CA: Academic Press.

Clark, H. H., & Clark, E. V. (1977). *Psychology and language*. New York: Harcourt Brace Jovanovich.

Clark, H. H., & Krych, M. A. (2004). Speaking while monitoring addressees for understanding. *Journal of Memory and Language, 50,* 62–81.

Clark, H. H., & Wasow, T. (1998). Repeating words in spontaneous speech. *Cognitive Psychology, 37,* 201–242.

Claus, B., & Kelter, S. (2006). Comprehending narratives containing flashbacks: Evidence for temporally organized representations. *Journal of Experimental Psychology: Learning, Memory, and Cognition, 32,* 1031–1044.

Cleary, A. M. (2008). Recognition memory, familiarity, and déjà vu experiences. *Current Directions in Psychological Science, 17,* 353–357.

Clifton, C., Jr., Carlson, K., & Frazier, L. (2006). Tracking the what and why of speakers' choices: Prosodic boundaries and the length of constituents. *Psychonomic Bulletin & Review, 13,* 854–861.

Clifton, C., & Frazier, L. (2004). Should given information come before new? Yes and no. *Memory & Cognition, 32,* 886–895.

Clifton, C., Jr., Traxler, M. J., Mohamed, M. T., Williams, R. S., Morris, R. K., & Rayner, K. (2003). The use of thematic role information in parsing: Syntactic processing autonomy revisited. *Journal of Memory and Language, 49,* 317–334.

Cohen, G. (1979). Language comprehension in old age. *Cognitive Psychology, 11,* 412–429.

Cokely, E. T., Kelley, C. M., & Gilchrist, A. L. (2006). Sources of individual differences in working memory capacity: Contributions of strategy to capacity. *Psychonomic Bulletin & Review, 13,* 991–997.

Colcombe, S. J., Kramer, A. F., Erickson, K. I., & Scalf, P. (2005). The implications of cortical recruitment and brain morphology for individual differences in inhibitory function in aging humans. *Psychology and Aging, 20,* 363–375.

Cole, G. G., & Kuhn, G. (2010). Attentional capture by object appearance and disappearance. *Quarterly Journal of Experimental Psychology, 63,* 147–159.

Colflesh, G. J. H., & Conway, A. R. A. (2007). Individual differences in working memory capacity and divided attention in dichotic listening. *Psychonomic Bulletin & Review, 14,* 699–703.

Colle, H. A., & Welsh, A. (1976). Acoustic masking in primary memory. *Journal of Verbal Learning and Verbal Behavior, 15,* 17–32.

Collins, A. M., & Loftus, E. F. (1975). A spreading-activation theory of semantic processing. *Psychological Review, 82,* 407–428.

Collins, A. M., & Quillian, M. R. (1969). Retrieval time from semantic memory. *Journal of Verbal Learning and Verbal Behavior, 8,* 240–247.

Collins, A. M., & Quillian, M. R. (1970). Does category size affect categorization time? *Journal of Verbal Learning and Verbal Behavior, 9,* 432–438.

Collins, A. M., & Quillian, M. R. (1972). How to make a language user. In E. Tulving & W. Donaldson (Eds.), *Organization of memory* (pp. 309–351). New York: Academic Press.

Collins, K. A., Pillemer, D. B., Ivcevic, Z., & Gooze, R. A. (2007). Cultural scripts guide recall of intensely positive life events. *Memory & Cognition, 35,* 651–659.

Coltheart, M. (1973). Readings in cognitive psychology. Toronto: Holt, Rinehart & Winston of Canada.

Comalli, P. E., Wapner, S., & Werner, H. (1962). Interference effects of Stroop color-word test in childhood, adulthood, and aging. *The Journal of Genetic Psychology: Research and Theory on Human Development, 100,* 47–53.

Coman, A., Manier, D., & Hirst, W. (2009). Forgetting the unforgettable through conversation: Socially shared retrieval-induced forgetting of September 11 memories. *Psychological Science, 20,* 627–633.

Connell, L., & Lynott, D. (2009). Is a bear white in the woods? Parallel representation of implied object color during language comprehension. *Psychonomic Bulletin & Review, 16,* 573–577.

Conrad, R., & Hull, A. (1964). Information, acoustic confusion, and memory span. *British Journal of Psychology, 55,* 75–84.

Conway, A. R. A., Cowan, N., & Bunting, M. F. (2001). The cocktail party phenomenon revisited: The importance of working memory capacity. *Psychonomic Bulletin & Review, 8,* 331–335.

Conway, M. A., Anderson, S. J., Larsen, S. F., Donnelly, C. M., McDaniel, M. A., McClelland, A. G. R., et al. (1994). The formation of flashbulb memories. *Memory & Cognition, 22,* 326–343.

Conway, M. A., Cohen, G., & Stanhope, N. (1991). On the very long-term retention of knowledge acquired through formal education: Twelve years of cognitive psychology. *Journal of Experimental Psychology: General, 120,* 395–409.

Conway, M. A., & Pleydell-Pearce, C. W. (2000). The construction of autobiographical memories in the self-memory system. *Psychological Review, 107,* 261–288.

Cook, A. E., & Myers, J. L. (2004). Processing discourse roles in scripted narratives: The influences of context and world knowledge. *Journal of Memory and Language, 50,* 268–288.

Cook, M. (1977). Gaze and mutual gaze in social encounters. *American Scientist, 65,* 328–333.

Cooke, N. J., & Breedin, S. D. (1994). Constructing naive theories of motion on the fly. *Memory & Cognition, 22,* 474–493.

Cooper, E. H., & Pantle, A. J. (1967). The total-time hypothesis in verbal learning. *Psychological Bulletin, 68,* 221–234.

Cooper, L. A., & Shepard, R. N. (1973). Chronometric studies of the rotation of mental images. In W. G. Chase (Ed.), *Visual information processing* (pp. 75–176). New York: Academic Press.

Copeland, D. E., Gunawan, K., & Bies-Hernandez, N. J. (2011). Source credibility and syllogistic reasoning. *Memory & Cognition, 39,* 117–127.

Copeland, D. E., & Radvansky, G. A. (2001). Phonological similarity in working memory. *Memory & Cognition, 29,* 774–776.

Copeland, D. E., & Radvansky, G. A. (2004a). Working memory and syllogistic reasoning. *Quarterly Journal of Experimental Psychology, 57A,* 1437–1457.

Copeland, D. E., & Radvansky, G. A. (2004b). Working memory span and situation model processing. *American Journal of Psychology, 117,* 191–213.

Copeland, D. E., Radvansky, G. A., & Goodwin, K. A. (2009). A novel study: Forgetting curves and the reminiscence bump. *Memory, 17,* 323–336.

Corballis, M. C. (1989). Laterality and human evolution. *Psychological Review, 96,* 492–505.

Corballis, M. C. (2004). The origins of modernity: Was autonomous speech a critical factor? *Psychological Review, 111,* 543–552.

Corder, M. (2004). Crippled but not crashed neural networks can help pilots land damaged planes. *Scientific American, 291,* 94–96.

Corley, M., Brockleburst, P. H., & Moat, H. S. (2011). Error biases in inner and overt speech: Evidence from tongue twisters. *Journal of Experimental Psychology: Learning, Memory, and Cognition, 37,* 162–175.

Coughlan, A. K., & Warrington, E. K. (1978). Word comprehension and word retrieval in patients with localised cerebral lesions. *Brain, 101,* 163–185.

Coulson, S., Federmeier, K. D., Van Petten, C., & Kutas, M. (2005). Right hemisphere sensitivity to word- and sentence-level context: Evidence from event-related brain potentials.

Journal of Experimental Psychology: Learning, Memory, and Cognition, 31, 127–147.

Courtney, S. M., Petit, L. Maisog, C. M., Ungerleider, L. G., & Haxby, J. V. (1998). An area specialized for spatial working memory in human frontal cortex. *Science, 279,* 1347–1351.

Cowan, N. (1995). *Attention and memory: An integrated framework.* New York: Oxford University Press.

Cowan, N. (2010). The magical mystery four: How is working memory capacity limited, and why? *Current Directions in Psychological Science, 19,* 51–57.

Cowan, N., & Morey, C. C. (2007). How can dual-task working memory retention limits be investigated? *Psychological Science, 18,* 686–688.

Cowan, N., Wood, N. L., Wood, P. K., Keller, T. A., Nugent, L. D., & Keller, C. V. (1998). Two separate verbal processing rates contributing to short-term memory span. *Journal of Experimental Psychology: General, 127,* 141–160.

Craik, F. I. M., & Byrd, M. (1982). Aging and cognitive deficits: The role of attentional resources. In F. I. M. Craik & S. Trehub (Eds.), *Aging and cognitive processes,* pp. 191–211. New York: Plenum Press.

Craik, F. I. M., Govoni, R., Naveh-Benjamin, M., & Anderson, N. D. (1996). The effects of divided attention on encoding and retrieval processes in human memory. *Journal of Experimental Psychology: General, 125,* 181–194.

Craik, F. I. M., & Lockhart, R. S. (1972). Levels of processing: A framework for memory research. *Journal of Verbal Learning and Verbal Behavior, 11,* 671–684.

Craik, F. I., & Tulving, E. (1975). Depth of processing and the retention of words in episodic memory. *Journal of experimental Psychology: General, 104*(3), 268–294.

Craik, F. I., & Watkins, M. J. (1973). The role of rehearsal in short-term memory. *Journal of verbal learning and verbal behavior, 12*(6), 599–607.

Cree, G. S., & McRae, K. (2003). Analyzing the factors underlying the structure and computation of the meaning of chipmunk, cherry, chisel, cheese, and cello (and many other such concrete nouns). *Journal of Experimental Psychology: General, 132,* 163–201.

Crosby, J. R., Monin, B., & Richardson, D. (2008). Where do we look during potentially offensive behavior? *Psychological Science, 19,* 226–228.

Crovitz, H. F., & Shiffman, H. (1974). Frequency of episodic memories as a function of their age. *Bulletin of the Psychonomic Society, 4,* 517–518.

Crowder, R. G. (1970). The role of one's own voice in immediate memory. *Cognitive Psychology, 1,* 157–178.

Crowder, R. G. (1972). Visual and auditory memory. In J. F. Kavanaugh & I. G. Mattingly (Eds.), *Language by ear and by eye: The relationships between speech and reading* (pp. 251–276). Cambridge, MA: MIT Press.

Crowder, R. G., & Morton, J. (1969). Precategorical acoustic storage (PAS). *Perception and Psychophysics, 5,* 365–373.

Cummins, D. D., Lubart, T., Alksnis, O., & Rist, R. (1991). Conditional reasoning and causation. *Memory & Cognition, 19,* 274–282.

Curran, T. (2000). Brain potentials of recollection and familiarity. *Memory & Cognition, 28,* 923–938.

Curtis, M. E., & Bharucha, J. J. (2009). Memory and musical expectation for tones in cultural context. *Music Perception, 26,* 365–375.

Dahan, D. (2010). The time course of interpretation in speech comprehension. *Current Directions in Psychological Science, 19,* 121–126.

Damasio, H., & Damasio, A. R. (1997). The lesion method in behavioral neurology and neuropsychology. In T. E. Feinberg & M. J. Farah (Eds.), *Behavioral neurology and neuropsychology* (pp. 69–82). New York: McGraw-Hill.

Daneman, M., & Carpenter, P. A. (1980). Individual differences in working memory and reading. *Journal of Verbal Learning and Verbal Behavior, 19,* 450–466.

Daneman, M., & Merikle, P. M. (1996). Working memory and language comprehension: A meta-analysis. *Psychonomic Bulletin & Review, 3,* 422–433.

Danziger, S., Kingstone, A., & Rafal, R. D. (1998). Orienting to extinguished signals in hemispatial neglect. *Psychological Science, 9,* 119–123.

Darwin, C. J., Turvey, M. T., & Crowder, R. G. (1972). An auditory analogue of the Sperling partial report procedure: Evidence for brief auditory storage. *Cognitive Psychology, 3,* 255–267.

Davachi, L., Mitchell, J. P., & Wagner, A. D. (2003). Multiple routes to memory: Distinct medial temporal lobe processes build item and source memories. *Proceedings of the National Academy of Sciences, 100,* 2157–2162.

Davelaar, E. J., Goshen-Gottstein, Y., Ashkenazi, A., Haarmann, H. J., & Usher, M. (2005). The demise of short-term memory revisited: Empirical and computational investigations of recency effects. *Psychological Review, 112,* 3–42.

Davis, M. (1997). Neurobiology of fear responses: The role of the amygdala. *Journal of Neuropsychiatry and Clinical Neurosciences, 9*, 382–402.

Davoli, C. C., Brockmole, J. R., & Goujon, A. (2012). A bias to detail: how hand position modulates visual learning and visual memory. *Memory & Cognition, 40*, 352–359.

Davoli, C. C., Brockmole, J. R., & Witt, J. K. (2012). Compressing perceived distance with remote tool-use: Real, imagined, and remembered. *Journal of Experimental Psychology: Learning, Memory, and Cognition, 38*, 80–89.

Davoli, C. C., Suszko, J. W., & Abrams, R. A. (2007). New objects can capture attention without a unique luminance transient. *Psychonomic Bulletin & Review, 14*, 338–343.

Day, S. B., & Gentner, D. (2007). Nonintentional analogical inference in text comprehension. *Memory & Cognition, 35*, 39–49.

DeCaro, M. S., Rotar, K. E., Kendra, M. S., & Beilock, S. L. (2010). Diagnosing and alleviating the impact of performance pressure on mathematical problem solving. *Quarterly Journal of Experimental Psychology, 63*, 1619–1630.

DeCaro, M. S., Thomas, R. D., Albert, N. B., & Beilock, S. L. (2011). Choking under pressure: Multiple routes to skill failure. *Journal of Experimental Psychology: General, 140*, 390–406.

Deese, J. (1959). On the prediction of occurrence of particular verbal intrusions in immediate recall. *Journal of Experimental Psychology, 58*, 17–22.

Debaene, S., Bossini, S., & Giraux, P. (1993). The mental representation of parity and number magnitude. *Journal of Experimental Psychology: General, 122*, 371–396.

de Hevia, M. D., & Spelke, E. S. (2010). Number-space mapping in human infants. *Psychological Science, 21*, 653–660.

Debon, H., & Brédart, S. (2004). False memories: Young and older adults think of semantic associates at the same rate, but young adults are more successful at source monitoring. *Psychology and Aging, 19*, 191–197.

Delany, P. F., Ericsson, K. A., & Knowles, M. E. (2004). Immediate and sustained effects of planning in a problem-solving task. *Journal of Experimental Psychology: Learning, Memory, and Cognition, 30*, 1219–1234.

Dell, G. S. (1986). A spreading-activation theory of retrieval in sentence production. *Psychological Review, 93*, 283–321.

Dell, G. S., & Newman, J. E. (1980). Detecting phonemes in fluent speech. *Journal of Verbal Learning and Verbal Behavior, 20*, 611–629.

Dell'acqua, R., & Job, R. (1998). Is object recognition automatic? *Psychonomic Bulletin & Review, 5*, 496–503.

DePaulo, B. M., & Bonvillian, J. D. (1978). The effect on language development of the special characteristics of speech addressed to children. *Journal of Psycholinguistic Research, 7*, 189–211.

Descartes, R. (1637). *Treatise on man* (T. S. Hall, Trans.). Cambridge, MA: Harvard University Press, 1972. (Original work published in 1637.)

Desmarais, G., Dixon, M. J., & Roy, E. A. (2007). A role for action knowledge in visual object identification. *Memory & Cognition, 35*, 1712–1723.

Deutsch, G., Bourbon, T., Papanicolaou, A. C., & Eisenberg, H. M. (1988). Visuospatial tasks compared via activation of regional cerebral blood flow. *Neuropsychologia, 26*, 445–452.

Deutsch, J. A., & Deutsch, D. (1963). Attention: Some theoretical considerations. *Psychological Review, 70*, 80–90.

de Vega, M., León, I., & Díaz, J. M. (1996). The representation of changing emotions in reading comprehension. *Cognition and Emotion, 10*, 303–321.

de Vega, M., Robertson, D. A., Glenberg, A. M., Kaschak, M. P., & Rinck, M. (2004). On doing two things at once: Temporal constraints on action in language comprehension. *Memory & Cognition, 32*, 1033–1043

deWinstanley, P. A., & Bjork, E. L. (2004). Processing strategies and the generation effect: Implications for making a better reader. *Memory & Cognition, 32*, 945–955.

Dewitt, L. A., & Samuel, A. G. (1990). The role of knowledge-based expectations in music perception: Evidence from musical restoration. *Journal of Experimental Psychology: General, 119*, 123–144.

Dewsbury, D. A. (2000). Comparative cognition in the 1930s. *Psychonomic Bulletin & Review, 7*, 267–283.

Diamond, A., & Gilbert, J. (1989). Development as progressive inhibitory control of action: Retrieval of a contiguous object. *Cognitive Development, 4*, 223–249.

Di Pelligrono, G., Fadiga, L., Fogassi, L., Galese, V., & Rizzolatti, G. (1992). Understanding motor events: A neurophysiological study. *Experimental Brain Research, 91*, 176–180.

Ditman, T., & Kuperberg, G. R. (2005). A source-monitoring account of auditory verbal hallucinations in patients with schizophrenia. *Harvard Review of Psychiatry, 13*, 280–299.

Dixon, R. A., Simon, E. W., Nowak, C. A., & Hultsch, D. F. (1982). Text recall in adulthood as a function of level of information, input modality, and delay interval. *Journals of Gerontology: Psychological Sciences, 37*, P358–P364.

Dodd, M. D., & MacLeod, C. M. (2004). False recognition without intentional learning. *Psychonomic Bulletin & Review, 11,* 137–142.

Dodd, M. D., Van der Stigchel, S., & Hollingworth, A. (2009). Inhibition of return and facilitation of return as a function of visual task. *Psychological Science, 20,* 333–339.

Dodson, C. S., & Krueger, L. E. (2006). I misremember it well: Why older adults are unreliable eyewitnesses. *Psychonomic Bulletin & Review, 13,* 770–775.

Dodson, C. S., & Schacter, D. L. (2002). When false recognition meets metacognition: The distinctiveness heuristic. *Journal of Memory and Language, 46,* 782–803.

Dolcos, F., Labar, K. S., & Cabeza, R. (2005). Remembering one year later: Role of the amygdala and the medial temporal lobe memory system in retrieving emotional memories. *Proceedings of the National Academy of Sciences, 102,* 2626–2631.

Donchin, E. (1981). Surprise! . . . Surprise? *Psychophysiology, 18,* 493–513.

Donders, F. C. (1969). *Over de snelheid van psychische processen [Speed of mental processes].* Onderzoekingen gedann in het Psysiologish Laboratorium der Utrechtsche Hoogeschool (W. G. Koster, Trans.). In W. G. Koster (Ed.), Attention and performance II. *Acta Psychologica, 30,* 412–431. (Original work published 1868)

Donley, R. D., & Ashcraft, M. H. (1992). The methodology of testing naive beliefs in the physics classroom. *Memory & Cognition, 20,* 381–391.

Dooling, D., & Lachman, R. (1971). Effects of comprehension on retention of prose. *Journal of Experimental Psychology, 88,* 216–222.

Dosher, B. A., & Ma, J.-J. (1998). Output loss or rehearsal loop? Output-time versus pronunciation-time limits in immediate recall for forgetting-matched materials. *Journal of Experimental Psychology: Learning, Memory, and Cognition, 24,* 316–335.

Drachman, D. A. (1978). Central cholinergic system and memory. In M. A. Lipton, A. D. Mascio, & K. F. Killam (Eds.), *Psychopharmacology: A generation of process.* New York: Raven.

Dresler, T., Mériau, K., Heekeren, H. R., & van der Meer, E. (2009). Emotional Stroop task: effect of word arousal and subject anxiety on emotional interference. *Psychological Research, 73,* 364–371.

Drolet, M., Schubotz, R. I., & Fischer, J. (2012). Authenticity affects the recognition of emotions in speech: Behavioral and fMRI evidence. *Cognitive, Affective & Behavioral Neuroscience, 12,* 140–150.

Drosopoulos, S., Schulze, C., Fischer, S., & Born, J. (2007). Sleep's function in the spontaneous recovery and consolidation of memories. *Journal of Experimental Psychology: General, 136,* 169–183.

Duchek, J. M. (1984). Encoding and retrieval differences between young and old: The impact of attentional capacity usage. *Developmental Psychology, 20,* 1173–1180.

Dunbar, K., & MacLeod, C. M. (1984). A horse race of a different color: Stroop interference patterns with transformed words. *Journal of Experimental Psychology: Human Perception and Performance, 10,* 622–639.

Duncan, E. M., & McFarland, C. E., Jr. (1980). Isolating the effects of symbolic distance and semantic congruity in comparative judgments: An additive-factors analysis. *Memory & Cognition, 8,* 612–622.

Duncan, J., Bundesen, C., Olson, A., Humphreys, G., Chavda, S., & Shibuya, H. (1999). Systematic analysis of deficits in visual attention. *Journal of Experimental Psychology: General, 128,* 450–478.

Duncan, J., & Humphreys, G. (1989). Visual search and stimulus similarity. *Psychological Review, 96,* 433–458.

Duncan, S. (1972). Some signals and rules for taking speaking turns in conversations. *Journal of Personality and Social Psychology, 23,* 283–292.

Duncker, K. (1945). On problem solving. *Psychological Monographs, 58* (Whole no. 270).

Dunlosky, J., & Hertzog, C. (2001). Measuring strategy production during associative learning: The relative utility of concurrent versus retrospective reports. *Memory & Cognition, 29,* 247–253.

Dunlosky, J., & Lipko, C. (2007). Metacomprehension: A brief history and how to improve its accuracy. *Current Directions in Psychological Science, 16,* 228–232.

Dunlosky, J., & Nelson, T. O. (1994). Does the sensitivity of judgments of learning (JOLs) to the effects of various activities depend on when the JOLs occur? *Journal of Memory and Language, 33,* 545–565.

Dyer, F. C. (2002). When it pays to waggle. *Nature, 419,* 885–886.

Dywan, J., Segalowitz, S. J., & Webster, L. (1998). Source monitoring: ERP evidence for greater reactivity to nontarget information in older adults. *Brain and Cognition, 36,* 390–430.

Eakin, D. K., Schreiber, T. A., & Sergent-Marshall, S. (2003). Misinformation effects in eyewitness memory: The presence and absence of memory impairment as a function of warning and misinformation accessibility. *Journal* *of Experimental Psychology: Learning, Memory, and Cognition, 29*, 813–825.

Ebbinghaus, H. (1885/1913). *Memory: A contribution to experimental psychology* (H. A. Ruger & C. E. Bussenius, Trans.). New York: Columbia University, Teacher's College. (Reprinted 1964, New York: Dover).

Ebbinghaus, H. (1908). *Abriss der Psychologie [Survey of psychology].* Leipzig: Veit & Comp. (Also cited as 1910.)

Edridge-Green, F. W. (1900). *Memory and its cultivation.* New York: Appleton & Co.

Edwards, D., & Potter, J. (1993). Language and causation: A discursive action model of description and attribution. *Psychological Review, 100*, 23–41.

Eerland, A., Guadalupe, T. M., & Zwaan, R. A. (2011). Leaning to the left makes the Eiffel Tower seem smaller: Posture-modulated estimation. *Psychological Science, 22*, 1511–1514.

Egan, P., Carterette, E. C., & Thwing, E. J. (1954). Some factors affecting multichannel listening. *Journal of the Acoustic Society of America, 26*, 774–782.

Eichenbaum, H., & Fortin, N. (2003). Episodic memory and the hippocampus: It's about time. *Current Directions in Psychological Science, 12*, 53–57.

Eimas, P. D. (1975). Speech perception in early infancy. In L. B. Cohen & P. Salapatek (Eds.), *Infant perception: From sensation to cognition: Vol. II. Perception of space, speech, and sound* (pp. 193–231). New York: Academic Press.

Einstein, G. O., & McDaniel, M. A. (1990). Normal aging and prospective memory. *Journal of Experimental Psychology: Learning, Memory, and Cognition, 16*, 717–726.

Einstein, G. O., & McDaniel, M. A. (2005). Prospective memory: Multiple retrieval processes. *Current Directions, 14*, 286–290.

Einstein, G. O., McDaniel, M. A., Richardson, S. L., Guynn, M. L., & Cunfer, A. R. (1995). Aging and prospective memory: Examining influences of self-initiated retrieval processes. *Journal of Experimental Psychology: Learning, Memory, and Cognition, 21*, 996–1007.

Ellis, H. D. (1983). The role of the right hemisphere in face perception. In A. W. Young (Ed.), *Functions of the right cerebral hemisphere* (pp. 33–64). New York: Academic Press.

Emery, N. J. (2000). The eyes have it: The neuroethology, function and evolution of social gaze. *Neuroscience and Biobehavioral Review, 24*, 581–604.

Engelhardt, P. E., Bailey, K. G. D., & Ferreira, F. (2006). Do speakers and listeners observe the Gricean maxim of quantity? *Journal of Memory and Language, 54*, 554–573.

Engelkamp, J., & Dehn, D. M. (2000). Item and order information in subject-performed tasks and experimenter-performed tasks. *Journal of Experimental Psychology: Learning, Memory, and Cognition, 26*, 671–682.

Engle, R. W. (2001). What is working memory capacity? In H. L. Roediger, J. S. Nairne, I. Neath, & A. M. Suprenant (Eds.), *The nature of remembering: Essays in honor of Robert G. Crowder* (pp. 297–314). Washington, DC: American Psychological Association Press.

Engle, R. W. (2002). Working memory capacity as executive attention. *Current Directions in Psychological Science, 11*, 19–23.

Epstein, R., & Kanwisher, N. (1998). A cortical representation of the local visual area. *Nature, 392*, 598–601.

Erdelyi, M. H. (2010). The ups and downs of memory. *American Psychologist, 65*, 623–633.

Erdfelder, E., & Buchner, A. (1998). Decomposing the hindsight bias: A multinomial processing tree model for separating recollection and reconstruction in hindsight. *Journal of Experimental Psychology: Learning, Memory, and Cognition, 24*, 387–414.

Erickson, T. D., & Mattson, M. E. (1981). From words to meanings: A semantic illusion. *Journal of Verbal Learning and Verbal Behavior, 20*, 540–551.

Ericsson, K. A., & Charness, N. (1994). Expert performance: Its structure and acquisition. *American Psychologist, 49*, 725–747.

Ericsson, K. A., Delaney, P. F., Weaver, G., & Mahadevan, R. (2004). Uncovering the structure of a memorist's superior "basic" memory capacity. *Cognitive Psychology, 49*, 191–237.

Ericsson, K. A., Krampe, R. T., & Tesch-Römer, C. (1993). The role of deliberate practice in the acquisition of expert performance. *Psychological Review, 100*, 363–406.

Ericsson, K. A., & Simon, H. A. (1980). Verbal reports as data. *Psychological Review, 87*, 215–251.

Ericsson, K. A., & Simon, H. A. (1993). *Protocol analysis: Verbal reports as data* (Rev. ed.). Cambridge, MA: MIT Press.

Ernst, G. W., & Newell, A. (1969). *GPS: A case study in generality and problem solving.* New York: Academic Press.

Estes, Z., Verges, M., & Barsalou, L. W. (2008). Head up, foot down: object words orient attention to the objects' typical location. *Psychological Science, 19*, 93–97.

Evans, J. St. B. T., Barston, J. L., & Pollard, P. (1983). On the conflict between logic and belief in syllogistic reasoning. *Memory & Cognition, 11,* 295–306.

Evans, J. St. B. T., Handley, S. J., Harper, C. N. J., & Johnson-Laird, P. H. (1999). Reasoning about necessity and possibility: A test of the mental model theory of deduction. *Journal of Experimental Psychology: Learning, Memory, and Cognition, 25,* 1495–1513.

Evans, J. St. B. T., Handley, S. J., Over, D. E., & Perham, N. (2002). Background beliefs in Bayesian inference. *Memory & Cognition, 30,* 179–190.

Fantz, R. L. (1963). Pattern vision in newborn infants. *Science, 140,* 296–297.

Farah, M. J., & McClelland, J. L. (1991). A computational model of semantic memory impairment: Modality specificity and emergent category specificity. *Journal of Experimental Psychology: General, 120,* 339–357.

Faroqi-Shah, Y., & Thompson, C. K. (2007). Verb inflections in agrammatic aphasia: Encoding of tense features. *Journal of Memory and Language, 56,* 129–151.

Fausey, C. M., & Boroditsky, L. (2011). Who dunnit? Cross-linguistic differences in eye-witness memory. *Psychonomic Bulletin & Review, 18,* 150–157.

Fechner, G. (1860). *Elements of psychophysics* (English ed. of Vol. 1; H. E. Adler, Trans., D. H. Howes & E. G. Boring, Eds.). New York: Holt, Rinehart & Winston, 1966.

Fedorenko, E., Gibson, E., & Rohde, D. (2006). The nature of working memory capacity in sentence comprehension: Evidence against domain-specific working memory resources. *Journal of Memory and Language, 54,* 541–553.

Feigenson, L., Debaene, S., & Spelke, E. (2004). Core systems of number. *Trends in Cognitive Science, 8,* 307–314.

Feldman, D. (1992). *When did wild poodles roam the earth? An Imponderables™ book.* New York: HarperCollins.

Feldman, J. (2003). The simplicity principle in human concept learning. *Current Directions in Psychological Science, 12,* 227–232.

Feng, J., Spence, I., & Pratt, J. (2007). Playing an action video game reduces gender differences in spatial cognition. *Psychological Science, 18,* 850–855.

Fenske, M. J., & Raymond, J. E. (2006). Affective influences of selective attention. *Current Directions in Psychological Science, 15,* 312–316.

Fernald, A., & Marchman, V. A. (2006). Language learning in infancy. In M. J. Traxler & M. A. Gernsbacher (Eds.), *Handbook of psycholinguistics* (2nd ed., pp.1027–1071). New York: Elsevier.

Ferreira, F., Henderson, J. M., Anes, M. D., Weeks, P. A., Jr., & McFarlane, D. K. (1996). Effects of lexical frequency and syntactic complexity in spoken-language comprehension: Evidence from the auditory moving-window technique. *Journal of Experimental Psychology: Learning, Memory, and Cognition, 22,* 324–335.

Ferreira, F., & Swets, B. (2002). How incremental is language production? Evidence from the production of utterances requiring the computation of arithmetic sums. *Journal of Memory and Language, 46,* 57–84.

Ferreira, V. S. (1996). Is it better to give than to donate? Syntactic flexibility in language production. *Journal of Memory and Language, 35,* 724–755.

Ferreira, V. S., & Dell, G. S. (2000). Effect of ambiguity and lexical availability on syntactic and lexical production. *Cognitive Psychology, 40,* 296–340.

Ferreira, V. S., & Firato, C. E. (2002). Proactive interference effects on sentence production. *Psychonomic Bulletin & Review, 9,* 795–800.

Ferreira, V. S., & Humphreys, K. R. (2001). Syntactic influences on lexical and morphological processing in language production. *Journal of Memory and Language, 44,* 52–80.

Fillenbaum, S. (1974). Pragmatic normalization: Further results for some conjunctive and disjunctive sentences. *Journal of Experimental Psychology, 102,* 574–578.

Fillmore, C. J. (1968). Toward a modern theory of case. In D. A. Reibel & S. A. Schane (Eds.), *Modern studies in English* (pp. 361–375). Englewood Cliffs, NJ: Prentice Hall.

Finke, R. A., & Freyd, J. J. (1985). Transformations of visual memory induced by implied motions of pattern elements. *Journal of Experimental Psychology: Learning, Memory, and Cognition, 11,* 780–794.

Finkenhauer, C., Luminet, O., Gisle, L., El-ahmadi, A., van der Linden, M., & Philipott, P. (1998). Flashbulb memories and the underlying mechanisms of their formation: Toward an emotional-integrative model. *Memory & Cognition, 26,* 516–531.

Finn, B., & Roediger, H. L. (2011). Enhancing retention through reconsolidation: Negative emotional arousal following retrieval enhances later recall. *Psychological Science, 22,* 781–786.

Fischer, M. H. (2008). Finger counting habits modulate spatial-numerical associations. *Cortex, 44,* 386–392.

Fischhoff, B. (1975). Hindsight does not equal foresight: The effect of outcome knowledge on judgment under uncertainty. *Journal of Experimental Psychology: Human Perception and Performance, 1,* 288–299.

Fischhoff, B., & Bar-Hillel, M. (1984). Diagnosticity and the base-rate effect. *Memory & Cognition, 12,* 402–410.

Fisk, J. E., & Sharp, C. (2002). Syllogistic reasoning and cognitive ageing. *Quarterly Journal of Experimental Psychology, 55A,* 1273–1293.

Fitzgerald, J. M. (2010). Culture, gender, and the first memories of black and white American students. *Memory & Cognition, 38,* 785–796.

Fleck, J. I., & Weisberg, R. W. (2004). The use of verbal protocols as data: An analysis of insight in the candle problem. *Memory & Cognition, 32,* 990–1006.

Fletcher, C. R., & Bloom, C. P. (1988). Causal reasoning in the comprehension of simple narrative texts. *Journal of Memory and Language, 27,* 235–244.

Flusberg, S. J., & Boroditsky, L. (2011). Are things that are hard to physically move also hard to imagine moving? *Psychonomic Bulletin & Review, 18,* 158–164.

Fodor, J. A., & Garrett, M. (1966). Some reflections on competence and performance. In J. Lyons & R. J. Wales (Eds.), *Psycholinguistic papers* (pp. 135–154). Edinburgh, Scotland: Edinburgh University Press.

Fong, G. T., & Nisbett, R. E. (1991). Immediate and delayed transfer of training effects in statistical reasoning. *Journal of Experimental Psychology: General, 120,* 34–45.

Forgus, R. H., & Melamed, L. E. (1976). *Perception: A cognitive-stage approach.* New York: McGraw-Hill.

Forsyth, D. K., & Burt, C. D. B. (2008). Allocating time to future tasks: The effect of task segmentation on planning fallacy bias. *Memory & Cognition, 36,* 791–798.

Foss, D. J., & Hakes, D. T. (1978). *Psycholinguistics: An introduction to the psychology of language.* Englewood Cliffs, NJ: Prentice Hall.

Franconeri, S. L., & Simons, D. J. (2003). Moving and looming stimuli capture attention. *Perception & Psychophysics, 65,* 999–1010.

Frazier, L., & Rayner, K. (1982). Making and correcting errors during sentence comprehension: Eye movements in the analysis of structurally ambiguous sentences. *Cognitive Psychology, 14,* 178–210.

Frazier, L., & Rayner, K. (1990). Taking on semantic commitments: Processing multiple meanings vs. multiple senses. *Journal of Memory and Language, 29,* 181–200.

Freedman, J. L., & Loftus, E. F. (1971). Retrieval of words from long-term memory. *Journal of Verbal Learning and Verbal Behavior, 10,* 107–115.

Freeman, J. E., & Ellis, J. A. (2003). The representation of delayed intentions: A prospective subject-performed task? *Journal of Experimental Psychology: Learning, Memory, and Cognition, 29,* 976–992.

Freud, S. (1899/1938). Childhood and concealing memories. In A. A. Brill (Ed.), *The Basic Writings of Sigmund Freud.* New York: Modern Library.

Freud, S. (1953/1905). Three essays on the theory of sexuality. In J. Strachey (Ed.), *The standard edition of the complete psychological works of Sigmund Freud* (Vol. 7, pp. 135–423). London: Hogarth. (Original work published in 1905.)

Freyd, J. J., & Finke, R. A. (1984). Representational momentum. *Bulletin of the Psychonomic Society, 23,* 443–446.

Freyd, J. J., & Jones, K. T. (1994). Representational momentum for a spiral path. *Journal of Experimental Psychology: Learning, Memory, and Cognition, 20,* 968–976.

Friederici, A. D., Hahne, A., & Mecklinger, A. (1996). Temporal structure of syntactic parsing: Early and late event-related brain potential effects. *Journal of Experimental Psychology: Learning, Memory, and Cognition, 22,* 1219–1248.

Friedman, A. (1978). Memorial comparisons without the "mind's eye." *Journal of Verbal Learning and Verbal Behavior, 17,* 427–444.

Friedman, A., & Brown, N. R. (2000). Reasoning about geography. *Journal of Experimental Psychology: General, 129,* 193–219.

Friedman, A., Brown, N. R., & McGaffey, A. P. (2002). A basis for bias in geographical judgments. *Psychonomic Bulletin & Review, 9,* 151–159.

Friedman, A., Kerkman, D. D., & Brown, N. R. (2002). Spatial location judgments: A cross-national comparison of estimation bias in subjective North American geography. *Psychonomic Bulletin & Review, 9,* 615–623.

Friedman, A., & Montello, D. R. (2006). Global-scale location and distance estimates: Common representations and strategies in absolute and relative judgments. *Journal of Experimental Psychology: Learning, Memory, and Cognition, 32,* 333–346.

Friedman, A., & Polson, M. C. (1981). Hemispheres as independent resource systems: Limited-capacity processing and cerebral specialization. *Journal of Experimental Psychology: Human Perception and Performance, 7,* 1031–1058.

Friedman, N. P., Miyake, A., Young, S. E., DeFries, J. C., Corley, R. P., & Hewitt, J. K. (2008). Individual differences in executive functions are almost entirely genetic in origin. *Journal of Experimental Psychology: General, 137,* 201–225.

Friedrich, F. J., Henik, A., & Tzelgov, J. (1991). Automatic processes in lexical access and spreading activation. *Journal of Experimental Psychology: Human Perception and Performance, 17*, 792–806.

Frieske, D. A., & Park, D. C. (1999). Memory for news in young and old adults. *Psychology and Aging, 14*, 90–98.

Frisson, S., & Pickering, M. J. (1999). The processing of metonymy: Evidence from eye movements. *Journal of Experimental Psychology: Learning, Memory, and Cognition, 25*, 1366–1383.

Frisson, S., & Wakefield, M. (2012). Psychological essentialist reasoning and perspective taking during reading: A donkey is not a zebra, but a plate can be a clock. *Memory & Cognition, 40*, 297–310.

Fromkin, V. A. (1971). The non-anomalous nature of anomalous utterances. *Language, 47*, 27–52.

Fromkin, V. A., & Rodman, R. (1974). *An introduction to language*. New York: Holt, Rinehart & Winston.

Frost, P. (2000). The quality of false memory over time: Is memory for misinformation "remembered" or "known"? *Psychonomic Bulletin & Review, 7*, 531–536.

Fukuda, K., Vogel, E., Mayr, U., & Awh, E. (2010). Quality, not quantity: the relationship between fluid intelligence and working memory capacity. *Psychonomic Bulletin & Review, 17*, 673–679.

Fung, H. H., Lai, P., & Ng, R. (2001). Age differences in social preferences among Taiwanese and Mainland Chinese: the role of perceived time. *Psychology and Aging, 16*, 351–356.

Galanter, E. (1962). Contemporary psychophysics. In R. Brown, E. Galanter, E. H. Hess, & G. Mandler (Eds.), *New directions in psychology* (Vol. 1, pp. 87–156). New York: Holt, Rinehart & Winston.

Galantucci, B., Fowler, C. A., & Turvey, M. T. (2006). The motor theory of speech perception reviewed. *Psychonomic Bulletin & Review, 13*, 361–377.

Gallo, D. A. (2010). False memories and fantastic beliefs: 15 years of the DRM illusion. *Memory & Cognition, 38*, 833–848.

Gallo, D. A., & Roediger, H. L. (2003). The effects of associations and aging on illusory recollection. *Memory & Cognition, 31*, 1036–1044.

Galton, F. (1879). Psychometric experiments. *Brain: A Journal of Neurology, II*, 149–162.

Garcia-Retamero, R., Wallin, A., & Dieckmann, A. (2007). Does causal knowledge help us be faster and more frugal in our decisions? *Memory & Cognition, 35*, 1399–1409.

Gardner, H. (1985). *The mind's new science: A history of the cognitive revolution*. New York: Basic Books.

Garrett, M. F. (1975). The analysis of sentence production. In G. H. Bower (Ed.), *The psychology of learning and memory* (Vol. 9, pp. 133–177). New York: Academic Press.

Garry, M., Manning, C. G., Loftus, E. F., & Sherman, S. J. (1996). Imagination inflation: Imagining a childhood event inflates confidence that it occurred. *Psychonomic Bulletin & Review, 3*, 208–214.

Garry, M., & Polaschek, D. L. L. (2000). Imagination and memory. *Current Directions in Psychological Science, 9*, 6–10.

Gates, A. I. (1917). Recitation as a factor in memorizing. *Archives of Psychology, 40*, 104.

Gazzaniga, M. S. (1995). Principles of human brain organization derived from split-brain studies. *Neuron, 14*, 217–228.

Gazzaniga, M. S., Ivry, R. B., & Mangun, G. R. (1998). *Cognitive neuroscience: The biology of the mind*. New York: W. W. Norton.

Gazzaniga, M. S., & Sperry, R. W. (1967). Language after section of the cerebral commissures. *Brain, 90*, 131–148.

Geary, D. C. (1992). Evolution of human cognition: Potential relationship to the ontogenetic development of behavior and cognition. *Evolution and Cognition, 1*, 93–100.

Geary, D. C. (1994). *Children's mathematical development: Research and practical applications*. Washington, DC: American Psychological Association.

Gennari, S. P. (2004). Temporal references and temporal relations in sentence comprehension. *Journal of Experimental Psychology: Learning, Memory, and Cognition, 30*, 877–890.

Gentner, D., & Collins, A. (1981). Studies of inference from lack of knowledge. *Memory & Cognition, 9*, 434–443.

Gentner, D., & Markman, A. B. (1997). Structure mapping in analogy and similarity. *American Psychologist, 52*, 45–56.

Gerard, L. D., Zacks, R. T., Hasher, L., & Radvansky, G. A. (1991). Age deficits in retrieval: The fan effect. *Journal of Gerontology, 46*, 131–136.

Gerhardstein, P., & Rovee-Collier, C. (2002). The development of visual search in infants and very young children. *Journal of Experimental Child Psychology, 81*, 194–215.

Gernsbacher, M. A. (1990). *Language comprehension as structure building*. Hillsdale, NJ: Erlbaum.

Gernsbacher, M. A. (1997). Two decades of structure building. *Discourse Processes, 23*, 265–304.

Gernsbacher, M. A., & Faust, M. E. (1991). The mechanism of suppression: A component of general comprehension skill. *Journal of Experimental Psychology: Learning, Memory, & Cognition, 17,* 245–262.

Gernsbacher, M. A., & Hargreaves, D. (1988). Accessing sentence participants: The advantage of first mention. *Journal of Memory and Language, 27,* 699–717.

Gernsbacher, M. A., Hallada, B. M., & Robertson, R. R. W. (1998). How automatically do readers infer fictional characters' emotional states? *Scientific Studies of Reading, 2,* 271–300.

Gernsbacher, M. A., Hargreaves, D., & Beeman, M. (1989). Building and accessing clausal representations: The advantage of first mention versus the advantage of clause recency. *Journal of Memory and Language, 28,* 735–755.

Gernsbacher, M. A., Keysar, B., Robertson, R. R. W., & Werner, N. K. (2001). The role of suppression and enhancement in understanding metaphors. *Journal of Memory and Language, 45,* 433–450.

Gernsbacher, M. A., & Robertson, R. R. W. (1992). Knowledge activation vs mapping when representing fictional characters' emotional states. *Language and Cognitive Processes, 7,* 337–353.

Gershkoff-Stowe, L., & Goldin-Meadow, S. (2002). Is there a natural order for expressing semantic relations? *Cognitive Psychology, 45,* 375–412.

Geschwind, N. (1967). The varieties of naming errors. *Cortex, 3,* 97–112.

Geschwind, N. (1970). The organisation of language and the brain. *Science, 170,* 940–944.

Gevers, W., Reynvoet, B., & Fias, W. (2004). The mental representation of ordinal sequences is spatially organised: Evidence from days of the week. *Cortex, 40,* 171–172.

Gevins, A., Smith, M. E., McEvoy, L., & Yu, D. (1997). High resolution EEG mapping of cortical activation related to working memory: Effects of task difficulty, type of processing, and practice. *Cerebral Cortex, 7,* 374–385.

Giambra, L. M. (1977). Adult male daydreaming across the life span: A replication, further analyses, and tentative norms based upon retrospective reports. *International Journal of Aging and Human Development, 8,* 197–228.

Giambra, L. M. (1989). Task-unrelated-thought frequency as a function of age: A laboratory study. *Psychology and Aging. 4,* 136–143.

Gick, M. L., & Holyoak, K. J. (1980). Analogical problem solving. *Cognitive Psychology, 12,* 306–355.

Gigerenzer, G. (1996). On narrow norms and vague heuristics: A reply to Kahneman and Tversky. *Psychological Review, 103,* 592–596.

Gigerenzer, G. (2004). Dread risk, September 11, and fatal traffic accidents. *Psychological Science, 15,* 286–287.

Gigerenzer, G. (2008). Why heuristics work. *Perspectives in Psychological Science, 3,* 20–29.

Gigerenzer, G., & Goldstein, D. G. (1996). Reasoning the fast and frugal way: Models of bounded rationality. *Psychological Review, 104,* 650–669.

Gilhooly, K. J., Philips, L. H., Wynn, V., Logie, R. H., & Della Sala, S. (1999). Planning processes and age in the five-disc tower of London task. *Thinking and Reasoning, 5,* 339–361.

Gilinsky, A. S., & Judd, B. B. (1994). Working memory and bias in reasoning across the life span. *Psychology and Aging, 9,* 356–371.

Gillihan, S. J., & Farah, M. J. (2005). Is the self special? A critical review of evidence from experimental psychology and cognitive neuroscience. *Psychological Bulletin, 131,* 76–97.

Gilovich, T., Vallone, R., & Tversky, A. (1985). The hot hand in basketball: On the misperception of random sequences. *Cognitive Psychology, 17,* 295–314.

Glanzer, M. (1972). Storage mechanisms in recall. In G. H. Bower & J. T. Spence (Eds.), *The psychology of learning and motivation* (Vol. 5, pp. 129–193). New York: Academic Press.

Glanzer, M., & Cunitz, A. R. (1966). Two storage mechanisms in free recall. *Journal of Verbal Learning and Verbal Behavior, 5,* 351–360.

Glass, A. L., & Holyoak, K. J. (1986). *Cognition* (2nd ed.). New York: Random House.

Glaze, J. A. (1928). The association value of nonsense syllables. *Journal of Genetic Psychology, 35,* 255–269.

Gleason, J. B. (1985). Studying language development. *The development of language.* Boston: Allyn & Bacon/Longman.

Glenberg, A. (2011). Introduction to the mirror neuron forum. *Perspectives on Psychological Science, 6,* 363–368.

Glenberg, A., & Adams, F. (1978). Type I rehearsal and recognition. *Journal of Verbal Learning and Verbal Behavior, 17,* 455–464.

Glenberg, A. M., & Lehmann, T. S. (1980). Spacing repetitions over 1 week. *Memory & Cognition, 8,* 528–538.

Glenberg, A., Smith, S. M., & Green, C. (1977). Type I rehearsal: Maintenance and more. *Journal of Verbal Learning and Verbal Behavior, 11*, 403–416.

Glück, J., & Bluck, S. (2007). Looking back across the life span: A life story account of the reminiscence bump. *Memory & Cognition, 35*, 1928–1939.

Glucksberg, S., & Danks, J. H. (1975). *Experimental psycholinguistics: An introduction.* Hillsdale, NJ: Erlbaum.

Glucksberg, S., & Keysar, B. (1990). Understanding metaphorical comparisons: Beyond similarity. *Psychological Review, 97*, 3–18.

Glucksberg, S., & McCloskey, M. (1981). Decisions about ignorance: Knowing that you don't know. *Journal of Experimental Psychology: Human Learning and Memory, 7*, 311–325.

Gobet, F., & Simon, H. A. (1996). Recall of random and distorted chess positions: Implications for the theory of expertise. *Memory & Cognition, 24*, 493–503.

Godden, D. B., & Baddeley, A. D. (1975). Context-dependent memory in two natural environments: On land and underwater. *British Journal of Psychology, 66*, 325–331.

Gogate, L. J., & Hollich, G. (2010). Invariance detection within an interactive system: A perceptual gateway to language development. *Psychological Review, 117*, 496–516.

Gold, P. E., Cahill, L., & Wenk, G. L. (2002). Ginkgo biloba: A cognitive enhancer? *Psychological Science in the Public Interest, 3*, 2–11.

Gold, P. E., Cahill, L., & Wenk, G. L. (2003). The lowdown on ginkgo biloba. *Scientific American, 288*, 86–92.

Goldin-Meadow, S. (1997). When gestures and words speak differently. *Psychological Science, 6*, 138–143.

Goldin-Meadow, S. (2006). Talking and thinking with our hands. *Current Directions in Psychological Science, 15*, 34–39.

Goldin-Meadow, S., & Beilock, S. L. (2010). Action's influence on thought: The case of gesture. *Perspectives on Psychological Science, 5*, 664–674.

Goldinger, S. D., Kleider, H. M., Azuma, T., & Beike, D. R. (2003). "Blaming the victim" under memory load. *Psychological Science, 14*, 81–85.

Goldstein, D. G., & Gigerenzer, G. (2002). Models of ecological rationality: The recognition heuristic. *Psychological Review, 109*, 75–90.

Goodglass, H., Kaplan, E., Weintraub, S., & Ackerman, N. (1976). The "tip-of-the-tongue" phenomenon in aphasia. *Cortex, 12*, 145–153.

Goodwin, D. W., Powell, B., Bremeer, D., Hoine, H., & Stern, J. (1969). Alcohol and recall: State-dependent effects in man. *Science, 163*, 2358–2360.

Goodwin, G. P., & Johnson-Laird, P. N. (2005). Reasoning about relations. *Psychological Review, 112*, 468–493.

Gordon, B., Hart, J., Jr., Boatman, D., & Lesser, R. P. (1997). Cortical stimulation (interference) during behavior. In T. E. Feinberg & M. J. Farah (Eds.), *Behavioral neurology and neuropsychology* (pp. 667–672). New York: McGraw-Hill.

Gordon, P. C., & Chan, D. (1995). Pronouns, passives, and discourse coherence. *Journal of Memory and Language, 34*, 216–231.

Gordon, P. C., & Scearce, K. A. (1995). Pronominalization and discourse coherence, discourse structure and pronoun interpretation. *Memory & Cognition, 23*, 313–323.

Goshen-Gottstein, Y., & Kempinski, H. (2001). Probing memory with conceptual cues at multiple retention intervals: A comparison of forgetting rates on implicit and explicit tests. *Psychonomic Bulletin & Review, 8*, 139–146.

Graesser, A. C. (1981). *Prose comprehension beyond the word.* New York: Springer.

Graesser, A. C., & Nakamura, G. V. (1982). The impact of a schema on comprehension and memory. In G. H. Bower (Ed.), *The psychology of learning and motivation* (pp. 59–109). New York: Academic Press.

Graesser, A. C., Singer, M., & Trabasso, T. (1994). Constructing inferences during narrative text comprehension. *Psychological Review, 101*, 371–395.

Graf, P., & Schacter, D. L. (1987). Selective effects of interference on implicit and explicit memory for new associations. *Journal of Experimental Psychology: Learning, Memory, and Cognition, 13*, 45–53.

Grafman, J., Pascual-Leone, A., Always, D., Nichelli, E., Gomez-Tortosa, E., & Hallett, M. (1994). Induction of a recall deficit by rapid-rate transcranial magnetic stimulation. *Neuroreport, 5*, 1157–1160.

Graham, E. R., & Burke, D. M. (2011). Aging increases inattention blindness to the gorilla in our midst. *Psychology and Aging, 26*, 162–166.

Gray, R., Beilock, S. L., & Carr, T. H. (2007). "As soon as the bat met the ball, I knew it was gone": Outcome prediction, hindsight bias, and the representation and control of action in expert and novice baseball players. *Psychonomic Bulletin & Review, 14*, 669–675.

Greenberg, J. H. (1978). Generalizations about numeral systems. In J. H. Greenberg (Ed.), *Universals of human* *language: Vol. 3. Word structure* (pp. 249–295). Stanford, CA: Stanford University Press.

Greenberg, S. N., Healy, A. F., Koriat, A., & Kreiner, H. (2004). The GO model: A reconsideration of the role of structural units in guiding and organizing text on line. *Psychonomic Bulletin & Review, 11,* 428–433.

Greene, R. L. (1986). Effects of intentionality and strategy on memory for frequency. *Journal of Experimental Psychology: Learning, Memory, and Cognition, 12,* 489–495.

Greeno, J. G. (1974). Hobbits and orcs: Acquisition of a sequential concept. *Cognitive Psychology, 6,* 270–292.

Greeno, J. G. (1978). Natures of problem-solving abilities. In W. K. Estes (Ed.), *Handbook of learning and cognitive processes: Vol. 5. Human information processing* (pp. 239–270). Hillsdale, NJ: Erlbaum.

Greenspan, S. L. (1986). Semantic flexibility and referential specificity of concrete nouns. *Journal of Memory and Language, 25,* 539–557.

Greenwald, A. G., Spangenberg, E. R., Pratkanis, A. R., & Eskenazi, J. (1991). Double-blind tests of subliminal self-help audiotapes. *Psychological Science, 2,* 119–122.

Grice, H. P. (1975). Logic and conversation. In P. Cole & J. L. Morgan (Eds.), *Syntax and semantics: Vol. 3. Speech acts* (pp. 41–58). New York: Seminar Press.

Griffin, D., & Tversky, A. (1992). The weighing of evidence and the determinants of confidence. *Cognitive Psychology, 24,* 411–435.

Griffin, T. D., Wiley, J., & Thiede, K. W. (2008). Individual differences, rereading, and self-explanation: Concurrent processing and cue validity as constraints on metacomprehension accuracy. *Memory & Cognition, 36,* 93–103.

Griffin, Z. M. (2003). A reversed word length effect in coordinating the preparation and articulation of words in speaking. *Psychonomic Bulletin & Review, 10,* 603–609.

Griffin, Z. M., & Bock, K. (2000). What the eyes say about speaking. *Psychological Science, 11,* 274–279.

Griffiths, T. L., Steyvers, M., & Tenebaum, J. B. (2007). Topics in semantic representation. *Psychological Review, 114,* 211–244.

Grill-Spector, K., & Kanwisher, N. (2005). Visual recognition: As soon as you know it is there, you know what it is. *Psychological Science, 16,* 152–160.

Grossman, M., Smith, E. E., Koenig, P., Glosser, G., DeVita, C., Moore, P., & McMillan, C. (2002). The neural basis for categorization in semantic memory. *Neuroimage, 17,* 1549–1561.

Gruppuso, V., Lindsay, D. S., & Masson, M. E. J. (2007). I'd know that face anywhere! *Psychonomic Bulletin & Review, 14,* 1085–1089.

Gupta, P., & Cohen, N. J. (2002). Theoretical and computational analysis of skill learning, repetition priming, and procedural memory. *Psychological Review, 109,* 401–448.

Gustafsson, B., & Wigstrom, H. (1988). Physiological mechanisms underlying long-term potentiation. *Trends in Neuroscience, 11,* 156–163.

Gutchess, A. H., Welsh, R. C., Boduroglu, A., & Park, D. C. (2006). Cultural differences in neural function associated with object processing. *Cognitive, Affective, & Behavioral Neuroscience, 6,* 102–109.

Gygax, P., Garnham, A., & Oakhill, J. (2004). Inferring characters' emotional states: Can readers infer specific emotions? *Language and Cognitive Processes, 19,* 613–639.

Haber, R. N., & Hershenson, M. (1973). *The psychology of visual perception.* New York: Holt, Rinehart & Winston.

Habib, R., Nyberg, L., & Tulving, E. (2003). Hemispheric asymmetries of memory: The HERA model revisited. *Trends in Cognitive Science, 7,* 241–245.

Hagmayer, Y., & Sloman, S. A. (2009). Decision makers conceive of their choices as interventions. *Journal of Experimental Psychology: General, 138,* 22–38.

Hahn, U., & Warren, P. A. (2009). Perceptions of randomness: Why three heads are better than four. *Psychological Review, 116,* 454–461.

Haines, R. F. (1991). A breakdown in simultaneous information processing. In G. Obrecht & L. W. Stark (Eds.), *Presbyopia research* (pp. 171–175). New York: Plenum Press.

Hall, J. F. (1971). *Verbal learning and retention.* Philadelphia: Lippincott.

Hambrick, D. Z. (2003). Why are some people more knowledgeable than others? A longitudinal study of knowledge acquisition. *Memory & Cognition, 31,* 902–917.

Hambrick, D. Z., & Engle, R. W. (2002). Effects on domain knowledge, working memory capacity, and age on cognitive performance: An investigation of the knowledge-is-power hypothesis. *Cognitive Psychology, 44,* 339–387.

Hambrick, D. Z., & Meinz, E. J. (2011). Limits on the predictive power of domain-specific experience and knowledge in skilled performance. *Current Directions in Psychological Science, 20,* 275–279.

Hanley, J. R., & Chapman, E. (2008). Partial knowledge in a tip-of-the-tongue state about two- and three-word proper names. *Psychonomic Bulletin & Review, 15,* 156–160.

Hannigan, S. L., & Reinitz, M. T. (2001). A demonstration and comparison of two types of inference-based memory errors. *Journal of Experimental Psychology: Learning, Memory, and Cognition, 27,* 931–940.

Hannigan, S. L., & Reinitz, M. T. (2003). Migration of objects and inferences across episodes. *Memory & Cognition, 31,* 434–444.

Hanson, C., & Hirst, W. (1988). Frequency encoding of token and type information. *Journal of Experimental Psychology: Learning, Memory, and Cognition, 14,* 289–297.

Harley, E. M., Carlsen, K. A., & Loftus, G. R. (2004). The "saw-it-all-along" effect: Demonstrations of visual hindsight bias. *Journal of Experimental Psychology: Learning, Memory, and Cognition, 30,* 960–968.

Harris, R. J., & Monaco, G. E. (1978). Psychology of pragmatic implication: Information processing between the lines. *Journal of Experimental Psychology, 107,* 1–22.

Hart, J. T. (1965). Memory and the feeling-of-knowing experience. *Journal of Educational Psychology, 56,* 208–216.

Hartley, J. T., Stojack, C. C., Mushaney, T. J., Annon, T. A. K., & Lee, D. W. (1994). Reading speed and prose memory in older and younger adults. *Psychology and Aging, 9,* 216–223.

Hartshorn, K., Rovee-Collier, C., Gerhardstein, P., Bhatt, R. S., Wondoloski, T. L., Klein, P., et al. (1998). The ontogeny of long-term memory over the first year-and-a-half of life. *Developmental Psychobiology, 32,* 69–89.

Hartsuiker, R. J., Anton-Mendez, I., & van Zee, M. (2001). Object attraction in subject-verb agreement construction. *Journal of Memory and Language, 45,* 546–572.

Hartsuiker, R. J., & Kolk, H. H. J. (2001). Error monitoring in speech production: A computational test of the perceptual loop theory. *Cognitive Psychology, 42,* 113–157.

Hasher, L., & Griffin, M. (1978). Reconstructive and reproductive processes in memory. *Journal of Experimental Psychology: Human Learning and Memory, 4,* 318–330.

Hasher, L., & Zacks, R. T. (1984). Automatic processing of fundamental information: The case of frequency of occurrence. *American Psychologist, 39,* 1372–1388.

Hasher, L., & Zacks, R. T. (1988). Working memory, comprehension, and aging: A review and a new view. In G. H. Bower (Ed.), *The psychology of learning and motivation* (Vol. 22, pp. 193–225). New York: Academic Press.

Hashtroudi, S., Johnson, M. K., & Chrosniak, L. D. (1990). Aging and qualitative characteristics of memories for perceived and imagined complex events. *Psychology and Aging, 5,* 119–126.

Haviland, S. E., & Clark, H. H. (1974). What's new? Acquiring new information as a process in comprehension. *Journal of Verbal Learning and Verbal Behavior, 13,* 512–521.

Hayes, J. R., & Simon, H. A. (1974). Understanding written problem instructions. In L. W. Gregg (Ed.), *Knowledge and cognition* (pp. 167–200). Hillsdale, NJ: Erlbaum.

Haywood, S. L., Pickering, M. J., & Branigan, H. P. (2005). Do speakers avoid ambiguities during dialogue? *Psychological Science, 16,* 362–366.

Heaps, C. M., & Nash, M. (2001). Comparing recollective experience in true and false autobiographical memories. *Journal of Experimental Psychology: Learning, Memory, and Cognition, 27,* 920–930.

Hecht, H., & Proffitt, D. R. (1995). The price of expertise: Effects of experience on the water-level task. *Psychological Science, 6,* 90–95.

Heil, M., Rolke, B., & Pecchinenda, A. (2004). Automatic semantic activation is no myth: Semantic context effects on the N400 in the letter-search task in the absence of response time effects. *Psychological Science, 15,* 852–857.

Hell, W., Gigerenzer, G., Gauggel, S., Mall, M., & Muller, M. (1988). Hindsight bias: An interaction of automatic and motivational factors? *Memory & Cognition, 16,* 533–538.

Hellyer, S. (1962). Frequency of stimulus presentation and short-term decrement in recall. *Journal of Experimental Psychology, 64,* 650.

Helsabeck, F., Jr. (1975). Syllogistic reasoning: Generation of counterexamples. *Journal of Educational Psychology, 67,* 102–108.

Henderson, J. M., & Anes, M. D. (1994). Roles of object-file review and type priming in visual identification within and across eye fixations. *Journal of Experimental Psychology: Human Perception and Performance, 20,* 826–839.

Henderson, J. M., & Hollingsworth, A. (2003). Global transsaccadic change in blindness during scene perception. *Psychological Science, 14,* 493–497.

Henkel, L. A. (2004). Erroneous memories arising from repeated attempts to remember. *Journal of Memory and Language, 50,* 26–46.

Henry, J. D., MacLeod, M. S., Philips, L. H., & Crawford, J. R. (2004). A meta-analytic review of prospective memory and aging. *Psychology and Aging, 19,* 27–39.

Herrera, A., Macizo, P., & Semenza, C. (2008). The role of working memory in the association between number magnitude and space. *Acta Psychologica, 128,* 225–237.

Hertwig, R., Barron, G., Weber, E. U., & Erev, I. (2004). Decision from experience and the effect of rare events in risky choice. *Psychological Science, 15*, 534–539.

Herz, R. S., & Engen, T. (1996). Odor memory: Review and analysis. *Psychonomic Bulletin & Review, 3*, 300–313.

Herz, R. S., & Schooler, J. W. (2002). A naturalistic study of autobiographical memories evoked by olfactory and visual cues: Testing the Proustian hypothesis. *American Journal of Psychology, 115*, 21–32.

Hess, T. M. (2005). Memory and aging in context. *Psychological Bulletin, 131*, 383–406.

Hicks, J. L., & Marsh, R. L. (2000). Toward specifying the attentional demands of recognition memory. *Journal of Experimental Psychology: Learning, Memory, and Cognition, 26*, 1483–1498.

Higham, P. A., & Garrard, C. (2005). Not all errors are created equal: Metacognition and changing answers on multiple-choice tests. *Canadian Journal of Experimental Psychology, 59*, 28–34.

Hildreth, E. C., & Ullman, S. (1989). The computational study of vision. In M. I. Posner (Ed.), *Foundations of cognitive science* (pp. 581–630). Cambridge, MA: Bradford.

Hinson, J. M., Jameson, T. L., & Whitney, P. (2003). Impulsive decision making and working memory. *Journal of Experimental Psychology: Learning, Memory, and Cognition, 29*, 298–306.

Hintzman, D. L. (1978). *The psychology of learning and memory*. San Francisco: Freeman.

Hirshman, E., & Durante, R. (1992). Prime identification and semantic priming. *Journal of Experimental Psychology: Learning, Memory, and Cognition, 18*, 255–265.

Hirshman, E., Whelley, M. M., & Palij, M. (1989). An investigation of paradoxical memory effects. *Journal of Memory and Language, 28*, 594–609.

Hirst, W., & Kalmar, D. (1987). Characterizing attentional resources. *Journal of Experimental Psychology: General, 116*, 68–81.

Hoch, S. J. (1984). Availability and interference in predictive judgment. *Journal of Experimental Psychology: Learning, Memory, and Cognition, 10*, 649–662.

Hoch, S. J. (1985). Counterfactual reasoning and accuracy in predicting personal events. *Journal of Experimental Psychology: Learning, Memory, and Cognition, 11*, 719–731.

Hoch, S. J., & Loewenstein, G. F. (1989). Outcome feedback: Hindsight and information. *Journal of Experimental Psychology: Learning, Memory, and Cognition, 15*, 605–619.

Hockett, C. F. (1960a). Logical considerations in the study of animal communication. In W. E. Lanyon & W. N. Tavolga (Eds.), *Animal sounds and communication* (pp. 392–430). Washington, DC: American Institute of Biological Sciences.

Hockett, C. F. (1960b). The origin of speech. *Scientific American, 203*, 89–96.

Hockett, C. F. (1966). The problem of universals in language. In J. H. Greenberg (Ed.), *Universals of language* (2nd ed., pp. 1–29). Cambridge, MA: MIT Press.

Holcomb, P. J. (1993). Semantic priming and stimulus degradation: Implications for the role of the N400 in language processing. *Psychophysiology, 30*, 47–61.

Holcomb, P. J., Kounios, J., Anderson, J. E., & West, W. C. (1999). Dual-coding, context availability, and concreteness effects in sentence comprehension: An electrophysiological investigation. *Journal of Experimental Psychology: Learning, Memory, and Cognition, 25*, 721–742.

Holtgraves, T. (1994). Communication in context: Effects of speaker status on the comprehension of indirect requests. *Journal of Experimental Psychology: Learning, Memory, and Cognition, 20*, 1205–1218.

Holtgraves, T. (1998). Interpreting indirect replies. *Cognitive Psychology, 37*, 1–27.

Holtgraves, T. (2008a). Automatic intention recognition in conversation processing. *Journal of Memory and Language, 58*, 627–645.

Holtgraves, T. (2008b). Conversation, speech acts, and memory. *Memory & Cognition, 36*, 361–374.

Holyoak, K. J., & Mah, W. A. (1982). Cognitive reference points in judgments of symbolic magnitude. *Cognitive Psychology, 14*, 328–352.

Holyoak, K. J., & Simon, D. (1999). Bidirectional reasoning in decision making by constraint satisfaction. *Journal of Experimental Psychology: General, 128*, 3–31.

Holyoak, K. J., & Thagard, P. (1997). The analogical mind. *American Psychologist, 52*, 35–44.

Holyoak, K. J., & Walker, J. H. (1976). Subjective magnitude information in semantic orderings. *Journal of Verbal Learning and Verbal Behavior, 15*, 287–299.

Hopkins, W. D., Russell, J. L., & Cantalupo, C. (2007). Neuroanatomical correlates of handedness for tool use in chimpanzees (*Pan troglodytes*): Implication for theories on the evolution of language. *Psychological Science, 18*, 971–977.

Horton, W. S., & Gerrig, R. J. (2002). Speakers' experiences and audience design: Knowing *when* and knowing *how* to adjust utterances to addressees. *Journal of Memory and Language, 47,* 589–606.

Hostetter, A. B., & Alibali, M. (2008). Visible embodiment: Gestures as simulated action. *Psychonomic Bulletin & Review, 15,* 495–514.

Hothersall, D. (1984). *History of psychology.* New York: Random House.

Hothersall, D. (1985). *Psychology.* Columbus, OH: Merrill.

Howe, M. L., & Courage, M. L. (1993). On resolving the enigma of infantile amnesia. *Psychological Bulletin, 113,* 305–326.

Hu, P., Stylos-Allan, M., & Walker, M. P. (2006). Sleep facilitates consolidation of emotional declarative memory. *Psychological Science, 17,* 891–898.

Huang, T-R., & Grossberg, S. (2010). Cortical dynamics of contextually cued attentive visual learning and search: Spatial and object evidence accumulation. *Psychological Review, 117,* 1080–1112.

Huang, Y. T., & Gordon, P. C. (2011). Distinguishing the time course of lexical and discourse processes through context, coreference, and quantified expressions. *Journal of Experimental Psychology: Learning, Memory, and Cognition, 37,* 966–978.

Hubbard, T. L. (1990). Cognitive representation of linear motion: Possible direction and gravity effects in judged displacement. *Memory & Cognition, 18,* 299–309.

Hubbard, T. L. (1995). Environmental invariants in the representation of motion: Implied dynamics and representational momentum, gravity, friction, and centripetal force. *Psychonomic Bulletin & Review, 2,* 322–338.

Hubbard, T. L. (1996). Representational momentum, centripetal force, and curvilinear impetus. *Journal of Experimental Psychology: Learning, Memory, and Cognition, 22,* 1049–1060.

Hubbard, T. L. (2005). Representational momentum and related displacements in spatial memory: A review of the findings. *Psychonomic Bulletin & Review, 12,* 822–851.

Hubbard, T. L., Hutchinson, J. L., & Courtney, J. R. (2010). Boundary extension: Findings and theories. *Quarterly Journal of Experimental Psychology, 63,* 1467–1494.

Huang, Y. T., & Gordon, P. C. (2011). Distinguishing the time course of lexical and discourse processes through context, coreference, and quantified expressions. *Journal of Experimental Psychology: Learning, Memory, and Cognition, 37,* 966–978.

Hubel, D. H., & Wiesel, T. N. (1962). Receptive fields, binocular interaction, and functional architecture in the cat's visual cortex. *Journal of Physiology, 160,* 106–154.

Huettel, S. A., Song, A. W., & McCarthy, G. (2004). *Functional magnetic resonance imaging.* Sunderland, MA: Sinauer Associates.

Hulme, C., Thomson, N., Muir, C., & Lawrence, A. (1984). Speech rate and the development of short-term memory span. *Journal of Experimental Child Psychology, 38,* 241–253.

Hunt, E., & Agnoli, F. (1991). The Whorfian hypothesis: A cognitive psychology perspective. *Psychological Review, 98,* 377–389.

Hunt, R. R., & Lamb, C. A. (2001). What causes the isolation effect? *Journal of Experimental Psychology: Learning, Memory, and Cognition, 27,* 1359–1366.

Hussain, Z., Sekuler, A. B., & Bennett, P. J. (2011). Superior identification of familiar visual patterns a year after learning. *Psychological Science, 22,* 724–730.

Hyman, I. E., Jr., Husband, T. H., & Billings, F. J. (1995). False memories of childhood experiences. *Applied Cognitive Psychology, 9,* 181–197.

Hyman, I. E., Jr., & Pentland, J. (1996). The role of mental imagery in the creation of false childhood memories. *Journal of Memory and Language, 35,* 101–117.

Inhoff, A. W. (1984). Two stages of word processing during eye fixations in the reading of prose. *Journal of Verbal Learning and Verbal Behavior, 23,* 612–624.

Intraub, H., & Richardson, M. (1989). Wide-angle memories of close-up scenes. *Journal of Experimental Psychology: Learning, Memory, and Cognition, 15,* 179–187.

Intriligator, J., & Cavanagh, P. (2001). The spatial resolution of visual attention. *Cognitive Psychology, 43,* 171–216.

Inzlicht, M., & Gutsell, J. N. (2007). Running on empty: Neural signals for self-control failure. *Psychological Science, 18,* 933–937.

Irwin, D. E. (1991). Information integration across saccadic eye movements. *Cognitive Psychology, 23,* 420–456.

Irwin, D. E. (1992). Memory for position and identity across eye movements. *Journal of Experimental Psychology: Learning, Memory, and Cognition, 18,* 307–317.

Irwin, D. E. (1996). Integrating information across saccadic eye movements. *Current Directions in Psychological Science, 5,* 94–100.

Irwin, D. E., & Brockmole, J. R. (2004). Suppressing where but not what: The effect of saccades on dorsal- and ventral-stream visual processing. *Psychological Science, 15,* 467–473.

Irwin, D. E., Yantis, S., & Jonides, J. (1983). Evidence against visual integration across saccadic eye movements. *Perception & Psychophysics, 34,* 49–57.

Jackendoff, R. S. (1992). *Languages of the mind: Essays on mental representation.* Cambridge, MA: MIT Press.

Jacobs, N., & Garnham, A. (2007). The role of conversational hand gestures in a narrative task. *Journal of Memory and Language, 56*(2), 291–303.

Jacoby, L. L. (1991). A process dissociation framework: Separating automatic from intentional uses of memory. *Journal of Memory and Language, 30,* 513–541.

Jacoby, L. L., & Dallas, M. (1981). On the relationship between autobiographical memory and perceptual learning. *Journal of Experimental Psychology: General, 110,* 306–340.

Jacoby, L. L., Toth, J. P., & Yonelinas, A. P. (1993). Separating conscious and unconscious influences of memory: Measuring recollection. *Journal of Experimental Psychology: General, 122,* 139–154.

Jacoby, L. L., Woloshyn, V., & Kelley, C. (1989). Becoming famous without being recognized: Unconscious influences of memory produced by dividing attention. *Journal of Experimental Psychology: General, 118,* 115–125.

James, W. (1890). *The principles of psychology.* New York: Dover.

January, D., & Kako, E. (2007). Re-evaluating evidence for linguistic relativity: Reply to Boroditsky (2001). *Cognition, 104,* 417–426.

Jared, D., Levy, B. A., & Rayner, K. (1999). The role of phonology in the activation of word meanings during readings: Evidence from proofreading and eye movements. *Journal of Experimental Psychology: General, 128,* 219–264.

Jefferies, E., Lambdon Ralph, M. A., & Baddeley, A. D. (2004). Automatic and controlled processing in sentence recall: The role of long-term and working memory. *Journal of Memory and Language, 51,* 623–643.

Jesse, A., & Massaro, D. W. (2010). Seeing a singer helps comprehension of the song's lyrics. *Psychonomic Bulletin & Review, 17,* 323–328.

Jenkins, J. G., & Dallenbach, K. M. (1924). Obliviscence during sleep and waking. *American Journal of Psychology, 35,* 605–612.

Jessberger, S., & Gage, F. H. (2008). Stem-cell-associated structural and functional plasticity in the aging hippocampus. *Psychology and Aging, 23,* 684–691.

Johnson, J. T., & Finke, R. A. (1985). The base-rate fallacy in the context of sequential categories. *Memory & Cognition, 13,* 63–73.

Johnson, M. K., Hashtroudi, S., & Lindsay, S. (1993). Source monitoring. *Psychological Bulletin, 114,* 3–28.

Johnson, N. F. (1970). The role of chunking and organization in the process of recall. In G. H. Bower (Ed.), *The psychology of learning and motivation* (Vol. 4, pp. 172–247). New York: Academic Press.

Johnson, S. K., & Anderson, M. C. (2004). The role of inhibitory control in forgetting semantic knowledge. *Psychological Science, 15,* 448–453.

Johnson-Laird, P. N. (1983). *Mental models: Towards a cognitive science of language, inference and consciousness.* Cambridge, MA: Harvard University Press.

Johnson-Laird, P. N., & Byrne, R. M. J. (2002). Conditionals: A theory of meaning, pragmatics, and inference. *Psychological Review, 109,* 646–678.

Johnson-Laird, P. N., Byrne, R. M. J., & Schaeken, W. (1992). Propositional reasoning by model. *Psychological Review, 99,* 418–439.

Johnson-Laird, P. N., Legrenzi, P., & Legrenzi, M. S. (1972). Reasoning and a sense of reality. *British Journal of Psychology, 63,* 395–400.

Johnston, J. C., McCann, R. S., & Remington, R. W. (1995). Chronometric evidence for two types of attention. *Psychological Science, 6,* 365–369.

Johnston, W. A., & Heinz, S. P. (1978). Flexibility and capacity demands of attention. *Journal of Experimental Psychology: General, 107,* 420–435.

Jones, D. M., Macken, W. J., & Nicholls, A. P. (2004). The phonological store of working memory: Is it phonological and is it a store? *Journal of Experimental Psychology: Learning, Memory, and Cognition, 30,* 656–674.

Jones, G. V. (1989). Back to Woodworth: Role of interlopers in the tip-of-the-tongue phenomenon. *Memory & Cognition, 17,* 69–76.

Jones, G. V., & Martin, M. (2006). Primacy of memory linkage in choice among valued objects. *Memory & Cognition, 34,* 1587–1597.

Jonides, J., & Jones, C. M. (1992). Direct coding for frequency of occurrence. *Journal of Experimental Psychology: Learning, Memory, and Cognition, 18,* 368–378.

Jonides, J., Lacey, S. C., & Nee, D. E. (2005). Processes of working memory in mind and brain. *Current Directions in Psychological Science, 14,* 2–5.

Jonides, J., Smith, E. E., Koeppe, R. A., Awh, E., Minoshima, S., & Mintun, M. A. (1993). Spatial working-memory in humans as revealed by PET. *Nature, 363,* 623–625.

Juhasz, B. J., & Rayner, K. (2003). Investigating the effects of a set of intercorrelated variables on eye fixation durations in reading. *Journal of Experimental Psychology: Learning, Memory, and Cognition, 29,* 1312–1318.

Just, M. A. (1976, May). *Research strategies in prose comprehension.* Paper presented at the meetings of the Midwestern Psychological Association, Chicago.

Just, M. A., & Carpenter, P. A. (1980). A theory of reading: From eye fixations to comprehension. *Psychological Review, 87,* 329–354.

Just, M. A., & Carpenter, P. A. (1987). *The psychology of reading and language comprehension.* Boston: Allyn & Bacon.

Just, M. A., & Carpenter, P. A. (1992). A capacity theory of comprehension. *Psychological Review, 99,* 122–149.

Just, M. A., Carpenter, P. A., Maguire, M., Diwadkar, V., & McMains, S. (2001). Mental rotation of objects retrieved from memory: A functional MRI study of spatial processing. *Journal of Experimental Psychology: General, 130,* 493–504.

Kaakinen, J. K., Hyona, J., & Keenan, J. M. (2003). How prior knowledge, WMC, and relevance of information affect eye fixations in expository text. *Journal of Experimental Psychology: Learning, Memory, and Cognition, 29,* 447–457.

Kahana, M. J., & Wingfield, A. (2000). A functional relation between learning and organization in free recall. *Psychonomic Bulletin & Review, 7,* 516–521.

Kahneman, D. (1968). Method, findings and theory in studies of visual masking. *Psychological Bulletin, 70,* 404–426.

Kahneman, D. (1973). *Attention and effort.* Englewood Cliffs, NJ: Prentice Hall.

Kahneman, D. (2003a). A perspective on judgment and choice: Mapping bounded rationality. *American Psychologist, 58,* 697–720.

Kahneman, D. (2003b). Experiences of collaborative research. *American Psychologist, 58,* 723–730.

Kahneman, D., Slovic, P., & Tversky, A. (Eds.) (1982). *Judgment under uncertainty: Heuristics and biases.* Cambridge, England: Cambridge University Press.

Kahneman, D., Triesman, A., & Gibbs, B. J. (1992). The reviewing of object files: Object-specific integration of information. *Cognitive Psychology, 24,* 175–219.

Kahneman, D., & Tversky, A. (1972). Subjective probability: A judgment of representativeness. *Cognitive Psychology, 3,* 430–454.

Kahneman, D., & Tversky, A. (1973). On the psychology of prediction. *Psychological Review, 80,* 237–251.

Kahneman, D., & Tversky, A. (1982). The simulation heuristic. In D. Kahneman, P. Slovic, & A. Tversky (Eds.), *Judgment under uncertainty: Heuristics and biases* (pp. 201–208). Cambridge, England: Cambridge University Press.

Kahneman, D., & Tversky, A. (Eds.) (2000). *Choice, values, and frames.* New York: Cambridge University Press.

Kail, R. (1991). Processing time declines exponentially during childhood and adolescence. *Developmental Psychology, 27,* 259–266.

Kail, R. (1997). Processing time, imagery, and spatial memory. *Journal of Experimental Child Psychology, 64,* 67–78.

Kalénine, S., & Bonthoux, F. (2008). Object manipulability affects children's and adults' conceptual processing. *Psychonomic Bulletin & Review, 15,* 667–672.

Kambe, G., Duffy, S. A., Clifton, C. Jr., & Rayner, K. (2003). An eye-movement-contingent probe paradigm. *Psychonomic Bulletin & Review, 10,* 661–666.

Kane, M. J., Brown, L. H., McVay, J. C., Silvia, P. J., Myin-Germeys, I., & Kwapil, T. R. (2007). For whom the mind wanders, and when. *Psychological Science, 18,* 614–621.

Kane, M. J., & Engle, R. W. (2000). Working memory capacity, proactive interference, and divided attention: Limits on long-term memory retrieval. *Journal of Experimental Psychology: Learning, Memory, and Cognition, 26,* 336–358.

Kane, M. J., & Engle, R. W. (2002). The role of prefrontal cortex in working-memory capacity, executive attention, and general fluid intelligence: An individual-differences perspective. *Psychonomic Bulletin & Review, 9,* 637–671.

Kane, M. J., & Engle, R. W. (2003). Working-memory capacity and the control of attention: The contributions of goal neglect, response competition and task set to Stroop interference. *Journal of Experimental Psychology: General, 132,* 47–70.

Kane, M. J., Hambrick, D. Z., Tuholski, S. W., Wilhelm, O., Payne, T. W., & Engle, R. W. (2004). The generality of working memory capacity: A latent-variable approach to verbal and visuospatial memory span and reasoning. *Journal of Experimental Psychology: General, 133,* 189–217.

Kanwisher, N. (1987). Repetition blindness: Type recognition without token individuation. *Cognition, 27,* 117–143.

Kanwisher, N. (1991). Repetition blindness and illusory conjunctions: Errors in binding visual types with visual tokens. *Journal of Experimental Psychology: Human Perception and Performance, 17*, 404–421.

Kanwisher, N., & Driver, J. (1992). Objects, attributes, and visual attention: Which, what, and where. *Psychological Science, 1*, 26–31.

Karpicke, J. D., & Roediger, H. L. (2007). Repeated during retrieval is the key to long-term retention. *Journal of Memory and Language, 57*, 151–162.

Kaschak, M. P., & Glenberg, A. M. (2000). Constructing meaning: The role of affordances and grammatical constructions in sentence comprehension. *Journal of Memory and Language, 43*, 508–529.

Kassam, K. S., Gilbert, D. T., Swencionis, J. K., & Wilson, T. D. (2009). Misconceptions of memory: The Scooter Libby effect. *Psychological Science, 20*, 551–552.

Kassam, K. S., Koslov, K., & Mendes, W. B. (2009). Decisions under distress: Stress profiles influence anchoring and adjustment. *Psychological Science, 20*, 1394–1399.

Kay, J., & Ellis, A. (1987). A cognitive neuropsychological case study of anomia: Implications for psychological models of word retrieval. *Brain, 110*, 613–629.

Kelley, C. M., & Jacoby, L. L. (1996). Memory attributions: Remembering, knowing, and feeling of knowing. In L. M. Reder (Ed.), *Implicit memory and metacognition* (pp. 287–308). Hillsdale, NJ: Erlbaum.

Kelley, C. M., & Lindsay, D. S. (1993). Remembering mistaken for knowing: Ease of retrieval as a basis for confidence in answers to general knowledge questions. *Journal of Memory and Language, 32*, 1–24.

Kelley, M. R., & Nairne, J. S. (2001). von Restorff revisited: Isolation, generation, and memory of order. *Journal of Experimental Psychology: Learning, Memory, and Cognition, 27*, 54–66.

Kelly, S. D., Barr, D. J., Church, R. B., & Lynch, K. (1999). Offering a hand to pragmatic understanding: The role of speech and gesture in comprehension and memory. *Journal of Memory and Language, 40*, 577–592.

Kelly, S. D., Özyürek, A., & Maris, E. (2010). Two sides of the same coin: Speech and gesture mutually interact to enhance comprehension. *Psychological Science, 21*, 260–267.

Kemmerer, D., Castillo, J. G., Talavage, T., Patterson, S., & Wiley, C. (2008). Neuroanatomical distribution of five semantic components of verbs: Evidence from fMRI. *Brain and Language, 107*, 16–43.

Kempen, G., & Hoekamp, E. (1987). An incremental procedural grammar for sentence formulation. *Cognitive Science, 11*, 201–258.

Kemper S. (1987). Life-span changes in syntactic complexity. *Journals of Gerontology: Psychological Sciences, 42*, P323–P328.

Kemper, S., & Thissen, D. (1981). Memory for the dimensions of requests. *Journal of Verbal Learning and Verbal Behavior, 20*, 552–563.

Kempton, W. (1986). Two theories of home heat control. *Cognitive Science, 10*, 75–90.

Kemtes, K. A., & Kemper, S. (1997). Younger and older adults' on-line processing of syntactically ambiguous sentences. *Psychology and Aging, 12*, 362–371.

Kennedy, Q., Mather, M., & Carstensen, L. L. (2004). The role of motivation in the age-related positivity effect in autobiographical memory. *Psychological Science, 15*, 208–214.

Kensinger, E. A. (2007). Negative emotion enhances memory accuracy: Behavioral and neuroimaging evidence. *Current Directions in Psychological Science, 16*, 213–218.

Kensinger, E. A. (2009). *Emotional memory across the adult lifespan*. New York: Psychology Press.

Kensinger, E. A., & Corkin, S. (2004). Two routes to emotional memory: Distinct neural processes for valence and arousal. *Proceedings of the National Academy of Sciences, 101*, 3310–3315.

Kensinger, E. A., Garoff-Eaton, R. J., & Schacter, D. L. (2006). Memory for specific visual details can be enhanced by negative arousing content. *Journal of Memory and Language, 54*, 99–112.

Kensinger, E. A., & Schacter, D. L. (2006). When the Red Socks shocked the Yankees: Comparing negative and positive memories. *Psychonomic Bulletin & Review, 13*, 757–763.

Keppel, G., & Underwood, B. J. (1962). Proactive inhibition in short-term retention of single items. *Journal of Verbal Learning and Verbal Behavior, 1*, 153–161.

Kershaw, T. C., & Ohlsson, S. (2004). Multiple causes of difficulty in insight: The case of the nine-dot problem. *Journal of Experimental Psychology: Learning, Memory, and Cognition, 30*, 3–13.

Kertesz, A. (1982). Two case studies: Broca's and Wernicke's aphasia. In M. A. Arbib, D. Caplan, & J. C. Marshall (Eds.), *Neural models of language processes* (pp. 25–44). New York: Academic Press.

Keysar, B., Shen, Y., Glucksberg, S., & Horton, W. S. (2000). Conventional language: How metaphorical is it? *Journal of Memory and Language, 43,* 576–593.

Kibbe, M. M., & Leslie, A. M. (2011). What do infants remember when they forget? Location and identity in 6-month-olds' memory for objects. *Psychological Science, 22,* 1500–1505.

Kim, N. S., & Ahn, W. (2002). Clinical psychologists' theory-based representations of mental disorders predict their diagnostic reasoning and memory. *Journal of Experimental Psychology: General, 131,* 451–476.

Kim, N. S., Yopchick, J. E., & de Kwaadsteniet, L. (2008). Causal diversity effects in information seeking. *Psychonomic Bulletin & Review, 15,* 81–88.

Kinder, A., & Shanks, D. R. (2003). Neuropsychological dissociations between priming and recognition: A single-system connectionist account. *Psychological Review, 110,* 728–744.

Kingstone, A., Smilek, D., Ristic, J., Friesen, C. K., & Eastwood, J. D. (2003). Attention, researchers! It is time to take a look at the real world. *Current Directions in Psychological Science, 12,* 176–180.

Kintsch, W. (1974). *The representation of meaning in memory.* Hillsdale, NJ: Erlbaum.

Kintsch, W. (2000). Metaphor comprehension: A computational theory. *Psychonomic Bulletin & Review, 7,* 257–266.

Kintsch, W., & Bates, E. (1977). Recognition memory for statements from a classroom lecture. *Journal of Experimental Psychology: Human Learning and Memory, 3,* 150–159.

Kintsch, W., & van Dijk, T. A. (1978). Toward a model of text comprehension and production. *Psychological Review, 85,* 363–394.

Kintsch, W., Welsch, D., Schmalhofer, F., & Zimny, S. (1987). Sentence memory: A theoretical analysis. *Journal of Memory and Language, 29,* 133–159.

Kishiyama, M. M., Yonelinas, A. P., & Lazzara, M. M. (2004). The von Restorff effect in amnesia: The contribution of the hippocampal system to novelty-related memory enhancements. *Journal of Cognitive Neuroscience, 16,* 15–23.

Kisilevsky, B. S., Hains, S. M. J., Lee, K., Xie, X., Huang, H., Ye, H. H., et al. (2003). Effects of experience on fetal voice recognition. *Psychological Science, 14,* 220–224.

Kissler, J., Herbert, C., Peyk, P., & Junghofer, M. (2007). Buzzwords: Early cortical response to emotional words during reading. *Psychological Science, 18,* 475–480.

Klatzky, R. L. (1980). *Human memory: Structures and processes* (2nd ed.). San Francisco: Freeman.

Klatzky, R. L., Pellegrino, J. W., McCloskey, B. P., & Doherty, S. (1989). Can you squeeze a tomato? The role of motor representations in semantic sensibility judgments. *Journal of Memory and Language, 28,* 56–77.

Klauer, K. C., Stahl, C., & Erdfelder, E. (2007). The abstract selection task: New data and an almost comprehensive model. *Journal of Experimental Psychology: Learning, Memory, and Cognition, 33,* 680–703.

Klayman, J., & Ha, Y.-W. (1989). Hypothesis testing in rule discovery: Strategy, structure, and content. *Journal of Experimental Psychology: Learning, Memory, and Cognition, 15,* 596–604.

Klein, D. V., & Murphy, G. L. (2002). Paper has been my ruin: conceptual relations of polysemous senses. *Journal of Memory and Language, 47,* 548–570.

Klein, R. (2000). Inhibition of return. *Trends in Cognitive Sciences, 4,* 138–147.

Klein, S. B., Robertson, T. E., & Delton, A. W. (2010). Facing the future: Memory as an evolved system for planning future acts. *Memory & Cognition, 38,* 13–22.

Kliegl, R., Nuthmann, A., & Engbert, R. (2006). Tracking the mind during reading: The influence of past, present, and future words on fixation durations. *Journal of Experimental Psychology: General, 135,* 12–35.

Knight, R. T. (1984). Decreased response to novel stimuli after prefrontal lesions in man. *Electroencephalography and Clinical Neurophysiology: Evoked Potentials Section, 59,* 9–20.

Koehler, J. J., & Macchi, L. (2004). Thinking about low-probability events: An exemplar-cuing theory. *Psychological Science, 15,* 540–546.

Köhler, W. (1927). *The mentality of apes.* New York: Harcourt, Brace.

Koivisto, M., & Revonsuo, A. (2007). How meaning shapes seeing. *Psychological Science, 18,* 845–849.

Kolers, P. A., & Roediger, H. L. III (1984). Procedures of mind. *Journal of Verbal Learning and Verbal Behavior, 23,* 425–449.

Kolodner, J. L. (1997). Educational implications of analogy: A view from case-based reasoning. *American Psychologist, 52,* 57–66.

Komeda, H., & Kusumi, T. (2006). The effect of a protagonist's emotional shift on situation model construction. *Memory & Cognition, 34,* 1548–1556.

Koriat, A. (1993). How do we know that we know? The accessibility model of the feeling of knowing. *Psychological Review, 100*, 609–639.

Koriat, A. (1995). Dissociating knowing and the feeling of knowing: Further evidence for the accessibility model. *Journal of Experimental Psychology: General, 124*, 311–333.

Koriat, A., Fiedler, K., & Bjork, R. A. (2006). Inflation of conditional predictions. *Journal of Experimental Psychology: General, 135*, 429–447.

Koriat, A., Levy-Sadot, R., Edry, E., & de Marcus, S. (2003). What do we know about what we cannot remember? Accessing the semantic attributes of words that cannot be recalled. *Journal of Experimental Psychology: Learning, Memory, and Cognition, 29*, 1095–1105.

Koriat, A., & Pearlman-Avnion, S. (2003). Memory organization of action events and its relationship to memory performance. *Journal of Experimental Psychology: General, 132*, 435–454.

Koriat, A., Sheffer, L., & Ma'ayan, H. (2002). Comparing objective and subjective learning curves: Judgments of learning exhibit increased underconfidence with practice. *Journal of Experimental Psychology: General, 131*, 147–162.

Kosslyn, S. M., Alpert, N. M., Thompson, W. L., Maljkovic, V., Weise, S. B., Chabris, C. F., et al. (1993). Visual mental imagery activates topographically organized visual cortex: PET investigations. *Journal of Cognitive Neuroscience, 5*, 263–287.

Kosslyn, S. M., & Pomerantz, J. P. (1977). Imagery, propositions, and the form of internal representations. *Cognitive Psychology, 9*, 52–76.

Kotovsky, K., Hayes, J. R., & Simon, H. A. (1985). Why are some problems hard? Evidence from Tower of Hanoi. *Cognitive Psychology, 17*, 248–294.

Kounios, J. (1996). On the continuity of thought and the representation of knowledge: Electrophysiological and behavioral time-course measures reveal levels of structure in semantic memory. *Psychonomic Bulletin & Review, 3*, 265–286.

Kounios, J., Frymiare, J. L., Bowden, E. M., Fleck, J. I., Subramaniam, K., Parrish, T. B., et al. (2006). The prepared mind: Neural activity prior to problem presentation predicts subsequent solution by sudden insight. *Psychological Science, 17*, 882–890.

Kounios, J., & Holcomb, P. J. (1992). Structure and process in semantic memory: Evidence from event-related brain potentials and reaction times. *Journal of Experimental Psychology: General, 121*, 459–479.

Kounios, J., & Holcomb, P. J. (1994). Concreteness effects in semantic processing: ERP evidence supporting dual-coding theory. *Journal of Experimental Psychology: Learning, Memory, and Cognition, 20*, 804–823.

Kousta, S-T., Vigliocco, G., Vinson, D. P., Andrews, M., & Campo, E. D. (2010). The representation of abstract words: Why emotion matters. *Journal of Experimental Psychology: General, 140*, 14–34.

Kozhevnikov, M., & Hegarty, M. (2001). Impetus beliefs as default heuristics: Dissociation between explicit and implicit knowledge about motion. *Psychonomic Bulletin & Review, 8*, 439–453.

Kozhevnikov, M., Louchakova, O., Josipovic, Z., & Motes, M. A. (2009). The enhancement of visuospatial processing efficiency through Buddhist Deity Meditation. *Psychological Science, 20*, 645–653.

Kraljik, T., Samuel, A. G., & Brennan, S. E. (2008). First impressions and last resorts: How listeners adjust to speaker variability. *Psychological Science, 19*, 332–338.

Kramer, A. F., Hahn, S., Irwin, D. E., & Theeuwes, J. (1999). Attention capture and aging: Implications for visual search performance and oculomotor control. *Psychology and Aging, 14*, 135–154.

Kramer, T. H., Buckout, R., & Eugenio, P. (1990). Weapon focus, arousal, and eyewitness memory. *Law and Human Behavior, 14*, 167–184.

Krawietz, S. A., Tamplin, A. K., & Radvansky, G. A. (2012). Aging and mind wandering during text comprehension. *Psychology and Aging, 27*, 951–958

Krist, H., Fieberg, E. L., & Wilkening, F. (1993). Intuitive physics in action and judgment: The development of knowledge about projectile motion. *Journal of Experimental Psychology: Learning, Memory, and Cognition, 19*, 952–966.

Kubilius, J., Wagemans, J., & Op de Beeck, H. P. (2011). Emergence of perceptual gestalts in the human visual cortex: The case of the configural superiority effect. *Psychological Science, 22*, 1296–1303.

Kucera, H., & Francis, W. N. (1967). *Computational analysis of present day American English*. Providence, RI: Brown University Press.

Kumon-Nakamura, S., Glucksberg, S., & Brown, M. (1995). How about another piece of pie? The allusional pretense theory of discourse irony. *Journal of Experimental Psychology: General, 124*, 3–21.

Kunar, M A., Carter, R., Cohen, M., & Horowitz, T. S. (2008). Telephone conversation impairs sustained visual attention via a central bottleneck. *Psychonomic Bulletin & Review, 15*, 1135–1140.

Kurtz, K. J., & Loewenstein, J. (2007). Converging on a new role for analogy in problem solving and retrieval: When two problems are better than one. *Memory & Cognition, 35,* 334–341.

Kutas, M., & Hillyard, S. A. (1980). Reading senseless sentences: Brain potentials reflect semantic incongruity. *Science, 207,* 203–205.

Kynski, T. R., & Tenebaum, J. B. (2007). The role of causality in judgment under uncertainty. *Journal of Experimental Psychology: General, 136,* 430–450.

Lachman, R., Lachman, J. L., & Butterfield, E. C. (1979). *Cognitive psychology and information processing: An introduction.* Hillsdale, NJ: Erlbaum.

Lachter, J., Forster, K. I., & Ruthruff, E. (2004). Forty-five years after Broadbent (1958): Still no identification without attention. *Psychological Review, 111,* 880–913.

Lakens, D., Schneider, I. K., Jostmann, N. B., & Schubert, T. W. (2011). Telling things apart: The distance between response keys influences categorization times. *Psychological Science, 22,* 887–890.

Lambert, W. E. (1990). Issues in foreign language and second language education. *Proceedings of the Research Symposium on Limited English Proficient Students' Issues* (1st, Washington, DC, September 10–12, 1990).

Lane, S. M., & Zaragoza, M. S. (2007). A little elaboration goes a long way: The role of generation in eyewitness suggestibility. *Memory & Cognition, 35,* 1255–1266.

Lang, J. W. B., & Lang, J. (2010). Priming competence diminishes the link between cognitive test anxiety and test performance: Implications for the interpretation of test scores. *Psychological Science, 21,* 811–819.

Larsen, A., & Bundesen, C. (2009). Common mechanisms in apparent motion perception and visual pattern matching. *Scandinavian Journal of Psychology, 50,* 526–534.

Lashley, K. D. (1950). In search of the engram. *Symposia for the Society for Experimental Biology, 4,* 454–482.

Laszlo, S., & Federmeier, K. D. (2009). A beautiful day in the neighborhood: An event-related potential study of lexical relationships and prediction in context. *Journal of Memory and Language, 61,* 326–338.

Lavaer, G. D, & Burke, D. M. (1993). Why do semantic priming effects increase in old age? A meta-analysis. *Psychology and Aging, 8,* 34–43.

Lavie, N. (2010). Attention, distraction, and cognitive control under load. *Current Directions in Psychological Science, 19,* 143–148.

LaVoie, D. J., & Malmstrom, T. (1998). False recognition effects in younger and older adults' memory for text passages. *Journals of Gerontology: Psychological Sciences, 53B,* P255–P262.

Lawson, R. (2006). The science of cycology: Failures to understand how everyday objects work. *Memory & Cognition, 34,* 1667–1675.

Leahey, T. H. (1992). The mythical revolutions of American psychology. *American Psychologist, 47,* 308–318.

Leahey, T. H. (2000). *A history of psychology: Main currents in psychological thought* (3rd ed.). Englewood Cliffs, NJ: Prentice Hall.

Leahey, T. H. (2003). Herbert A. Smith Nobel Prize in economic sciences, 1978. *American Psychologist, 58,* 753–755.

LeDoux, J. E. (2000). Emotion circuits in the brain. *Annual Review of Neuroscience, 23,* 155–184.

Lee, C.-L., & Federmeier, K. D. (2009). Wave-ering: An ERP study of syntactic and semantic context effects on ambiguity resolution for noun/verb homographs. *Journal of Memory and Language, 61,* 538–555.

Lee, H.-W., Rayner, K., & Pollatsek, A. (1999). The time course of phonological, semantic, and orthographic coding in reading: Evidence from the fast-priming technique. *Psychonomic Bulletin & Review, 6,* 624–634.

Lee, J. J., & Pinker, S. (2010). Rationales for indirect speech: The theory of the strategic speaker. *Psychological Review, 117,* 785–807.

LeFevre, J., Bisanz, J., Daley, K. E., Buffone, L., Greenham, S. L., & Sadesky, G. S. (1996). Multiple routes to solution of single-digit multiplication problems. *Journal of Experimental Psychology: General, 125,* 284–306.

Lehman, D. R., Lempert, R. O., & Nisbett, R. E. (1988). The effects of graduate training on reasoning. *American Psychologist, 43,* 431–442.

Leonesio, R. J., & Nelson, T. O. (1990). Do different metamemory judgments tap the same underlying aspects of memory? *Journal of Experimental Psychology: Learning, Memory, and Cognition, 16,* 464–470.

LePine, J. A., LePine, M. A., & Jackson, C. L. (2004). Challenge and hindrance stress: Relationships with exhaustion, motivation to learn, and learning performance. *Journal of Applied Psychology, 89,* 883–891.

Levy, B. (1996). Improving memory in old age through implicit self-stereotyping. *Journal of Personality and Social Psychology, 71,* 1092–1107.

Levy, D. A., Stark, C. E. L., & Squire, L. R. (2004). Intact conceptual priming in the absence of declarative memory. *Psychological Science, 15,* 680–686.

Levy, J., Pashler, H., & Boer, E. (2006). Central interference in driving: Is there any stopping the psychological refractory period? *Psychological Science, 17,* 228–235.

Lewandowsky, S., Stritzka, W. G. K., Oberauer, K., & Morales, M. (2005). Memory for fact, fiction, and misinformation. *Psychological Science, 16,* 190–195.

Lewis, J. L. (1970). Semantic processing of unattended messages using dichotic listening. *Journal of Experimental Psychology, 85,* 225–228.

Lewontin, R. C. (1990). The evolution of cognition. In D. N. Osherson & E. E. Smith (Eds.), *Thinking: An invitation to cognitive science* (Vol. 3, pp. 229–246). Cambridge, MA: MIT Press.

Li, X., Schweickert, R., & Gandour, J. (2000). The phonological similarity effect in immediate recall: Positions of shared phonemes. *Memory & Cognition, 28,* 1116–1125.

Libby, L. K. (2003). Imagery perspective and source monitoring in imagination inflation. *Memory & Cognition, 31,* 1072–1081.

Liberman, A. M. (1957). Some results of research on speech perception. *Journal of the Acoustical Society of America, 29,* 117–123.

Liberman, A. M., Cooper, F. S., Shankweiler, D. P., & Studdert-Kennedy, M. (1967). Perception of speech code. *Psychological Review, 74,* 431–461.

Liberman, A. M., Harris, K. S., Hoffman, H. S., & Griffith, B. C. (1957). The discrimination of speech sounds within and across phoneme boundaries. *Journal of Experimental Psychology, 54,* 358–368.

Liberman, A. M., & Mattingly, I. G. (1985). The motor theory of speech perception revised. *Cognition, 21,* 1–36.

Libkuman, T. M., Nichols-Whitehead, P., Griffith, J., & Thomas, R. (1999). Source of arousal and memory for detail. *Memory & Cognition, 27,* 166–190.

Light, L. L., & Anderson, P. A. (1983). Memory for scripts in young and older adults. *Memory & Cognition, 11*(5), 435–444.

Light, L. L., & Capps, J. L. (1986). Comprehension of pronouns in young and older adults. *Developmental Psychology, 22,* 580–585.

Lindberg, M. A. (1980). Is knowledge base development a necessary and sufficient condition for memory development? *Journal of Experimental Child Psychology, 30,* 401–410.

Linder, I., Echterhoff, G., Davidson, P. S. R., & Brand, M. (2010). Observation inflation: Your actions become mine. *Psychological Science, 21,* 1291–1299.

Lidji, P., Kolinsky, R., Lochy, A., & Morais, J. (2007). Spatial associations for musical stimuli: A piano in the head? *Journal of Experimental Psychology: Human Perception and Performance, 33,* 1189–1207.

Lindsay, D. S., Allen, B. P., Chan, J. C. K., & Dahl, L. C. (2004). Eyewitness suggestibility and source similarity: Intrusions of details from one event into memory reports of another event. *Journal of Memory and Language, 50,* 96–111.

Lindsay, D. S., Hagen, L., Read, J. D., Wade, K. A., & Garry, M. (2004). True photographs and false memories. *Psychological Science, 15,* 149–154.

Lindsay, P. H., & Norman, D. A. (1977). *Human information processing: An introduction to psychology.* New York: Academic Press.

Lindsley, J. R. (1975). Producing simple utterances: How far ahead do we plan? *Cognitive Psychology, 7,* 1–19.

Linek, J. A., Kroll, J. F., & Sunderman, G. (2010). Losing access to the native language while immersed in a second language: Evidence for the role of inhibition in second-language learning. *Psychological Science, 20,* 1507–1515.

Linton, M. (1975). Memory for real-world events. In D. A. Norman & D. E. Rumelhart (Eds.), *Explorations in cognition* (pp. 376–404). San Francisco: Freeman.

Linton, M. (1978). Real world memory after six years: An *in vivo* study of very long term memory. In M. M. Gruneberg, P. E. Morris, & R. N. Sykes (Eds.), *Practical aspects of memory* (pp. 69–76). Orlando, FL: Academic Press.

Liszkowski, U., Schäfer, M., Carpenter, M., & Tomasello, M. (2010). Prelinguistic infants, but not chimpanzees, communicate about absent entities. *Psychological Science, 20,* 654–660.

Litman, D. J., & Allen, J. F. (1987). A plan recognition model for subdialogues in conversation. *Cognitive Science, 11,* 163–200.

Livesey, E. J., Harris, I. M., & Harris, J. A. (2009). Attentional changes during implicit learning: Signal validity protects target stimulus from the attentional blink. *Journal of Experimental Psychology: Learning, Memory, and Cognition, 35,* 408–422.

Löckenhoff, C. E., & Carstensen, L. L. (2007). Aging, emotion, and health-related decision strategies: motivational manipulations can reduce age differences. *Psychology and Aging, 22,* 134–146.

Lockridge, C. B., & Brennan, S. E. (2002). Addressees' needs influence speakers' early syntactic choices. *Psychonomic Bulletin & Review, 9,* 550–557.

Loftus, E. F. (1971). Memory for intentions: The effect of presence of a cue and interpolated activity. *Psychonomic Science, 23,* 315–316.

Loftus, E. F. (1991). Made in memory: Distortions in recollection after misleading information. In G. H. Bower (Ed.), *The psychology of learning and motivation* (Vol. 27, pp. 187–215). New York: Academic Press.

Loftus, E. F. (1993). The reality of repressed memories. *American Psychologist, 48,* 518–537.

Loftus, E. F. (2003). Make-believe memories. *American Psychologist, 58,* 867–873.

Loftus, E. F. (2004). Memories of things unseen. *Current Directions in Psychological Science, 13,* 145–147.

Loftus, E. F., & Coan, D. (1994). The construction of childhood memories. In D. Peters (Ed.), *The child witness in context: Cognitive, social, and legal perspectives.* New York: Kluwer.

Loftus, E. F., Donders, K., Hoffman, H. G., & Schooler, J. W. (1989). Creating new memories that are quickly accessed and confidently held. *Memory & Cognition, 17,* 607–616.

Loftus, E. F., & Hoffman, H. G. (1989). Misinformation and memory: The creation of new memories. *Journal of Experimental Psychology: General, 118,* 100–104.

Loftus, E. F., & Ketcham, K. (1991). *Witness for the defense.* New York: St. Martin's Press.

Loftus, E. F., & Palmer, J. C. (1974). Reconstruction of automobile destruction: An example of the interaction between language and memory. *Journal of Verbal Learning and Verbal Behavior, 13,* 585–589.

Loftus, G. R., & Hanna, A. M. (1989). The phenomenology of spatial integration: Data and models. *Cognitive Psychology, 21,* 363–397.

Loftus, G. R., & Irwin, D. E. (1998). On the relations among different measures of visible and informational persistence. *Cognitive Psychology, 35,* 135–199.

Loftus, G. R., & Loftus, E. F. (1974). The influence of one memory retrieval on a subsequent memory retrieval. *Memory & Cognition, 2,* 467–471.

Logan, G. D. (1988). Toward an instance theory of automatization. *Psychological Review, 95,* 492–527.

Logan, G. D. (1990). Repetition priming and automaticity: Common underlying mechanisms? *Cognitive Psychology, 22,* 1–35.

Logan, G. D. (2003). Executive control of thought and action: In search of the wild homunculus. *Current Directions in Psychological Science, 12,* 45–48.

Logan, G. D., & Crump, M. J. C. (2009). The left hand doesn't know what the right hand is doing: the disruptive effects of attention to the hands in skilled typewriting. *Psychological Science, 20,* 1296–1300.

Logan, G. D., & Etherton, J. L. (1994). What is learned during automatization? The role of attention in constructing an instance. *Journal of Experimental Psychology: Learning, Memory, and Cognition, 20,* 1022–1050.

Logan, G. D., & Klapp, S. T. (1991). Automatizing alphabet arithmetic: I. Is extended practice necessary to produce automaticity? *Journal of Experimental Psychology: Learning, Memory, and Cognition, 17,* 179–195.

Logie, R. H., Zucco, G., & Baddeley, A. D. (1990). Interference with visual short-term memory. *Acta Psychologica, 75,* 55–74.

Long, D. L., & De Ley, L. (2000). Implicit causality and discourse focus: The interaction of text and reader characteristics in pronoun resolution. *Journal of Memory and Language, 42,* 545–570.

Long, D. L., Golding, J., Graesser, A. C., & Clark, L. F. (1990). Inference generation during story comprehension: A comparison of goals, events, and states. In A. C. Graesser & G. H. Bower (Eds.), *The psychology of learning and motivation* (Vol. 25). New York: Academic Press.

Long, D. L., Oppy, B. J., & Seely, M. R. (1997). Individual differences in readers' sentence- and text-level representations. *Journal of Memory and Language, 36,* 129–145.

Lorch, R. F. Jr., Lorch, E. P., & Matthews, P. D. (1985). On-line processing of the topic structure of a text. *Journal of Memory and Language, 24,* 350–362.

Lourenco, S. F., & Longo, M. R. (2010). General magnitude representation in human infants. *Psychological Science, 21,* 873–881.

Lozano, S. C., & Tversky, B. (2006). Communicative gestures facilitate problem solving for both communicators and recipients. *Journal of Memory and Language, 55,* 47–63.

Lu, S., & Zhou, K. (2005). Stimulus-driven attentional capture by equiluminent color change. *Psychonomic Bulletin & Review, 12,* 567–572.

Luchins, A. S. (1942). Mechanization in problem solving. *Psychological Monographs, 54* (Whole no. 248).

Luo, L., & Craik, F. I. M. (2009). Age differences in recollection: Specificity effects at retrieval. *Journal of Memory and Language, 60,* 421–436.

Lustig, C., & Hasher, L. (2001). Implicit memory is vulnerable to proactive interference. *Psychological Science, 12,* 408–412.

Lutz, M. E., & Radvansky, G. A. (1997). The fate of completed goal information. *Journal of Memory and Language, 36,* 293–310.

Lynchard, N. A., & Radvansky, G. A. (2012). Age-related perspectives and emotion processing. *Psychology and Aging, 27,* 934–939.

Maass, A., & Köhnken, G. (1989). Simulating the "weapon effect." *Law and Human Behavior, 13,* 397–408.

Mack, A. (2003). Inattentional blindness: looking without seeing. *Current Directions in Psychological Science, 12,* 180–184.

Mack, A., & Rock, I. (1998). *Inattentional blindness.* Cambridge, MA: MIT Press.

Mackworth, N. H. (1948). The breakdown of vigilance during prolonged visual search. *Quarterly Journal of Experimental Psychology, 1,* 6–21.

MacLean, K. A., Ferrer, E., Aichele, S. R., Bridwell, D. A., Zanesco, A. P., Jacobs, T. L., et al. (2010). Intensive meditation training improves perceptual discrimination and sustained attention. *Psychological Science, 21,* 829–839.

MacLeod, C. M. (1988). Forgotten but not gone: Savings for pictures and words in long-term memory. *Journal of Experimental Psychology: Learning, Memory, and Cognition, 14,* 195–212.

MacLeod, C. M. (1991). Half a century of research on the Stroop effect: An integrative review. *Psychological Bulletin, 109,* 163–203.

MacLeod, C. M. (1992). The Stroop task: The "gold standard" of attentional measures. *Journal of Experimental Psychology: General, 121,* 12–14.

MacLeod, C. M. (2011). I said, you said: The production effect gets personal. *Psychonomic Bulletin & Review, 18,* 1197–1202.

MacLeod, C. M., Gopie, N., Hourihan, K. L., Neary, K. R., & Ozubko, J. D. (2010). The production effect: Delineation of a phenomenon. *Journal of Experimental Psychology. Learning, Memory, and Cognition, 36,* 671–685.

MacLeod, M. D., & Macrae, C. N. (2001). Gone but not forgotten: The transient nature of retrieval-induced forgetting. *Psychological Science, 12,* 148–152.

MacLeod, M. D., & Saunders, J. (2008). Retrieval inhibition and memory distortion. *Current Directions in Psychological Science, 17,* 26–30.

MacPherson, S. E., Phillips, L. H., & Sala, S. D. (2002). Age, executive functioning, and social decision making: A dorsolateral prefrontal theory of cognitive aging. *Psychology and Aging, 17,* 598–609.

MacQueen, G. M., Tipper, S. P., Young, L. T., Joffe, R. T., & Levitt, A. J. (2000). Impaired distractor inhibition on a selective attention task in unmedicated, depressed subjects. *Psychological Medicine, 30,* 557–564.

Madden, D. J., Turkington, J. M., Provenzale, J. M., Denny, L. L., Langley, L. K., Hawk, T. C., et al. (2002). Aging and attentional guidance during visual search: Functional neuroanatomy by positron emission tomography. *Psychology and Aging, 17,* 24–43.

Madigan, S., & O'Hara, R. (1992). Short-term memory at the turn of the century: Mary Whiton Calkins's memory research. *American Psychologist, 47,* 170–174.

Magliano, J. P., Miller, J., & Zwaan, R. A. (2001). Indexing space and time in film understanding. *Applied Cognitive Psychology, 15,* 533–545.

Magliano, J. P., Taylor, H. A., & Kim, H. J. (2005). When goals collide: Monitoring the goals of multiple characters. *Memory & Cognition, 33,* 1357–1367.

Magliano, J. P., Trabasso, T., & Graesser, A. C. (1999). Strategic processing during comprehension. *Journal of Educational Psychology, 91,* 615–629.

Magno, E., & Allan, K. (2007). Self-reference during explicit memory retrieval: An event-related potential analysis. *Psychological Science, 18,* 672–677.

Mahmood, D., Manier, D., & Hirst, W. (2004). Memory for how one learned of multiple deaths from AIDS: Repeated exposure and distinctiveness. *Memory & Cognition, 32,* 125–134.

Maier, N. R. F. (1931). Reasoning in humans: II. The solution of a problem and its appearance in consciousness. *Journal of Comparative Psychology, 12,* 181–194.

Maki, R. H. (1989). Recognition of added and deleted details in scripts. *Memory & Cognition, 17,* 274–282.

Maloney, E. A., Ansari, D., & Fugelsang, J. A. (2011). The effect of mathematics anxiety on the processing of numerical magnitude. *Quarterly Journal of Experimental Psychology, 64,* 10–16.

Malt, B. C. (1985). The role of discourse structure in understanding anaphora. *Journal of Memory and Language, 24,* 271–289.

Malt, B. C., Sloman, S. A., & Gennari, S. P. (2003). Universality and language specificity in object naming. *Journal of Memory and Language, 49,* 20–42.

Mandel, D. R., & Lehman, D. R. (1996). Counterfactual thinking and ascriptions of cause and preventability. *Journal of Personality and Social Psychology, 71,* 450–463.

Mandler, G. (1967). Organization and memory. In K. W. Spence & J. T. Spence (Eds.), *The psychology of learning and motivation* (Vol. 1, pp. 327–372). New York: Academic Press.

Mandler, G. (1972). Organization and recognition. In E. Tulving & W. Donaldson (Eds.), *Organization of memory* (pp. 139–166). New York: Academic Press.

Mandler, G. (1989). Affect and learning: Causes and consequences of emotional interactions. In D. B. McLeod & V. M. Adams (Eds.), *Affect and mathematical problem solving* (pp. 3–19). New York: Springer.

Mandler, G. (2007). *A history of modern experimental psychology: From James and Wundt to cognitive science.* Cambridge, MA: MIT Press.

Mandler, J. M., & Mandler, G. (1969). The diaspora of experimental psychology: The Gestaltists and others. In D. Fleming & B. Bailyn (Eds.), *The intellectual migration: Europe and America, 1930–1960* (pp. 371–419). Cambridge, MA: Harvard University Press.

Manwell, L. A., Roberts, M. A., & Besner, D. (2004). Single letter coloring and spatial cuing eliminates a semantic contribution to the Stroop effect. *Psychonomic Bulletin & Review, 11,* 458–462.

Marchman, V. A., & Fernald, A. (2008). Speed of word recognition and vocabulary knowledge in infancy predict cognitive and language outcomes in later childhood. *Developmental Science, 11,* 1–14.

Marcel, A. J. (1980). Conscious and preconscious recognition of polysemous words: Locating the selective effects of prior verbal context. In R. S. Nickerson (Ed.), *Attention and performance VIII* (pp. 435–457). Hillsdale, NJ: Erlbaum.

Marcel, A. J. (1983). Conscious and unconscious perception: Experiments on visual masking and word recognition. *Cognitive Psychology, 15,* 197–237.

Marcus, G. F. (1996). Why do children say "breaked"? *Current Directions in Psychological Science, 5,* 81–85.

Marian, V., & Neisser, U. (2000). Language-dependent recall of autobiographical memories. *Journal of Experimental Psychology: General, 129,* 361–368.

Markman, A. B., Taylor, E., & Gentner, D. (2007). Auditory presentation leads to better analogical retrieval than written presentation. *Psychonomic Bulletin & Review, 14,* 1101–1106.

Markovits, H., & Doyon, C. (2004). Information processing and reasoning with premises that are empirically false: Interference, working memory, and processing speed. *Memory & Cognition, 32,* 592–601.

Markovits, H., & Potvin, F. (2001). Suppression of valid inferences and knowledge structures: The curious effect of producing alternative antecedents on reasoning with causal conditionals. *Memory & Cognition, 29,* 736–744.

Marler, P. (1967). Animal communication signals. *Science, 35,* 63–78.

Marschark, M., & Paivio, A. (1979). Semantic congruity and lexical marking in symbolic comparisons: An expectancy hypothesis. *Memory & Cognition, 7,* 175–184.

Marsh, E. J. (2007). Retelling is not the same as recalling. *Current Directions in Psychological Science, 16,* 16–20.

Marsh, E. J., Meade, M. L., Roediger, H. L. III (2003). Learning facts from fiction. *Journal of Memory and Language, 49,* 519–536.

Marsh, E. J., Roediger, H. L., Bjork, R. A., & Bjork, E. L. (2007). The memorial consequences of multiple-choice testing. *Psychonomic Bulletin & Review, 14,* 194–199.

Marsh, R. L., Cook, G. I., Meeks, J. T., Clark-Foos, A., & Hicks, J. L. (2007). Memory for intention-related material presented in a to-be-ignored channel. *Memory & Cognition, 35,* 1197–1204.

Marsh, R. L., & Hicks, J. L. (1998). Event-based prospective memory and executive control of working memory. *Journal of Experimental Psychology, 24,* 336–349.

Marsh, R. L., Hicks, J. L., & Cook, G. I. (2005). On the relationship between effort toward an ongoing task and cue detection in event-based prospective memory. *Journal of Experimental Psychology: Learning, Memory, and Cognition, 31,* 68–75.

Marshall, P. J. (2009). Relating psychology and neuroscience. *Perspectives on Psychological Science, 4,* 113–125.

Marslen-Wilson, W. D., & Welsh, A. (1978). Processing interactions and lexical access during word recognition in continuous speech. *Cognitive Psychology, 30,* 509–517.

Martin, R. C. (2000). Contribution from the neuropsychology of language and memory to the development of cognitive theory. *Journal of Memory and Language, 43,* 149–156.

Martindale, C. (1991). *Cognitive psychology: A neural-network approach.* Pacific Grove, CA: Brooks/Cole.

Mason, R. A., Just, M. A., Keller, T. A., & Carpenter, P. A. (2003). Ambiguity in the brain: What brain imaging reveals about the processing of syntactically ambiguous sentences.

Journal of Experimental Psychology: Learning, Memory, and Cognition, 29, 1319–1338.

Masson, M. E. J. (1984). Memory for the surface structure of sentences: Remembering with and without awareness. *Journal of Verbal Learning and Verbal Behavior, 23,* 579–592.

Masson, M. E. J. (1995). A distributed memory model of semantic priming. *Journal of Experimental Psychology: Learning, Memory, and Cognition, 21,* 3–23.

Masters, R. S. W. (1992). Knowledge, knerves and know-how: The role of explicit versus implicit knowledge in the breakdown of a complex motor skill under pressure. *British Journal of Psychology, 83,* 343–358.

Mata, R., & Nunes, L. (2010). When less is enough: Cognitive aging, information search, and decision quality in consumer choice. *Psychology and Aging, 25,* 289–298.

Mata, R., Schooler, L. J., & Reiskamp, J. (2007). The aging decision maker: Cognitive aging and the adaptive selection of decision strategies. *Psychology and Aging, 22,* 796–810.

Mather, M., Shafir, E., & Johnson, M. K. (2000). Misremembrance of options past: Source monitoring and choice. *Psychological Science, 11,* 132–138.

Mather, M., & Sutherland, M. R. (2011). Arousal-based competition in perception and memory. *Perspectives on Psychological Science, 6,* 114–133.

Mathis, K. M. (2002). Semantic interference from objects both in and out of scene context. *Journal of Experimental Psychology: Learning, Memory, and Cognition, 28,* 171–182.

Matlin, M. (1983). *Cognition.* New York: Holt.

Matlin, M. (2002). *Cognition* (5th ed.). New York: Wiley.

Mayr, S., & Buchner, A. (2006). Evidence for episodic retrieval of inadequate prime responses in auditory negative priming. *Journal of Experimental Psychology: Human Perception and Performance, 32,* 932–943.

Mazzoni, G., & Cornoldi, C. (1993). Strategies in study time allocation: Why is study time sometimes not effective? *Journal of Experimental Psychology: General, 122,* 47–60.

Mazzoni, G., & Memon, A. (2003). Imagination can create false autobiographical memories. *Psychological Science, 14,* 186–188.

McCabe, D. P. (2010). The influence of complex working memory span task administration methods on prediction of higher level cognition and metacognitive control of response times. *Memory & Cognition, 38,* 868–882.

McCabe, D. P., Smith, A. D., & Parks, C. M. (2007). The role of working memory capacity in reducing memory errors. *Memory & Cognition, 35,* 231–241.

McCabe, J. (2011). Metacognitive awareness of learning strategies in undergraduates. *Memory & Cognition, 39,* 462–476.

McCandliss, B. D., Posner, M. I., & Givon, T. (1997). Brain plasticity in learning visual words. *Cognitive Psychology, 33,* 88–110.

McCarley, J. S., Kramer, A. F., Wickens, C. D., Vidoni, E. D., & Boot, W. R. (2004). Visual skills in airport security screening. *Psychological Science, 15,* 302–306.

McCarthy, R. A., & Warrington, E. K. (1984). A two route model of speech production: Evidence from aphasia. *Brain, 107,* 463–485.

McCarthy, R. A., & Warrington, E. K. (1990). *Cognitive neuropsychology: A clinical introduction.* San Diego: Academic Press.

McClelland, J. L. (1979). On the time relations of mental processes: An examination of systems of processes in cascade. *Psychological Review, 86,* 287–330.

McClelland, J. L., & Elman, J. L. (1986). The TRACE model of speech perception. *Cognitive Psychology, 18,* 1–86.

McClelland, J. L., & Rumelhart, D. E. (1981). An interactive activation model of context effects in letter perception: Part 1. An account of basic findings. *Psychological Review, 88,* 375–407.

McClelland, J. L., Rumelhart, D. E., & Hinton, G. E. (1986). The appeal of parallel distributed processing. In D. E. Rumelhart, J. L. McClelland, & PDP Research Group (Eds.), *Parallel distributed processing* (Vol. 1, pp. 3–44). Cambridge, MA: MIT Press.

McCloskey, M. (1983). Naive theories of motion. In D. Gentner & A. L. Stevens (Eds.), *Mental models* (pp. 299–324). Hillsdale, NJ: Erlbaum.

McCloskey, M. (1992). Cognitive mechanisms in numerical processing: Evidence from acquired dyscalculia. *Cognition, 44,* 107–157.

McCloskey, M., Caramazza, A., & Green, B. (1980). Curvilinear motion in the absence of external forces: Naive beliefs about the motion of objects. *Science, 210,* 1139–1141.

McCloskey, M., Wible, C. G., & Cohen, N. J. (1988). Is there a special flashbulb-memory mechanism? *Journal of Experimental Psychology: General, 117,* 171–181.

McCloy, R., & Byrne, R. M. (2000). Counterfactual thinking about controllable events. *Memory & Cognition, 28,* 1071–1078.

McCrae, C. S., & Abrams, R. A. (2001). Age-related differences in object- and location-based inhibition of return of attention. *Psychology and Aging, 16,* 437–449.

McDaniel, M. A., Maier, S. F., & Einstein, G. O. (2002). "Brain-specific" nutrients: A memory cure? *Psychological Science in the Public Interest, 31,* 12–38.

McDaniel, M. A., Roediger, H. L., & McDermott, K. B. (2007). Generalized test-enhanced learning from the laboratory to the classroom. *Psychonomic Bulletin & Review, 14,* 200–206.

McDonald, J. L., & MacWhinney, B. (1995). The time course of anaphor resolution: Effects of implicit verb causality and gender. *Journal of Memory and Language, 34,* 543–566.

McGeoch, J. A. (1932). Forgetting and the law of disuse. *Psychological Review, 39,* 352–370.

McKoon, G., & Macfarland, T. (2002). Event templates in the lexical representations of verbs. *Cognitive Psychology, 45,* 1–44.

McKoon, G., & Ratcliff, R. (1986). Inferences about predictable events. *Journal of Experimental Psychology: Learning, Memory, and Cognition, 12,* 82–91.

McKoon, G., & Ratcliff, R. (1989). Inferences about contextually defined categories. *Journal of Experimental Psychology: Learning, Memory, and Cognition, 15,* 1134–1146.

McKoon, G., & Ratcliff, R. (1992). Inference during reading. *Psychological Review, 99,* 440–466.

McKoon, G., & Ratcliff, R. (2007). Interactions of meaning and syntax: Implications for models of sentence comprehension. *Journal of Memory and Language, 56,* 270–290.

McNamara, D. S., & McDaniel, M. A. (2004). Suppressing irrelevant information: Knowledge activation or inhibition? *Journal of Experimental Psychology: Learning, Memory, and Cognition, 30,* 465–482.

McNamara, T. P. (1992). Priming and constraints it places on theories of memory and retrieval. *Psychological Review, 99,* 650–662.

McNeill, D. (1992). *Hand and mind: What gestures reveal about thought.* Chicago: University of Chicago Press.

McRae, K., & Boisvert, S. (1998). Automatic semantic similarity priming. *Journal of Experimental Psychology: Learning, Memory, and Cognition, 24,* 558–572.

McRae, K., de Sa, V. R., & Seidenberg, M. S. (1997). On the nature and scope of featural representations of word meaning. *Journal of Experimental Psychology: General, 126,* 99–130.

Meade, M. L., & Roediger, H. L. III. (2002). Explorations in the social contagion of memory. *Memory & Cognition, 30,* 995–1009.

Meade, M. L., Watson, J. M., Balota, D. A., & Roediger, H. L. (2007). The roles of spreading activation and retrieval mode in producing false recognition in the DRM paradigm. *Journal of Memory and Language, 56,* 305–320.

Medin, D. L. (1989). Concepts and conceptual structure. *American Psychologist, 44,* 1469–1481.

Medin, D. L., & Atran, S. (2004). The native mind: Biological categorization and reasoning in development and across cultures. *Psychological Review, 111,* 960–983.

Medin, D. L., & Bazerman, M. H. (1999). Broadening behavioral decision research: Multiple levels of cognitive processing. *Psychonomic Bulletin & Review, 6,* 533–546.

Medin, D. L., Coley, J. D., Storms, G., & Hayes, B. K. (2003). A relevance theory of induction. *Psychonomic Bulletin & Review, 10,* 517–532.

Medin, D. L., & Edelson, S. M. (1988). Problem structure and the use of base-rate information from experience. *Journal of Experimental Psychology: General, 117,* 68–85.

Medin, D. L., Goldstone, R. L., & Gentner, D. (1993). Respects for similarity. *Psychological Review, 100,* 254–278.

Medin, D. L., Lynch, E. B., Coley, J. D., & Atran, S. (1997). Categorization and reasoning among tree experts: Do all roads lead to Rome? *Cognitive Psychology, 32,* 49–96.

Mehler, J., Morton, J., & Jusczyk, P. W. (1984). On reducing language to biology. *Cognitive Neuropsychology, 1,* 83–116.

Melton, A. W. (1963). Implications of short-term memory for a general theory of memory. *Journal of Verbal Learning and Verbal Behavior, 2,* 1–21.

Metcalfe, J. (1986). Feeling of knowing in memory and problem solving. *Journal of Experimental Psychology: Learning, Memory, and Cognition, 12,* 288–294.

Metcalfe, J. (2002). Is study time allocated selectively to a region of proximal learning? *Journal of Experimental Psychology: General, 131,* 349–363.

Metcalfe, J., & Finn, B. (2008). Evidence that judgments of learning are causally related to study choice. *Psychonomic Bulletin & Review, 15,* 174–179.

Metcalfe, J., & Kornell, N. (2003). The dynamics of learning and allocation of study time to a region of proximal learning. *Journal of Experimental Psychology: General, 132,* 530–542.

Metcalfe, J., & Wiebe, D. (1987). Intuition in insight and noninsight problem solving. *Memory & Cognition, 15,* 238–246.

Metzing, C., & Brennan, S. E. (2003). When conceptual pacts are broken: Partner-specific effects on the comprehension of referring expressions. *Journal of Memory and Language, 49,* 201–213.

Meyer, A. S., & Bock, K. (1992). The tip-of-the-tongue phenomenon: Blocking or partial activation? *Memory & Cognition, 20,* 715–726.

Meyer, B. J. F., & Rice, G. E. (1981). Information recalled from prose by young, middle, and old adult readers. *Experimental Aging Research, 7,* 253–268.

Meyer, D. E., & Schvaneveldt, R. W. (1971). Facilitation in recognizing pairs of words: Evidence of a dependence between retrieval operations. *Journal of Experimental Psychology, 90,* 227–234.

Meyer, D. E., Schvaneveldt, R. W., & Ruddy, M. G. (1975). Loci of contextual effects on visual word-recognition. In P. M. A. Rabbitt & S. Dornic (Eds.), *Attention and performance* (Vol. 5, pp. 98–118). London: Academic Press.

Milham, M. P., Erickson, K. I., Banich, M. T., Kramer, A. F., Webb, A., Wszalek, T., et al. (2002). Attentional control in the aging brain: Insights from an fMRI study of the Stroop task. *Brain and Cognition, 49,* 277–296.

Miller, D. T., & McFarland, C. (1986). Counterfactual thinking and victim compensation: A test of norm theory. *Personality and Social Psychology Bulletin, 12,* 513–519.

Miller, G. A. (1956). The magical number seven, plus or minus two: Some limits on our capacity for processing information. *Psychological Review, 63,* 81–97.

Miller, G. A. (1973). Psychology and communication. In G. A. Miller (Ed.), *Communication, language, and meaning: Psychological perspectives* (pp. 3–12). New York: Basic Books.

Miller, G. A. (1977). Practical and lexical knowledge. In P. N. Johnson-Laird & P. C. Wason (Eds.), *Thinking: Readings in cognitive science* (pp. 400–410). Cambridge, England: Cambridge University Press.

Miller, G. A., Galanter, E., & Pribram, K. H. (1960). *Plans and the structure of behavior.* New York: Holt.

Miller, G. A., & Isard, S. (1963). Some perceptual consequences of linguistic rules. *Journal of Verbal Learning and Verbal Behavior, 2,* 217–228.

Millis, K. K., & Graesser, A. C. (1994). The time-course of constructing knowledge-based inferences for scientific texts. *Journal of Memory and Language, 33,* 583–599.

Millis, K. K., & Just, M. A. (1994). The influence of connectives on sentence comprehension. *Journal of Memory and Language, 33,* 128–147.

Milner, B., Corkin, S., & Teuber, H. L. (1968). Further analysis of the hippocampal amnesic syndrome: 14–year follow up study of H. M. *Neuropsychologia, 6,* 215–234.

Minsky, M. L. (1986). *The society of mind.* New York: Simon & Schuster.

Mishkin, M., & Appenzeller, T. (1987). The anatomy of memory. *Scientific American, 256,* 80–89.

Mishkin, M., Ungerleider, L., & Macko, K. A. (1983). Object vision and spatial vision: Two cortical pathways. *Trends in Neurosciences, 6,* 414–417.

Mitchell, D. B. (2006). Nonconscious priming after 17 years. *Psychological Science, 17,* 925–929.

Mitchell, D. C., & Holmes, V. M. (1985). The role of specific information about the verb in parsing sentences with local structural ambiguity. *Journal of Memory and Language, 24,* 542–559.

Mitchell, K. J., & Zaragoza, M. S. (1996). Repeated exposure to suggestion and false memory: The role of contextual variability. *Journal of Memory and Language, 35,* 246–260.

Mitchell, K. J., & Zaragoza, M. S. (2001). Contextual overlap and eyewitness suggestibility. *Memory & Cognition, 29,* 616–626.

Mitterschiffthaler, M. T., Williams, S. C. R., Walsh, N. D., Cleare, A. J., Donaldson, C., Scott, J., et al. (2008). Neural basis of the emotional Stroop interference effect in major depression. *Psychological Medicine, 38,* 24–256.

Miyake, A., Friedman, N. P., Emerson, M. J., Witzki, A. H., Howerter, A., & Wager, T. D. (2000). The unity and diversity of executive functions and their contributions to complex "frontal lobe" tasks: A latent variable analysis. *Cognitive Psychology, 41,* 49–100.

Miyake, A., Just, M. A., & Carpenter, P. A. (1994). Working memory constraints on the resolution of lexical ambiguity: Maintaining multiple interpretations in neutral contexts. *Journal of Memory and Language, 33,* 175–202.

Miyake, A., & Shah, P. (Eds.). (1999). *Models of working memory: Mechanisms of active maintenance and executive control.* New York: Cambridge University Press.

Moldoveanu, M., & Langer, E. (2002). False memories of the future: A critique of the applications of probabilistic reasoning to the study of cognitive processes. *Psychological Review, 109,* 358–375.

Monaghan, P., & Pollmann, S. (2003). Division of labor between the hemispheres for complex but not simple tasks: An implemented connectionist model. *Journal of Experimental Psychology: General, 132,* 379–399.

Monaghan, P., & Shillcock, R. (2004). Hemispheric asymmetries in cognitive modeling: connectionist modeling of unilateral visual neglect. *Psychological Review, 111,* 283–308.

Moore, A. B., Clark, B. A., & Kane, M. J. (2008). Who shalt not kill? Individual differences in working memory capacity, executive control, and moral judgment. *Psychological Science, 19,* 549–557.

Moray, N. (1959). Attention in dichotic listening: Affective cues and the influence of instructions. *Quarterly Journal of Experimental Psychology, 11,* 56–60.

Moray, N., Bates, A., & Barnett, T. (1965). Experiments on the four-eared man. *Journal of the Acoustical Society of America, 38,* 196–201.

Moreno, S., Bialystok, E., Barac, R., Schellenberg, E. G., Cepeda, N. J., & Chau, T. (2011). Short-term music training enhances verbal intelligence and executive function. *Psychological Science, 22,* 1425–1433.

Morey, C. C., & Cowan, N. (2004). When visual and verbal memories compete: Evidence of cross-domain limits in working memory. *Psychonomic Bulletin & Review, 11,* 296–301.

Morris, A. L., & Harris, C. L. (2002). Sentence context, word recognition, and repetition blindness. *Journal of Experimental Psychology: Learning, Memory, and Cognition, 28,* 962–982.

Morrow, D. G., Greenspan, S. L., & Bower, G. H. (1987). Accessibility and situation models in narrative comprehension. *Journal of Memory and Language, 26,* 165–187.

Morrow, D. G., Leirer, V. O., Altieri, P. A., & Fitzsimmons, C. (1994). Age differences in creating spatial models from narratives. *Language & Cognitive Processes, 9,* 203–220.

Morrow, D. G., Stine-Morrow, E. A. L., Leirer, V. O., Andrassy, J. M., & Kahn, J. (1997). The role of reader age and focus of attention in creating situation models from narratives. *Journals of Gerontology, 52B,* P73–P80.

Morton, J. (1979). Facilitation in word recognition: Experiments causing change in the logogen models. In P. A. Kolers, M. E. Wrolstad, & H. Bouma (Eds.), *Processing of visible language* (Vol. 1, pp. 259–268). New York: Plenum.

Moscovitch, M. (1979). Information processing and the cerebral hemispheres. In M. S. Gazzaniga (Ed.), *Handbook of behavioral neurobiology: Vol. 2. Neuropsychology* (pp. 379–446). New York: Plenum.

Moshinsky, A., & Bar-Hillel, M. (2002). Where did 1850 happen first—in America or in Europe? A cognitive account for a historical bias. *Psychological Science, 13,* 20–26.

Most, S. B., Scholl, B. J., Clifford, E. R., & Simons, D. J. (2005). What you see is what you set: Sustained inattentional blindness and the capture of awareness. *Psychological Review, 112,* 217–242.

Moyer, R. S. (1973). Comparing objects in memory: Evidence suggesting an internal psychophysics. *Perception and Psychophysics, 13,* 180–184.

Moyer, R. S., & Bayer, R. H. (1976). Mental comparison and the symbolic distance effect. *Cognitive Psychology, 8,* 228–246.

Mueller, S. T., Seymour, T. L., Kieras, D. E., & Meyer, D. E. (2003). Theoretical implications of articulatory duration, phonological similarity, and phonological complexity in verbal working memory. *Journal of Experimental Psychology: Learning, Memory, and Cognition, 29,* 1353–1380.

Murdock, B. B., Jr. (1962). The serial position effect of free recall. *Journal of Experimental Psychology, 64,* 482–488.

Murphy, G. L. (1985). Processes of understanding anaphora. *Journal of Memory and Language, 24,* 290–303.

Murphy, G. L., & Medin, D. L. (1985). The role of theories in conceptual coherence. *Psychological Review, 92,* 289–316.

Murphy, M. C., Steele, C. M., & Gross, J. J. (2007). Signaling threat: How situational cues affect women in math, science, and engineering settings. *Psychological Science, 18,* 879–885.

Murray, D. J. (1967). The role of speech responses in short-term memory. *Canadian Journal of Psychology, 21,* 263–276.

Myers, E. B., Blumstein, S. E., Walsh, E., & Eliassen, J. (2009). Inferior frontal regions underlie the perception of phonetic category invariance. *Psychological Science, 20,* 895–903.

Myerson, J., Ferraro, F. R., Hale, S., & Lima, S. D. (1992). General slowing in semantic priming and word recognition. *Psychology and Aging, 7,* 257–270.

Myerson, J., Hale, S., Wagstaff, D., Poon, L. W., & Smith, G. A. (1990). The information loss model: A mathematical theory of age-related cognitive slowing. *Psychological Review, 97,* 475–487.

Nadel, L., & Zola-Morgan, S. (1984). Infantile amnesia: A neurobiological perspective. In M. Moscovitch (Ed.), *Infant memory.* New York: Plenum Press.

Nairne, J. S., Pandeirada, N. S., & Thompson, S. R. (2008). Adaptive memory: The comparative value of survival processing. *Psychological Science, 19,* 176–180.

Nairne, J. S., Thompson, S. R., & Pandeirada, N. S. (2007). Adaptive memory: Survival processing enhances retention.

Journal of Experimental Psychology: Learning, Memory, and Cognition, 33, 263–273.

Navon, D. (1984). Resources: A theoretical soup stone? *Psychological Review, 91,* 216–234.

Neath, I., Surprenant, A. M., & Crowder, R. G. (1993). The context-dependent stimulus suffix effect. *Journal of Experimental Psychology: Learning, Memory and Cognition, 19,* 698–703.

Nee, D. E., & Jonides, J. (2008). Dissociable interference control processes in perception and memory. *Psychological Science, 19,* 490–500.

Neely, J. H. (1977). Semantic priming and retrieval from lexical memory: Roles of inhibitionless spreading activation and limited-capacity attention. *Journal of Experimental Psychology: General, 106,* 226–254.

Neill, W. T. (1977). Inhibition and facilitation processes in selective attention. *Journal of Experimental Psychology: Human Perception & Performance, 3,* 444–450.

Neill, W. T., Valdes, L. A., & Terry, K. M. (1995). Selective attention and the inhibitory control of cognition. In F. N. Dempster & C. J. Brainerd (Eds.), *New perspectives on interference and inhibition in cognition* (pp. 207–261). New York: Academic Press.

Neisser, U. (1964). Visual search. *Scientific American, 210,* 94–102.

Neisser, U. (1967). *Cognitive psychology.* New York: Appleton-Century-Crofts.

Neisser, U. (1976). *Cognition and reality.* San Francisco: Freeman.

Neisser, U. (1981). John Dean's memory: A case study. *Cognition, 9,* 1–22.

Neisser, U. (1982). *Memory observed: Remembering in natural contexts.* San Francisco: Freeman.

Neisser, U., Novick, R., & Lazar, R. (1963). Searching for ten targets simultaneously. *Perceptual and Motor Skills, 17,* 955–961.

Nelson, K. (1993). The psychological and social origins of autobiographical memory. *Psychological Science, 4,* 7–14.

Nelson, K., & Fivush, R. (2004). The emergence of autobiographical memory: A social cultural developmental theory. *Psychological Review, 111,* 486–511.

Nelson, T. O. (1978). Savings and forgetting from long-term memory. *Journal of Verbal Learning and Verbal Behavior, 10,* 568–576.

Nelson, T. O. (1985). Ebbinghaus's contribution to the measurement of retention: Savings during relearning. *Journal of Experimental Psychology: Learning, Memory, and Cognition, 11,* 472–479.

Nelson, T. O. (1988). Predictive accuracy of the feeling of knowing across different criterion tasks and across different subject populations and individuals. In M. Gruneberg, P. Morris, & R. Sykes (Eds.), *Practical aspects of memory: Current research and issues* (Vol. 1, pp. 190–196). New York: Wiley.

Nelson, T. O. (1993). Judgments of learning and the allocation of study time. *Journal of Experimental Psychology: General, 122,* 269–273.

Nelson, T. O., & Leonesio, R. J. (1988). Allocation of self-paced study time and the "labor-in vain effect." *Journal of Experimental Psychology: Learning, Memory, and Cognition, 14,* 676–686.

Nelson, T. O., McSpadden, M., Fromme, K., & Marlatt, G. A. (1986). Effects of alcohol intoxication on metamemory and on retrieval from long-term memory. *Journal of Experimental Psychology: General, 115,* 247–254.

Neuschatz, J. S., Benoit, G. E., & Payne, D. G. (2003). Effective warnings in the Deese–Roediger–McDermott false-memory paradigm: The role of identifiability. *Journal of Experimental Psychology: Learning, Memory, and Cognition, 29,* 35–41.

Newell, A., Shaw, J. C., & Simon, H. A. (1958). Elements of a theory of human problem solving. *Psychological Review, 65,* 151–166.

Newell, A., & Simon, H. A. (1972). *Human problem solving.* Englewood Cliffs, NJ: Prentice Hall.

Newell, B. R., & Shanks, D. R. (2003). Take the best or look at the rest? Factors influencing "one-reason" decision making. *Journal of Experimental Psychology: Learning, Memory, and Cognition, 29,* 53–65.

Newell, B. R., & Shanks, D. R. (2004). On the role of recognition in decision making. *Journal of Experimental Psychology: Learning, Memory, and Cognition, 30,* 923–935.

Nickerson, R. S. (2001). The projective way of knowing: A useful heuristic that sometimes misleads. *Current Directions in Psychological Science, 10,* 168–172.

Nickerson, R. S. (2002). The production and perception of randomness. *Psychological Review, 109,* 330–357.

Nickerson, R. S., & Adams, M. J. (1979). Long-term memory for a common object. *Cognitive Psychology, 11,* 287–307.

Nisbett, R. E., Krantz, D. H., Jepson, C., & Kunda, Z. (1983). The use of statistical heuristics in everyday inductive reasoning. *Psychological Review, 90,* 339–363.

Nisbett, R. E., & Masuda, T. (2003). Culture and point of view. *Proceedings of the National Academy of Sciences, 100,* 11163–11170.

Nisbett, R. E., Peng, K., Choi, I., & Norenzayan, A. (2001). Culture and systems of thought: Holistic versus analytic cognition. *Psychological Review, 108,* 291–310.

Nob, S. R., & Stine-Morrow, E. A. L. (2009). Age differences in tracking characters during narrative comprehension. *Memory & Cognition, 37,* 769–778.

Noice, H., & Noice, T. (1999). Long-term retention of theatrical roles. *Memory, 7,* 357–382.

Noice, H., & Noice, T. (2001). Learning dialogue with and without movement. *Memory and Cognition, 29,* 820–827.

Norman, D. A. (1981). Categorization of action slips. *Psychological Review, 88,* 1–15.

Norman, D. A. (1986). Reflections on cognition and parallel distributed processing. In J. L. McClelland, D. E. Rumelhart, & PDP Research Group (Eds.), *Parallel distributed processing: Explorations in the microstructure of cognition: Vol. 2. Psychological and biological models* (pp. 531–546). Cambridge, MA: MIT Press.

Norman, D. A., & Rumelhart, D. E. (Eds.). (1975). *Explorations in cognition.* San Francisco: Freeman.

Norman, K. A., & Schacter, D. L. (1997). False recognition in younger and older adults: Exploring the characteristics of illusory memories. *Memory & Cognition, 25,* 838–848

Norris, D., McQueen, J. M., Cutler, A., & Butterfield, S. (1997). The possible-word constraint in the segmentation of continuous speech. *Cognitive Psychology, 34,* 191–243.

Nosofsky, R. M. (1986). Attention, similarity, and the identification-categorization relationship. *Journal of Experimental Psychology: General, 115,* 39–57.

Novick, L. R. (1988). Analogical transfer, problem similarity, and expertise. *Journal of Experimental Psychology: Learning, Memory, and Cognition, 14,* 510–520.

Nyberg, L., Cabeza, R., & Tulving, E. (1996). PET studies of encoding and retrieval: The HERA model. *Psychonomic Bulletin & Review, 3,* 135–148.

Nyberg, L., McIntosh, A. R., & Tulving, E. (1998). Functional brain imaging of episodic and semantic memory with positron emission tomography. *Journal of Molecular Medicine, 76,* 48–53.

Oberfeld, D., Hecht, H., & Gamer, M. (2010). Surface lightness influences perceived room height. *The Quarterly Journal of Experimental Psychology, 63,* 1999–2011.

O'Brien, E. J., Albrecht, J. E., Hakala, C. M., & Rizzella, M. L. (1995). Activation and suppression of antecedents during reinstatement. *Journal of Experimental Psychology: Learning, Memory, and Cognition, 21,* 626–634.

O'Brien, E. J., & Myers, J. L. (1987). The role of causal connections in the retrieval of text. *Memory & Cognition, 15,* 419–427.

O'Brien, E. J., Plewes, P. S., & Albrecht, J. E. (1990). Antecedent retrieval processes. *Journal of Experimental Psychology: Learning, Memory, and Cognition, 16,* 241–249.

Ofshe, R. J. (1992). Inadvertent hypnosis during interrogation: False confession due to dissociative state, misidentified multiple personality, and the satanic cult hypothesis. *International Journal of Clinical and Experimental Hypnosis, 40,* 125–156.

Öhman, A., Flykt, A., & Esteves, F. (2001). Emotion drives attention: Detecting the snake in the grass. *Journal of Experimental Psychology: General, 130,* 466–478.

Ojemann, G. A. (1982). Models of the brain organization for higher integrative functions derived with electrical stimulation techniques. *Human Neurobiology, 1,* 243–250.

Ojemann, G. A., & Creutzfeldt, O. D. (1987). Language in humans and animals: Contribution of brain stimulation and recording. In *Handbook of physiology: The nervous system* (Vol. 5). Bethesda, MD: American Physiological Society.

Olafson, K. M., & Ferraro, F. R. (2001). Effects of emotional state on lexical decision performance. *Brain and Cognition, 45,* 15–20.

Oosterwijk, S., Winkielman, P., Pecher, D., Zeelenberg, R., Rottveel, M., & Fischer, A. H. (2012). Mental states inside out: Switching costs for emotional and nonemotional sentences that differ in internal and external focus. *Memory & Cognition, 40,* 93–100.

Oppenheim, G. M., & Dell, G. S. (2010). Motor movement matters: The flexible abstractness of inner speech. *Memory & Cognition, 38,* 1147–1160.

O'Seaghdha, P. G. (1997). Conjoint and dissociable effects of syntactic and semantic context. *Journal of Experimental Psychology: Learning, Memory, and Cognition, 23,* 807–828.

Osterhout, L., Allen, M. D., McLaughlin, J., & Inoue, K. (2002). Brain potentials elicited by prose-embedded linguistic anomalies. *Memory & Cognition, 30,* 1304–1312.

Osterhout, L., & Holcomb, P. J. (1992). Event-related brain potentials elicited by syntactic anomaly. *Journal of Memory and Language, 31,* 785–806.

Özyürek, S. (2002). Do speakers design their cospeech gestures for their addressees? The effects of addressee location on representational gestures. *Journal of Memory and Language, 46,* 688–704.

Pachur, T., Mata, R., & Schooler, L. J. (2007). Cognitive aging and the adaptive use of recognition in decision making. *Psychology and Aging, 24,* 901–915.

Paivio, A. (1971). *Imagery and verbal processes.* New York: Holt.

Paivio, A. (1990). *Mental representations: A dual coding approach.* New York: Oxford University Press.

Palermo, D. S. (1978). *Psychology of language.* Glenview, IL: Scott, Foresman.

Palmer, S. E. (1975). The effects of contextual scenes on the identification of objects. *Memory & Cognition, 3,* 519–526.

Park, D. C., Hertzog, C., Kidder, D. P., Morrell, R. W., & Mayhorn, C. B. (1997). Effect of age on event-based and time-based prospective memory. *Psychology and Aging, 12,* 314–327.

Park, D. C., & Huang, C-M. (2010). Culture wires the brain: A cognitive neuroscience perspective. *Perspectives on Psychological Science, 5,* 391–400.

Pashler, H. (1994). Dual-task interference in simple tasks: Data and theory. *Psychological Bulletin, 116,* 220–244.

Pashler, H., & Johnson, J. C. (1998). Attentional limitations in dual-task performance. In H. Pashler (Ed.), *Attention* (pp. 155–189). Hove, England: Psychology Press.

Pashler, H., Rohrer, D., Cepeda, N. J., & Carpenter, S. K. (2007). Enhancing learning and retarding forgetting: Choices and consequences. *Psychonomic Bulletin & Review, 14,* 187–193.

Paul, S. T., Kellas, G., Martin, M., & Clark, M. B. (1992). Influence of contextual features on the activation of ambiguous word meanings. *Journal of Experimental Psychology: Learning, Memory, and Cognition, 18,* 703–717.

Payne, D. G., Toglia, M. P., & Anastasi, J. S. (1994). Recognition performance level and the magnitude of the misinformation effect in eyewitness memory. *Psychonomic Bulletin & Review, 1,* 376–382.

Payne, J. D., & Kensinger, E. A. (2010). Sleep's role in the consolidation of emotional episodic memories. *Psychological Science, 19,* 290–295.

Pearlmutter, N. J., Garnsey, S. M., & Bock, K. (1999). Agreement processes in sentence comprehension. *Journal of Memory and Language, 41,* 427–456.

Pecher, D., Zeelenberg, R., & Barsalou, L. W. (2003). Verifying different modality properties for concepts produces switching costs. *Psychological Science, 14,* 119–124.

Pedone, R., Hummel, J. E., & Holyoak, K. J. (2001). The use of diagrams in analogical problem solving. *Memory & Cognition, 29,* 214–221.

Pell, M. D. (1999). Fundamental frequency encoding of linguistic and emotional prosody by right hemisphere-damaged speakers. *Brain and Language, 69,* 161–192.

Penfield, W. (1958). *The excitable cortex in conscious man.* Liverpool, UK: Liverpool University Press.

Penfield, W., & Jasper, H. H. (1954). *Epilepsy and the functional anatomy of the human brain.* Boston: Little, Brown.

Penfield, W., & Milner, B. (1958). Memory deficit produced by bilateral lesions in the hippocampal zone. *Archives of Neurology and Psychiatry, 79,* 475–497.

Perea, M., Duñabeitia, J. A., & Carreiras, M. (2008). Masked associative/semantic priming effects across languages with highly proficient bilinguals. *Journal of Memory and Language, 58,* 916–930.

Peretz, I., Radeau, M., & Arguin, M. (2004). Two-way interactions between music and language: Evidence from priming recognition of tune and lyrics in familiar songs. *Memory & Cognition, 32,* 142–152.

Perfect, T. J., Andrade, J., & Eagan, I. (2011). Eye closure reduces the cross-modal memory impairment caused by auditory distraction. *Journal of Experimental Psychology: Learning, Memory, and Cognition, 37,* 1008–1013.

Peterson, R. R., Burgess, C., Dell, G. S., & Eberhard, K. M. (2001). Dissociation between syntactic and semantic processing during idiom comprehension. *Journal of Experimental Psychology: Learning, Memory, and Cognition, 27*(5), 1223.

Peterson, L. R., & Peterson, M. J. (1959). Short-term retention of individual items. *Journal of Experimental Psychology, 58,* 193–198.

Petrusic, W. M., & Baranski, J. V. (2003). Judging confidence influences decision processing in comparative judgments. *Psychonomic Bulletin & Review, 10,* 177–183.

Pexman, P. M., Holyk, G. G., & Monfils, M. (2003). Number-of-features effects and semantic processing. *Memory & Cognition, 31,* 842–855.

Piaget, J. (1967). *Six psychological studies* (A. Tenzer, Trans.). New York: Random House.

Pickering, M. J., & Traxler, M. J. (1998). Plausibility and recovery from garden paths: An eye-tracking study. *Journal of Experimental Psychology: Learning, Memory, and Cognition, 24,* 940–961.

Piercey, C. D., & Joordens, S. (2000). Turning an advantage into a disadvantage: Ambiguity effects in lexical decision versus reading tasks. *Memory & Cognition, 28,* 657–666.

Pinker, S. (1994). *The language instinct: How the mind creates language.* New York: Morrow.

Pitt, M. A., & Samuel, A. G. (1995). Lexical and sublexical feedback in auditory word recognition. *Cognitive Psychology, 29,* 149–188.

Pittenger, C., & Kandel, E. R. (2003). In search of general mechanisms for long-lasting plasticity: Aplysia and the hippocampus. *Philosophical Transactions of the Royal Society of London, 358,* 757–763.

Plude, D. J., & Doussard-Roosevelt, J. A. (1989). Aging, selective attention, and feature integration. *Psychology and Aging, 4,* 98–105.

Poldrack, R. A., & Wagner, A. D. (2004). What can neuroimaging tell us about the mind? *Current Directions in Psychological Science, 13,* 177–181.

Polk, T. A., & Farah, M. J. (2002). Functional MRI evidence for an abstract, not perceptual, word-form area. *Journal of Experimental Psychology: General, 131,* 65–72.

Pollack, I., & Pickett, J. M. (1964). Intelligibility of excerpts from fluent speech: Auditory vs. structural context. *Journal of Verbal Learning and Verbal Behavior, 3,* 79–84.

Pollatsek, A., Konold, C. E., Well, A. D., & Lima, S. D. (1984). Beliefs underlying random sampling. *Memory & Cognition, 12,* 395–401.

Polya, G. (1957). *How to solve it.* Garden City, NY: Doubleday/Anchor.

Posner, M. I., & Cohen, Y. (1984). Components of visual orienting. In H. Bouma & D. G. Bouwhuis (Eds.), *Attention and performance X* (pp. 531–556). Hillsdale, NJ: Erlbaum.

Posner, M. I., Kiesner, J. Thomas-Thrapp, L., McCandliss, B., Carr, T. H., & Rothbart, M. K. (1992, November). *Brain changes in the acquisition of literacy.* Paper presented at the meetings of the Psychonomic Society, St. Louis.

Posner, M. I., Nissen, M. J., & Ogden, W. C. (1978). Attended and unattended processing modes: The role of set for spatial location. In H. L. Pick & I. J. Saltzman (Eds.), *Modes of perceiving and processing information* (pp. 137–157). Hillsdale, NJ: Erlbaum.

Posner, M. I., & Rothbart, M. K. (2007). Research on attention networks as a model for the integration of psychological science. *Annual Review of Psychology, 58,* 1–23.

Posner, M. I., & Snyder, C. R. R. (1975). Facilitation and inhibition in the processing of signals. In P. M. A. Rabbitt & S. Dornic (Eds.), *Attention and performance V* (pp. 669–682). New York: Academic Press.

Posner, M. I., Snyder, C. R. R., & Davidson, B. J. (1980). Attention and the detection of signals. *Journal of Experimental Psychology: General, 109,* 160–174.

Postman, L., & Underwood, B. J. (1973). Critical issues in interference theory. *Memory & Cognition, 1,* 19–40.

Prado, J., Van der Henst, J-B., & Noveck, I. A. (2008). Spatial associations in relational reasoning: Evidence for a SNARC-like effect. *Quarterly Journal of Experimental Psychology, 61,* 1143–1150.

Pratt, J., Radulescu, P. V., Guo, R. M., & Abrams, R. A. (2010). It's alive! Animate motion captures visual attention. *Psychological Science, 21,* 1724–1730.

Price, R. H. (1987). *Principles of psychology.* Glenview, IL: Scott Foresman.

Prince, S. E., Tsukiura, T., & Cabeza, R. (2007). Distinguishing the neural correlates of episodic encoding and semantic retrieval. *Psychological Science, 18,* 144–151.

Pritchard, R. M. (1961). Stabilized images on the retina. *Scientific American, 204,* 72–78.

Proffitt, D. R. (2006). Embodied perception and the economy of action. *Perspectives on Psychological Science, 1,* 110–122.

Proffitt, D. R., Kaiser, M. K., & Whelan, S. M. (1990). Understanding wheel dynamics. *Cognitive Psychology, 22,* 342–373.

Protopapas, A., Archonti, A., & Skaloumbakas, C. (2007). Reading ability is negatively related to Stroop interference. *Cognitive Psychology, 54,* 251–282.

Provins, K. A. (1997). Handedness and speech: A critical reappraisal of the role of genetic and environmental factors in the cerebral lateralization of function. *Psychological Review, 104,* 554–571.

Queen, T. L., & Hess, T. M. (2010). Age differences in the effects of conscious and unconscious thought in decision making. *Psychology and Aging, 25,* 251–261.

Quillian, M. R. (1968). Semantic memory. In M. Minsky (Ed.), *Semantic information processing* (pp. 216–270). Cambridge, MA: MIT Press.

Quillian, M. R. (1969). The teachable language comprehender: A simulation program and theory of language. *Communications of the ACM, 12,* 459–476.

Quinn, P. C., Eimas, P. D., & Rosenkrantz, S. L. (1993). Evidence for representations of perceptually similar natural categories by 3-month-old and 4-month-old infants. *Perception, 22,* 463–475.

Rader, A. W., & Sloutsky, V. M. (2002). Processing of logically valid and logically invalid conditional inferences in discourse comprehension. *Journal of Experimental Psychology: Learning, Memory, and Cognition, 28,* 59–68.

Radvansky, G. A., & Copeland, D. E. (2006a). Memory retrieval and interference: Working memory issues. *Journal of Memory and Language, 55,* 33–46.

Radvansky, G. A., & Copeland, D. E. (2006b). Walking through doorways causes forgetting. *Memory & Cognition, 34,* 1150–1156.

Radvansky, G. A., Copeland, D. E., & Zwaan, R. A. (2003). Aging and functional spatial relations in comprehension and memory. *Psychology and Aging, 18,* 161–165.

Radvansky, G. A., & Dijkstra, K. (2007). Aging and situation model processing. *Psychonomic Bulletin & Review, 14,* 1027–1042.

Radvansky, G. A., Gerard, L. D., Zacks, R. T., & Hasher, L. (1990). Younger and older adults' use of mental models as representations for text materials. *Psychology and Aging, 5,* 209–214.

Radvansky, G. A., Krawietz, S. A., & Tamplin, A. K. (2011). Walking through doorways causes forgetting: Further explorations. *Quarterly Journal of Experimental Psychology, 64,* 1632–1645.

Radvansky, G. A., Spieler, D. H., & Zacks, R. T. (1993). Mental model organization. *Journal of Experimental Psychology: Learning, Memory, and Cognition, 19,* 95–114.

Radvansky, G. A., Tamplin, A. K., & Krawietz, S. A. (2010). Walking through doorways causes forgetting: Environmental integration. *Psychonomic Bulletin & Review, 17,* 900–904.

Radvansky, G. A., & Zacks, R. T. (1991). Mental models and the fan effect. *Journal of Experimental Psychology: Learning, Memory, and Cognition, 17,* 940–953.

Radvansky, G. A., Zwaan, R. A., Curiel, J. M., & Copeland, D. E. (2001). Situation models and aging. *Psychology and Aging, 16,* 145–160.

Radvansky, G. A., Zwaan, R. A., Federico, T., & Franklin, N. (1998). Retrieval from temporally organized situation models. *Journal of Experimental Psychology: Learning, Memory, and Cognition, 24,* 1224–1237.

Rafal, R. D. (1997). Hemispatial neglect: Cognitive neuropsychological aspects. In T. E. Feinberg & M. J. Farah (Eds.), *Behavioral neurology and neuropsychology* (pp. 319–336). New York: McGraw-Hill.

Ramachandran, V. S. (2011). *The tell-tale brain: A neuroscientist's quest for what makes us human.* New York: Norton.

Ramsey-Rennels, J. L., & Langlois, J. H. (2007). How infants perceive and process faces. In A. Slater & M. Lewis (Eds.), *Introduction to infant development* (pp. 191–232). Oxford, England: Oxford University Press.

Ranganath, C. (2010). Binding items and contexts: The cognitive neuroscience of episodic memory. *Current Directions, 19,* 131–137.

Ranganath, C., & Pallar, K. A. (1999). Frontal brain activity during episodic and semantic retrieval: Insights from event-related potentials. *Journal of Cognitive Neuroscience, 11,* 598–609.

Rapp, B., & Goldrick, M. (2000). Discreteness and interactivity in spoken word production. *Psychological Review, 107,* 460–499.

Rasch, B., & Born, J. (2008). Reactivation and consolidation of memory during sleep. *Current Directions in Psychological Science, 17,* 188–192.

Ratcliff, G., & Newcombe, F. (1982). Object recognition: Some deductions from the clinical evidence. In A. W. Ellis (Ed.), *Normality and pathology in cognitive functions* (p. 162). London: Academic Press.

Ratcliff, R., & McKoon, G. (1988). A retrieval theory of priming in memory. *Psychological Review, 95,* 385–408.

Raven, J. C. (1941). Standardization of progressive matrices, 1938. *British Journal of Medical Psychology, 19,* 137–150.

Rayner, K. (1998). Eye movements in reading and information processing: 20 years of research. *Psychological Bulletin, 124,* 372–422.

Rayner, K., Carlson, M., & Frazier, L. (1983). The interaction of syntax and semantics during sentence processing: Eye movements in the analysis of semantically biased sentences. *Journal of Verbal Learning and Verbal Behavior, 22,* 358–374.

Rayner, K., & Clifton, C., Jr. (2002). Language comprehension. In D. L. Medin (Ed.), *Steven's handbook of experimental psychology* (Vol. X, pp. 261–316). New York: Wiley.

Rayner, K., & Duffy, S. A. (1988). On-line comprehension processes and eye movements in reading. In M. Daneman, G. E. MacKinnon, & T. G. Waller (Eds.), *Reading research: Advances in theory and practice* (pp. 13–66). New York: Academic Press.

Rayner, K., & Frazier, L. (1989). Selection mechanisms in reading lexically ambiguous words. *Journal of Experimental Psychology: Learning, Memory, and Cognition, 15,* 779–790.

Rayner, K., Inhoff, A. W., Morrison, P. E., Slowiaczek, M. L., & Bertera, J. H. (1981). Masking of foveal and parafoveal vision during eye fixations in reading. *Journal of Experimental Psychology: Human Perception and Performance, 7,* 167–179.

Rayner, K., Pollatsek, A., & Binder, K. S. (1998). Phonological codes and eye movements in reading. *Journal of Experimental Psychology: Learning, Memory, and Cognition, 24,* 476–497.

Rayner, K., Warren, T., Juhasz, B. J., & Liversedge, S. P. (2004). The effect of plausibility on eye movements in reading. *Journal of Experimental Psychology: Learning, Memory, and Cognition, 30,* 1290–1301.

Rayner, K., & Well, A. D. (1996). Effects of contextual constraint on eye movements in reading: A further examination. *Psychonomic Bulletin & Review, 3,* 504–509.

Rayner, K., White, S. J., Johnson, R. L., & Liversedge, S. P. (2006). Raeding wrods with jumbled letters: There is a cost. *Psychological Science, 17,* 192–193.

Reason, J. (1990). *Human error.* New York: Cambridge University Press.

Reder, L. M., & Kusbit, G. W. (1991). Locus of the Moses illusion: Imperfect encoding, retrieval, or match? *Journal of Memory and Language, 30,* 385–406.

Reed, S. K. (1992). *Cognition: Theory and applications* (3rd ed.). Pacific Grove, CA: Brooks/Cole.

Reed, S. K., & Hoffman, B. (2004). Use of temporal and spatial information in estimating event completion time. *Memory & Cognition, 32,* 271–282.

Reeves, L. M., & Weisberg, R. W. (1993). Abstract versus concrete information as the basis for transfer in problem solving: Comment on Fong and Nisbett (1991). *Journal of Experimental Psychology: General, 122,* 125–128.

Rehder, B. (2003). A causal-model theory of conceptual representation and categorization. *Journal of Experimental Psychology: Learning, Memory, and Cognition, 29,* 1141–1159.

Rehder, B., & Burnett, R. C. (2005). Feature inference and the causal structure of categories. *Cognitive Psychology, 50,* 264–314.

Reichle, E. D., Carpenter, P. A., & Just, M. A. (2000). The neural bases of strategy and skill in sentence–picture verification. *Cognitive Psychology, 40,* 261–295.

Reichle, E. D., Pollatsek, A., Fisher, D. L., & Rayner, K. (1998). Eye movements during mindless reading. *Psychological Science, 21,* 1300–1310.

Reichle, E. D., Reineberg, A. E., & Schooler, J. W. (2010). Toward a model of eye movement control in reading. *Psychological Review, 105,* 125–157.

Reingold, E. M., Charness, N., Pomplun, M., & Stampe, D. M. (2001). Visual span in expert chess players: Evidence from eye movements. *Psychological Science, 12,* 48–55.

Reiser, B. J., Black, J. B., & Abelson, R. P. (1985). Knowledge structures in the organization and retrieval of autobiographical memories. *Cognitive Psychology, 17,* 89–137.

Reuter-Lorenz, P. A., & Cappell, K. A. (2008). Neurocognitive aging and the compensation hypothesis. *Current Directions in Psychological Science, 17,* 177–182.

Reyna, V. F. (2004). How people make decisions that involve risk. *Current Directions in Psychological Science, 13,* 60–67.

Riley, K. P. (1989). Psychological interventions in Alzheimer's disease. In G. C. Gilmore, P. J. Whitehouse, & M. R. Wykle (Eds.), *Memory, aging and dementia.* New York: Springer.

Rips, L. J. (1975). Inductive judgments about natural categories. *Journal of Verbal Learning and Verbal Behavior, 14,* 665–681.

Rips, L. J. (1989). Similarity, typicality, and categorization. In S. Vosniadou & A. Ortony (Eds.), *Similarity and analogical reasoning* (pp. 21–59). Cambridge, England: Cambridge University Press.

Rips, L. J. (1998). Reasoning and conversation. *Psychological Review, 105,* 411–441.

Rips, L. J. (2001). Two kinds of reasoning. *Psychological Science, 12,* 129–134.

Rips, L. J., & Collins, A. (1993). Categories and resemblance. *Journal of Experimental Psychology: General, 122,* 468–486.

Rips, L. J., & Marcus, S. L. (1977). Supposition and the analysis of conditional sentences. In M. A. Just & P. A. Carpenter (Eds.), *Cognitive processes in comprehension* (pp. 185–220). Hillsdale, NJ: Erlbaum.

Rips, L. J., Shoben, E. J., & Smith, E. E. (1973). Semantic distance and the verification of semantic relations. *Journal of Verbal Learning and Verbal Behavior, 12,* 1–20.

Roberson, D., Davies, I., & Davidoff, J. (2000). Color categories are not universal: Replications and new evidence from a Stone-Age culture. *Journal of Experimental Psychology: General, 129,* 369–398.

Robertson, D. A., Gernsbacher, M. A., Guidotti, S. J., Robertson, R. R. W., Irwin, W., Mock, B. J., et al. (2000). Functional neuroanatomy of the cognitive process of mapping during discourse comprehension. *Psychological Science, 11,* 255–260.

Robins, R. W., Gosling, S. D., & Craik, K. H. (1999). An empirical analysis of trends in psychology. *American Psychologist, 54,* 117–128.

Roediger, H. L. III. (1996). Memory illusions. *Journal of Memory and Language, 35,* 76–100.

Roediger, H. L. III, & Crowder, R. G. (1976). A serial position effect in recall of United States presidents. *Bulletin of the Psychonomic Society, 8*(4), 275–278.

Roediger, H. L. III, Jacoby, D., & McDermott, K. B. (1996). Misinformation effects in recall: Creating false memories through repeated retrieval. *Journal of Memory and Language, 35,* 300–318.

Roediger, H. L., & Karpicke, J. D. (2006). The power of resting memory: Basic research and implications for educational practice. *Perspectives on Psychological Science, 1,* 181–210.

Roediger, H. L. III, Marsh, E. J., & Lee, S. C. (2002). Kinds of memory. In D. Medin (Ed.), *Stevens' handbook of experimental psychology, Vol. 2* (3rd ed., pp. 1–42). New York: Wiley.

Roediger, H. L. III, & McDermott, K. B. (1995). Creating false memories: Remembering words not presented in lists. *Journal of Experimental Psychology: Learning, Memory, and Cognition, 21,* 803–814.

Roediger, H. L. III, & McDermott, K. B. (2000). Tricks of memory. *Current Directions in Psychological Science, 9,* 123–127.

Roediger, H. L. III, Meade, M. L., & Bergman, E. T. (2001). Social contagion of memory. *Psychonomic Bulletin & Review, 8,* 365–371.

Roediger, H. L. III, Stadler, M. L., Weldon, M. S., & Riegler, G. L. (1992). Direct comparison of two implicit memory tests: Word fragment and word stem completion. *Journal of Experimental Psychology: Learning, Memory, and Cognition, 18,* 1251–1269.

Roese, N. J. (1997). Counterfactual thinking. *Psychological Bulletin, 121,* 133–148.

Roese, N. J. (1999). Counterfactual thinking and decision making. *Psychonomic Bulletin & Review, 6,* 570–578.

Rogers, T. B., Kuiper, N. A., & Kirker, W. S. (1977). Self-reference and the encoding of personal information. *Journal of Personality and Social Psychology, 35,* 677–688.

Rogers, T. T., Lambon Ralph, M. A., Gerrard, P., Bozeat, S., McClelland, J. L., Hodges, J. R., et al. (2004). Structure and deterioration of semantic memory: A neuropsychologi-cal and computational investigation. *Psychological Review, 111,* 205–235.

Rohrer, D. (2003). The natural appearance of unnatural incline speed. *Memory & Cognition, 31,* 816–826.

Rönnlund, M., Nyberg, L., Bäckman, L., & Nilsson, L-G. (2005). Stability, growth, and decline in adult life span development of declarative memory: Cross-sectional and longitudinal data from a population-based study. *Psychology and Aging, 20,* 3–18.

Rosch, E. H. (1978). Principles of categorization. In E. H. Rosch & B. B. Lloyd (Eds.), *Cognition and categorization* (pp. 27–48). Hillsdale, NJ: Erlbaum.

Rosch, E. H., & Mervis, C. B. (1975). Family resemblances: Studies in the internal structure of categories. *Cognitive Psychology, 7,* 573–605.

Rosch-Heider, E. (1972). Universals in color naming and memory. *Journal of Experimental Psychology, 93,* 10–21.

Rosen, V. M., & Engle, R. W. (1997). The role of working memory capacity in retrieval. *Journal of Experimental Psychology: General, 126,* 211–227.

Rosler, F., Pechmann, T., Streb, J., Roder, B., & Henni-ghausen, E. (1998). Parsing of sentences in a language with varying word order: Word-by-word variations of processing demands are revealed by event-related brain potentials. *Journal of Memory and Language, 38,* 150–176.

Ross, B. H. (1987). This is like that: The use of earlier problems and the separation of similarity effects. *Journal of Experimental Psychology: Learning, Memory, and Cognition, 13,* 629–640.

Ross, B. H., & Murphy, G. L. (1999). Food for thought: Cross-classification and category organization in a complex real-world domain. *Cognitive Psychology, 38,* 495–553.

Ross, M., & Wang, Q. (2010). Why we remember and what we remember: Culture and autobiographical memory. *Perspectives on Psychological Science, 5,* 401–409.

Roy, M., Shohamy, D., & Wager, T. D. (2012). Ventromedial prefrontal-subcortical systems and the generation of affective meaning. *Trends in Cognitive Sciences, 16,* 147–156.

Rubin, D. C. (2007). A basic-systems model of episodic memory. *Perspectives on Psychological Science, 1,* 277–311.

Rubin, D. C., & Berntsen, D. (2003). Life scripts help to maintain autobiographical memories of highly positive, but not highly negative, events. *Memory & Cognition, 31,* 1–14.

Rubin, D. C., Rahhal, T. A., & Poon, L. W. (1998). Things learned in early adulthood are remembered best. *Memory & Cognition, 26,* 3–19.

Rubin, D. C., Schrauf, R. W., & Greenberg, D. L. (2003). Belief and recollection of autobiographical memories. *Memory and Cognition, 31,* 887–901.

Ruff, C. C., Kristkjánsson, Á., & Driver, J. (2007). Readout from iconic memory and selective spatial attention involve similar neural processes. *Psychological Science, 18,* 901–909.

Rugg, M. D., & Coles, M. G. H. (Eds.). (1995). *Electrophysiology of mind: Event-related brain potential and cognition.* New York: Oxford University Press.

Rumelhart, D. E. (1989). The architecture of mind: A connectionist approach. In M. I. Posner (Ed.), *Foundations of cognitive science* (pp. 133–159). Cambridge, MA: MIT Press.

Rumelhart, D. E., Lindsay, P. H., & Norman, D. A. (1972). A process model for long-term memory. In E. Tulving & W. Donaldson (Eds.), *Organization of memory* (pp. 197–246). New York: Academic Press.

Rumelhart, D. E., & McClelland, J. L. (1986). *Parallel distributed processing: Explorations in the microstructure of cognition: Vol. 1. Foundations.* Cambridge, MA: Bradford.

Rundus, D. (1971). Analysis of rehearsal processes in free recall. *Journal of Experimental Psychology, 89,* 63–77.

Rundus, D., & Atkinson, R. C. (1970). Rehearsal processes in free recall: A procedure for direct observation. *Journal of Verbal Learning and Verbal Behavior, 9,* 99–105.

Russo, J. E., Johnson, E. J., & Stephens, D. L. (1989). The validity of verbal protocols. *Memory & Cognition, 17,* 759–769.

Rypma, B., Prabbakaran, V., Desmond, J. E., & Gabriei, D. E. (2001). Age differences in prefrontal cortical activity in working memory. *Psychology and Aging, 16,* 371–384.

Sachs, J. S. (1967). Recognition memory for syntactic and semantic aspects of connected discourse. *Perception & Psychophysics, 2,* 437–442.

Sachs, J. (1983). Talking about the there and then: The emergence of displaced reference in parent-child discourse. In K. E. Nelson (Ed.), *Children's language* (Vol. 3, pp. 1–28). Hillsdale, NJ: Erlbaum.

Sacks, H., Scbegloff, E. A., & Jefferson, G. (1974). A simplest systematics for the organization of turntaking for conversation. *Language, 50,* 696–735.

Sacks, O. (1970). *The man who mistook his wife for a hat.* New York: Harper & Row.

Safer, M. A., Christiansen, S-A., Autry, M. W., & Österlund, K. (1998). Tunnel memory for traumatic events. *Applied Cognitive Psychology, 12,* 99–117.

Sakaki, M., Niki, K., & Mather, M. (2012). Beyond arousal and valence: The importance of the biological versus social relevance of emotional stimuli. *Cognitive Affective & Behavioral Neuroscience, 12,* 115–139.

Salame, P., & Baddeley, A. D. (1982). Disruption of short-term memory by unattended speech: Implications for the structure of working memory. *Journal of Verbal Learning and Verbal Behavior, 21,* 150–164.

Saltbouse, T. A. (1984). Effects of age and skill in typing. *Journal of Experimental Psychology: General, 113,* 345–371.

Saltbouse, T. A. (1996). The processing-speed theory of adult age differences in cognition. *Psychological Review, 103*(3), 403–427.

Saltbouse, T. A., & Pink, J. E. (2009). Why is working memory related to fluid intelligence? *Psychonomic Bulletin & Review, 15,* 364–371.

Saltz, E., & Donnenwertb-Nolan, S. (1981). Does motoric imagery facilitate memory for sentences? A selective interference test. *Journal of Verbal Learning and Verbal Bebavior, 20,* 322–332.

Samuel, A. G. (2001). Knowing a word affects the fundamental perception of the sounds within it. *Psychological Science, 12,* 348–351.

Samuel, D. (1999). *Memory: How we use it, lose it and can improve it.* New York: New York University Press.

Sanchez, C. A. (2012). Enhancing visuospatial performance through video game training to increase learning in visuospatial science domains. *Psychonomic Bulletin & Review, 19,* 58–65.

Sanchez, C. A., & Wiley, J. (2006). An examination of the seductive details effect in terms of working memory capacity. *Memory & Cognition, 34,* 344–355.

Sanna, L. J., & Schwartz, N. (2006). Human judgment: The case of the hindsight bias and its debiasing. *Current Directions in Psychological Science, 15,* 172–176.

Santens, S., & Gevers, W. (2008). The SNARC effect does not imply a mental number line. *Cognition, 108,* 263–270.

Sara, S. J. (2000). Retrieval and reconsolidation: toward a neurobiology of remembering. *Learning and Memory, 7,* 73–84.

Sarter, M., Berntson, G. G., & Cacioppo, J. T. (1996). Brain imaging and cognitive neuroscience: Toward strong inference in attributing function to structure. *American Psychologist, 51,* 13–21.

Sattler, J. M. (1982). *Assessment of children's intellectual and special abilities* (2nd ed.). Boston: Allyn & Bacon.

Sayette, M. A., Reichle, E. D., & Schooler, J. W. (2009). Lost in the sauce: The effects of alcohol on mind wandering. *Psychological Science, 20,* 747–752.

Sayette, M. A., Schooler, J. W., & Reichle, E. D. (2010). Out for a smoke: The impact of cigarette craving on zoning out during reading. *Psychological Science, 21,* 26–30.

Schab, F. R. (1990). Odors and the remembrance of things past. *Journal of Experimental Psychology: Learning, Memory, and Cognition, 16,* 648–655.

Schacter, D. L. (1987). Implicit memory: History and current status. *Journal of Experimental Psychology: Learning, Memory, and Cognition, 13,* 501–518.

Schacter, D. L. (1989). Memory. In M. I. Posner (Ed.), *Foundations of cognitive science* (pp. 683–725). Cambridge, MA: MIT Press.

Schacter, D. L. (1996). *Searching for memory.* New York: Basic Books.

Schacter, D. L. (1999). The seven sins of memory: Insights from psychology and cognitive neuroscience. *American Psychologist, 54,* 182–203.

Schacter, D. L., & Badgaiyan, R. D. (2001). Neuroimaging of priming: New perspectives on implicit and explicit memory. *Current Directions in Psychological Science, 10,* 1–4.

Schank, R. C. (1972). Conceptual dependency: A theory of natural language understanding. *Cognitive Psychology, 3,* 552–631.

Schank, R. C. (1977). Rules and topics in conversation. *Cognitive Science, 1,* 421–441.

Schank, R. C., & Abelson, R. P. (1977). *Scripts, plans, goals and understanding.* Hillsdale, NJ: Erlbaum.

Schiller, P. H. (1966). Developmental study of color-word interference. *Journal of Experimental Psychology, 72,* 105–108.

Schilling, H. E. H., Rayner, K., & Chumbley, J. I. (1998). Comparing naming, lexical decision, and eye fixation times: Word frequency effects and individual differences. *Memory & Cognition, 26,* 1270–1281.

Schmader, T. (2010). Stereotype threat deconstructed. *Current Directions in Psychological Science, 19,* 14–18.

Schmeichel, B. J. (2007). Attention control, memory updating, and emotion regularity temporarily reduce the capacity for executive control. *Journal of Experimental Psychology: General, 136,* 241–255.

Schmidt, J. R., & Thompson, V. A. (2008). "At least one" problem with "some" formal reasoning paradigms. *Memory & Cognition, 36,* 217–229.

Schmidt, S. R. (1985). Encoding and retrieval processes in the memory for conceptually distinctive events. *Journal of Experimental Psychology: Learning, Memory, and Cognition, 11,* 565–578.

Schmidt, S. R. (1994). Effects of humor on sentence memory. *Journal of Experimental Psychology: Learning, Memory, and Cognition, 20,* 953–967.

Schmidt, S. R. (2004). Autobiographical memories for the September 11th attacks: Reconstructive errors and emotional impairment of memory. *Memory & Cognition, 32,* 443–454.

Schmolck, H., Buffalo, E. A., & Squire, L. R. (2000). Memory distortions develop over time: Recollections of the O. J. Simpson trial verdict after 15 and 32 months. *Psychological Science, 11,* 39–45.

Schneider, V. I., Healy, A. F., & Bourne, L. E., Jr. (2002). What is learned under difficult conditions is hard to forget: Contextual interference effects in foreign vocabulary acquisition, retention, and transfer. *Journal of Memory and Language, 46,* 419–440.

Schneider, W., & Shiffrin. R. M. (1977). Controlled and automatic human information processing: I. Detection, search, and attention. *Psychological Review, 84,* 1–66.

Schnorr, J. A., & Atkinson, R. C. (1969). Repetition versus imagery instructions in the short- and long-term retention of paired associates. *Psychonomic Science, 15,* 183–184.

Schooler, J. W., Ohlsson, S., & Brooks, K. (1993). Thoughts beyond words: When language overshadows insight. *Journal of Experimental Psychology: General, 122,* 166–183.

Schrauf, R. W., & Rubin, D. C. (1998). Bilingual autobiographical memory in older adult immigrants: A test of cognitive explanations of the reminiscence bump and the linguistic encoding of memories. *Journal of Memory and Language, 39,* 437–457.

Schrauf, R. W., & Rubin, D. C. (2000). Internal languages of retrieval: The bilingual encoding of memories for the personal past. *Memory & Cognition, 28,* 616–623.

Schreiber, T. A., & Sergent, S. D. (1998). The role of commitment in producing misinformation effects in eyewitness memory. *Psychonomic Bulletin & Review, 5,* 443–448.

Schustack, M. W., Ehrlich, S. F., & Rayner, K. (1987). Local and global sources of contextual facilitation in reading. *Journal of Memory and Language, 26,* 322–340.

Schutzwohl, A. (1998). Surprise and schema strength. *Journal of Experimental Psychology: Learning, Memory, and Cognition, 24,* 1182–1199.

Schwartz, D. L., & Black, T. (1999). Inferences through imagined actions: Knowing by simulated doing. *Journal of*

Experimental Psychology: Learning, Memory, and Cognition, 25, 116–136.

Scullin, M. K., & McDaniel, M. A. (2010). Remembering to execute a goal: Sleep on it! *Psychological Science, 21,* 128–1035.

Seamon, J. G., Philbin, M. M., & Harrison, L. G. (2006). Do you remember proposing marriage to the Pepsi machine? False recollections from a campus walk. *Psychonomic Bulletin & Review, 13,* 752–756.

Searle, J. R. (1969). *Speech acts.* Cambridge, England: Cambridge University Press.

Sederberg, P. B., Schulze-Bonhage, A., Madsen, J. R., Bromfield, E. B., Litt, B., Brandt, A., et al. (2007). Gamma oscillations distinguish true from false memories. *Psychological Science, 18,* 927–932.

See, J. E., Howe, S. R., Warm, J. S., & Dember, W. N. (1995). Meta-analysis of the sensitivity decrement in vigilance. *Psychological Bulletin, 2,* 230–249.

Sehulster, J. R. (1989). Content and temporal structure of autobiographical knowledge: Remembering twenty-five seasons at the Metropolitan Opera. *Memory & Cognition, 17,* 590–606.

Seidenberg, M. S. (1993). Connectionist models and cognitive theory. *Psychological Science, 4,* 228–235.

Seifert, C. M., Robertson, S. P., & Black, J. B. (1985). Types of inferences generated during reading. *Journal of Memory and Language, 24,* 405–422.

Selfridge, O. G. (1959). Pandemonium: A paradigm for learning. In *The mechanisation of thought processes.* London: H. M. Stationery Office.

Senkfor, A. J., & Van Petten, C. (1998). Who said what? An event-related potential investigation of source and item memory. *Journal of Experimental Psychology: Learning, Memory, and Cognition, 24,* 1005–1025.

Serences, J. T., Shomstein, S., Leber, A. B., Golay, X., Egeth, H. E., & Yantis, S. (2005). Coordination of voluntary and stimulus-driven attentional control in human cortex. *Psychological Science, 16,* 114–122.

Sereno, S. C., Brewer, C. C., & O'Donnell, P. J. (2003). Context effects in word recognition: Evidence for early interactive processing. *Psychological Science, 14,* 328–333.

Shafir, E., & Tversky, A. (1992). Thinking through uncertainty: Nonconsequential reasoning and choice. *Cognitive Psychology, 24,* 449–474.

Shaki, S., & Fischer, M. H. (2008). Reading space into numbers—A cross-linguistic comparison of the SNARC effect. *Cognition, 108,* 590–599.

Shallice, T., Fletcher, P., & Dolan, R. (1998). The functional imaging of recall. In M. A. Conway, S. E. Gathercole, and C. Cornoldi (Eds.), *Theories of memory* (Vol. II, pp. 247–258). Hove, England: Psychology Press.

Shallice, T., & Warrington, E. K. (1970). Independent functioning of the verbal memory stores: A neuropsychological study. *Quarterly Journal of Experimental Psychology, 22,* 261–273.

Shand, M. A. (1982). Sign-based short-term coding of American Sign Language signs and printed English words by congenitally deaf signers. *Cognitive Psychology, 14,* 1–12.

Sharkey, N. E., & Mitchell, D. C. (1985). Word recognition in a functional context: The use of scripts in reading. *Journal of Memory and Language, 24,* 253–270.

Sharot, T., Martorella, E. A., Delgado, M. R., & Phelps, E. A. (2007). How personal experience modulates the neural circuitry of memories of September 11. *Proceedings of the National Academy of Science, 104,* 389–394.

Shaw, J. S. III. (1996). Increases in eyewitness confidence resulting from postevent questioning. *Journal of Experimental Psychology: Applied, 2,* 126–146.

Shaw, J. S. III, Bjork, R. A., & Handal, A. (1995). Retrieval-induced forgetting in an eyewitness–memory paradigm. *Psychonomic Bulletin & Review, 2,* 249–253.

Shaywitz, S. E., Mody, M., & Shaywitz, B. A. (2006). Neural mechanisms in dyslexia. *Current Directions in Psychological Science, 15,* 278–281.

Shelton, A. L., & McNamara, T. P. (2001). Visual memories from nonvisual experiences. *Psychological Science, 12,* 343–347.

Shelton, J. T., Elliott, E. M., Matthews R. A., Hill, B. D., & Gouvier, W. D. (2010). The relationships of working memory, secondary memory, and general fluid intelligence: Working memory is special. *Journal of Experimental Psychology: Learning, Memory, and Cognition, 36,* 813–820.

Shepard, R. N., & Metzler, J. (1971). Mental rotation of three-dimensional objects. *Science, 171,* 701–703.

Sherman, G., & Visscher, P. K. (2002). Honeybee colonies achieve fitness through dancing. *Nature, 419,* 920–922.

Shiffrin, R. M., & Schneider, W. (1977). Controlled and automatic human information processing: II. Perceptual learning, automatic attending, and a general theory. *Psychological Review, 84,* 127–190.

Shintel, H., & Keysar, B. (2007). You said it before and you'll say it again: Expectations and consistency in communication. *Journal of Experimental Psychology: Learning, Memory, and Cognition, 33,* 357–369.

Shoben, E. J., Sailor, K. M., & Wang, M.-Y. (1989). The role of expectancy in comparative judgments. *Memory & Cognition, 17,* 18–26.

Siegler, R. S. (2000). Unconscious insights. *Current Directions in Psychological Science, 9,* 79–83.

Siegler, R. S., & Stern, E. (1998). A microgenetic analysis of conscious and unconscious strategy discoveries. *Journal of Experimental Psychology: General, 127,* 377–397.

Simion, F., Regolin, L., & Bulf, H. (2008). A predisposition for biological motion in the newborn baby. *Proceedings of the National Academy of Sciences, 105,* 809–813.

Simon, H. A. (1975). The functional equivalence of problem solving skills. *Cognitive Psychology, 7,* 268–288.

Simon, H. A. (1979). *Models of thought.* New Haven, CT: Yale University Press.

Simon, H. A. (May, 1995). *Thinking in words, pictures, equations, numbers: How do we do it and what does it matter?* Invited address presented at the meeting of the Midwestern Psychological Association, Chicago.

Simons, D. J., & Ambinder, M. S. (2005). Change blindness: Theory and consequences. *Current Directions in Psychological Science, 14,* 44–48.

Simpson, G. B. (1981). Meaning dominance and semantic context in the processing of lexical ambiguity. *Journal of Verbal Learning and Verbal Behavior, 20,* 120–136.

Simpson, G. B. (1984). Lexical ambiguity and its role in models of word recognition. *Psychological Bulletin, 96,* 316–340.

Simpson, G. B., Casteel, M. A., Peterson, R. R., & Burgess, C. (1989). Lexical and sentence context effects in word recognition. *Journal of Experimental Psychology: Learning, Memory, and Cognition, 15,* 88–97.

Singer, M. (1990). *Psychology of language: An introduction to sentence and discourse processes.* Hillsdale, NJ: Erlbaum.

Singer, M., Andrusiak, P., Reisdorf, P., & Black, N. L. (1992). Individual differences in bridging inference processes. *Memory & Cognition, 20,* 539–548.

Singer, M., Graesser, A. C., & Trabasso, T. (1994). Minimal or global inference during reading. *Journal of Memory and Language, 33,* 421–441.

Sitaran, N., Weingartner, H., Caine, E. D., & Gillin, J. C. (1978). Choline: Selective enhancement of serial learning and encoding of low imagery words in man. *Life Sciences, 22,* 1555–1560.

Sitton, M., Mozer, M. C., & Farah, M. J. (2000). Superadditive effects of multiple lesions in a connectionist architecture: Implications for the neuropsychology of optic aphasia. *Psychological Review, 107,* 709–734.

Skinner, B. F. (1957). *Verbal behavior.* New York: Appleton-Century-Crofts.

Slamecka, N. J. (1968). An examination of trace storage in free recall. *Journal of Experimental Psychology, 4,* 504–513.

Slamecka, N. J. (1985). Ebbinghaus: Some associations. *Journal of Experimental Psychology: Learning, Memory, and Cognition, 11,* 414–435.

Slamecka, N. J., & Graf, P. (1978). The generation effect: delineation of a phenomenon. *Journal of Experimental Psychology: Human Learning and Memory, 4,* 592–604.

Sloman, S. A. (1998). Categorical inference is not a tree: The myth of inheritance hierarchies. *Cognitive Psychology, 35,* 1–33.

Small, B. J., Dixon, R. A., Hultsch, D. F., & Hertzog, C. (1999). Longitudinal changes in quantitative and qualitative indicators of word and story recall in young-old and old-old adults. *Journal of Gerontology: Psychological Sciences 54B,* P107–P115.

Smallwood, J., Davies, J. B., Heim, D., Finnigan, F., Sudberry, M. V., O'Connor, R. C., et al. (2004). Subjective experience and the attentional lapse. Task engagement and disengagement during sustained attention. *Consciousness and Cognition, 4,* 657–690.

Smallwood, J., Fishman, D. J., & Schooler, J. W. (2007). Counting the cost of an absent mind: Mind wandering as an unrecognized influence on educational performance. *Psychonomic Bulletin & Review, 14,* 230–236.

Smallwood, J., McSpadden, M., & Schooler, J. W. (2007). The lights are on but no one's home: Meta-awareness and the decoupling of attention when the mind wanders. *Psychonomic Bulletin & Review, 14,* 527–533.

Smallwood, J., & Schooler, J. W. (2006). The restless mind. *Psychological Bulletin, 132,* 946–958.

Smilek, D., Carriere, J. S. A., & Cheyne, J. A. (2010). Out of mind, out of sight: Eye blinking as indicator and embodiment of mind wandering. *Psychological Science, 21,* 786–789.

Smith, D. A., & Graesser, A. C. (1981). Memory for actions in scripted activities as a function of typicality, retention interval, and retrieval task. *Memory & Cognition, 9,* 550–559.

Smith, E. E. (2000). Neural bases of human working memory. *Current Directions in Psychological Science, 9,* 45–49.

Smith, E. E., & Jonides, J. (1999). Storage and executive processes in the frontal lobes. *Science, 283,* 1657–1661.

Smith, E. E., Rips, L. J., & Shoben, E. J. (1974). Semantic memory and psychological semantics. In G. H. Bower (Ed.), *The psychology of learning and motivation* (Vol. 8, pp. 1–45). New York: Academic Press.

Smith, J. D., Redford, J. S., Washburn, D. A., & Tagliatela, L. A. (2005). Specific-token effects in screening tasks: Possible implications for aviation security. *Journal of Experimental Psychology: Learning, Memory, and Cognition, 31,* 1171–1185.

Smith, L. (2003). Learning to recognize objects. *Psychological Science, 14,* 244–250.

Smith, M. C., Bentin, S., & Spalek, T. M. (2001). Attention of semantic activation during visual word recognition. *Journal of Experimental Psychology: Learning, Memory, and Cognition, 27,* 1289–1298.

Smith, R. E. (2003). The cost of remembering to remember in event-based prospective memory: Investigating the capacity demands of delayed intention performance. *Journal of Experimental Psychology: Learning, Memory, and Cognition, 29,* 347–361.

Smith, R. E., & Bayen, U. J. (2004). A multinomial model of event-based prospective memory. *Journal of Experimental Psychology: Learning, Memory, and Cognition, 30,* 756–777.

Smith, R. E., Lozito, J. P., & Bayen, U. J. (2005). Adult age differences in distinctive processing: the modality effect on false recall. *Psychology and Aging, 20,* 486–492.

Smith, S. M. (1995). Getting into and out of mental ruts: A theory of fixation, incubation, and insight. In R. J. Sternberg & J. E. Davidson (Eds.), *The nature of insight* (pp. 229–251). Cambridge, MA: MIT Press.

Smith, S. W., Rebok, G. W., Smith, W. R., Hall, S. E., & Alvin, M. (1983). Adult age differences in the use of story structure in delayed free recall. *Experimental Aging Research, 9*(3), 191–195.

Snow, C. (1972). Mother's speech to children learning language. *Child Development, 43,* 549–565.

Snow, C., & Ferguson, C. (Eds.). (1977). *Talking to children: Language input and acquisition.* Cambridge, England: Cambridge University Press.

Solso, R. L. (1995). *Cognitive psychology* (4th ed.). Boston: Allyn & Bacon.

Solso, R. L. (1998). *Cognitive psychology* (5th ed.). Boston: Allyn & Bacon.

Son, L. K. (2004). Spacing one's study: Evidence for a metacognitive control strategy. *Journal of Experimental Psychology: Learning, Memory, and Cognition, 30,* 601–604.

Son, L. K., & Metcalfe, J. (2000). Metacognitive and control strategies in study-time allocation. *Journal of Experimental Psychology: Learning, Memory, and Cognition, 26,* 204–221.

Song, H., & Schwarz, N. (2009). If it's difficult to pronounce, it must be risky: Fluency, familiarity, and risk perception. *Psychological Science, 20,* 135–138.

Spaniol, J., Madden, D. J., & Voss, A. (2006). A diffusion model analysis of adult age differences in episodic and semantic long-term memory retrieval. *Journal of Experimental Psychology: Learning, Memory, and Cognition, 32,* 101–117.

Speer, N. K., Zacks, J. M., & Reynolds, J. R. (2007). Human brain activity time-locked to narrative event boundaries. *Psychological Science, 18,* 449–455.

Speer, S. R., & Clifton, C., Jr. (1998). Plausibility and argument structure in sentence comprehension. *Memory & Cognition, 26,* 965–978.

Spelke, E., Hirst, W., & Neisser, U. (1976). Skills of divided attention. *Cognition, 4,* 215–230.

Spellman, B. A., & Busey, T. A. (2010). Emerging trends in psychology and law: An editorial overview. *Psychonomic Bulletin & Review, 17,* 141–142.

Spellman, B. A., & Holyoak, K. J. (1996). Pragmatics in analogical mapping. *Cognitive Psychology, 31,* 307–346.

Spellman, B. A., & Mandel, D. R. (1999). When possibility informs reality: Counterfactual thinking as a cue to causality. *Current Directions in Psychological Science, 8,* 120–123.

Spence, C., & Read, L. (2003). Speech shadowing while driving: On the difficulty of splitting attention between eye and ear. *Psychological Science, 14,* 251–256.

Sperling, G. (1960). The information available in brief visual presentations. *Psychological Monographs, 74* (Whole No. 48).

Sperling, G. (1963). A model for visual memory tasks. *Human Factors, 5,* 9–31.

Sperry, R. W. (1964). The great cerebral commissure. *Scientific American, 210,* 42–52.

Spieth, W., Curtis, J. F., & Webster, J. C. (1954). Responding to one of two simultaneous messages. *Journal of the Acoustical Society of America, 26,* 391–396.

Spilich, G. J. (1983). Life-span components of text processing: structural and procedural differences. *Journal of Verbal Learning and Verbal Behavior, 22,* 231–244.

Spivey, M. J., Tanenhaus, M. K., Eberhard, K. M., & Sedivy, J. C. (2002). Eye movements and spoken language comprehension: Effects of visual context on syntactic ambiguity resolution. *Cognitive Psychology, 45,* 447–481.

Squire, L. R. (1986). Mechanisms of memory. *Science, 232* (4578), 1612–1619.

Squire, L. R. (1987). *Memory and brain.* New York: Oxford University Press.

Squire, L. R. (1993). The organization of declarative and non-declarative memory. In T. Ono, L. R. Squire, M. E. Raichle, D. I. Perrett, & M. Fukuda (Eds.), *Brain mechanisms of perception and memory: From neuron to behavior* (pp. 219–227). New York: Oxford University Press.

Stadler, M. A., Roediger, H. L. III., & McDermott, K. B. (1999). Norms for word lists that create false memories. *Memory & Cognition, 27,* 494–500.

Stallings, L. M., MacDonald, M. C., & O'Seagbdlba, P. G. (1998). Phrasal ordering constraints in sentence production: Phrase length and verb disposition in heavy-NP shift. *Journal of Memory and Language, 39,* 392–417.

Stark, L., & Perfect, T. J. (2008). The effects of repeated idea elaboration on unconscious plagiarism. *Memory & Cognition, 36,* 65–73.

Stazyk, E. H., Ashcraft, M. H., & Hamann, M. S. (1982). A network approach to simple multiplication. *Journal of Experimental Psychology: Learning, Memory, and Cognition, 17,* 355–376.

Stebbins, G. T., Carrillo, M. C., Dorfman, J., Dirksen, C., Desmond, J. E., Turner, D. A., et al. (2002). Aging effects on memory encoding in the frontal lobes. *Psychology and Aging, 17,* 44–55.

Steblay, N. M. (1992). A meta-analytic review of the weapon focus effect. *Law and Human Behavior, 16,* 413–424.

Stefanucci, J. K., & Storbeck, J. (2009). Don't look down: Emotional arousal elevates height perception. *Journal of Experimental Psychology: General, 131,* 131–145.

Sternberg, R. J. (1996). *Cognitive psychology.* Fort Worth, TX: Harcourt Brace.

Sternberg, S. (1966). High-speed scanning in human memory. *Science, 153,* 652–654.

Sternberg, S. (1969). The discovery of processing stages: Extensions of Donder's method. In W. G. Koster (Ed.), *Attention and performance II. Acta Psychologica, 30,* 276–315.

Sternberg, S. (1975). Memory scanning: New findings and current controversies. *Quarterly Journal of Experimental Psychology, 27,* 1–32.

Stine, E. A. L., Cheung, H., & Henderson, D. (1995). Adult age differences in the on-line processing of new concepts in discourse. *Aging & Cognition, 2,* 1–18.

Stine, E. A. L., & Hindman, J. (1994). Age differences in reading time allocation for propositionally dense sentences. *Aging & Cognition, 1,* 2–16.

Stine, E. A. L., & Wingfield, A. (1988). How much do working memory deficits contribute to age differences in discourse memory? *European Journal of Cognitive Psychology, 2,* 289–304.

Stine-Morrow, E. A. L., Gagne, D. D., Morrow, D. G., & DeWall, B. H. (2004). Age differences in rereading. *Memory & Cognition, 32,* 696–710.

Storm, B. C. (2011). The benefit of forgetting in thinking and remembering. *Current Directions in Psychological Science, 20,* 291–295.

Strayer, D. L., & Drews, F. A. (2007). Cell-phone-induced driver distraction. *Current Directions in Psychological Science, 16,* 128–131.

Strayer, D. L., & Johnston, W. A. (2001). Driven to distraction: Dual-task studies of stimulated driving and conversing on a cellular phone. *Psychological Science, 12,* 462–466.

Stroop, J. R. (1935). Studies of interference in serial verbal reactions. *Journal of Experimental Psychology, 18,* 643–662.

Struiksma, M. E., Noordzij, M. L., & Postma, A. (2011). Embodied representation of the body contains veridical spatial information. *Quarterly Journal of Experimental Psychology, 64,* 1124–1137.

Sub, S. Y., & Trabasso, T. (1993). Inferences during reading: Converging evidence from discourse analysis, talk-aloud protocols, and recognition priming. *Journal of Memory and Language, 32,* 279–300.

Sulin, R. A., & Dooling, D. J. (1974). Intrusion of a thematic idea in retention of prose. *Journal of Experimental Psychology, 103,* 255–262.

Sullivan, S. J., Mikels, J. A., & Carstensen, L. L. (2010). You never lose the ages you've been: Affective perspective taking in older adults. *Psychology and Aging, 25,* 229–234.

Sun, X., Punjabi, P. V., Greenberg, L. T., & Seamon, J. G. (2009). Does feigning amnesia impair subsequent recall? *Memory & Cognition, 37,* 81–89.

Svartvik, J., & Quirk, R. (Eds.). (1980). *A corpus of English conversation.* Lund, Sweden: CWK Gleerup.

Symons, C. S., & Johnson, B. T. (1997). The self-reference effect in memory: A meta-analysis. *Psychological Bulletin, 121,* 371–394.

Tabor, W., & Hutchins, S. (2004). Evidence for self-organized sentence processing: Digging-in effects. *Journal of Experimental Psychology: Learning, Memory, and Cognition, 30,* 431–450.

Takahashi, M., Shimizu, H., Saito, S., & Tomoyori, H. (2006). One percent ability and ninety-nine percent perspiration: A study of a Japanese memorist. *Journal of Experimental Psychology: Learning, Memory, and Cognition, 32,* 1195–1200.

Talarico, J. M., LaBar, K. S., & Rubin, D. C. (2004). Emotional intensity predicts autobiographical memory experience. *Memory & Cognition, 32,* 1118–1132.

Talarico, J. M., & Rubin, D. C. (2003). Confidence, not consistency, characterizes flashbulb memories. *Psychological Science, 14,* 455–461.

Talmi, D., & Garry, L. M. (2012). Accounting for immediate emotional memory enhancement. *Journal of Memory and Language, 66,* 93–108.

Talmi, J. M., Schimmack, U., Paterson, T., & Moscovitch, M. (2007). The role of attention and relatedness in emotionally enhanced memory. *Emotion, 7,* 89–102.

Tamplin, A. K., Krawietz, S. A., Copeland, D. E., & Radvansky, G. A. (in press). Event memory and moving in a well-known environment. *Memory & Cognition.*

Tanaka, J. T., & Curran, T. (2001). A neural basis for expert object recognition. *Psychological Science, 12,* 43–47.

Tanenhaus, M. K., & Trueswell, J. C. (1995). Sentence comprehension. In J. Miller & P. Eiman (Eds.), Handbook of perception and cognition: Speech, language, and communication (2nd ed., Vol. 11, pp. 217–262). San Diego: Academic Press.

Tang, Y., Zhang, W., Chen, K., Feng, S., Ji, Y., Shen, J., et al. (2006). Arithmetic processing in the brain shaped by cultures. *Proceedings of the National Academy of Sciences, 103,* 10775–10780.

Taraban, R., & McClelland, J. L. (1988). Constituent attachment and thematic role assignment in sentence processing: Influences of content-based expectations. *Journal of Memory and Language, 27,* 597–632.

Taylor, S. F., Liberzon, I., & Koeppe, R. A. (2000). The effect of graded aversive stimuli on limbic and visual activation. *Neuropsychologia, 38,* 1415–1425.

Teller, D. Y., Morse, R., Borton, R., & Regal, D. (1974). Visual acuity for vertical and diagonal gratings in human infants. *Vision Research, 14,* 1433–1439.

Thapar, A., & Greene, R. L. (1994). Effects of level of processing on implicit and explicit tasks. *Journal of Experimental Psychology: Learning, Memory, and Cognition, 20,* 671–679.

Theeuwes, J., Kramer, A. F., Hahn, S., & Irwin, D. E. (1998). Our eyes do not always go where we want them to go: Capture of the eyes by new objects. *Psychological Science, 9,* 379–385.

Thiede, K. W. (1999). The importance of monitoring and self-regulation during multitrial learning. *Psychonomic Bulletin & Review, 6,* 662–667.

Thomas, A. K, Bulevich, J. B., & Loftus, E. F. (2003). Exploring the role of repetition and sensory elaboration in the imagination inflation effect. *Memory & Cognition, 31,* 630–640.

Thomas, A. K., & Dubois, S. J. (2011). Reducing the burden of stereotype threat eliminates age differences in memory distortion. *Psychological Science, 22,* 1515–1517.

Thomas, J. C., Jr. (1974). An analysis of behavior in the hobbits–orcs problem. *Cognitive Psychology, 6,* 257–269.

Thomas, M. H., & Wang, A. Y. (1996). Learning by the keyword mnemonic: Looking for long-term benefits. *Journal of Experimental Psychology: Applied, 2,* 330–342.

Thompson, R. F. (1986). The neurobiology of learning and memory. *Science, 233,* 941–947.

Thompson, V. A., & Byrne, R. M. J. (2002). Reasoning counterfactually: Making inferences about things that didn't happen. *Journal of Experimental Psychology: Learning, Memory, and Cognition, 28,* 1154–1170.

Thomson, D. M., & Tulving, E. (1970). Associative encoding and retrieval: Weak and strong cues. *Journal of Experimental Psychology, 86,* 255–262.

Thorndike, E. L. (1914). *The psychology of learning.* New York: Teachers College.

Tillman, B., & Dowling, W. J. (2007). Memory decreases for prose but not for poetry. *Memory & Cognition, 35,* 628–639.

Tipper, S. P. (1985). The negative priming effect: Inhibitory priming with to be ignored objects. *The Quarterly Journal of Experimental Psychology, 37A,* 571–590.

Tipper, S. P. (2010). From observation to action simulation: The role of attention, eye-gaze, emotion, and body state. *The Quarterly Journal of Experimental Psychology, 63,* 2081–2105.

Tolman, E. C. (1948). Cognitive maps in rats and men. *Psychological Review, 55,* 189–208.

Tourangeau, R., & Rips, L. (1991). Interpreting and evaluating metaphors. *Journal of Memory and Language, 30,* 452–472.

Townsend, J. T., & Wenger, M. J. (2004). The serial-parallel dilemma: A case study in a linkage of theory and method. *Psychonomic Bulletin & Review, 11,* 391–418.

Trabasso, T., & Bartolone, J. (2003). Story understanding and counterfactual reasoning. *Journal of Experimental Psychology: Learning, Memory, and Cognition, 29,* 904–923.

Trawley, S. L., Law, A. S., & Logie, R. H. (2011). Event-based prospective remembering in a virtual world. *Quarterly Journal of Experimental Psychology, 64,* 2181–2193.

Treccani, B., Argyri, E., Sorace, A., & Della Salla, S. (2009). Spatial negative priming in bilingualism. *Psychonomic Bulletin & Review, 16,* 320–327.

Treisman, A. M. (1960). Contextual cues in selective listening. *Quarterly Journal of Experimental Psychology, 12,* 242–248.

Treisman, A. M. (1964). Monitoring and storage of irrelevant messages in selective attention. *Journal of Verbal Learning and Verbal Behavior, 3,* 449–459.

Treisman, A. M. (1965). The effects of redundancy and familiarity on translating and repeating back a foreign and a native language. *British Journal of Psychology, 56,* 369–379.

Treisman, A. (1982). Perceptual grouping and attention in visual search for features and for objects. *Journal of Experimental Psychology: Human Perception and Performance, 8,* 194–214.

Treisman, A. (1988). Features and objects: The Fourteenth Bartlett Memorial Lecture. *Quarterly Journal of Experimental Psychology, 40A,* 201–237.

Treisman, A. (1991). Search, similarity, and integration of features between and within dimensions. *Journal of Experimental Psychology: Human Perception and Performance, 17,* 652–676.

Treisman, A., & Gelade, G. (1980). A feature integration theory of attention. *Cognitive Psychology, 12,* 97–136.

Treisman, A. M., Russell, R., & Green, J. (1975). Brief visual storage of shape and movement. In P. M. A. Rabbitt & S. Dornic (Eds.), *Attention and performance* (Vol. 5, pp. 699–721). New York: Academic Press.

Trigg, G. L., & Lerner, R. J. (Eds.). (1981). *Encyclopedia of physics.* Reading, MA: Addison-Wesley.

Tucker, M., & Ellis, R. (1998). On the relations between seen objects and components of potential actions. *Journal of Experimental Psychology: Human Perception and Performance, 24,* 830–846.

Tuholski, S. W., Engle, R. W., & Baylis, G. C. (2001). Individual differences in working memory capacity and enumeration. *Memory & Cognition, 29,* 484–492.

Tulving, E. (1962). Subjective organization in free recall of "unrelated" words. *Psychological Review, 69,* 344–354.

Tulving, E. (1972). Episodic and semantic memory. In E. Tulving & W. Donaldson (Eds.), *Organization of memory* (pp. 381–403). New York: Academic Press.

Tulving, E. (1983). *Elements of episodic memory.* Oxford, England: Clarendon.

Tulving, E. (1989). Remembering and knowing the past. *American Scientist, 77,* 361–367.

Tulving, E. (1993). What is episodic memory? *Current Directions in Psychological Science, 2,* 67–70.

Tulving, E., & Pearlstone, Z. (1966). Availability versus accessibility of information in memory for words. *Journal of Verbal Learning and Verbal Behavior, 5,* 381–391.

Tulving, E., & Thompson, D. M. (1973). Encoding specificity and retrieval processes in episodic memory. *Psychological Review, 80,* 352–373.

Tun, P. A. (1989). Age differences in processing expository and narrative text. *Journals of Geronology: Psychological Sciences, 44,* P9–P15.

Turner, M. L., & Engle, R. W. (1989). Is working memory capacity task dependent? *Journal of Memory and Language, 28,* 127–154.

Tversky, A., & Kahneman, D. (1973). Availability: A heuristic for judging frequency and probability. *Cognitive Psychology, 5,* 207–232.

Tversky, A., & Kahneman, D. (1974). Judgment under uncertainty: Heuristics and biases. *Science, 185,* 1124–1131.

Tversky, A., & Kahneman, D. (1980). Causal schemas in judgments under uncertainty. In M. Fishbein (Ed.), *Progress in social psychology* (Vol. 1, pp. 49–72). Hillsdale, NJ: Erlbaum.

Tversky, A., & Kahneman, D. (1983). Extensional versus intuitive reasoning: The conjunction fallacy in probability judgment. *Psychological Review, 90,* 293–315.

Tyler, L. K., Voice, J. K., & Moss, H. E. (2000). The interaction of meaning and sound in spoken word recognition. *Psychonomic Bulletin & Review, 7,* 320–326.

Tzelgov, J., Yehene, V., Kotler, L., & Alon, A. (2000). Automatic comparisons of artificial digits never compared: Learning linear ordering relations. *Journal of Experimental Psychology: Learning, Memory, and Cognition, 26,* 103–120.

Underwood, B. J. (1957). Interference and forgetting. *Psychological Review, 64,* 49–60.

Underwood, B. J., Keppel, G., & Schulz, R. W. (1962). Studies of distributed practice: XXII. Some conditions which enhance retention. *Journal of Experimental Psychology, 64,* 112–129.

Underwood, B. J., & Schulz, R. W. (1960). *Meaningfulness and verbal learning*. Philadelphia: Lippincott.

Ungerleider, L. G., & Haxby, J. V. (1994). "What" versus "where" in the human brain. *Current Opinion in Neurobiology, 4*, 157–165.

Unsworth, N. (2007). Individual differences in working memory capacity and episodic retrieval: The dynamics of delayed and continuous distractor free recall. *Journal of Experimental Psychology: Learning, Memory, and Cognition, 33*, 1020–1034.

Unsworth, N., & Engle, R. W. (2007). The nature of individual differences in working memory capacity: Active maintenance in primary memory and controlled search from secondary memory. *Psychological Review, 114*, 104–132.

Unsworth, N., Heitz, R. P., & Parks, N. A. (2008). The importance of temporal distinctiveness for forgetting over the short-term. *Psychological Science, 19*, 1078–1081.

Unsworth, N., & Spillers, G. J, (2010). Working memory capacity: Attention control, secondary memory, or both? A direct test of the dual component model. *Journal of Memory and Language, 62*, 392–406.

Unsworth, N., Spillers, G. J., & Brewer, G. A. (2012). Dynamics of context-dependent recall: An examination of internal and external context change. *Journal of Memory and Language, 66*, 1–16.

Vachon, F., Hughes, R. W., & Jones, D. M. (2012). Broken expectations: Violation of expectancies, not novelty, captures auditory attention. *Journal of Experimental Psychology: Learning, Memory, and Cognition, 38*, 164–177.

Vallar, G., & Baddeley, A. D. (1984). Fractionation of working memory: Neuropsychological evidence for a phonological short-term store. *Journal of Verbal Learning and Verbal Behavior, 23*, 151–161.

Vallée-Tourangeau, F., Euden, G., & Hearn, V. (2011). Einstellung defused: Interactivity and mental set. *Quarterly Journal of Expermental Psychology, 64*, 1889–1895.

Van Berkum, J. J. A. (2008). Understanding sentences in context: What brain waves can tell us. *Current Directions in Psychological Science, 17*, 376–380.

Van Berkum, J. J. A., Brown, C. M., & Hagoort, P. (1999). Early referential context effects in sentence processing: Evidence from event-related brain potentials. *Journal of Memory and Language, 41*, 147–182.

Van Dijk, T. A., & Kintsch, W. (1983). *Strategies in discourse comprehension*. New York: Academic Press.

van Elk, M., & Blanke, O. (2011). The relation between body semantics and spatial body representations. *Acta Psychologica, 138*, 347–358.

van Hell, J. G., & Dijkstra, T. (2002). Foreign language knowledge can influence native language performance in exclusively native contexts. *Psychonomic Bulletin & Review, 9*, 780–789.

VanLehn, K. (1989). Problem solving and cognitive skill acquisition. In M. I. Posner (Ed.), *Foundations of cognitive science* (pp. 527–579). Cambridge, MA: MIT Press.

Van Overschelde, J. P., Rawson, K. A., & Dunlosky, J. (2004). Category norms: An updated and expanded version of the Battig and Montague (1969) norms. *Journal of Memory and Language, 50*, 289–335.

Vasta, R., & Liben, L. S. (1996). The water-level task: An intriguing puzzle. *Current Directions in Psychological Science, 5*, 171–177.

Vecera, S. P., Behrmann, M., & McGoldrick, J. (2000). Selective attention to the parts of an object. *Psychonomic Bulletin & Review, 7*, 301–308.

Vergauwe, E., Barrouillet, P., & Camos, V. (2010). Do mental processes share a domain-general resource? *Psychological Science, 21*, 384–390.

Verfaille, K., & Y'dewalle, G. (1991). Representational momentum and event course anticipation in the perception of implied motions. *Journal of Experimental Psychology: Learning, Memory, and Cognition, 17*, 302–313.

Verhaeghen, P. (2011). Aging and executive control: Reports of a demise greatly exaggerated. *Psychological Science, 20*, 174–180.

Verhaeghen, P., Cerella, J., & Basak, C. (2004). A working memory workout: How to expand the focus of serial attention from one to four items in 10 hours or less. *Journal of Experimental Psychology: Learning, Memory, and Cognition, 30*, 1322–1337.

Verhaeghen P., & Meersman, L. D. (1998). Aging and the Stroop effect: A meta-analysis. *Psychologya and Aging, 13*, 120–126.

Virtue, S., van den Broek, P., & Linderholm, T. (2006). Hemispheric processing of inferences: the effects of textual constraint and working memory capacity. *Memory & Cognition, 34*, 1341–1354.

Vivas, A. B., Humphreys, G. W., & Fuentes, L. J. (2006). Abnormal inhibition of return: A review and new data on patients with parietal lobe damage. *Cognitive Neuropsychology, 23*, 1049–1064.

von Frisch, K. (1967). *The dance language and orientation of honeybees*. Cambridge, MA: Harvard University Press.

von Restorff, H. (1933). Über die Wirkung von Bereichsbildungen im Spurenfeld [On the effect of sphere formations in the trace field]. *Psychologische Forschung, 18*, 299–342.

Vredeveldt, A., Hitch, G. J., & Baddeley, A. D. (2011). Eyeclosure helps memory by reducing cognitive load and enhancing visualization. *Memory & Cognition, 39,* 1253–1263.

Vu, H., Kellas, G., Metcalf, K., & Herman, R. (2000). The influence of global discourse on lexical ambiguity resolution. *Memory & Cognition, 28,* 236–252.

Vuilleumeir, P. (2005). How brains beware: Neural mechanisms of emotional attention. *Trends in Cognitive Sciences, 9,* 585–594.

Vuilleumeir, P., & Huang, Y-M. (2009). Emotional attention: Uncovering the mechanisms of affective biases in perception. *Current Directions in Psychological Science, 18,* 148–152.

Vul, E., & Pashler, H. (2007). Incubation benefits only after people have been misdirected. *Memory & Cognition, 35,* 701–710.

Wade, K. A., Garry, M., Read, J. D., & Lindsay, S. (2002). A picture is worth a thousand lies: Using false photographs to create false childhood memories. *Psychonomic Bulletin & Review, 9,* 597–603.

Wagar, B. M., & Thagard, P. (2004). Spiking Phineas Gage: A neurocomputational theory of cognitive-affective integration in decision making. *Psychological Review, 111,* 67–79.

Wagenaar, W. A. (1986). My memory: A study of autobiographical memory over six years. *Cognitive Psychology, 18,* 225–252.

Waltz, J. A., Knowlton, B. J., Holyoak, K. J., Boone, K. B., Mishkin, F. S., Santos, M. M., et al. (1999). A system for relational reasoning in human prefrontal cortex. *Psychological Science, 10,* 119–125.

Waltz, J. A., Lau, A., Grewal, S. K., & Holyoak, K. J. (2000). The role of working memory in analogical mapping. *Memory & Cognition, 28,* 1205–1212.

Warm, J. S. (1984). An introduction to vigilance. In J. S. Warm (ed.), *Sustained attention in human performance* (pp. 1–14). Chichester, England: Wiley.

Warm, J. S., & Jerison, H. J. (1984). The psychophysics of vigilance. In J. S. Warm (ed.), *Sustained attention in human performance* (pp. 15–60). Chichester, England: Wiley.

Warren, R. M. (1970). Perceptual restoration of missing speech sounds. *Science, 167,* 392–393.

Warren, R. M., & Warren, R. P. (1970). Auditory illusions and confusions. *Scientific American, 223,* 30–36.

Warrington, E. K., & James, M. (1988). Visual apperceptive agnosia: A clinico-anatomical study of three cases. *Cortex, 24,* 13–32.

Warrington, E. K., & McCarthy, R. (1983). Category specific access dysphasia. *Brain, 106,* 859–878.

Warrington, E. K., & Shallice, T. (1969). The selective impairment of auditory verbal short-term memory. *Brain, 92,* 885–896.

Warrington, E. K., & Shallice, T. (1984). Category specific semantic impairments. *Brain, 107,* 829–854.

Warrington, E. K., & Weiskrantz, L. (1970). The amnesic syndrome: Consolidation or retrieval? *Nature, 228,* 628–630.

Wason, P. C., & Johnson-Laird, P. N. (1972). *Psychology of reasoning: Structure and content.* Cambridge, MA: Harvard University Press.

Wassenburg, S. I., & Zwaan, R. A. (2010). Readers routinely represent implied object rotation: The role of visual experience. *Quarterly Journal of Experimental Psychology, 63,* 1665–1670.

Watson, J. B. (1913). Psychology as the behaviorist sees it. *Psychological Review, 20,* 158–177.

Watson, J. M., McDermott, K. B., & Balota, D. A. (2004). Attempting to avoid false memories in the Deese–Roediger–McDermott paradigm: Assessing the combined influence of practice and warnings in young and old adults. *Memory & Cognition, 32,* 135–141.

Watson, R. I. (1968). *The great psychologists from Aristotle to Freud.* New York: Lippincott.

Waugh, N. C., & Norman, D. A. (1965). Primary memory. *Psychological Review, 72,* 89–104.

Weaver, C. A. III. (1993). Do you need a "flash" to form a flashbulb memory? *Journal of Experimental Psychology: General, 122,* 39–46.

Webster's New World dictionary of the American language. (1980). 2nd college edition. Cleveland: William Collins.

Weinstein, Y., Bugg, J. M., & Roediger, H. L. (2008). Can the survival recall advantage be explained by basic memory processes? *Memory & Cognition, 36,* 913–919.

Weisberg, R. (1995). Prolegomena to theories of insight in problem solving: A taxonomy of problems. In R. J. Sternberg & J. E. Davidson (Eds.), *The nature of insight* (pp. 157–196). Cambridge, MA: MIT Press.

Wells, G. L., Olson, E. A., & Charman, S. D. (2002). The confidence of eyewitnesses in their identifications from lineups. *Current Directions in Psychological Science, 11,* 151–154.

Wenger, M. J., & Payne, D. G. (1995). On the acquisition of mnemonic skill: Application of skilled memory theory. *Journal of Experimental Psychology: Applied, 1,* 194–215.

Werner, H. (1935). Studies on contour. *American Journal of Psychology, 47,* 40–64.

Wertheimer, M. (1912). Experimentelle Studien über das Sehen von Bewegung [Experimental studies on the seeing of motion]. *Zeitschrift für Psychologie und Physiologie der Sinnesorgane, 61,* 161–265.

West, R. F., & Stanovich, K. E. (1986). Robust effects of syntactic structure on visual word processing. *Memory & Cognition, 14,* 104–112.

Westmacott, R., & Moscovitch, M. (2003). The contribution of autobiographical significance to semantic memory. *Memory & Cognition, 31,* 761–774.

Whaley, C. P. (1978). Word–nonword classification time. *Journal of Verbal Learning and Verbal Behavior, 17,* 143–154.

Wharton, C. M., Grafman, J., Flitman, S. S., Hansen, E. K., Brauner, J., Marks, A., et al. (2000). Toward neuroanatomical models of analogy: A positron emission tomography study of analogical mapping. *Cognitive Psychology, 40,* 173–197.

Whitney, P. (1998). *The psychology of language.* Boston: Houghton Mifflin.

Whorf, B. L. (1956). Science and linguistics. In J. B. Carroll (Ed.), *Language, thought, and reality: Selected writings of Benjamin Lee Whorf* (pp. 207–219). Cambridge, MA: MIT Press.

Wickelgren, W. A. (1974). *How to solve problems.* San Francisco: Freeman.

Wickens, D. D. (1972). Characteristics of word encoding. In A. W. Melton & E. Martin (Eds.), *Coding processes in human memory* (pp. 191–215). New York: Winston.

Wickens, D. D., Born, D. G., & Allen, C. K. (1963). Proactive inhibition and item similarity in short-term memory. *Journal of Verbal Learning and Verbal Behavior, 2,* 440–445.

Wiener, E. L. (1984). Vigilance and inspection. In J. S. Warm (ed.), *Sustained attention in human performance* (pp. 207–246). Chichester, England: Wiley.

Wiggs, C. L., Weisberg, J., & Martin, A. (1999). Neural correlates of semantic and episodic memory retrieval. *Neuropsychologia, 37,* 103–118.

Wiley, J. (1998). Expertise as mental set: The effects of domain knowledge in creative problem solving. *Memory & Cognition, 26,* 716–730.

Wiley, J., & Rayner, K. (2000). Effects of titles on the processing of text and lexically ambiguous words: Evidence from eye movements. *Memory & Cognition, 28,* 1011–1021.

Willander, J., & Larsson, M. (2006). Smell your way back to childhood. *Psychonomic Bulletin & Review, 13,* 240–244.

Willander, J., & Larsson, M. (2007). Olfaction and emotion: The case of autobiographical memory. *Memory & Cognition, 35,* 1659–1663.

Williams, J. M. G., Mathews, A., & MacLeod, C. (1996). The emotional Stroop task and psychopathology. *Psychological Bulletin, 120,* 3–24.

Willems, R. M., Hagoort, P., & Casasanto, D. (2010). Body-specific representations of action verbs: Neural evidence from right- and left-handers. *Psychological Science, 21,* 67–74.

Willems, R. M. Labruna, L., D'Espisito, M., Ivry, R., & Casasanto, D. (2011). A functional role for the motor system in language understanding: Evidence from theta-burst transcranial magnetic stimulation. *Psychological Science, 22,* 849–854.

Williams, R. W., & Herrup, K. (1988). The control of neuron number. *Annual Review of Neuroscience, 11,* 423–453.

Williamson, V. J., Baddeley, A. D., & Hitch, G. J. (2010). Musicians' and nonmusicians' shortterm memory for verbal and musical sequences: Comparing phonological similarity and pitch proximity. Memory & Cognition, *38,* 163–175.

Wilkes-Gibbs, D., & Clark, H. H. (1992). Coordinating beliefs in conversation. *Journal of Memory and Language, 31,* 183–194.

Wilson, M., & Emmorey, K. (2006). Comparing sign language and speech reveals a universal limit on short-term memory capacity. *Psychological Science, 17,* 682–683.

Wilson, M., & Fox, G. (2007). Working memory for language is not special: Evidence for an articulatory loop for novel stimuli. *Psychonomic Bulletin & Review, 14,* 470–473.

Wilson, M., & Knoblich, G. (2005). The case for motor involvement in perceiving conspecifics. *Psychological Bulletin, 131,* 460–473.

Wilson, M., & Wilson, T. P. (2005). An oscillator model of the timing of turn-taking. *Psychonomic Bulletin & Review, 12,* 957–968.

Windschitl, P. D., & Weber, E. U. (1999). The interpretation of "likely" depends on the context, but "70%" is 70%—right? The influence of associative processes on perceived certainty. *Journal of Experimental Psychology: Learning, Memory, and Cognition, 25,* 1514–1533.

Winer, G. A., Cottrell, J. E., Gregg, V., Fournier, J. S., & Bica, L. A. (2002). Fundamentally misunderstanding visual perception: Adults' belief in visual emissions. *American Psychologist, 57,* 417–424.

Wingfield, A., Goodglass, H., & Lindfield, K. C. (1997). Separating speed from automaticity in a patient with focal brain atrophy. *Psychological Science, 8,* 247–249.

Winograd, E., & Killinger, W. A., Jr. (1983). Relating age at encoding in early childhood to adult recall: Development of flashbulb memories. *Journal of Experimental Psychology: General, 112*, 413–422.

Witt, J. K. (2011). Action's effect on perception. *Current Directions in Psychological Science, 20*, 201–206.

Witt, J. K., Proffitt, D. R., & Epstein, W. (2005). Tool use affects perceived distance, but only when you intend to use it. *Journal of Experimental Psychology: Human Perception and Performance, 31*, 880–888.

Wixted, J. T. (2004). On common ground: Jost's (1897) law of forgetting and Ribot's (1881) law of retrograde amnesia. *Psychological Review, 111*, 864–879.

Wixted, J. T. (2005). A theory about why we forget what we once knew. *Current Directions in Psychological Science, 14*, 6–9.

Wixted, J. T., & Ebbesen, E. B. (1991). On the form of forgetting. *Psychological Science, 2*, 409–415.

Wood, N. L., & Cowan, N. (1995a). The cocktail party phenomenon revisited: Attention and memory in the classic selective listening procedure of Cherry (1953). *Journal of Experimental Psychology: General, 124*, 243–262.

Wood, N., & Cowan, N. (1995b). The cocktail party phenomenon revisited: How frequent are attention shifts to one's name in an irrelevant auditory channel? *Journal of Experimental Psychology: Learning, Memory, and Cognition, 21*, 255–260.

Woodworth, R. S., & Schlosberg, H. (1954). *Experimental psychology* (Rev. ed.). New York: Holt, Rinehart & Winston.

Worthy, D. A., Gorlick, M. A., Pacheco, J. L., Schnyer, D. M., & Maddox, W. T. (2011). With age comes wisdom: Decision making in younger and older adults. *Psychological Science, 22*, 1375–1380.

Wraga, M., Swaby, M., & Flynn, C. M. (2008). Passive tactile feedback facilitates mental rotation of handheld objects. *Memory & Cognition, 36*, 271–281.

Wright, A. A., & Roediger, H. L. III. (2003). Interference processes in monkey auditory list memory. *Psychonomic Bulletin & Review, 10*, 696–702.

Wurm, L. H. (2007). Danger and usefulness: An alternative framework for understanding rapid evaluation effects in perception. *Psychonomic Bulletin & Review, 14*, 1218–1225.

Wurm, L. H., & Seaman, S. R. (2008). Semantic effects in naming and perceptual identification but not in delayed naming: Implications for models and tasks. *Journal of Experimental Psychology: Learning, Memory, and Cognition, 34*, 381–398.

Yamauchi, T., & Markman, A. B. (2000). Inference using categories. *Journal of Experimental Psychology: Learning, Memory, and Cognition, 26*, 776–795.

Yang, S-J., & Beilock, S. L. (2011). Seeing and doing: Ability to act moderates orientation effects in object perception. *Quarterly Journal of Experimental Psychology, 64*, 639–648.

Yantis, S. (2008). The neural basis of selective attention. *Current Directions in Psychological Science, 17*, 86–90.

Yantis, S., & Jonides, J. (1984). Abrupt visual onsets and selective attention: Evidence from visual search. *Journal of Experimental Psychology: Human Perception and Performance, 10*, 601–621.

Yarbus, A. L. (1967). *Eye movements and vision* (B. Haigh, Trans.). New York: Plenum.

Yates, M., Locker, L., Jr., & Simpson, G. B. (2003). Semantic and phonological influences on the processing of words and pseudohomophones. *Memory & Cognition, 31*, 856–866.

Yechiam, E., Kanz, J. E., Bechara, A., Stout, J. C., Busemeyer, J. R., Altmaier, E. M., et al. (2008). Neurocognitive deficits related to poor decision making in people behind bars. *Psychonomic Bulletin & Review, 15*, 44–51.

Yonelinas, A. P. (2002). The nature of recollection and familiarity: A review of 30 years of research. *Journal of Memory and Language, 46*, 441–517.

Yu, C., & Smith, L. B. (2011). What you learn is what you see: using eye movements to study infant cross- situational word learning. *Developmental Science, 14*(2), 165–180.

Yuille, J. C., & Paivio, A. (1967). Latency of imaginal and verbal mediators as a function of stimulus and response concreteness-imagery. *Journal of Experimental Psychology, 75*, 540–544.

Zacks, J. L., & Zacks, R. T. (1993). Visual search times assessed without reaction times: A new method and an application to aging. *Journal of Experimental Psychology: Human Perception and Performance, 19*, 798–813.

Zacks, J. M., Braver, T. S., Sheridan, M. A., Donaldson, D. I., Snyder, A. Z., Ollinger, J. M., et al. (2001). Human brain activity time-locked to perceptual event boundaries. *Nature Neuroscience, 4*, 651–655.

Zacks, J. M., Speer, N. K., Swallow, K. M., Braver, T. S., & Reynolds, J. R. (2007). Event perception: A mind/brain perspective. *Psychological Bulletin, 133*, 273–293.

Zaragoza, M. S., & Lane, S. M. (1994). Source misattributions and the suggestibility of eyewitness memory. *Journal of Experimental Psychology: Learning, Memory, and Cognition, 20*, 934–945.

Zaragoza, M. S., McCloskey, M., & Jamis, M. (1987). Misleading postevent information and recall of the original event: Further evidence against the memory impairment hypothesis. *Journal of Experimental Psychology: Learning, Memory, and Cognition, 13*, 36–44.

Zaragoza, M. S., Payment, K. E., Ackil, J. K., Drivdahl, S. B., & Beck, M. (2001). Interviewing witnesses: Forced confabulation and confirmatory feedback increase false memories. *Psychological Science, 12,* 473–477.

Zaromb, F. M., Karpicke, J. D., & Roediger, H. L. (2010). Comprehension as a basis for metacognitive judgments: Effects of effort after meaning on recall and metacognition. *Journal of Experimental Psychology: Learning, Memory, and Cognition, 36,* 552–557.

Zbrodoff, N. J., & Logan, G. D. (1986). On the autonomy of mental processes: A case study of arithmetic. *Journal of Experimental Psychology: General, 115,* 118–130.

Zechmeister, E. B., & Shaughnessy, J. J. (1980). When you think that you know and when you think that you know but you don't. *Bulletin of the Psychonomic Society, 15,* 41–44.

Zeelenberg, R., Wagenmakers, E., & Rotteveel, M. (2006). The impact of emotion on perception: Bias or enhanced processing? *Psychological Science, 17,* 287–291.

Zelinski, E. M., & Stewart, S. T. (1998). Individual differences in 16-year memory changes. *Psychology and Aging, 13,* 622–630.

Zhang, W., & Luck, S. J. (2009). Sudden death and gradual decay in visual working memory. *Psychological Science, 20,* 423–428.

Zola-Morgan, S., Squire, L., & Amalral, D. G. (1986). Human amnesia and the medial temporal region: Enduring memory impairment following a bilateral lesion limited to field CA1 of the hippocampus. *Journal of Neuroscience, 6,* 2950–2967.

Zwaan, R. A. (1996). Processing narrative time shifts. *Journal of Experimental Psychology: Learning, Memory, and Cognition, 22,* 1196–1207.

Zwaan, R. A., Langston, M. C., & Graesser, A. C. (1995). The construction of situation models in narrative comprehension: An event-indexing model. *Psychological Science, 6,* 292–297.

Zwaan, R. A., Magliano, J. P., & Graesser, A. C. (1995). Dimensions of situation model construction in narrative comprehension. *Journal of Experimental Psychology: Learning, Memory, and Cognition, 21,* 386–397.

Zwaan, R. A., & Radvansky, G. A. (1998). Situation models in language comprehension and memory. *Psychological Bulletin, 123,* 162–185.

Zwaan, R. A., Stanfield, R. A., & Yaxley, R. H. (2002). Language comprehenders mentally represent the shapes of objects. *Psychological Science, 13,* 168–171.

PHOTO CREDITS

Chapter 1 p. 9: © Bettmann/Corbis; p. 10: Bettmann/Corbis; p. 11: Antman Archives/The Image Works; p. 13: Purestock/ Alamy; p. 15: SASCHA SCHUERMANN/Newscom.

Chapter 2 p. 44: Layland Masuda/Shutterstock.com; p. 52: (R) IvicaNS/Shutterstock; p. 52: (L) Patrick J. Lynch/Science Source p. 53: Deco/Alamy.

Chapter 3 p. 68: Fesus Robert/Shutterstock.com; p. 81: Aleksey Stemmer/Shutterstock.; p. 82: Paul Lampard/Fotolia.

Chapter 4 p. 119: PhotoAlto/Alamy; p. 120: Steve Debenport/Getty Images; p. 131: Eileen Langsley Olympic Images/ Alamy; p. 132: Mark Antman/The Image Works; p. 134: Ariwasabi, 2010/Used under license from Shutterstock.com.

Chapter 5 p. 139: Thomas Del Brase/Getty; p. 161: Larry Lilac/Alamy.

Chapter 6 p. 182: Sergejs Rahunoks/Fotolia LLC; p. 199: Moviestore collection Ltd/Alamy; p. 201: intoit/Shutterstock.

Chapter 7 p. 216: Science Source; p. 217: Steve Taylor ARPS/Alamy.

Chapter 8 p. 266: Lon C. Diehl/PhotoEdit; p. 280: Jose Luis Pelaez Inc/Blend Images/Getty Images.

Chapter 9 p. 289: Huntstock, Inc/Alamy; p. 280: Elena Efimova/Shutterstock.com; p. 296: Steve Bloom Images/Alamy, p. 313: Bernal Revert/Alamy Limited.

Chapter 10 p. 338: Dragon Images/Shutterstock; p. 339: Network Photographers/Alamy; p. 366: Digital Vision/Getty Images.

Chapter 11 p. 389: nutsiam/Fotolia LLC; p. 397: Pearson Education/PH College; p. 418: Libby Welch/Alamy.

Chapter 12 p. 431: Intelligenzprüfungen an Menschenaffen. By Wolfgang Kohler. Tafel IV. © 1921 Verlag Von Julius Springer in Berlin; p. 439: Huntstock, Inc/Alamy; p. 463: peshkova/Fotolia LLC; p. 465: AVAVA/Shutterstock.

Chapter 13 p. 474: Denkou Images/Alamy; p. 475: Asti Suwandi/Shutterstock.com; p. 481: Everett Collection Historical/ Alamy; p. 481: ZUMA Press, Inc./Alamy.

Chapter 14 p. W-8: Nadezda Cruzova/Shutterstock.com; p. W-13: iofoto/Shutterstock.com; p. W-20: Monkey Business Images/shutterstock.com; p. W-23: Diego Cervo/Shutterstock.com.

TEXT CREDITS

Chapter 1 Entry for "cognition" from AMERICAN HERITAGE DICTIONARY OF THE ENGLISH LANGUAGE 4th edition. Copyright © 2000 by Houghton Mifflin Company. Reproduced by permission of Houghton Mifflin Company. **Chapter 1** Definitions of "memory and language" from WEBSTER'S NEW WORLD COLLEGE DICTIONARY 4th edition ed. by Michael E. Agnes. Copyright © 2008 by Wiley Publishing Inc., Cleveland, OH. Reprinted by permission of John Wiley & Sons, Inc.

Illustration and Table Credits

Figure 1-2 Data from Campbell, J. I. D., & Graham, D. J. (1985). Mental multiplication skill: Structure, process, and acquisition. Canadian Journal of Psychology, 39, 338–366. **Figure 1-4** Atkinson, R. C., & Shiffrin, R. M. (1971). The control of short-term memory. Scientific American, 225, 82–90. and Atkinson, R. C., & Shiffrin, R. M. (1968). Human memory: A proposed system and its control processes. In W. K. Spence & J. T. Spence (Eds.), The psychology of learning and motivation: Advances in research and theory (Vol. 2, pp. 89–195). New York: Academic Press. **Figure 1-5** Adapted from Sternberg, S. (1969). The discovery of processing stages: Extensions of Donder's method. In W. G. Koster (Ed.), Attention and performance II. Acta Psychologica, 30, 276–315. **Figure 2-10** Davachi, L., Mitchell, J. P., & Wagner, A. D. (2003). Multiple routes to memory: Distinct medial temporal lobe processes build item and source memories. Proceedings of the National Academy of Sciences, 100, 2157–2162. Copyright © 2003. National Academy of Sciences, U.S.A. **Figure 2-11** Liverpool University Press **Figure 3-4** Data from Sperling, G. (1960). The information available in brief visual presentations. Psychological Monographs, 74 (Whole No. 48). **Figure 3-10** Adapted from Selfridge, O. G. (1959). Pandemonium: A paradigm for learning. In The mechanisation of thought processes, National Physical Laboratory, London: H. M. Stationery Office. **Figure 3-15** Osherson, Daniel N., Stephen M. Kosslyn, and John Hollerbach, eds., An Invitation to Cognitive Science, Volume 2: Visual Cognition and Action, Figure 3-15: Geons and the objects they make, © 1990 Massachusetts Institute of Technology, by permission of The MIT

Press. **Figure 3-16** Biederman, I. (1987). Recognition by components: A theory of human image understanding. Psychological Review, 94, 115–147. **Figure 3-17** SOURCE: Biederman, I. (1987). Recognition by components: A theory of human image understanding. Psychological Review, 94, 115–147. **Figure 3-18** Tucker,M. & Ellis, R. (1998). On the relations of seen objects and components of potential actions. Journal of Experimental Psychology: Human Perception and Performance, 24, 830–846. **Figure 3-20** Price, R.H., Principles of Psychology, 1st Ed., © 1987. Reprinted and Electronically reproduced by permission of Pearson Education, Inc., Upper Saddle River, New Jersey. **Figure 4a-b** Chris Madden/Alamy **Figure 4-3** Posner, M. I., Snyder, C. R. R., & Davidson, B. J. (1980). Attention and the detection of signals. Journal of Experimental Psychology: General, 109, 160–174. **Figure 4-6** Solso, R. L., Cognitive Psychology, 5th Ed., © 1998. Reprinted and Electronically reproduced by permission of Pearson Education, Inc., Upper Saddle River, New Jersey. **Figure 4-7** From: Brain, Mind, and Behavior, 2/e by F.E. Bloom, and A. Lazerson. Copyright © 1998 Used with permission of W.H. Freeman and Company. **Figure 4-9** Adapted from Broadbent, D. E. (1958). Perception and communication. London: Pergamon. **Figure 4-10** Adapted from Lindsay, p. H., & Norman, D. A. (1977). Human information processing: An introduction to psychology. New York: Academic Press. **Figure 4-11** Data from Barshi, I., & Healy, A. F. (1993). Checklist procedures and the cost of automaticity. Memory & Cognition, 21, 496–505. **Figure 5-1** Peterson, L. R., & Peterson, M. J. (1959). Short-term retention of individual items. Journal of Experimental Psychology, 58, 193–198. **Figure 5-6** Adapted from Sternberg, S. (1969). The discovery of processing stages: Extensions of Donder's method. In W. G. Koster (Ed.), Attention and performance II. Acta Psychologica, 30, 276–315. **Figure 5-14** Rosen, V. M., & Engle, R. W. (1997). The role of working memory capacity in retrieval. Journal of Experimental Psychology: General, 126, 211–227. **Figure 6-1** Squire and Zola-Morgan (1991). Source: Squire, L. R., & Zola-Morgan, S. (1991). The medial temporal lobe memory system. Science, 253, 1380–1386. Reprinted with permission from AAAS. **Figure 6-2** Ebbinghaus, H. (1885/1913). Memory: A contribution to experimental psychology (H. A. Ruger & C. E. Bussenius, Trans.). New York: Columbia University, Teacher's College. (Reprinted 1964, New York: Dover) **Figure 6-10** After Blakemore, C. (1977). Mechanics of the mind. Cambridge, U.K.: Cambridge University Press. **Table 6-4** Adapted from Bower, G. H., Clark, M. C., Lesgold, A. M., & Winzenz, D. (1969). Hierarchical retrieval schemes in recall of categorical word lists. Journal of Verbal Learning and Verbal Behavior, 8, 323–343. **Figure 7-13** Neely, J. H. (1977). Semantic priming and retrieval from lexical memory: Roles of inhibitionless spreading activation and limited-capacity attention. Journal of Experimental Psychology: General, 106, 226–254. **Table 7-3** Meyer, D. E., & Schvaneveldt, R. W. (1971). Facilitation in recognizing pairs of words: Evidence of a dependence between retrieval operations. Journal of Experimental Psychology, 90, 227–234. **Table 7-5** SOURCE: Bartlett, F. C. (1920). Some Experiments on the Reproduction of Folk-Stories. From the Psychological Laboratory, University of Cambridge. **Table 7-6** Bartlett, F. C. (1932). Remembering: A study in experimental and social psychology. Reprinted by permission of Cambridge University Press. **Table 7-7** Bransford, J. D. (1979). Human cognition: Learning, understanding and remembering. Belmont, CA: Wadsworth. **Table 7-13** Neely, J. H. (1977). Semantic priming and retrieval from lexical memory: Roles of inhibitionless spreading activation and limited-capacity attention. Journal of Experimental Psychology: General, 106, 226–254. **Table 8-1** Schacter, D. L. (1999). The seven sins of memory: Insights from psychology and cognitive neuroscience. American Psychologist, 54, 182–203. **Figure 9-3** Reprinted by permission from Journal of Acoustical Society of America, 29, 117(1957). Copyright 1957, Acoustical Society of America. **Figure 9-4** Reprinted by permission from Journal of Acoustical Society of America, 29, 117(1957). Copyright 1957, Acoustical Society of America. **Figure 9-6** Foss & Hakes, Psycholinguistics: An Introduction to the Psychology of Language., 1st Ed., © 1978. Reprinted and Electronically reproduced by permission of Pearson Education, Inc., Upper Saddle River, New Jersey. **Figure 9-8** Lachman, R., Lachman, J. L., & Butterfield, E. C. (1979). Cognitive psychology and information processing: An introduction. Hillsdale, NJ: Erlbaum. Reprinted by permission of Copy Clearance Center. **Figure 9-9** Adapted from Figures 3 and 4 in Holcomb, p. J., Kounios, J., Anderson, J. E., & West, W. C. (1999). Dual-coding, context availability, and concreteness effects in sentence comprehension: An electrophysiological investigation. Journal of Experimental Psychology: Learning, Memory, and Cognition, 25, 721–742. **Figure 9-11** Fillenbaum, S. (1974). Pragmatic normalization: Further results for some conjunctive and disjunctive sentences. Journal of Experimental Psychology, 102, 574–578. **Figure 9-13** Data from Rayner, K., Carlson, M., & Frazier, L. (1983). The interaction of syntax and semantics during sentence processing: Eye movements in the analysis of semantically biased sentences. Journal of Verbal Learning and Verbal Behavior, 22, 358–374. **Table 9-4** Fromkin, V. A. (1971). The non-anomalous nature of anomalous utterances. Language, 47, 27–52. **Figure 10-1** Network Photographers/Alamy **Figure 10-2** Pascal Goetgheluck/Science Source. **Figure 10-3** Rayner, K. (1998). Eye movements in reading and information processing: 20 years of research. Psychological Bulletin, 124, 372–422. **Figure 10-4** Figure 2-1 (p. 27). Credited to Buswell, G. T. (1937). How adults read. Chicago: Chicago University Press, Plates II and IV, pp. 6, 7. **Figure 10-5** Just, M. A., & Carpenter, p. A. (1980). A theory of reading: From eye fixations to comprehension. Psychological Review, 87, 329–354. **Figure 10-9A** wollertz/Fotolia **Figure 10-9B** searagen/Fotolia. **Table 10-3** Just, M. A., & Carpenter, p. A. (1980). A theory of reading: From eye fixations to comprehension. Psychological Review, 87, 329–354. **Figure 11-5** Banks, W. P., Fujii, M., & Kayra-Stuart, F. (1976). Semantic congruity effects in comparative judgments of magnitude of digits. Journal of Experimental Psychology: Human Perception and Performance, 2, 435–447. **Figure 11-7** Goldstein, D. G., & Gigerenzer, G. (2002). Models of ecological rationality: The recognition heuristic. Psychological Review, 109, 75–90. **Figure 11-12** Waltz, J. A., Knowlton, B. J., Holyoak, K. J., Boone,

K. B., Mishkin, F. S., Santos, M. M., Thomas, C. R., & Miller, B. L. (1999). A aystem for relational reasoning in human prefrontal cortex. Psychological Science, 10, 119–125, Figure 2. **Table 11-2** Rader, A. W., & Sloutsky, V. M. (2002). Processing of logically valid and logically invalid conditional inferences in discourse comprehension. Journal of Experimental Psychology: Learning, Memory, and Cognition, 28, 59–68, Tables 2 and 4 (pp. 61, 65).**Table 11-4** Kahneman, D., & Tversky, A. (1982). The simulation heuristic. In D. Kahneman, p. Slovic, & A. Tversky (Eds.), Judgment under uncertainty: Heuristics and biases (pp. 201–208). Reprinted with the permission of Cambridge University Press. **Table 11-5** Adapted from Gigerenzer, G. (2008). Why heuristics work. Perspectives in Psychological Science, 3, 20–29. **Table 11-6** Tversky, A., & Kahneman, D. (1983). Extensional versus intuitive reasoning: The conjunction fallacy in probability judgment. Psychological Review, 90, 293–315. **Figure 12-2** Data from Metcalfe, J., & Wiebe, D. (1987). Intuition in insight and noninsight problem solving. Memory & Cognition, 15, 238–246. **Figure 12-5** Bowden, E. M., & Beeman, M. J. (1998). Getting the right idea: Semantic activation in the right hemisphere may help solve insight problems. Psychological Science, 9, 435–440. **Figure 12-7** SOURCE: Adapted from Wickelgren, W. A. (1974). How to solve problems. San Francisco: Freeman. **Figure 12-13** Adapted from Ericsson, K. A., Krampe, R. T., & Tesch-Römer, C. (1993). The role of deliberate practice in the acquisition of expert performance. Psychological Review, 100, 363–406. **Table 12-4** SOURCE: Based on Gick, M. L., & Holyoak, K. J. (1980). Analogical problem solving. Cognitive Psychology, 12, 306–355. **Table 12-6** After Gick, M. L., & Holyoak, K. J. (1980). Analogical problem solving. Cognitive Psychology, 12, 306–355. **Figure 14-2** Schiller, p. H. (1966). Developmental study of color-word interference. Journal of Experimental Psychology, 72, 105–108. **Figure 14-3** Hartshorn, K., Rovee-Collier, C., Gerhardstein, P., Bhatt, R.S., Wondoloski, T.L., Klein, P., Gilch, J., Wurtzel, N., & Campos-de-Carvalho, M. (1998). The ontogeny of long-term memory over the first year-and-a-half of life. Developmental Psychobiology, 32, 69–89. **Figure 14-4** K. Hartshorn, et al., (1998). The ontogeny of long-term memory over the first year-and-a-half of life. Developmental Psychobiology, 32, 69–89. **Figure 14-6** Derived from Lynchard, N. A., & Radvansky, G. A. (2012). Age-related perspectives and emotion processing. Psychology and Aging, 27, 934–939. **Table 14-2** Light, L. L., & Capps, J. L. (1986). Comprehension of pronouns in young and older adults. Developmental Psychology, 22, 580–585.

NAME INDEX

SUBJECT INDEX